Wielding the Pen

∽

Writings on Authorship by American Women of the Nineteenth Century

EDITED BY ANNE E. BOYD

The Johns Hopkins University Press | Baltimore

To Beverly Anne Hall Rude

© 2009 The Johns Hopkins University Press
All rights reserved. Published 2009
Printed in the United States of America on acid-free paper
9 8 7 6 5 4 3 2 1

The Johns Hopkins University Press
2715 North Charles Street
Baltimore, Maryland 21218-4363
www.press.jhu.edu

Library of Congress Cataloging-in-Publication Data

Wielding the pen : writings on authorship by American women of the
nineteenth century / edited by Anne E. Boyd.
    p. cm.
  Includes indexes.
  ISBN-13: 978-0-8018-9274-5 (alk. paper)
  ISBN-10: 0-8018-9274-0 (alk. paper)
  ISBN-13: 978-0-8018-9275-2 (pbk. : alk. paper)
  ISBN-10: 0-8018-9275-9 (pbk. : alk. paper)
    1. American literature—Women authors. 2. Authorship. 3. American
literature—19th century. 4. Women—Literary collections. 5. Voice in
literature. I. Boyd, Anne E., 1969–
  PS508.W7W45 2009
  810.8'0357—dc22   2008042177

A catalog record for this book is available from the British Library.

*Special discounts are available for bulk purchases of this book. For more informa-
tion, please contact Special Sales at 410-516-6936 or specialsales@press.jhu.edu.*

Page 437 constitutes an extension of this copyright page.

Contents

INTRODUCTION

When Nathaniel Hawthorne wrote to his publisher in 1855, he could hardly have anticipated that his words would be used by generations of scholars to sum up the field of women writers of his day.

> America is now wholly given over to a d_____d mob of scribbling women, and I should have no chance of success while the public taste is occupied with their trash—and should be ashamed of myself if I did succeed. What is the mystery of these innumerable editions of the Lamplighter, and other books neither better nor worse?—worse they could not be, and better they need not be, when they sell by the 100,000.[1]

This invective has so informed critical perceptions of the field that scholars working on the recovery of women writers are still trying to overcome Hawthorne's contempt. Yet it remains the most frequently quoted statement about nineteenth-century American women writers. It is understandable why Hawthorne's quip about the "damned mob of scribbling women" has been so popular. On the one hand, it forecast the critical disdain that for decades dismissed legions of presumably insignificant female scribblers, when they were alluded to at all. On the other hand, it conveyed Hawthorne's (and other men's) anxiety about the threat women posed to the male preserve of authorship and the cultural power it enshrined, as well as the tactics male writers would use to discourage women from writing in the first place.

The opinions of nineteenth-century women writers on their incursion into the literary world have not been as available or as often quoted as Hawthorne's omnipresent reproof. How did women writers, popular and unknown, feel about their entrance into the print culture of the nineteenth century? Although his letter was not made public until 1910, Hawthorne's attitudes were echoed in the mid-nineteenth-century press by many other male authority figures. How did women respond? Did they internalize such censure or fashion alternative perceptions of female authorship? How much were women affected by the derision of their male critics? Did they simply make excuses for their trespass on the male realm of literature or the supposed lesser quality of their writings compared to the great male authors? Or did they fight back and assert their right to authorship as well as the value of their contributions to a national culture? Did they perhaps adopt different strategies at different times in their careers or during different parts of the century?

No comprehensive effort to answer these questions has been undertaken. This anthology of primary materials—the words of American women writers on the act of authorship and their participation in the literary cultures of the nineteenth century—seeks to redress this imbalance. For women were anything but silent on the momentous question of whether or not they should enter the public sphere with their pens and how they should go about the business and art of authorship. What they had to say suggests they were quite conscious of the effect their authorial acts had on discourses of gender, literature, democracy, and nationalism.

Nineteenth-century women's voices on authorship were in no way uniform, yet taken as a whole they do evince the power of self-representation and self-definition for women writers, a power that they claimed in the popular press of their day but that largely has been denied them by subsequent scholars and editors of anthologies. This is not to say that women's perceptions of authorship have been completely absent from the scholarly studies and classroom anthologies that shape current perceptions of the field. However, those texts generally taken as representative of women's attitudes about authorship could be summed up by Fanny Fern's famous phrase from her novel *Ruth Hall* (1855): "no happy woman ever writes." When Ruth's daughter suggests that she might someday write books like her mother, Ruth answers in horror, "From Harry's grave sprang Floy," meaning that only the death of her husband and the ensuing deprivations suffered by herself and her daughters drove her to the desperate (although wildly successful) enterprise of a literary career.[2] God forbid that her daughter, who already exhibits unusual talents, should actually seek out such a career; rather, she should marry, have children, and pray that she is never forced to sell her brains for her bread.

Similar denunciations of public authorship or failures of women to achieve their goals as writers occur in other texts widely circulated in today's anthologies, such as Catharine Maria Sedgwick's "Cacoethes Scribendi," Emily Dickinson's "Publication - is the Auction / Of the Mind of Man -" (Poem 788), Constance Fenimore Woolson's "'Miss Grief,'" and Mary Wilkins Freeman's "A Poetess." The student of nineteenth-century American women writers is left with the impression that women wrote only reluctantly or painfully and that they would have preferred to keep their writing to themselves. Another famous quote from Harriet Beecher Stowe that "God wrote" her masterpiece *Uncle Tom's Cabin* has also contributed to the notion that women were loathe to portray themselves as writers at all. In essence, the answer to Hawthorne's diatribe has seemed to be a rather fatalistic one. In her foundational essay, "The 'Scribbling Women' and Fanny Fern: Why Women Wrote," Ann D. Wood declared, "In masking and hallowing their activity, these women writers reached the paradoxical point where, by a mysterious transmutation, they were somehow hardly writing at all."[3]

Feminist scholarship since Wood has focused quite a bit on the inherently conflicted and contradictory aspects of women's authorship. Understandably, as scholars sought to explain the absence of women writers from the canon, they focused on how they were constrained and discouraged from picking up the pen. "Shakespeare's sister," first imagined by Virginia Woolf in "A Room of One's Own," or, in an American context, "Melville's sister," was an attractive concept for early feminist scholars eager to find evidence of such a talented woman but also aware of the insurmountable odds against a woman developing her genius.[4] The fact that Emily Dickinson, who appeared to be an exception to the rule, could subvert the prohibitions against her sex only by secreting her poetry away seemed to prove the theory of women's silencing. Sandra Gilbert and Susan Gubar's *Madwoman in the Attic* (1979) argued that women who attempted to pick up the pen were "evidently infected or sickened by just the feelings of self-doubt, inadequacy, and inferiority that their education in 'femininity' almost seems to have been designed to induce." When women did write and publish, as Hawthorne's quote reminds us they did in great numbers, they relegated themselves to a smaller, lesser sphere, as Wood and, most influentially, Mary Kelley in *Private Woman, Public Stage* (1984) argued. Kelley's literary history of the female fiction writers who ruled the marketplace highlighted their feelings of shame, fear, ambivalence, and self-deprecation about adopting "the male roles of public figure, economic provider, and creator of culture."[5]

In my own research, I certainly have been swayed by such depictions of women's writing. In the late 1990s, I came across an essay by one "S. E. Wallace," published by *Harper's* in 1867, which seemed to sum up women's defeated attitudes toward authorship. As I prepared the table of contents for this anthology, I knew that this piece must be included. In fact, powerful expressions like hers had given me the impetus to create this collection in the first place. Hers was the voice of a woman who ached for literary success but was unable to achieve it. She was in some ways a real live Betsey Dole from Freeman's "A Poetess," who burned her works in shame after the negative judgment of male literary authorities. How ironic that Wallace's one significant publication, the work that allowed her to break into the hallowed pages of *Harper's Monthly*, should be a renunciation of authorship, not only for herself but for all women. After confessing to her "crime" of secret writing, she concludes by telling her female readers who may harbor aspirations such as hers, "Bury pen and paper at once."[6] Her words seemed to be perfect proof of how not only male critics like Hawthorne stifled women but also of how women had silenced themselves, lending credence to the view promoted by feminist scholars such as Wood, Gilbert, Gubar, and Kelley.

In the course of my work on this anthology, however, I was pleasantly surprised to discover dozens of women writers who did anything but silence themselves on the subject of authorship. Some were famous, but quite a few of them I had never heard of before; others I knew only vaguely by name. I quickly realized that many female authors were self-reflective about their ventures into print and did not try to hide their desires for expression, respect, and recognition. They stood up for their right to authorship against the slings and arrows of male criticism. They redefined the maligned image of the bluestocking, asserting the nobility of their ambitions and disavowing women writers' lack of seriousness. And they rejected the idea that authorship lay outside of women's sphere, declaring the value of their contributions to the national culture.

Most importantly, their voluminous writings remind us that whatever anxieties or misgivings they may have felt about becoming authors, they continued to write, many of them successfully. Perhaps the most astonishing example is S. E. Wallace herself. Imagine my surprise—and delight—to discover, in the final stages of my work on this book, that the person shrouded behind these initials was not, in fact, completely obscure, unpublished, and unknown. Indeed, she was Susan Elston Wallace, the wife of Lew Wallace, author of perhaps the most popular novel by a man in the nineteenth century: *Ben Hur* (1880). More notable was that a decade after she had supposedly abandoned her ambitions and her writing materials for good (having published a few stories and poems), she returned to writing and publishing in 1879, producing at least six books, most of them collections of travel essays, and numerous essays in the *Atlantic Monthly* and elsewhere. She may have buried pen and paper, but only for a while.

The other turning point for me as I edited this collection was the discovery of Catharine Maria Sedgwick's virtually unknown work "A Sketch of a Blue Stocking" (1832), reprinted here for the first time. It offers a very different view of women's authorship than her often-anthologized story "Cacoethes Scribendi" (1830), which has for decades been seen as emblematic of women's authorial anxieties. In spite of Sedgwick's own success as a novelist, the story sympathizes with the young Alice who "would as soon have stood in a pillory as appeared in print." As María Carla Sánchez has written, it "mocks its own published format and satirizes the emergence of women writers."[7] Yet "A Sketch of a Blue Stocking," which may well be a companion piece to this story, presents the reader with the kind of figure that feminist critics have long searched for in vain in nineteenth-century women's writings: a successful writer who is also happy, married, and even a mother. Sedgwick clearly wrote the sketch to counter popular perceptions of the dreaded bluestocking as a "mannish" "literary Amazon." Why, one wonders, has the negative story been so often republished when the more positive one has been forgotten?

Another common notion that women were not self-reflective about their method of writing or their aesthetic values is also challenged by many of the texts included here. Although few women writers engaged in the kind of extended self-examinations of their authorial roles that we find in Hawthorne's and Henry James's prefaces, throughout the century they reflected on the act of literary or artistic production by themselves or other women, as well as on the field of American literature generally. Thus the texts collected here by Alice Cary, Sarah Hale, Harriet Beecher Stowe, Sarah Orne Jewett, Elizabeth Stuart Phelps, Anna Julia Cooper, Victoria

Earle Matthews, and Pauline Hopkins belie the prevalent assumption, and sometimes their own self-portrayal, that women's writing was simply a natural, even un-self-conscious act and therefore void of theoretical underpinning. Famous female authors were asked to write autobiographies reflecting on their long careers. Successful writers published advice essays for the benefit of aspiring ones. Especially as the century came to a close, women wrote historical overviews of white or African American women's accomplishments in literature. Throughout the century, they wrote prefaces explaining the circumstances or motivations behind their works or situating them in the context of prevailing discourses of literary aesthetics and value. They often used fiction as an opportunity to challenge patriarchal assumptions about female authorship or literature. Their poetry participated in metalyric traditions, musing on the nature of inspiration or on how gender complicated the poet's role. Their private letters reveal the ambitions they sometimes hid from the public. And the periodical press abounds with examples of women's critical analyses of the literary world.

Writing is at once the most solitary and the most communal of acts. Putting pen to paper can arouse the keenest self-awareness as well as the profoundest sense of interacting with the outside world. Because women were routinely encouraged to stifle their individuality and refrain from participating in the public sphere, it may seem a wonder that they ever picked up their pens to begin with. Nonetheless, for many, the urge to create, comment, observe, or reflect was a natural part of their lives and simply too strong to stifle. They therefore developed a number of strategies for legitimating their supposed trespasses on male territory, just as male writers adopted a variety of authorial poses that were, scholars have argued, formulated in partial response to women's perceived prominence in the literary marketplace.[8]

In the women's texts collected here, we can see, in addition to sentimental constructions of authorship as a moral duty and an extension of the family circle, strains of republican nation-building, evangelical Protestantism's emphasis on individual vocation, romantic notions of artistic genius, Transcendentalist individualism, more modern theories of professionalization, the realist's approach to collecting everyday materials, as well as desires to contribute to racial uplift or women's advancement or regional pride. In texts by successful white writers, unknown authors, young female factory workers, middle-class African Americans, freed or escaped slaves, Native Americans, immigrants, and women from the Northeast, South, Midwest, and West, writing is portrayed variously as hard work, pastime, disease, habit, calling, financial necessity, lifesaver and/or sanity-preserver, religious act, natural force, art, foolish or vain endeavor, moral imperative, business venture, and guilty pleasure. A single composite portrait of women's authorship in nineteenth-century America does not emerge from these texts (many of them reprinted for the first time since their original publications). Instead, taken together, these texts represent a multifaceted debate that was carried on throughout the century about the justifications for and merits or liabilities of female authorship. The terms of the debate shifted in interesting ways over the course of the century as women's general access to education and their confidence as authors and contributors to a national culture gained momentum, yet many central issues persisted.

The Itch to Write

Especially after the 1830s, as book and periodical publishing became a lucrative business and an increasingly literate (and among the middle- and upper-classes, leisured) populace demanded more and more reading material, the opportunities for writing and publishing abounded. The unprecedented access of women (Euro-American and African American) to the written word as producers and consumers, coupled with the explosive growth of the publishing industry, was a revolutionary event in human history. Publishing provided an outlet and a platform for women's voices and the most potent tool they had to shape their own lives and their society. As Linda Grasso has noted, "Excluded from institutionalized avenues of power, women writers use the literary realm to claim self, home, educational opportunity, racial equality, economic security, and imaginative autonomy in a nation that denies them their rights and privileges as citizens."[9] Therefore, when we examine women's roles as authors, we investigate the ways that women challenged (implicitly or explicitly) their exclusion from the rights of democratic and cultural citizenship. To be a published author meant fundamentally to be a participant in the life of the nation.

The magazine industry was particularly important to women's growing access to authorship, and, as Amy Beth Aronson has written, "Through formal dynamics, discursive practices, and popular presence, [women's] magazines created the first viable opportunities [for women] to subvert and redress the problems of women's silence in the public realm."[10] Helen Gray Cone concluded in 1890, "The encouragement of the great magazines, from the first friendly to women writers, is an important factor in their development." Cone singled out the high literary periodicals, *Harper's Monthly* and the *Atlantic*, but the proliferation of regional, women's, and African American magazines also provided steady work for female writers and editors. The editor of *Godey's Lady's Book*, Sarah Josepha Hale, was the most influential woman editor of the nineteenth century, using her "Editor's Table" column to set standards for women's roles as well as for men's and women's literature. But she was not alone. Patricia Okker has discovered six hundred female editors of nineteenth-century American magazines, many of whom wrote much of the content.[11] Many of the authors represented in this anthology were editors or editorial assistants as well.

As Okker's numbers suggest, writing and publishing comprised a field of cultural production to which women had significant access. "The boundaries of the cultural field," in the words of Richard S. Lowry, "are much more permeable than those of other fields; there are no established career tracks, no partnerships or degrees that confirm one's professional success."[12] Thus, it is not surprising to find women seizing the economic and cultural opportunities that the publishing business, more than any other profession or field of culture, provided to them without requiring the kind of rigorous, extended education that elite males received. It is also not surprising that some male writers were annoyed to find so many women competing with them for an audience and therefore for money and cultural authority; such competition occurred in virtually no other occupation or industry.

It is impossible to gauge the number of men and women who published in the nineteenth century if we include aspiring and anonymous writers. But as more female names (real or pseudonymous) were found among magazine contributors' lists, and their identities became public knowledge, women's desire to write and publish spread. The rhetoric of disease used in discussions about the rise of authorship suggests the anxieties attendant upon such an increase, as in this quip from *The Southern Literary Messenger*: "In these days, . . . the press is constantly teeming, and the cacoethes scribendi is a disease so wide-spread, as to call loudly for some Jenner who may suggest a preventive like vaccination." The term *cacoethes scribendi,* meaning the "itch to write," derives from the Latin *cacoethes,* meaning "an ill habit or propensity."[13]

While many men, in addition to Hawthorne, lamented the outbreak of female authorship, it is at first glance ironic how many women, themselves successful authors, did as well, most notably, Judith Sargent Murray in her poem "The Rage for Writing" (1801) and Sedgwick in her story "Cacoethes Scribendi" (1830). But even those pieces that portray women writers as silly or foolish or warn young women against taking up the pen can be read as implicit efforts to set the writer apart from such popular images of female authorship, much like George Eliot's famous essay "Silly Novels by Lady Novelists" (1856).[14] Many such works are not necessarily critical of women's writing per se but critical of certain kinds of women's writing, such as Margaret Fuller's review "Miss Barrett's Poems" (1848), Alice B. Neal's essay "American Female Authorship" (1852), Mary E. Bryan's "How Should Women Write?" (1870), Mary Kyle Dallas's "Women in Literature" (1871), and Phoebe Cary's "Advice Gratis to Certain Women" (1873). These texts suggest that not only male critics were concerned about preserving literature as an exclusive, if not exactly elite, activity. The numerous articles and stories warning foolish or inexperienced women away from the field of authorship or informing them of the hard work required for a successful career should be understood not merely as ironic acts but as efforts to preserve the status these writers had achieved. They understood that women writers were often categorized as a group, or even a "mob," and feared the diminution of the status of all women writers as the field of authorship widened. They may not have wished to close the gates on other women aspiring to join their ranks, but they seem to have desired to keep their ranks relatively small and thus more esteemed. To be a member of a "damned mob," they undoubtedly understood, meant certain banishment to literary obscurity.

Some even directly challenged the notion that women were in fact invading the arena of print culture in large numbers, as Caroline Kirkland did in her essay "Literary Women" (1850): "How many literary women has any one person ever seen? How many has the world seen? . . . The spite which is generally nourished against these unhappy ladies implies great respect; for their numbers are too insignificant to attract notice." But by 1867, Elizabeth Stuart Phelps, in her essay, "What Shall They Do?" painted a very different picture: "It is not strange, but it is sorrowful, to see in what crowds the women, married and unmarried, flock to the gates of authorship. Here and there you see them with white hands of command turning back the ponderous golden hinges and entering in where the palms are, and the crowns. Down below they are turning away in great sad groups, shut out." Instead of an unruly mob attacking or threatening the field of literature, women are portrayed as being turned away in great numbers. While a few have gained entrance through the pearly gates, the invading mob that Hawthorne described has instead been "shut out" and told to go home. In both cases, Kirkland and Phelps challenged the male construction of women's entrance into the literary field and thereby helped preserve the notion that their achievements were rare and thus valuable.

Answering the Critics

Many women's texts on authorship reveal the extent to which the acts of writing and publication challenged nineteenth-century American culture's most fundamental ideas about women and how seriously female authors took their critics' objections. One writer for the *North American Review* claimed in 1851 that "the time is gone by for" "some gruff remark upon misdirected talents, and the concocting of puddings being the appropriate sphere of feminine intellect."[15] Yet, as late as 1895, the western writer Kate Cleary spoofed the still-common portrayal of women writers: "'She is prouder of her pork pies than of her poems.'" Throughout the century women felt compelled to justify to themselves and their readers the motivations behind their ventures into print, the value of their works, and their right to devote their private time to writing and to publish their works for public consumption. Particularly in the 1850s, just as critics had reached the conclusion that too many women had ventured into print, female writers felt the need to defend themselves against the accusations emanating from the periodical press. In some cases, they were overtly defensive, such as Ann S. Stephens in "Women of Genius" (1839), "Leila" in her essay "Critics and Criticism" (1855), or Thrace Talmon, who responded to Thomas De Quincey's assertion that a woman would never produce great art in

"The Latest Crusade. Lady Authors and Their Critics" (1857). In a few cases, a writer took the offensive, as did Fanny Fern in her mock review of her own book, *Fresh Leaves* (1857). In most cases, however, we can see the more subtle influence of years of invectives against the bluestocking, that ever-present scarecrow, the "unfeminine and arrogant Amazon"[16] with which nearly all women writers feared being equated. To be "literary" or "learned" meant somehow to be less of a woman, a charge that female writers battled throughout the century.

Another effective attack was to claim the futility of women's aspirations, such as the following statement from a writer hiding behind the nom de plume "Il Sectario": "It is strictly true that the entire mass of what female authorship has produced, might be struck out of existence without ever being missed in the permanent learning of the world."[17] Such pejorative rhetoric clearly affected many women who aspired to recognition, and some were inclined to accept the judgment against them. Susan Elston Wallace gave up writing in part, she claimed, because "I do not believe the world will ever produce a feminine Shakspeare [*sic*] or Milton." Sarah Hale concurred but with a difference in *Godey's Lady's Book* (1857). While disclaiming that women were the competitors of men in the literary field, she staked out a different and, she believed, superior field for women writers, concluding, "Why should women wish to be or to do or to write like men? Is not the feminine genius the most angel-like?" In another refutation of women's literary inferiority, Stowe assured her female readers in "How Shall I Learn to Write?" (1869) that they "may have subject matter of peculiar weight and importance—subject matter which woman, and only woman, could possibly be able to present." By the 1880s, however, Helen Gray Cone would declare that the day for such separate literary spheres was at an end. Women, she believed, had fully entered into the mainstream of American literature: "the distinction of sex is lost in the distinction of schools." Her assessment may have been overly optimistic, but it certainly represents an altered perception of women's place in the field of letters.

The business side of the literary enterprise also posed a problem for women, particularly middle- and upper-class white women, as prevailing notions of the feminine dictated aloofness from such endeavors. Although the act of publication was often construed as an entrance into the male terrain of the "public sphere" and the world of business, women writers found a variety of ways to overcome this barrier. Some, like Fern in "A Practical Blue-Stocking," countered such perceptions by portraying women writers who could succeed in the business of publishing while maintaining their femininity. Others disavowed agency in the act of publishing. If their works had been spirited away by others and later appeared in print, how could they be to blame? Or, they could claim financial necessity as their primary motivation, as did Lydia Sigourney, E.D.E.N. Southworth, and Rose Terry Cooke's fictional Matilda Muffin. Gail Hamilton refused to fall back on such justifications when she wrote to the editor of the *National Era* asking him to employ her as a contributor: "It is quite useless to mention the agency of friends in inducing me to this step, as you have probably heard that a thousand times, and moreover all the friends in the world could not move me to it against my own sweet will. Neither do I write entirely for money, . . . I want an end and aim in life, and see no other way to obtain it." Yet, she insisted on retaining her anonymity: "my happiness in life will be blotted out forever if this circumstance should ever come to the eyes or ears of any of my friends."

The desire for privacy among women writers was widespread, in large part as a way to shield oneself from the disdain directed at one who, in the words of Grace Greenwood, in "Letter I. To an Unrecognized Poetess," "turns out the 'silver lining' of her soul to the world's gaze." The numbers of women who published anonymously or under pseudonyms is impossible to determine, but it is clear that it was quite large. Sedgwick published nearly all of her works without her name on them. Sigourney published anonymously for eighteen years, until her identity became known. Maria Cummins, author of the runaway best seller *The Lamplighter* (which Hawthorne specifically castigated), also published anonymously. Many also took pseudonyms: Marion Harland (Mary Virginia Terhune), Elizabeth Wetherell (Susan Warner), Gail Hamilton (Mary Abigail Dodge), Fanny Fern (Sara Payson Willis Parton), Grace Greenwood (Sara Jane Clarke Lippincott), and Charles Egbert Craddock (Mary Murfree) were some of the most famous. Other writers included in this anthology who adopted pseudonyms or published anonymously include Judith Sargent Murray, Caroline Kirkland, Harriet Jane Farley, Alice B. Neal, Thrace Talmon, Zitkala-Ša, Eliza Earle, Elizabeth Oakes Smith, and Adah Isaacs Menken, as well as the poets who signed themselves "Tabitha," "Ella," and "Egeria" and thus remain hidden to this day.

Such widespread desire for anonymity is emblematic of what Mary Kelley has deemed "an implicit recognition of wrongdoing, of guilt, perhaps of shame" by "secret writers" who wanted to remain private women even as their works were carried into the public marketplace. By crafting a public persona for their works, however, female authors were also managing their careers. *The Lamplighter, The Wide, Wide World,* and *Ruth Hall* elicited widespread speculation about their authors' identities that boosted sales.[18] While Fern, in particular, had good reasons to want to remain undiscovered, it is also well known that she chose her pseudonym as a kind of spoof of the flowery, alliterative names adopted by many women writers, which were themselves a kind of branding. Cooke's story about Matilda Muffin pokes fun at this tradition by claiming that this is actually her real name, not made up as her readers suppose. Other writers certainly enjoyed the shield that anonymity provided to allow them to chart new territories in their work. Hamilton and Fern used the freedom their pen names afforded to write more forthrightly and satirically than any other women writers of their era. Others, like Harriet Prescott Spofford and Rebecca Harding Davis published break-out stories in the *Atlantic Monthly*, which in its early years published all pieces anonymously, affording Spofford and Davis a space to publish stories that were atypical for women writers of their day.

The issue of anonymity was often more crucial for African American women writers, some of whom fictionalized their autobiographies, created personas under other names, and wrote in the third person in order to hide their identities and "resist commodification."[19] For both Harriet Jacobs—who used the name Linda Brent for her autobiography, *Incidents in the Life of a Slave Girl*—and Harriet Wilson—who called herself "Frado" in her novelized account of her servitude, *Our Nig*—the discovery of their identities could have meant further persecution for themselves or their friends. So successful were their disguises that only in recent years have their authorship and the autobiographical nature of their narratives been established.

Some white female authors attempted to circumvent prescriptions for women's texts by adopting male personas, as did Lydia Maria Child in the preface to her first novel, *Hobomok* (1824). Yet the phenomenon of adopting a male pen name was a relatively uncommon occurrence in America as compared to the famous examples of George Sand, Currer Bell, and George Eliot abroad. The most successful disguise was that of Mary Murfree, who for years had convinced her editors and the public that she was Charles Egbert Craddock, author of rough stories set in the Tennessee mountains. Others included Elizabeth Oakes Smith (Ernest Helfenstein), Helen Hunt Jackson (Saxe Holm and the ambiguous H.H.), Louisa May Alcott (A. M. Barnard), and Harriet Beecher Stowe (Christopher Crowfield).

In addition to working against the presumption that the artist must be male, women writers of color had to confront the prejudice that the artist or author must be white. For these authors, the weight of critical prejudice was an even heavier burden to overcome. Assertions of accomplishment by their sister-writers were prevalent in African American women's writings and can be seen as a response to critics who discount the possibility of women of color producing literature of value as well as a spur to younger writers to create works that will elicit the admiration of the mainstream culture. Frances Harper's sketch "Fancy Etchings" (1873) and her poem "Songs for the People" (1895), as well as essays by Anna Julia Cooper (1892) and Victoria Earle Matthews (1895), insist that literary pursuits are not solely for one's own pleasure or gain but for the benefit of one's race. While white women writers challenged men's negative portrayals of bluestockings and "strong-minded" ladies, women writers of color also countered the stereotypical or maligned depictions of Native American and African American women and men. Examples in this anthology include the pseudonymous "Leila" writing for the *Cherokee Rose Buds* (1855), Anna Julia Cooper's "The Negro as Presented in American Literature" (1892),

E. Pauline Johnson's "A Strong Race Opinion: On the Indian Girl in Modern Fiction" (1892), and Priscilla Jane Thompson's poem "The Song" (1900). For these writers, the power of self-representation is central to the act of authorship.

The charge leveled by cultural critics that women's appearance in print was the result of a self-seeking and vain desire for notoriety was especially damaging to their sense of femininity as well as their claim to respect as authors and thus was most vigorously challenged. Women writers asserted time and again in their prefaces and autobiographical writings that others encouraged them to publish, that they had little hope of success, that they did not believe their work had much merit but if it could do any good, and so on. But perhaps the most compelling argument against women writers' vanity was the claim of divine inspiration, an assertion that stemmed from the evangelical Christian beliefs pervading nineteenth-century American culture. Rather than demand their right to pursue individual fulfillment or recognition, many women drew strength from evangelical Protestantism, which encouraged self-determination, perfectionism, and a one-on-one relationship with God.

The high value placed on discovering one's vocation or special God-given talents within evangelical Protestantism led many women to look beyond their domestic duties for their higher calling. In her study of spinsterhood in nineteenth-century New England, Zsuzsa Berend found that many women who chose to remain single did not do so out of a modern desire for self-actualization; rather, they sought a vocation instead of marriage as a way of "exercising the autonomy of a moral agent, responsible to her God . . . Female self-direction, in the world of nineteenth-century spinsters, was not an ultimate good but a stepping stone to a life of usefulness and service, a life in accordance with God's purposes."[20] This same emphasis on the right to pursue authorship because it is one's duty to develop her God-given capabilities in the service of humanity fueled the careers of women writers of all races. "The pen is ours to wield," the white Quaker poet Eliza Earle proclaimed; to write was a solemn responsibility granted by God. As Frances Smith Foster has shown, African American women "who converted to Christianity (and virtually every extant text was written by a professed Christian) took seriously the biblical injunction to 'write the vision, and make it plain' (Hab. 2:2). They used the Word as both a tool and a weapon to correct, to create, and to confirm their visions of life as it was and as it could become."[21] Maria Stewart's introduction to "Religion and the Pure Principles of Morality, the Sure Foundation on Which We Must Build" (1835) is a prime example.

Perhaps the most famous example of divine inspiration comes from Harriet Beecher Stowe, who claimed in her 1879 preface to *Uncle Tom's Cabin,* "I did not write it. God wrote it. I merely did his dictation." This quote, and others like it, often have been dismissed by critics as evidence of self-effacement and the minimizing of artistic ambition. Seen another way, however, the claims that Stowe and many other women writers made to divine inspiration bespeak not merely humility but the belief in oneself and one's access to creative powers. The many tributes to a divine muse written by female poets—the claim to a mysterious, otherworldly source of inspiration that can be found in poems by Sigourney, Dickinson, Elizabeth Stoddard, Adah Isaacs Menken, and Henrietta Cordelia Ray, all of whom drew at least in part on romantic constructions of the poet—and the many prefaces by women declaring a higher authority for their creations, stake out a territory for women writers beyond the reach of men, or, in the case of African American women writers, beyond the reach of white critics. Reminiscent of Margaret Fuller's argument in *Woman in the Nineteenth Century* that "to one Master only are [women] accountable"—namely, God, not man—this maneuver is a way of sidestepping men's or mainstream culture's influence and criticism in favor of a higher authority.[22]

The authors in this anthology also often describe creativity as a natural force under pressure—even volcanic (much like the imagery in many of Dickinson's poems)—which cannot be suppressed. For instance, Adah Isaacs Menken declared in her poem "Genius" (1873),

> I hear people speak of "unfortunate genius," of "poets who never penned their inspirations;" that
> "Some mute inglorious Milton here may rest;"
> of "unappreciated talent," and "malignant stars," and other contradictory things.
> It is all nonsense.
> Where power exists, it cannot be suppressed any more than the earthquake can be smothered.
> As well attempt to seal up the crater of Vesuvius as to hide God's given power of the soul.

By naturalizing the creative impulse, these writers recast the terms about what comprised woman's inherent nature and thus her appropriate sphere. Stephens, in "Women of Genius," and Harper, in "Fancy Etchings," also celebrate creative power for its own sake, as a natural resource for women, one that does not make them more like men but is simply an integral part of their identities that cannot be denied.

During and after the Civil War, as women from many backgrounds ventured into previously male realms of public space—acting as postmistresses, running businesses, working in hospitals—and increasing numbers of women did not have the opportunity to marry or simply chose not to, the fact of women's authorship became more acceptable. Many women writers strayed from claims of religious or moral authority, choosing devotion to art over service to others and aspiring to participate in the high literary culture that Hawthorne helped initiate. The bifurcation between high/masculine and low/feminine literary culture, which his epithet against the "damned mob" encapsulates for many scholars, was not yet firmly established in the middle decades of the century. By the 1860s, many women desired the recognition that had been achieved by a few illustrious women of genius, the "white hands of command" that Phelps described as having entered "where the palms are, and the crowns." In addition to Harriet Beecher Stowe's cultural legacy, Phelps was no doubt referring to Charlotte Brontë, Elizabeth Barrett Browning, and George Eliot in England, as well as Madame de Staël and George Sand in France. The many tributes written to these authors and their Greek predecessor Sappho—as in work by "Egeria," Elizabeth Oakes Smith, Dickinson, Phelps, and Margaret Junkin Preston—attest to their profound influence in providing another model of the female author, one predicated on de Staël's claim that "genius has no sex." Such a view, an inheritance from Enlightenment ideologies of sexual equality as well as romantic conceptions of an androgynous genius, had inspired American women as early as the late eighteenth century; however, it also took the ferment of democratic rhetoric, Protestant evangelicalism, American exceptionalism, Transcendental idealism, and the rise of a literary print culture (with prestigious periodicals such as *Harper's Monthly* and the *Atlantic*) for women to perceive of their authorial identities as taking precedence over their roles as wives and mothers.[23] Thus the women writers who responded to the exclusion of women from the *Atlantic Monthly*'s celebration of poet John Greenleaf Whittier's seventieth birthday in 1877 (see "Mr. Houghton's Mistake" and "The Atlantic-Whittier Dinner—A Woman's Thoughts Thereof") both claim that women had earned the right to be seated next to men at the banquet table as well as in the upper echelons of the literary establishment.

Domesticity and Authorship

At the heart of many discussions of female authorship—by men and women—was the issue of whether or not women could conduct careers as authors and still fulfill their duties as wives and mothers, duties upon which the cohesiveness of society was deemed to depend. In the antebellum era, while male critics used this issue as their primary argument against women's writing, many women responded vociferously that they could be simultaneously mothers, wives, and authors. Ann S. Stephens wrote in 1839, "That the distinguished women of our country are remarkable for domestic qualities, admits of proof, from many brilliant examples. Most of those who stand foremost in our world of letters, perform the duties of wives, mothers and housekeepers, in connexion with the pursuits of mind." The strategy of domesticating the woman writer was designed to allay fears that as women became authors they would abandon their domestic posts. Sedgwick's and Fern's bluestocking sketches also depict literary women who maintain their femininity and keep happy homes.

However, while this argument certainly seems like capitulation to the dominant ideology of true womanhood, it was also a powerful claim to the right to authorship. For to indicate otherwise would be to mark the realm of literature as off-limits to the vast majority of women who did marry and have children. Rather than proclaim a literary career as accessible to only a select few women who had the time and energy to devote to it, many claimed that writing could be woven into the fabric of women's everyday lives. The metaphor here is an apt one, as many female poets, such as Sigourney, Lucy Larcom, Harriet Prescott Spofford, Stoddard, Preston, and Cooke, used weaving, spinning, and sewing as allegories of women's writing. In her autobiography, Sigourney also described her method of composing as complementary to the act of knitting: "How to obtain time to appease editorial appetites, and not neglect my housekeeping tactics, was a study. I found the employment of knitting congenial to the contemplation and treatment of the slight themes that were desired, and, while completing fifteen or sometimes twenty pairs of stockings yearly for our large family, or for the poor, stopped the needles to arrest the wings of a flying thought or a flowing stanza."

As the century wore on, more women began to declare that the combination of domestic responsibilities and authorship was impossible. Phelps's novel *The Story of Avis* (1877) sparked a firestorm of debate for its portrayal of the downfall of a woman artist's ambition with her surrender to a man who promised to honor her work but failed to support her.[24] Postbellum stories in this collection by Stoddard, Rebecca Harding Davis, and Dunbar-Nelson all posit women's literary or artistic careers as impossible within the context of household duties or marriage. The point here was not capitulation to conservative critics; rather, growing pessimism on this score suggests a shift in conceptions of authorship as more women saw writing as either an art that requires tremendous concentration or a career demanding much more time and energy than a mother can spare. While Sigourney claimed that a woman could find snatches of time to write, she also admitted that her mode of writing was "fatal to literary ambition. It prevents that labor of thought by which intellectual eminence is acquired." Alice Williams Brotherton's poem "To E. M. T." (1887) suggests a similar equation of motherhood with a lesser form of literary accomplishment: "A brief way up Parnassus's slope, / Only, I may go: / Held by clasp of little fingers." Augusta Jane Evans wrote to her friend Rachel Lyons in 1860, "No loving Wife and Mother can sit down and serve two Masters; Fame and Love." She thus claimed she would never marry, although she did eight years later.

Many female authors who did marry declined in literary productivity after their marriages, as Evans did. In some cases, husbands' disapproval affected their careers, as in the case of Sigourney, Preston, and Julia Ward Howe. Others devoted themselves to literary careers only after their husbands' deaths, as did Alice B. Neal, Hale, Harper, Fern, Cooper, Kate Chopin, and Southworth (in her case, after her husband abandoned her). Many, however, wrote significant works while they were married, including Child, Stephens, Elizabeth Oakes Smith, Frances Osgood, Caroline Kirkland, Caroline Lee Hentz, Spofford, Stoddard, Piatt, Stowe, Susette La

Flesche Tibbles, Davis, Mary Hallock Foote, Elia Wilkinson Peattie, Gertrude
Bustill Mossell, and Annie Nathan Meyer. Some were even inspired and supported
by their husbands. However, many of the more ambitious women writers of the
postbellum generation eschewed traditional marriages, some choosing to remain
single for their entire lives (Sedgwick, the Cary sisters, Hamilton, Alcott, Dickinson, Larcom, Lazarus, Woolson, Henrietta Cordelia Ray, and Grace King), others
marrying late (Fuller, Phelps, Cooke, Evans, and Mary Wilkins Freeman) or engag-
ing in "Boston marriages" with like-minded women (such as Sarah Orne Jewett's
with Annie Fields). In virtually all cases, however, the choices women writers made
about their relationships and household arrangements were pivotal to their careers
and influenced their literary works.

Editorial Decisions

I have selected texts using a variety of criteria. First and foremost, I have striven
for diversity in content, genre, and authors. My aim is to do justice to the historical record and to recreate the broad spectrum of voices that proliferated in the
nineteenth-century press. Voices private and public; conservative and progressive;
outspoken and diffident; religious and secular; upper-, middle- and lower-class;
mainstream and outsider; famous, unknown, and anonymous; Anglo, immigrant,
Native, African American, and Asian American; professional and amateur; northern, southern, and western are all represented here.

The deeper into this project I waded, the more overwhelmed I was by the sheer
number of women's texts on the subject of authorship. I collected hundreds of texts,
only 153 of which made the final cut. The choices I have had to make have been in
some cases quite difficult. I have chosen not to include excerpts of novels, such as
Fern's *Ruth Hall* (1854), Phelps's *The Story of Avis* (1877), Evans's *St. Elmo* (1866),
Helen Hunt Jackson's *Mercy Philbrick's Choice* (1876), Alcott's *Little Women* (1868),
Chopin's *The Awakening* (1899), and Harper's *Iola Leroy* (1892). All of these novels,
with the exception of Jackson's, are available in reprint editions and would make
excellent supplements to this anthology.

In the reproduction of texts, I have chosen to present them exactly as they were
originally published. In the case of misspellings or in other instances in which the
reader may perceive that an error has been introduced, I have inserted [*sic*] into the
text. I have tried, whenever possible, to reproduce texts in their entirety. However,
due to space considerations and a desire to include as many different texts as possible, I have excised portions of some. In making cuts, however, I have tried to select
redundant or tangential passages that do not contribute to the overall interest or
meaning of the text.

Overall, this anthology reflects my desire to give readers access to lesser-known
texts and voices alongside more familiar ones and thereby offer a broader spectrum

of women's attitudes toward authorship than the prevailing perception of "no happy woman ever writes." Such choices, I hope, will offer a corrective to the assumption that to write and publish was necessarily a painful or stressful activity for nine-teenth-century American women. Certainly, there is still plenty of grief in these pages. But what I hope readers will see is that women writers employed many ratio-nales for their ventures into print and reacted to their fame or failure in a variety of ways. As Susan S. Williams has argued, it is time to acknowledge the multiple authorial roles that women adopted, sometimes even at different times in their careers (and, I would argue, sometimes within the very same work).[25]

Again, Susan Elston Wallace's career after she had convinced herself to "bury pen and paper at once" is instructive. In the preface to her collection of travel sketches, *The Storied Sea* (1883), she wrote of her "dear" readers who have been "a constant companion grown into an abiding presence."[26] The confidence and plea-sure this preface exhibits suggests Wallace had come a long way since the nadir of her "weak-minded" days. The discovery of her later fulfillment as an author has taught me that no single statement can sum up how women felt about writing, not even for the individual who wrote it. While so many nineteenth-century women expressed ambivalence or even defeatism about their projects as authors, the sheer number and variety of their literary productions convey their ultimate triumph over those who would condemn them as a "damned mob of scribbling women."

Notes

1. Nathaniel Hawthorne, Letter to William D. Ticknor, Jan. 19, 1855, in *Hidden Hands: An Anthology of American Women Writers, 1790–1870,* ed. Lucy M. Freibert and Barbara A. White (New Brunswick, NJ: Rutgers University Press, 1985), 356–57.

2. Fanny Fern, *Ruth Hall and Other Writings,* ed. Joyce Warren (New Brunswick, NJ: Rutgers University Press, 1986), 175.

3. Ann D. Wood, "The 'Scribbling Women' and Fanny Fern: Why Women Wrote," *American Quarterly* 23 (Spring 1971): 7.

4. See *Shakespeare's Sisters: Feminist Essays on Women Poets,* ed. Sandra M. Gilbert and Susan Gubar (Bloomington: Indiana University Press, 1979). On "Melville's sister," see Elaine Showalter, "American Gynocriticism," *American Literary History* 5, no. 1 (1993): 113–15.

5. Sandra Gilbert and Susan Gubar, *Madwoman in the Attic: The Woman Writer and the Nineteenth-Century Literary Imagination,* 2d ed. (New Haven, CT: Yale University Press, 2000), 60. Mary Kelley, *Private Woman, Public Stage: Literary Domesticity in Nineteenth-Century America* (New York: Oxford University Press, 1984), 111. In a similar vein, Tillie Olsen's *Silences* (New York: Delacorte, 1978) examined the forces that limited women's liter-ary production or creativity in the nineteenth century.

6. Susan Elston Wallace, "Another Weak-Minded Woman. A Confession," *Harper's* (1867). This essay and the other nineteenth-century women's texts mentioned in the intro-duction are included in this anthology, unless otherwise noted.

xxx Introduction

7. María Carla Sánchez, "'Prayers in the Market Place': Women and Low Culture in Catharine Sedgwick's 'Cacoethes Scribendi,'" *American Transcendental Quarterly* 16, no. 2 (2002): 106.

8. See, for instance, Richard S. Lowry, *"Littery Man": Mark Twain and Modern Authorship* (New York, Oxford University Press, 1996), 85.

9. Linda Grasso, *The Artistry of Anger: Black and White Women's Literature in America, 1820–1860* (Chapel Hill: University of North Carolina Press, 2002), 23.

10. Amy Beth Aronson, *Taking Liberties: Early American Women's Magazines and Their Readers* (Westport, CT: Praeger, 2002), 12.

11. Patricia Okker, *Our Sister Editors: Sarah J. Hale and the Tradition of Nineteenth-Century American Women Editors* (Athens: University of Georgia Press, 1995).

12. Lowry, *"Littery Man,"* 8.

13. "The Literary Miser," *Southern Literary Messenger* 13 (Dec. 1847): 759. *Putnam's Home Cyclopedia,* vol. 2: *Hand-Book of Literature and the Fine Arts,* ed. George Ripley and Bayard Taylor (New York: G. P. Putnam, 1852), 50.

14. George Eliot, "Silly Novels by Lady Novelists," *Westminster Review* 66 (Oct. 1856): 442–61.

15. "Female Authors," *North American Review* 72 (Jan. 1851): 152.

16. "Editor's Easy Chair," *Harper's* 68 (March 1884): 640.

17. Il Sectario, "American Letters: Their Character and Advancement," *American Whig Review* 1 (June 1845): 577. (This page is numbered wrong; it comes after page 580.)

18. Kelley, *Private Woman, Public Stage,* 128. For a discussion of the "open secret" of Cummins's authorship of *The Lamplighter,* see Susan S. Williams, *Reclaiming Authorship: Literary Women in America, 1850–1900* (Philadelphia: University of Pennsylvania Press, 2006), 73–74.

19. Carla L. Peterson, *"Doers of the Word": African-American Women Speakers and Writers in the North, 1830–1880* (New York: Oxford University Press, 1995), 152.

20. Zsuzsa Berend, "'The Best or None!' Spinsterhood in Nineteenth-Century New England," *Journal of Social History* 33, no. 4 (2000): 942.

21. Frances Smith Foster, *Written By Herself: Literary Production by African American Women, 1746–1892* (Bloomington: Indiana University Press, 1993), 2.

22. Margaret Fuller, "Woman in the Nineteenth Century," in *The Essential Margaret Fuller,* ed. Jeffrey Steele (New Brunswick, NJ: Rutgers University Press, 1992), 261.

23. I develop these claims at length in *Writing for Immortality: Women and the Emergence of High Literary Culture in America* (Baltimore: Johns Hopkins University Press, 2004). Naomi Sofer, in *Making the "America of Art": Cultural Nationalism and Nineteenth-Century Women Writers* (Columbus: Ohio State University Press, 2005), also discusses women's artistic ambitions in the 1860s and after.

24. Elizabeth Stuart Phelps, *The Story of Avis,* ed. Carol Farley Kessler (1878; New Brunswick, NJ: Rutgers University Press, 1985).

25. Williams, *Reclaiming Authorship.*

26. Susan E. Wallace, *The Storied Sea* (Boston: James R. Osgood, 1883), v.

Wielding the Pen

🌿 Judith Sargent Murray (1751–1820)

Born into a wealthy seafaring family in Gloucester, Massachusetts, Judith Sargent received little formal education compared to her brother, who went to Harvard. In 1769 she married John Stevens, who died in 1787. The following year, she married John Murray, and they had one daughter, born in 1791. She had published her first work, a theological treatise, in 1782, albeit anonymously and only at the urging of friends. In the 1790s, she began to publish in earnest, many of the pieces having been written in the previous decade. She published essays on women's rights, plays, and poetry under the pen name Constantia. Murray was an ardent supporter of women's education, not only as preparation for the roles of wife and mother but also as a means to fit women for independence of thought and self-support. The following poem, on the same topic as Catharine Maria Sedgwick's short story "Cacoethes Scribendi" (1830), ridicules women who venture into print without sufficient education or intelligence.

The Rage for Writing

"Cacœthes Scribendi,"[1] is the rage,
And she's a genius, who can fill a page,
All to the field with the conscious strength repair,
With brains congenial to the arms they wear;
"Fire in each eye, and papers in each hand,
"They rave, recite, and madden round the land,"[2]
Alike professing all the self same end,
Vice to reform, and Virtue to defend;
Alike all strive each other to excell,
And most do *ill,* who *seem* intending well,
To whom is given a moderate share of sense,
To spell and write (tho' badly) shall commence
An "*Author,*" and the better to succeed,
In the first essay publishes a creed,
That passes current, and by which we guess
The principles, this riddle *would* express.
But so desultory seems the motley scrawl,
The maudlin meaning so equivocal,
That we might well these farrago's[3] regard

---

1. Latin: the itch to write.
2. Lines from Alexander Pope's *An Epistle to Dr. Arbuthnot* (1735).
3. A *farrago* is a confused medley of persons or things.

As written, and baptized afterward.
Writers like these would sooner gain their end
By writing *'gainst* the cause they would defend.

Source: Boston Gazette (1801)

ᛥ MERCY OTIS WARREN (1728–1814)

Mercy Otis received an exceptional education; she was tutored alongside her brothers, who were being prepared to attend Harvard. Her male family members and her husband, James Warren, whom she married in 1754 and with whom she had five sons, served in the Massachusetts House of Representatives and were vocal leaders of the American Revolution. Encouraged by her family as well as John Adams to use her considerable rhetorical talents in the service of the Revolution, Mercy anonymously published satiric and propagandistic letters, poems, and plays. As the following preface to her three-volume history of the Revolution indicates, her close associations with the era's leaders made her an important chronicler as well as contributor to the events that founded the nation. Yet she felt the need to pardon her intrusion into the male field of history.

An Address to the Inhabitants of the United States of America

At a period when every manly arm was occupied, and every trait of talent or activity engaged, either in the cabinet or the field, apprehensive, that amidst the sudden convulsions, crowded scenes, and rapid changes, that flowed in quick succession, many circumstances might escape the more busy and active members of society, I have been induced to improve the leisure Providence had lent, to record as they passed, in the following pages, the new and unexperienced events exhibited in a land previously blessed with peace, liberty, simplicity, and virtue.

As circumstances were collected, facts related, and characters drawn, many years antecedent to any history since published, relative to the dismemberment of the colonies, and to American independence, there are few allusions to any later writers.

Connected by nature, friendship, and every social tie, with many of the first patriots, and most influential characters on the continent; in the habits of confidential and epistolary intercourse with several gentlemen employed abroad in the most distinguished stations, and with others since elevated to the highest grades of rank and distinction, I had the best means of information, through a long period that the colonies were in suspense, waiting the operation of foreign courts, and the success of their own enterprising spirit.

The solemnity that covered every countenance, when contemplating the sword uplifted, and the horrors of civil war rushing to habitations not inured to scenes of rapine and misery; even to the quiet cottage, where only concord and affection had reigned; stimulated to observation a mind that had not yielded to the assertion, that all political attentions lay out of the road of female life.

It is true there are certain appropriate duties assigned to each sex; and doubtless it is the more peculiar province of masculine strength, not only to repel the bold invader of the rights of his country and of mankind, but in the nervous style of manly eloquence, to describe the blood-stained field, and relate the story of slaughtered armies.

Sensible of this, the trembling heart has recoiled at the magnitude of the undertaking, and the hand often shrunk back from the task; yet, recollecting that every domestic enjoyment depends on the unimpaired possession of civil and religious liberty, that a concern for the welfare of society ought equally to glow in every human breast, the work was not relinquished. The most interesting circumstances were collected, active characters portrayed, the principles of the times developed, and the changes marked; nor need it cause a blush to acknowledge, a detail was preserved with a view of transmitting it to the rising youth of my country, some of them in infancy, others in the European world, while the most interesting events lowered over their native land.

Conscious that truth has been the guide of my pen, and candor, as well as justice, the accompaniment of my wishes through every page, I can say, with an ingenious writer, "I have used my pen with the liberty of one, who neither hopes nor fears, nor has any interest in the success or failure of any party, and who speaks to posterity—perhaps very far remote." . . .

Not indifferent to the opinion of the world, nor servilely courting its smiles, no further apology is offered for the attempt, though many may be necessary, for the incomplete execution of a design, that had rectitude for its basis, and a beneficent regard for the civil and religious rights of mankind, for its motive. . . .

Source: History of the Rise, Progress and Termination of the American Revolution (1805)

❧ "Tabitha" (?–?)

The poem below, signed simply "Tabitha," was prefaced with: "The following verses in a female hand, are gladly welcomed, and obtain a ready place in the Evening Post. The editor laments that the fair authoress should consider his remarks in Saturday's paper, that 'masculine vigor' is rather to be looked for from man than woman, as intended to undervalue the female understanding. Her's [sic] is the empire of persuasion and blandishments, of smiles and tears, and as long as she is irresistible here, why should she desire also to show her superior prowess elsewhere?" At the conclusion of the poem, the editor included Thomas Moore's translation of the Greek poet Anacreon's "Ode 24," which "will better and fully express my meaning, and I hope make my peace with the indignant poetress [sic]." The concluding lines of Anacreon's poem are, "Woman! be fair, we must adore thee; / Smile, and a world is weak before thee."

Advice to Female Poets

Occasioned by the Editorial remarks on the lines signed Harriet, in Saturday's Evening Post.[1]

In vain thy numbers sweetly flow;
   In vain the rays of genius shine;
For where so e'er thy verses go,
   Where e'er they shed their beams Divine,

From thee, the bay shall be withheld,
   And man shall steal the meed of praise;
The female mind to earth is fell'd,
   Depriv'd of all its heav'nly rays.

If meagre runs thy feeble line,
   Constrain'd, and heavy, void of grace;
Proud man will own the verses thine,
   But wisely, show thee out of place.

---

1. "Sonnet" (a tribute to Lord Byron) by "Harriet" appeared in the *New York Evening Post* with the following editorial preface: "The following beautiful lines, received this morning, from some unknown hand, evince the spirit of true poetry; but are, I think, dictated by a masculine vigor, hardly reconcileable [*sic*] with their signature."

Then take a hint of heavenly lore,
    If weak, be humble and retir'd,
And if thou own'st a richer store,
    Conceal, nor hope to be admir'd.

Source: New York Evening Post (1817)

❧ "Ella" (?–?)

The following poem, signed only "Ella,"[1] imparts a familiar argument made in favor of women's intellectual development in the Early Republic, namely, that an era of enlightenment would enable women to reach their potential in order to better fulfill their roles as mothers. Thus education for women would not challenge the existing social order.

Female Literature

The voice of Sidney[2] is not raised in vain—
A sympathising muse resumes the strain,
"That female genius, female talents claim,
An equal right to culture and to fame;"
To share the praise of every mental grace,
That raises and adorns the human race.

O for an age of chivalry again,
To renovate the race of generous men!
Of men whose favorite and peculiar care
Was to protect and elevate the fair;
Their rights assert, their virtues, talents raise
And crown their merit with appropriate praise.

In feudal times, tho' other virtues failed,
Respectful, tender deference prevailed
For woman's worth. Not as in Greece and Rome,
Was she degradingly confined *at home;*
But both in *social bower* and *sumptuous ball*
Was seen, admired, and reverenced by all.

From the fair hand of some distinguished dame,
Umpire of valor, arbitress of fame,
Each northern knight respectfully received
The prize his gallantry in arms achieved;

---

1. One source suggests that this poem, also published in the *Literary and Musical Magazine* (Philadelphia), could have been written by Margaretta Van Wyck Bleecker Faugères, who published under the pseudonym "Ella." However, Faugères died in 1801.
2. Sir Philip Sidney (1554–1586) was a British author as well as a loyal courtier during the reign of Elizabeth I. Source of the following quote is unknown.

Of toil and danger the reward and crown,
Her smile was *triumph,* her applause *renown.*

Nor Fame's bright palm did she alone dispense
At *galas, festivals* and *tournaments;*
For feudal records prove, her talents, zeal,
In council oft, advanced her country's weal;
Her judgment, penetration and address,
Promoting *public, social, private,* happiness.

Admired, esteemed, distinguished and carest,
Her proper station, woman then possest;
And had the light of *classic* letters shone,
Among the nations of the northern zone,
With taste, discernment, influence combined,
The zeal of woman had the world refined.

And are there not some noble spirits still,
That with the *power,* possess the generous *will*
To advocate the cause of woman's mind,
And raise it to the height by heaven design'd;
A height from which her virtue may dispense
The most auspicious and diffusive influence?

Such spirits are: and one bright period more,
Outshining all that ever shone before,
Shall shed its pleasing light and influence kind,
On every cloud and envious shade of mind;
Till mental gloom, expelled Virginia's shore,
Shall darken female intellect no more.

Such is the period which our hopes await,
The pleasant change our wishes advocate;
When female genius may display its powers
From lisping infancy's delightful hours,
To youth's developement, when nature kind
Unfold the charms and graces of the mind.

No more imprisoned, *like fair Chinese feet.*
To keep them down, *diminutively neat,*
The female mind, its fetters shall escape,

And beauteous rise into *its natural shape:*
Its opening talents man shall raptured view,
Acknowledge, prize—and profit by them too.

Enlightened taste with fond parental care
Shall then illustrate the domestic sphere;
Maternal love shall make man's infant powers,
As genial spring awakes the nascent flowers;
Youth's opening bud, *maternal light* illume,
Till intellect expand its highest, richest bloom.

Source: Alexandria Gazette and Daily Advertiser (1819)

🐚 Lydia Maria Child (1802–1880)

Lydia Francis, born into a middle-class family in Massachusetts, was encouraged by her brother, Convers, to write her first novel, Hobomok *(1824). Although published anonymously, in her preface to this work, Lydia posed as a man. In 1828, after she had become a famous author of two historical novels and editor of the first children's magazine, she married David Child, editor and publisher of the* Massachusetts Journal, *for which Lydia subsequently wrote. She also wrote children's books and domestic advice manuals, including her famous* The Frugal Housewife *(1829), to supplement her husband's meager income. The couple had no children. In her fiction as well as nonfiction, written over five decades, she was a prominent advocate for the rights of Native Americans, African Americans, and women. The preface to her novel* Philothea *(1836) expresses her desire to write creatively after a long period of reformist and practical-minded writing. She wrote only one more novel, and in 1861, she helped Harriet Jacobs edit and publish her slave narrative,* Incidents in the Life of a Slave Girl.

Preface to *Hobomok*

In the summer of 1823, my friend ******* entered my study with an air which indicated he had something to communicate.

"Frederic," says he, "do you know I have been thinking of a new plan lately?"

"A wise one, no doubt," replied I; "but, prithee, what is it?"

"Why, to confess the truth, your friend P******'s remarks concerning our early history, have half tempted me to write a New England novel."

"A novel!" quoth I—"when Waverly is galloping over hill and dale, faster and more successful than Alexander's conquering sword?[1] Even American ground is occupied. 'The Spy' is lurking in every closet,—the mind is every where supplied with 'Pioneers' on the land, and is soon likely to be with 'Pilots' on the deep."[2]

"I know that," replied he; "Scott wanders over every land with the same proud, elastic tread—free as the mountain breeze, and majestic as the bird that bathes in the sunbeams. He must always stand alone—a high and solitary shrine, before which minds of humbler mould are compelled to bow down and worship. I did not mean," added he, smiling, "that my wildest hopes, hardly my wildest wishes, had placed me even within sight of the proud summit which has been gained either by

---

1. Scottish writer Sir Walter Scott's novel *Waverly* (1814) was very popular in America. Alexander the Great, military leader of ancient Greece, was known for his vast empire.

2. James Fenimore Cooper's popular novels *The Spy* (1821), *The Pioneers* (1823), and *The Pilot* (1823).

Sir Walter Scott, or Mr. Cooper. I am aware that the subject which called forth your friend's animated observations, owed its romantic coloring almost wholly to his own rich imagination. Still, barren and uninteresting as New England history is, I feel there is enough connected with it, to rouse the dormant energies of my soul; and I would fain deserve some other epitaph than that 'he lived and died.'"

I knew that my friend, under an awkward and unprepossessing appearance, concealed more talents than the world was aware of. I likewise knew that when he once started in the race, "the de'il take the hindmost" was his favorite motto. So I e'en resolved to favor the project, and to procure for him as many old, historical pamphlets as possible.

A few weeks after, my friend again entered my apartment, and gave me a package, as he said, "Here are my MSS., and it rests entirely with you, whether or not to give them to the public. You, and every one acquainted with our earliest history, will perceive that I owe many a quaint expression, and pithy sentence, to the old and forgotten manuscripts of those times.

"The ardour with which I commenced this task, has almost wholly abated.

"Seriously, Frederic, what chance is there that I, who so seldom peep out from 'the loop-holes of retreat,'[3] upon a gay and busy world, can have written any thing which will meet their approbation? Besides, the work is full of faults, which I have talents enough to see, but not to correct. It has indeed fallen far short of the standard which I had raised in my own mind. You well know that state of feeling, when the soul fixes her keen vision on distant brightness, but in vain stretches her feeble and spell-bound wing, for a flight so lofty. The world would smile," continued he, "to hear me talk thus, concerning a production, which will probably never rise to the surface with other ephemeral trifles of the day;—but painful, anxious timidity must unavoidably be felt by a young author in his first attempt. However, I will talk no more about it. 'What is writ, is writ—would it were worthier.'[4]

"If I succeed, the voice of praise will cheer me in my solitude. If I fail, thank Heaven, there is no one, but yourself, can insult me with their pity."

Perhaps the public may think me swayed by undue partiality,—but after I had read my friend's MS. I wrote upon the outside, "Send it to the Printer."

Source: Hobomok, A Tale of Early Times (1824)

---

3. "'Tis pleasant through the loop-holes of retreat / To peep at such a world." These often-quoted lines from William Cowper's *The Task* (1785) were associated with the seclusion of the author from the social and commercial world.

4. Lines from Lord Byron's *Childe Harold's Pilgrimage* (1812).

Preface to *Philothea*

This volume is purely romance; and most readers will consider it romance of the wildest kind. A few kindred spirits, prone to people space "with life and mystical predominance,"[5] will perceive a light *within* the Grecian Temple.

For such I have written it. To minds of different mould, who may think an apology necessary for what they will deem so utterly useless, I have nothing better to offer than the simple fact that I found delight in doing it.

The work has been four or five years in its progress; for the practical tendencies of the age, and particularly of the country in which I lived, have so continually forced me into the actual, that my mind has seldom obtained freedom to rise into the ideal.

The hope of extended usefulness has hitherto induced a strong effort to throw myself into the spirit of the times; which is prone to neglect beautiful and fragrant flowers, unless their roots answer for vegetables, and their leaves for herbs. But there have been seasons when my soul felt restless in this bondage,—like the Pegasus[6] of German fable, chained to a plodding ox, and offered in the market; and as that rash steed, when he caught a glimpse of the far blue sky, snapped the chain that bound him, spread his wings, and left the earth beneath him—so I, for a while, bid adieu to the substantial fields of utility, to float on the clouds of romance.

The state of mind produced by the alternation of thoughts, in their nature so opposite, was oddly pictured by the following dream, which came before me in my sleep, with all the distinctness of reality, soon after I began to write this work.

I dreamed that I arose early in the morning, and went into my garden, eager to see if the crocus had yet ventured to peep above the ground. To my astonishment, that little spot, which the day before had worn the dreary aspect of winter, was now filled with flowers of every form and hue! With enthusiastic joy I clapped my hands, and called aloud to my husband to come and view the wonders of the garden. He came; and we passed from flower to flower, admiring their marvellous beauty. Then, with a sudden bound, I said, "Now come and see the sunshine on the water!"

We passed to the side of the house, where the full sea presented itself, in all the radiance of morning. And as we looked, lo! there appeared a multitude of boats, with sails like the wings of butterflies—which now opened wide, and reposed on the surface of the water; and now closed, like the motions of weary insects in July;—and ever as they moved, the gorgeous colors glittered in the sunshine.

I exclaimed, "These must have come from fairy land!" As I spoke, suddenly we

---

5. Line from Samuel Taylor Coleridge's translation of Friedrich Schiller's *The Piccolomini, or The First Part of Wallenstein, A Drama in Five Acts* (1800).

6. Winged horse. The fable of Pegasus yoked to an ox is a metaphor for the incompatibility of romance and realism.

saw among the boats a multitude of statues, that seemed to be endowed with life; some large and majestic, some of beautiful feminine proportions, and an almost infinite variety of lovely little cherubs. Some were diving, some floating, and some undulating on the surface of the sea; and ever as they rose up, the water-drops glittered like gems on the pure white marble.

We could find no words to express our rapture, while gazing on a scene thus clothed with the beauty of other worlds. As we stood absorbed in the intensity of delight, I heard a noise behind me, and turning round, saw an old woman with a checked apron, who made an awkward courtesy [*sic*], and said, "Ma'am, I can't afford to let you have that brisket for eight pence a pound."

When I related this dream to my husband, he smiled and said, "The first part of it was dreamed by Philothea; the last, by the Frugal Housewife."

Source: Philothea. A Romance (1836)

❧ Maria Gowen Brooks (1795?–1845)

Born in Massachusetts, Abigail Gowen later changed her name to Maria. Her marriage to John Brooks at the age of about fifteen, precipitated by her father's death, was unsatisfying, and she fell for a Canadian officer while living with her husband in Portland, Maine. After the anonymous publication of a small volume of poems and the death of her husband, she pursued a relationship with the Canadian officer. Having no success with him, she went to Cuba, where she had inherited a plantation. There she began her most famous work, the epic poem Zophiel, *which is based on the story of Sara in the apocryphal Book of Tobit. She published the first canto in 1825 under the name Mrs. Brooks and subsequently gained the admiration of British poet laureate Robert Southey, who facilitated the publication of the complete work in London in 1833 under the name Maria del Occidente, which he had given her. Although her work was never popular,* Zophiel *was widely considered the most ambitious and erudite work of poetry by an American woman.*

Preface to *Zophiel*

Wishing to make a continued effort, in an art which, though almost in secret, has been adored and assiduously cultivated from earliest infancy, it was my intention to have chosen some incident from Pagan history, as the foundation of my contemplated poem. But, looking over the Jewish annals, I was induced to select for my purpose, one of their well-known stories which besides its extreme beauty, seemed to open an extensive field for the imagination which might therein avail itself not only of important and elevated truths but pleasing and popular superstitions.

Having finished one Canto I left the United States for the West Indies in the hope of being able to sail thence for Great Britain, where I might submit what I had done to the candour of some able writer; publish it, if thought expedient; and obtain advice and materials for the improvement and prosecution of my work. But as events have transpired to frustrate that intention I have endeavored to make it as perfect, as with the means I have access to, is possible.

It is, now, far beneath what might have been done, under the influence of more decided hopes and more auspicious circumstances. Yet, as it is, I am induced to place it before the public, with that anxiety which naturally attends the doubtful accomplishment of any favourite object, on the principle that no artist can make the same improvement, or labour with so much pleasure to himself, in private, as when comparing his efforts with those of others, and listening to the opinions of critics and the remarks of connoisseurs. The beauty, though she may view herself, in her mirror, from the ringlets of her hair to the sole of her slipper, and appear most lovely to her own gaze, can never be certain of her power to please until the suffrage of society confirm the opinion formed in seclusion; and "Qu'est ce que la beauté s'elle ne touche pas?"[1]

Literary employments are necessary to the happiness and almost to the vitality of those who pursue them with much ardour; and though the votaries of the muses are, too often, debased by faults, yet, abstractedly considered, a taste for any art, if well directed, must seem a preservative not only against melancholy, but even against misery and vice.

Genius, whatever its bent, supposes a refined and delicate moral sense and though sometimes perverted by sophistry or circumstance, and sometimes failing through weakness; can always, at least, comprehend and feel, the grandeur of honour and the beauty of virtue.

As to the faults of those to whom the world allows the possession of genius, there are, perhaps, good grounds for the belief that they have actually fewer than those employed about ordinary affairs; but the last are easily concealed and the first carefully dragged to light.

The miseries too, sometimes attendant on persons of distinguished literary attainments, are often held forth as a subject of "warn and scare" but Cervantes and Camoëns would both have been cast into prison even though unable to read or write, and Savage,[2] though a mechanic or scrivener, would probably have possessed the same failings and consequently have fallen into the same, or a greater degree of poverty and suffering. Alas! how many, in the flower of youth and strength, perish in the loathsome dungeons of this island, and, when dead, are refused a decent grave; who, in many instances, were their histories traced by an able pen would be wept by half the civilized world.

Although I can boast nothing but an extreme and unquenchable love for the art to which my humble aspirations are confined, my lyre has been a solace when every thing else has failed; soothing when agitated, and when at peace furnishing that exercise and excitement without which the mind becomes sick, and all her faculties retrograde when they ought to be advancing. Men, when they feel that nature has kindled in their bosoms a flame which must incessantly be fed, can cultivate eloquence and exert it, in aid of the unfortunate before the judgment seats of their country; or endeavour to "lure to the skies" such as enter the temples of their god; but woman, alike subject to trials and vicissitudes and endowed with the same wishes, (for the observation, "there is no sex to soul,"[3] is certainly not untrue,)

1. French: What does beauty not touch?

2. Miguel de Cervantes, Spanish author, claimed to have conceived of *Don Quixote* (1605–1615) while in jail for keeping improper records as a purveyor for the Spanish Armada. Luis Vaz de Camoëns (1524–1580), Portuguese poet, was imprisoned for wounding an officer of the king's cavalry in 1552. British poet Richard Savage (1697–1743) died in prison for not paying his debts.

3. The idea that "there is no soul in sex" was often discussed among early modern feminists in Europe as well as among women of the new American republic.

condemned, perhaps, to a succession of arduous though minute duties in which, oftentimes, there is nothing to charm and little to distract, unless she be allowed the exercise of her pen must fall into melancholy and despair, and perish, (to use the language of Mad. de Staël,) "consumed by her own energies."[4]

Thus do we endeavour to excuse any inordinate or extreme attachment by labouring to show in their highest colours the merits of its object.

Zophiel may or may not be called entirely a creature of imagination, as comports with the faith of the reader; he is not, however, endowed with a single miraculous attribute; for which the general belief of ages, even among christians [sic], may not be produced as authority.

The stanza in which his story is told though less complicate [sic] and beautiful than the Spencerian [sic],[5] is equally ancient; and favorable to a pensive melody, is also susceptible of much variety.

The marginal notes will be useless to such as have read much.

San Patricio, Island of Cuba, March 30, 1825.

Source: Zophiel, A Poem (1825)

4. Anne Louise Germaine Necker de Staël, known as Madame de Staël (1766–1817). The quote likely comes from her novel *Corinne* (1807), which depicted a failed woman artist.

5. Edmund Spenser (1552–1599), British poet, author of *The Faerie Queen* (1590). His innovative and challenging meter was widely copied in the eighteenth and nineteenth centuries.

❧ CATHARINE MARIA SEDGWICK (1789–1867)

Catharine Maria Sedgwick, member of a wealthy family in Stockbridge, Massachusetts, lost her parents when she was young. As an adult, she remained single, dividing her time among the households of her four brothers. Her brothers spurred on her career and even encouraged her to devote herself to literature instead of a husband. One wrote to her in 1827, "I look forward to the exertion of your literary talents as a great national blessing." Indeed, she was considered one of the founders of a national literature. Her historical novels, including Redwood *(1824) and* Hope Leslie *(1827), helped to construct the young nation's view of its origins. Her widely anthologized story "Cacoethes Scribendi" (1830) depicts the mortification of a young woman upon discovering that her mother has ushered her private writings into print. The lesser-known story, "A Sketch of a Blue Stocking" (1832) presents a more sympathetic view of women's authorship. Together they suggest the complex feelings women had about venturing into the literary marketplace.*

Cacoethes Scribendi

Glory and gain the industrious tribe provoke.—Pope.[1]

The little secluded and quiet village of H. lies at no great distance from our "literary emporium." It was never remarked or remarkable for any thing, save one mournful preeminence, to those who sojourned within its borders—it was duller even than common villages. The young men of the better class all emigrated. The most daring spirits adventured on the sea. Some went to Boston; some to the south; and some to the west; and left a community of women who lived like nuns, with the advantage of more liberty and fresh air, but without the consolation and excitement of a religious vow. Literally, there was not a single young gentleman in the village—nothing in manly shape to which these desperate circumstances could give the form and quality and use of a beau. Some dashing city blades, who once strayed from the turnpike to this sequestered spot, averred that the girls stared at them as if, like Miranda, they would have exclaimed—

> "What is't? a spirit?
> Lord, how it looks about! Believe me, sir,
> It carries a brave form:—But 'tis a spirit."[2]

A peculiar fatality hung over this devoted place. If death seized on either head of a family, he was sure to take the husband; every woman in H. was a widow or maiden;

1. From Alexander Pope's *The Dunciad* (1728).
2. From William Shakespeare's *The Tempest* (1611).

and it is a sad fact, that when the holiest office of the church was celebrated, they were compelled to borrow deacons from an adjacent village. But, incredible as it may be, there was no great diminution of happiness in consequence of the absence of the nobler sex. Mothers were occupied with their children and housewifery, and the young ladies read their books with as much interest as if they had lovers to discuss them with, and worked their frills and capes as diligently, and wore them as complacently, as if they were to be seen by manly eyes. Never were there pleasanter gatherings or parties (for that was the word even in their nomenclature) than those of the young girls of H. There was no mincing—no affectation—no hope of passing for what they were not—no envy of the pretty and fortunate—no insolent triumph over the plain and demure and neglected,—but all was good will and good humour. They were a pretty circle of girls—a garland of bright fresh flowers. Never were there more sparkling glances,—never sweeter smiles—nor more of them. Their present was all health and cheerfulness; and their future, not the gloomy perspective of dreary singleness, for somewhere in the passage of life they were sure to be mated. Most of the young men who had abandoned their native soil, as soon as they found themselves *getting along,* loyally returned to lay their fortunes at the feet of the companions of their childhood.

The girls made occasional visits to Boston, and occasional journeys to various parts of the country, for they were all enterprising and independent, and had the characteristic New England avidity for seizing a "privilege"; and in these various ways, to borrow a phrase of their good grandames, "a door was opened for them," and in due time they fulfilled the destiny of women.

We spoke strictly, and à la lettre, when we said that in the village of H. there was not a single *beau.* But on the outskirts of the town, at a pleasant farm, embracing hill and valley, upland and meadow land; in a neat house, looking to the south, with true economy of sunshine and comfort, and overlooking the prettiest winding stream that ever sent up its sparkling beauty to the eye, and flanked on the north by a rich maple grove, beautiful in spring and summer, and glorious in autumn, and the kindest defence in winter;—on this farm and in this house dwelt a youth, to fame unknown, but known and loved by every inhabitant of H., old and young, grave and gay, lively and severe. Ralph Hepburn was one of nature's favourites. He had a figure that would have adorned courts and cities; and a face that adorned human nature, for it was full of good humour, kindheartedness, spirit, and intelligence; and driving the plough or wielding the scythe, his cheek flushed with manly and profitable exercise, he looked as if he had been moulded in a poet's fancy—as farmers look in Georgics and Pastorals.[3] His gifts were by no means all external. He wrote verses in every album in the village, and very pretty album verses they were, and numerous too—for the number of albums was equivalent to the whole female

3. Poems about rustic occupations or rural life, often idealized.

population. He was admirable at pencil sketches; and once with a little paint, the refuse of a house painting, he achieved an admirable portrait of his grandmother and her cat. There was, to be sure, a striking likeness between the two figures, but he was limited to the same colours for both; and besides, it was not out of nature, for the old lady and her cat had purred together in the chimney corner, till their physiognomies[4] bore an obvious resemblance to each other. Ralph had a talent for music too. His voice was the sweetest of all the Sunday choir, and one would have fancied, from the bright eyes that were turned on him from the long line and double lines of treble and counter singers, that Ralph Hepburn was a note book, or that the girls listened with their eyes as well as their ears. Ralph did not restrict himself to psalmody. He had an ear so exquisitely susceptible to the "touches of sweet harmony," that he discovered, by the stroke of his axe, the musical capacities of certain species of wood, and he made himself a violin of chestnut, and drew strains from it, that if they could not create a soul under the ribs of death, could make the prettiest feet and the lightest hearts dance, an achievement far more to Ralph's taste than the aforesaid miracle. In short, it seemed as if nature, in her love of compensation, had showered on Ralph all the gifts that are usually diffused through a community of beaux. Yet Ralph was no prodigy; none of his talents were in excess, but all in moderate degree. No genius was ever so good humoured, so useful, so practical; and though, in his small and modest way, a Crichton,[5] he was not, like most universal geniuses, good for nothing for any particular office in life. His farm was not a pattern farm—a prize farm for an agricultural society, but in wonderful order considering—his miscellaneous pursuits. He was the delight of his grandfather for his sagacity in hunting bees—the old man's favourite, in truth his only pursuit. He was so skilled in woodcraft that the report of his gun was as certain a signal of death as the tolling of a church bell. The fish always caught at his bait. He manufactured half his farming utensils, improved upon old inventions, and struck out some new ones; tamed partridges—the most untameable of all the feathered tribe; domesticated squirrels; rivalled Scheherazade[6] herself in telling stories, strange and long—the latter quality being essential at a country fireside; and, in short, Ralph made a perpetual holiday of a life of labour.

Every girl in the village street knew when Ralph's wagon or sleigh traversed it; indeed, there was scarcely a house to which the horses did not, as if by instinct, turn up while their master greeted its fair tenants. This state of affairs had continued for two winters and two summers since Ralph came to his majority and, by the death

4. Physical features, particularly of the face.

5. General term for one of many accomplishments, derived from James Crichton of Clunie (1560–1585?), a Scottish prodigy.

6. The female narrator of the *Arabian Nights,* who each night convinces the King to let her live another day to tell another of her spellbinding stories.

of his father, to the sole proprietorship of the "Hepburn farm,"—the name his patrimonial acres had obtained from the singular circumstance (in our *moving* country) of their having remained in the same family for four generations. Never was the matrimonial destiny of a young lord, or heir just come to his estate, more thoroughly canvassed than young Hepburn's by mothers, aunts, daughters, and nieces. But Ralph, perhaps from sheer good heartedness, seemed reluctant to give to one the heart that diffused rays of sunshine through the whole village.

With all decent people he eschewed the doctrines of a certain erratic female lecturer on the odious monopoly of marriage, yet Ralph, like a tender hearted judge, hesitated to place on a single brow the crown matrimonial which so many deserved, and which, though Ralph was far enough from a coxcomb, he could not but see so many coveted.

Whether our hero perceived that his mind was becoming elated or distracted with this general favour, or that he observed a dawning of rivalry among the fair competitors, or whatever was the cause, the fact was, that he by degrees circum-scribed his visits, and finally concentrated them in the family of his aunt Courland.

Mrs. Courland was a widow, and Ralph was the kindest of nephews to her, and the kindest of cousins to her children. To their mother he seemed their guardian angel. That the five lawless, daring little urchins did not drown themselves when they were swimming, nor shoot themselves when they were shooting, was, in her eyes, Ralph's merit; and then "he was so attentive to Alice, her only daughter—a brother could not be kinder." But who would not be kind to Alice? she [*sic*] was a sweet girl of seventeen, not beautiful, not handsome perhaps,—but pretty enough—with soft hazel eyes, a profusion of light brown hair, always in the neatest trim, and a mouth that could not but be lovely and loveable, for all kind and tender affections were playing about it. Though Alice was the only daughter of a doting mother, the only sister of five loving boys, the only niece of three single, fond aunts, and, last and greatest, the only cousin of our only beau, Ralph Hepburn, no girl of seventeen was ever more disinterested, unassuming, unostentatious, and unspoiled. Ralph and Alice had always lived on terms of cousinly affection—an affection of a neutral tint that they never thought of being shaded into the deep dye of a more tender passion. Ralph rendered her all cousinly offices. If he had twenty damsels to escort, not an uncommon case, he never forgot Alice. When he returned from any little excursion, he always brought some graceful offering to Alice.

He had lately paid a visit to Boston. It was at the season of the periodical inun-dation of annuals.[7] He brought two of the prettiest to Alice. Ah! little did she think

7. Literary annuals or "gift books" were produced yearly for the Christmas season, chiefly from the 1820s to the 1850s. They were beautifully bound and contained sentimental poetry, stories, and essays. *The Atlantic Souvenir,* in which this story first appeared, was a literary annual.

they were to prove Pandora's box to her.[8] Poor simple girl! she sat down to read them, as if an annual were meant to be read, and she was honestly interested and charmed. Her mother observed her delight. "What have you there, Alice?" she asked. "Oh the prettiest story, mamma!—two such tried faithful lovers, and married at last! It ends beautifully: I hate love stories that don't end in marriage."

"And so do I, Alice," exclaimed Ralph, who entered at the moment, and for the first time Alice felt her cheeks tingle at his approach. He had brought a basket, containing a choice plant he had obtained for her, and she laid down the annual and went with him to the garden to see it set by his own hand.

Mrs. Courland seized upon the annual with avidity. She had imbibed a literary taste in Boston, where the best and happiest years of her life were passed. She had some literary ambition too. She read the North American Review[9] from beginning to end, and she fancied no conversation could be sensible or improving that was not about books. But she had been effectually prevented, by the necessities of a narrow income, and by the unceasing wants of five teasing boys, from indulging her literary inclinations; for Mrs. Courland, like all New England women, had been taught to consider domestic duties as the first temporal duties of her sex. She had recently seen some of the native productions with which the press is daily teeming, and which certainly have a tendency to dispel our early illusions about the craft of authorship. She had even felt some obscure intimations, within her secret soul, that she might herself become an author. The annual was destined to fix her fate. She opened it—the publisher had written the names of the authors of the anonymous pieces against their productions. Among them she found some of the familiar friends of her childhood and youth.

If, by a sudden gift of second sight, she had seen them enthroned as kings and queens, she would not have been more astonished. She turned to their pieces, and read them, as perchance no one else ever did, from beginning to end—faithfully. Not a sentence—a sentence! not a word was skipped. She paused to consider commas, colons, and dashes. All the art and magic of authorship were made level to her comprehension, and when she closed the book, she *felt a call* to become an author, and before she retired to bed she obeyed the call, as if it had been, in truth, a divinity stirring within her. In the morning she presented an article to *her* public, consisting of her own family and a few select friends. All applauded, and every voice, save one, was unanimous for publication—that one was Alice. She was a modest, prudent girl; she feared failure, and feared notoriety still more. Her mother laughed at her childish scruples. The piece was sent off, and in due time graced the pages of

8. In Greek mythology, Pandora released all the evils of the world when she opened the box Zeus had warned her not to open.

9. The *North American Review*, published in Boston from 1815, was the most distinguished literary magazine in the United States at the time. It was written primarily for an elite male audience.

an annual. Mrs. Courland's fate was now decided. She had, to use her own phrase, started in the career of letters, and she was no Atalanta[10] to be seduced from her straight onward way. She was a social, sympathetic, good hearted creature too, and she could not bear to go forth in the golden field to reap alone.

She was, besides, a prudent woman, as most of her countrywomen are, and the little pecuniary equivalent for this delightful exercise of talents was not overlooked. Mrs. Courland, as we have somewhere said, had three single sisters—worthy women they were—but nobody ever dreamed of their taking to authorship. She, however, held them all in sisterly estimation. Their talents were magnified as the talents of persons who live in a circumscribed sphere are apt to be, particularly if seen through the dilating medium of affection.

Miss Anne, the oldest, was fond of flowers, a successful cultivator, and a diligent student of the science of botany. All this taste and knowledge, Mrs. Courland thought, might be turned to excellent account; and she persuaded Miss Anne to write a little book entitled "Familiar Dialogues on Botany." The second sister, Miss Ruth, had a turn for education ("bachelor's wives and maid's children are always well taught"), and Miss Ruth undertook a popular treatise on that subject. Miss Sally, the youngest, was the saint of the family, and she doubted about the propriety of a literary occupation, till her scruples were overcome by the fortunate suggestion that her coup d'essai[11] should be a Saturday night book entitled "Solemn Hours,"— and solemn hours they were to their unhappy readers. Mrs. Courland next besieged her old mother. "You know, mamma," she said, "you have such a precious fund of anecdotes of the revolution and the French war, and you talk just like the 'Annals of the Parish,' and I am certain you can write a book fully as good."

"My child, you are distracted! I write a dreadful poor hand, and I never learned to spell—no girls did in my time."

"Spell! that is not of the least consequence—the printers correct the spelling." But the honest old lady would not be tempted on the crusade, and her daughter consoled herself with the reflection that if she would not write, she was an admirable subject to be written about, and her diligent fingers worked off three distinct stories in which the old lady figured.

Mrs. Courland's ambition, of course, embraced within its widening circle her favourite nephew Ralph. She had always thought him a genius, and genius in her estimation was the philosopher's stone. In his youth she had laboured to persuade his father to send him to Cambridge, but the old man uniformly replied that Ralph "was a smart lad on the farm, and steady, and by that he knew he was no genius."

---

10. In Greek mythology, Atalanta was a female hunter and athlete who participated in many male activities. She would only marry the man who could beat her in a foot race. Hippomenes was able to win by rolling three golden apples in her path.

11. First attempt.

As Ralph's character was developed, and talent after talent broke forth, his aunt re-newed her lamentations over his ignoble destiny. That Ralph was useful, good, and happy—the most difficult and rare results achieved in life—was nothing, so long as he was but a farmer in H. Once she did half persuade him to turn painter, but his good sense and filial duty triumphed over her eloquence, and suppressed the han-kerings after distinction that are innate in every human breast, from the little ragged chimneysweep that hopes to be a *boss,* to the political aspirant whose bright goal is the presidential chair.

Now Mrs. Courland fancied Ralph might climb the steep of fame without quit-ting his farm; occasional authorship was compatible with his vocation. But alas! she could not persuade Ralph to pluck the laurels that she saw ready grown to his hand. She was not offended, for she was the best natured woman in the world, but she heartily pitied him, and seldom mentioned his name without repeating that stanza of Gray's, inspired for the consolation of hopeless obscurity:

"Full many a gem of purest ray serene," &c.[12]

Poor Alice's sorrows we have reserved to the last, for they were heaviest. "Alice," her mother said, "was gifted; she was well educated, well informed; she was every thing necessary to be an author." But Alice resisted; and, though the gentlest, most complying of all good daughters, she would have resisted to the death—she would as soon have stood in a pillory[13] as appeared in print. Her mother, Mrs. Courland, was not an obstinate woman, and gave up in despair. But still our poor heroine was destined to be the victim of this *cacoethes scribendi;* for Mrs. Courland divided the world into two classes, or rather parts—authors and subjects for authors; the one active, the other passive. At first blush one would have thought the village of H. rather a barren field for such a reaper as Mrs. Courland, but her zeal and indefati-gableness worked wonders. She converted the stern scholastic divine of H. into as much of a La Roche as she could describe; a tall wrinkled bony old woman, who reminded her of Meg Merrilies, sat for a witch; the school master for an Ichabod Crane;[14] a poor half witted boy was made to utter as much pathos and sentiment and wit as she could put into his lips; and a crazy vagrant was a God-send to her. Then every "wide spreading elm," "blasted pine," or "gnarled oak," flourished on her pages. The village church and school house stood there according to their actual dimensions. One old *pilgrim* house was as prolific as haunted tower or ruined abbey.

12. Thomas Gray's "An Elegy Wrote in a Country Churchyard" (1751).

13. Device used for public punishment in which the head and hands are confined by rings or holes. Its use was abolished in England in 1837 but in Delaware not until 1905.

14. Francois VI, Duke de la Rochefoucauld (1613–1680), French classical author known for the maxime, or epigram. Meg Merrilies is the gypsy witch in Sir Walter Scott's novel *Guy Mannering* (1815). Ichabod Crane is the protagonist of Washington Irving's story "The Legend of Sleepy Hol-low" (1820).

It was surveyed outside, ransacked inside, and again made habitable for the reim-bodied spirits of its founders.

The most kind hearted of women, Mrs. Courland's interests came to be so at variance with the prosperity of the little community of H., that a sudden calamity, a death, a funeral, were fortunate events to her. To do her justice she felt them in a twofold capacity. She wept as a woman, and exulted as an author. The days of the calamities of authors have passed by. We have all wept over Otway and shivered at the thought of Tasso.[15] But times are changed. The lean sheaf is devouring the full one. A new class of sufferers has arisen, and there is nothing more touching in all the memoirs Mr. D'Israeli[16] has collected, than the trials of poor Alice, tragi-comic though they were. Mrs. Courland's new passion ran most naturally in the worn channel of maternal affection. Her boys were too purely boys for her art—but Alice, her sweet Alice, was preeminently lovely in the new light in which she now placed every object. Not an incident of her life but was inscribed on her mother's memory, and thence transferred to her pages, by way of precept, or example, or pathetic or ludicrous circumstance. She regretted now, for the first time, that Alice had no lover whom she might introduce among her dramatis personæ. Once her thoughts did glance on Ralph, but she had not quite merged the woman in the author; she knew instinctively that Alice would be particularly offended at being thus paired with Ralph. But Alice's *public life* was not limited to her mother's pro-ductions. She was the darling niece of her three aunts. She had studied botany with the eldest, and Miss Anne had recorded in her private diary all her favourite's clever remarks during their progress in the science. This diary was now a mine of gold to her, and faithfully worked up for a circulating medium. But, most trying of all to poor Alice, was the attitude in which she appeared in her aunt Sally's "solemn hours." Every aspiration of piety to which her young lips had given utterance was there *printed*. She felt as if she were condemned to say her prayers in the market place. Every act of kindness, every deed of charity, she had ever performed, were produced to the public. Alice would have been consoled if she had known how small that public was; but, as it was, she felt like a modest country girl when she first enters an apartment hung on every side with mirrors, when, shrinking from obser-vation, she sees in every direction her image multiplied and often distorted; for, notwithstanding Alice's dutiful respect for her good aunts, and her consciousness of their affectionate intentions, she could not but perceive that they were unskilled painters. She grew afraid to speak or to act, and from being the most artless, frank, and, at home, social little creature in the world, she became as silent and as stiff as

15. Thomas Otway (1652–1685), English dramatist who suffered severe poverty. Torquato Tasso (1544–1595), Italian poet driven mad by the church's censorship of his work.

16. Issac D'Israeli (1766–1848), British writer best known for his *Curiosities of Literature* (6 vols., 1791–1824), a compilation of anecdotes about famous authors.

a statue. And, in the circle of her young associates, her natural gaiety was constantly checked by their winks and smiles, and broader allusions to her multiplied portraits; for they had instantly recognized them through the thin veil of feigned names of persons and places. They called her a blue stocking[17] too; for they had the vulgar notion that every body must be tinged that lived under the same roof with an author. Our poor victim was afraid to speak of a book—worse than that, she was afraid to touch one, and the last Waverley novel actually lay in the house a month before she opened it. She avoided wearing even a blue ribbon, as fearfully as a forsaken damsel shuns the colour of green.

It was during the height of this literary fever in the Courland family, that Ralph Hepburn, as has been mentioned, concentrated all his visiting there. He was of a compassionate disposition, and he knew Alice was, unless relieved by him, in solitary possession of their once social parlour, while her mother and aunts were driving their quills in their several apartments.

Oh! what a changed place was that parlour! Not the tower of Babel, after the builders had forsaken it, exhibited a sadder reverse; not a Lancaster school, when the boys have left it, a more striking contrast. Mrs. Courland and her sisters were all "talking women," and too generous to encroach on one another's rights and happiness. They had acquired the power to hear and speak simultaneously. Their parlour was the general gathering place, a sort of village exchange, where all the innocent gossips, old and young, met together. "There are tongues in trees,"[18] and surely there seemed to be tongues in the very walls of that vocal parlour. Every thing there had a social aspect. There was something agreeable and conversable in the litter of netting and knitting work, of sewing implements, and all the signs and shows of happy female occupation.

Now, all was as orderly as a town drawing room in company hours. Not a sound was heard there save Ralph's and Alice's voices, mingling in soft and suppressed murmurs, as if afraid of breaking the chain of their aunt's ideas, or, perchance, of too rudely jarring a tenderer chain. One evening, after tea, Mrs. Courland remained with her daughter, instead of retiring, as usual, to her writing desk.—"Alice, my dear," said the good mother, "I have noticed for a few days past that you look out of spirits. You will listen to nothing I say on that subject; but if you would try it,

---

17. The term *bluestocking* was used widely and usually derogatively in the early nineteenth century to refer to a learned or intellectual woman, suggesting that she had pretensions beyond her abilities. The name derives from an influential women's literary club that met in London during the last half of the eighteenth century. A visitor who could not afford formal black silk stockings was told, "come in your blue stockings," referring to the informal blue worsted stockings traditionally worn at home.

18. From William Shakespeare's *As You Like It* (ca. 1599): "and this our life, exempt from public haunt, / Finds tongues in trees, books in the running brooks, / Sermons in stones, and good in everything."

my dear, if you would only try it, you would find there is nothing so tranquillizing as the occupation of writing."

"I shall never try it, mamma."

"You are afraid of being called a blue stocking. Ah! Ralph, how are you?"—Ralph entered at this moment.—"Ralph, tell me honestly, do you not think it a weakness in Alice to be so afraid of blue stockings?"

"It would be a pity, aunt, to put blue stockings on such pretty feet as Alice's."

Alice blushed and smiled, and her mother said—"Nonsense, Ralph; you should bear in mind the celebrated saying of the Edinburgh wit—'no matter how blue the stockings are, if the petticoats are long enough to hide them.'"

"Hide Alice's feet! Oh aunt, worse and worse!"

"Better hide her feet, Ralph, than her talents—that is a sin for which both she and you will have to answer. Oh! you and Alice need not exchange such significant glances! You are doing yourselves and the public injustice, and you have no idea how easy writing is."

"Easy writing, but hard reading, aunt."

"That's false modesty, Ralph. If I had but your opportunities to collect materials"—Mrs. Courland did not know that in literature, as in some species of manufacture, the most exquisite productions are wrought from the smallest quantity of raw material—"There's your journey to New York, Ralph," she continued, "you might have made three capital articles out of that. The revolutionary officer would have worked up for the 'Legendary;' the mysterious lady for the 'Token;' and the man in black for the 'Remember Me;'[19]—all founded on fact, all romantic and pathetic."

"But mamma," said Alice, expressing in words what Ralph's arch smile expressed almost as plainly, "you know the officer drank too much; and the mysterious lady turned out to be a runaway milliner; and the man in black—oh! what a theme for a pathetic story!—the man in black was a widower, on his way to Newhaven, where he was to select his third wife from three *recommended* candidates."

"Pshaw! Alice: do you suppose it is necessary to tell things precisely as they are?"

"Alice is wrong, aunt, and you are right; and if she will open her writing desk for me, I will sit down this moment, and write a story—a true story—true from beginning to end; and if it moves you, my dear aunt, if it meets your approbation, my destiny is decided."

Mrs. Courland was delighted; she had slain the giant, and she saw fame and fortune smiling on her favourite. She arranged the desk for him herself; she prepared a folio sheet of paper, folded the ominous margins; and was so absorbed in her bright visions, that she did not hear a little by-talk between Ralph and Alice,

---

19. Titles of literary annuals.

nor see the tell-tale flush on their cheeks, nor notice the perturbation with which Alice walked first to one window and then to another, and finally settled herself to that best of all sedatives—hemming a ruffle. Ralph chewed off the end of his quill, mended his pen twice, though his aunt assured him "printers did not mind the penmanship," and had achieved a single line when Mrs. Courland's vigilant eye was averted by the entrance of her servant girl, who put a packet into her hands. She looked at the direction, cut the string, broke the seals, and took out a periodical fresh from the publisher. She opened at the first article—a strangely mingled current of maternal pride and literary triumph rushed through her heart and brightened her face. She whispered to the servant a summons to all her sisters to the parlour, and an intimation, sufficiently intelligible to them, of her joyful reason for interrupting them.

Our readers will sympathize with her, and with Alice too, when we disclose to them the secret of her joy. The article in question was a clever composition written by our devoted Alice when she was at school. One of her fond aunts had preserved it; and aunts and mother had combined in the pious fraud of giving it to the public, unknown to Alice. They were perfectly aware of her determination never to be an author. But they fancied it was the mere timidity of an unfledged bird; and that when, by their innocent artifice, she found that her pinions could soar in a literary atmosphere, she would realize the sweet fluttering sensations they had experienced at their first flight. The good souls all hurried to the parlour, eager to witness the coup de théatre.[20] Miss Sally's pen stood emblematically erect in her turban; Miss Ruth, in her haste, had overset her inkstand, and the drops were trickling down her white dressing, or, as she now called it, writing gown; and Miss Anne had a wild flower in her hand, as she hoped, of an undescribed species, which, in her joyful agitation, she most unluckily picked to pieces. All bit their lips to keep impatient congratulation from bursting forth. Ralph was so intent on his writing, and Alice on her hemming, that neither noticed the irruption; and Mrs. Courland was obliged twice to speak to her daughter before she could draw her attention.

"Alice, look here—Alice, my dear."

"What is it, mamma? something new of yours?"

"No; guess again, Alice."

"Of one of my aunts, of course?"

"Neither, dear, neither. Come and look for yourself, and see if you can then tell whose it is."

Alice dutifully laid aside her work, approached and took the book. The moment her eye glanced on the fatal page, all her apathy vanished—deep crimson overspread her cheeks, brow, and neck. She burst into tears of irrepressible vexation, and threw the book into the blazing fire.

20. French: surprising turn of events, as in a play.

The gentle Alice! Never had she been guilty of such an ebullition of temper. Her poor dismayed aunts retreated; her mother looked at her in mute astonishment; and Ralph, struck with her emotion, started from the desk, and would have asked an explanation, but Alice exclaimed—"Don't say any thing about it, mamma—I cannot bear it now."

Mrs. Courland knew instinctively that Ralph would sympathize entirely with Alice, and quite willing to avoid an éclaircissement,[21] she said—"Some other time, Ralph, I'll tell you the whole. Show me now what you have written. How have you begun?"

Ralph handed her the paper with a novice's trembling hand.

"Oh! how very little! and so scratched and interlined! but never mind—'c'est le premier pas qui coute.' "[22]

While making these general observations, the good mother was getting out and fixing her spectacles, and Alice and Ralph had retreated behind her. Alice rested her head on his shoulder, and Ralph's lips were not far from her ear. Whether he was soothing her ruffled spirit, or what he was doing, is not recorded. Mrs. Courland read and re-read the sentence. She dropped a tear on it. She forgot her literary aspirations for Ralph and Alice—forgot she was herself an author—forgot every thing but the mother; and rising, embraced them both as her dear children, and expressed, in her raised and moistened eye, consent to their union, which Ralph had dutifully and prettily asked in that short and true story of his love for his sweet cousin Alice.

In due time the village of H. was animated with the celebration of Alice's nuptials: and when her mother and aunts saw her the happy mistress of the Hepburn farm, and the happiest of wives, they relinquished, without a sigh, the hope of ever seeing her an AUTHOR.

Source: Atlantic Souvenir (1830)

A Sketch of a Blue Stocking[23]

Mrs. Laight, till the respectable age of fifty, devoted her time and talents to the ordinary occupations of those ladies of our country who are favored with a numerous progeny; that is, to minute care of her children, and thrifty management of her household concerns. She was the daughter of a President of one of our literary

21. French: clarification or explanation.
22. Sedgwick means the French proverb, "Ce n'est que la premier pas qui coute," meaning it is only the first step that costs, or, only the beginning is difficult.
23. Perjorative term for an intellectual or learned woman.

institutions, and had early imbibed a taste for literary pursuits, which was apparent in a slight tinge of pedantry, though she was prevented from indulging it by the pressure of domestic affairs. This taste revived with renewed force, when, by the death of her husband, and the control of an abundant income, she became mistress of her time and inclinations; and it received a fresh impetus from a visit to the place of her nativity, where, as she said, all her mental powers had been restored, by inhaling her native atmosphere, and reviving her intimacies with the literary associates of her youth. Among these, was a lady whom I shall take the liberty to call Mrs. Rosewell. Her friendship was Mrs. Laight's highest ambition, and she returned to *Lawrentum* (the classic name she had recently bestowed on her place, situated in the centre of a compact village), flushed with the expectation of a visit from her distinguished friend. Nothing could have been much more appalling to the younger members of her family than the annunciation of the approaching honor—Mrs. Laight's daughters—she has half a dozen of them—are pretty, intelligent, sufficiently well instructed, and very charming girls, but they have not—not one of them (for their mother's sake I grieve to say it), a literary bias; and the ardor with which her ruling passion had recently broken forth, had inspired them with a horror of *blue stockingism*. Frank Laight, their eldest brother, a spirited young man, just returned from a successful voyage to South America, foresaw that his glad holiday at home was to be overclouded. His younger brothers perceived that a universal *géne* was expected; and their imaginations presented it in the form of the sacrifice of their fishing and sporting pleasures with Frank. Anne Milnor, a lovely girl, a guest at *Lawrentum,* who was secretly cherishing a well-requited tenderness for Frank, timidly shrunk from the observation of a learned lady, whose opinion, as she anticipated, would confirm that which she feared, with too much reason, Mrs. Laight had already conceived against her. All were malecontents [*sic*], but the most anxious among them, and with most reason, was Leonard Clay. Mrs. Rosewell was the friend of Professor Lowe; he was to attend her to *Lawrentum,* and the Professor was an admirer of Sarah Laight, a dangerous rival to Leonard; for, in addition to qualities that commended him to a young lady's favor, the Professor had Latin, Greek, science, and erudition, appliances and means to win the mother.

The mind of the majority of *Lawrentum* was unfavorable to poor Mrs. Rosewell, but the majority did not rule there; and, happily for her, hospitality was the genius of the place, and the whole family were perfectly amiable and dutiful to their mother.

"Heaven preserve us! Clay, are *you* reading a review?" asked Frank Laight, who found his friend in his mother's library, poring over a tri-monthly publication, with a most doleful aspect.

"I am trying to read it; crawling through it. Your mother says we must be prepared with some topics suitable to this Mrs. Rosewell, and she has set me down here to a rigmarole article, written by the lady herself."

"Pshaw! my dear fellow, you are irretrievably lost, if you undertake to meet these literary Amazons[24] on their own ground. The only way to manage them is to talk them down on subjects they know nothing about. Take them *out* of books, Leonard, and they are as ignorant as you and I are *in* them. I'll lay a wager, I'll run this blue aground with rodomontade about my voyage, before she has been a day in the house; and do you rattle away on fishing and sporting. I'll answer for it; you'll *tree* her. Hang it! it is too absurd to be afraid of a woman, just because she happens to be a *mannish* writer of reviews."—Frank was interrupted by his mother's entrance. She requested the young men to leave the library, as she had scarcely time to put it in proper trim for Mrs. Rosewell's reception.

Frank and Leonard found the young ladies just going out to walk, and joined them. "Well, Anne," asked Frank of Miss Milnor, "have you prepared high converse for this benign cerulean?"[25]

"Not I—I shall not open my lips before her."

"You are right, Anne," replied Frank, and then added, in a low tone of earnest compliment, "modesty is the prettiest device in the world for the seal of a young lady's lips—speaking of lips, girls," he continued, raising his voice, "what sort of a looking person do you take this Mrs. Rosewell to be?"

"Of course," replied Sarah Laight, "she has what is called an intellectual fine face."

"That is to say," retorted Frank, "rolling black eyes, or deep-set gray ones, a nose like the tower of Lebanon, and cheeks ploughed with lines of thought, and furrows of reflection; in short, a *striking countenance*. Thank Heaven, Leonard we have bright, round, dimpled cheeks, to refresh and repose our eyes upon; but have a care, Sarah, do n't [*sic*] you see that horse is frightened by your parasol? put it down, child!" A horse and chaise were rapidly passing. Sarah attempted, as bidden, to lower the parasol, but the wind, which was blowing freshly, took it up, and carried it under the horse's feet. He sheared, reared, and floundered, and would inevitably have overturned the chaise if Leonard Clay had not adroitly seized the bridle. He succeeded in holding the horse while a lady jumped from the chaise, and then springing in himself, he received the reins from the willing hands of the unskilled driver, and succeeded in subduing the terrified animal before such exclamation as, "Oh! Leonard, do n't [*sic*] get into the chaise!" "Leonard! Leonard!" "Mr. Clay!" "Let Leonard alone; he can manage the horse." "Heavens! Sarah, how pale you are!" Before such exclamations had well parted from the lips of his companions, another moment passed, and the young ladies' eyes were asking "who this stranger could be," that had so suddenly descended among them? A lady she was, whose manner

24. In Greek mythology, the Amazons were female warriors who lived apart from men and were alleged to be "men killers."
25. A shade of deep blue.

had that beautiful combination of grace, refinement, unaffectedness, and gentility, that is best described by the comprehensive word ladylike. Her countenance was bright, lovely, and still retained its symmetry and much of its early beauty, though the bloom and roundness of youth had long been gone. The stranger's dress, a circumstance that first strikes a female eye, was arranged with taste, and just up to the suitable and becoming point of fashion, a very critical matter, one of the nicest of all the *fine arts* of women. "Who can she be?" was plainly spoken by the glances of our young friends, and answered immediately by the lady's companion, who, with a confession, that requires both courage and magnanimity, of his incompetency to manage his horse, alighted from the chaise, and was recognised by Sarah Laight as Professor Lowe. The lady, of course—the lady, who, at first sight, had captivated the bright eyes and warm hearts of the young people, was no other than the dreaded blue-stocking, the "benign cerulean," the veritable author, the perpetrator of full-sized volumes, and, as Frank Laight had called her, the writer of *mannish reviews*— our friend, Mrs. Rosewell! For a moment her sunbeams broke through the clouds of prejudice, that had settled over the minds of the group, but they had been too long gathering to be so suddenly dispersed. Frank proposed to Miss Milnor to hasten home with him, to announce Mrs. Rosewell's arrival to his mother; and by this pretext, as he thought, and said, "got his neck out of the scrape for the present." He had, however, the grace to remark to Anne, the little resemblance Mrs. Rosewell bore to the figure he had sketched, and to confess she had the sweetest blue eye he had ever seen, save one. Anne Milnor assented to his opinion, by putting in a blushing, smiling demurrer to the exception. Sarah Laight, never less propitious to the Professor than at this moment, when he had resigned the post of honor and of danger to Leonard Clay, clung to her sister's arm; and Miss Laight, though on ordinary occasions a young lady of exemplary propriety, only replied in monosyllables to Mrs. Rosewell's efforts to sustain a conversation, so that she and the Professor were finally condemned to a stately walk, and a dull *tête à tête*,[26] for a distance of half a mile to *Lawrentum*. Arrived there, the fervid and circumstanced reception of Mrs. Laight was even more oppressive to her friend than the reserve of the young people. But Mrs. Rosewell was a lady of resources, and she took refuge with the children. They had their prejudices too, but the prejudices of childhood vanished before a genial influence, like the dews of a summer's morning. In the first hour's acquaintance, Mrs. Rosewell had been conducted by the two little girls to the extremity of the garden, to try a new swing, hung for them by Leonard Clay. Hal had given her a ride on his new rocking-horse, and the little slattern, Bessie, had slunk away from her mother's reproving eye, and in the most confiding manner, thrust her foot into Mrs. Rosewell's lap to get her shoe tied! Dinner was soon announced, and, as philosophers, philanthropists, savans, and blue-stockings, at a dinner table,

26. French: a private conversation.

fall or rise to the level of ordinary mortals, the admiration and awe of mother and children were forgotten in the common courtesies of the table; and when the suspended conversation began to revive, it flowed on naturally, in spite of Mrs. Laight's efforts (to borrow her own ambitious phrase) to season it with Attic salt. Frank Laight found himself quite unexpectedly involved, and interested, too, in giving Mrs. Rosewell a sketch of the modes of living among the South Americans, which somehow ended in Mrs. Rosewell's asking Leonard Clay if he liked macaroni? Clay never happened to have heard the name. Macaroni sounded like Italian. He encountered Frank's eye; he fancied that his ever-ready smile was archly hovering on his lips; he was not yet disabused of the notion that an author must always talk of books; and, resolving not to be ashamed of his ignorance, he said, manfully, "I have never seen the work, Madam; I do not read Italian." Frank Rosewell shouted; Sarah blushed to her fingers ends, and poor Clay would have been thoroughly chagrined, if Mrs. Rosewell had not graciously and gracefully assumed all the disgrace of the mistake to her blue-stocking reputation. Afterwards, when the parties came to understand one another better, Clay's blunder was the occasion of many a merry allusion among them.

When they rose from the table, Mrs. Laight conducted her friend to the library. Her children, as soon as they were left to the free interchange of their impressions of their dreaded visiter [sic], exclaimed:—"How unaffected she is!" "How very agreeable!" "I entirely forgot that she was anything uncommon!" "Who would suspect she had ever published a book!" "Or ever read one!" These may sound like equivocal compliments, but so Mrs. Rosewell did not esteem them; and any unpretending fellow-sufferer, who has been invested with the repulsive name of blue-stocking, would prefer them to fifty diplomas from as many learned societies.

Mrs. Laight had put her library into complete order for her friend's reception. Alas! what a labor lost it was! Books of scholastic divinity and philosophy, over which her father, the Doctor, had withered and dried away, body and spirit, for forty years, had been brought forth from the quiet oblivion which they had shared with their old proprietor, and were ostentatiously arranged on shelves where they bore the same relative interest to the fresh, tempting, unbound, and dog-eared volumes of modern writers, that mummies do to a beautiful piece of living and glowing humanity. "This apartment," said Mrs. Laight, looking around her with a serene smile of enviable self-complacency, "this apartment is yours; your sanctum sanctorum; your imperium in imperio,[27] as my dear father would have said. Here are books, a mine of wealth; and here, my dear," opening a writing-desk, "are materials for more books; pens in abundance; ink and folio paper. By the way, do tell me what was your last work?"

27. Latin. *Sanctum sanctorum*: holy of holies, or most sacred spot. *Imperium in imperio*: a state within a state, such as the Vatican.

"My *last* work; really; I do not remember!" replied Mrs. Rosewell, hesitating and half smiling.

"Not remember? that's impossible!"

"Pardon me; I do; my last work was cutting out some vests for my boys."

The good lady looked crest-fallen, and replied so meekly, that Mrs. Rosewell was conscience-stricken.

"It is very natural, I know it is, my dear, that you should think my knowledge limited to such *works* as you have mentioned; but I assure you, I have always had a literary taste, and if I had been a man I should have devoted myself to books; but women, at least most of us, are condemned to obscure, if not useless, lives."

"My good friend, you do your lot injustice; your life, according to Napoleon's estimate in his celebrated reply to Madame de Stael, has been illustrious."[28]

"How? what do you mean?" asked Mrs. Laight, eagerly, hoping for some new revelation on her past destiny.

"Why, have you not given twelve children to the state?" Poor Mrs. Laight's countenance fell; her friend proceeded; "I cannot think there is any great merit in number, but a mother, who has twelve *such* children as yours, may make a Cornelian[29] boast of them, and ought to be hailed as a benefactress to her country."

The mother (Mrs. Laight was a true-hearted one), for a moment, prevailed over her ruling passion. "They are good children," she said, "all of them; kind, affectionate, and dutiful, and I ought to be satisfied with them; but it is a disappointment, that not one of them takes after me; that not one of them has the least literary turn. Sarah, indeed—Sarah has, I think, a *latent* talent. She writes a pretty letter; she has quite a knack at quotation, and, if she were to get into the right kind of society, her ambition might be roused. Once a reader, she might become a writer."

"Ah! these possibilities look well for my friend, the Professor."

"How?" exclaimed Mrs. Laight, and after turning the key of the door and drawing close to her friend, she added, "do you think the Professor is attached to Sarah?"

"Not precisely attached, but if he believed he might gain her affections, and your approbation, he would soon be irretrievably in love."

"My approbation!" exclaimed the good lady, "he has it already; it is the very thing. To tell you the truth, I have long had a secret hope this might be. How delightful for us again to be connected with the college! You have my consent to give the Professor a hint that he will meet with no opposition."

"None from you, I perceive; but has he nothing to fear in another quarter? We have heard alarming rumors of an attachment between young Clay and Sarah, and I fancied I perceived some indications that confirmed them."

28. When Madame de Staël, fishing for a compliment, asked Napoleon Bonaparte who was the greatest woman, he responded, "She who bears the most children to the state."

29. The Cornelius family was one of the most prolific and illustrious of ancient Rome.

"Oh, that's nothing; a mere childish predilection, which has kept alive by Frank's intimacy with Leonard; Sarah knows my opinion of Leonard."

"He is a very pleasing young man. Is there any objection to him?"

"Very pleasing! *You* cannot think so. Recollect his blunder about the macaroni! a specimen of his ignorance, my dear. He has not one particle of erudition. He was, to be sure, a great favorite with my husband, because he was a lad of integrity, intelligent about affairs, and successful in managing his own. The young people like him because he is good humored and amiable. But he is no reader; and as to writing, I do not believe he ever wrote a paragraph for a newspaper—in short, my dear friend, he has nothing of what you and I should call *mind.*"

The scale by which Mrs. Rosewell graduated *mind* was different from her friend's. She thought it was best demonstrated by the wise and successful conduct of life; and conceiving a good opinion of Clay, and guessing truly at the real position of affairs, she placed the subject in the most favorable light to the mother; and so adroitly used her influence, that she obtained Mrs. Laight's acquiescence in the propriety of giving a hint to the Professor (whose affections were too precious to put to hazard), to make a timely retreat.

This subject dismissed, and by Mrs. Laight, with a sigh of disappointment, she, after a misty preface, introduced another topic, still nearer to her heart. The preface I omit. The topic was a manuscript production, which no eye had yet seen, "on the intellectual faculties, comprising a view of their essence—modus operandi[30] (a scrap of Latin from her father of blessed memory)—of their sublimity and beauty, and of their use to society in general."

Mrs. Rosewell's heart sank within her, as she read the ominous title, and promised her friend that she would examine the closely written pages to which it was prefixed, and would give her *honest* opinion as to their publication.

I promised my readers a sketch; and I do not mean to take them in for a story; a sketch of a *blue-stocking,* falsely so called, and I have merely given a few circumstances, to illustrate the common impressions against those who are unfairly branded with an odious name. They are shown off as lions by the little flutterers (willing to scorch their own wings in a blaze), when they would rather pass for a sheep, or any other "very gentle beast, and of a good conscience."[31] I can at least answer for my friend, Mrs. Rosewell. She has all the most lovely qualities of her sex. She has well done those humble duties that lie in the obscure recesses of domestic life. She has genius without eccentricity, knowledge without pedantry, and enthusiasm without extravagance. Her colloquial gifts are hardly surpassed, yet I never detected her in the vanity of talking to display them. Her manners are so gentle and

---

30. Mode of operation.
31. Lines from William Shakespeare's *A Midsummer Night's Dream* (ca. 1595–1596).

feminine, that she seems rather to ask sufferance than to claim admiration. None are impassive to her influence. It resembles the fabled effect of the sun on Memnon's statue,[32] eliciting melody from the cold and silent. This is by no miracle, but by the steady application of her powers to their legitimate objects. She loves her fellow creatures, and takes a benevolent interest in whatever elevates or makes them happier. She looks on the bright side of characters, as well as of events. She finds good in everything. I have sometimes thought she gave undue encouragement to the vanity of others, but it must be confessed to be difficult to raise to a sudden elevation, without causing dizziness.

Mrs. Rosewell is literary, and—a blue-stocking. I cannot deny it; if the most ardent devotion to knowledge and talent, even though they chance to be found in books; if a love of science; if an occasional communication to the public of the result of her studies and observations, constitutes a *blue-stocking*. But if being the most honored and beloved of wives; the most tender and capable of mothers; the most efficient and least bustling of housewives; the truest of friends, and the most attractive of women, can rescue her from this repulsive name, she deserves it no more than the veriest ignoramus in the land. If any doubt the truth of my portrait, I appeal to our friends of *Lawrentum*. In a visit of a month she worked wonders there. She entered heartily into the views of the young people, and what was more important, brought their mother to their point of sight. Sarah was permitted to plight her troth to Leonard Clay, and Frank, his to the pretty orphan, Anne Milnor, without one sigh from their mother over their unlettered destiny. She even confessed, that her girls had talents, though not a literary turn; and that her boys were clever, in their way, though they preferred fishing and sporting to books. She ceased to express her surprise (never I believe to feel it), that Mrs. Rosewell loved better to ramble over the country, or romp with the children, than to immure herself in the library with the Doctor's rare books. My friend's greatest achievement, she deems it her *chef d'œuvre*,[33] was inducing Mrs. Laight to suppress her metaphysical essay, and that, too, without wounding her vanity, or materially abating her self-complacency. Mrs. Rosewell's conquest over the junior members of the family, if not as surprising, was as complete. The girls confided to her their most romantic sentiments. Leonard Clay secretly begged her to prescribe a course of reading to him; that would qualify him to elicit Sarah's *latent* talents; and Frank was detected in purchasing the books she had published to beguile the tediousness of his next voyage.

I have not ventured to grace my portrait with those minute touches that would

---

32. The statue of Memnon, son of Aurora, at Thebes was said to produce a sound like the snap of a musical string when the rays of the morning sun (or Aurora) fell upon it.

33. French: Masterpiece of literature or art.

have identified it, but I doubt not that its verisimilitude will be acknowledged by those who are familiar with any of the circles of the cultivated, useful, and happy women of our country.

Source: Token and Atlantic Souvenir (1832)

Maria Miller was born in Hartford, Connecticut, and orphaned when she was five. For ten years she was a servant in a clergyman's family. Thereafter she was a domestic in other homes and attended a Sabbath school, the main source of her education. When she was twenty-three she married the middle-class businessman James W. Stewart but was widowed three years later. She subsequently experienced a religious conversion, and at twenty-eight she became the first American woman to speak in public. Her public speaking career ended in 1833, when she left Boston for New York and became a teacher. From there she moved to Baltimore and then Washington, D.C., where she died. The introductory section to her first publication, which initially appeared in The Liberator *in 1831, is reprinted below. In this piece, she encourages her African American audience in their pursuit of literacy, which she saw as leading to their public agitation against slavery, an act justified by Christianity.*

Introduction to "Religion and the Pure Principles of Morality, the Sure Foundation on Which We Must Build"

Feeling a deep solemnity of soul, in view of our wretched and degraded situation, and sensible of the gross ignorance that prevails among us, I have thought proper thus publicly to express my sentiments before you. I hope my friends will not scrutinize these pages with too severe an eye, as I have not calculated to display either elegance or taste in their composition, but have merely written the meditations of my heart as far as my imagination led; and have presented them before you, in order to arouse you to exertion, and to enforce upon your minds the great necessity of turning your attention to knowledge and improvement. . . .

All the nations of the earth are crying out for Liberty and Equality. Away, away with tyranny and oppression! And shall Afric's [*sic*] sons be silent any longer? Far be it from me to recommend to you, either to kill, burn, or destroy. But I would strongly recommend to you, to improve your talents; let not one lie buried in the earth. Show forth your powers of mind. Prove to the world, that

> Though black your skins as shades of night,
> Your hearts are pure, your souls are white.

This is the land of freedom. The press is at liberty. Every man has a right to express his opinion. Many think, because your skins are tinged with a sable hue, that you are an inferior race of beings; but God does not consider you as such. He hath formed and fashioned you in his own glorious image, and hath bestowed upon you reason and strong powers of intellect. He hath made you to have dominion over the beasts of the field, the fowls of the air, and the fish of the sea. He hath crowned you with glory and honor; hath made you but a little lower than the angels; and, according to the Constitution of these United States, he hath made all men free and equal. Then why should one worm say to another, "Keep you down there, while I sit up yonder; for I am better than thou?" It is not the color of the skin that makes the man, but it is the principles formed within the soul.

Many will suffer for pleading the cause of oppressed Africa, and I shall glory in being one of her martyrs; for I am firmly persuaded, that the God in whom I trust is able to protect me from the rage and malice of mine enemies, and from them that will rise up against me; and if there is no other way for me to escape, he is able to take me to himself, as he did the most noble, fearless, and undaunted David Walker.[1]

NEVER WILL VIRTUE, KNOWLEDGE, AND TRUE POLITENESS BEGIN TO FLOW,
    TILL THE PURE PRINCIPLES OF RELIGION AND MORALITY ARE PUT INTO
    FORCE.

MY RESPECTED FRIENDS,

I feel almost unable to address you; almost incompetent to perform the task; and, at times, I have felt ready to exclaim, O that my head were waters, and mine eyes a fountain of tears, that I might weep day and night, for the transgressions of the daughters of my people. Truly, my heart's desire and prayer is, that Ethiopia might stretch forth her hands unto God. But we have a great work to do. Never, no, never will the chains of slavery and ignorance burst, till we become united as one, and cultivate among ourselves the pure principles of piety, morality and virtue. I am sensible of my ignorance; but such knowledge as God has given to me, I impart to you. I am sensible of former prejudices; but it is high time for prejudices and animosities to cease from among us. I am sensible of exposing myself to calumny and reproach; but shall I, for fear of feeble man who shall die, hold my peace? shall I for fear of scoffs and frowns, refrain my tongue? Ah, no! I speak as one that must give an account at the awful bar of God; I speak as a dying mortal, to dying mortals. O, ye daughters of Africa, awake! awake! arise! no longer sleep nor slumber, but distinguish yourselves. Show forth to the world that ye are endowed with noble and exalted faculties. O, ye daughters of Africa! what have ye done to immortalize your names beyond the grave? what examples have ye set before the rising generation? what foundation have ye laid for generations yet unborn? where are our union and love? and where is our sympathy, that weeps at another's wo [sic], and hides the faults we see? And our daughters, where are they? blushing in innocence and virtue? And our sons, do they bid fair to become crowns of glory to our hoary heads?

---

1. David Walker (1785–1830) was a free black who wrote the *Appeal, In Four Articles: Together With A Preamble To The Coloured Citizens Of The World, But In Particular, And Very Expressly, To Those Of The United States Of America* (1829) to arouse the slaves of the South to rebellion.

Where is the parent who is conscious of having faithfully discharged his duty, and at the last awful day of account, shall be able to say, here, Lord, is thy poor, unworthy servant, and the children thou hast given me? And where are the children that will arise, and call them blessed? Alas, O God! forgive me if I speak amiss; the minds of our tender babes are tainted as soon as they are born; they go astray, as it were, from the womb. Where is the maiden who will blush at vulgarity? and where is the youth who has written upon his manly brow a thirst for knowledge; whose ambitious mind soars above trifles, and longs for the time to come, when he shall redress the wrongs of his father, and plead the cause of his brethren? Did the daughters of our land possess a delicacy of manners, combined with gentleness and dignity; did their pure minds hold vice in abhorrence and contempt, did they frown when their ears were polluted with its vile accents, would not their influence become powerful? would not our brethren fall in love with their virtues? Their souls would become fired with a holy zeal for freedom's cause. They would become ambitious to distinguish themselves. They would become proud to display their talents. Able advocates would arise in our defence. Knowledge would begin to flow, and the chains of slavery and ignorance would melt like wax before the flames. I am but a feeble instrument. I am but as one particle of the small dust of the earth. You may frown or smile. After I am dead, perhaps before, God will surely raise up those who will more powerfully and eloquently plead the cause of virtue and the pure principles of morality than I am able to do. . . .

I have been taking a survey of the American people in my own mind, and I see them thriving in arts, and sciences, and in polite literature. Their highest aim is to excel in political, moral and religious improvement. They early consecrate their children to God, and their youth indeed are blushing in artless innocence; they wipe the tears from the orphan's eyes, and they cause the widow's heart to sing for joy! and their poorest ones, who have the least wish to excel, they promote! And those that have but one talent, they encourage. But how very few are there among them that bestow one thought upon the benighted sons and daughters of Africa, who have enriched the soils of America with their tears and blood: few to promote their cause, none to encourage their talents. Under these circumstances, do not let our hearts be any longer discouraged; it is no use to murmur nor to repine; but let us promote ourselves and improve our own talents. And I am rejoiced to reflect that there are many able and talented ones among us, whose names might be recorded on the bright annals of fame. But, *"I can't,"* is a great barrier in the way. I hope it will soon be removed, and *"I will,"* resume its place. . . .

I have never taken one step, my friends, with a design to raise myself in your esteem, or to gain applause. But what I have done, has been done with an eye single to the glory of God, and to promote the good of souls. I have neither kindred nor friends. I stand alone in your midst, exposed to the fiery darts of the devil, and to the assaults of wicked men. But though all the powers of earth and hell were to combine against me, though all nature should sink into decay, still would I trust in the Lord, and joy in the God of my salvation. For I am fully persuaded, that he will bring me off conqueror, yea, more than conqueror, through him who hath loved me and given himself for me.

Source: Productions of Mrs. Maria Stewart, Presented to the First African Baptist Church and Society (1835)

&. ELIZA EARLE (1807–1846)

A white Quaker, Eliza Earle was a teacher and participant in the abolitionist move-ment. She inherited her love of literature from her mother, Patience, who published her poetry in local newspapers. Eliza published many poems under the pseudonym "Ada," which is the first female name in the Old Testament, until she married William Hacker in 1840 and began using her own name. She likely died due to complications from the birth of her third child. This poem, signed by "Ada," was for many years mistakenly attributed to African American poet Sara Forten, who also wrote under this pseudonym. It includes the often-quoted line "The pen is ours to wield," an assertion of women's right to participate with their pens in public discussions of slavery.

Lines

Suggested on Reading "An Appeal to Christian Women of the South," by A. E. Grimke.[1]

My spirit leaps in joyousness tow'rd thine,
My gifted sister, as with gladdened heart
My vision flies along thy "speaking pages."
Well hast thou toiled in Mercy's sacred cause;
And thus another strong and lasting thread
Is added to the woof our sex is weaving,
With skill and industry, for Freedom's garb.
Precious the privilege to labor here,—
Worthy the lofty mind and handy-work
Of Chapman, Chandler, Child, and Grimke too.[2]
There's much in woman's influence, ay much,
To swell the rolling tide of sympathy,
And aid those champions of a fettered race,
Now laboring arduous in the moral field.
We may not "cry aloud," as they are bid,
And lift our voices in the *public* ear;
Nor yet be mute. The pen is ours to wield,
The heart to will, and hands to execute.

1. Angelina Grimké (1805–1879), a Quaker originally from South Carolina, lived in Philadel-phia. She was an abolitionist and one of the first American women to speak in public. Her tract *An Appeal to the Christian Women of the South* (1836) was burned in the South and caused a public outcry in the North.

2. Maria Weston Chapman (1806–1885), Elizabeth Margaret Chandler (1807–1834), Lydia Maria Child (1802–1880), and Grimké all published antislavery writings.

And more the gracious promise gives to all—
Ask, says the Saviour, and ye shall receive.
In concert then, Father of love, we join,
To wrestle with thy presence, as of old
Did Israel, and will not let thee go
Until thou bless. The cause is thine—for 'tis
Thy guiltless poor who are oppressed, on whom
The sun of Freedom may not cast his beams,
Nor dew of heavenly knowledge e'er descend.
And for their fearless advocates we ask
The wisdom of the serpent—above all,
Our heavenly Father, clothe, oh clothe them with
The dove-like spirit of thine own dear Son:
Then are they safe, tho' Persecution's waves
Dash o'er their bark, and furious winds assail—
Still they are safe.
————Yes, this *is* woman's work,
Her own appropriate sphere; and nought should drive
Her from the mercy seat, till Mercy's work
Be finished.
    Whose is that wail, piercing the ear
Of night, with agony too deep for words
To give it birth? 'Tis woman's—she of Ramah—
Another Rachel, weeping for her babes,
And will not be consoled, for they are not.[3]
Oh! slavery, with all its withering power,
Can never wholly quench the flame of love,
Nor dry the stream of tenderness that flows
In breasts maternal. A *mother's love!* deep grows
That plant of Heaven, fast by the well of life,
And nought can pluck it thence till woman cease
To be.—Then, long as mother's hearts are breaking
Beneath the hammer of the auctioneer,
And ruthless Avarice tears asunder bonds,
That the fiat of the Almighty joined,
So long should woman's melting voice be heard,

3. Jeremiah 31:15: "Thus saith the LORD; A voice was heard in Ramah, lamentation, and bitter weeping; Rachel weeping for her children refused to be comforted for her children, because they were not."

In intercession strong and deep, that this
Accursed thing, this Achan[4] in our camp,
May be removed.

Source: Liberator (1836)

4. In the book of Joshua, Achan's crimes are believed to have caused God's wrath and the fall of Jericho.

🍂 Maria James (1793–1868)

Born in Wales, Maria James immigrated to the United States in 1803. At the age of ten, she entered domestic service in the Garrison family of Dutchess County, New York. Professor Alonzo Potter, a friend of the family, edited and wrote a lengthy introduction to a volume of her verses in 1839. When her first poem, "What is Poetry?" was published in The United States Democratic Review *in 1838, the following footnote appeared: "The above lines . . . are from the pen of Maria James, of Rhinebeck, New York, a young woman of very high merit, in every aspect of character and conduct, whose life has been spent from childhood in domestic service. To those of our readers who participate in the profound interest with which the truly sincere American democrat watches every scintillation of the light of educated and refined civilization flashing up from the depths, . . . these lines will not be without a lively interest."*

What Is Poetry?

A lambent flame within the breast;
A thought harmoniously express'd;
A distant meteor's glimmering ray;
A light that often leads astray;
A harp, whose ever-varying tone
Might waken to the breeze's moan;
A lake, in whose transparent face
Fair nature's lovely form we trace;
A blooming flower, in gardens rare,
Yet found in deserts bleak and bare;
A charm o'er every object thrown;
A bright creation of its own;
A burst of feeling, warm and wild,
From nature's own impassion'd child.

Thoughts
On Receiving a Blank Book

New, blank, and all so neatly bound,
There's inspiration in the sound;
Sure none might see, but fain would write,—
Would mar the pure, unsullied white,
And clothe the pages, in their turn,

"With thoughts that breathe and words that burn"—[1]
Here rescue from destruction's power
Some withering leaf—some fading flower—
Or sketch the rainbow's passing dyes,
Ere swift they vanish from the skies,—
Or call from memory's lonely waste
Some fleeting vision of the past,
As, uncontroll'd, the Muse again
Shall roam through fancy's wide domain.

Is there a heart by grief oppress'd,
An anxious, care-worn, aching breast,—
A load by day, no tongue can tell,
By night a sleepless sentinel?—
There may she speed, and with her bring
A balmy healing in her wing,—
A light the darkness to illume,—
A ray to penetrate the gloom;
Where misery's cup is still the share,
Infuse one drop of comfort there.

Would ills long past afflict the soul?
There bid oblivion's surges roll—
While looks and words, in kindness given,
Are treasur'd with our hopes of heaven.
Be this her aim, her object still,
To cherish virtue—banish ill—
To prove, what endless years shall prove—
'Tis man who errs,—that God is love.

Source: Wales: And Other Poems (1839)

1. Thomas Gray, "The Progress of Poesy" (1754).

❧ ANN S. STEPHENS (1810–1886)

Ann Sophia Winterbotham was a native of Connecticut, but after her marriage to Edward Stephens in 1831, she moved to Portland, Maine, where she edited and he published the Portland Magazine *from 1834 to 1836. She was a pioneer in the professionalization of literature for women, going on to author over forty volumes and serve as editor, co-editor, or associate editor for seven different magazines, including the* Ladies' Companion *(1837–1841),* Peterson's *(1849–1853), and* Mrs. Stephens' New Monthly *(1856–1858). She was a popular author of historical romances and domestic fiction and conducted a famous literary salon in New York after moving there in 1837. After her husband's death in 1862, she supported herself and two children by writing novels at the rate of more than one a year for the next twenty-four years. In the following essay, she asserts women's right to careers as authors and denies that literary pursuits unfit women to perform their domestic duties.*

Women of Genius

"What is genius but deep feeling,
Wakening to glorious revealing?
And what is feeling but to be
Alive to every misery!"—L. E. L.[1]

"I revere talent in any form," said a young friend in conversation, the other evening, "but, in selecting a wife, I should never think of choosing a woman of genius!"

"And why not," I inquired, expecting to hear him advance the usual list of objections to literary women—their want of domestic habits—eccentricities, carelessness of fashion, and the thousand unjust charges urged against a class of women as little understood as any upon the face of the earth. My friend was a man of no inconsiderable talent, and from him, the sentiment seemed strange and ungenerous. It was probably the first time that he had ever been called upon to think seriously upon the subject. He seemed puzzled how to make a fitting reply.

"Why," he said, after a moment's hesitation, "my *beau ideal* is somewhat like that of Byron's.[2] My wife should have talent enough to be able to understand and value mine, but not sufficient to be able to shine herself. I could never love a woman who was entirely occupied with literature. I want feeling, affection, devotion to

---

1. Lines from "The Golden Violet," in *The Golden Violet, With Its Tales of Romance and Chivalry; And Other Poems* (1827), by English writer L. E. L., or Letitia Elizabeth Landon (1802–1838).

2. In *Don Juan* (1819), Byron famously wrote, "Oh! ye lords of ladies intellectual, / Inform us truly, have they not hen-peck'd you all?"

myself—a domestic woman who would think my approbation sufficient for her happiness, and would have no desire for greater admiration. I could never be happy with an ambitious woman."

On my return home, the injustice of my friend's speech haunted me. He wanted feeling, affection, domestic qualities in a wife, and, *therefore,* would not seek one in a woman of genius. Byron's *beau ideal* was as purely a creature of the imagination as his Haidée or Zuleika.[3] He seems to have forgotten that to understand and value talent, is one of the highest attributes of genius; that no person ever thoroughly appreciated a feeling or a property of the intellect which she did not possess in a degree, at least. A less selfish man, instead of requiring mediocrity and a worshipper in the place of a companion, would only have wished that the beautiful delicacy which nature has implanted in the female mind to chasten and refine her genius, should be preserved, and that in her pursuits and feelings, she should be *womanly* and true to her sex.

Pen and paper lay convenient, and in fancy, I went on discoursing and putting questions, as if the culprit had been present in person.

Have you been thoroughly acquainted with a woman of undoubted genius—one who stands high in any department of our literature? Have you been domesticated with one—seen her at all seasons—entered into the sanctuary of her thoughts; have you been the brother, husband, father, or even friend of one?

You say no, and yet without knowledge, decide that they are not fit objects of domestic affection; that because certain uncommon powers are granted to them by the Most High for his own good purpose, the common attributes which form the loveliness and beauty of womanhood are withheld. You would hedge them round with respect and reverence, and yet fear to give them the affection which is to none more precious, by none more thirsted for, or more keenly appreciated. You would smother the spark which must kindle all that is worthy of love in the genius of woman. You would build to her an altar of marble, cold as the grave, and bow down your intellect before it in the homage which mind renders to mind, without one thought that beneath her mental wealth are affections in proportionate strength, which gush up at the call of sympathy, and tinge the mind with hues of beauty, as the sun forms a rainbow by weaving its light among the water-drops of a summer shower. Deep and sensitive feelings alone give that delicacy and pathos which will ever distinguish the creations of a truly feminine author from those of men. The very word genius comprehends all that makes the loveliness of woman. It signifies but the power to feel, deeply combined with an intellect capable of embodying feelings into language, and of conveying images of truth and beauty from the heart of the writer to the heart of the reader.

3. Haidée is from *Don Juan* (1819). Zuleika is from *The Bride of Abydos* (1813).

Why then should you refuse to gather the mantle of domestic love about the woman of genius?

Ambitious, are they? Else, why do they write—why publish?

Why do they write? Why does the bird sing but that its little heart is gushing over with melody? Why does the flower blossom but that it has been drenched with dew, and kindled up by the sunshine, till its perfume bursts the petals and lavishes its sweetness on the air? Why does the artist become restless with a yearning want as the creatures of his fancy spring to life beneath his pencil? When his ideal has taken to itself a form of beauty, does he rest till some kindred eye has gazed with his upon the living canvass? His heart is full of a strange joy, and he would impart something of that joy to another. Is this vanity? No, it is a beautiful desire for sympathy. The feeling may partake of a love of praise, but it is one which would be degraded by the title of ambition.

Ask any woman of genius why she writes, and she will tell you it is because she cannot help it; that there are times when a power which she can neither comprehend nor resist, impels her to the sweet exercise of her intellect; that at such moments, there is happiness in the very exertion—a thrilling excitement which makes the action of thought "its own exceeding reward;" that her heart is crowded with feelings which pant for language and for sympathy, and that ideas gush up from the mind unsought and uncalled for, as waters leap from their fount when the earth is deluged with moisture. I am almost certain that the most beautiful things that enrich our literature, have sprung to life from the sweet, irresistible impulse for creation, which pervaded the heart of the author without motive and without aim.

The motives which urge literary women to publish, are probably as various as those which lead persons to any other calling. Many may place themselves before the world from a natural and strictly feminine thirst for sympathy; from the same feeling which prompts a generous boy to call his companions about him, when he has found a robin's nest hid away among the blossoming boughs of an old apple-tree, or a bed of ripe strawberries melting in their own ruby light through the grass, on a hill-side. The discovery would be almost valueless could he find none to gaze on the blue eggs exposed in the bottom of the nest, or to revel with him in the luscious treasure of the strawberry-bed; so the enjoyment of a mental discovery is enhanced by companionship and appreciation.

That women sometimes publish, from the impulses of vanity, it were useless to deny; but, in such cases, the effort is usually worthy of the motive: it touches no heart, because it emanates from none; it kindles no pure imagination—it excites no holy impulses—because, the impulse from which it originated, is neither lofty nor worthy. It may be safely asserted, that no woman, who has written or published, from the promptings of ambition or vanity, alone, was ever successful, or ever will be. She may gain notoriety, but that is a consequence of authorship, which must ever be painful to a woman of true genius, unless is added to it that public respect and private affection, which can never be secured by one who writes from a wish to shine, and from that wish alone.

Literature is an honorable profession, and, that women devote a portion of their time to it, requires neither excuse nor palliation, so long as they preserve the delicacy and gentleness which are the attributes of their sex. It would be folly to assert that there is any thing in the nature of genius, which incapacitates its possessor for usefulness, or that a literary woman may not be, in the strictest sense of the word, a domestic one.

That the distinguished women of our country are remarkable for domestic qualities, admits of proof, from many brilliant examples. Most of those who stand foremost in our world of letters, perform the duties of wives, mothers and housekeepers, in connexion with the pursuits of mind. It is a mistaken idea, that literature must engross the entire time or attention, even of those who make authorship a profession. It is to be doubted if the most industrious female writer among us spends more hours out of the twenty-four, at her desk, than the fashionable belle devotes to the adornment of her person.

There are few American women, except those who labor for their daily bread, who, by a systematic arrangement of time, cannot command three or four hours out of each day, without encroaching on her household duties, the claims of society, or the little season of domestic enjoyment, when her household seeks companionship and relaxation at home. These hours devoted to authorship, at a moderate computation, would produce four duodecimo volumes[4] a year. Thus, by a judicious management of time, she has produced a property more or less valuable, enriched and strengthened her own mind, carried the sunshine of thought to thousands, and all without necessarily sacrificing one domestic duty—without the least degree of personal publicity, which need shock the most fastidious delicacy.

Cast not a shadow, even, of implied reproach on a class of women, who are quietly and steadily exerting a healthy influence in domestic life; rather let men of power—and, in this country, there is no power like that of intellect—extend to them such aid and encouragement, as will best preserve the purity of female literature. So long as the dignity and delicacy of sex is preserved, there *can* be no competition between men and women of genius. In literature, as in every thing else, the true woman will feel how much better it is to owe something to the protection, generosity, and forbearance of the stronger and sterner sex, than to enter into an unnatural strife in the broad arena which men claim for the trial of masculine intellect. Open the fountains of domestic love to her, and there is little danger that her genius will stray from the sunny nooks of literature, or that she will forsake the pure wells of affection, to leap into the high road of politics—to lose her identity in the smoke of a battle-field, or to gather up popular applause and unsatisfactory admira-

4. Small books, usually the format for popular literature.

tion, in place of tenderness, and all those home comforts which cling so naturally around the feminine heart.

It has been beautifully said, that the heart is woman's dominion. Cast her not forth, then, from the little kingdom which she may do so much to purify and embellish. Her gentle culture has kept many of those rugged passes green, where sterner laborers might have left them sterile and blossomless.

If you would cultivate genius aright, cherish it among the most holy of your household gods. Make it a domestic plant. Let its roots strike deep in your home, nor care that its perfume floats to a thousand casements besides your own, so long as the greenness and its blossoms are for you. Flowers of the sweetest breath give their perfume most lavishly to the breeze, and, yet, without exhausting their own delicate urns.

Source: Ladies' Companion (1839)

The following poem was published with the signature "Egeria." At least nine more poems were signed with this pseudonym and the words "Clark's Mills, Ohio" in The Southern Literary Messenger, *from 1839 to 1840. Egeria was the name of the wife of Numa Pompilius, Rome's second king. The name also belonged to a fourth-century pilgrim who wrote a letter describing her journey to the Holy Land, a fragment of which survived. This Egeria was believed to be a nun, which probably accounts for the anonymous poet's use of the name. In this poem, although the speaker laments solitude as the price of fame, she convinces herself of the worthiness of her sacrifice.*

The Poet and the Sybil

"And bought alone by gifts beyond all price—
The trusting heart's repose, the paradise
Of home with all its loves—doth fate allow
The crown of glory unto woman's brow."[1]

I.

I have sought thee oft, in the starless night—
    I have left a cheerful hearth,
When the lightning-flash was the only light
    That fell on the trembling earth.

I have sought thee beside the foamy sea,
    As its wild waves wash'd the strand,
When the whirlwind was sweeping flower and tree,
    With the besom of rage from the land.

I sought thee there, for they say thou dost love
    The night that is shrouded in storm,
When the sable clouds that are fleeting above,
    Wear a dark and a terrible form.

II.

"What would'st thou with me?" the Sybil[2] replied,
    "Thou wearest a wreath of fame;

1. From "Joan of Arc, in Rheims" (1828) by Felicia Hemans (1793–1835).
2. Prophetess associated with holy sites in ancient Greece.

What would'st thou of one whom fate has denied
    E'en the boon of a virtuous name?

I love not the night, nor the whirlwind, more
    Than thou, in whose youthful breast
The tempest-crash and the ocean-roar,
    Find types of their own unrest.

Do the happy, the gay, and the beautiful seek
    The loveliest spot that nature e'er made,
When the glow of contentment is bright on the cheek,
    Or hope on the heart like a gem-gift is laid?

When the heart that has sigh'd for a glorious name,
    And wasted its youth in the labor of years,
And the pale brow above wears the green wreath of fame;
    Why sighs it for solitude, silence, and tears?

The light of thy song is shed over the sea,
    And in isles afar off they are singing thy lays—
In ages to come, fame will point unto thee:
    Then what can'st thou wish for?—*thou hast the world's* PRAISE."

III.

Alas! alas! it is indeed too true;
    I've dreamed the first fresh hours of life away:
My hours of bliss have been but brief and few,
    And I have sought in fame a broken stay;
But is there not, (and hope beamed in her eye,)
    Some hope of happiness still left for me?
It cannot be that I am thus to die,
    So sad, and lonely—No, it *cannot* be;
Oh! I would give my fame, my glorious art,
    To win one pure and undivided heart.

IV.

Sad one! Genius is around thee—
    What hast thou to do with love?
With a mystic chain he's bound thee;
    Turn then, turn thy heart above!
Spells of night around thee lieth—

A mournful gift he made thy own,
And when thy heart oft sadly sigheth,
  Thou can'st not hear an answering tone.
Turn thy heart to things above thee,
  Thou hast given love for fame—
Would'st thou give for *one* to love thee,
  Thine own glory-circled name?
Go, sit thee down on earth's green bosom,
  And gaze upon the deep blue sky;
Go, watch the wild-flowers bud and blossom,
  Whose beauties with the pale stars vie.
Go forth at night, when stars are keeping
  Their solemn watch o'er quiet earth,
And heaven her pearly tears is weeping,
  As if she mourn'd the planet's birth.
Go, sit beside the gushing fountain,
  And listen to the night-wind's moan—
Go, climb the steep and hoary mountain:
  Thy spirit will not be alone.
Those are the treasures of the spirit
  Which barters human love for fame—
And *these* the gifts it must inherit;
  A broken heart and deathless name.

Source: Southern Literary Messenger (1840)

🍂 LYDIA SIGOURNEY (1791–1865)

Arguably the most popular American poet of the nineteenth century alongside Henry Wadsworth Longfellow and once considered the most important female poet after the British writer Felicia Hemans, Lydia Sigourney is almost forgotten today. Born Lydia Howard Huntley in Connecticut, she published her first book of poetry in 1815. Four years later she married Charles Sigourney, who did not approve of women conducting public careers as authors. However, as his business failed, she turned again to writing, publishing anonymously until her identity became known in 1833. One of the most prolific and best paid poets of her day, she was the first American woman to support herself as a professional writer, yet she always ranked her domestic duties uppermost. Sigourney published fifty books of poetry and prose, including educational and advice books. Her poetry defies easy categorization: sentimental treatments of death and love mingle with public and political themes. The excerpts from her autobiography below describe how she managed the conflict between home life and writing as well as the demands her editors and the reading public placed on her.

The Sacred Poet

Art thou a mouth for the immortal mind?—
A voice that shall be heard when ages sleep
In cold oblivion? when the rich man's pomp,
And all the ambitious strivings of the crowd
Shall be forgotten? art thou well convinc'd
That such a gift is thine?
                              Bow thee to dust,
And take this honour from the hand of God,
In deep humility, worm as thou art,
And all unworthy: ask for nought beside,
Thou, having this, hast all.
                              Prosperity,
Such as earth names, what are its gaudes to thee?
Accustom'd to the crystal and the gold
Of poesy, that, like a sea of glass,
Doth compass thee around.   Look up! look up!
Baptized and set apart for Heaven's high will,
Cast not thy pearls to groundlings, lest they rend
Thy lavish hand; but list when trembling dawn
Instructs Aurora; muse when night to night
Doth show forth knowledge, when the folded flower

Taketh its lesson of the dews that steal
Into its bosom, like the mother's hymn
O'er the tir'd infant; and thine ear shall drink
A music-tone to solace every wound
That earth has made.
                              Then strike thy hallow'd harp
For unborn ages, and with trumpet-tone
Wake the immortal mind to highest hopes,
And be the teacher of what cannot die.
Yea, wear thy birth-right nobly on thy brow,
And nerve thy wing for God.

To a Shred of Linen

Would they swept cleaner!—
                              Here's a littering shred
Of linen left behind—a vile reproach
To all good housewifery. Right glad am I
That no neat lady, train'd in ancient times
Of pudding-making, and of sampler-work,[1]
And speckless sanctity of household care,
Hath happened here to spy thee. She, no doubt,
Keen looking through her spectacles, would say,
"This comes of reading books:"—or some spruce beau,
Essenc'd and lily-handed, had he chanc'd
To scan thy slight superfices, 'twould be,
"This comes of writing poetry."—Well—well—
Come forth—offender!—hast thou aught to say?
Canst thou by merry thought, or quaint conceit,
Repay this risk that I have run for thee?
——Begin at alpha, and resolve thyself
Into thine elements. I see the stalk
And bright, blue flower of flax, which erst o'erspread
That fertile land where mighty Moses stretch'd
His rod miraculous. I see thy bloom
Tinging, too scantly, these New England vales.
But, lo! the sturdy farmer lifts his flail,

---

1. Young women were taught to embroider decorative samplers, which often included the alphabet and religious or moral sayings, as proof of their skill with the needle.

To crush thy bones unpitying, and his wife
With 'kerchief'd head, and eyes brimful of dust,
Thy fibrous nerves, with hatchel-tooth divides.
—I hear a voice of music—and, behold!
The ruddy damsel singeth at her wheel,
While by her side the rustic lover sits.
Perchance, his shrewd eye secretly doth count
The mass of skeins which, hanging on the wall,
Increaseth day by day. Perchance his thought
(For men have deeper minds than women—sure!)
Is calculating what a thrifty wife
The maid will make; and how his dairy shelves
Shall groan beneath the weight of golden cheese
Made by her dexterous hand, while many a keg
And pot of butter, to the market borne,
May, transmigrated, on his back appear
In new thanksgiving coats.

                              Fain would I ask,
Mine own New England, for thy once loved wheel,
By sofa and piano quite displac'd.
Why dost thou banish from thy parlour-hearth
That old Hygeian[2] harp, whose magic rul'd
Dyspepsia,[3] as the minstrel-shepherd's skill
Exorcis'd Saul's[4] ennui? There was no need,
In those good times, of trim callisthenics,
And there was less of gadding, and far more
Of home-born, heart-felt comfort, rooted strong
In industry, and bearing such rare fruit
As wealth might never purchase.

                              But come back,
Thou shred of linen. I did let thee drop,
In my harangue, as wiser ones have lost
The thread of their discourse. What was thy lot
When the rough battery of the loom had stretch'd
And knit thy sinews, and the chemist sun
Thy brown complexion bleach'd?

                              Methinks I scan

2. Hygeia was the Greek goddess of health.
3. Indigestion.
4. Saul, the first king of Israel, was entertained by David's harp.

Some idiosyncrasy, that marks thee out
A defunct pillow-case.—Did the trim guest,
To the best chamber usher'd, e'er admire
The snowy whiteness of thy freshen'd youth
Feeding thy vanity? or some sweet babe
Pour its pure dream of innocence on thee?
Say, hast thou listen'd to the sick one's moan,
When there was none to comfort?—or shrunk back
From the dire tossings of the proud man's brow?
Or gather'd from young beauty's restless sigh
A tale of untold love?
                              Still, close and mute!—
Wilt tell no secrets, ha?—Well then, go down,
With all thy churl-kept hoard of curious lore,
In majesty and mystery, go down
Into the paper-mill, and from its jaws,
Stainless and smooth, emerge.—Happy shall be
The renovation, if on thy fair page
Wisdom and truth, their hallow'd lineaments
Trace for posterity. So shall thine end
Be better than thy birth, and worthier bard
Thine apotheosis immortalize.

Source: Pocahontas, and Other Poems (1841)

The Muse

They say that the cell of the poet should be
Like the breast of the shell that remembers the sea,
Quiet and still, save a murmuring sigh
Of the far-rolling wave to the summer-lit sky;
Tasteful and polished, as coralline bowers,
Remote from intrusion, and fragrant with flowers.

'Twould be beautiful, surely, but as for me,
Nothing like this I expect to see,
For I've written my poetry, sooth to say,
In the oddest of places, by night or by day,
Line by line, with a broken chain,
Interrupted, and joined again.

I, if paper were wanting, or pencils had fled,
Some niche in the brain, spread a storehouse instead,
And Memory preserved, in her casket of thought,
The embryo rhymes, till the tablets were brought:
At home or abroad, on the land or the sea,—
Wherever it came, it was welcome to me.

When first it would steal o'er my infantine hour,
With a buz [*sic*] or a song, like a bee in a flower,
With its ringing rhythm, and its measured line,
What it was I could scarce divine,
Calling so oft, from my sports and play,
To some nook in the garden, away, away,
To a mound of turf which the daisies crown,
Or a vine-wreathed summer-house, old and brown,
On a lilac's green leaf, with a pin, to grave
The tinkling chime of the words it gave.

At dewy morn, when to school I hied,
Methought like a sister it went by my side,
Well pleased o'er the fresh lanes to gambol and stray,
Or gather the violets that grew by the way,
Or turn my lessons to rhyme, and bask
In a rose, 'till I finished my needle's task.

When Winter in frost did the landscape enfold,
And my own little study was cheerless and cold,
A humble resource from the exigence rose,
And a barn was my favourite place to compose;
For there I could stow myself snugly away,
With my pencil and slate, on a nice mow of hay;
While with motherly face peeping out from her rack,
The cow munched her food, with a calf at her back;
And the fancies that there in that solitude wrought,
Were as chainless and bright as the palace-born thought.

When school years were o'er, and the tremulous ray
Of the young dawn of life took the tinting of day,
With ardour and pride I delighted to share,
By the side of my mother, her sweet household care.
My callisthenics followed each morning, with zeal,

Were the duster and broom, and the great spinning-wheel;
No curve of the spine in that region was feared,
And of nervous diseases we seldom had heard.
So, singing along, with a buoyant tread
I drew out a line, as I drew out a thread.
Bees and bluebirds the casement flew by,
Yet none were so busy or happy as I;
The voice of my wheel, like a harp in my ear,
And the Muse keeping time with her melody clear,
And the joy of my heart overflowing the lay,
And my parent's approval each toil to repay.

A season there was when the viol grew sweet,
And the maze of the dance was a charm to my feet,
For Youth and Joy, with their measures gay,
Beckoned me onward both night and day;
Yet oft in the soul was a secret tone
Winning away to my chamber lone,
And, lingering there, was a form serene
With a mild reproof on her pensive mien;
And though I feigned from her sway to start,
Having music enough in my own merry heart,
Yet her quiet tear on my brow that fell,
Was more dear than the dance or the viol's swell.

When life's mantling pleasures their climax attained,
And the sphere of a wife and a mother was gained,
When that transport awoke, which no language may speak,
As the breath of my first-born stole soft o'er my cheek,
While she slept on my breast, in the nursery fair,
A smothered lyre would arrest me there,
Half complaining of deep neglect,
Half demanding its old respect;
And if I mingled its cadence mild
With the tuneful tones of the rosy child,
Methought 'twas no folly such garlands to twine,
As could brighten life's cares, and its pleasures refine.

And now, though my life from its zenith doth wane,
And the wreaths of its morning grow scentless and vain,
And many a friend who its pilgrimage blest,

Have fallen from my heart and gone down to their rest,
Yet still by my side, unforgetful and true,
Is the being that walked with me all the way through.
She doth cling to the High Rock wherein is my trust,
Let her chant to my soul when I go to the dust;
Hand in hand with the faith that my Saviour hath given
Let her kneel at His feet mid the anthems of Heaven.

Source: The Western Home and Other Poems (1854)

Letters of Life [Excerpts]

There was a long period, after I became a writer for the public, when periodical literature flourished abundantly. . . .

On this sea of miscellany I was allured to embark, and, having set sail, there was no return. I think now with amazement, and almost incredulity, of the number of articles I was induced by the urgency of editors to furnish. Before I ceased to keep a regular catalogue, they had amounted to more than two thousand. Some of these were afterwards comprehended in selections, though enough for several volumes must still be floating about, like sea-weed among the noteless billows. They were divided among nearly three hundred different publications, from the aristocratic "Keepsake" of the Countess of Blessington, and the classic "Athenæum" and "For-get-Me-Not" of London, to the "Coachmakers' Magazine," the "Herald of the Upper Mississippi," the "Buckeye Blossom" of the West, and the "Rose-Bud" of the factory girls at Lowell. Promptitude was the life-blood of these contributions. Hungering presses must be fed, and not wait. How to obtain time to appease editorial appetites, and not neglect my housekeeping tactics, was a study. I found the employment of knitting congenial to the contemplation and treatment of the slight themes that were desired, and, while completing fifteen or sometimes twenty pairs of stockings yearly for our large family, or for the poor, stopped the needles to arrest the wings of a flying thought or a flowing stanza. Still, I always corrected, and rewrote more than once, these extemporaneous effusions, not considering it decorous to throw crude matter at the head of the public.

This habit of writing *currente calamo*[5] is fatal to literary ambition. It prevents that labor of thought by which intellectual eminence is acquired. Miss Edgeworth,[6] however, thinks fit thus to commend it: "Few persons of genius have possessed what Mrs. Sigourney appears to have—the power of writing extempore on passing sub-

---

5. With a running pen, without planning or revision.
6. Maria Edgeworth (1768–1849), British author of domestic novels of manners.

jects, and at the moment they chance to be called for. She must have great command over her own mind, or what a celebrated physician used to call 'voluntary attention,' in which most people are so lamentably deficient, that they can never write any thing well when called upon for it, or when the subject is suggested and the effort bespoken. Those powers are twice as valuable that can well accomplish their purpose on demand. Certainly, as it respects poetic gifts, those who give promptly give twice. How few, even of professed and eminent poets, have been able to produce any effusion worthy of their reputation, or even worth reading on what the French call 'des sujets de commande,' or what we English describe as on the 'spur of the moment!' Gray could not—Addison could not. Mrs. Sigourney's friends will doubtless be ready to bear testimony that she can."

With the establishment of a poetic name came a host of novel requisitions. Fame gathered from abroad cut out work at home. The number and nature of consequent applications were alike remarkable. Churches requested hymns, to be sung at consecrations, ordinations, and installations; charitable societies, for anniversaries; academies and schools, for exhibitions. Odes were desired for the festivities of New Year and the Fourth of July, for silver and golden weddings, for the voyager wherewith to express his leave-taking, and the lover to propitiate his mistress. Epistles from strangers often solicited elegies and epitaphs; and though the voice of bereavement was to me a sacred thing, yet I felt the inefficiency of balm thus offered to a heart that bled. Sometimes I consoled myself that the multitude of these solicitations bespoke an increasing taste for poetry among the people. But to gratify all was an impossibility. They would not only have covered the surface of one life, but of as many as ancient fable attributed to the feline race. I undertook at one time to keep a statement of the solicitations that showered upon me. A good-sized manuscript book was thus soon filled. It was commenced during what dear Mrs. Hemans used to call the "album persecution." It was then the fashion for school-girls, other youthful personages, and indeed people of every age, to possess themselves of a neatly-bound blank book, which was sent indiscriminately to any one whom they chose, with the request, or exaction, of a page or more in their own handwriting.

Of those who were so unfortunate as to be known as rhymers, it was expressly stipulated that it must be original. Sometimes there would be a mass of these cormorant tax-gatherers in the house at the same time. To refuse compliance was accounted an offence, or an insult. I commuted the matter with my imperative engagements as well as I could, by setting aside a peculiar portion of time for these enforced subsidies. Happily this custom is now obsolete, having been merged in the slighter impost of autographs. . . .

If there is any kitchen in Parnassus,[7] my Muse has surely officiated there as a woman of all work, and an aproned waiter. Lacking firmness to say no, I consented

7. Mountain in Delphi; home of the Muses in Greek mythology.

so frequently, that the right of refusal began to be counted invidious. Those who requested but a few verses considered them, what they appeared to be, a trifle. Yet "trifles make up the sum of human things," and this trifle involved thought, labor, and time. This habit of yielding to persuasion occasionally led to the curtailment of sleep, and of meals, as the poems which were to be sung in public audiences must be ready at a specified period, and frequently a very brief notice was accorded me. Sometimes I have been urged to send copies of long printed poems to strangers, that they might possess them in my own handwriting. Though there is always a degree of pleasure connected with obliging others, yet the extent of my own facility or folly in this respect might be rebuked by the common sense displayed in other occupations.

Do we go to a milliner, and say, "You have earned a good name in your line. Make me a bonnet and a dress. I should prize them as proofs of your skill?" Do we tell the carpet manufacturer, "You assort your colors better than others. Weave me a carpet for my study?" Do we address the professed cook with "You have a high reputation. I am to have a party. Come and make my jellies and confections?" Would those functionaries, think ye, devote time, toil, and material to such proposals, without compensation? I trow not. But a truce to this diffuse matter of custom-work.

My epistolary intercourse is extensive, and exceeds a yearly exchange of two thousand letters. It includes many from strangers, who are often disposed to be tenacious of replies, and to construe omission as rude neglect. I have no aid from amanuensis or copyist since the marriage of my loved daughter, or any listening friend to whom I may take the liberty of reading an unpublished production. Yet, if ever inclined to account so large a correspondence burdensome, I solace myself with the priceless value of the epistles of long-tried friendship, with the warm vitality often breathing from young hearts, and the hope of disseminating through this quiet vehicle, some cheering thought or hallowed principle.

My literary course has been a happy one. Its encouragements have exceeded both my expectations and deserts. Originating in impulse, and those habits of writing that were deepened by the solitary lot of an only child, it gradually assumed a financial feature which gave it both perseverance and permanence.

This, which at first supplied only my indulgences, my journeyings, or my charities, became eventually a form of subsistence; and now, through the income of its accumulated savings, gives ease to the expenditure of my widowhood, and the means of mingling with the benevolent enterprises of the day. Pecuniary gain has flowed in upon me rather from abroad than at home. With the exception of the initiatory volume, sheltered under the patronage of my venerated friend, Mr. Wadsworth, scarcely any profit has accrued to my literary labors in this vicinity, or indeed in the whole of my own New England. On the contrary, some severe losses have occurred. To the States of New York and Pennsylvania I am mainly indebted for the remuneration of intellectual toil, and gratefully acknowledge them as bene-factors.

Fame, as a ruling motive, has not stimulated me to literary effort. It has ever seemed to have too flimsy a wing for sustained and satisfactory flight. Candid criti-cism, and the voice of friendship, have been coveted correctives and tonics. Still the only adequate payment [*sic*] are the hope and belief that, by enforcing some salu-tary precept, or prompting some hallowed practice, good may have been done to our race.

I ought to speak with more emphasis of the encouragement kindly addressed to me since first, as a timid waif, I ventured into regions then seldom traversed by the female foot. It has breathed upon me from highways and hedges, from boughs where nesting birds reared their young, from the crested billows, and the islands of the sea. Thanks be to Him who hath thus touched the hearts of my fellow-creatures with kindness toward me!

Letters of appreciation have reached me from crowned heads—from the King of Prussia, the Empress of Russia, and the late Queen of France; marks of favor from nobles of high degree; and what was to me still more animating, from mon-archs in the realm of mind. I have felt humbled by such distinctions, as transcend-ing my merits. Some degree of chastening counterpoise has arisen from the marked indifference of my native city, which I have loved almost with the fervor of the ancient Jews for Zion. Neither by word nor smile can I recollect that she has fos-tered the mental labors of the child who went out from her fair borders, leaving her heart behind. Sweet hospitalities she extends to me, but in the point where I yearn for her sympathy, or would fain lay my honors at her feet, she keeps silence. I wrote, by request, a lyric to be sung at the anniversary of her favorite academy, which the chief musician scornfully declined to perform, and it was read among the prose exercises. I prepared poems with my whole heart, for her beautiful bi-centennial birthday, and they were refused admission into the fair volume that described the festivity.

I mention these trifling circumstances, not by way of complaint, for they are unworthy of it, but simply as facts to prove that I have no other claim to the title of prophet, save the absence of honor in my own country, and with some slight thrill of the sadness of a child, whose filial love has failed of reciprocity.

Yes, my literary course has indeed been a most happy one. At an age surpassing threescore and ten, I still pursue it with unimpaired delight and unspectacled eyes. Through its agency, and the Divine blessing, I feel no loneliness, though my house-hold contains only servants, with the exception of occasional guests. Praise be unto Him who hath led me all my life long unto this day; and if any good fruit shall ever spring from the seed He hath enabled me to sow, to His name be all the glory.

Source: Letters of Life (1866)

❧ Harriet Jane Farley (1812–1907)

Harriet Jane Farley went to work at age fourteen and entered the textile factories in Lowell, Massachusetts, when she was twenty-five. Despite working up to thirteen hours a day, she began writing (under a variety of pseudonyms) for the Lowell Offering *in 1840 and became its editor in 1842. The magazine was solely the product of young women working in the Lowell mills, which brought it notoriety as well as the attention of Charles Dickens and Harriet Martineau. Farley's defensive editorial below suggests the skepticism and reproach under which she and her fellow writers labored. (The excerpts of Lucy Larcom's* A New England Girlhood *included in this anthology also discuss the magazine's early days.) Farley served as publisher and editor of the* New England Offering *from 1847 to 1850. After marrying John Intaglio Donlevy in 1854, she continued to write occasionally but devoted herself more to her family, which included one daughter and one stepdaughter.*

Conclusion of the Volume

In seating myself to write the article which is to conclude the first volume of the Offering, my mind reverts involuntarily to the commencement of our enterprize. Our periodical was sent into the literary world with many doubts and misgivings, and the Offering was humbly laid upon the altar of literature. A success which we hardly dared anticipate, has crowned our labors. From distant parts of our own land, from many respected and valuable authorities, and even from beyond the great waters, has the voice of praise and encouragement been wafted to our ears; and truly grateful has it been to us—for *all* have not been thus indulgent. We have gone on "through *evil* report" as well as "through *good* report;" and the voice of censure has mingled with the tones of approbation.

We are well aware of the circumstances which have procured for us so cheering a welcome. We know that the new star, which appeared in the literary firmament, was hailed with joy, not so much because it was bright and beautiful, as because it appeared where no star had shone before, and where none had dared to look for an illuminating ray. The joyous shout went up, because that little star could penetrate so thick a cloud. The wonder has been, that in the passage along the stream of life, those who are toiling at the oars have found time and capacities to pluck a few of the beautiful flowers which are blooming on the banks, the privilege of culling which had been generally conceded to the leisure passengers of the bark; and the astonishment, that some taste has been displayed in the selection of the blossoms, has been heightened by the reflection that they were plucked in *twilight* hours. We experience some pleasure in the knowledge that the blossoms, so prettily arranged in this *boquet*, were gathered by ourselves; and though another hand occasionally removed a withered leaf, or cast aside an unsightly stalk, yet what is left is *ours*.

We will now glance at some of the objections which have been urged against our publication.

We have been accused by those who seem to wish us no ill, of disingenuousness, and unfaithfulness to ourselves, as exponents of the general character and state of feeling among the female population of this city. They say the Offering, if indeed it be the organ of the factory girls, is not a *true* organ. It does not expose all the evils, and miseries, and mortifications, attendant upon a factory life. It speaks, they say, on only one side of the question; and they compare us to poor, caged birds, singing of the flowers which surround our prison bars, and apparently unconscious that those bars exist. We however challenge any one to prove that we have made false assertions, and happy indeed are we, if our minds can turn involuntarily to the sunny side of the objects which arrest our gaze. May it not be supposed that we have written of these flowers, because so many assert that they do not exist, and that

"No more for us the violet shall bloom,
Nor modest daisy rear its humble head"?

And perhaps we have written of the bright sky above us, because so many think our sun is always obscured by gloomy clouds.

And who will say that had the Offering been but the medium of the foreboding and discontented, and the instrument for the conveyance of one long, dismal wail throughout the land, that it would have been more useful, or a more correct exponent of the state of feeling amongst us?

We are not generally miserable, either in point of fact, or in the prospect of a dreadful future. This may be the result of our ignorance—for it should be observed that the objections brought against the manufacturing system, are usually founded on analogies from foreign lands. Neither are we philosophical enough to deduce the long chain of dreadful effects which many think will be consequent upon the simple causes which we see in operation around us. But more than this: we see not how we can be accused of disingenuousness when we have never, either through our Editor, or in any other way, pledged ourselves to disseminate a knowledge of every petty evil and inconvenience of the manufacturing system. The Offering has faithfully sustained its character, as A REPOSITORY OF ORIGINAL ARTICLES, WRITTEN BY FEMALES EMPLOYED IN THE MILLS. In the words of one of our own number, we,

"desired to show
What factory girls had power to do."

Still we might have portrayed the evils of a manufacturing system, had it not been a picture so often presented to the public, and painted, too, in colors black as the Stygian[1] waves. Something surely was needed to counteract the false impression made by others.

It has also been asserted that we are tools, dupes, decoys, &c. Now those who are acquainted with the circumstances in which this periodical originated, will certainly exonerate us from aspersions of this character; and if our publication has an influence, similar to that which has been attributed to it, it must be merely the incidental result of the removal of an unwarranted prejudice. And if that alone has restrained individuals from coming here, let there be henceforth no barrier.

We do not feel guilty of misleading others, by false representations. We have never said that confinement was less irksome, or labor less tedious here, than in any other place. We have never said that money could compensate for loss of health, or that exciting amusements were better than innocent pleasures. We have also so much confidence in the good sense of our countrywomen, as to feel assured that they will usually know when they have amended their condition. And should the time arrive when the great congregation of operatives here will cause a reduction of their wages, I fear not for the crust of black bread, the suppliant voice, and bended knee; for then the inducement to remain will be withdrawn. Our broad and beautiful country will long present her spreading prairies, verdant hills, and smiling vales, to all who would rather work than starve; and when that time shall no more exist, it will not be found that all wisdom and benevolence perished with the philanthropic of this age.

But those who have brought no other charge against us, say that our communications are too light, nonsensical, &c.

Now we never expected to be considered oracles, instructors, modern Minervas,[2] &c. We did not write for the Offering, thinking our assistance was needed to enlighten the community upon lofty or abstruse themes. Still we know that the solid metal, which would sink if alone, may be buoyed upon the waters by the light and otherwise useless pith of a tree; and so we may sometimes convey a useful moral in an amusing tale, which would have been passed unnoticed in a wise essay.

Yet if our "romantic stories" and "nonsense" have not even this redeeming quality, they are certainly an innocent amusement for those who are too toil-worn to engage after their day's labor in profound disquisitions, or deep investigations. May we not be allowed a harmless recreation? The Vicar of Wakefield[3] gave his daughters money to pay an old fortune-teller, saying, that he was "tired of being always wise;" and if the old and learned will sometimes indulge in pleasantries, may not *we* be

1. Of the River Styx in Greek mythology, hence, hellish.
2. Roman goddess of wisdom.
3. Novel by Oliver Goldsmith from 1766.

allowed this privilege? And those who can make a publication of this nature interesting without "nonsense" or "romantic stories," are gifted with talents for pleasing, superior to ours.

We will now take leave of our opponents, with the feeling that even their injustice would be no excuse for us, should we harbor malice or ill will; and gladly we turn to our friends and patrons.

A merry Christmas we wish them all, and a bounteous share of the blessings they so well deserve. May Providence ever smile upon their earthly path, and kindly hearts and hands be ever near, to cheer and aid their onward way.

To the Editor of this work we would also tender our thanks, for the patience, assiduity, and cheerfulness with which he has accomplished his arduous task. To him we are indebted for support and encouragement when our feelings were sorely tried. His was the cheering assurance that hostility would be of short duration; and though that hope was but a meteor light, it illuminated the gloom when the dark cloud hung nearest. He has the consciousness of projecting a noble work; and while we remember a stream which flowed on in almost unbroken darkness, we cannot forget *whose hand first* removed the overshadowing boughs, and showed a deriding world that those waters could flash and sparkle, when open to the sun's bright beams.

His opinion is also *ours*, that, spite of the aspersions cast upon us, no discredit has been done to *ourselves,* THE MANCHESTER[4] OF AMERICA, OR THE MODEL REPUBLIC itself, by the publication of THE LOWELL OFFERING.

Source: Lowell Offering (1841)

4. Industrial center of England.

❧ Lydia Jane Peirson (1802–1862)

A native of Connecticut, Lydia Jane Peirson married at age seventeen and moved to the Pennsylvania woods. Her collections of poetry were titled Forest Leaves *(1845) and* The Forest Minstrel *(1846). In the 1850s, she became active in the women's rights movement and was a corresponding editor for* The Woman's Advocate. *Caroline May, who included Peirson in her anthology of* American Female Poets *(1853), wrote, "Her muse has, indeed, been disciplined in the school of sorrow; she has had little leisure for study, and her poems have been generally 'written by the flickering lamp of midnight, with a weary hand, and yet more weary heart.' " Cut off from the literary centers of Boston and New York and consumed by domestic duties, Peirson was not able to sustain a career as a writer.*

My Muse

Born of the sunlight and the dew,
   That met amongst the flow'rs,
That on the river margin grew
   Beneath the willow bow'rs;
Her earliest pillow was a wreath
   Of violets newly blown,
And the meek incense of their breath
   Became at once her own.

Her cradle hymn the river sung
   In that same liquid tone,
With which it gave, when earth was young,
   Praise to the Living One;
The breeze that lay upon its breast
   Responded with a sigh,
And the sweet ring-dove from her nest
   Warbled her lullaby.

The only nurse she ever knew
   Was Nature, free and wild:
Such was her birth; and so she grew
   A moody, wayward child,
Who loved to climb the rocky steep,
   To wade the mountain stream;
To lie beside the sounding deep
   And weave the enchanted dream.

She lov'd the paths with shadows dim
   Beneath the dark-leav'd trees,
Where Nature's feather'd seraphim
   Mingled their melodies;
To dance amongst the pensile stems
   Whose blossoms bright and sweet,
Threw diamonds from their diadems
   Upon her fairy feet.

She lov'd to watch the day-star float
   Upon the aerial sea,
Till morning sunk his pearly boat
   In floods of brilliancy;
To see the angel of the storm
   Upon his wind-wing'd car,
With dark clouds wrapt around his form
   Come shouting from afar;

And pouring treasures rich and free,
   The pure refreshing rain,
Till every weed and forest tree
   Could boast its diamond chain;
Then rising with the hymn of praise
   That swell'd from hill and dale,
Leave a rainbow—sign of peace—
   Upon his misty veil.

She lov'd the wave's deep utterings,
   And gaz'd with frenzied eye
When night shook lightning from his wings,
   And winds went sobbing by.
Full oft I chid the wayward child
   Her wanderings to restrain,
And sought her airy limbs to bind
   With prudence's worldly chain.

I bade her stay within my cot
   And ply the housewife's art;
She heard me, but she heeded not;
   Oh who can bind the heart!
I told her she had none to guide

Her inexperienced feet,
To where through Tempe's valley glide
    Castalia's[1] waters sweet.

No son of fame to take her hand
    And lead her blushing forth,
Proclaiming to a laurel'd[2] band
    A youthful sister's worth;
That there was none to help her climb
    The steep and toilsome way,
To where, above the mists of time
    Shines genius' living ray.

Where wreath'd with never-fading flow'rs
    The Harp immortal lies,
Filling the souls that reach those bow'rs
    With heavenly melodies.
I warn'd her of the cruel foes
    That throng that rugged path,
Where many a thorn of misery grows,
    And tempests wreak their wrath.

I told her of the serpent's dread
    With malice-pointed fangs;
The yellow-blossom'd weeds that shed
    Derision's maddening pangs;
And of the broken moulderling lyres
    Thrown carelessly aside,
Telling the winds with shivering wires
    How noble spirits died.

I said her sandals were not meet
    Such journey to essay,
There should be gold beneath the feet
    That tempt Fame's toilsome way.
But while I spoke, her burning eye

1. A Greek nymph who gave her name to the Delphic spring at the base of Mount Parnassus. Its waters were a source of inspiration for the Muses, who resided there.
2. To be laurelled, or crowned with a laurel wreath, is a sign of recognition for greatness in poetry. Laurel was sacred to the Greek sun god Apollo, the patron of music and poetry.

Was flashing in the light
That shone upon that mountain high,
    Insufferably bright.

And soft upon the balmy air
    Castalia's murmurs came,
And gentle spirits hymning there
    Breath'd forth her humble name.
And bending from the dizzy height
    The blossom'd laurel seem'd,
And wreaths of bloom divinely bright
    Like crowns of glory gleamed;

While streaming from the Eternal Lyre,
    Like distant echoes, came
A strain that wrapp'd her soul in fire,
    And thrill'd her trembling frame.
She sprang away, that wayward child,
    The Harp! the Harp! she cried.
And still she climbs and warbles wild
    Along the mountain's side.

Source: *Southern Literary Messenger* (1842)

Sing On!

"Sing on!—You will win the wreath of Fame: if not in life, it will bloom gloriously over your
tomb."—*Friendly Correspondence.*

'Tis not for Fame: I know I may not win
A wreath from high Parnassus, for my name
Is written on the page of humble life,
From which the awarders of the laurel wreath
Avert their eyes with scorning.
                                        I have felt
The mildew of affliction, the east wind
Of withering contempt, the pelting storms
Of care, and toil, and bitterness, and wo [*sic*],
In almost every form. I too have known
The darkness of bereavement, and keen pangs

Which woman may not utter, though her heart
Consume amid their fierceness, and her brain
Burn to a living cinder; though the wound
Which is so hard to bear, lie festering deep
Within her outraged spirit; though her sighs
Disturb the quiet of the blessed night,
While sweet dews cool and soothe the fever'd breast
Of every other mourner; though she pour
The flood of life's sweet fountain out in tears
Along her desert pathway; while the blooms
Of health, and hope, and joy, that should have fed
Upon its gushing waters and rich dew,
Lie wither'd in her bosom, breathing forth
The odours of a crush'd and wasted heart,
That cannot hope for soothing or redress,
Save in the quiet bosom of the grave,
And in the heaven beyond.
                              'Tis not for Fame
That I awaken with my simple lay
The echoes of the forest. I but sing
As sings the bird, that pours her native strain,
Because her soul is made of melody;
And lingering in the bowers, her warblings seem
To gather round her all the tuneful forms,
Whose bright wings shook rich incense from the flowers,
And balmy verdure of the sweet young spring,
O'er which the glad day shed his brightest smile,
And night her purest tears. I do but sing
Like that sad bird, who in her loneliness
Pours out in song the treasures of her soul,
Which else would burst her bosom, which has nought
On which to lavish the warm streams that gush
Up from her trembling heart, and pours them forth
Upon the sighing winds, in fitful strains.

   Perchance one pensive spirit loves the song,
And lingers in the twilight near the wood
To list her plaintive sonnet, which unlocks
The sealed fountain of a hidden grief.—
That pensive listener, or some playful child,
May miss the lone bird's song, what time her wings

Are folded in the calm and silent sleep,
Above her broken heart. Then, though they weep
In her deserted bower, and hang rich wreaths
Of ever-living flowers upon her grave,
What will it profit her who would have slept
As deep and sweet without them?
                                        Oh! how vain
With promised garlands for the sepulchre,
To think to cheer the soul, whose daily prayer
Is but for bread and peace!—whose trembling hopes
For immortality ask one green leaf
From off the healing trees that grow beside
The pure bright river of Eternal Life.

Source: American Female Poets, ed. Caroline May (1853)

&. Elizabeth Oakes Smith (1806–1893)

At sixteen, Elizabeth Oakes married Seba Smith, editor of a Portland, Maine, newspaper to which she contributed poetry. After the couple was bankrupted in the Panic of 1837, they moved with their five sons to New York City, where they belonged to the circle of literati that included the Cary sisters, Margaret Fuller, and Edgar Allan Poe. Smith was a prolific writer of stories, poems, novels, and gift books published under the names "Mrs. Seba Smith" or "Ernest Helfenstein." She is primarily know for her poem "The Sinless Child," considered a classic of sentimental literature, although she was also a vocal defender of women's rights. The poems below disavow a desire for fame because the presumed cost of love was too great.

Poesy

With no fond, sickly thirst for fame, I kneel,
Oh, goddess, of the high-born art to thee;
Not unto thee with semblance of a zeal
I come, oh, pure and heaven-eyed Poesy!
Thou art to me a spirit and a love,
Felt ever from the time, when first the earth,
In its green beauty, and the sky above
Informed my soul with joy too deep for mirth.
I was a child of thine before my tongue
Could lisp its infant utterance unto thee,
And now, albeit from my harp are flung
Discordant numbers, and the song may be
That which I would not, yet I know that thou
The offering wilt not spurn, while thus to thee I bow.

An Incident

A simple thing, yet chancing as it did,
When life was bright with its illusive dreams,
A pledge and promise seemed beneath it hid;
The ocean lay before me, tinged with beams,
That lingering draped the west, a wavering stir,
And at my feet there fell a worn, grey quill;
An eagle, high above the darkling fir,
With steady flight, seemed there to take his fill

Of that pure ether breathed by him alone.
O! noble bird! why didst thou loose for me
Thy eagle plume? still unessayed, unknown
Must be that pathway fearless winged by thee;
I ask it not, no lofty flight is mine,
I would not soar like thee, in loneliness to pine!

Source: The Sinless Child and Other Poems (1843)

Ode to Sappho[1]

Bright, glowing Sappho! child of love and song!
    Adown the blueness of long-distant years
Beams forth thy glorious shape, and steals along
    Thy melting tones, beguiling us to tears.
        Thou priestess of great hearts,
           Thrilled with the secret fire
      By which a god imparts
        The anguish of desire—
  For meaner souls be mean content—
  Thine was a higher element.
Over Leucadia's[2] rock thou leanest yet,
    With thy wild song, and all thy locks outspread;
The stars are in thine eyes, the moon hath set—
    The night dew falls upon thy radiant head;
      And thy resounding lyre—
        Ah! not so wildly sway:
    Thy soulful lips inspire
        And steal our hearts away!
    Swanlike and beautiful, thy dirge
    Still moans along the Ægean surge.
No unrequited love filled thy lone heart,
    But thine infinitude did on thee weigh,
And all the wildness of despair impart,
    Stealing the down from Hope's own wing away.

1. Greek lyric poet of the sixth century B.C., widely considered the greatest female poet before the modern era.
2. In some legends, after Phaon rejected her, Sappho is said to have killed herself by jumping from the cliffs of Leucas, a Greek Ionian sea.

Couldst thou not suffer on,
Bearing the direful pang,
While thy melodious tone
Through wondering cities rang?
Couldst thou not bear thy godlike grief?
In godlike utterance find relief?
Devotion, fervor, might upon thee wait:
But what were these to thine? all cold and chill,
And left thy burning heart but desolate;
Thy wondrous beauty with despair might fill
The worshipper who bent
Entranced at thy feet:
Too affluent the dower lent
Where song and beauty meet!
Consumed by a Promethean fire
Wert thou, O daughter of the lyre!
Alone, above Leucadia's wave art thou,
Most beautiful, most gifted, yet alone!
Ah! what to thee the crown from Pindar's[3] brow!
What the loud plaudit and the garlands thrown
By the enraptured throng,
When thou in matchless grace
Didst move with lyre and song,
And monarchs gave thee place?
What hast thou left, proud one? what token?
Alas! a lyre and heart—both broken!

Source: *Female Poets of America,* ed. by Rufus Griswold (1849)

3. Ancient Greek lyric poet. Unlike Sappho, much of his poetry, as well as information about his life, has survived.

🐚 GRACE GREENWOOD (1823–1904)

Born Sara Jane Clark in Pompey, New York, she later adopted the pen name "Grace Greenwood," which she also used in her personal life. Although a writer of poetry, stories, and children's literature, she was known primarily as one of the first female writers to establish a career as a newspaper correspondent, publishing letters from her travels in Europe and the American West in the New York Tribune *and other papers. Although she has been associated with sentimentalism and conservative attitudes toward women's authorship, she also promoted progressive causes, including women's suffrage and abolition. Greenwood resided for many years in Washington, D.C., and wrote on politics for the* Saturday Evening Post. *In 1853, she began an unhappy marriage with Leander K. Lippincott; they had one daughter. In the following letter, Greenwood argues that fame is a poor substitute for a happy home life. She cautions against literary and intellectual pursuits if they exclude "the thrill of home-music."*

Letter I.
To an Unrecognized Poetess

June, 1846

Well, has old Time been playing any impertinent tricks with the face I love, since we parted, a whole long year ago? Ah, no; I dare take an oath on—the "Book of Beauty," that your golden curls are not yet put soberly back from your brow; that you have not yet refused your countenance to smiles and laughter; that the dimples are yet playing "Puss-in-the-corner" about your mouth, or cradled in your cheeks, peeping out occasionally, like young loves from roses.

I suppose it is foolishness in me, but I cannot think of you as one who will ever change and grow old. Your face is so bathed in radiance, that in the pleasant May-time, when you were born, the flowers, the *other* flowers, should have brought a complaint against it for a monopoly of their rightful sunshine. It is a soft, rosy, *morning* light which tinges your cheek and lip, but your eyes, sweetest, must have opened first on the mid-day sun, for they are full of its summer fire. It was this which first revealed to me the *genius* alive within you; coursing through your entire nature, as richly as ran royal blood through the veins of Mary Stuart. I soon found that you had a nightingale imprisoned in your breast, singing for you alone. I believed that you must have known many restless aspirations, and intense longings for the power of giving full and passionate expression to the deep, sad, wild and beautiful things which were confined, compressed and sealed up within you. For *your own sake,* as well as ours, I at last implored you to let the tide of your destiny have way, even at the risk of its bearing you onward into the rough sea of letters.

You thus respond to my appeal: "I confess, dear Grace, that F—— F——'s[1] share of public admiration would make me a proud and happy girl. From my childhood, my dreams have been of honors and distinction; I have often said, and *thought,* that I would willingly resign all social and domestic ties, and live lonely and unloved, if only I might possess a tithe of Mrs. Hemans's[2] genius and reputation. Fame's clarion voice has been to me 'the voice of a charmer,' and when I have spoken contemptuously of popularity, and with approbation of a woman's holy and humble office, *my heart was not with it;* 'twas because I found myself grown up to womanhood, without evincing that the fire of genius ever existed in my soul."

Ah, my sadly mistaken little maiden, "fling away ambition," indeed, if glory is to be won at such a sacrifice. In the first place, such a fame as you would ask, could only be yours after years of waiting, longing, and earnest endeavor; when you were beyond "proud and happy" girlhood. But should it be suddenly bestowed, without your care or toil, fall at your feet like a star, you might joy over it with a dizzy exultation for a while, but you would soon hunger for the simplest home-pleasures, and pant for affection, "as the hart panteth after the water-brook."

The intellectual woman should be *richest* in "social and domestic ties;" she should have along her paths a guard of friendship, and about her life a breastwork of love. True feminine genius is ever timid, doubtful, and clingingly dependent; a perpetual childhood. A true woman shrinks instinctively from greatness, and it is "against her very will and wish transgressing," and in sad obedience to an inborn and mighty influence, that she turns out the "silver lining" of her soul to the world's gaze; permits all the delicate workings of her inner nature to be laid open; her heart passed round, and peered into as a piece of curious mechanism. In her loftiest soarings, when we almost think to see the swift play of her pinion lost in the distant heaven, even then, her wildest and most exulting strains come down to us with a delicious thrill of home-music. The radiant realms of her most celestial visions have always a ladder leading earthward. Her ways and words have nothing of the lofty and severe; over her face, sun-gleams and shadows succeed each other momently; her eyes are alternately dreamy and tender, and their intensest fire quivers through tears. Her lips, moulded in love, are tremulously full of the glowing softness they borrow from the heart, and electrically obedient to its impulses.

I have outlined genius incarnated in a lovable woman; such an one as would be loved adoringly, *malgré*[3] her fame; such an one as, dear L——, I could wish you to be.

The fact of your having grown up to womanhood without your genius being

---

1. Most likely Fanny Fern, included in this volume, or Fanny Forester, a popular sentimental writer whose real name was Emily C. Judson (1817–1854).

2. Felicia Hemans (1793–1835), British female poet.

3. French: in spite of.

recognized, amounts to nothing; or rather, it is better as it is. There will now be no girlish sentimentalism to dilute the rich, sparkling poetry of the woman. Let song and love be twin-born in your existence.

But if you go to starving your heart, if you "resign social and domestic ties," and stake your life on ambition, then at last "Fame's clarion voice" will be to you sadder than a death-knell; her wreath a crown of thorns, and her goblet "gall and vinegar." Never *unsex* yourself for greatness. The worship of one true heart is better than the wonder of the world. Don't trample on the flowers, while longing for the stars. Live up to the full measure of life; give way to your impulses, loves, and enthusiasms; sing, smile, labor, and be happy. Adore poetry for its own sake; yearn for, strive after, *excellence;* rejoice when others attain it; feel for your contemporaries a loving envy; steal into your country's heart; glory in its greatness, exult in its power; honor its gallant men and immortalize its matchless women. Then shall that grateful country throw around you a fame which shall be like the embrace of fond arms; a joy to cheer, and a strength to support you.

There is a joy which must, I think, be far more deep and full, than any which the million can bestow; one which precedes, and is independent of, the fame which sometimes results rather from the caprice than the justice of the world. This is *the joy of inspiration.* I have elsewhere expressed my meaning thus:

> Oh, when the heaven-born soul of song is blending
>> With the rapt poet's, in his burning strains,
> 'Tis like the wine drank on Olympus, sending
>> Divine intoxication through the veins!

But this is for the *masters* of the lyre; it can never be felt by woman with great intensity; at least can never *satisfy* her. I repeat that *her* well-spring of joy is in the heart.

You are familiar, I am sure, with "Undine."[4] I have been re-reading it lately, and I see in it a (to me) new and mournful meaning. Undine is the woman of genius, wedded to one unendowed with that scarce earthly gift. How humanly loveable was the ocean-spirit; how child-like in her fondness; how feminine in her dependence! and yet, with her supernatural power, with her strange, though marvellously beautiful organization, she was to her lord a humiliating mystery; she bewildered him, and he *feared* rather than loved her. The pure-spirited Hemans, the impulsive Landon,[5] and the queenly Norton,[6] they have been Undines.

It is an enchanting June evening; the whip-poor-will has begun his plaint, and

---

4. Story by Friedrich de la Motte Fougué (1811); undines are mythological water sprites who marry earthly men and thus give up their immortality.
5. Letitia Elizabeth Landon (1802–1838), British poet, novelist, and reviewer.
6. Caroline Norton (1808–1877), British society hostess and politically influential poet.

the moonlight is abroad. How tempting looks that garden-walk! but so does my pillow; and I, thank Heaven, am not enough of a poetess to risk taking my death-cold by wandering about in the dew-burdened grass; and so,

Good night, good night to thee, azure-eyed maiden,
  And sweet may thy sleep in thine innocence be;
May every pure star-beam come down blessing-laden,
  And every night-breeze bear a rose-breath to thee!

May thy sisters, the angels, watch over thy slumbers,
  With shining wings shelter the couch of thy rest,
And breathe in thy dreaming ear silver-voiced numbers,
  And fill thy rapt soul with the joys of the blest!

If thy heart weights to earth, and thou would'st not be soaring,
  May *love's* purple morn-light blush over thy skies!
And one whom "afar off" thou art meekly adoring,
  Gaze into thy soul with his passionate eyes!

Good night! good night!

Source: Greenwood Leaves (1849)

Frances Osgood (1811–1850)

Remembered today primarily for the scandal created by her literary courtship with Edgar Allan Poe, Frances Osgood was a notable poet in her own right. She began to publish at the age of fourteen and went on to receive accolades in Britain and America for her sentimental and sometimes piquant poetry. A celebrated member of New York literary circles, she was married to the artist Samuel Osgood. They had three children, all of whom died of tuberculosis, as did she. Osgood depended on the income she received from her writing and thus had to conform to marketplace expectations for female poets. Her poems about poetry acknowledge these limitations and suggest the desire to write outside of them.

To the Spirit of Poetry

Leave me not yet! Leave me not cold and lonely,
    Thou dear Ideal of my pining heart!
Thou art the friend—the beautiful—the only,
    Whom I would keep, tho' all the world depart!
Thou, that dost veil the frailest flower with glory,
    Spirit of light and loveliness and truth!
Thou that didst tell me a sweet, fairy story,
    Of the dim future, in my wistful youth!
Thou, who canst weave a halo round the spirit,
    Thro' which naught mean or evil dare intrude,
Resume not yet the gift, which I inherit
    From Heaven and thee, that dearest, holiest good!
Leave me not now! Leave me not cold and lonely,
    Thou starry prophet of my pining heart!
Thou art the friend—the tenderest—the only,
    With whom, of all, 'twould be despair to part.

Thou that cam'st to me in my dreaming childhood,
    Shaping the changeful clouds to pageants rare,
Peopling the smiling vale, and shaded wildwood,
    With airy beings, faint yet strangely fair;
Telling me all the sea-born breeze was saying,
    While it went whispering thro' the willing leaves,
Bidding me listen to the light rain playing
    Its pleasant tune, about the household eaves;
Tuning the low, sweet ripple of the river,

Till its melodious murmur seem'd a song,
A tender and sad chant, repeated ever,
  A sweet, impassion'd plaint of love and wrong!
Leave me not yet! Leave me not cold and lonely,
  Thou star of promise o'er my clouded path!
Leave not the life, that borrows from thee only
  All of delight and beauty that it hath!

Thou, that when others knew not how to love me,
  Nor cared to fathom half my yearning soul,
Didst wreathe thy flowers of light, around, above me,
  To woo and win me from my grief's control.
By all my dreams, the passionate, and holy,
  When thou hast sung love's lullaby to me,
By all the childlike worship, fond and lowly,
  Which I have lavish'd upon thine and thee.
By all the lays my simple lute was learning,
  To echo from thy voice, stay with me still!
Once flown—alas! for thee there's no returning!
  The charm will die o'er valley, wood, and hill.
Tell me not Time, whose wing my brow has shaded,
  Has wither'd spring's sweet bloom within my heart,
Ah, no! the rose of love is yet unfaded,
  Tho' hope and joy, its sister flowers, depart.

Well do I know that I have wrong'd thine altar,
  With the light offerings of an idler's mind,
And thus, with shame, my pleading prayer I falter,
  Leave me not, spirit! deaf, and dumb, and blind!
Deaf to the mystic harmony of nature,
  Blind to the beauty of her stars and flowers
Leave me not, heavenly yet human teacher,
  Lonely and lost in this cold world of ours!
Heaven knows I need thy music and thy beauty
  Still to beguile me on my weary way,
To lighten to my soul the cares of duty,
  And bless with radiant dreams the darken'd day:
To charm my wild heart in the worldly revel,
  Lest I, too, join the aimless, false, and vain;
Let me not lower to the soulless level
  Of those whom now I pity and disdain!

Leave me not yet!—leave me not cold and pining,
   Thou bird of paradise, whose plumes of light,
Where'er they rested, left a glory shining;
   Fly not to heaven, or let me share thy flight!

A Reply
To One Who Said, "Write from Your Heart"

   Ah! woman still
   Must veil the shrine,
Where feeling feeds the fire divine,
   Nor sing at will,
   Untaught by art,
The music prison'd in her heart!

   Still gay the note,
   And light the lay,
The woodbird warbles on the spray,
   Afar to float;
   But homeward flown,
Within his nest, how changed the tone!

   Oh! none can know,
   Who have not heard
The music-soul that thrills the bird,
   The carol low,
   As coo of dove
He warbles to his woodland-love!

   The world would say
   'Twas vain and wild,
Th' impassion'd lay of Nature's child;
   And Feeling, so
   Should veil the shrine,
Where softly glow her fires divine!

Aspirations

I waste no more in idle dreams my life, my soul away;
I wake to know my better self,—I wake to watch and pray.
Thought, feeling, time, on idols vain, I've lavish'd all too long:
Henceforth to holier purposes I pledge myself, my song!

Oh! still within the inner veil, upon the spirit's shrine,
Still unprofaned by evil, burns the one pure spark divine
Which God has kindled in us all, and be it mine to tend
Henceforth with vestal thought and care, the light that lamp may lend.

I shut mine eyes in grief and shame upon the dreary past,
My heart, my soul pour'd recklessly on dreams that could not last.
My bark has drifted down the stream, at will of wind or wave,
An idle, light, and fragile thing, that few had cared to save.

Henceforth the tiller Truth shall hold, and steer as Conscience tells,
And I will brave the storms of Fate, tho' wild the ocean swells.
I know my soul is strong and high, if once I give it sway;
I feel a glorious power within, tho' light I seem and gay.

Oh! laggard soul! unclose thine eyes. No more in luxury soft
Of joy ideal waste thyself! awake, and soar aloft!
Unfurl this hour those falcon wings which thou dost fold too long;
Raise to the skies thy lightning gaze, and sing thy loftiest song.

Source: Poems (1846)

To a Slandered Poetess

My brilliant Blue Belle! droop no more;
   But let them mock, and mow, and mutter!
I marvel, though a whirlwind roar,
   Your eagle soul should deign to flutter!

So low the pigmies aim'd the dart,
   (Ah, yes! your looks of scorn reveal it,)
You must have *stoop'd* your haughty heart,
   O wilful, wayward child!—to feel it.

My dark-eyed darling! don't you know,
    If you were homely, cold, and stupid,
Unbent for you were Slander's bow?
    Her shafts but follow those of Cupid.

'Tis but the penalty you pay
    For wit so rare and grace so peerless;
So let the snarlers say their say,
    And smile to hear them, free and fearless.

Nay! hear them *not!* Oh, you should listen
    To spheral tunes! the angels love you!
The stars with kindred beauty glisten;—
    No "evil eye" can lower *above* you!

Dear child of Genius! strike the lyre,
    And drown with melody delicious,
Soft answering to your touch of fire,
    The envious hint—the sneer malicious.

Remember it is Music's law,
    Each *pure, true* note, though low you sound it,
Is heard through Discord's wildest war
    Of rage and madness, storming round it.

You smile!—Nay, raise your queenly head;
    Braid up your hair, lest I upbraid it;
Be that last coward tear unshed,
    Or in your dancing dimple shed it!

Serenely go your glorious way,
    Secure that every footstep onward
Will lead you from *their* haunts away,
    Since you go *up,* and they go—*down*ward.

You from your love-lit, heavenly flight,
    Some pity dole to those who blame you;
You only can forgive them quite,
    You only smile while they defame you.

Oh! think how poor in all the wealth
   That makes *your* frame a fairy palace—
The mind's pure light,—the heart's sweet health,—
   Are they whose dearest joy is malice.

Source: Poems (1850)

❧ MARGARET FULLER (1810–1850)

Margaret Fuller, born and raised in Massachusetts, began to read Latin when she was six and became the most comprehensively educated woman of her day. Her most lasting accomplishment was the publication of the first feminist treatise in America, Woman in the Nineteenth Century *(1845). However, she also was known for leading an influential series of conversations for women in Boston and for contributing to the founding of American Transcendentalism, alongside Ralph Waldo Emerson and Henry David Thoreau. In 1844, Fuller moved to New York to write for the* New York Tribune, *which sent her to Europe two years later. In Italy, which was undergoing a civil war, she met Giovanni Angelo Ossoli, a marquis and revolutionary. Fuller had a son in September 1848, and it is not clear whether she and Ossoli ever married. The family was returning to America in 1850 when their ship sank. Emerson, William Henry Channing, and James Freeman Clarke published her memoirs (heavily edited) in 1852. These memoirs reveal the depth of her ambition as well as the conflicts she felt about being a woman intellectual. Even more difficult, she felt, would be the role of the artist, an identity inextricably tied to maleness in her view. Her greater comfort as a critic is reflected in her review of Elizabeth Barrett Browning's* A Drama of Exile: And Other Poems *(1845), which applauds the poet for soaring higher than any previous female poet.*

Miss Barrett's Poems[1]

What happiness for the critic when, as in the present instance, his task is, mainly, how to express a cordial admiration; to indicate an intelligence of beauties, rather than regret for defects!

We have read these volumes with feelings of delight far warmer than the writer, in her sincerely modest preface, would seem to expect from any reader, and cannot hesitate to rank her, in vigour and nobleness of conception, depth of spiritual experience, and command of classic allusion, above any female writer the world has yet known.

In the first quality, especially, most female writers are deficient. They do not grasp a subject with simple energy, nor treat it with decision of touch. They are, in general, most remarkable for delicacy of feeling, and brilliancy or grace in manner.

In delicacy of perception, Miss Barrett may vie with any of her sex. She has what is called a true woman's heart, although we must believe that men of a fine conscience and good organization will have such a heart no less. Signal instances

---

1. Review of *A Drama of Exile: And Other Poems* (1845) by Elizabeth Barrett Browning (1806–1861), the publication that established her as one of the greatest then-living poets.

occur to us in the cases of Spenser, Wordsworth and Tennyson.[2] The woman who reads them will not find hardness or blindness as to the subtler workings of thoughts and affections.

If men are often deficient on this score; women, on the other hand, are apt to pay excessive attention to the slight tokens, the little things of life. Thus, in conduct or writing, they tend to weary us by a morbid sentimentalism. From this fault Miss Barrett is wholly free. Personal feeling is in its place; enlightened by Reason, ennobled by Imagination. The earth is no despised resting place for the feet, the heaven bends wide above, rich in starry hopes, and the air flows around exhilarating and free.

The mournful, albeit we must own them tuneful, sisters of the lyre might hush many of their strains at this clear note from one who has felt and conquered the same difficulties. . . .

In the "Drama of Exile" and the "Vision of Poets," where she aims at a Miltonic flight or Dantesque grasp[3]—not in any spirit of rivalry or imitation, but because she is really possessed of a similar mental scope—her success is far below what we find in the poems of feeling and experience; for she has the vision of a great poet, but little in proportion of his plastic power. She is at home in the Universe; she sees its laws; she sympathises with its motions. She has the imagination all compact— the healthy archetypal plant from which all forms may be divined, and, so far as now existent, understood. Like Milton, she sees the angelic hosts in real presence; like Dante, she hears the spheral concords and shares the planetary motions. But she cannot, like Milton, marshal the angels so near the earth as to impart the presence other than by sympathy. He who is near her level of mind may, through the magnetic sympathy, see the angels with her. Others will feel only the grandeur and sweetness she expresses in these forms. Still less can she, like Dante, give, by a touch, the key which enables ourselves to play on the same instrument. She is singularly deficient in the power of compression. There are always far more words and verses than are needed to convey the meaning, and it is a great proof of her strength, that the thought still seems strong, when arrayed in a form so Briarean[4] clumsy and many-handed.

We compare her with those great poets, though we have read her preface and see how sincerely she deprecates any such comparison, not merely because her theme is the same as theirs, but because, as we must again repeat, her field of vision and nobleness of conception are such, that we cannot forbear trying her by the same high standard to see what she lacks. . . .

2. Edmund Spenser (1552–1599), William Wordsworth (1770–1850), and Lord Alfred Tennyson (1809–1892).

3. John Milton (1608–1674) and Dante Alighieri (1265–1321).

4. Resembling Briareus, a giant with a hundred hands in Greek mythology.

Of the greatest of Grecian sages it was said that he acquired such power over the lower orders of nature, through his purity and intelligence, that wild beasts were abashed and reformed by his admonitions, and that, once, when walking abroad with his disciples, he called down the white eagle, soaring above him, and drew from her willing wing a quill for his use.

We have seen women use with skill and grace, the practical goose-quill, the sentimental crow-quill, and even the lyrical, the consecrated feathers of the swan. But we have never seen one to whom the white eagle would have descended; and, for a while, were inclined to think that the hour had now, for the first time, arrived. But, upon full deliberation, we will award to Miss Barrett one from the wing of the sea-gull. That is also a white bird, rapid, soaring, majestic, and which can alight with ease, and poise itself upon the stormiest wave.

Source: Papers on Literature and Art, Part II (1848)

Memoirs of Margaret Fuller Ossoli [Excerpts]

When I look at my papers, I feel as if I had never had a thought that was worthy the attention of any but myself; and 'tis only when, on talking with people, I find I tell them what they did not know, that my confidence at all returns.

My verses,—I am ashamed when I think there is scarce a line of poetry in them,—all rhetorical and impassioned, as Goethe said of De Stael.[5] However, such as they are, they have been overflowing drops from the somewhat bitter cup of my existence.

How can I ever write with this impatience of detail? I shall never be an artist; I have no patient love of execution; I am delighted with my sketch, but if I try to finish it, I am chilled. Never was there a great sculptor who did not love to chip the marble.

I have talent and knowledge enough to furnish a dwelling for friendship, but not enough to deck with golden gifts a Delphi[6] for the world.

Then a woman of tact and brilliancy, like me, has an undue advantage in conversation with men. They are astonished at our instincts. They do not see where we

5. Johann Wolfgang von Goethe (1749–1832), German poet and dramatist, and Anne Louise Germaine Necker de Staël, known as Madame de Staël (1766–1817), French author of *Corinne* (1807).
6. In ancient Greece, those seeking a favorable prophesy brought gifts to the oracle at Delphi.

got our knowledge; and, while they tramp on in their clumsy way, we wheel, and fly, and dart hither and thither, and seize with ready eye all the weak points, like Saladin[7] in the desert. It is quite another thing when we come to write, and, without suggestion from another mind, to declare the positive amount of thought that is in us. Because we seemed to know all, they think we can tell all; and, finding we can tell so little, lose faith in their first opinion of us, *which, nathless, was true. . . .*

For all the tides of life that flow within me, I am dumb and ineffectual, when it comes to casting my thought into a form. No old one suits me. If I could invent one, it seems to me the pleasure of creation would make it possible for me to write. What shall I do, dear friend? I want force to be either a genius or a character. One should be either private or public. I love best to be a woman; but womanhood is at present too straitly-bounded to give me scope. At hours, I live truly as a woman; at others, I should stifle; as, on the other hand, I should palsy, when I would play the artist.

Source: Memoirs of Margaret Fuller Ossoli, ed. Ralph Waldo Emerson, William Henry Channing, and James Freeman Clarke (1852)

7. Sultan of Egypt who recaptured Jerusalem in 1187.

❧ CAROLINE KIRKLAND (1801–1864)

Caroline Stansbury, born in New York City, was well educated and was a teacher for many years until she married William Kirkland in 1828. After moving to frontier Michigan in 1835, she wrote letters to friends and family back East. With their encouragement, she wrote A New Home—Who'll Follow? *(1839), published under the pseudonym Mrs. Mary Clavers. The book caused "an undoubted sensation," in the words of Edgar Allan Poe, for its realistic and humorous depiction of frontier life. Caroline Kirkland returned to New York City in 1840 and continued her literary career, which, along with teaching, supported her and her four children after William's death in 1846. For a year and a half she edited the* Union Magazine of Literature and Art, *later called* Sartain's Union Magazine of Literature and Art. *After her editorship ended, she continued to contribute essays and reviews to the magazine, and she was a prominent figure in the New York literary world for the rest of her life. In the following essay, Kirkland satirically defends women writers against their critics.*

Literary Women

Let it not be for a moment supposed that we are about to attempt a crusade in defence of blue-stockings![1] Better undertake, single-handed, to lay a T rail to the Pacific, tunnelling the Rocky Mountains. Whether the prejudice entertained against this class—is it numerous enough to claim the title of a class?—be just or not, it is most potent; and, like the deaf adder, it stoppeth its ears. We hardly know of one more obstinate, unless it be that against old maids,—or that other, perhaps worse one, against stepmothers.

. . . Now-a-days, to be betrayed into the quixotism of defending blue-stockings, is to allow one's self to be suspected of wearing them. The utmost extent to which our courage will carry us is some little examination, after the natural-history fashion; some search into growth and properties, aims, destiny, and uses or no-uses. And to keep very clear of all ungenerous imputations of sympathy, we shall take care to deal with the subject after the desultory, unsystematic, and feminine manner. We repudiate learning; we disclaim accuracy; we abjure logic. We shall aim only at the pretty prattle which is conceded to our sex as a right, and admired as a charm.

How many literary women has any one person ever seen? How many has the world seen? How would the list compare in length with that of the pretty triflers who never in the whole course of their mortal lives took up a book with the least intention of obtaining any information from it? The spite which is generally nour-

---

1. Pejorative term for an intellectual or learned woman.

ished against these unhappy ladies implies great respect; for their numbers are too insignificant to attract notice, if the individuals were not of consequence. And it may be noticed here, as being particularly curious, that the man who declaims loudest against the ideal of a writing woman, is sure to be most vain-glorious of the smallest literary performance on the part of his wife or daughter. The gift of a place does not sooner silence a vehement patriot, than the first essay or magazine story produced by a lady of his family, does the indignant definer of "woman's sphere," with a pudding and a shirt for its two poles.

But as to the comparative scarcity of literary ladies. It seems strange to a simple looker-on that they should not be prized, at least on the principle of the Queen Anne's farthing, which, valueless in itself, became precious because there were but four struck. There is not even yet a "mob of gentle[*women*] [*sic*] that write with ease." Women are said to be peculiarly favoured in the possession of the quality called "passive courage," (fortitude?) [*sic*] one of the benevolent provisions of nature for need—but they have always, as a body, shown a good deal of cowardice in this matter. The risks are too fearful. So that really the number is kept down as low as prudence can desire. It would require no Briareus[2] to count on his fingers all that have dabbled in ink during the last century. No fear of usurpation; no danger that the pen will be snatched from strong hands and wielded in defiance, or even in self-defence. A handful of chimney swallows might as well be suspected of erecting their quills against the eagles—or owls. Swallows! literary ladies are hardly more abundant than dodos.[3]

Now let us ask what is the distinguishing mark of the literary woman of our day. Is it inky fingers—corrugated brows—unkempt locks—unrighteous stockings—towering talk—disdain of dinner—aspirations after garments symbolical of authority—any or all of these? Who pretends anything of the kind? One could almost wish there were some startling peculiarities, even though exhibited by only a few individuals, to break up the uniformity of society. What a treat it would be to see a blue enter a party with the suitable airs, and cross the awful space of carpet which sometimes intervenes between the door and the hostess, with gown pinned up from the mud, or one black slipper and one white one, the unconscious head all the while nodding graciously on either side, secure of the due effect of the *entrée!* But alas! no literary lady, since Mrs. Ann Royall,[4] has borne about with her the least outward token of the dreaded power within. Curls, ribbons, bracelets, bouquets, fans—not an item lacking; all correct, to the very shoe-tie. . . .

But we have hitherto neglected to inquire what it is that entitles a woman to the

2. One of the three one-hundred-handed sons of the Greek deities Gaia (earth) and Uranus (sky).

3. Birds that became extinct by the late seventeenth century.

4. Anne Newport Royall (1769–1854) exposed political corruption in Washington, D.C., in her papers *Paul Pry* (1831–1836) and *The Huntress* (1836–1854).

appellation of literary; or perhaps we should express the matter better, if we should say, what fastens upon her that imputation. Must she have written a book? Phœbus Apollo![5] how few then have claims upon a *tabouret*[6] at thy court! And must the size of the book be taken into account? Then those who dilate most unscrupulously will sit highest. Or will the number of volumes settle precedence? There will, in that case, be little room for any but Mrs. Ellis,[7] Mrs. Gore,[8] and their immediate sister-hood. But to the point. If not a book, will a poem be sufficient? or an essay? or a magazine article? Then more of us are included in the glory or odium of female authorship. Or does writing letters make one literary? In these Californian days it is to be hoped not, lest some of our fair friends should be tempted to neglect their absent brothers rather than be liable to misconstruction, in so important a particular. Writing letters sometimes ends in writing books, as more than Madame de Sevigné[9] can testify. How is it with keeping a journal? Does that come within the canon? Might it not be maliciously interpreted to be writing a book in disguise?

Does the toleration for which a female writer may hope depend in any degree upon the class of subjects which may engage her pen? We have an idea that some gentlemen would award a palm (no pun, positively,) to her who writes a Cook's Oracle,[10] where a rod or a fool's cap would be the doom of a lady who should presume to touch political economy. Next to a family receipt-book,[11] one would suppose books of instruction for children would be most popular in female hands; but there is no doubt that some men think Mrs. Barbauld[12] wore, or should have worn, a beard, and would be surprised to see a picture of Mrs. Trimmer[13] in petticoats. The novel of fashionable life, provided it have no suspicion of a moral, and make no pretension to teach anything whatever, may pass as feminine, without detracting from the fame of its author; but a novel with the least bit of bone in it is "mannish"— a very different term from "manly." Poetry, provided it be of the sigh-away, die-away cast, does not injure a lady's reputation; acrostic-making[14] is considered quite an accomplishment, and so are watch-paper verses[15]; but poetry which some un-

---

5. Apollo, also known as Phoebus Apollo, was the Greek god of the sun as well as music, the arts, and poetry.

6. A stool used in the presence of royalty.

7. Sarah Stickney Ellis (1812–1872), conservative British author of *The Wives of England, Their Relative Duties, Domestic Influence, and Social Obligations* (1843).

8. Catherine Gore (1799–1861), prolific British "silver-fork" novelist who portrayed elite society.

9. Marie de Sevigné (1626–1696), French woman whose published correspondence made her famous.

10. William Kitchiner's *The Cook's Oracle* (1825) was a popular cookbook.

11. Recipe book.

12. Anna Laetitia Barbauld (1743–1825), popular British writer.

13. Sarah Trimmer (1741–1810), British children's author.

14. An acrostic is a short poem in which the first letters of each line, taken in sequence, spell out a word or phrase.

15. Verses on a small piece of paper fitted into the inside face of a pocket watch.

thinking, out-of-the-world critics praise as "masculine" for vigour and freshness, is insufferable. If we could show to some objectors the delicate Elizabeth Barrett Browning[16]—the minutest, most fragile, most ethereal creature the sun ever shone upon, with a voice like a ring-dove's, we might swear in vain to her identity as the author of some of the strongest and bravest poetry that has appeared in our day; so obstinate a conviction exists in some minds of the close connexion between mental power and masculine coarseness.

It seems a little inconsistent that anybody should venture in our day to put such dangerous weapons as the *ologies* into the hands of a sex to whose peculiar charms too much mind is known to be so fatal. Why not leave a girl in the hands of the nurse until she is fit to be transferred to those of the seamstress, the pastry-cook, the dancing-master, the teacher of music, in succession? Why occupy precious hours and risk fine eyes over even French and Italian, which could be learned in colloquy with these artists? Why not adapt means to ends? Is it certain that school-knowledge will pass in at one ear and out at the other? If not, how far safer not to impart it! Considering the advantage that may be taken of it, the unsexing and unsphering that may ensue upon an indiscreet use of it, surely it were best to send Grammar and History, Philosophy and Mathematics, to the limbo of forgotten things, as far as females are concerned. If Madame de Stael[17] had been brought up only to sing and dance, regulate household affairs, and tend children, would she have written the books which provoked Napoleon to banish her from Paris? If Mrs. Somerville[18] had spent years sitting with her feet in the stocks and her arms pinioned in a back-board to make her genteel, while her eyes were employed in counting bead-work, or devising stitches in crochet, could she ever have lowered herself by writing about the geography of the heavens? Prevention is certainly better than cure. Choke the fountain rather than have to dam the river (no pun will be suspected here). Shut up our schools for young ladies; bid the teachers "go spin!" Use the copy-books for recipes or papillottes;[19] the learned treatises popularized "for the use of schools" to kindle fires less to be dreaded than those of literary ambition: and if our daughters should not thereafter be "like polished stones at the corners of the temple," they will at least make kitchen-hearths, which we all know to be a far more obviously useful part of the social edifice.

One great duty of woman, if not the greatest, is to be agreeable. Now, if teaching her to think for herself, and so putting her upon the temptation of expressing her thoughts, imperil in the least degree this her high vocation, we vote for the

---

16. Elizabeth Barrett Browning (1806–1861), British poet, compared in her day to Milton.

17. Anne Louise Germaine Necker de Staël, the French writer known as Madame de Staël (1766–1817), was admired and feared by her male contemporaries. She wrote *Corinne* (1807), a female Künstlerroman.

18. Mary Somerville (1780–1872), Scottish scientist and writer.

19. Papers for curling hair or cooking food.

instant abandonment of female cultivation, and would advocate a heavier fine on selling to a female under forty, unaccompanied by parent or guardian, a card of Joseph Gillott's[20] pens, than for allowing a paper of poison to go from the shop unlabelled. We would be the very Jack Cade[21] of legislators for such offenders. To be sure there may be question as to the universality of the feeling on which our zeal is predicated. Some men openly profess to like intelligent women, and there are doubtless others who in secret do not altogether reprobate the use of the pen in female hands, although they may for harmony's sake refrain from the avowal of such liberality, except, as we have hinted, the case fall within the limits of their own family circle, when they usually go beyond mere toleration. It is very desirable that unanimity be obtained in this matter. The natural desire to be agreeable will be quite strong enough to set things right after they are fully understood. To stand well with all men will far outweigh the penurious and timid praise of a few. So true is this that Madame de Stael herself confessed that she would gladly give her intellect and her fame for beauty!

But is beauty always the alternative? Ah, there is an important question. Many scandals have been uttered against the outward charms of literary ladies. "Ugly!" said a celebrated poet in our own hearing, on this very topic; "ugly, yes—they *all* are!" Which must mean that lines of thought are disadvantages to the peculiar charm of the female face—an equivocal compliment, rather. But waiving this delicate point—is the face, which has no lines of thought, on that account beautiful? If not, how fearful the risk of leaving the head unfurnished! If the face may be vacant yet not lovely—if we may neglect the brain without securing the beauty—how difficult becomes the decision of the parent. In old times—happy times!—when fairies attended at the birth of daughters, and offered choice of gifts, the balance between beauty and good sense was easily struck. It was understood that to select the one, precluded all chance of obtaining the other, without a new and more compulsive spell. Now, without any great insight into futurity, and with only a little fat beginning of a face, with a button nose and twinkling eyes to guide our estimate of probabilities of comeliness, while on the other hand frowns the fear lest furnishing the brain may, by giving a superabundance of meaning to the face, mar the promise of beauty,—how anxious must be the deliberation. A critical survey of society might lead one to suppose that with some parents a decision proves impossible, the poor child being left to grow up without either beauty or brains!

Our own convictions on this subject were rendered unalterable some years since in the course of a lecture by a young gentleman, before a debating society, at whose sitting we were so happy as to assist. The question was one not unfrequently discussed on those occasions—the comparative education of the sexes. Our friend was

20. Joseph Gillott (1799–1872), British pen maker.
21. Jack Cade (?–1450), Irish rebel, led an uprising against Henry VI.

warm against sharing the sciences with women. His picture of the ideal blue-stock-ing, a hideous man-woman, with high-crowned cap and spectacles, hoarse voice and masculine stride, still haunts our imagination, and has ever proved an effectual scare-crow in that field. On the other hand, his fancy's sketch of a charming young person was such as to leave in one's mind a somewhat confused mass of roses, lilies, smiles, blushes, pearls, snow, raven's wings, and Aurora's fingers, very fascinating, though suggestive of despair to most of the sex. But what made the most distinct impression on our memory was the question, repeated in various forms as different branches of knowledge were examined with reference to their fitness for female use—"Will it render her more *alluring?*" Here lay the key—far more potent than Blue Beard's, which locked up only women literally headless—to the whole popular philosophy of female claims on the score of intellect. This hint as to the object of woman's being, solved a world of doubts. Here was a touchstone by which to try any pursuit; a test to determine the value of any talent. Whatever does not conduce to the grand aim must be, if not noxious, at best indifferent. Whoever contends that an education regulated by this principle would leave woman insignificant and unhappy, shows only his ignorance of the world; for do we not see every day splen-did people who avow it, consciously or unconsciously? and can splendid people be unhappy or insignificant?

There is one potent argument against allowing women in habits of literary employment—the injury that would arise to the great cause of public amusements. Our theatres would be worse filled even than they are at present, and the opera would cease its languishing existence at once, if the fair eyes that now are fain to let down the "fringed curtains" as a veil against the intensity of floods of gas-light, should learn to prefer the shaded study-lamp at home, and the singing of the quiet fire to the louder efforts of the cantatrice. Dancing, except in horrible sobriety, after the piano, would become obsolete, waltzing might be studied in the abstract, or as an illustration of the revolution of the heavenly bodies, but "certain stars" would no longer "shoot madly from their spheres" to join the giddy round in person. Parties would break up at eleven; for eyes and nerves would so rise in value if put to serious use, that any wilful [*sic*] expenditure of their powers would soon be voted *mauvais ton*,[22] and if that should ever happen, adieu to suppers and champagne! There is really no end to the overturn that might result from an innovation of this sort. Imagination pictures the splendid fabric of Fashion tottering to its fall—under-mined by that seemingly impotent instrument, the pen, wielded by female hands. We shrink from our own picture of so mournful a reversal of the present happy state of things. It is one of the perversities of the imagination to torment itself with delin-eations of what can never by any possibility occur, and this is truly a case in point.

The truth being conceded that no women but those who are ugly and un-

22. French: vulgar manners.

attractive should or do write, a thought suggests itself with respect to the limited duration of the beauty which is so justly considered the most desirable of female possessions, and the most natural and proper bar to any extensive cultivation of the mind. As none but very robust beauty lasts beyond fifty, would it not be advisable to establish schools, especially fitted for that age, in which the remains of a lovely woman might have an opportunity of some education suited to the twenty years which may be supposed still to lie before her? It would be irksome to pass so long a period in silence, and mortifying to continue to talk nonsense without rosy lips to set it off. Here a certain amount of knowledge might be communicated by those whom inexorable plainness of person had condemned to intellectual exercise in early life; and the circumstances might prove mutually beneficial, since the husbands of the once beautiful would undoubtedly be willing to pay liberally for having some ideas infused into their minds, as provision for the conversation of old age. The face could no longer be injured, while the head, and perhaps the heart, too, might gain materially.

> Teeth for the toothless, ringlets for the bald,
> And roses for the cheeks of faded age—[23]

would be valueless, compared with this more potent elixir of life. The practice of the old surgeons, who sometimes filled the shrunken veins of decrepitude with the rich blood of bounding youth, might be considered a precedent for such efforts as we propose. Scruples were sometimes entertained as to the lawfulness of that mode of repairing the decay of Nature; but to the attempt to make education the substitute for beauty, we are sure, society will not object, even though the result should be that "dim horror"—a literary woman.

Source: Sartain's Union Magazine of Literature and Art (1850)

23. From *The Task* (1785) by William Cowper (1731–1800).

♨ ALICE CARY (1820–1871)

Alice Cary's first collection of stories, Clovernook *(1852–1853), was based on the farming community where she was raised, eight miles from Cincinnati, Ohio. She began to publish poetry at eighteen, and by the time she was thirty, she had published frequently in eastern magazines. In 1850, Alice and her sister Phoebe, also a poet, published a volume of their verse and traveled to Boston and New York. Alice decided to make a permanent move to New York to devote herself to a literary career, with Phoebe following the next year. Neither sister married, and together they held a popular literary salon that attracted the city's literary elite until both died in 1871. The following preface and conclusion to* Clovernook *convey Cary's pioneering American realism and her responses to critics who found her work too dark, a particularly objectionable and unusual quality in a woman's work. Despite these criticisms, Cary was widely considered one of the foremost female writers of her generation. The poem below, "To the Spirit of Song. Apology," which served as a preface to* Ballads, Lyrics, and Hymns *(1865), declares the gifts of poetry greater than those conventionally associated with womanhood.*

Preface to *Clovernook*

The pastoral life of our country has not been a favorite subject of illustration by painters, poets, or writers of romance. Perhaps it has been regarded as wanting in the elements of beauty; perhaps it has been thought too passionless and even; or it may have been deemed too immediate and familiar. I have had little opportunity for its observation in the eastern and northern states, and in the south there is no such life, and in the far west where pioneers are still busy with felling the opposing trees, it is not yet time for the reed's music; but in the interior of my native state, which was a wilderness when first my father went to it, and is now crowned with a dense and prosperous population, there is surely as much in the simple manners, and the little histories every day revealed, to interest us in humanity, as there can be in those old empires where the press of tyrannous laws and the deadening influence of hereditary acquiescence necessarily destroy the best life of society.

Without a thought of making a book, I began to recall some shadows and sunbeams that fell about me as I came up to womanhood, incidents for the most part of so little apparent moment or significance that they who live in what is called the world would scarcely have marked them had they been detained with me while they were passing, and before I was aware, the record of my memories grew to all I now have printed.

Looking over the proof sheets, as from day to day they have come from my publisher, the thought has frequently been suggested that such experiences as I have endeavored to describe will fail to interest the inhabitants of cities, where, however

much there may be of pity there is surely little of sympathy for the poor and humble, and perhaps still less of faith in their capacity for those finer feelings which are
too often deemed the blossoms of a high and fashionable culture. The masters of
literature who at any time have attempted the exhibition of rural life, have, with
few exceptions, known scarcely anything of it from participation, and however brilliant may have been their pictures, therefore, they have seldom been true. Perhaps
in their extravagance has been their greatest charm. For myself, I confess I have no
invention, and I am altogether too poor an artist to dream of any success which
may not be won by the simplest fidelity. I believe that for these sketches I may challenge of competent witnesses at least this testimony, that the circumstances have a
natural and probable air which should induce their reception as honest relations
unless there is conclusive evidence against them. Having this merit, they may perhaps interest if they do not instruct readers who have regarded the farming class as
essentially different and inferior, and entitled only to that peculiar praise they are
accustomed to receive in the resolutions of political conventions.

Source: Clovernook; or, Recollections of Our Neighborhood in the West (1852)

Conclusion to *Clovernook, Second Series*

. . . It has been objected by some critics to the former series of these sketches of
Western rural life, that they are of too sombre a tone; that a melancholy haze, an
unnatural twilight, hangs too continually over every scene; but I think it is not so;
if my recollections of "Clovernook" fail to suggest as much happiness as falls to the
common lot, my observation has been unfortunate. I have not attempted any descriptions of the gay world; others—nearly all indeed of those writers of my sex who
have essayed to amuse or instruct society—have apparently been familiar only with
wealth and splendor, and such joys or sorrows as come gracefully to mingle with the
refinements of luxury and art; but my days have been passed with the humbler
classes, whose manners and experiences I have endeavored to exhibit in their customary lights and shadows, and in limiting myself to that domain to which I was
born, it has never been in my thoughts to paint it as less lovely or more exposed to
tearful influences than it is. If among those whose attention may be arrested by
these unambitious delineations of scenes in "our neighborhood," there be any who
have climbed through each gradation of fortune or consideration up to the stateliest
distinctions, let them judge whether the "simple annals of the poor" are apt to be
more bright, and the sum of enjoyment is greater in even those elevations, to attain
to which is so often the most fondly cherished hope of youth and maturity.

In our country, though all men are not "created equal," such is the influence of
the sentiment of liberty and political equality, that

> "All thoughts, all passions, all delights,
>   Whatever stirs this mortal frame,"

may with as much probability be supposed to affect conduct and expectation in the log cabin as in the marble mansion; and to illustrate this truth, to dispel that erroneous belief of the necessary baseness of the "common people" which the great masters in literature have in all ages labored to create, is a purpose and an object in our nationality to which the finest and highest genius may wisely be devoted; but which may be effected in a degree by writings as unpretending as these reminiscences of what occurred in and about the little village where I from childhood watched the pulsations of surrounding hearts.

Source: Clovernook; or, Recollections of Our Neighborhood in the West, Second Series (1853)

To the Spirit of Song
Apology

O ever true and comfortable mate,
  For whom my love outwore the fleeting red
Of my young cheeks, nor did one jot abate,
  I pray thee now, as by a dying bed,
Wait yet a little longer! Hear me tell
  How much my will transcends my feeble powers:
  As one with blind eyes feeling out in flowers
Their tender hues, or, with no skill to spell
  His poor, poor name, but only makes his mark,
  And guesses at the sunshine in the dark,
So I have been. A sense of things divine
  Lying broad above the little things I knew,
The while I made my poems for a sign
  Of the great melodies I felt were true.
Pray thee accept my sad apology,
  Sweet master, mending, as we go along,
  My homely fortunes with a thread of song,
That all my years harmoniously may run;
  Less by the tasks accomplished judging me,
Than by the better things I would have done.
  I would not lose thy gracious company
Out of my house and heart for all the good

Besides, that ever comes to womanhood,—
    And this is much: I know what I resign,
    But at that great price I would have thee mine.

Source: Ballads, Lyrics, and Hymns (1865)

❧ Louise Amelia Knapp Smith Clappe (1819–1906)

Louise Amelia Knapp Smith was the daughter of a New Jersey schoolmaster. After her family moved to Massachusetts in 1832, she was educated at the Amherst Academy. In 1849, at the height of the California Gold Rush, she headed west with her new husband, Fayette Clapp, a doctor. Writing under the name "Dame Shirley," she published twenty-three letters to her sister Molly in the Pioneer, *a California literary magazine. (Bret Harte gained much greater fame than she by mining the literary material first uncovered in her letters.) After a divorce in 1857, she kept Clapp's name, adding the e. She was a teacher, writer, and lecturer for the rest of her life, residing in San Francisco; Columbia, Missouri; and New York. Her letters, widely regarded as important historical documents of the Gold Rush, also demonstrate how letter writing served as a literary outlet and springboard to publication for many women. They also show how many westward-migrating women took their literary ambitions with them, as Mary Hallock Foote and Ina Coolbrith later did in the 1880s.*

Letter the Fifteenth (1852)

From our Log Cabin, Indian Bar, *April* 10, 1852

I have been haunted all day, my dear M., with an intense ambition to write you a letter which shall be dreadfully commonplace and severely utilitarian in its style and contents. Not but that my epistles are *always* commonplace enough (spirits of Montague and Sévigné, forgive me!), but hitherto I have not really *tried* to make them so. Now, however, I *intend* to be stupidly prosy, with malice aforethought, and without one mitigating circumstance, except, perchance, it be the temptations of that above-mentioned ambitious little devil to palliate my crime.

You would certainly wonder, were you seated where I now am, how any one with a quarter of a soul *could* manufacture herself into a bore amid such surroundings as these. The air is as balmy as that of a midsummer's day in the sunniest valleys of New England. It is four o'clock in the evening, and I am sitting on a cigar-box outside of our cabin. From this spot not a person is to be seen, except a man who is building a new wing to the Humboldt. Not a human sound, but a slight noise made by the aforesaid individual in tacking on a roof of blue drilling to the room which he is finishing, disturbs the stillness which fills this purest air. I confess that it is difficult to fix my eyes upon the dull paper, and my fingers upon the duller pen with which I am soiling it. Almost every other minute I find myself stopping to listen to the ceaseless river-psalm, or to gaze up into the wondrous depths of the California heaven; to watch the graceful movements of the pretty brown lizards jerking up their impudent little heads above a moss-wrought log which lies before me, or to mark the dancing water-shadow on the canvas door of the bakeshop opposite; to follow with childish eyes the flight of a golden butterfly, curious to know if it will crown with a capital of winged beauty that column of nature's carving, the pine stump rising at my feet, or whether it will flutter down (for it is dallying coquettishly around them both) upon that slate-rock beyond, shining so darkly lustrous through a flood of yellow sunlight; or I lazily turn my head, wondering if I know the blue or red shirted miner who is descending the precipitous hill behind me. In sooth, Molly, it is easy to be commonplace at all times, but I confess that, just at present, I find it difficult to be utilitarian; the saucy lizards, the great orange-dotted butterflies, the still, solemn cedars, the sailing smoke-wreath, and the vaulted splendor above, are wooing me so winningly to higher things.

But, as I said before, I have an ambition that way, and I *will* succeed. You are such a good-natured little thing, dear, that I know you will meekly allow yourself to be victimized into reading the profound and prosy remarks which I shall make in my efforts to initiate you into the mining polity of this place. Now, you may rest assured that I shall assert nothing upon the subject which is not perfectly correct; for have I not earned a character for inquisitiveness (and you know that does *not* happen to be one of my failings) which I fear will cling to me through life, by my persevering questions to all the unhappy miners from whom I thought I could gain any information? Did I not martyrize myself into a human mule by descending to the bottom of a dreadful pit (suffering mortal terror all the time, lest it should cave in upon me), actuated by a virtuous desire to see with my own two eyes the process of underground mining, thus enabling myself to be stupidly correct in all my statements thereupon? Did I not ruin a pair of silk-velvet slippers, lame my ankles for a week, and draw a "browner horror" over my already sunburnt face, in a wearisome walk, miles away, to the head of the ditch, as they call the prettiest little rivulet (though the work of men) that I ever saw? Yea, verily, this have I done for the express edification of yourself and the rest of your curious tribe, to be rewarded, probably, by the impertinent remark, "What! *does* that little goose Dame Shirley think that *I* care about such things?" But, madam, in spite of your sneer, I shall proceed in my allotted task. . . .

Letter the Twentieth (1852)

From our Log Cabin, Indian Bar, *September 4, 1852*

If I could coax some good-natured fairy or some mischievous Puck[1] to borrow for me the pen of Grace Greenwood, Fanny Forester, or Nathaniel P. Willis,[2] I might

---

1. Mischievous spirit believed to haunt the countryside.
2. All popular American authors of the day. Greenwood is included in this volume. Fanny Forester was the pseudonym of Emily C. Judson (1817–1854). Nathaniel Parker Willis (1806–1867) was also an editor and the brother of Fanny Fern.

be able to weave my stupid nothings into one of those airy fabrics the value of which depends entirely upon the skillful work, or rather penmanship, which distinguishes it. I have even fancied that if I could steal a feather from the living opal swinging like a jeweled pendulum from the heart of the great tiger-lily which nods its turbaned head so stately within the mosquito-net cage standing upon the little table, my poor lines would gather a certain beauty from the rainbow-tinted quill with which I might trace them. But as there is nobody magician enough to go out and shoot a fairy or a brownie and bind it by sign and spell to do my bidding, and as I have strong doubts whether my coarse fingers would be able to manage the delicate pen of a humming-bird even if I could have the heart to rob my only remaining pet of its brilliant feathers, I am fain to be content with one of "Gillott's Best,"—no, of "C. R. Sheton's Extra Fine,"[3] although I am certain that the sentences following its hard stroke will be as stiff as itself. If they were only as bright, one might put up with the want of grace, but to be stiff and stupid both, is *too* provoking, is it not, dear M.? However, what must be, must be; and as I have nothing to write about, and do not possess the skill to make that nothing graceful, and as you will fret yourself into a scold if you do not receive the usual amount of inked pages at the usual time, why, of course I am bound to act (my first appearance on *any* stage, I flatter myself in *that* character) the very original part of the *bore,* and you must prepare to be bored with what philosophy you may.

But, without further preface, I will begin with one of the nothings. . . .

On our return we called to see Yank's cub, which is fast rising into young grizzly-bearhood. It is about the size of a calf, very good-natured, and quite tame. Its acquirements, as yet, are few, being limited to climbing a pole. Its education has not been conducted with that care and attention which so intelligent a beast merits, but it is soon, I hear, to be removed to the valley and placed under teachers capable of developing its wonderful talents to the utmost.

We also stopped at a shanty to get a large gray squirrel which had been promised to me some days before; but I certainly am the most unfortunate wretch in the world with pets. This spiteful thing, on purpose to annoy me I do believe, went and got itself drowned the very night before I was to take it home. It is always so.

I never had two humming-birds,
  With plumage like a sunset sky,
But one was sure to fly away,
  And the other one was sure to die.

I never nursed a flying-squirrel,
  To glad me with its soft black eye,

3. Types of pens.

But it always ran into somebody's tent,
  Got mistaken for a rat and killed!

There, M.; there is poetry for you. "Oh, the second verse does n't rhyme."—
"Does n't?"—"And it ain't original, is it?" Well, *I* never heard that rhyme was necessary to make a poet, any more than colors to make a painter. And what if Moore
did say the same thing twenty years ago? I am sure any writer would consider himself lucky to have an idea which has been anticipated but *once*. I am tired of being
a "mute inglorious Milton,"[4] and, like that grand old master of English song, would
gladly write something which the world would not willingly let die; and having
made that first step, as witness the above verses, who knows what will follow?

Last night one of our neighbors had a dinner-party. He came in to borrow a
teaspoon. "Had you not better take them all?" I said. "Oh, no," was the answer;
"that would be too much luxury. My guests are not used to it, and they would think
that I was getting aristocratic, and putting on airs. One is enough; they can pass it
round from one to the other."

A blacksmith—not the learned one—has just entered, inquiring for the Doctor, who is not in, and he is obliged to wait. Shall I write down the conversation
with which he is at this moment entertaining me? "Who writ this 'ere?" is his first
remark, taking up one of my most precious books, and leaving the marks of his
irreverent fingers upon the clean pages. "Shakespeare," I answer, as politely as possible. "Did Spokeshave write it? He was an almighty smart fellow, that Spokeshave,
I 've hear'n tell," replies my visitor. "I must write hum and tell our folks that this
'ere is the first carpet I 've seen sin' I came to Californy, four year come next month,"
is his next remark. For the last half-hour he has been entertaining me with a wearisome account of the murder of his brother by an Irishman in Boston, and the chief
feeling which he exhibits is a fear that the jury should only bring in a verdict of
manslaughter. But I hear F.'s step, and his entrance relieves me from the bore.

I am too tired to write more. Alas, dear M.! this letter is indeed a stupid one—a
poor return for your pregnant epistles. It is too late to better it. The express goes at
eight in the morning. The midnight moon is looking wonderingly in at the cabin
window, and the river has a sleepy murmur that impels me irresistibly bedward.

*Source: The Shirley Letters from California Mines in 1851–1852: Being a Series of
Twenty-Three Letters from Dame Shirley (Mrs. Louise Amelia Knapp Smith Clappe) to
her Sister in Massachusetts and now Reprinted from the Pioneer Magazine of 1854–1855*
(1922)

4. Thomas Gray, "An Elegy Wrote in a Country Churchyard" (1751).

🍂 HARRIET JACOBS (1813–1897)

Harriet Jacobs was born a slave in Edenton, North Carolina, where her mistress taught her to read and write. At eleven, Jacobs was willed to the daughter of Dr. James Norcom, who subjected her to repeated sexual harassment. By giving birth to another white man's child, she hoped her master would no longer harass her. But her desperate plan failed. After a seven-year seclusion in her grandmother's attic, she escaped to the North and worked as a domestic. There she met the abolitionist Amy Post, who encouraged Jacobs to write her autobiography. But Jacobs was loath to make public the details of her story, particularly her out-of-wedlock children. She considered asking Harriet Beecher Stowe to write her story. After nearly a decade, in which Jacobs worked in the home of Nathan-iel Parker Willis (brother of Fanny Fern), she finally completed Incidents in the Life of a Slave Girl *(1861), which she published under the pseudonym Linda Brent. For years it was believed to be a novel by Lydia Maria Child, who helped Jacobs edit the work. Finally, in the 1980s, Jean Fagan Yellin determined the veracity of the slave narrative and the identity of its author.*

Letters to Amy Post

[1852?]

My Dear Friend

. . . your proposal to me has been thought over and over again but not without some most painful rememberances [*sic*] dear Amy if it was the life of a Heroine with no degradation associated with it far better to have been one of the starving poor of Ireland whose bones had to bleach on the highways than to have been a slave with the curse of slavery stamped upon yourself and Children your purity of heart and kindly sympathies won me at one time to speak of my children it is the only words that has passed my lips since I left my Mothers door I had determined to let others think as they pleased but my lips should be sealed and no one had a right to question me for this reason when I first came north I avoided the Antislavery people as much as possible because I felt that I could not be honest and tell the whole truth often have I gone to my poor Brother with my grieved and mortified spirits he would mingle his tears with mine while he would advise me to do what was right my conscience approved it but my stubborn pride would not yeild [*sic*] I have tried for the last two years to conquer it and I feel that God has helped me or I never would consent to give my past life to any one for I would not do it without giving the whole truth if it could help save another from my fate it would be selfish and unchristian in me to keep it back situated as I am I do not see any way that I could put it forward Mrs Willis thinks it would do much good in Mrs Stowe hand but I

106

could not ask her to take any step Mr W is too proslavery he would tell me that it was very wrong and that I was trying to do harm or perhaps he was sorry for me to undertake it while I was in his family Mrs Willis thinks if is not done in my day it will [be] a good legacy for my children to do it after my death but now is the time when their [sic] is so much excitement everywhere Mrs Hallowell said in her letter that you thought of going to New York in the course of a few weeks if you will let me know when I will meet you there I can give you my Ideas much better than write them

If the Antislavery society could prapare [sic] this I would be willing to exert myself in any way that they thought best for the welfare of the cause

They do not know me they have heard of me as John Jacobs sister

my dear friend would you be willing to make this proposal I would rather have you do it than any one else you could do it better I should be [scratched out] happier in remembering it was you if Mrs Stowe would under take it I should like to be with her a Month I should want the History of my childhood and the first five years in one volume and the next three and my home in the northern states in the secont [sic] besids [sic] I could give her some fine sketches for her pen on slavery give my love to your dear Husband and sons kiss Willie for me love to all God bless Yours Harriet

June 21st [1857]

My Dear Friend

A heart full of thanks for your kind and welcome letter which would have been answered immediately but for want of time to think a moment. I would dearly love to talk with you as it would be more satisfactory—but as I cannot I will try to explain myself on paper as well as I can—

I have My dear friend [scratched out] Striven faithfully to give a true and just account of my own life in slavry [sic]— God knows I have tried to do it in a Christian spirit — there are somethings that I might have made plainer I know - woman can whisper — her cruel wrongs into the ear of a very dear friend - much easier than she can record them for the world to read — I have left nothing out but what I thought — the world might believe that a Slave woman was too willing to pour out - that she might gain their sympathies I ask nothing - I have placed myself before you to be judged as a woman whether [scratched out] I deserve your pity or contempt - I have another object in view - it is to come to you just as I am a poor slave Mother - not to tell you what I have heard but what I have seen - and what I have suffered - and if their [sic] is any sympathy to give - let it be given to the thousands - of of [sic] Slave Mothers that are still in bondage—suffering far more than I have - let it plead for their helpless Children that they may enjoy the same liberties that my Children now enjoy — Say anything of me that you have had from a truthful source that you think best — ask me any question you like - in regard to the father of my Children I think I have stated all perhaps I did not tell you - that he was a member of Congress - at that time all ~~that~~ of this I have written [*sic*]— I think it would be best for you to begin with our acquaintance and the length of time that I was in your family you [*sic*] advice ~~about~~ about giving the history of my life in Slavry [*sic*] mention that I lived at service all the while that I was striving to get the Book out but do not say with whom I lived as I would not use the Willis name neither would I like to have people think that I was living an Idle life - and had got this book out merely to make money - my kind friend I do not restrict you in anything for you know far better than I do what to say I am only too happy to think that I am going to have it from you -

I have been thinking that I would so like to go away and sell my Book - I could then secure a copywright to sell it both here and in England - and by identifying myself with it I might do something for the Antislavry [*sic*] Cause - to do this I would have to ~~have of~~ get letters of introduction. from some of the leading Abolitionist of this Country to those of the Old - when you write tell me what you think of it I must stop for I am in the only spot where I can have a light - and the mosquitoes have taken possession of me - much love to all my friends - and Willie - and believe me ever yours Harriet

Source: Post Family Papers, Department of Rare Books and Special Collections, University of Rochester Library

Preface by the Author to *Incidents in the Life of a Slave Girl*

Reader, be assured this narrative is no fiction. I am aware that some of my adventures may seem incredible; but they are, nevertheless, strictly true. I have not exaggerated the wrongs inflicted by Slavery; on the contrary, my descriptions fall far short of the facts. I have concealed the names of places, and given persons fictitious names. I had no motive for secrecy on my own account, but I deemed it kind and considerate towards others to pursue this course.

I wish I were more competent to the task I have undertaken. But I trust my readers will excuse deficiencies in consideration of circumstances. I was born and reared in Slavery; and I remained in a Slave State twenty-seven years. Since I have been at the North, it has been necessary for me to work diligently for my own support, and the education of my children. This has not left me much leisure to make up for the loss of early opportunities to improve myself; and it has compelled me to write these pages at irregular intervals, whenever I could snatch an hour from household duties.

When I first arrived in Philadelphia, Bishop Paine advised me to publish a sketch of my life, but I told him I was altogether incompetent to such an undertaking. Though I have improved my mind somewhat since that time, I still remain of the same opinion; but I trust my motives will excuse what might otherwise seem presumptuous. I have not written my experiences in order to attract attention to myself; on the contrary, it would have been more pleasant to me to have been silent about my own history. Neither do I care to excite sympathy for my own sufferings. But I do earnestly desire to arouse the women of the North to a realizing sense of the condition of two millions of women at the South, still in bondage, suffering what I suffered, and most of them far worse. I want to add my testimony to that of abler pens to convince the people of the Free States what Slavery really is. Only by experience can any one realize how deep, and dark, and foul is that pit of abominations. May the blessing of God rest on this imperfect effort in behalf of my persecuted people!

LINDA BRENT.

Source: Incidents in the Life of a Slave Girl (1861)

🏵 ALICE B. NEAL (HAVEN) (1827–1863)

Emily Alice Bradley Neal Haven published under a variety of names, including Clara Cushman, Alice Gordon Lee, Alice G. Lee, Mrs. Joseph B. Neal, Alice B. Neal, Alice B. Haven, and "Cousin Alice." She sent her first story to the Philadelphia paper Neal's Saturday Gazette *using a pseudonym, in acquiescence to her sister's wishes. The editor, Joseph Neal, married her in 1846; at his request she adopted the name Alice. When Joseph died after seven months of marriage, Alice took over editorship of his paper and began to write to support herself. In 1853, she married Samuel Livermore Haven and moved back to New York, her home state. She published twenty-two books and was a frequent contributor to* Godey's Lady's Book, Graham's American Monthly Magazine of Literature and Art, *and* Harper's Monthly. *She died a month after the birth of her fifth child. The following essay suggests Neal's own literary ambitions, which often conflicted with her sense of propriety and duty for women. Similar in some respects to George Eliot's famous essay "Silly Novels by Lady Novelists" (1856), it is much more encouraging to aspiring women writers.*

American Female Authorship

That "the fashion of this world passeth away," is quite as noticeable in the change of domestic amusements as in any style of dress or equipage. The tapestry of the early ages that employed the busy fingers, and suggested the delicious reveries of maidens waiting with patience the return of the lover long exiled to the Holy Land—the embroidery and tent-stitch of our grandmothers, the sampler-making of the last generation, and the net-work and crochet of this—all are by turns the rage, copied, discussed, exhibited, and forgotten. But just now the needle seems to be for the first time threatened by a powerful rival; the work-box is replaced by the desk, and the portfolio has usurped the corner sacred to the tambour-frame. In other words, authorship is the mania of our ladies, and an ambition for literary distinction becomes even in childhood the *grande passion*.

We can remember the time when we gazed on proof sheets with awe, and wondered at the cabalistic characters traced on the margin. "Copy" was a word unknown to ears polite, and ladies had their portraits painted only for their friends. But now "proof-reading" forms a regular branch of education; the fairest fingers are more or less soiled with printer's ink—metaphorically, of course—and

> "Touching verses
> Take now the place of birthday purses."

Every country newspaper has its quota of "our charming correspondents," and the magazines shine in the steady brilliancy of a constellation of fixed stars—names conspicuous on the cover, and sure to be quoted in a notice of the number.

Well, and what is there to urge against it? Nothing, dear ladies, of itself; for we, too, have suffered *cacoethes scribendi,*[1] and therefore can speak feelingly of its approach. Our school-girl days were haunted with visions of magazine covers, and a niche—in the appendix, we humbly said—of a collection of prose or poets. How eagerly we listened to every anecdote connected with those already made so glorious! how we longed to see their pictured semblances, and studied every feature when they came! And we can still remember the delightful flutter when a poem with our *nom de plume*—we won't say of *our own*—was actually in print, and we laid it by the bedside, as children do their dolls, to be conned over again at earliest day. And when one was copied—really copied, with a dozen printer's mistakes, and one line omitted—that was still more charming, and we wondered our classmates did not acknowledge the access of dignity attained, even though we gained the foot of the algebra class, and received black marks for Latin syntax.

It was a strange chance that made us, soon, very soon, co-editor of the very journal that had so befriended our youthful indiscretions; and it was in the exercise of the power, thus our duty, that we watched the rapid growth of the taste for authorship to which we have alluded. It was this experience which had led us to embody some of the rules we were so constantly called on to give, in an article that will reach most of those whose hopes, fears, and anxieties we have known. So if you choose, we invite you to enter our *sanctum,* and go over with us the pile of communications that crowd the basket devoted to their reception, that, instead of a dry disquisition, we may have our criticism in a more chatty and sociable form.

In the first place, as we sort the documents into prose and verse, we remark that nine out of the ten poets expect to be paid for their verses, and all to have the publication gratis. Two tales have the modest request, "Please publish next week," and their notes inform you that the authors themselves have very miserable opinions of the article inclosed [sic], but are over-persuaded to offer it by admiring friends. One modest little sketch has not even a word commending it to our care; and another we welcome at the first glance, for we see by the broad margin, the separated pages, written only on one side, and carefully numbered, that there is experience, if not force of talent, in the hand from whence it comes.

Shall we commence with the prose, then, leaving the poetry by way of dessert, and see some symptoms of the mania now epidemic? The letter is dated "Rosewood Seminary;" it is in a fine crow-quill hand, with pale ink, on satin paper. Our eyes are strained to decipher it; and yet we do so, and find that "Mignon Mignonette"— the authoress of the tale submitted to our judgment—"has already a considerable reputation in local prints," conducts the "Rose-Bud," a manuscript school periodical, and writes letters for the "Home Journal," but forgets to mention whether accepted or not. She does not write for money. "Fame," she tells us, "is all the reward

1. Latin: the itch to write.

she wants," and "ambition is her angel." So we are introduced to "her darling pet of all she has written—'Lilla Lenister: a Tale of Myrtle Dell.'"

"'Come to me, my angel child,' said Mrs. Lenister, on a warm, bright summer afternoon, when the sun was slowly sinking to its western couch, and the flowers bent languidly on their stalks, thirsting for the pearly, cooling drops of heaven; 'I am about to depart for "that bourne from whence no traveler returns," and I would fain give thee my parting counsel. Thou art too lovely for this cold, false world, dearest one; thine eyes droop to behold its agony, thy fair cheek pales at its ingratitude.'

"'Oh, my idol mother! do not speak such cruel words of foreboding!' And the young girl clasped her hands in agony over her throbbing temples, until the blood seemed oozing through her waxen fingers."

So much for the first half page of "Mignon," and it is quite enough to make us certain that, whatever might be the interest or variety of the plot, the ambitious style would quite destroy its pretensions to our pages. In the first place, the description of nature has a redundancy of adjectives, a fault most common with young writers. Then, again, no person feeling the solemn realities of such a departure, would stop to quote the very trite line with which she prefaces her remarks, or talk blank verse at such a moment. Moreover, the "blood oozing through the waxen fingers" is certainly suggestive of a very delicate and beautiful hand, but one that certainly would unfit its possessor for the hard realities of this bitter world.

This brings us to the first element of tale writing, or, indeed, of any description—naturalness; forgetting this, the charm is destroyed, be the language ever so well chosen, or the thoughts daintily expressed. People in stories should talk, as much as possible, like people in real life. They are expected to be properly dressed, not in Cherubino's[2] Grecian drapery, but as neatly and tastefully as their situation or position would require. The costume, language, and actions must be in keeping with the character intended to be portrayed, and the incidents should ensue in natural order. This is apt to be lost sight of by young writers, who consider imagination the only talent to be cultivated, and, laying the reins on the neck of their favorite hobby, neither know nor care to what cloud-land he takes his flight. We often find an admirable plot spoiled by this very "playing at stilts," in the conversation of the actors. This often results from a lack of observation on the subject, but too frequently from the mistaken idea that people in books should have a different vernacular from the well-bred in society around us. For instance, in a declaration which should express as much natural feeling as possible, how often we find the exalted language of Sir Charles Grandison[3] put in the mouth of a modern watering-place lover, who perhaps has never seen the lady but three times before in his life,

2. The young lover in Mozart's *The Marriage of Figaro* (1786).
3. Samuel Richardson's novel *The History of Sir Charles Grandison* (1753–1754).

and proposes for the same reason that he drinks wine at dinner—because every one around him does. Modern story writers—it must be understood that we allude entirely to novices—never allow the hero or heroine to think seriously upon what is involved in such a step. They meet a pretty girl in their morning walks, and propose without the slightest hint of the question Willis[4] so thoughtfully propounds—

"Who is thy progenitor, fair girl?
What doeth he for lucre?"

Cruel fathers are overcome in a breath, and send a check for $1000 for bridal expenses, and inexorable mammas faint, use a vinaigrette, and add their blessing to the naughty young couple. They are launched into matrimony with no hope of being taken into the firm, or the least hint to the reader as to how the housekeeping is to go on. To be sure, we would not have a dry detail of these important facts, but a blending of the real with the ideal should at all times be insisted on. Let us have enough of human nature to excuse the blind devotion in all cases represented.

But we forget to mention that this last disquisition on prospects has arisen from certain passages in the successor of "Lilla Lenister," a tale of twenty-five foolscap pages, in which the very novel incident of marrying a poor girl against the wishes of the hero's father, the elopement, and subsequent reconciliation on most honorable terms, is served up. However, we would first state that an equally novel incident disposes of the fair Lilla: A rich uncle arrives from India, seeks out the orphan child of his only sister, who proves her claims to his consideration by the possession of a certain locket, and protects her from "the agony and ingratitude of this cold, false world."

Therefore commonplace or stereotyped incident should be avoided. Hackneyed plots are as much out of favor with the public as unnatural language or positions. Think what you have known, if in real life—imagine what would be most probably said by people you are acquainted with, situated as your hero and heroine are, and do not give three pages of description to one of action. Remember that a most delicate touch and long practice are needed by every landscape painter, before he can produce agreeable pictures. Artists of eminence aim to copy nature alone, and those who approach most nearly stand highest in their profession. Suppose, for instance, they were distinguished for imagination, and choose to give us a red sky at noonday, bright yellow foliage in spring, blue trees, and pink cattle. It might be a very showy and striking picture, one that would arrest the attention, no doubt, but no delicacy of touch could harmonize or cover such deformities. Again, if all things were their proper hue, but the parts of the scene were patched together, an Italian

4. Nathaniel Parker Willis (1806–1867), brother of Fanny Fern. His poem, "To The Lady in the Chemisette With Black Buttons" (1849) is quoted, with slight alteration, below.

sky with New Hampshire granite hills, tropical foliage and Swiss peasant girls, every one would cry out at the strange admixture, and turn with commendation to the modest delineation of a simple, unpretending landscape. A clump of trees well executed will receive more praise than the grandest sunset, and a cool, gray rock give more pleasure than Alps on Alps of ultra-marine hills with pink summits.

It is by these very touches that we judge of the "capabilities and improvabilities" of a young writer. Though the handling is rough, if they have preserved correctness of outline, even if they have chosen an artistic point without the least skill in its delineation, we know that there is real taste, and a true perception of the beautiful to be encouraged and fostered. And this we are ever ready cheerfully to do. For its own sake, the happiness which the power of expression confers, and for the good it may be the medium of conveying to others, real talent should never be neglected by its possessor. Not in vanity or self-seeking, but with a still thankfulness for the great gift Heaven has thought you worthy to receive, and a deep realization of the responsibility which attends it. Were talent thus regarded, and thus cultivated, we should have less flippant tales presented to our notice, and fewer poems to reject for their utter lack of novelty or thought.

Therefore, to sum up our simple rules, in tale-writing the plot and incident should be probable, at least possible, and arranged with a thought to the ordinary sequence of events; the descriptions of natural scenery few and delicately handled— we say few, because readers generally are not interested in a geographical description of mountains and valleys that never existed, and that do not increase the excitement of the plot, or hasten the development of character. It is a form of amplification that too often serves only as a cloak for poverty of material. The conversations should be spirited or thoughtful, as the case may be, but always remember that they are conversations, and in real life; one rarely moralizes a whole page without even a comment or ejaculation from the listener. Nor does a colloquial style often admit of sentences Johnsonian[5] in length and finish. It is, more properly, characterized by abrupt transitions, terse opinions, or brilliant sallies. Look, for example, at the animated repartee of Beatrice, or the gentle thoughtfulness, the childlike simplicity of Miranda, or the eagerness of Ferdinand. There is a tenderness in the elevated and womanly thoughts of Portia naturally expressed, and the very trifling of Rosalind has more meaning than the most labored assurance of returned affection could convey.[6]

To return once more to our parallel, as the painter goes forth to the woods and fields to study nature in its varied phases, and while reproducing with magic skill the broad sweep of the landscape, does not fail in most careful heed to its minutest

5. Ben Jonson (1572–1637), dramatist, contemporary of Shakespeare.
6. The characters mentioned here are all from Shakespeare: Beatrice, *Much Ado About Nothing* (1598); Miranda and Ferdinand, *The Tempest* (1611); Portia, *The Merchant of Venice* (1596–1597); Rosalind, *As You Like It* (1599–1600).

detail, twining carefully a tuft of foliage, or copying, with patient skill, the circles of the rough bark he intends to portray, or imitates with minute exactness the gray moss that drapes the fallen tree—so those who would represent social grace or human loveliness, or even trace the follies and weakness too often its startling contrast, must not neglect the most trivial point that can contribute to the air of reality which gives it the greatest charm. . . .

Authorship, in the absence of varied employment for our sex, is of late looked to as a means of subsistence by many whose naturally refined and well cultivated minds make them shrink from actual contact with business life. The belief has gone abroad that all who have acquired any reputation are winning fortunes as well, and that the harvest is still broad and waiting for reapers. Many, thrown by unexpected reverses upon their own resources, scarcely question the possibility of failure, to meet only with a bitter disappointment which they cannot comprehend, and which a wounded spirit construes into personal insult or neglect. But to look soberly at the fact. There are perhaps ten or twelve ladies in our own country who have adopted literature as a profession. Six of these—we speak of what we know—by giving all their time and energy to their labors, by an industry which few professional men dream of and few ladies can imitate, realize a comfortable, barely comfortable, income, as a reward of years passed in battling with disappointments and patient waiting upon the fancies of a capricious public. One of our most finished and elegant writers, quoted by European critics and upheld by our own, teaches for many hours of every day to supply deficiency of income, which ought not to exist where so much talent is displayed in books eagerly read, but meagerly paid for.

Besides those who have earned their position and established their claims to a magazine hearing, there are many writing equally well perhaps, but without the *éclat* of a name, who get a communication accepted now and then. This leaves but little opening for a new and utterly unknown author, who may have graceful fancies, but crudely expressed, and whose manuscript, carefully written and tied with a white ribbon, betrays inexperience at once to a practised eye. A hearing even is difficult to be obtained; and then is it natural that a publisher should reject a finished article by an author already well known, to make room for one that is mediocre, to say the least? Not until publishers have more unselfishness than distinguishes common mortals.

Book writing is even worse; the market, so to speak, being equally crowded, and the stamp of magazine approval having come to be considered almost essential. It is an avenue closed to all but those who are content to serve a laborious apprenticeship, or who can afford to print as well as write, asking no remuneration. Of course, there are exceptions to all that we have here stated. "Friends at court" now and then gain audience for those who prove worthy of an introduction. Some there have been who at once, by force of originality, can adopt the standard of Miss Mary Maria Quiggs, and "write at once for the greatest glory and the highest pay." But these exceptions only prove the general rule, that authorship, as a profession, is the last to be chosen, if speedy or ample remuneration is expected; for the salary of many a governess equals, if not exceeds, the largest income we have ever known an American authoress to receive.

We have said nothing of simple literary ambition, because we do not recognize it as a worthy motive. It savors too much of vanity, and its returns are too often only "vexation of spirit." We commenced a playful criticism upon a topic forced daily upon our consideration, but, if it has become subdued or practical, it is because the subject seemed to demand the transition. We gladly welcome to the sisterhood those who are earnest and trustful in their vocation, for we owe it to them as a debt of gratitude to those whose hands and hearts were so kindly opened to us; but we would also shield others from painful disappointments and harsh experiences which are almost inevitable.

Source: Godey's Lady's Book (1852)

❧ HARRIET BEECHER STOWE (1811–1896)

Harriet Beecher was born into a prominent religious family in Litchfield, Connecticut. Her father, Lyman Beecher, and her brother Henry were the two most famous preachers of the nineteenth century. Harriet's fame, however, overshadowed theirs. She was known throughout the world as the author of Uncle Tom's Cabin *(1852), the most popular book of the century, credited by many with contributing to the sectional split that would result in the Civil War. After an extensive education and an early teaching career, she married Calvin Stowe in 1836, had seven children, and published more than thirty books in the course of her career. At seventy, she received the honor of an* Atlantic *birthday party (the only one given to a woman), at which the publisher counted her as one of "the creators of American literature." Stowe's discussion of slavery in the preface to* Uncle Tom's Cabin *can be read alongside Caroline Lee Hentz's preface to* The Planter's Northern Bride. *Her advice essay, which appeared in a journal Stowe edited,* Hearth and Home, *holds up Hawthorne as a model and counsels women to write about what they know, namely their domestic lives.*

Preface to *Uncle Tom's Cabin*

The scenes of this story, as its title indicates, lie among a race hitherto ignored by the associations of polite and refined society; an exotic race, whose ancestors, born beneath a tropic sun, brought with them, and perpetuated to their descendants, a character so essentially unlike the hard and dominant Anglo-Saxon race, as for many years to have won from it only misunderstanding and contempt.

But, another and better day is dawning; every influence of literature, of poetry and of art, in our times, is becoming more and more in unison with the great master chord of Christianity, "good will to man."

The poet, the painter, and the artist, now seek out and embellish the common and gentler humanities of life, and, under the allurements of fiction, breathe a humanizing and subduing influence, favorable to the development of the great principles of Christian brotherhood.

The hand of benevolence is everywhere stretched out, searching into abuses, righting wrongs, alleviating distresses, and bringing to the knowledge and sympathies of the world the lowly, the oppressed, and the forgotten.

In this general movement, unhappy Africa at last is remembered; Africa, who began the race of civilization and human progress in the dim, gray dawn of early time, but who, for centuries, has lain bound and bleeding at the foot of civilized and Christianized humanity, imploring compassion in vain.

But the heart of the dominant race, who have been her conquerors, her hard masters, has at length been turned towards her in mercy; and it has been seen how far nobler it is in nations to protect the feeble than to oppress them. Thanks be to God, the world has at last outlived the slave-trade!

The object of these sketches is to awaken sympathy and feeling for the African race, as they exist among us; to show their wrongs and sorrows, under a system so necessarily cruel and unjust as to defeat and do away the good effects of all that can be attempted for them, by their best friends, under it.

In doing this, the author can sincerely disclaim any invidious feeling towards those individuals who, often without any fault of their own, are involved in the trials and embarrassments of the legal relations of slavery.

Experience has shown her that some of the noblest of minds and hearts are often thus involved; and no one knows better than they do, that what may be gathered of the evils of slavery from sketches like these, is not the half that could be told, of the unspeakable whole.

In the northern states, these representations may, perhaps, be thought caricatures; in the southern states are witnesses who know their fidelity. What personal knowledge the author has had, of the truth of incidents such as here are related, will appear in its time.[1]

It is a comfort to hope, as so many of the world's sorrows and wrongs have, from age to age, been lived down, so a time shall come when sketches similar to these shall be valuable only as memorials of what has long ceased to be.

When an enlightened and Christianized community shall have, on the shores of Africa, laws, language and literature, drawn from among us, may then the scenes of the house of bondage be to them like the remembrance of Egypt to the Israelite,— a motive of thankfulness to Him who hath redeemed them!

For, while politicians contend, and men are swerved this way and that by conflicting tides of interest and passion, the great cause of human liberty is in the hands of one, of whom it is said:

"He shall not fail nor be discouraged
Till He have set judgment in the earth."
"He shall deliver the needy when he crieth,
The poor, and him that hath no helper."
"He shall redeem their soul from deceit and violence,
And precious shall their blood be in His sight."[2]

Source: Uncle Tom's Cabin, Or, Life Among the Lowly (1852)

1. In 1853, Stowe published *The Key to Uncle Tom's Cabin; Presenting The Original Facts and Documents Upon Which the Story is Founded.*
2. Isaiah 42:4; Psalms 27:12; Psalms 27:14.

How Shall I Learn to Write?

We have presupposed, in our former article, that there is a great deal of ability for good writing lying dormant in the community. This is particularly the case among women.

It is our opinion that certain gifts of expression, and certain graces and facilities of style, belong more naturally to women than to men. As far as the two sexes study together in our normal and high schools, is it not a fact that the very best compositions come from the female pupils? Why is it, then, that the best writing is done by men? This is the reason: The education of the woman stops short at the point where the boy's education really begins. At the age that the boy enters college for an arduous and mature course, the girl comes home and addresses herself to going into company; and the five or six years following, that her brother spends in severe intellectual drill, she fritters away in what is called society.

The result of all this is that women are deficient in the very first requisite of a good writer—namely, something to say which is worth saying.

A man who is educated to any purpose goes around a certain circle of human knowledge, and if he improves his advantages, gets thus a solid basis of ideas and opinions on which he can profitably and instructively build in after life; while the woman is spending the same four or five years in forgetting all that she has learned during her school education.

But it is a fact that the experiences of woman in real life, in all that comes to her in her domestic capacity as mistress of a family, sister, daughter, wife, and mother, do furnish a class of subjects wherein a woman, trained to think wisely and justly, may find a great deal to say that is worth saying. She may have subject matter of peculiar weight and importance—subject matter which woman, and only woman, could possibly be able to present.

Let us suppose, then, a woman with something to say, about which she is truly and really in earnest. How is she to get the gift of expression?

The manner of saying things to make them vivid and clear and interesting, is a fine art. It is a thing that may be studied; it is a thing that *must* be practised.

The differences between a natural writer and a person who is not, is not so great as people often imagine. It amounts simply to this: the natural writer has a passion for writing which leads him, in youth and immaturity, to go through a great deal of practice—and practice in this, as in everything else, makes perfect.

Now, the kind of writing for which there is a call in our paper, HEARTH AND HOME, is writing about domestic and rural subjects, and subjects of a practical nature, such as lie more fully within the sphere of woman's knowledge and observation than in that of ordinary men.

Some of the most celebrated and most admired writing in the world has been bestowed on the dullest and most unpromising subjects. Washington Irving's description of the barnyard of a country inn on a rainy day is a case exactly in point.

There is a great deal of writing, very charming, very acceptable, and much in demand, which consists simply in painting by means of words the simple and homely scenes of every-day life.

The most commonplace object, well represented in a painting, often commands an artist's price. In the same manner, the most commonplace object or scene, well painted by words, has an artistic value.

The greatest artist of this sort that we have ever had in America is Hawthorne. To every young writer, who wishes to study how to learn to use language so as to make every-day scenes and things picturesque and charming, we recommend a thorough and diligent study of his writings.

The sketch called "The Old Apple Dealer" is a specimen of what can be done by a thoughtful and careful study of apparently the most uninteresting subject in the world. A poor, stupid, commonplace old man is made the theme of one of his most wonderful pieces of writing.

Many have supposed that writing comes by fits and starts, and by dashes—by bursts and inspirations. But there is no good writing that has ever come without great labor, great study, and incessant practice.

The publication of *Passages from the American Note-Books of Nathaniel Hawthorne* has done a great service to all who wish to learn to write, in opening before their view all the processes by which the greatest American writer formed that inimitable style, whose sheeny gloss and exquisite word-painting are so astonishing.

We can see in these books that he studied nature day by day; going out to study, as a painter goes out with pallet and brushes, only that instead of pallet and brushes, he used the words of the English language.

The young writer can see in these note-books how in this daily process of walking, studying, and writing, he accumulated that wonderful store of imagery which is reflected in all he says.

It also illustrates what we say—that he excelled in writing because his love for it led him to practise it constantly.

These note-books are but a small specimen of volumes after volumes filled with minute descriptions of all that he saw and all that he did. Just as a gymnast becomes graceful by a constant use of his muscles, so Hawthorne, by a constant dealing with words and a constant daily habit of writing, acquired flexibility and versatility of style.

Many young writers imagine that the vivid dreams and romantic visions and conceptions that come to them are evidence of a talent for writing. Alas! my dear young friend, your vision and your dream has got to be translated into the English language, and it is only by seeing that your words and phrases will reproduce the same vision and the same enthusiasm in other minds that you are to feel that you have succeeded.

The greatest modern French novelist, De Balzac, says:

"To imagine is easy enough. It is merely to smoke enchanted cigarettes, which, after all, may dissolve in air. The real work consists in the bringing out into language these airy conceptions." . . .

Source: Hearth and Home (1869)

✿ FANNY FERN (1811–1872)

Born Sarah Willis, in Portland, Maine, Fanny Fern attended the famous Beecher Seminary, where Catharine Beecher taught her to write. After Sara's husband's death in 1846, the failure of another short-lived marriage, and the realization that neither sewing nor teaching could support her and her two daughters, Sara began to write, using the pseudonym Fanny Fern. She quickly gained fame as a writer of witty, colloquial newspaper columns that challenged conventional pieties about women's roles. Her autobiographical novel Ruth Hall *(1855) chronicles her troubles, culminating in a successful literary career. Its popularity led Robert Bonner, publisher of the* New York Ledger, *to offer her one hundred dollars a week to write for his paper, making her the highest paid newspaper writer in America. Fern was happily married in 1856 and wrote a regular column in the* Ledger *until her death. Her story "A Practical Blue-Stocking" disputes pejorative stereotypes about women writers' domestic ineptitude, much as Catharine Maria Sedgwick's "A Sketch of Blue Stocking" did two decades earlier. Yet the "Soliloquy of a Literary Housekeeper," written in Fern's own voice, laments the domestic concerns that take time and energy away from her work. The satirical review of her own book,* Fresh Leaves, *is typical of her style and wit. Although it was signed with her name, readers likely would have begun reading it as an example of male criticism of "strong-minded" women writers like Fern.*

A Practical Blue-Stocking

"Have you called on your old friend, James Lee, since your return?" said Mr. Seldon to his nephew.

"No, sir; I understand he has the misfortune to have a blue-stocking for a wife, and whenever I have thought of going there, a vision with inky fingers, frowzled hair, rumpled dress, and slip-shod heels has come between me and my old friend,—not to mention thoughts of a disorderly house, smoky puddings, and dirty-faced children. Defend me from a wife who spends her time dabbling in ink, and writing for the papers. I'll lay a wager James has n't [*sic*] a shirt with a button on it, or a pair of stockings that is not full of holes. Such a glorious fellow as he used to be, too!" said Harry soliloquizingly, "so dependent upon somebody to love him. By Jove, it's a hard case."

"Harry, will you oblige me by calling there?" said Mr. Seldon with a peculiar smile.

"Well, yes, if you desire it; but these married men get so metamorphosed by their wives, that it's a chance if I recognize the melancholy remains of my old friend. A literary wife!" and he shrugged his shoulders contemptuously.

At one o'clock the next afternoon, Harry might have been seen ringing the bell of James Lee's door. He had a very ungracious look upon his face, as much as to say,—"My mind is made up for the worst, and I must bear it for Jemmy's sake."

The servant ushered him into a pretty little sitting-room, not expensively furnished, but neat and tasteful. At the further end of the room were some flowering plants, among which a sweet-voiced canary was singing. Harry glanced round the room; a little light-stand or Chinese table stood in the corner, with pen, ink, and papers scattered over it.

"I knew it," said Harry; "there's the sign! horror of horrors! an untidy, slatternly blue-stocking! how I shall be disgusted with her! Jemmy's to be pitied."

He took up a book that lay upon the table, and a little manuscript copy of verses fell from between the leaves. He dropped the book as if he had been poisoned; then picking up the fallen manuscript with his thumb and forefinger, he replaced it with an impatient pshaw! Then he glanced round the room again,—no! there was not a particle of dust to be seen, even by his prejudiced eyes; the windows were transparently clean; the hearth-rug was longitudinally and mathematically laid down; the pictures hung "plumb" upon the wall; the curtains were fresh and gracefully looped; and, what was a greater marvel, there was a child's dress half finished in a dainty little work-basket, and a thimble of fairy dimensions in the immediate neighborhood thereof. Harry felt a perverse inclination to examine the stitches, but at the sound of approaching footsteps he braced himself up to undergo his mental shower-bath.

A little lady tripped lightly into the room, and stood smilingly before him; her glossy black hair was combed smoothly behind her ears, and knotted upon the back of a remarkably well-shaped head; her eyes were black and sparkling, and full of mirth; her dress fitted charmingly to a very charming little figure; her feet were unexceptionably small, and neatly gaitered; the snowy fingers of her little hand had not the slightest "soupçon" of ink upon them, as she extended them in token of welcome to her guest.

Harry felt very much like a culprit, and greatly inclined to drop on one knee, and make a clean breast of a confession, but his evil bachelor spirit whispered in his ear,—"Wait a bit, she's fixed up for company; cloven foot will peep out by and by!"

Well, they sat down! The lady knew enough,—he heard that before he came;—he only prayed that he might not be bored with her book-learning, or blue-stockingism. It is hardly etiquette to report private conversations for the papers,—so I will only say that when James Lee came home, two hours after, he found his old friend Harry in the finest possible spirits, tête-à-tête with his "blue" wife. An invitation to dinner followed. Harry demurred,—he had begun to look at the little lady through a very bewitching pair of spectacles, and he hated to be disenchanted,—and a blue-stocking dinner!

However, his objections, silent though they were, were over-ruled. There was no fault to be found with that table-cloth, or those snowy napkins; the glasses were clean, the silver bright as my lady's eyes; the meats cooked to a turn, the gravies and sauces perfect, and the dessert well got up and delicious. Mrs. Lee presided with ease and elegance; the custards and preserves were of her own manufacture, and the little prattler, who was introduced with them, fresh from her nursery bath, with moist ringlets, snowy robe, and dimpled shoulders, looked charmingly well cared for.

As soon as the two gentlemen were alone, Harry seized his friend's hand, saying, with a half smile, "James, I feel like an unmitigated scoundrel! I have heard your wife spoken of as a 'blue-stocking,' and I came here prepared to pity you as the victim of an unshared heart, slatternly house, and indigestible cooking; but may I die an old bachelor if I don't wish that woman, who has just gone out, was my wife."

James Lee's eyes moistened with gratified pride. "You don't know half," said he. "Listen;—some four years since I became involved in business; at the same time my health failed me; my spirits were broken, and I was getting a discouraged man. Emma, unknown to me, made application as a writer to several papers and magazines. She soon became very popular; and not long after placed in my hands the sum of three hundred dollars, the product of her labor. During this time, no parental or household duty was neglected; and her cheerful and steady affection raised my drooping spirits, and gave me fresh courage to commence the world anew. She still continues to write, although, as you see, my head is above water. Thanks to her as my guardian angel, for she says, 'We must lay up something for a rainy day.' God bless her sunshiny face!"

The entrance of Emma put a stop to any further eulogy, and Harry took his leave in a very indescribable and penitential frame of mind, doing ample penance for his former unbelieving scruples, by being very uncomfortably in love with a "Blue-Stocking.["]

Source: Fern Leaves from Fanny's Portfolio (1853)

Soliloquy of a Literary Housekeeper

"Spring cleaning!" Oh misery! Ceilings to be whitewashed, walls to be cleaned, paint to be scoured, carpets to be taken up, shaken, and put down again; scrubbing women, painters, and whitewashers, all engaged for months a-head, or beginning on your house to secure the job, and then running off a day to somebody else's to secure another. Yes, spring cleaning to be done; closets, bags, and baskets to be disemboweled; furs and woolens to be packed away; children's last summer clothes to be inspected (not a garment that will fit—all grown up like Jack's bean-stalk); spring cleaning, sure enough. I might spring my feet off and not get all that done. When is that book of mine to get written, I'd like to know? It's Ma'am, will you have this? and Ma'am, will you have that? and Ma'am, will you have the other thing? May I be kissed if I hadn't more time to write when I lived in an attic on salt and potatoes, and scrubbed the floor myself. Must I turn my house topsy-turvy, and inside out, once a year, because my grandmother did, and send my MSS. flying to the four winds, for this traditionary "spring cleaning." Spring fiddlestick! Must I buy up all Broadway to be made into dresses, because all New York women go fashion-mad? What's the use of having a house, if you can't do as you like in it? What's the use of being an authoress, if you can't indulge in the luxury of a shabby bonnet, or a comfortable old dress? What's the use of dressing when your cook can outshine you? What is the use of dragging brocade and velvet through ferry-boats and omnibusses, to serve as mats for market-baskets and dirty boots? "There goes Lily Larkspur, the authoress, in that everlasting old black silk." Well—what's the use of being well off, if you can't wear old clothes. If I was poor, as I was once, I couldn't afford it. Do you suppose I'm going to wrinkle up my face, scowling at unhappy little boys for treading on a five-hundred-dollar silk? or fret myself into a fever because some *gentleman* throws a cigar-stump on its lustrous trailing folds? no, no; life is too short, for that, and much too earnest. Give me good health—the morning for writing, and no interruptions, plenty of fresh air afterwards, and an old gown to enjoy it in, and you may mince along in your peacock dry-goods till your soul is as shriveled as your body.

Source: Fresh Leaves (1857)

Review of *Fresh Leaves*

This little volume has just been laid upon our table. The publishers have done all they could for it, with regard to outward adorning. No doubt it will be welcomed by those who admire this lady's style of writing; we confess ourselves not to be of that number. We have never seen Fanny Fern, nor do we desire to do so. We imagine her, from her writings, to be a muscular, black-browed, grenadier-looking female, who would be more at home in a boxing gallery than in a parlor,—a vociferous, demonstrative, strong-minded horror,—a woman only by virtue of her dress. Bah! the very thought sickens us. We have read, or, rather, tried to read, her halloo-there effusions. When we take up a woman's book we expect to find gentleness, timidity, and that lovely reliance on the patronage of our sex which constitutes a woman's greatest charm. We do not wish to be startled by bold expressions, or disgusted with exhibitions of masculine weaknesses. We do not desire to see a woman wielding the scimetar [*sic*] blade of sarcasm. If she be, unfortunately, endowed with a gift so dangerous, let her—as she values the approbation of our sex—fold it in a napkin. Fanny's strong-minded nose would probably turn up at this inducement.

Thank heaven! there are still women who *are* women—who know the place Heaven assigned them, and keep it—who do not waste floods of ink and paper, brow-beating men and stirring up silly women;—who do not teach children that a game of romps is of as much importance as Blair's Philosophy;—who have not the presumption to advise clergymen as to their duties, or lecture doctors, and savans;—who live for something else than to astonish a gaping, idiotic crowd. Thank heaven! there are women writers who do not disturb our complacence or serenity; whose books lull one to sleep like a strain of gentle music; who excite no antagonism, or angry feeling. Woman never was intended for an irritant: she should be oil upon the troubled waters of manhood—soft and amalgamating, a necessary but unobtrusive ingredient;—never challenging attention—never throwing the gauntlet of defiance to a beard, but softly purring beside it lest it bristle and scratch.

The very fact that Fanny Fern has, in the language of her admirers, "elbowed her way through unheard of difficulties," shows that she is an antagonistic, pugilistic female. One must needs, forsooth, get out of her way, or be pushed one side, or trampled down. How much more womanly to have allowed herself to be doubled up by adversity, and quietly laid away on the shelf of fate, than to have rolled up her sleeves, and gone to fisticuffs with it. Such a woman may conquer, it is true, but her victory will cost her dear; it will neither be forgotten nor forgiven—let her put that in her apron pocket.

As to Fanny Fern's grammar, rhetoric, and punctuation, they are beneath criticism. It is all very well for her to say, those who wish commas, semi-colons and periods, must look for them in the printer's case, or that she who finds ideas must not be expected to find rhetoric or grammar, for our part, we should be gratified if we had even found any ideas!

We regret to be obliged to speak thus of a lady's book: it gives us great pleasure, when we can do so conscientiously, to pat lady writers on the head; but we owe a duty to the public which will not permit us to recommend to their favorable notice an aspirant who has been unwomanly enough so boldly to contest every inch of ground in order to reach them—an aspirant at once so high-stepping and so ignorant, so plausible, yet so pernicious. We have a conservative horror of this pop-gun, torpedo female; we predict for Fanny Fern's "Leaves" only a fleeting autumnal flutter.

Source: The New York Ledger (1857)

❧ Sarah Josepha Hale (1788–1879)

Born Sarah Josepha Buell in New Hampshire, Hale was educated at home by her mother and her brother, who attended Dartmouth. She began to publish after her husband's death in 1822. Based on the success of her first novel, Northwood *(1827), she was offered the editorship of the* Ladies' *Magazine and Literary Gazette. In 1837, she became editor of the most popular magazine in America,* Godey's Lady's Book, *publishing important male and female writers and promoting the development of a national literature. Her influence as an editor before the Civil War was certainly as great as William Dean Howells's was after the war. Indeed, many of her admonitions to would-be writers, such as those in the "Editor's Table," are similar to Howells's later warnings against frivolous, sensationalist fiction. She also promoted the idea of "separate spheres" for men and women, believing that women were morally superior and thus better suited to the work of educating the populace as mothers and as writers. Hale considered her most important work to be* Woman's Record; or, Sketches of All Distinguished Women from "The Beginning" Till A.D. 1850 *(1853), which included 1,650 biographical sketches and began with her own brief autobiography.*

Untitled Autobiographical Sketch

A few words respecting the influences which have, probably, caused me to become the Chronicler of my own sex, may not be considered egotistical. I was mainly educated by my mother, and strictly taught to make the Bible the guide of my life. The books to which I had access were few, very few, in comparison with the number given children now-a-days; but they were such as required to be studied—and I did study them. Next to the Bible and The Pilgrim's Progress,[1] my earliest reading was Milton, Addison, Pope, Johnson, Cowper, Burns, and a portion of Shakspeare [*sic*]. I did not obtain all his works till I was nearly fifteen. The first regular novel I read was "The Mysteries of Udolpho,"[2] when I was quite a child. I name it on account of the influence it exercised over my mind. I had remarked that of all the books I saw, few were written by Americans, and none by *women*. Here was a work, the most fascinating I had ever read, always excepting "The Pilgrim's Progress," written by a woman! How happy it made me! The wish to promote the reputation of my own sex, and do something for my own country, were among the earliest mental emotions I can recollect. These feelings have had a salutary influence by directing my thoughts to a definite object; my literary pursuits have had an aim beyond self-seeking of any kind. The mental influence of woman over her own sex,

1. Christian allegory by John Bunyan, published in 1678.
2. Novel by Ann Radcliffe, published in 1794.

which was so important in my case, has been strongly operative in inclining me to undertake this my latest work, "Woman's Record." I have sought to make it an assistant in home education; hoping the examples shown and characters portrayed, might have an inspiration and a power in advancing the moral progress of society. Yet I cannot close without adverting to the ready and kind aid I have always met with from those men with whom I have been most nearly connected. To my brother[3] I owe what knowledge I possess of the Latin, of the higher branches of mathematics, and of mental philosophy. He often lamented that I could not, like himself, have the privilege of a college education. To my husband I was yet more deeply indebted. He was a number of years my senior, and far more my superior in learning. We commenced, soon after our marriage, a system of study and reading which we pursued while he lived. The hours allowed were from eight o'clock in the evening till ten; two hours in the twenty-four: how I enjoyed those hours! In all our mental pursuits, it seemed the aim of my husband to enlighten my reason, strengthen my judgment, and give me confidence in my own powers of mind, which he estimated much higher than I. But this approbation which he bestowed on my talents has been of great encouragement to me in attempting the duties that have since become my portion. And if there is any just praise due to the works I have prepared, the sweetest thought is—that *his name* bears the celebrity.

Source: Woman's Record; or, Sketches of All Distinguished Women, From "The Beginning" Till A.D. 1850 (1853)

Editor's Table

She was like me in lineaments; her eyes,
Her air, her features, all, to the very tone
Even of her voice, they said were like to mine,
But softened all, and tempered into beauty.
She had the same lone thoughts and wonderings,
The quest of hidden knowledge, and a mind
To comprehend the universe; nor these
Alone, but with them gentler powers than mine—
Pity, and smiles, and tears—which I had not;
And tenderness—but that I had for her;
Humility—and that I never had.
Her faults were mine; her virtues were her own.

BYRON's *Manfred*

3. The late Judge Buell, of Glen's Falls, New York [Hale's note].

"Genius has no sex,"[4] is a phrase which has captivated the imagination of some sensible women, impatient of supposed inferiority when literature is discussed. Yet we do not hesitate to say that the proposition, "Genius has no sex," is preposterous as well as false; nor do we disparage the feminine mind by this assertion, as we shall show while demonstrating the contrary of this proposition, that "genius has no sex."

Is it a disparagement to the rose that it differs from the acorn? Would the peach choose to be identical with the potato? Nature gives the kindly "fruits of the earth" their uses and virtues, all different and all good. With mankind it is similar. Men and women differ as essentially in their minds or modes of thought as in their forms. Men might as well set up for

"The vermeil-tinted lip and tresses like the morn,"

as women for man's strong frame, his muscular arm, and his power

"To shake alike the senate and the field."[5]

We have, it is true, seen "The Bearded Lady" (a frightful sight); we have seen women who have attempted to shine in the rostrum; and we have heard of a *woman* who officiated as *constable* in some Western State. Still, we doubt if these were the best specimens of human nature. We cannot suppose them lovely as women, or respectable as men. As to the lady orators, whatever may be their care and pains to efface the stamp of womanhood, there will still lurk about their manner, their phrases, their thoughts, those little refinements, spiritualities, and graces to which man's rougher nature is a stranger. In vain do these women strive to dress up their minds in broadcloth. You see the delicate feminine predominance of a silken texture in the turn of every idea, and you recognize it in the cadence and inflexion of every tone.

A foreign *authoress* has truly observed that a certain saying, applied to men and women in the same words, by the different notions it inspires, shows what a difference there is in the moral existence or nature of the sexes.

"*He* has been a good deal talked about:" this said of a man awakens at once the idea that he is a person of political, or literary, or professional celebrity. It is fame to him.

But, when you say of a woman, "*She* has been a good deal talked about," no person thinks the better of her. It is blame to her.

Sir Walter Scott tells us, in the preface to his earliest novel, "Waverly," that he was first induced to attempt that kind of delineation of Scottish manners by read-

4. Quote most frequently attributed to Madame de Staël.
5. Alexander Pope, "Epilogue to the Satires" (1738).

ing the admirable Irish sketches of Miss Edgeworth.[6] How he succeeded, it is needless to describe here; but the widely different manner in which he has accomplished the same object, with that of the charming *authoress* of "Patronage" and "Belinda," shows more clearly than anything we could say that the genius of the sexes is different. Both these writers have abundance of wit and humor, both copy from nature, both began to write at a mature age, both had well-balanced minds, and, with much generous enthusiasm, were quite free from bigotry or unbending prejudices. Yet, in Miss Edgeworth's writings, there are little delicacies of thought, tender, but nicely discriminating touches of feminine feelings, that no man could ever think of or describe; while, in Sir Walter's works, there are vigorous touches of manly qualities that no woman could portray, and illustrations of manly character that no woman of herself could penetrate. These differences, in two excellent, moral, imaginative, and useful writers, imply no inferiority in either. Both are delightful. As they esteemed and admired each other, so the reading public esteems and admires both. Miss Edgeworth's works are the most useful, for a good woman naturally tends to moral utility more than a good man. This is one of the distinguishing traits of the feminine mind. The early guidance and moral training of children devolve on the mother; her office is to mould the heart, "out of which are the issues of life," and thus exalt the race. Therefore women have an instructive readiness to "paint a moral" when they "adorn a tale."

Even those women who have, in action, education, and thought, seemed most like men, write in a way that could never confound them with the other sex. The unfortunate Madame Dudevant (George Sand)[7] tried by every means to abjure her sex; but nature, stronger than all the seemings she could surround herself with, has guided her pen in descriptions of thought and character not only impossible, but inimitable by men. Compare her "Letters of a Traveler" and "True Love" with any writings of Eugene Sue or Dumas;[8] the superior moral sense of the woman is clearly discerned. Madame De Stael is another illustration of this point. From infancy brought forward among political and literary celebrities, she was educated at a period when everybody seemed privileged to try and make himself something for which birth or nature had not intended him. Madame de Stael, so far from being held in the comparative seclusion of women's usual life, was more versed in political debates, political intrigues, and public matters, to say nothing of her literary notoriety, than nine-tenths of the men who, in our country, or in any other, now hold the reins of political power, and devote their energies to public life. Yet, read her

6. Maria Edgeworth's (1768–1849) domestic novels of manners, set in Ireland, influenced Sir Walter Scott's (1771–1832) historical novels.

7. George Sand was the pseudonym of Armantine-Aurore-Lucile Dupin (1804–1876), a French novelist. She was widely considered the most important female literary genius of her generation.

8. Eugene Sue (1804–1857), the most popular male French novelist of the 1830s–1850s. Alexandre Dumas, pére (1802–1870), wrote *The Three Musketeers* (1844), among numerous other works.

books, and you will see that she had not the mind or aspirations of man. Her woman's nature is as clearly defined in her writings as it could have been in the form of her hand, or in the tone of her voice.

In poetry we see the same distinction. Thomas Moore and Mrs. Norton,[9] though widely apart in years, wrote contemporaneously. Both were elegant, imaginative, tender writers; and neither has written very long poems. With both, their shorter pieces are beautifully finished; both are admirable, but with a marked difference. Take, for example, a song of each, lamenting a buried affection:—

"I saw thy form in youthful prime,"

of Moore; and

"When poor in all but youth and love,"

of Mrs. Norton. Compare these sweet and tender songs; you will see, and feel too, the difference of sex in the genius of these two writers. The same remarks will apply to the totally different Scotch songs of Robert Burns and Joanna Baillie.[10]

Our subject has a wide bearing on the most important questions of the day— the progress of humanity and the moral improvement of the race. These we shall not now discuss; but we would like to have those of our lady readers, if we have any who believe that "genius has no sex," to reflect on the instances we have given; and also to consider these propositions:—

Why was woman made to differ from man in her external appearance, and in the duties assigned her by nature (maternity, for instance), if she were identical with him in her genius or mental gifts?

Is not moral power better than mechanical invention? Is not the love, which purifies the heart and makes the sanctity of home, stronger even than the "red right arm of war?"

Why should women wish to be or to do or to write like men? Is not the feminine genius the most angel-like?

Source: Godey's Lady's Book (1857)

9. Thomas Moore (1779–1852), Irish Romantic poet. Caroline Norton (1808–1877), British Romantic poet, as well as novelist and essayist.

10. Robert Burns (1759–1796), national poet of Scotland. Joanna Baillie (1762–1851), Scottish Romantic poet and playwright. Both wrote Scottish folk songs.

ᔥ ANONYMOUS

Students at the Cherokee National Female Seminary published a monthly magazine in Cherokee and English from 1854 to 1857. Initially called Cherokee Rose Buds, *it became* A Wreath of Rose Buds *in 1855. The magazine created an internal literary community while also addressing itself to the larger white culture; some of its poetry and articles were reprinted in the mainstream* Youth's Companion. *Some of the pieces were written as school assignments and included news items, editorials, essays, and poetry. Under the influence of white Christian teachers, the magazine promoted conservative feminine values yet encouraged students to develop their literary and intellectual abilities.*

Our Wreath of Rose Buds

I.

We offer you a wreath of flowers
Culled in recreation hours,
Which will not wither, droop, or die,
Even when days and months pass by.

II.

Ask you where these flowers are found?
Not on sunny slope, or mound;
Not on prairies bright and fair
Growing without thought or care.

III.

No, our simple wreath is twined
From the garden of the mind;
Where bright thoughts like rivers flow
And ideas like roses grow.

IV.

The tiny buds which here you see
Ask your kindly sympathy;
View them with a lenient eye,
Pass each fault, each blemish by.

V.

Warmed by the sunshine of your eyes,
Perhaps you'll find to your surprise,
Their petals fair will soon unclose,
And every bud become—a Rose.

VI.

Then take our wreath, and let it stand
An emblem of our happy band;
The *Seminary*, our *garden* fair,
And *we*, the *flowers* planted there.

VII.

Like roses bright we hope to grow,
And o'er our home such beauty throw
In future years—that all may see
Loveliest of lands,—the Cherokee.

CORRINNE.

Source: Cherokee Rose Buds (1854)

Untitled Editorial

Another Spring term has drawn to a close, and we present you again with a collection of ROSE BUDS, gathered from our Seminary Garden. If on examining them, you chance to find a withered or dwarfish bud, please pass it by; attributing the deficiency to the *drought* which prevailed in the early part of the Spring.

We hope our friends out of the Nation will bear in mind how few have been the literary advantages we possessed, until lately. Only four or five years ago, some of our number knew very little of the English language, and although they have now obtained a good idea of it, and are making progress in some branches of English literature, yet we hope for lenient judgment, when our efforts are compared with those of our white sisters.

Critics and Criticism

How many things there are in the world to find fault with. According to some people, every thing is wrong. But nothing is more vexatious than *criticism*. In the literary world, no writer can put his thoughts before the public, but what his work is pounced upon by some merciless *critic*, who takes delight in bringing out, not the beauties of a piece, but its defects. The best of poets and writers have had their feelings lacerated by these severe attacks; and it has even caused the death of some. It is doubtful if the critics possess half the genius of those whose literary efforts they attack.

Even our poor little *Rose Bud* cannot escape, but has to receive its full share of criticism. "Well, that's copied, I know," when they don't know any thing about it;

or, "She must have been to the upper regions;" or, "She has tried very hard to have a little touch of sublimity." Or, perhaps they please themselves with some slight grammatical blunder.

> We have faults, to be sure,
> We very well know it;
>   We don't expect to vie
> With proser and poet.

[That *poetry* was not stolen from any one.] But if these terrible fault-finders could only be here on "composition" day, and note the deep lines of care on the countenances of those who are trying to grasp some thought, or the despairing looks of others as they find, after all their efforts, bright thoughts have taken to themselves wings, I think they would be more sparing of their cutting remarks, and inclined to speak a word of encouragement, instead of withering the Rose Bud with their icy breath.   LELIA.

Source: A Wreath of Cherokee Rose Buds (1855)

🌸 Phoebe Cary (1824–1871)

Throughout her life, Phoebe lived and worked with her sister, Alice Cary, who was also a popular poet and author of sketches about their rural youth in Ohio. The two began publishing poetry in their teens, with the encouragement of their father. In 1850 and 1851, the two sisters moved to New York to be closer to the literary world they had entered from afar. They quickly became prominent figures in the city's literary salons and themselves hosted one on Sunday evenings. Although Alice was more successful, the two committed their lives to literature and were often referred to as "the Cary sisters." Phoebe's first volume of poetry, Poetry and Parodies *(1854), was a combination of sentimental poems and parodies of serious male poets, which elicited indignation from the male critical establishment. She wrote for a living but also as an outlet for her considerable wit, creating work both conventional and unpredictable.*

The Soiree

This is the Soiree: from grate to entrance,
   Like milliners' figures, stand the lovely girls;
But from their silent lips no merry sentence
   Disturbs the smoothness of their shining curls.

Ah! what will rise, how will they rally,
   When shall arrive the "gentlemen of ease"!
What brilliant repartee, what witty sally,
   Will mingle with their pleasant symphonies!

I hear even now the infinite sweet chorus,
   The laugh of ecstasy, the merry tone,
That through the evenings that have gone before us
   In long reverberations reach our own.

From round-faced Germans come the guttural voices,
   Through curling *moustache* steals the Italian clang,
And, loud amidst their universal noises,
   From distant corners sounds the Yankee twang.

I hear the editor, who from his office
   Sends out his paper, filled with praise and puff,
And holy priests, who, when they warn the scoffers,
   Beat the fine pulpit, lined with velvet stuff.

The tumult of each *saqued,* and charming maiden,
   The idle talk that sense and reason drowns,
The ancient dames with jewelry o'erladen,
   And trains depending from the brocade gowns,—

The pleasant tone, whose sweetness makes us wonder,
   The laugh of gentlemen, and ladies too,
And ever and anon, in tones of thunder,
   The diapason of some lady *blue,*—[1]

Is it, O man, with such discordant noises,
   With pastimes so ridiculous as these,
Thou drownest Nature's sweet and kindly voices,
   And jarrest the celestial harmonies?

Were half the wealth that fills the world with ladies,
   Were half the time bestowed on caps and lace,
Given to the home, the husbands, and the babies,
   There were no time to visit such a place.

Source: Poems and Parodies (1854)

Advice Gratis to Certain Women
By a Woman

O, my strong-minded sisters, aspiring to vote,
And to row with your brothers, all in the same boat,
When you come out to speak to the public your mind,
Leave your tricks, and your airs, and your graces behind!

For instance, when you by the world would be seen
As reporter, or editor (first-class, I mean),
I think—just to come to the point in one line—
What you write will be finer, if 'tis not too fine.

Pray, don't let the thread of your subject be strung
With "golden," and "shimmer," "sweet," "filter," and "flung;"

1. *Diapason*: a deep outburst of sound; *blue* is a reference to a blue-stocking.

Nor compel, by your style, all your readers to guess
You've been looking up words Webster marks *obs.*

And another thing: whatever else you may say,
Do keep personalities out of the way;
Don't try every sentence to make people see
What a dear, charming creature the writer must be!

Leave out affectations and pretty appeals;
Don't "drag yourself in by the neck and the heels,"
Your dear little boots, and your gloves; and take heed,
Nor pull your curls over men's eyes while they read.

Don't mistake me; I mean that the public's not home,
You must do as the Romans do, when you're in Rome;
I would have you be womanly, while you are wise;
'Tis the weak and the womanish tricks I despise.

On the other hand: don't write and dress in such styles
As astonish the natives, and frighten the isles;
Do look, on the platform, so folks in the show
Needn't ask, "Which are lions, and which tigers?" you know!

'Tis a good thing to write, and to rule in the state,
But to be a true, womanly woman is great:
And if ever you come to be that, 'twill be when
You can cease to be babies, nor try to be men!

Source: A Memorial of Alice and Phoebe Cary: With Some of Their Later Poems (1873)

❧ Caroline Lee Hentz (1800–1856)

Perhaps most well-known today as the author of The Planter's Northern Bride *(1854),
a novel intended to counter the depiction of slavery in Harriet Beecher Stowe's* Uncle
Tom's Cabin *(1852), Hentz also wrote seven other novels and several collections of stories.
She supported her family with her writing after her husband became an invalid in 1849.
Although she and her husband never owned slaves and she herself was born in Massachusetts, Hentz was a vocal apologist of the southern institution as well as an ardent
proponent of preserving the union. A popular writer of sentimental fiction, Hentz understood her authorial role as possessing political influence, as the following preface attests.*

Preface to *The Planter's Northern Bride*

It was the intention of the author to have given this book to the world during the
course of the past season, but unforeseen occurrences have prevented the accomplishment of her purpose. She no longer regrets the delay, as she believes it will meet
a more cordial reception at the present time.

When individual or public feeling is too highly wrought on any subject, there
must inevitably follow a reaction, and reason, recovering from the effects of tran-
sient inebriation, is ready to assert its original sovereignty.

Not in the spirit of egotism, do we repeat wha[t] was said in the preface of a
former work, that we were born at the North, and though destiny has removed us
far from our native scenes, we cherish for them a sacred regard, an undying attachment.

It cannot therefore be supposed that we are actuated by hostility or prejudice,
in endeavouring to represent the unhappy consequences of that intolerant and
fanatical spirit, whose fatal influence we so deeply deplore.

We believe that there are a host of noble, liberal minds, of warm, generous,
candid hearts, at the North, that will bear us out in our views of Southern character,
and that feel with us that our *national* honour is tarnished, when a portion of our
country is held up to public disgrace and foreign insult, by those, too, whom every
feeling of patriotism should lead to defend it from ignominy and shield it from
dishonour. The hope that they will appreciate and do justice to our motives, has
imparted enthusiasm to our feelings, and energy to our will, in the prosecution of
our literary labour.

When we have seen the dark and horrible pictures drawn of slavery and exhibited to a gazing world, we have wondered if we were one of those favoured individuals to whom the fair side of life is ever turned, or whether we were created with
a moral blindness, incapable of distinguishing its lights and shadows. One thing is
certain, and if we were on judicial oath we would repeat it, that during our resi-

dence in the South, we have never *witnessed* one scene of cruelty or oppression, never beheld a chain or a manacle, or the infliction of a punishment more severe than parental authority would be justified in applying to filial disobedience or transgression. This is not owing to our being placed in a limited sphere of observation, for we have seen and studied domestic, social, and plantation life, in Carolina, Alabama, Georgia, and Florida. We have been admitted into close and familiar communion with numerous families in each of these States, not merely as a passing visiter, but as an indwelling guest, and we have never been pained by an inhuman exercise of authority, or a wanton abuse of power.

On the contrary, we have been touched and gratified by the exhibition of affectionate kindness and care on one side, and loyal and devoted attachment on the other. We have been especially struck with the cheerfulness and contentment of the slaves, and their usually elastic and buoyant spirits. From the abundant opportunities we have had of judging, we give it as our honest belief, that the negroes of the South are the happiest *labouring class* on the face of the globe; even subtracting from their portion of enjoyment all that can truly be said of their trials and sufferings. The fugitives who fly to the Northern States are no proof against the truth of this statement. They have most of them been made disaffected by the influence of others—tempted by promises which are seldom fulfilled[.] Even in the garden of Eden, the seeds of discontent and rebellion were sown; surely we need not wonder that they sometimes take root in the beautiful groves of the South.

In the large cities we have *heard* of families who were cruel to their slaves, as well as unnaturally severe in the discipline of their children. (Are there no similar instances at the North?) But the indignant feeling which any known instance of inhumanity calls forth at the South, proves that they are not of common occurrence.

We have conversed a great deal with the coloured people, feeling the deepest interest in learning their own views of their peculiar situation, and we have almost invariably been delighted and affected by their humble devotion to their master's family, their child-like, affectionate reliance on their care and protection, and above all, with their genuine cheerfulness and contentment. . . .

The history of Crissy and the circumstances of her abduction are true.

The character of Dr. Darley is drawn from life. . . .

Many of the circumstance [*sic*] we have recorded in these pages are founded on truth. The plot of the insurrection, the manner in which it was instigated and detected, and the brief history of Nat, the giant, with his domestication in a Northern family, are literally true.

If any one should think the affection manifested by the slaves of Moreland for their master is too highly coloured, we would refer them to the sketch of Thomas Jefferson's arrival at Monticello on his return from Paris, after an absence of five years. It is from the pen of his daughter, and no one will doubt its authenticity.

"The negroes discovered the approach of the carriage as soon as it reached Shadwell, and such a scene I never witnessed in my life. They collected in crowds around it, and almost drew it up the mountain by hand. The shouting, &c., had been sufficiently obstreperous before, but the moment the carriage arrived on the top it reached the climax. When the door of the carriage was opened, they received him in their arms and bore him into the house, crowding around, kissing his hands and feet, some blubbering and crying, others laughing. It appeared impossible to satisfy their eyes, or their anxiety to touch, and even to kiss the very earth that bore him. These were the first ebullitions of joy for his return, after a long absence, which they would of course feel; but it is perhaps not out of place to add here, that they were at all times very devoted in their attachment to their master. They believed him to be one of the greatest, and they knew him [t]o be one of the best of men, and kindest of masters. They spoke to him freely, and applied confidingly to him in all their difficulties and distresses; and he watched over them in sickness and health; interested himself in all their concerns; advising them, and showing esteem and confidence in the good, and indulgence to all."

We can add nothing to this simple, pathetic description. Monticello is hallowed ground, and the testimony that proceeds from its venerated retreat should be listened to with respect and confidence. The same accents might be heard from Mount Vernon's august shades, where the grave of Washington has been bedewed by the tears of the grateful African.

But we have done.

If we fail to accomplish the purpose for which we have written, we shall at least have the consolation of knowing that our motives are disinterested, and our aim patriotic and true.

Should no Northern heart respond to our earnest appeal, we trust the voice of the South will answer to our own, not in a faint, cold, dying echo, but in a full, spontaneous strain, whose reverberations shall reach to the green hills and granite cliffs of New England's "rock-bound coast."

Source: The Planter's Northern Bride (1854)

❧ Julia Ward Howe (1819–1910)

Although self-educated, Julia Ward Howe was one of the most intellectual women of her age. She grew up in New York and moved to Boston in 1843 when she married the physician and reformer Samuel Gridley Howe. They edited the abolitionist newspaper the Commonwealth *(1851–1853), but they clashed over her desire for a public career as a reformer and writer. When her first volume of poetry,* Passion-Flowers, *was published anonymously in 1854, the identity of the author of such sensual, personal poems was soon revealed and all of Boston was scandalized (Nathaniel Hawthorne wrote to his publisher that "she ought to have been soundly whipt for publishing them"), leading to a greater rift between the couple. With the publication of her poem, "Battle Hymn of the Republic," in the* Atlantic Monthly *in 1862, Howe received the recognition of America's most illustrious writers, as described in the excerpt from her autobiography below. She went on to become a prominent member of the women's rights movement, and a prolific writer of verse and travel essays, as well as the author of a biography of Margaret Fuller.*

Sybil

Your head is wild with books, Sybil,[1]
   But your heart is good and kind—
I feel a new contentment near you,
   A pleasure of the mind.

Glad should I be to sit beside you,
   And let long hours glide by,
Reading, through all your sweet narrations,
   The language of your eye.

Since the maternal saint I worshipped
   Did look and love her last,
No woman o'er my wayward spirit
   Such gentle spell has cast.

Oh! tell me of your varied fortunes,
   For you know not, from your face

---

1. The sibyls of ancient Greece were prophetesses associated with holy sites. Here the sibyl is likely Margaret Fuller (1810–1850). In her introduction to *Love-Letters of Margaret Fuller* (1903), Howe wrote, "Among the titles bestowed on women of unusual gifts, that of Sibyl appears to me to suit best with what we know of her."

Looks out strange sadness, lit with rapture,
   And melancholy grace.

You are a gem, whose native brilliance
   Could never wholly reign,
An opal, whose prismatic fire
   A white cloud doth restrain.

And thus, the mood to which you move me
   Is never perfect, quite,
'Tis pity, wonderment, and pleasure,
   Opacity and light.

Bear me then in your presence, Sybil,
   And leave your hand in mine,
For, though human be my nature,
   You've made it half divine.

Mother Mind

I never *made* a poem, dear friend—
I never sat me down, and said,
This cunning brain and patient hand
Shall fashion something to be read.

Men often came to me, and prayed
I should indite a fitting verse
For fast, or festival, or in
Some stately pageant to rehearse.
(As if, than Balaam[2] more endowed,
I of myself could bless or curse.)

Reluctantly I bade them go,
Ungladdened by my poet-mite;
My heart is not so churlish but
It loves to minister delight.

But not a word I breathe is mine
To sing, in praise of man or God;

2. A prophet of the Old Testament.

My Master calls, at noon or night,
I know his whisper and his nod.

Yet all my thoughts to rhythms run,
To rhyme, my wisdom and my wit?
True, I consume my life in verse,
But wouldst thou know how *that* is writ?

'Tis thus—through weary length of days,
I bear a thought within my breast
That greatens from my growth of soul,
And waits, and will not be expressed.

It greatens, till its hour has come,
Not without pain, it sees the light;
'Twixt smiles and tears I view it o'er,
And dare not deem it perfect, quite.

These children of my soul I keep
Where scarce a mortal man may see,
Yet not unconsecrate, dear friend,
Baptismal rites they claim of thee.

Source: Passion-Flowers (1854)

Our Orders

Weave no more silks, ye Lyons looms,[3]
　To deck our girls for gay delights!
The crimson flower of battle blooms,
　And solemn marches fill the nights.

Weave but the flag whose bars to-day
　Drooped heavy o'er our early dead,
And homely garments, coarse and gray,
　For orphans that must earn their bread!

Keep back your tunes, ye viols sweet,
　That pour delight from other lands!

3. Lyons, France, was famous for its silk trade and manufacture.

Rouse there the dancer's restless feet,—
    The trumpet leads our warrior bands.

And ye that wage the war of words
    With mystic fame and subtle power,
Go, chatter to the idle birds,
    Or teach the lesson of the hour!

Ye Sibyl Arts, in one stern knot
    Be all your offices combined!
Stand close, while Courage draws the lot,
    The destiny of humankind!

And if that destiny could fail,
    The sun should darken in the sky,
The eternal bloom of Nature pale,
    And God, and Truth, and Freedom die!

Source: Atlantic Monthly (1861)

A Visit to C. H.[4]

Let us sit with you, sister, before the low fire,
The scanty rag-carpet sufficing our feet:
You cannot command, and we need not require,
The window well shaded and soft-cushioned seat.

The children of pride scarcely come to your door,
And we who have entered walk not in their ways;
But experience brings to the rich and the poor
One value abiding in life's changeful days.

You are homely in breeding? Some one of your race
Had a spark of high blood, to immortals akin:
You are loath to be seen in this desolate place?
What honor may lack where the Muse is within?

---

4. C. H. could be Caroline Healy (Dall) (1822–1912). Howe and Dall both attended Margaret
Fuller's conversations in 1841. She married Charles Dall in 1844.

A presence I feel in the God-lightened air,
The spell of the art I have followed so long;
In your calico garment and rough-twisted hair
Let us speak of your queendom, poor sister of song.

For, well may we know it, the tap that you hear,
When you lay down the needle, and take up the pen,
Is the summons august that the highest revere,
The greatest that visits the children of men.

The fountain of song in your bosom arose
When the small baby pillow was tenantless left?
You share with all mortals life's burthen of woes;
But all have not music, when grieved and bereft.

You dream o'er the wash-tub, strive vainly to fix
Your thought on the small household matter in hand?
Some spices, no doubt, in your condiments mix,
Some flavors your neighbors can scarcely command.

The world is so hard, and the world is so cold?
And the dear-bought deliverance comes scanty and slow?
Say, whether is better,—its frosts to behold,
Or to share its heart winter, and shed no more glow?

I have found a rich blossom astray on the heath;
In sordid surroundings, an altar of love;
Or lashed in a cart, beyond beauty and breath,
The steed that should carry the bidding of Jove.

The town that hums near us has rich folk, besure,—
Its man of the Congress, its Mayor with his state,
Its lords of the spindle who pillage the poor,
Its pampered young people who quarrel and mate.

But not for their scanning I come here to-day;
The rich and the proud are forever the same:
My feet, poet sister, have found out this way,
Unsought and unsummoned, your kinship to claim.

Source: Later Lyrics (1866)

Reminiscences [Excerpts]

It would be impossible for me to say how many times I have been called upon to rehearse the circumstances under which I wrote the "Battle Hymn of the Republic." I have also had occasion more than once to state the simple story in writing. As this oft-told tale has no unimportant part in the story of my life, I will briefly add it to these records. I distinctly remember that a feeling of discouragement came over me as I drew near the city of Washington at the time already mentioned. I thought of the women of my acquaintance whose sons or husbands were fighting our great battle; the women themselves serving in the hospitals, or busying themselves with the work of the Sanitary Commission. My husband, as already said, was beyond the age of military service, my eldest son but a stripling; my youngest was a child of not more than two years. I could not leave my nursery to follow the march of our armies, neither had I the practical deftness which the preparing and packing of sanitary stores demanded. Something seemed to say to me, "You would be glad to serve, but you cannot help any one; you have nothing to give, and there is nothing for you to do." Yet, because of my sincere desire, a word was given me to say, which did strengthen the hearts of those who fought in the field and of those who languished in the prison.

We were invited, one day, to attend a review of troops at some distance from the town. While we were engaged in watching the manœuvres, a sudden movement of the enemy necessitated immediate action. The review was discontinued, and we saw a detachment of soldiers gallop to the assistance of a small body of our men who were in imminent danger of being surrounded and cut off from retreat. The regiments remaining on the field were ordered to march to their cantonments. We returned to the city very slowly, of necessity, for the troops nearly filled the road. My dear minister was in the carriage with me, as were several other friends. To beguile the rather tedious drive, we sang from time to time snatches of the army songs so popular at that time, concluding, I think, with

"John Brown's body lies a-mouldering in the ground;
   His soul is marching on."[5]

The soldiers seemed to like this, and answered back, "Good for you!" Mr. Clarke said, "Mrs. Howe, why do you not write some good words for that stirring tune?" I replied that I had often wished to do this, but had not as yet found in my mind any leading toward it.

I went to bed that night as usual, and slept, according to my wont, quite soundly. I awoke in the gray of the morning twilight; and as I lay waiting for the dawn, the

5. John Brown (1800–1859) was a militant abolitionist who was hung for his 1859 raid on the federal armory at Harper's Ferry, Virginia.

long lines of the desired poem began to twine themselves in my mind. Having thought out all the stanzas, I said to myself, "I must get up and write these verses down, lest I fall asleep again and forget them." So, with sudden effort, I sprang out of bed, and found in the dimness an old stump of a pen which I remembered to have used the day before. I scrawled the verses almost without looking at the paper. I had learned to do this when, on previous occasions, attacks of versification had visited me in the night, and I feared to have recourse to a light lest I should wake the baby, who slept near me. I was always obliged to decipher my scrawl before another night should intervene, at it was only legible while the matter was fresh in my mind. At this time, having completed my writing, I returned to bed and fell asleep, saying to myself, "I like this better than most things that I have written."

The poem, which was soon after published in the "Atlantic Monthly," was somewhat praised on its appearance, but the vicissitudes of the war so engrossed public attention that small heed was taken of literary matters. I knew, and was content to know, that the poem soon found its way to the camps, as I heard from time to time of its being sung in chorus by the soldiers.

As the war went on, it came to pass that Chaplain McCabe, newly released from Libby Prison, gave a public lecture in Washington, and recounted some of his recent experiences. Among them was the following: He and the other Union prisoners occupied one large, comfortless room, in which the floor was their only bed. An official in charge of them told them, one evening, that the Union arms [sic] had just sustained a terrible defeat. While they sat together in great sorrow, the negro who waited upon them whispered to one man that the officer had given them false information, and that the Union soldiers had, on the contrary, achieved an important victory. At this good news they all rejoiced, and presently made the walls ring with my Battle Hymn, which they sang in chorus, Chaplain McCabe leading. The lecturer recited the poem with such effect that those present began to inquire, "Who wrote this Battle Hymn?" It now became one of the leading lyrics of the war. In view of its success, one of my good friends said, "Mrs. Howe ought to die now, for she has done the best that she will ever do." I was not of this opinion, feeling myself still "full of days' works," although I did not guess at the new experiences which then lay before me.

While the war was still at its height, I received a kind letter from Hon. George Bancroft, conveying an invitation to attend a celebration of the poet Bryant's seventieth birthday, to be given by the New York Century Club,[6] of which Mr. Bancroft was the newly-elected president. He also expressed the hope that I would bring with me something in verse or in prose, to add to the tributes of the occasion. . . .

6. The Century Club was a private, all-male club for New York artists and authors founded in 1847. William Cullen Bryant (1794–1878) was a Romantic poet and editor of the *New York Evening Post*. George Bancroft (1800–1891) was author of the ten-volume *History of the United States, From the Discovery of the American Continent* (1854–1878).

The assemblage was indeed a notable one. The fashion of New York was well represented, but its foremost artists, publicists, and literary men were also present. Mr. Emerson had come on from Concord. Christopher Cranch united with other artists in presenting to the venerable poet a portfolio of original drawings, to which each had contributed some work of his own. I afterwards learned that T. Buchanan Read had arrived from Washington, having in his pocket his newly composed poem on "Sheridan's Ride," which he would gladly have read aloud had the committee found room for it on their programme. A letter was received from the elder R. H. Dana, in which he excused his absence on account of his seventy-seven years and consequent inability to travel. Dr. Holmes read his verses very effectively.[7] Mr. Emerson spoke rather vaguely. For my part in the evening's proceedings, I will once more quote from the diary:—

"Mr Bryant, in his graceful reply to Mr. Bancroft's address of congratulation, spoke of me as 'she who has written the most stirring lyric of the war.' After Mr. Emerson's remarks my poem was announced. I stepped to the middle of the platform, and read it well, I think, as every one heard me, and the large room was crammed. The last two verses were applauded. George H. Boker,[8] of Philadelphia, followed me, and Dr. Holmes followed him. This was, I suppose, the greatest public honor of my life. I record it here for my grandchildren." . . .

Source: Reminiscences, 1819–1899 (1899)

7. Ralph Waldo Emerson (1803–1822), American Transcendentalist and resident of Concord, Massachusetts; Christopher Cranch (1813–1892), minor Transcendentalist poet and a landscape painter of the Hudson River School; Thomas Buchanan Read (1822–1872), poet and portrait painter; Richard Henry Dana (1815–1882), U.S. Attorney during the Civil War and author of the popular sea adventure *Two Years Before the Mast* (1840); and Oliver Wendell Holmes, Sr. (1809–1894), eminent physician and one of the most beloved American poets of the nineteenth century.
    8. George H. Boker (1823–1890), poet and playwright.

🍃 E.D.E.N. Southworth (1819–1899)

Emma Dorothea Eliza Nevitte, born in Washington, D.C., first experienced financial hardship at the age of four when her father died. After her mother remarried, Emma received an education but little love and affection. In 1840, after five years as a teacher, she married Frederick Hamilton Southworth and moved with him to Wisconsin. After his desertion of her in 1844, she returned to teaching in Washington. Five years later she turned to writing for support, the ordeal of which is recorded in the autobiographical sketch below. Her portrayal of her route to authorship is similar to that of Fanny Fern, who claimed in Ruth Hall *(1855) that "no happy woman ever writes." Southworth would go on to earn ten thousand dollars a year as one of the nation's most popular and prolific authors, writing more than sixty novels, most of which appeared serially in the* New York Ledger. *Her novels depict the fortitude of disadvantaged heroines as they confront the vicissitudes of life in a world controlled by often unfeeling men.*

Untitled Autobiographical Sketch

Let me pass over in silence the stormy and disastrous days of my wretched girlhood and womanhood—days that stamped upon my brow of youth the furrows of fifty years—let me come at once to the time when I found myself broken in spirit, health, and purse—a widow in fate but not in fact—with my babes looking up to me for a support I could not give them. It was in these darkest days of my *woman's* life, that my *author's* life commenced. I wrote and published "Retribution," my first novel, under the following circumstances.

In January, 1849, I had been appointed teacher of the Fourth District Primary School. The school was kept in the two largest rooms in my house—those upon the ground floor. I had eighty pupils. A few months previous to this I had written a few short tales and sketches for the National Era. It was while I was organizing my new school that Dr. Bailey applied to me for *another* story. I promised one that should go through two papers. I called up several subjects of a profoundly moral and philosophical nature upon which the very trials and sufferings of my own life had led me to reflect, and from among them selected that of *moral retribution,* as I understood it. I designed to illustrate the idea by a short tale. I commenced, and, somehow or other, my head and heart were teeming with thought and emotion, and the idea that had at first but glimmered faintly upon my perceptions, blazed into a perfect glory of light—but which I fear I have not been able to transmit to others with the brightness with which it shone upon myself—no, it was dimmed by the dullness of the medium. My story grew into a volume. Every week I would supply a portion to the paper, until weeks grew into months, and months into quarters, before it was finished.

The circumstances under which this, my first novel, was written, and the success that afterwards attended its publication, is a remarkable instance of "sowing in tears and reaping in joy;" for, in addition to that bitterest sorrow with which I may not make you acquainted—that great life-sorrow—I had many minor troubles. My small salary was inadequate to our comfortable support. My school numbered eighty pupils, boys and girls, and I had the whole charge of them myself. Added to this, my little boy fell dangerously ill and was confined to his bed in perfect helplessness until June. He would suffer no one to move him but myself—in fact no one else *could* do so without putting him in pain. Thus my time was passed between my housekeeping, my school-keeping, my child's sick-bed, and my literary labours. The time devoted to writing was the hours that should have been given to sleep or to fresh air. It was too much for me. It was too much for any human being. My health broke down. I was attacked with frequent hemorrhage of the lungs. Still I persevered. I did my best by my house, my school, my sick child, and my publisher. Yet neither child, nor school, nor publisher received justice. The child suffered and complained—the patrons of the school grew dissatisfied, annoying and sometimes insulting me—and as for the publisher, he would reject whole pages of that manuscript which was written amid grief, and pain, and toil that he knew nothing of (pages, by the way, that were restored in the republication).

This was indeed the very *melee* of the "Battle of Life." I was forced to keep up struggling when I only wished for death and for rest.

But look you how it terminated. That night of storm and darkness came to an end, and morning broke on me at last—a bright glad morning, pioneering a new and happy day of life. First of all, it was in this very tempest of trouble that my "life-sorrow" was, as it were, carried away—or *I* was carried away from brooding over it. Next, my child, contrary to my own opinion and the doctor's, got well. Then my book, written in so much pain, published besides in a newspaper, and, withal, being the *first* work of an obscure and penniless author, was, contrary to all probabilities, accepted by the first publishing house in America, was published and (subsequently) noticed with high favour even by the cautious English reviews. Friends crowded around me—offers for contributions poured in upon me. And I, who six months before had been poor, ill, forsaken, slandered, *killed* by sorrow, privation, toil, and friendliness [sic], found myself born as it were into a new life; found independence, sympathy, friendship, and honour, and an occupation in which I could delight. All this came very suddenly, as after a terrible storm, a sun burst.

Source: Female Prose Writers of America (1855)

❧ GAIL HAMILTON (1833–1896)

Gail Hamilton was the pseudonym of Mary Abigail Dodge, who grew up in Hamilton, Massachusetts, and graduated from Ipswich Female Seminary in 1850. Determined to support herself rather than marry, she pursued a teaching career until she was able to break into publishing. From 1856 to 1860, while she wrote for Gamaliel Bailey of the National Era, *she also was a governess to his children in Washington, D.C., where she found ample material for her satirical pen. After Bailey's death, she returned to Hamilton and went on to produce twenty-five volumes of travel writing, poetry, fiction, and, primarily, essays. In the late 1860s and early 1870s, she waged a public battle with the publishing industry on behalf of young, particularly female, authors, whom she thought were not paid fairly. In* A Battle of the Books *(1870) and other essays, she demystified the business of authorship and ridiculed gender inequities in the literary world. Hamilton's daring entrance into the business of literature is described in the letters below, as is her determination to keep her identity from the public.*

Letters

HARTFORD, CONN., January 17, 1856.

MR. BAILEY: *Sir,*—If you are not in a mood to be disturbed I beg you to take out the postage stamp which I enclose with this—burn the whole package, and send me word immediately that you have done so. Direct, if you please, to Box No. 747, Hartford, Conn.

If, on the other hand, I may be allowed to occupy a half hour of your valuable time—allow me to say at once that I desire to become a contributor to the "Era," if I am worthy. It is quite useless to mention the agency of friends in inducing me to this step, as you have probably heard that a thousand times, and moreover all the friends in the world could not move me to it against my own sweet will. Neither do I write entirely for money, as at this particular juncture I am tolerably well off, though an income of five hundred dollars and an expenditure of one thousand will sometimes produce embarrassment. But I wish to measure myself by a new standard. I have been flattered from my youth up till I have perhaps learned to flatter myself. May I beg that your practised eye glance over the pages that accompany this and see whether they be of sufficient merit to interest your readers, or whether the hand that wrote them is capable of producing anything of real worth?

I hope I am not misunderstood. I do not ask for charity, nor for a friendly judgment, but for a just one. If you think the pieces worthless, you will not hesitate to say so and I promise not to drown myself thereupon. If you think they are good, but not adapted to your paper, I shall be glad to know even that.

If you consider them worth insertion, but not worth remuneration, I shall be glad also and willing to send more on the same terms as long as you think best—or as shortly.

If they are worth being paid for I shall be happy to receive their market value.

I want an end and aim in life, and see no other way to obtain it.

May I request an answer, even if you should decline any farther [*sic*] communication?

I have occasionally "rushed into print," but have never made any stated engagement. The prose article was written more than a year ago and has been seen by several persons. If you print it at all, pray say nothing whatever about it, and of all things do not say anything about this to anybody in public or private, as my happiness in life will be blotted out forever if this circumstance should ever come to the eyes or ears of any of my friends. The utmost secrecy is the only thing which I insist on. I should be very glad to withhold my name, but if it is at all necessary to the transaction of business, I will divulge at once. If you would not deem it impertinent, may I request a reply as soon as your convenience will allow?

I am a woman, twenty-two years old. Direct to Box 747, Hartford, Conn.

Yours respectfully,

SEVEN FORTY-SEVEN

JANUARY 17, '56.

(P.S.) I do not take the "National Era" and have not seen it for a year. If my articles are published, will you send me a copy? Do not fail to reply privately to this letter even if your engagements give you time only to say "no" and I shall be placed under everlasting obligations.

The printed *morceau*[1] was printed without my knowledge or consent, but I have seen it copied into four different papers in as many States, which was one encouragement for me to make this attack on you. Will you be so good as to return it to me, as I borrowed it from a friend.

February 15, 1856

MY DEAR SISTER: I am going to tell you a story. You know I went to Meriden a few weeks ago. You know also that our cousin is somewhat of a literary person. She wanted me to write—for the public; thought it was a sin that I should not improve my talents, etc. I said[,] Well, what shall I do? She said, "Write at once to Dr. Bailey of the 'National Era.'" I thought upon her words, and after I came home wrote to the gentleman aforesaid. I sent a copy of "Hair," and several pieces of

---

1. A short literary composition or fragment.

poetry. Well, one, two, three weeks passed away and I came to the conclusion that my letter and its valuable contents were consigned to oblivion, but last night I took a letter from my box addressed to "Seven Forty-Seven" and mailed "Washington, D.C." You see I had not told my real name, but directed him to address Box 747. I walked leisurely home, went upstairs quietly, lit my gas composedly, and then—I opened the letter and read:

"Seven Forty Seven" must pardon the delay in answering her delightfully independent letter. My answer will be a short one. Your contributions are acceptable and accepted worthy of a place in the "Era," and filed for insertion. But the compensation is another thing. For cogent reasons, which I need not now specify, I have been obliged for the last year to be rigidly economical. The same reasons compel me to pursue the same course the present year.

After that I shall be easy and be prepared once more to be liberal. If you can afford to wait I will on the first week of next December send you a remittance of fifty dollars, for which you may send me whatever you please in your best style of prose sketches, at any time between this and then. When I tell you that I have on hand articles already paid for enough to fill fifty columns, and that my list of paid contributors is never crowded, you will not wonder at my proposition. But the truth is, your pen is not a commonplace one.

I hope now that "Seven Forty-Seven" will introduce herself to me with her own name, which I am sure must be a worthy one.

With friendly sentiments,
I remain, yours etc.,
G. BAILEY.

This is the substance of the letter. I was quite overwhelmed by such an answer, besides being frightened out of my senses. I never can write fifty dollars' worth between now and December, for I don't have time. I am just as busy as I can be with school duties from morning till night. But don't you think it a generous offer? You see they say I may send just when I please. I ought to send enough to make it about five dollars a column, I think. Now don't tell anybody of this. I hesitated about telling you, but finally concluded I would as a proof of my love for you and confidence in you. I have told Mr. —— and shall tell A. R., because she induced me to do it. You may send this to father and mother, and upon no account is anybody else to know anything about it at present. I have also entered into an engagement to write for the "Independent," for which they will pay me three dollars a column. The first piece was published a week or two ago. I sent the paper to mother. Mr. —— says it is too little, but I am perfectly satisfied. A. R. says the honor of writing for the "Independent" is enough without any money. If I once get my name up you know I can do anything. This, too, is a profound secret. I did not tell A. R. Now don't suppose I shall do any great things all of a sudden. With all I have to do it is impossible for me to write much, but it is something to have an outlet provided in case I do overflow. The "National Era" is no mean paper. Grace Greenwood and John G. Whittier[2] write for it, and Mrs. Stowe's "Uncle Tom's Cabin" first appeared in it, and *I* feel quite complimented to be received so cordially on my own recommendation. If I had time I think I could do something in the way of writing.

HARTFORD, CONN., February 18, 1856.

MR. BAILEY:

DEAR SIR: I am astonished! I am overwhelmed! I am on my knees to you (metaphysically)! I am blushing furiously at the savage ferocity of my last letter. I can never write fifty dollars' worth in the world. I must say, sir, I think you have made a very rash bargain. I don't believe you consulted Mrs. Bailey. Why, suppose now I choose to send only one article between now and next December, don't you see you will have to pay all the same? I have always considered myself a genius. My friends have uniformly cherished the same belief, but now this temple of faith is shaken to its very foundations, and I am under the calamitous necessity of classing myself with the common money-making herd. For Sir, Genius is always repulsed, always Genius goes clad in russet fluttering with rags, only Mediocrity rustles in silk. When Genius is the centre of the wheel of life, gold has a far greater centrifugal than centripetal attraction. But if Gold and Grandeur are to be my fate, I will endeavor to beat it with a very great degree of Christian resignation.

I have not the slightest objection to waiting till next December. I am in no particular need of money. But I am really afraid I shall not come up to what you desire. I have no idea what my "best style" is—in fact I am quite unconscious of having any style at all. The cordiality and kindness of your letter, for which I do assure you I thank you most heartily, have quite banished every thought from my head and left it in the precise state of a squeezed orange, but I will do my best, and if you are not satisfied it shall be all the same as if you had never written—only you won't have poetry—that is too bad, for it is a thousand times easier to write than prose.

If you really have any curiosity to know my name I will tell you, but it is a shocking one. I mean to change it as soon as possible. It is, however, a consolation to reflect that if the name confers no honor on "my family," "my family" make the name respectable.

And I remain, sir, yours very truly,
MARY ABBY DODGE—but don't tell.

2. John Greenleaf Whittier (1807–1892), esteemed abolitionist Quaker poet.

Miss Hunt took me aside yesterday and said she had something to tell me—that she had seen two pieces of mine in the "National Era," that her sister knew they were mine because one of them had appeared in the school paper and they both had the same signature. As my articles are printed, or being printed, I shall have to bestir myself to get something more ready for forwarding. One of our old graduates has just called on me. I cannot yet tell how matters and things will go in the school, but at present they wear a promising aspect. I should like a hot brown-bread cake for breakfast, if you please, with good fresh butter melted in and a good deal of it. Good-night, my dear father and mother. The mother of two of our pupils called while I was gone, told how much their boys liked the teachers, and "as for Miss Dodge—she was an oracle."

There's something for you to sleep on.

Yours very affectionately,
Abby.

Source: Gail Hamilton's Life in Letters, ed. H. Augusta Dodge (1901)

🍂 Thrace Talmon (1830–1900)

Thrace Talmon was the pseudonym of the novelist and children's writer Ellen Tryphosa Harrington Putnam, who was a native of Massachusetts. She authored a series of advice articles for the Ladies' Repository *and also wrote on religious and literary subjects for that magazine in the late 1850s and early 1860s. She also published under her own full name as well as Mrs. E. T. H. Putnam. Her first husband was Charles A. V. Putnam, editor of the* Boston Museum; *they had one son. Talmon later married George Harvey, likely in 1875, when she stopped publishing, and moved to Saratoga Springs, New York, and then to Brooklyn, where she lived until her death. The following essay, comparable to Fanny Fern's writings in its anger if not its wit, is one of the most direct counterattacks against male critics of women writers produced in the nineteenth century.*

The Latest Crusade. Lady Authors and Their Critics

"The New York *Observer* is out upon what it calls the mob of novels that have flooded the country within the last three years or so, mostly written by women. It has been lately told that the demand for these books and the sale has almost ceased, and thinks the fact should encourage the ladies to stop. 'Go out washing,' it says to them, 'take in sewing, attend to the children, nurse the sick, do anything honest and useful, but do stop writing wishy-washy, namby-pamby, milk-and-water, sentimental love stories.'"—*Traveller.*

Dr. Bailey: Through your columns we beg leave to reply to the reverend gentleman of the New York *Observer,* and of some other editors, who of late have been indulging in a similar tone.

We see them now at their desks, complacent and thriving, in view of the condition of their affairs, spiritual and temporal; we also see the objects of their sage criticism, at their desks, nine out of ten of them pale, harrowed, and sad—pale, for want of plenty and rest; harrowed, for the cries for bread from their children, sweet and beloved; sad, in view of a coming time, when, with broken health and spirits, they will have to look to friends or strangers for a home in which to die.

Women do not often take to authorship simply to gratify pride or malice prepense. There are such instances, but they are the exceptions.

"Ah, well-a-day—true—true. We know this, like many another, is a hungry generation. The poor we have with us always. But the poor women who *write* for a living had better 'go out washing,' 'take in sewing,' &c. That would be reasonable."

But why not come out with the truth, the *whole* truth? Is not *this* truth in your hearts? "These women-writers are not so respectful to the clergymen as they ought to be; in their namby-pamby, milk-and-water stories. They take off our friends, with all their little, harmless peccadilloes, in such a provoking way, we can't say a word, only wince most uncomfortably. These *thin* coats fit us to a squeeze. These triflers earn too much, (wo, the day!) They get out of their sphere. They get high-notional, so as to dare fault *us,* the higher power. They dare animadvert upon a great many things, which makes us uncomfortable. Women should be kept down like negroes, and like those of the sex to whom we forward missionaries. If they don't happen to be wealthy, if they are not *our* daughters or sisters, they should be hewers of wood and drawers of water," &c.

We should infer that men who write of women, like the editor of the New York *Observer,* would be in favor of slavery in more ways than one.

We believe in wrong and right. We believe in the Bible, and in "a judgment to come"—*especially* for those scribes who love greetings in the markets, and the highest seats in the synagogues, and the chief rooms at feasts; who devour widows' houses, and for a pretence make long prayers. We think we are sufficiently orthodox to satisfy the New York *Observer,* or any other paper, albeit we are a novel-writer, now and then; (one, by the way, who has not had to write for *bread,* like many, with whom we truly sympathize.) . . .

We do not know whether the New York *Observer* and other papers which condemn novel-writers approve of this whitewashing course; but do they "cry aloud and spare not" against it, as they do against novels? If they would take up their pens to castigate existing evils in various ranks, and often as they carp at poor, weak, struggling women-writers, on whom is imposed the burden of ills "too numerous to mention," they would be acting more in accordance with the dictates of reason and common humanity. If they think to repair the crumbling foundations of ecclesiastical power and pomp, by making war upon women who work with their brains for a living, they must sometime discover that such sin cannot be daubed over with untempered mortar.

A word about novels apart from critics. We do not think the novel is the highest class of writing—at least, not always. But if the people will not be spoken to in any other way, what can the author do? For some years past, and even at present, but a very few essays or poems have sold, or will sell at all, and these in a moderate ratio. Publishers of periodicals and books pronounce them "not available," or "a drug in the market."

Of what use is it to write what nobody will buy or read? So long as the public demand fiction, so long there will be a supply; and the fault, if fault there is, will not be attributable to the manufacturers, who write to provide themselves with a modicum of life. . . .

Reverend gentlemen—you well know that a great and a powerful work has been effected in the garb of *fiction,* through all of the ages. How did Christ speak unto the people? At one time, it is said, that without a parable spake he not unto them. A parable, as everybody knows is a fable, illustrative of truth. So is a good novel.

It strikes us that your philippics against all novels are not in good taste or good sense. We say this, after having read your good *notices*, in past times, of many novels which have done a great work in the purification of society. We say this, after having *observed* your notices of some of the worst evils in the world—as, for instance, *Slavery*.

After all, we do not believe that you really *mean* all that you say against novels and women-writers. If you do, you are deplorably ignorant, to say the least. You are besottedly presumptuous, to level your most cutting shafts against women, and then let the guilty go with a sugar-plum, in which is hidden away a coriander seed of reproof, or with a sly wink, whisper, "They are gentlemen of the first water, and it won't do for us to come down upon them. We shall *lose* by it."

We *were* inclined to think highly of you, "for your work's sake;" we even approved of your condemnation of many books of the day—for that many *ought* to be condemned, few will dispute; but when you come out with such sweeping denunciations against *all* novels, (as some of you have done,) and when you bid a woman, educated, delicately nurtured, highly gifted, who chances not to have the means of getting a good living like yourselves, to "*go out washing*," &c., we would remind you that there must come a time when the wrongs which women have suffered, do suffer, and may suffer, will be *judged!*

There will come a day of last things, when tyrants will no longer have it in their power to gloat over the miseries of the oppressed. You may now treat us as though we were *fools*. We will bear that with the most becoming submission. We will respectfully listen to a man like De Quincy,[1] who, with a superciliousness which affects us like ipecacuanha,[2] observes: "Woman, sister—there are some things which you do not execute as well as your brother, man; no, nor ever will. Pardon me, if I doubt whether you will ever produce a great poet from your choirs, or a Mozart, or a Phidias,[3] or a Michael Angelo, or a great philosopher, or a great scholar." Pardon me, brother De Quincy, have not *women* produced the greatest *novels* which the world have ever read? novels which have rung through the ranks of every caste; been quoted by great men on the highest of our public forums, and been registered among those works which the world will not let die through all the coming ages?

That women are inferior to your sex, I am ready to concede, even in the face of a long array of *facts* to the contrary. But *never* will I allow that woman, gifted and

---

1. Thomas de Quincey (1785–1859), British Romantic writer most famous for *Confessions of an English Opium-Eater* (1821). The quote that follows is from an essay on Joan of Arc published in 1847.

2. Syrup of ipecac, which induces vomiting, is made from this plant.

3. Phidias (fifth century B.C.) is widely regarded as the greatest Greek sculptor. He directed the construction of the Parthenon.

cultured, was designed by her Creator for the *slave,* which the editor of the New York *Observer* would make his readers believe!

Thanks to Heaven! all men are not of this ilk. Chivalry was not blown out of the world with the breath of Don Quixote. There are *gentlemen* who respect and esteem the worthy of our sex, who speak and write honorably of them. There have been such in all ages. Such there will be, ever. God bless them with good wives and daughters, fair as "Jemima, Kezia, and Kerenhappuch!"[4]

Source: The National Era (1857)

4. Job's beautiful daughters. See Job 42:13–15.

🔖 HARRIET WILSON (1825–1900)

Harriet "Hattie" E. Adams Wilson, the author of one of the first novels by an African American, was a free mulatto born in Milford, New Hampshire. Abandoned by her mother when she was six, she lived and worked in the home of a family that treated her as an indentured servant or even a slave, physically and mentally abusing her. In 1851, Harriet married Thomas Wilson, a free man of color, who soon deserted her, leaving her to bear a son in a house for the poor. Her motivation for writing Our Nig *was to support herself and her child, as she explains in the preface below. Sadly, he died the following year and Wilson made little money from the book. She does not appear to have tried her hand at writing again. From 1867 until her death in 1900 she worked in the Boston area as a spiritualist, lecturer, and housekeeper, vocations apparently more accessible to her and more lucrative than authorship.*

Preface to *Our Nig*

In offering to the public the following pages, the writer confesses her inability to minister to the refined and cultivated, the pleasure supplied by abler pens. It is not for such these crude narrations appear. Deserted by kindred, disabled by failing health, I am forced to some experiment which shall aid me in maintaining myself and child without extinguishing this feeble life. I would not from these motives even palliate slavery at the South, by disclosures of its appurtenances North. My mistress was wholly imbued with *southern* principles. I do not pretend to divulge every transaction in my own life, which the unprejudiced would declare unfavorable in comparison with treatment of legal bondmen; I have purposely omitted what would most provoke shame in our good anti-slavery friends at home.

My humble position and frank confession of errors will, I hope, shield me from severe criticism. Indeed, defects are so apparent it requires no skilful [*sic*] hand to expose them.

I sincerely appeal to my colored brethren universally for patronage, hoping they will not condemn this attempt of their sister to be erudite, but rally around me a faithful band of supporters and defenders.

H. E. W.

Source: Our Nig; or, Sketches from the Life of a Free Black, In a Two-Story White House, North. Showing That Slavery's Shadows Fall Even There. *By "Our Nig." (1859)*

❧ LOUISA MAY ALCOTT (1832–1888)

The beloved author of the most popular girls' book of the nineteenth century, Little Women *(1868), received remarkable encouragement and opportunities for a girl of her day. Her parents, members of the Transcendentalist circle in Concord, Massachusetts, instilled in their four daughters the belief that each individual possessed unique talents as well as the right to develop them to their fullest potential. Alcott, however, also felt compelled to provide income for her family while her father pursued his Transcendentalist philosophies and struggled to put bread on the table. She began her career writing sensational stories published under the pseudonym A. M. Barnard, at the same time laboring intensively on her serious romantic novel* Moods *(1864). The journals excerpted below show Alcott's deep involvement with* Moods *and her efforts to make money as a writer, as well as her doubts about writing a book for girls.*

Journals [Excerpts]

April [1860].— . . . Sent "Cinderella" to the "Atlantic,"[1] and it was accepted. Began "By the River," and thought that this was certainly to be a lucky year; for after ten years hard climbing I had reached a good perch on the ladder, and could look more hopefully into the future, while my paper boats sailed gaily over the Atlantic. . . .

August.—"Moods." Genius burned so fiercely that for four weeks I wrote all day and planned nearly all night, being quite possessed by my work. I was perfectly happy, and seemed to have no wants. Finished the book, or a rough draught of it, and put it away to settle. Mr. Emerson[2] offered to read it when Mother told him it was "Moods" and had one of his sayings for motto.

Daresay nothing will ever come of it; but it *had* to be done, and I'm the richer for a new experience.

September.— Received $75 of Ticknor[3] for "Cinderella," and feel very rich. Emerson praised it, and people wrote to me about it and patted me on the head. Paid bills, and began to simmer another. . . .

October.— . . . Mother went to see Uncle S. J. May, and I was housekeeper. Gave my mind to it so energetically that I dreamed dip-toast, talked apple-sauce, thought pies, and wept drop-cakes. Read my book to Nan, who came up to cheer me in my struggles; and she laughed and cried over it and said it was "good." So I felt encouraged, and will touch it up when duty no longer orders me to make a burnt-offering of myself. . . .

1. "A Modern Cinderella" was published in the *Atlantic Monthly* in October 1860.
2. Ralph Waldo Emerson (1803–1882) was her neighbor and the foremost member of the Transcendentalist circle that included her father, Bronson Alcott (1799–1888).
3. William Ticknor of Ticknor and Fields, publishers of the *Atlantic Monthly.*

February [1861]. — Another turn at "Moods," which I remodelled. From the 2d to the 25th I sat writing, with a run at dusk; could not sleep, and for three days was so full of it I could not stop to get up. Mother made me a green silk cap with a red bow, to match the old green and red party wrap, which I wore as a "glory cloak." Thus arrayed I sat in groves of manuscripts, "living for immortality," as May said. Mother wandered in and out with cordial cups of tea, worried because I could n't eat. Father thought it fine, and brought his reddest apples and hardest cider for my Pegasus[4] to feed upon. All sorts of fun was going on, but I did n't care if the world returned to chaos if I and my inkstand only "lit" in the same place.

It was very pleasant and queer while it lasted; but after three weeks of it I found that my mind was too rampant for my body, as my head was dizzy, legs shaky, and no sleep would come. So I dropped the pen, and took long walks, cold baths, and had Nan up to frolic with me. Read all I had done to my family; and Father said: "Emerson must see this. Where did you get your metaphysics?" Mother pronounced it wonderful, and Anna laughed and cried, as she always does, over my works, saying, "My dear, I'm proud of you."

So I had a good time, even if it never comes to anything; for it was worth something to have my three dearest sit up till midnight listening with wide-open eyes to Lu's first novel.

I planned it some time ago, and have had it in my mind ever so long; but now it begins to take shape. . . .

October [1863].—Thought much about going to Port Royal to teach contrabands. Fields[5] wanted the letters I should write, and asked if I had no book. Father spoke of "Moods," and he desired to see it. So I fell to work, and finished it off, thinking the world must be coming to an end, and all my dreams getting fulfilled in a most amazing way. If there was ever an astonished young woman, it is myself; for things have gone on so swimmingly of late I don't know who I am. A year ago I had no publisher, and went begging with my wares; now *three* have asked me for something, several papers are ready to print my contributions, and F. B. S.[6] says "any publisher this side of Baltimore would be glad to get a book." There is a sudden hoist for a meek and lowly scribbler who was told to "stick to her teaching," and never had a literary friend to lend a helping hand! Fifteen years of hard grubbing may be coming to something after all; and I may yet "pay all the debts, fix the

4. Winged horse of Greek mythology, symbol of poetic inspiration.

5. Port Royal, South Carolina, was abandoned by Confederate troops and white planters in November 1861, leaving behind 8,000 slaves. Northern benevolent societies sent abolitionists to teach the contraband slaves there. Alcott considered going but ultimately did not participate in the "Port Royal Experiment." After the success of her *Hospital Sketches* (1863), letters about her experiences nursing soldiers, James T. Fields, editor of the *Atlantic Monthly,* was interested in the letters she might write from Port Royal.

6. Frank B. Sanborn (1831–1917), member of the Transcendentalist circle in Concord.

house, send May to Italy, and keep the old folks cosey," as I've said I would so long, yet so hopelessly.

May began to take anatomical drawing lessons of Rimmer.[7] I was very glad to be able to pay her expenses up and down and clothe her neatly. Twenty dollars more from Redpath[8] on account. . . .

February [1864].— . . .Redpath came flying up on the 4th to get "Moods," promising to have it out by May. Gave it to him with many fears, and he departed content. The next day received a telegram to come down at once and see the printers. Went, and was told the story was too long for a single volume, and a two-volume novel was bad to begin with. Would I cut the book down about half? No, I would n't, having already shortened it all it would bear. So I took my "opus" and posted home again, promising to try and finish my shorter book in a month. . . .

April.—At Father's request I sent "Moods" to T.,[9] and got a very friendly note from him, saying they had so many books on hand that they could do nothing about it now. So I put it back on the shelf, and set about my other work. Don't despair, "Moods," we'll try again by and by!

[Alas! we did try again.—L.M.A.]

Wrote the first part of a story for Professor C. called "Love and Loyalty,"—flat, patriotic, and done to order. Wrote a new fairy tale, "Nelly's Hospital."

May.—Had a letter from Mrs. Gildersleeve, asking for my photograph and a sketch of my life, for a book called "Heroic Women" which she was getting up. Respectfully refused. Also a letter and flattering notice from "Ruth Hall,"[10] and a notice from a Chicago critic with a long extract from "Rose Family." My tale "Enigmas"[11] came out, and was much liked by readers of sensation rubbish. Having got my $50, I was resigned. . . .

September.—Mrs. D.[12] made a visit, and getting hold of my old book of stories liked them, and insisted on taking "Moods" home to read. As she had had experience with publishers, was a good business woman, and an excellent critic, I let her have it, hoping she might be able to give the poor old book the lift it has been waiting for all these years. She took it, read it, and admired it heartily, saying that "no American author had showed so much promise; that the plan was admirable, the execution unequal, but often magnificent; that I had a great field before me, and my book must be got out."

7. Alcott's youngest sister May (1840–1879) was an artist. She took lessons with Dr. William Rimmer in Boston.

8. James Redpath (1833–1891), publisher of Alcott's *Hospital Sketches* (1863).

9. Probably Howard Ticknor, who took over the firm Ticknor and Fields after his father, William Ticknor, died suddenly April 10, 1864.

10. Fanny Fern (Sarah Payson Parton) (1811–1872).

11. Alcott, *The Rose Family: A Fairy Tale* (1864). "Enigmas" was published in *Frank Leslie's Illustrated.*

12. Caroline Healy Dall (1822–1912), Boston author and reformer.

Mrs. D. sent it to L.,[13] who liked it exceedingly, and asked me to shorten it if I could, else it would be too large to sell well. Was much disappointed, said I'd never touch it again, and tossed it into the spidery little cupboard where it had so often returned after fruitless trips. . . .

October.—Wrote several chapters of "Work,"[14] and was getting on finely, when, as I lay awake one night, a way to shorten and arrange "Moods" came into my head. The whole plan laid itself smoothly out before me, and I slept no more that night, but worked on it as busily as if mind and body had nothing to do with one another. Up early, and began to write it all over again. The fit was on strong, and for a fortnight I hardly ate, slept, or stirred, but wrote, wrote, like a thinking machine in full operation. When it was all rewritten without copying, I found it much improved, though I'd taken out ten chapters, and sacrificed many of my favorite things; but being resolved to make it simple, strong, and short, I let every thing else go, and hoped the book would be better for it.

[It was n't. 1867.]

Sent it to L.; and a week after, as I sat hammering away at the parlor carpet,— dusty, dismal, and tired—a letter came from L. praising the story more enthusiastically than ever, thanking me for the improvements, and proposing to bring out the book at once. Of course we all had a rapture, and I finished my work "double quick," regardless of weariness, toothache, or blue devils.

Next day I went to Boston and saw L. A brisk, business-like man who seemed in earnest and said many complimentary things about "Hospital Sketches" and its author. It was agreed to bring out the book immediately, and Mrs. D. offered to read the proof with me.

Was glad to have the old thing under way again, but did n't quite believe it would ever come out after so many delays and disappointments. . . .

November.—Proof began to come, and the chapters seemed small, stupid, and no more my own in print. I felt very much afraid that I'd ventured too much and should be sorry for it. But Emerson says "that what is true for your own private heart is true for others."[15] So I wrote from my own consciousness and observation and hope it may suit some one and at least do no harm. . . .

December.—Earnings, 1864,—$476.

On Christmas Eve received ten copies of "Moods" and a friendly note from L. The book was hastily got out, but on the whole suited me, and as the inside was considered good I let the outside go. For a week wherever I went I saw, heard, and talked "Moods;" found people laughing or crying over it, and was continually told how well it was going, how much it was liked, how fine a thing I'd done. I was glad

13. Aaron K. Loring (1826–1911) of Boston, best known for publishing Horatio Alger.

14. Alcott's novel *Work: A Story of Experience,* a novel for adults, was not published until 1873.

15. In his essay "Self-Reliance" (1841), Emerson wrote, "To believe your own thought, to believe that what is true for you in your private heart is true for all men—that is genius."

but not proud, I think, for it has always seemed as if "Moods" grew in spite of me, and that I had little to do with it except to put into words the thoughts that would not let me rest until I had. Don't know why.

By Saturday the first edition was gone and the second ready. Several booksellers ordered a second hundred, the first went so fast, and friends could not get it but had to wait till more were ready. . . .

January, 1865.— . . . Notices of "Moods" came from all directions, and though people did n't understand my ideas owing to my shortening the book so much, the notices were mostly favorable and gave quite as much praise as was good for me. I had letters from Mrs. Parker, Chadwick, Sanborn, E. B. Greene, the artist, T. W. Higginson[16] and some others. All friendly and flattering.

Saw more notices of "Moods" and received more letters, several from strangers and some very funny. People seemed to think the book finely written, very promising, wise, and interesting; but some fear it is n't moral, because it speaks freely of marriage. . . .

May.— . . . Had a fine letter from Conway,[17] and a notice in the "Reader,"—an English paper. He advised sending copies to several of the best London papers. English people don't understand "transcendental literature," as they call "Moods." My next book shall have no *ideas* in it, only facts, and the people shall be as ordinary as possible; then critics will say it is all right. . . .

May, 1868.—Father saw Mr. Niles[18] about a fairy book. Mr. N. wants a *girls' story,* and I begin "Little Women." Marmee, Anna, and May all approve of my plan. So I plod away, though I don't enjoy this sort of thing. Never liked girls or knew many, except my sisters; but our queer plays and experiences may prove interesting, though I doubt it.

[Good joke.—L. M. A.]

June.—Sent twelve chapters of "L. W." to Mr. N. He thought it *dull;* so do I. But work away and mean to try the experiment; for lively, simple books are very much needed for girls, and perhaps I can supply the need. . . .

July 15th.—Have finished "Little Women," and sent it off,—402 pages. May is designing some pictures for it. Hope it will go, for I shall probably get nothing for "Morning Glories."

Very tired, head full of pain from overwork, and heart heavy about Marmee, who is growing feeble.

---

16. Lydia Parker, wife of Theodore Parker; perhaps John White Chadwick (1840–1904); Frank B. Sanborn; E. B. Greene, woman illustrator; and Thomas Wentworth Higginson (1823–1911), an editor at the *Atlantic Monthly.*

17. Moncure Conway (1832–1907), follower of the Transcendentalists.

18. Thomas Niles (1825–1894), Alcott's editor and publisher at Roberts Brothers, which published *Little Women* (1868) and most of Alcott's subsequent works.

[Too much work for one young woman. No wonder she broke down. 1876.—
L. M. A.]

August.—Roberts Bros. made an offer for the story, but at the same time advised
me to keep the copyright; so I shall.

[An honest publisher and a lucky author, for the copyright made her fortune,
and the "dull book" was the first golden egg of the ugly duckling. 1885.—L. M. A.]

August 26th.—Proof of whole book came. It reads better than I expected. Not a
bit sensational, but simple and true, for we really lived most of it; and if it succeeds
that will be the reason of it. Mr. N. likes it better now, and says some girls who have
read the manuscripts say it is "splendid!" As it is for them, they are the best critics,
so I should be satisfied. . . .

[*October*] *30th.*—Saw Mr. N. of Roberts Brothers, and he gave me good news of
the book. An order from London for an edition came in. First edition gone and
more called for. Expects to sell three or four thousand before the New Year.

Mr. N. wants a second volume for spring. Pleasant notices and letters arrive,
and much interest in my little women, who seem to find friends by their truth to
life, as I hoped.

November 1st.—Began the second part of "Little Women." I can do a chapter a
day, and in a month I mean to be done. A little success is so inspiring that I now
find my "Marches" sober, nice people, and as I can launch into the future, my fancy
has more play. Girls write to ask who the little women marry, as if that was the only
end and aim of a woman's life. I *won't* marry Jo to Laurie to please any one. . . . [19]

Source: Life, Letters, and Journals of Louisa May Alcott, ed. Ednah Cheney (1889)

---

19. *Little Women* was published in two parts. After the publication of the first volume, readers
wrote to Alcott requesting that her autobiographical heroine Jo March marry her neighbor and
friend Laurie. Instead, Alcott married Laurie to Jo's sister Amy and, under pressure, introduced a
new love interest for Jo, Professor Baehr.

☙ ROSE TERRY COOKE (1827–1892)

A resident of Connecticut for most of her life, Rose Terry was educated at the Hartford Female Seminary. After her graduation, she taught and served as a governess until she received an inheritance from her uncle and was able to devote her time to writing. She was a prolific short story writer and poet from the 1840s until her death. She published the lead story in the first issue of the Atlantic Monthly *in 1857 and was a frequent contributor to* Harper's, Galaxy, *and other high culture magazines. Along with Harriet Beecher Stowe, her Hartford friend and neighbor, she pioneered the tradition of women's regionalism that would flourish in the 1880s and 90s. After her marriage to Rollin Cooke in 1873, she was under increasing pressure to support her profligate husband. For her, literature was a business as much as an art. The following story displays Cooke's considerable wit and humorously portrays the challenges of celebrity and anonymity for women writers.*

The Memorial of A. B., or Matilda Muffin

THE MEMORIAL OF A. B.

Humbly Showeth:—

Ladies and gentlemen,—enlightened public,—kind audience,—dear readers,—or whatever else you may be styled,—whose eyes, from remote regions of east, west, or next door, solace themselves between the brown covers of this magazine, making of themselves flowers to its lunar brilliancy,—I wish to state, with all humility and self-disgust, that I am what is popularly called a literary woman.

In the present state of society, I should feel less shame in declaring myself the elect lady of Dunderhed Van Nudel, Esquire, that wealthy Dutch gentleman, aged seventy, whom we all know. It is true, that, as I am young and gay and intelligent, while he is old and stupid and very low Dutch indeed, such an announcement would be equivalent to saying that I was bought by Mr. Van Nudel for half a million of dollars; but then that is customary, and you would all congratulate me.

Also, I should stand a better chance of finding favor in your eyes, if I declared myself to be an indigent tailoress; for no woman should use her head who can use her hands,—a maxim older than Confucius.

Or even if I were a school-ma'am! (blessed be the man who has brought them into fashion and the long path!) In that case, you might say, "Poor thing! isn't she interesting? quite like *the* schoolmistress!"—And I am not averse to pity, since it is love's poor cousin, nor to belonging to a class mentioned in Boston literary society. I really am not!

But the plain truth is, I earn my living by writing. Sewing does not pay. I have no "faculty" at school-keeping; for I invariably spoil all the good children, and pet all the pretty ones,—a process not conducive, as I am told, to the development of manners or morals;—so I write: just as Mr. Jones makes shoes, Mr. Peters harangues the jury, Mr. Smith sells calico, or Mr. Robinson rolls pills.

For, strange as it may seem, when it is so easy to read, it is hard work to write,— *bonâ fide,* undeniable hard work. Suppose my head cracks and rings and reels with a great ache that stupefies me? In comes Biddy with a letter.

> "The editor of the 'Monthly Signpost' would be much obliged to Miss Matilda Muffin for a tale of four pages, to make up the June number, before the end of next week.
> "Very respectfully, etc., etc."

Miss Muffin's head looks her in the face, (metaphorically,) and says, "You can't!"—but her last year's bonnet creaks and rustles from the bandbox, finally lifts the lid and peeps out. Gracious! the ghost in Hamlet was not more of an "airy nothing" than that ragged, faded, dilapidated old structure of crape and blonde. The bonnet retires to the sound of slow music; the head slinks back and holds its tongue; Miss Muffin sits down at her table; scratch, scratch, scratch, goes the old pen, and the ideas catch up with it, it is so shaky; and the words go tumbling over it, till the *t*s go out without any hats on, and the eyes—no, the *is* (*is* that the way to pluralize them?)—get no dots at all; and every now and then the head says, softly, "Oh, dear!" Miss Muffin goes to something called by novel-writers "repose," toward one o'clock that night, and the next night, and the next; she obliges the "Monthly Signpost" with a comic story at a low price, and buys herself a decent little bonnet for Sundays, replenishing her wardrobe generally by the same process; and the head considers it work, I assure you.

But this is not the special grievance to which I direct this Memorial. I like to work; it suits me much better to obtain my money by steady, honest effort than it would to depend on anybody else for one round cent. If I had a thousand dollars unexpectedly left me by some unknown benefactor, I don't think it would be worth five cents on the dollar, compared with what I earn; there is a healthy, trustworthy pleasure in that, never yet attained by gifted or inherited specie. Neither is it the publicity of the occupation that I here object to. I knew that, before I began to write; and many an hour have I cried over the thought of being known, and talked about, and commented on,—having my dear name, that my mother called me by, printed on the cover of a magazine, seeing it in newspapers, hearing it in whispers, when Miss Brown says to Miss Black under her breath,—"That girl in the straw bonnet is Matilda Muffin, who writes for the 'Snapdragon' and the 'Signpost.'"

I knew all this, as I say. I dreaded and hated it. I hate it now. But I had to work, and this was the only way open to me; so I tried to be brave, and to do what I ought, and let the rest go. I cannot say I am very brave yet, or that I don't feel all this; but I do not memorialize against it, because it is necessary to be borne, and I must bear it. When I go to the dentist's to have a tooth out, I sit down, and hold the chair tight, and open my mouth as wide as it will open, but I always say, "Oh! don't, doctor! I can't! I can't possibly!" till the iron what-d'you-call-it enters my soul and stops my tongue.

Yes, when I began to write, I knew I should some day see my name in print. I knew people would wonder who and what I was, and how I looked;—I had done it myself. I knew that I should be delivered over to be the prey of tongues and the spoil of eyes. I was aware, I think, I am aware now, of every possible "disagreeable" that can befall the state. I am accustomed to hear people say, if I venture a modest opinion about a dinner, "Dear me! as if a literary woman knew anything about cooking!"—I endure that meekly, sustained by the inner consciousness that I *can* cook much better than any artist in that line I ever yet encountered. Likewise I am used to hear people say, "I suppose you don't waste your valuable time in sewing?" when a look at my left forefinger would insure me a fraternal grip from any member of the Seamstress's Friends Society anywhere. I do not either scold or cry when accidentally some visitor discovers me fitting my dress or making my bonnet, and looks at me with a "fearful joy," as if I were on a tight-rope. I even smile when people lay my ugly shawl or *passé* bonnet, that I bought because they were cheap, and wear for the same reason, at the door of the "eccentricities of genius." And I am case-hardened to the instantaneous scattering and dodging of young men that ensue the moment I enter a little party, because "gentlemen are so afraid of literary women." I don't think gentlemen are; I know two or three who never conceal a revolver in the breast of their coat when they talk to me, and who sometimes even offer to go home with me from a tea-party all alone, and after dark too. It is true, one or two of these are "literary" themselves; the others I knew before I was dyed blue; which may account for it. Also I am impervious to anonymous letters, exhorting me to all kinds of mental and moral improvement, or indulging in idle impertinences about my private affairs, the result of a knowledge about me and the aforesaid affairs drawn solely from my "Pieces in Prose and Verse."

Then as to the matter of the romantic stories that are afloat concerning me, I am rather amused than otherwise by them. I have a sentimental name, by the religious and customary ordinance of baptism, legally my own; and at first, being rather loath to enter the great alliterative ranks of female writers by my lawful title of Matilda Muffin, I signed my writings "A. B."

Two reprobatory poems addressed to those initials came to me through the medium of the "Snapdragon," immediately after my having printed in that spicy paper a pensive little poem called "The Rooster's Cry": one, in Spenserian measure,[1] rebuking me for alluding lightly to serious subjects,—a thing I never do, I am sure,

---

1. Edmund Spenser (1552–1599), British poet, author of *The Faerie Queen* (1590). His innovative and challenging meter was widely copied in the eighteenth and nineteenth centuries.

and I can't imagine what "J. H. P." meant; and another, in hexameter, calling upon me to "arouse," and "smile," and "struggle on," and, in short, to stop crying and behave myself,—only it was said in figures. I'm much obliged to "Quintius" for the advice; but I should like to explain, that I am subject to the toothache, and when it is bad I cannot possibly write comic poetry. I must be miserable, but it's only toothache, thank you!

Then I have heard several times, in the strictest confidence, the whole history of "A. B., who writes for the 'Snapdragon.'" Somebody told me she was a lady living on the North River, very wealthy, very haughty, and very unhappy in her domestic relations. Another said she was a young widow in Alabama, whose mother was extremely tyrannical, and opposed her second marriage. A third person declared to me that A. B. was a physician in the navy,—a highly educated man, but reduced in circumstances. I think that was a great compliment,—to be actually taken for a man! I felt it to be "the proudest moment of my life," as ship-captains say, when they return thanks for the silver teapot richly chased with nautical emblems, presented by the passengers saved from the wreck, as a token of gratitude for the hencoops thrown overboard by the manly commander. However, I called myself a woman in the very next contribution, for fear of the united wrath of the stronger sex, should I ever be discovered to have so imposed upon the public; although I know several old women who remain undiscovered to this day, simply because they avail themselves of a masculine signature.

There were other romances, too tedious to mention, depicting me sometimes as a lovely blonde, writing graceful tales beneath a bower of roses in the warm light of June; sometimes as a respectable old maid, rather sharp, fierce, and snuffy; sometimes as a tall, delicate, aristocratic, poetic looking creature, with liquid dark eyes and heavy tresses of raven hair; sometimes as a languishing, heart-broken woman in the prime of life, with auburn curls and a slow consumption.

Perhaps it may be as well to silence all conjecture at once, by stating that I am a woman of——no, I won't say how old, because everybody will date me from this time forward, and I shall not always be willing to tell how old I am! I am not very young now, it is true; I am more than sixteen and less than forty; so when our clergyman requested all between those ages to remain after service for the purpose of forming a week-day Bible-class, I sat still, and so did everybody else except Mrs. Van Doren, whose great-grandchild was christened in the morning;—our church is a new one.

However, this is digressing. I am not very tall, nor very short; I am rather odd-looking, but decidedly plain. I have brown hair and eyes, a pale light complexion, a commonplace figure, pretty good taste in dress, and a quick sense of the ludicrous, that makes me laugh a great deal, and have a good time generally.

I live at home, in the town of Blank, in a quiet by-street. My parents are both living, and we keep one Irish girl. I go to church on Sundays, and follow my trade week-days.

I write everything I do write in my own room, which is not so pleasant as a bower of roses in some respects, but is preferable in regard to earwigs and caterpillars, which are troublesome in bowers. I have a small pine table to write on, as much elderly furniture as supplies me places for sleep and my books, a small stove in winter, (which is another advantage over bowers,) and my "flowing draperies" are blue chintz, which I bought at a bargain; some quaint old engravings of Bartolozzi's in black and gilt frames; a few books, among which are prominently set forth a volume of "The Doctor,"—Nicolò de' Lapi, in delightful bindings of white parchment,—Thomas à Kempis,—a Bible, of English type and paper,—and Emerson's Poems, bound in Russia leather.[2] Not that I have no other books,—grammars, and novels, and cook-books, in gorgeous array,—but these are within reach from my pillow, when I want to read myself asleep; and a plaster cast of Minerva's owl[3] mounts guard above them, curious fowl that it is.

The neighbors think I am a pretty nice girl, and my papa secretly exults over me as a genius, but he don't say much about it. And there, dear public, you have Matilda Muffin as she is, which I hope will quash the romances, amusing though they be.

But when, after much editorial correspondence, and persevering whispers of kind friends who had been told the facts in confidence, A. B. became only the pretext of a mystery, and I signed myself by my full name, the question naturally arose,—"Who *is* Matilda Muffin?"

Now, for the first time in my life, do I experience the benefits of a sentimental name, which has rather troubled me before, as belonging to a quite unsentimental and commonplace person, and thereby raising expectations, through hearsay, which actual vision dispelled with painful suddenness. But now I find its advantage, for nobody believes it is my own, but confidently expects that Ann Tubbs or Susan Bucket will appear from a long suppression, like a Jack-in-a-box, and startle the public as she throws back the cover.

Indeed, I am told that not long since a circle of literary experimentalists, discussing a recent number of a certain magazine, and displaying great knowledge of *noms-de-plume,* ran aground all at once upon "Who is Matilda Muffin?"—even as, in the innocent faith of childhood, I pondered ten minutes upon "Who was the

2. Francesco Bartolozzi (1727–1815), famous Italian engraver who lived in London. *The Doctor,* a seven-volume novel (1843–1847) by Robert Southey (1774–1843). *Niccolò de' Lapi* (1841), a historical novel by Massimo Tapparelli D'Azeglio (1798–1866). Thomas à Kempis (ca. 1380–1471), German monk and author of *Imitation of Christ.* Ralph Waldo Emerson (1803–1882), American Transcendentalist philosopher, poet, and essayist. This list suggests that Matilda is an intellectual.
3. Minerva was the Roman goddess of wisdom and the arts. The owl was her symbol.

father of Zebedee's[4] children?" and at last "gave up." But these professional gentlemen, nowise daunted by the practical difficulties of the subject, held on, till at last
one, wiser in his generation than the rest, confidently announced that he knew
Matilda Muffin's real name, but was not at liberty to disclose it. Should this little
confidence ever reach the eyes of those friends, I wish to indorse that statement in
every particular; that gentleman does know my name; and know all men, by these
presents, I give him full leave to disclose it,—or rather, to save him the trouble, I
disclose it myself. My name, my own, that would have been printed in the mar-
riage-list of the "Snapdragon" before now, if it had not appeared in the list of contributors, and which will appear in its list of deaths some day to come,—my name,
that is called to breakfast, marked on my pocket-handkerchiefs, written in my
books, and done in yellow paint on my trunk, *is*—Matilda Muffin. "Only that, and
nothing more!" And "A. B.," which I adopted once as a species of veil to the aforesaid alliterative title, did not mean, as was supposed, "A Beauty," or "Any Body," or
"Another Barrett," or "Anti Bedott,"[5] or "After Breakfast," but only "A. B.," the first
two letters of the alphabet. Peace to their ashes—let them rest!

But, dear me! I forgot the Memorial! As I have said, all these enumerated troubles do not much move me, nor yet the world-old cry of all literary women's being,
in virtue of their calling, unfeminine. I don't think anybody who knows me can say
that about me; in fact, I am generally regarded by my male cousins as a "little
goose," and a "foolish child," and "a perfectly absurd little thing,"—epithets that
forbid the supposition of their object being strong-minded or having Women's
Rights;—and as for people who don't know me, I care very little what they think.
If I want them to like me, I can generally make them,—having a knack that way.

But there is one thing against which I do solemnly protest and uplift my voice,
as a piece of ridiculous injustice and supererogation,—and that is, that every new
poem or fresh story I write and print should be supposed and declared to be part
and parcel of my autobiography. Good gracious! Goethe[6] himself, "many-sided" as
the old stone Colossus[7] might have been, would have retreated in dismay from such
a host of characters as I have appeared in, according to the announcement of admiring friends.

My dear creatures, do just look at the common sense of the thing! Can I have
been, by any dexterity known to man, of mind or body, such a various creature,
such a polycorporate animal, as you make me to be? Because I write the anguish

---

4. In the Bible, Zebedee is the father of Jesus' disciples John and James.

5. Elizabeth Barrett Browning (1806–1861), the most highly esteemed female British poet of the
nineteenth century. The Widow Bedott was a popular, humorous, uncouth character created by
Frances Miriam Whitcher (1814–1852).

6. Johann Wolfgang von Goethe (1749–1832), foremost German Romantic writer and author of
Faust (1808 and 1832).

7. The Colossus of Rhodes, a gigantic statue of the Greek God Helios, was one of the seven
wonders of the ancient world.

and suffering of an elderly widow with a drunken husband, am I therefore meek and of middle age, the slave of a rum-jug? I have heard of myself successively as figuring in the character of a strong-minded, self-denying Yankee girl,—a broken-hearted Georgia beauty,—a fairy princess,—a consumptive school-mistress,—a young woman dying of the perfidy of her lover,—a mysterious widow; and I daily expect to hear that a caterpillar which figured as hero in one of my tales was an allegory of myself, and that a cat mentioned in "The New Tobias" is a travesty of my heart-experience.

Now this is rather more than "human natur" can stand. It is true that in my day and generation I have suffered as everybody does, more or less. It is likewise true that I have suffered from the same causes that other people do. I am happy to state that in the allotments of this life authoresses are not looked upon as "literary," but simply as women, and have the same general dispensations with the just and the unjust; therefore, in attempting to excite other people's sympathies, I have certainly touched and told many stories that were not strange to my own consciousness; I do not know very well how I could do otherwise. And in trying to draw the common joys and sorrows of life, I certainly have availed myself of experience as well as observation; but I should seem to myself singularly wanting in many traits which I believe I possess, were I to obtrude the details of my own personal and private affairs upon the public. And I offer to those who have so interpreted me a declaration which I trust may relieve them from all responsibility of this kind in future; I hereby declare, asseverate, affirm, and whatever else means to swear, that I never have offered and never intend to offer any history whatever of my personal experience, social, literary, or emotional, to the readers of any magazine, newspaper, novel, or correspondence whatever. Nor is there any one human being who has ever heard or ever will hear the whole of that experience,—no, not even Dunderhed Van Nudel, Esquire, should he buy me tomorrow!

Also, I wish to relieve the minds of many friendly readers, who, hearing and believing these reports, bestow upon me a vast amount of sympathy that is worthy of a better fate. My dear friends, as I said before, it is principally toothache; poetry is next best to clove-oil, and less injurious to the enamel. I beg of you not to suppose that every poet who howls audibly in the anguish of his soul is really afflicted in the said soul; but one must have respect for the dignity of High Art. Answer me now with frankness, what should you think of a poem that ran in this style?—

"The sunset's gorgeous wonder
    Flashes and fades away;
But my back-tooth aches like thunder,
    And I cannot now be gay!"

Now just see how affecting it is, when you "change the venue," as lawyers say:—

"The sunset's gorgeous wonder
    Flashes and fades away;
But I hear the muttering thunder,
    And my sad heart dies like the day."

I leave it to any candid mind, what would be the result to literature, if such a course were pursued?

Besides, look at the facts in the case. You read the most tearful strains of the most melancholy poet you know; if you took them *verbatim,* you would expect him to be found by the printer's—boy, sent for copy, "by starlight on the north side of a tombstone," as Dr. Bellamy[8] said, enjoying a northeaster without any umbrella, and soaking the ground with tears, unwittingly antiseptic, in fact, as Mr. Mantalini expressed himself, "a damp, moist, unpleasant body."[9] But where, I ask, does that imp find the aforesaid poet, when he goes to get the seventh stanza of the "Lonely Heart"? Why, in the gentlemen's parlor of a first-class hotel, his feet tilted up in the window, his apparel perfectly dry and shiny with various ornamental articles appended, his eyes half open over a daily paper, his parted lips clinging to a cigar, his whole aspect well-to-do and comfortable. And aren't you glad of it? I am; there is so much real misery in the world, that don't know how to write for the papers, and has to have its toothache all by itself, when a simple application of bread and milk or bread and meat would cure it, that I am glad to have the apparent sum of human misery diminished, even at the expense of being a traitor in the camp.

And still further, for your sakes, dear tender-hearted friends, who may suppose that I am wearing this mask of joy for the sake of deluding you into a grim and respectful sympathy,—you, who will pity me whether or no,—I confess that I have some material sorrows for which I will gladly accept your tears. My best bonnet is very unbecoming. I even heard it said the other day, striking horror to my soul, that it looked literary! And I'm afraid it does! Moreover, my only silk dress that is presentable begins to show awful symptoms of decline and fall; and though you may suppose literature to be a lucrative business, between ourselves it is not so at all, (very likely the "Atlantic" gentlemen will omit that sentence, for fear of a libel-suit from the trade,—but it's all the same a fact, unless you write for the "Dodger,")—and I'm likely to mend and patch and court-plaster the holes in that old black silk, another year at least: but this is my solitary real anguish at present.

I do assure all and sundry my reporters, my sympathizers, and my readers, that all that I have stated in this present Memorial is unvarnished fact, whatever they may say, read, or feel to the contrary,—and that, although I am a literary woman, and labor under all the liabilities and disabilities contingent thereto, I am yet sound

8. New England minister. According to Harriet Beecher Stowe, his saying here quoted "circulated about us in our childhood" (*Stories, Sketches and Studies* [1896]).
9. Quote from Mr. Mantalini in Charles Dickens's *Nicholas Nickleby* (1839).

in mind and body, (except for the toothache,) and a very amusing person to know, with no quarrel against life in general or anybody in particular. Indeed, I find one advantage in the very credulous and inquisitive gossip against which I memorialize; for I think I may expect fact to be believed, when fiction is swallowed whole; and I feel sure of seeing, directly on the publication of this document, a notice in the "Snapdragon," the "Badger," or the "Coon," (whichever paper gets that number of the magazine first,) running in this wise:—

> "Matilda Muffin.—We welcome in the last number of the 'Atlantic Monthly' a brief and spirited autobiography of this lady, whose birth, parentage, and home have so long been wrapt in mystery. The hand of genius has rent asunder the veil of reserve, and we welcome the fair writer to her proper position in the Blank City Directory, and post-office list of boxes."

After which, I shall resign myself tranquilly to my fate as a unit, and glide down the stream of life under whatever skies shine or scowl above, always and forever nobody but

Matilda Muffin.

Blank, 67 *Smith Street.*

Source: Atlantic Monthly (1860)

Arachne[10]

I watch her in the corner there,
    As restless, bold, and unafraid,
She slips and floats along the air,
    Till all her subtile house is made.

Her home, her bed, her nets for food,
    All from that inward store she draws;
She fashions it and knows it good
    By instinct's sure and sacred laws.

No silver threads to weave her nest
    She seeks and gathers far or near,
But spins it from her fruitful breast,
    Renewing still till leaves are sere.

10. In Greek mythology, the mortal Arachne, a gifted weaver, claimed to possess greater ability than Athena, the goddess of weaving. After a contest, Athena destroyed Arachne's tapestry and loom. Arachne hung herself, but Athena took pity on her and brought her back to life as a spider.

Till, worn with toil and tired of life,
   In vain her shining traps are set,
For frost hath stilled the insect strife,
   And gilded flies her charm forget.

Then, swinging on the shroud she spun,
   She sways to every wintry wind,
Her joy, her toil, her errand done,
   Her corse the sport of storms unkind.

Poor sister of the spinster[11] clan!
   I too, from out my store within,
My daily life and living plan,
   My home, my rest, my pleasure spin.

I know thy heart when heartless hands
   Sweep all that hard-earned web away,
Destroy its pearled and glittering bands,
   And leave thee homeless by the way.

I know thy peace when all is done,—
   Each anchored thread, each tiny knot
Soft shining in the autumn sun,
   A sheltered, silent, tranquil spot.

I know what thou hast never known,
   Sad foresight to a soul allowed,—
That not for life I spin alone,
   But day by day I spin my shroud.

Source: The Atlantic Monthly (1881)

11. This word for an unmarried woman originated as a word for a woman who spins, or makes yarn or thread.

❧ Augusta Jane Evans (1835–1909)

Augusta Jane Evans was the most popular southern woman author of the nineteenth century. Born into a wealthy planter family in Georgia, she spent four years of her youth in frontier Texas and settled in 1849 in Mobile, Alabama. Her national fame began with the publication of Beulah *(1859), a novel about an orphan, and continued with* Macaria *(1864), a pro-Confederacy novel. Her greatest success came with the novel* St. Elmo *(1867), whose intellectual heroine renounces authorship in order to reform and marry the rakish hero. The novel was one of the three most popular of the century and spawned a slew of plantations, railroad cars, towns, and children named after its protagonists. In 1868, Evans married Colonel Lorenzo Madison Wilson, and while she devoted herself to domestic pursuits, she went on to publish four more novels, two after her husband's death in 1891. Although her novels preached the superiority of the roles of wife and mother over literary pursuits, her own career and the following letters suggest how conflicted intellectual women were about their right to utilize their God-given talents.*

Letters to Rachel Lyons

Mobile July 30, 1860

My darling Rachel

Your welcome letter saddened me, for I had not heard of the severe affliction that has fallen on my kind friend Mr. Moses. How very sorry I am to know that the circumstances were so melancholy. Yes dear, I did wonder why you wrote me no letters this long while and thought that painted spectre <u>Fame</u> has taken bodily possession of you, and set you to grinding at that everlasting mill, yclept[1]—"<u>Novel-writing.</u>" Rachel darling, I rather think you should not "unbutton yourself" (as Seaver[2] says) to that same treacherous worthy afore-said. <u>Fame</u> <u>don't</u> <u>pay</u>:—well—I take that back; but the <u>payments</u> are in beautiful <u>looking</u> print, of an ancient variety,—first discovered on the margin of the <u>Dead</u> <u>Sea</u> and thence imported by all lands and people—; luscious looking, glossy, rosy, fragrant <u>Apples</u> <u>of</u> <u>Sodom.</u>[3] Most folks swallow the bitter dust, smiling all the time, and praising its <u>sweet</u> <u>juiciness;</u> N'importe![4] But jesting aside my dear far-off, longed for friend; I knew you did not write "<u>Rutledge.</u>"[5] I believe you would have told me—Now Rachel—what are you

---

1. Old English for "named" or "called." [Editor's note.]
2. The editor of *Harper's New Monthly Magazine* and a friend of AEW. [Editor's note.]
3. The deceptive apples of Sodom grow in the area of the Dead Sea in Israel and look edible but turn to dust if grasped.
4. French: No matter!
5. Novel by Miriam Coles Harris, published in 1860.

living for? What do you suppose your Creator gave you "good gifts" for? I have often wondered why you <u>did</u> <u>not</u> <u>write</u>—Of course you know you <u>could</u> if you would; and my darling you have <u>such</u> a glorious field stretching out before you. Your—nationality—; your grand ancestral rights, all of the sublime, that clusters around God's "<u>chosen</u> <u>people</u>."[6] Rachel write a Jewish tale; and make it a substratum on which to embroider your views of life, men, women, Art, Literature. You can do this: Give the world another Raphael Aben Ezra![7] Your surroundings and education have familiarized you with all the mystic points of your creed, and you might weave a tale of marvellous power. Understand me though, darling; literary women have trials that the world knows not of; are called on to make sacrifices whose incense floats not before the public; but Rachel, beloved, though our Sisterhood work in dark lonely corners, we have joys and encouragements peculiar to the vocation—I speak not now of mere <u>gratified</u> <u>ambition;</u> I point you to the nobler arm [*sic*] of doing <u>God's</u> <u>work.</u> There is a calm sweet reward, arising from the discharge of duty like this, such as no one can take from us. I have thought much of all this, and my deliberate conviction is, that while literary women as a class, are <u>not</u> <u>as</u> happy, as women who have Husbands and Children to engage their attention and monopolize their affections; yet in the faithful employment of their talents, they experience a deep peace and satisfaction, and are crowned with a glory such as marriage never gave. I have spoken of the two as antagonistic; I believe them to be so. No loving Wife and Mother can sit down and serve two Masters; Fame and Love. It is almost impossible. If you were happily married, I would say from the deeps [*sic*] of my heart—"Bless you dear Rachel; you are wise." But so long as you are not married, I wish you would <u>write</u>—<u>Do.</u> Now don't tell me you can't; Humbug! <u>Try</u> <u>Rachel</u> <u>try.</u> And now about my humble self. You "hear I am to marry soon"!!! You want to know about it; very natural you should. Rachel my darling; I may walk up the pyramids of Egypt, but I am not going to <u>marry</u> anybody. Do you believe me? Truly and solemnly my friend, <u>I</u> <u>am</u> <u>not</u> <u>engaged;</u> <u>nor</u> <u>shall</u> <u>I</u> <u>ever</u> <u>be.</u> What ever you may have heard, give it <u>no</u> <u>credit.</u> I am telling you the truth. You know I would not deceive you. I shall <u>live</u> and <u>die,</u> <u>Augusta</u> <u>Evans.</u> Write to me soon. Give me a <u>long</u> <u>letter.</u>

Your own
AJE

6. The Jews. Rachel was Jewish. [Editor's note.]

7. Aben-Ezra (1119–1194), a Spanish Jew and an eminent authority and commentator on the Scriptures. [Editor's note.]

Mobile Nov 15 1860

My dear Rachel—

. . . I have been particularly anxious to write to you, that I might tell you how exceedingly glad I was to learn from your last letter, that you <u>really</u> contemplated <u>writing.</u> Do persevere dear Rachel; let nothing discourage you; at all events make the attempt! Elaborate your plot, trace clearly to the end, your grand leading aim, before you write a <u>line</u> and then you will find no trouble I think, in weaving the details, arranging your—chiaroscuro—in fine—polishing the whole. Let me beg of you not to waver in this project; set to work, and your labor will gather wonderful charms for you. I know you <u>can write,</u> and I believe you will, if you only <u>once</u> set about it. Once [*sic*] thing more, be sure to <u>select</u> the <u>very</u> <u>highest</u> <u>types</u> of character for the standard has sadly deteriorated of late in works of fiction. In a too close imitation of <u>Nature</u> many of our novelists have fallen into the error of patronizing coarseness, vulgarity, and ignorance. I make this suggestion, because I think that it's [*sic*] truth is strikingly exemplified in "<u>Adam</u> <u>Bede</u>"[8] the <u>most</u> <u>popular</u> <u>book</u> of the age. The world needs <u>elevating</u> and it is the peculiar province of the Novelist to present the very highest <u>noblest</u> <u>types</u> of human nature. I know my dear Rachel you will not misunderstand my motive in making these affectionate suggestions, or think for one instant I presume to advise or dictate. I offer them as I would to one of my own sisters as the result of my own experience and observation. . . .

Source: A Southern Woman of Letters: The Correspondence of Augusta Jane Evans Wilson, ed. Rebecca Grant Sexton (2002)

8. Novel by George Eliot, published in 1859, which focuses on the lives of working-class characters and was influential in the development of realism. It also features an illegitimate birth and the mother's subsequent abandonment of the child.

⁊ ELIZABETH STODDARD (1823–1902)

Elizabeth Drew Barstow, born and raised in Mattapoisett, Massachusetts, was inspired not only to write but to strive for serious recognition by her husband, the poet and critic Richard Stoddard, and his circle of professional friends. With higher ambitions than most of the women writers she knew from the literary salons of New York City, she never gained the widespread appreciation that she craved, although reviewers compared her to Balzac, Hawthorne, and the Brontë sisters. By the time "Collected by a Valetudinarian" (1870), a story about a solitary woman committed to the pursuit of literary genius, was published, Stoddard had all but given up her hopes of gaining fame as a writer. She devoted more time to her son and husband while publishing occasional stories or poems. Her novels were republished to critical acclaim in the 1880s and 1890s, and Houghton Mifflin published a volume of her poetry in 1895. Nonetheless, she was again quickly forgotten until the 1980s, when Lawrence Buell and Sandra Zagarell rescued her from obscurity and republished her remarkable female Bildungsroman The Morgesons *(1862).*

The Poet's Secret

The poet's secret I must know,
　　If that will calm my restless mind.
I hail the seasons as they go,
　　I woo the sunshine, brave the wind.

I scan the lily and the rose,
　　I nod to every nodding tree,
I follow every stream that flows,
　　And wait beside the rolling sea.

I question melancholy eyes,
　　I touch the lips of women fair;
Their lips and eyes may make me wise,
　　But what I seek for is not there.

In vain I watch the day and night,
　　In vain the world through space may roll;
I never see the mystic light,
　　Which fills the poet's happy soul.

To hear through life a rhythm flow,
　　And into song its meaning turn—

The poet's secret I must know:—
   By pain and patience shall I learn?[1]

Source: Harper's New Monthly Magazine (1860)

Before the Mirror

Now, like the Lady of Shalott,[2]
   I dwell within an empty room,
And through the day, and through the night,
   I sit before an ancient loom.

And like the Lady of Shalott,
   I look into a mirror wide,
Where shadows come, and shadows go,
   And ply my shuttle as they glide.

Not as she wove the yellow wool,
   Ulysses's wife, Penelope;[3]
By day a queen among her maids,
   But in the night a woman, she,

Who, creeping from her lonely couch,
   Unraveled all the slender woof;
Or, with a torch, she climbed the towers,
   To fire the fagots on the roof!

But weaving with a steady hand,
   The shadows, whether false or true,

1. Altered final stanza from *Poems* (1895):
Through life I hear the rhythmic flow
   Whose meaning into song must turn;
Revealing all he longs to know,
   The secret each alone must learn.

2. The title character of Alfred Lord Tennyson's poem "The Lady of Shalott" (1833) is cursed to weave a magic web in a secluded tower and to view the outside world only through a mirror. When she leaves the tower in search of Sir Lancelot, whose image in the mirror she has fallen in love with, she dies. The figure summed up for many women writers the tension they felt between art and love.

3. Penelope, the wife of Homer's Odysseus, was also a weaver. She was known for her faithfulness during her husband's long travels. When other suitors came to her, assuming Odysseus was dead, she told them she would not decide until she was done making her father-in-law's shroud, which she wove during the day and unraveled each night.

I put aside a doubt which asks,
    "Among these phantoms what are you?"

For not with altar, tomb, or urn,
    Or long-haired Greek with hollow shield,
Or dark-prowed ship with banks of oars,
    Or banquet in the tented field;

Or Norman knight in armor clad,
    Waiting a foe where four roads meet;
Or hawk and hound in bosky dell,
    Where dame and page in secret greet;

Or rose and lily, bud and flower,
    My web is broidered. Nothing bright
Is woven here: the shadows grow
    Still darker in the mirror's light!

And as my web grows darker too,
    Accursed seems this empty room;
I know I must forever weave
    These phantoms by this hateful loom.

Source: Harper's New Monthly Magazine (1860)

Collected by a Valetudinarian[4]

Traveling this year in search of something lost, *i. e.,* health, and to appease a heart disquieted by grief, I revisited an old village on our sea-board for the first time in many years. Its mild and melancholy atmosphere accorded with my mood, and I determined to remain as long as the perturbed ghosts, my present rulers, would permit. The docks were empty, the wharves fallen to decay, the streets were bordered with burdock and plantain, and, for the most part, the houses looked as if life and thought had gone away:

> "Through the windows I might see
> The nakedness and vacancy
> Of the dark, deserted house."[5]

4. Person in ill health, an invalid.
5. Lord Alfred Tennyson, "The Deserted House" (1830).

At intervals an ox team dragged its slow length along the roads, or a dilapidated chaise rumbled by, or the butcher's cart rattled on. A child, a dog, a cat sometimes made themselves visible and brightened the scene; an occasional woman, shawl wrapped, now and then appeared; and a few men, either with or without business, moved here and there; a sailor, a carpenter, the doctor, an old man with a cane, and the young gentleman of the place in a smart dress and with a preoccupied air.

It was already May, warm enough on sunny days to go into the pastures where the anemone was blowing—spring's earliest flower this way—lovely with its feathery foliage and tinted blossom; and the stunted blue violet, just breaking through the cold, gray sod; curious grasses also were springing up beside the rivulets and ditches, almost flower-like in form and color. I engaged a room at the lonesome hotel—with an ignominious rear and an imposing Doric or Corinthian front—which was managed by Mr. Binks, a retired stage-driver. As I settled my belongings I attempted to make myself cheerful by recalling early associations, and testing them in a philosophical crucible. However old *I* had grown, and whatever *my* past had been, surely the material universe must have remained the same as of yore, and it ought to prove a resource to the seeker. I remembered the words of a sad and sensitive writer, Châteaubriand. "It is," he said "a natural instinct of the unhappy to seek to recall visions of happiness by the remembrance of their past pleasures. When I feel my heart dried up by intercourse with other men I turn away and give a sigh of regret to the past. It is in the midst of the immense forests of America that I have tasted to the full these enchanting meditations, these secret and ineffable delights of a mind rejoicing in itself. When I have found myself alone in an ocean of forests a change took place in me. I said, 'Here there are no more roads to follow, no more towns, no narrow houses, no presidents, no republics, or kings; above all, no more laws and no more men.' "[6]

Though neither oak nor maple leaf was unfolded, and the boughs were thin and brown, I could lose myself in the pine woods, which gave the northern part of the country a verdant, grand, and solitary expression. How well I knew them and their sand barrens, where were found arrow-heads, and the Indian skulls which premeditated them! I fondly wished for all the books written on solitude, retirement, communion with nature, and upon that text which the medieval Balzac calls *"Hide your life."* It was he who said, so ingeniously, that when he had any auditors about him he cried with all his might: "Let us go and live in the country; not only to make sure of rest, but also to make sure of salvation. Let us seek Jesus Christ in the way that He himself has directed us. He did not say that He was the gold of the

---

6. Quote from François-Auguste-René de Chateaubriand (1768–1848), published as here translated with the title "A Night Among the Savages in America" in *Half-Hours With the Best French Authors* (1867).

palace, the purple of the court. He said that He was the flower of the field, and the lily of the valley." 7

Who has written better on solitude, and the pleasures of the past, than the true Parisian authors—the fops and rakes of fashion and the court?

But I brought no books; indeed a bookish reminiscence was a resuscitation, for it had been months since I had read a printed page.

Yes, I had chosen the right spot; neither laws nor men could trouble a solitary stranger. Of the present generation inhabiting the village of course I knew nothing. Feeling as I did, it was no regret that my contemporaries had passed away. The very house I was in proved that every body who might have any knowledge of me was either dead or moved into some other place. It had been built and occupied by a family with which my own had been connected in a commercial way. As a child I had visited the old family. The house was worse than a ruin now, in my opinion, for it had been "fixed up" by a vulgar taste, which dictated monstrosities in form and color; scroll patterns every where in red and yellow. Happily my room, on one side of the house, had not been retouched; the old paper was on the walls, a satin gray with pink dots, and the chimney-place had not been bricked up according to modern fashion for an ugly stove. Mr. Binks was astonished at my choice of a room, and still more astonished when I proposed having a wood-fire. Nobody had wood-fires in the whole place, he insisted. I persisted; I wanted to watch the blaze, and I wanted to arrange and disarrange the sticks and brands at my own good pleasure and that of the tongs.

"A willful woman must have her way," he said; "and I expect you are sick, and maybe won't stay long." So he gave way, and made my room cheerful with birch and hickory fires, and after a little owned that it was the neatest spot in the house.

"It's dreadful dull out the window here," he remarked. "A crow or a robin is all you'll see."

"Swallows, and the grass, and the sky over the fields, also, Mr. Binks, and the three tall pines yonder."

"Well, I'll give up! You are too much for me, marm; them 'ere pines are about as aged as any thing since the flood."

All necessity for exertion being over, no demand of any sort to be made upon me, I fell into a lethargy; thought nothing and felt nothing for several days; dozed over my fire, or stared vacantly at the fields. Mr. Binks had a housekeeper; but she remained in the dark and backward abysm of the kitchen, and he waited upon me with a magisterial air which dignified the tray he brought to my door three times a day, with a kind, set little speech.

"Here is your meal, marm; may you relish it! The weather is softening; the wind is milder—more favorable for invalids. Sartinly you will be round by to-morrow."

---

7. Jean-Louis Guez de Balzac (ca. 1597–1654). Quotation as here translated was published as "On Retirement" in *Half-Hours With the Best French Authors* (1867).

At last I did get round; that is, I crept down stairs, and Mr. Binks dragged his housekeeper into the parlor to look at me.

"Didn't I say so, Mary Jane? Ain't she down stairs? She hasn't died on my hands, has she?"

"Mr. Binks," said Mary Jane, "always looks on the bright side of things, and you must excuse him."

If he was glad to have me down stairs, he was more rejoiced to have me sit at his table. There, to my surprise, I discovered another boarder, who bore a shadowy resemblance to myself, inasmuch as she was dressed in mourning, and looked delicate and feeble. When she saw a purpose of introduction in Mr. Binks's eye, she fluttered and turned her head, but in vain. In a loud voice he said:

"This is Mrs. Hobson; been with me, off and on, nigh to six years—haven't you, Mrs. Hobson?—and going all the time."

"Yes, Mr. Binks," she answered, gently inclining her head toward me, with a twinkle of humor in her eyes.

"Birds of a feather flock together," added Mr. Binks. "By your looks I conclude you have them 'ere mysterious complaints which make women so unaccountable. My wife was the same; first and last, she cost me a couple of hundred in patent medicines. She would try every individual one."

Mrs. Hobson and I exchanged looks, and both of us laughed; the laugh melted the frost between us, and we became friends. Take her for all in all, she was the most self-contained, heroic, patient creature I ever knew. She had come to that pass in life when nothing comes from nothing; consequently she reconstructed trifles into matters which filled up the hours—those slow serpents to people who have exhausted or lived out all illusion and enchantment. She had learned, she told me, to be more interested in a flower-pot than in a garden; to derive more satisfaction in the chairs and tables in her own room than she had formerly felt in setting up a whole house.

"Every small thing tells," she said, "when one becomes isolated; the soul comes out of it under observation. As for change, that which is good for us we have; it is in the atmosphere—its storms and sunshine; in the sky—its sunrise and sunset, its trailing clouds of glory and of gloom. In the sea too—so fixed and ever-varying."

Mrs. Hobson never told me her history; I never asked it. Having no wish to reveal mine, why should I demand hers? Mr. Binks, uneducated as he was, and as native as an oyster to the place which gave him birth, was delicate and refined in his care of her. He told me, soon after I made her acquaintance, that if ever there was a saint upon earth, she was one; that when she died she ought to have a monument equal to Washington's; that she had come to his house in the dead of winter, accompanied by a young man he thought to be a lawyer's clerk, and a great deal of baggage. In conclusion, he said: "Mrs. Sinclair, marm, I expect you have guessed I am an inquisitive man, but I never asked Mrs. Hobson a question, and I am never going to. She is as good as gold, and as sick as Lazarus.[8] I don't mean that she has any irruption, for she hasn't. She gives fifty dollars every New-Year's to the poor, and pays me every Saturday, reg'lar as clock-work. She has property here."

When I began to ramble about the country, Mrs. Hobson accompanied me. She professed gratitude for an opening in her accustomed ways; the small area of wood and field surrounding the village she had never explored. I taught her the names and habits of wild flowers; how to gather and preserve various delicate plants, and how to watch the various and minute laws which are opened to the eye of the student in the book of Nature, which I had learned from *ennui*. It was "Eliza" and "Helen" between us soon. One day, when perhaps infected by my enthusiasm at the discovery in the woods of a fragrant and delicious flower, she said:

"Eliza, you should have known my cousin Alicia Raymond. Of all the persons I ever knew, you might have understood and aided her. I am foolish that I have never told you the chief reason of my coming to this wild place after my widowhood. Here for some years lived, and died, a woman of genius. Behind yonder point on which stands the lighthouse is an old house, belonging to me now, where she lived. To-morrow we will go there."

"Alicia Raymond! surely I have heard the name. Is she not in some literary complication [*sic*]—a book of the time—or literary dictionary?"

"I dare say; her father, Commodore Raymond, was proud of her, and published some of her childish performances. His house was frequented by all the distinguished people of his time; but when he died she was forgotten. Talk about Chatterton and Keats[9]—if they did not live in their lifetime, they do now, while Alicia's memory only exists in mine and that of her brother. Mr. Binks continually says, one half the world does not know how the other half lives. I say, what a mockery the life of genius is! What half of a community knows it? What does even the nearest neighboring soul know of it?"

Helen's passion astonished me. A hectic flush rose in her cheek, and she gesticulated with vehemence.

"It is all luck," she cried. "After old Brontë had lived a starving life—and God knows what his wife passed through in suffering, aspiration, and contemplation!—and after the daughters had starved every way—most of all, starved for Beauty—fame came to them. Eliza, what a tragedy was the life of Charlotte Brontë![10] Do you

---

8. In the parable of Lazarus and Dives (Luke 16: 19–31), the beggar Lazarus is covered with sores, hence the reference to "irruption," and is rewarded for his sufferings with eternal life in heaven, while the rich man (Dives) goes to hell.

9. John Keats (1795–1821) and Thomas Chatterton (1752–1770) were often invoked as examples of poetic geniuses who suffered the neglect of their contemporaries.

10. Elizabeth Gaskell's *The Life of Charlotte Brontë* (1857) had popularized the story of the Brontë sisters as geniuses who suffered the deprivations of a restricted country life. Stoddard was moved by Gaskell's biography and wrote about it in her *Daily Alta California* column.

know that I have a scrap of her handwriting? She did not have paper enough to scribble on—think of that! But I am convinced, from my own experience in this narrowish way of life, where there is nothing which may be called rank, where no one possesses fortune, where all the paraphernalia of living is limited to that which supplies bread and clothing, that this gifted woman, Alicia, discerned a world of beauty and truth that made an everlasting happiness for her great soul, as did Charlotte Brontë."

"Dear Helen, how shall we idlers be taught this ideal happiness?"

"As soon as we can be made to believe that what is called material or positive happiness is no more truthful or exact than that named visionary or romantic happiness."

Mr. Binks, without being aware of a sense of the comic, called us a "game pair," when he met us strolling the by-roads; and so we were to the ordinary eye, for who would have guessed that any fire burned in our ashes? We were a couple of faded, middle-aged women, clad in black garments. Why should such indulge in aspirations for happiness, or the expectation of doing any farther work in this gay world?

In a day or two after Helen's mention of Alicia Raymond, on a calm, sombre afternoon, we took our way toward the light-house.

"We will go," said Helen, simply, "to the house Alicia last lived in. She gave it to me; the spot, worthless as it is, has chained me; the ground about it is barren; nobody would think of bringing it under cultivation, for it is a mixture of swamp and sandy beach; mullein, briers, sedge, and the beach pea dispute pre-eminence. Suppose, Eliza"—and Helen brightened at the thought—"that you and I should occupy the house?"

"But we should have to leave out the genius which has made such an impression upon you, and, I confess, upon me also. I have a lively curiosity concerning this Alicia and her surroundings."

We toiled in silence among the coarse pebbles of the beach, and climbed over the boulders scattered here and there on our way. The village grew distant, and the landscape solitary; on the left were swampy pastures, wild thickets, and borders of desolate woods; on the right, the wide bay, with distant headlands and islands uprising in the air. The waves came from afar, spent in their sounding fury, and fell in soft foam round the rocks and the pale smooth sand. The beautiful sea-swallow hovered near us, uttering its wild cry, and the little sand birds ran fearlessly before us.

"No wonder she lived here, Helen!"

"I knew you would like the scene; we are almost there—see!"

We had turned the point now on which the light-house stood, and I saw a large old-fashioned house standing in the middle of a natural lawn; two or three cherry-trees were in front of it, and a few fir-trees, indigenous to the soil, twisted and gnarled, but vigorous, were scattered over it. Helen took a key from her pocket as we went up a little path.

"How thick the butter-cups are!" she said, gayly; but I saw that she was deeply moved.

"Yes," I replied; "and the woodpecker is busy also; look at the hole under the eaves by the window-frame! How rank the flags are by the granite step! the ugly things flourish every where. No matter what happens, year after year their dull yellow flowers vulgarly blow."

"Year after year," she repeated, turning the key and opening the door. "So uniform was Alicia's life that it seemed eternal till it came to an end; then it was like a vision. Come in now; you will not see bats nor owls, for after a while it became my recreation to keep the house in order. I have given it sun and air; in the summer I pass half my time here. Has it not an occupied air?"

It was a plain common house; on one side a small parlor, on the other a large one. There was little furniture in either room. A table, a few chairs, book-cases with wide gaps in the shelves, a sofa, a desk, and some portraits on the dingy walls of literary people. I was surprised, however, to see the excellence of said portraits—Raeburn's Scott, Holmes's portrait of Byron—the one Byron himself preferred—Severn's portrait of Keats, a fine engraving of George Sand by Calomme,[11] one of the young Mozart, one of the boy Chatterton, and a few delightful water-colors.

"Do you mean to say," I asked, "that your friend Alicia was perfectly obscure?"

"Except to a few men and women of letters with whom she corresponded. Look over this desk, please; you may comprehend her taste. She *was* happy without fame, I believe."

"I might take her life for a text, and preach a sermon for these crusading days, when women assume so much, and so ardently desire that every assumption should be made public."

"Do so, if you dare. Every day of Alicia's life was made beautiful for the sake of beauty. She taxed all things for this purpose. A bit of moss, a bird's feather, an autumn leaf, a spray of grass served her. Her means went far to suit her artistic habits and tastes. She lived here six years in all. Her only brother returned from the East Indies with an obstinate disease, and was ordered to pass a year or two in the country. He selected this, where his mother was born."

"This desk is curious," I said; "have you examined it?"

"Only in a general way; but look over it. I think, now, I'll give up the place,

---

11. Scottish Romantic painter Henry Raeburn (1756–1823) produced portraits of the Scottish author Sir Walter Scott (1771–1832) in 1808, 1809, and 1823. English artist James Holmes (1777–1860) made a miniature portrait of Byron in 1815. English painter Joseph Severn (1793–1879) produced many portraits of Keats. The portrait of George Sand (1804–1876) was perhaps the one the *New York Times* credited to the Italian engraver Luigi Calamatta (1802–1869) and called "the best portrait of George Sand, in the dress of a man" (Feb. 25, 1890).

having been long enough sentimental over it; and it is a trouble to fight with mould and moth."

I opened some little drawers; they were full of nick-nacks, ivory boxes, ornaments in agate and marble, pearl and shell carvings, paper-knives, gypsum figures, clay vases and boxes, Chinese toys, bits of fine china, engravings, and a hundred other articles. One of the prettiest was a green crystal basket in a gold frame. A minute nest was in the basket, and several rose-colored eggs with chocolate spots; a bit of paper was tied to the handle, on which was written—"Robbed May 20, '64."

"They were a queer couple, this brother and sister," said Helen.

Poking into the deep pigeon-holes of the ancient desk, I came upon a book with a brass lock; it was fastened, but on the cover was printed with a pen:

"He who does not run may read."[12]

"Where is the key, Helen?"

"I have it, and you may read the diary; I never have. Let us go back, it is nightfall nearly. Mr. Binks thinks my mind is unsettled about this house; he will come for us with a lantern if we wait."

As we walked slowly homeward, Helen gave me some particulars of her cousin's life. If she had a mania, it was for composition; there were several manuscript volumes in existence, upon which months of labor had been bestowed. Her literary habits were as industrious and methodical as if her work had the market value of a Thackeray or a Dickens.[13] But she had the most self-contained, self-sustaining soul that ever existed, requiring neither praise nor appreciation to feed an ambition perfectly pure and lofty in its aims. If she had lived, she might have given her work to the world.

"Look over the little diary by yourself," Helen said, while we were at our supper, and beamed upon by the genial Binks. In my room I opened Alicia's volume, and soon felt its fresh, natural atmosphere.

April 22, 1864.[14]—House on the beach at Bront's Point just taken possession of by Brother Alton and myself, in the township where our beautiful mother died in our childhood. Nothing threatens recollection of our last city campaign. One Julia—sweet girl—may enter into *his* dreams; *my* vision will be disturbed by no apparition of tulle, Neapolitan ice-cream, or the waltz band. I know he left the pretty creature to be with me. Ten rooms, up stairs and down, every one shabby and

12. Hab. 2:2. "And the LORD answered me, and said, Write the vision, and make it plain upon tables, that he may run that readeth it." Often quoted to refer to literature that may be read easily and quickly, and thus is popular or widely disseminated. Alicia is saying the opposite about her diary.

13. English novelists William Makepeace Thackeray (1811–1863) and Charles Dickens (1812–1870) were among the most prolific and famous writers of their era.

14. Alicia's journal entries were adapted from Stoddard's own journal.

delightful. The rude lawn is full of clover and blooming grasses, and under the lonely stone walls, old as Adam, nicest brambles grow. We pulled down the paling this afternoon before the front of the house. Put up our Mexican hammock between the door and cherry-tree. Such a pretty view from said hammock: the lawn running to the beach, which is smooth, for it is the edge of the cove rounding in between two gravelly points, and looks quite lake-like; near the shore it is blue and smooth, when outside it is gray and rough under the beating winds.

The waves curve in and fall upon the sand, leaving soft bubbles and silky weeds, bits of drift-wood, snowy and silvery shells, and all the mysterious *débris* of the sea, daily tossed upon a hundred shores by the relentless tide. On each side of this secluded, fairy-like cove are groups of richly stained rocks. Above all this sea and shore I can watch the sunrise and sunset. But what civilized being ever sees a sunrise? The room with windows commanding this view I have named my own—this where I at this moment am. Funny gray paper on the walls, with sepia pictures—elegant fox-hunters on high-bred horses, hounds, whippers-in, a pleasant wood, and an impossible fountain. I have hung red curtains before the windows, and filled the mantel-piece with Indian china; matting is laid upon the floor, and the furniture is covered with Alton's Indian chintz—peacocks, parrots, birds of paradise, all so lively that I expect them to scream at any moment. A wood-fire burns in the chimney; Alton sits on the brick hearth beside it, a novel in his hand, his booted legs crossed, and he tugs at his mustache perfectly abstracted. "*Julia,*" I cry, from some impulse of mischief. He starts, drops his book, and says:

"Confound you, Alicia! Is she at the shutters? I thought I heard a woman whimper."

"It is only the water lapping the shore, Alton; better music than that of a woman's tongue."

"Shut yours, then, and go on with your pen. Its scratching is an opiate. I dare say what you write would prove a sleeping-draught to your reader."

Alton picks up his book, rustles a page or two, then lights a cigar, and resumes his musings. As I scribble on he rouses once more, winking his long black eyelashes, and says:

"Sis Alicia, literary people, after all, are only coral worms. It takes a million to make a little reef in the ocean."

"But the reef is there, Alton."

"Yes; and how much drifts to the patient minute structure!—weeds; all the refuse of the violence of the deep; weary sea-birds, with seeds of plants in their crops; the tangle of strong currents from pole to pole—and a world is made! I have half a mind to call you Coralline."

"Go to bed, my boy, or how shall I ever write a proper description of this house!"

"I'll go, my love, and snore to the breakers of Bront's Point. The air is superb coming through the shattered panes. And I shall be so hungry in the morning. What have you in the larder?"

"Nothing; I will watch for a fisherman."

Exit Alton with a grimace and loud yawn. Yes, this room suits me—at midnight—the present hour. Here is my new patent inkstand, which promises to be a failure, and a paper-weight with a bird on it unlike any known species of bird, and my comfortable port-folio under the shaded lamp. I have filled up the china closet with illustrated books. Their gold, red, and green backs glisten behind the glass door. What friends they are! A dead author is better than a live friend: the one can not change nor fail, the other may. Rogers, Gray, Bloomfield, Goldsmith, Béranger,[15] Tennyson, my goodly company! The last brand has fallen on the hearth, and the white ashes cover the coals. The bay gives tongue under the moon. A journal is a good thing—to express that which is neither in the heart nor brain! By-the-way, in rummaging my brain to-day I believe that I thanked God for suddenly feeling virile; I mean that I emerged from my fog. Why is Alton tramping overhead? Pooh! what is the feeling of a restless heart?

April 28.—East wind. The chimneys have smoked. We had trout for dinner to-day. Alton caught them in a brook a mile above us, on the other side of the high hill at the back of the house, where the sun seems to sit down and rags of clouds gather and hide. Spying inside and outside of myself for the fashion of my novel. The hero is vital. What name can I give him—Greek, Oriental, or English? Cleon, Hafiz, John! Come, let me clutch thee! Lonely old town this. Nobody comes to see us; evidently there is no social system in vogue. Somebody went by, though, to-day—a man with a horse, cart, and pitchfork; all went over our lawn straight to the beach. When I saw his purpose—that of gathering sea-weed—I went out and helped him; that is, I poked over the long green ribbons dashed up by the tide, and discovered shelly creatures on their first voyage from home, bright and smooth pebbles, and umber tufts of fat weeds. I hope Helen Hobson will visit us soon. So much of society as she can give I require.

I laid the diary down and sought Helen.

"I have left off at the mention of your name, Helen."

"Do you wonder at my permitting you to read a private record? I shrink from it. Will you go through with it? Since you came I have decided to settle my affairs so far as that old place is concerned. When Alicia's papers are looked over and every thing removed, I will sell the house. When you leave the town I will go also, for I can no longer endure it. We will not precisely play Naomi and Ruth,[16] but I trust we may not live far apart."

15. English writers Samuel Rogers (1763–1855), Thomas Gray (1716–1771), Robert Bloomfield (1766–1823), Oliver Goldsmith (1730–1774), and French poet Pierre Jean de Béranger (1780–1857).

16. In the Book of Ruth in the Old Testament, Ruth is Naomi's daughter-in-law. When Ruth's husband dies, she refuses to return to her own mother and devotes herself to Naomi.

"What about the brother Alton?"

"He will never return here. Nothing could induce him to look at any thing which might remind him of the lost Alicia, the sister he loved so wonderfully well. The delay is owing to him. Many letters have passed between us on the subject of Alicia's papers and possessions, and the house which she gave me. He has refused over and over again to have any thing to do with them, and at last, thanks to you, I have decided for myself. Read the fragmentary journal, and then give me your opinion whether any of her manuscript should be published."

"I should not imagine her a solitary or eccentric person from the little I have read."

"She was alive and at home with every thing except human companionship; but I never understood her."

"I dare say; no one understood her. Have you thought of that as a reason for her isolation? What should drive one into solitude, if a lack of comprehension of one's sincerest feelings and motives can not? And then, what strange modes of expression pride of soul will take! There are those, even in this jostling, crowded world, whose virgin hearts take alarm at the least approach to or necessity for revelation. They wait for some other world to be developed in—some unknown deity to govern them. I like this Alicia; she has her own atmosphere. Maybe I am sent here to be aided by her."

Helen's eyes glistened.

"Be, then," she exclaimed, "my atonement. Your mind is nearer hers than my futile, vacillating one was. Alicia is one of my dearest memories. Teach me to hope that she forgave me for every shortcoming of obtuseness, ignorance, and habit. What wretchedly imperfect, unfinished creatures we are! The flood did not wash us right, after all."

Some occult influence led me the next calm, cloudy afternoon to the old house by the sea, Alicia's home. I was glad to be alone. The grass on the lawn waved me a welcome; butter-cups glistened in it; bees and butterflies hummed and hovered every where. The wind sounded a fitful melody round the eaves, and shook the tall cherry-trees before the door. I had Alicia's diary with me. Taking a seat on the granite gate-sill, I opened it; as I read, shadows flickered over the page, the wind fluttered the leaves, stalks and unripe cherries fell into my lap, and birds constantly twittered over my head. I was Alicia, or I was the dream of myself—which? I looked toward the vague, blue horizon where land and water blended, and should not have been surprised to see a colossal reflection of either uprising in the distance.

May 6.—My birthday. Alicia, the child of an unhappy mother, is twenty-eight to-day. Sho! The gray water laps the paler sand, glimmers and trembles; the purple clouds glide by. Insidious Spirit of Beauty, dark or bright, you lurk every where.

May 8.—Poor fellow! his grave is nameless. So shall mine be.

May 10.—Happy again under this sky, before this sea. Is happiness atmospheric? Read Victor Hugo's novel, "The Toilers of the Sea." A Greek poem in French. Greek—a little distracted.

May 15.—Happier perhaps for being wrapped in a cloud of illness. Civilized people for the most part have nurses when they are ill. The black woman in the kitchen does not care for me, and while I suffer Alton stays in the woods. There is a deep frown on his face; I know what it means. He does not know how to approach me.

June 3.—I am gay. A box of books came to-day. So much good reading in so much good solitude. I see why Alton likes "Faith Unwin."[17] The lonely, pathetic, simple tenor of human feeling suits him. Alas! why and for what should I torture my genius? Let it be in its afrite[18] box—small, neat, compact. It need not rise in a cloud of smoke and assume in some kindred imaginative mind shape and meaning.

June 10.—I watched the road for Helen Hobson this morning. She did not come. Walked out and picked field flowers, so gay now every where.

June 11.—Helen came with a pair of amethyst ear-rings for me, a sketch by M'Entee[19]—so like my friend—a bower of trees, a glimpse of blue, and a solitary wanderer beneath the boughs. Art is better than nature. We talked, at first, about newspapers and religion. Helen ate a great deal. Next day we "parted at the gates of Ispahan"[20]—that is, Alton drove us to the railway station, six miles away. He made us swallow a mouthful of whisky from his flask, and muttered something which made Helen color. I did not understand him; but a moment after I discovered tears on my face. Suppose I was intoxicated. Heavens! What does it all mean? Are we wretched? What are we playing at, in this mechanical way? Shadows over the scene—death-ripples, gliding over the surface so glassy and hard! All forgetfulness must be intoxication.

June 12.—Summer drops in for a few hours on our bleak coast daily. Threw stones into the water to-day. Saw in the sand vermilion spiders, and black, swift-gaited ones. The blue scentless violet still blooms near the dead sea-weed, and the vivid yellow cinque-foil. Read the cook-book. Dashed into the opening of my novel. First line—very striking: "*On an autumn morning—*"

June 20.—I like old boggy fields. The sweetest flowers grow there, the greenest moss; there birds congregate, and the frog doth flourish. I brought home from said bogginess a bunch of delicious white violets, and put them to Alton's nose. He was lying in the hammock, with his hat pulled over his eyes. He caught my hands, and drew my face to his.

17. *Faith Unwin's Ordeal* (1865), popular novel by Georgiana Marion Craik (1831–1895).
18. Evil demon in Muslim mythology.
19. American landscape painter Jervis McEntee (1828–1891).
20. Ispahan, or Esfahan, is a province in central Iran as well as Iran's third largest city.

"Alicia, my love, how are you? Tell me, do you suffer?

"One way, yes; two ways, no. And how are you, master?"

"Bored one way; two ways, no."

"How handsome you are, my dear!"

"Ain't I? Bring out the big looking-glass, quick!"

He kept my violets; where they went to I could not discover. No letters have come to him. Where is that heartless girl? Pooh! She is not heartless.

June 21.—The sea is awfully full to-night. "It runneth here, it runneth there,"[21] crowding round all the points, pressing up every pier, and wave kisses wave. Read "Tom Cringle's Log"[22]—a first-rate nautical novel.

June 27.—Telegram scared us to-day. Alton is summoned to the city upon some Indian business. He looked so wistfully at me when he came for a good-by that I said, "See Julia, by all means, and give her my love."

"Can you love her?" he asked, eagerly.

"I'll try."

"You never will, Alicia; I am a fool to ask it."

Cried, and made a beautiful loaf of cake after he left. Then fell to reading. Wordsworth is a good doctor for the mind.

June 28.—It struck me just now that I should never be happier. I am alone with my own power. What I decide to be, that I am for myself. So long as I am solitary, how can I be convicted of error? Last night I sat in Alton's deserted room and watched the orange sunset waning slow. The moon rose, and I saw spectral sails gliding down the bay and vanishing beyond a range of purple cloud. The sea grew wild as the moon rode up the sky; its tumult filled the air. Nothing in nature can be finer than these scenes in these hours. From nature, went to Wordsworth[23] again; he is a teacher, as many painters and musicians are.

July 1.—Droning on my novel with faith and a tormented conscience. Shall I dare tell the truth about men and women? Can any wild invention excuse me for bringing to light that which exists with reason and with passion? Who may speak if I can not? I fear not my un-born publisher. No feat of my mind can deprive me of the fixed income which provides me bread; nothing can separate me from my sole living love—Alton—nothing from my sole friendship with Helen Hobson. As for opinion, criticism, admirers, enemies—how can I be reached *here,* or farther on— the grave? One may be egotistical on waste paper, as this is; and I assert that I have an experience in the life of love, enjoyment, and suffering which, frankly expressed and described, should teach timid and ignorant hearts their capacities and their

21. From a poem about how man stumbles blindly through life in *Sunday Acrostics. Selected From Names or Words in the Bible* (1867) by Eliza Ogilvy (1822–1912), a friend of Robert and Elizabeth Barrett Browning.

22. Novel by Scottish writer Michael Scott (1789–1835), published in 1829–1833.

23. William Wordsworth (1770–1850), English Romantic poet.

limits. Have I the power? Shall I build better than I know, if I go on? *On,* I mean so; but must leave my pen and paper behind me, then.

July 2.—My woodland walks are perfect now. The lady's-slipper is blooming above the pine needles; its pink-veined hanging bells, between two pointed green leaves, looked so pretty in the dry underbrush this afternoon. I dreamed away several hours under an aged, flat-topped yellow pine; the air was indescribably delicious; every time I looked about me found some new flower, among them the dwarf Solomon's-seal—an emerald, grooved leaf, with tiny dots of white flowers on the tiny stalk. Numerous grasses are in bloom, attractive in form, and dull, delicate in shade. Came home and found Alton drinking claret out of the pale Bohemian glasses, that is, one glass. Talk about writing novels and speaking the truth! Here we two were together, kindred souls at that, in utter ignorance of each other's moods and circumstances, having been parted a day or two, and as shy as strangers.

"Where have you been, Alicia?"

"In the woods."

"You mean tree woods?"

"Yes; the breezy, aromatic, uninterfering woods."

"Go with me now there; sunset will not come off this two hours. Besides, there is no more beautiful moment than that when the sun's last rays drop below the level trunks. The birds sing their even song; and the insects, creatures of night, begin their oratorio. Then, for greeting, too, the shrubs send up odors to mingle with the flying crimson clouds."

So we started. I continually said to myself, "Poor moth, glow-worm, vain-banging beetle, seeking the light and prating about novels!" Whatever Alton's thoughts were, he showed no disturbance, looked from right to left, and at last said, "Hist, hush!" We stood still, and presently heard the whir of wings and stifled chirps.

"Come out of the path, under the scrub oaks," he said; "it is dry. Here is the moss, with its red eyes. See here, with such things in it, Alicia, the world is pretty."

I looked into a holly-bush, as he directed, and close to the ground was a thrush's nest—four little chocolate-colored birds in it. The father and mother, with square cinnamon tails, kept near us, with distressing cries.

July 6.—Read Emerson, who makes apparent the originality of other authors. Read the "Simon" of George Sand.[24] Her case gives me despair. I was alone in to-night's deepening dusk, still and unoccupied; the walls of an invisible, fearful destiny I felt to be slowly closing round me. The cold gray sea, monotonously roaring, typified it. Horrible existence, now serene enough to contemplate inevitable death.

July 8.—The tissue complains to the brain. One's organs will not be subservient

24. Ralph Waldo Emerson (1803–1882), Transcendentalist philosopher. *Simon* (1836), a novel by Sand.

to intellectual action. They shall be, though. Wish I could get some black ink. Made a raid in the shops on Main Street for it, and that put me in better spirits. Saw blue yarn, eggs, but no ink. Lighted on a piece of lovely chintz, and bought it for Alton's windows.

July 10.—Two military officers arrived. Wore my violet grenadine and black lace. Alton's eyes beamed when I came in to dinner. Had roasted chickens, and the gold brand Champagne. The ice was slightly troubled with roots. Wondered whether they were the filaments of the Arethusa pink, or the adder's-tongue. Officers talked about icebergs being at the north yet. Also cursed war movements. Ate up all the dinner. Smoked terribly, and went away with inane compliments.

July 18.—"My days go on." No motive for writing. The moth-millers distract me. The beetles fly about greatly o' nights also. Full-blooded summer swells the sea and is in my veins. Let me sew a womanly seam. Who am I to summon giants? I remember a fine, sacred soul—vanished. He had the best of mine, yet left me. Eternally my heart is his. How frail and rapid my memorials recalling him—the western wind blowing after sunset, when the sky is still emerald and amber, and distant shrub and flowers send their odors to me, when the white water is motionless, and the crescent moon gives me silvered beams, where we often were, Arnold and I.

July 20.—The fields are wonderful, a mass of white, yellow, and blue blossoms in the deep, waving beds of green. Alton makes my heart ache. His eye passes me by, even when his smile is most pleasant, his voice most kind. Somebody sent me a bunch of white roses to-day. A friend came unexpectedly. Alton is playing cards with him in the east room. I saw this friend for the first time in November last. What is he here for? I wish I could fall in love with him. It might amuse us this summer weather.

Two hours afterward.

"Sir—Mr. Dresden," I asked, "do cards amuse you?"

"Not in the least. I came all these miles to see your ladyship, and your indifference is killing."

"So I was afraid. I wish to make amends, and beg you to talk to me. Alton, go away. Leave Mr. Dresden and myself together. I am forgetting human beings, among all these waves, grass, and insects."

Shrugging his shoulders, and giving a pitying smile to Dresden, he sauntered off, candle in hand.

Mr. Dresden and I looked at each other and laughed.

"Tell and teach me, Miss Alicia," he begged. "I am but a baby of thirty-five, you know. You can mention insects."

"I am old too. Look at my hair."

With sudden passion he kissed the band on my forehead.

"Oh, Alicia, do not be such a heavenly icicle. What can I do to please you? Give up your dreadful isolation, or let me share it with you. Come; let me carry your camp-stool and your umbrella. I'll mend your pens to my dying day, learn bot-any—any thing. Or, better—" and here he caught my hands—"come out into my world, be my wife! Don't you know that my father has lately left me a large fortune? Alton knows it. I have his best wishes. We three shall never separate. I love you, Alicia. I am worthy even you."

"What! Does Alton know that you would marry me? Will he give me away?"

"No away about it. Visionary, Quixotic[25] girl, yes! My love, let us go to the Old World, cities whose legends enchant you, to the birth-place of the genius you worship, the cradle of the arts you revere."

Oh, the pictures that flashed across my soul as he spoke the glowing vision of life without being aware of it! I put my hand in his; he saw tears in my eyes.

"Alton!" he shouted.

Instantly, like a ghost, Alton stood in the doorway.

"Do you mean for me to marry Dresden?" I asked.

"I mean that you shall do as you choose to do," he answered, stamping his foot. "But I like Dresden; he is good, strong."

"I can not die abroad. Somehow I can not fall in love, either. I wished most seriously to love you, Mr. Dresden. What's the matter with me? I *am* fond of you. But you must leave me."

"Alicia, you are a fool!" said Alton. "Come away, Dresden."

"Not I; I intend to talk with Alicia; you can take leave again of me. I begin to understand your sister."

And we did talk deep into the night. I like him better, much better; but what would become of my literary career? A strong man's love must interfere with my hero; and my heroine might interfere with him.

July 23.—He has gone. I feel free. What a perfect sunset we had!—purple drifts, crimson bars suffusing the sea, and then grew clearest light in the sky, with Venus, red and diamond-pointed, beside the young moon. I found to-day a great lunar moth sticking to a bush; splendid creature; hid him in my handkerchief, brought him home, administered chloroform, and pinned him on the curtain.

"Poor Dresden," said Alton, who was watching me.

"Kiss me, brother dear; I am lonely."

He complied, and then heaved a sigh. I continued:

"It need make no difference to you—"

Alton put his hand over my mouth.

"Hush! the lunar is kicking still, Alicia."

July 30.—Brought home a bunch of the wax-like flowers of the round-leafed winter-green. It has a penetrating odor, resembling that of the tuberose. More than "the glory in the grass, the splendor in the flower,"[26] I long for; their beauty suggests

25. Not practical, pursuing unrealistic dreams.
26. Slightly misquoted from Wordsworth's "Ode: Intimations of Immortality" (1807).

that which I require. The evening is profoundly quiet; the shield of the full moon shines in the water. Alton is floating upon it; I see the sail of his boat on the edge of the moon's wake, where the water is dark; the sail is motionless. I am going out to walk—have had the heartache before in moonlight nights, and out-of-doors too. After a while my heart will be uplifted; something from the mysterious stars, far off as they are in the void, will come down to my aid.

August 1.—Gathered fresh immortelles to-day from the sand-banks between here and Gilford. Filled Arnold's glass—the one he drank from last—which I keep by me always. Arnold! Why should I dream of other love, either in speaking or writing? By-the-way, Alton and I have read six novels this week, full of conventional white-kid love.

August 21.—Blank to me, and all out-of-doors looked blank.

September 3.—Dog-days.

Goethe says: "The highest problem of every art is, by means of appearances, to produce the illusion of a loftier reality. That is, however, a false effort which, in giving reality to the appearance, goes so far as to leave in it nothing but the common everyday actual."[27] Wordy, this; and yet when I think how I lie about *Lucretia,* the heroine of my novel—that is, how I enlarge and diverge from the slender stock of the real experience from which I derive my *Lucretia*—I perceive that Goethe, the calculating, is right. I *am* afraid, after all. Or do I follow the principle governing the universe, that every flower must have an ugly root—that behind or back of all beauty is the black, rough, coarse structure? Who has ever looked thoroughly into the lining of things? First rough beams to support our dwellings; then rough laths and mortar; then delicate, beautifully colored papers, or fresco painting; and upon that pictures, the culmination of art!

September 10.—Dog-days have a merit of their own, a variety. Excellent aromatic fogs; vivid sunshine to ripen wild, luscious berries; heavy dews to comfort the dying grass and hardy, lowly herbs, and to moisten the painted leaf before it drops to the cold, waiting earth. I wander on; pretend to be artistic and intellectual, and all that, when I know that Alton's life beats loudly for Julia, the woman he loves. I shall have to send for her. If she has a heart she must love this spot. I say that, although it is on the New England coast, near Plymouth Rock—throne of the exalted Puritans—it is beautiful. Yes, I would have her here already. I cough so, I suppose that I must die soon, and I do not want to leave Alton alone. For, let him start at the hour of my death, for any spot on any continent, he would be alone unless some kind, loving woman should accompany him, to watch and guard him.

September 20.—Autumn days, autumn fields—*not* happy autumn fields. The days that are no more are not between us yet. We tremble, we suffer; still our eyes

---

27. From *The Auto-Biography of Goethe. Truth and Poetry; From My Life, Third Part* (1847), edited by Parke Godwin. Johann Wolfgang von Goethe (1749–1832), German Romantic.

behold them. What trivial things we say to each other daily—about the wind, weather, flowers, each other! Oh, my poor boy—my brother!

September 26.—Marsh marigold, and golden-rod, and wild asters, star-like, white, and lavender blossoms thickly strewing every path. Well, flowers make me believe in God. In the most secret and waste places they bloom. In the ditch, thicket, swamp, beneath the trees choked with thorns and thistles. Still, God need not convict us if we do not choose to watch and follow nature. Oh, miserable, canting generation, groveling in the ignorance of your forefathers! And why should the forefathers be reproached? Cain killed Abel, and nobody has excused Cain. Where did his vice come from?

September 28.—Now the days are inclined to thin mist. The crows are busy between shore and wood, cawing perpetually. The crickets chirp day and night; they creep into the house, under the hearth, into the wall, into every crevice. I like the unfeeling cricket. If we are very sad, we do not heed his voice; if we are merry, we say, "how sociable and friendly the cricket is." The grass has changed. The sedge through which the tide washes is brown and sere. All these months gone, with bud, blossom, and fruit, and I have done nothing. Thirty chapters in my novel—all wrong, maybe. At any rate, I walked the room and felt my eyes water over the last one. Here's my journal, any how. How may we impart to each other the *ineffable?*— poor, poor word! How shall we help our neighbor souls with our nameless self-exaltations, which, noble and generous, do not seem to belong to our personality? They are not actions, nor resolves even. Yet, what moves and governs the world? By this prating I do not mean to say that I have done the ineffable with my pen.

September 30.—The brake along our rough granite walls is rich red-brown, pale amber, yellow-brown. Cheery autumn, dying so richly—loving summer, while reaching toward winter. This ineffectual record must end. Helen Hobson may read it; perchance, some person she loves, for Helen never liked trouble of any sort. October is at hand. Leaves lie on the grass already with decay's many tints.

"You shall not stay beyond the first frost, Alicia," orders my dear Alton, this evening.

"Oh, my darling, think of the Indian summer; let me stay!"

"I have written to Dresden. We are all going to the country you have dreamed of—Italy."

I pretended not to hear him.

"Won't you shoot any this month? Somebody says—

"For solemn autumn came with yellow wing."[28]

I take it to be snipe or plover; black wings and yellow legs, you know."

"Dear Alicia, I love you so that I will allow you to kiss me. Poor Dresden—a better fellow than I am; got more money."

28. This line from "Life" by Thomas Miller appeared in *Friendship's Offering* (1837).

I pull the boy's yellow mustache, and he nips my cheek.

"Don't be a goose," he continues, "but get ready and go, just as any sensible girl would.

> " 'Let you and I, fair sister, look
> Into the future's radiant book,
> And learn its lessons, and the scope
> It offers to the hearts that hope;
> And *we* will hope; for, sister, mark,
> To-morrow is not always dark!' "29

"Alton, Alton!"

In a moment I am in his arms, and we are weeping together. We say no more about departure. I determine to send for Julia Beaufort. How can I endure her? I must, though, for she will come.

October 8.—A delicate frost. It gave me a cold. Alton has been savage to-day. Pulled a few autumn-stained maple leaves at eve, and saw that the lady-birch was growing yellow fast. The children brought us berries—the last, they said. I asked Alton should I preserve them for his sweet tooth. He answered, "Yes," and I went to him. Tears were in his beautiful eyes.

"Alicia, darling, am I a brute?"

"No, dear; you are angry because I can not live."

"You shall live, by Heaven! you shall live. What does God mean by all this daily agony? My love, ever since we have been in this secluded spot, do you know that I have seen young men and women, idols to somebody, dying with your insidious, treacherous, terrible disease? I *can not* bear it. There is no reason about it. Talk about 'chastening' and 'discipline;' these things, destroying life and happiness, make us infidels."

"Yes, I know it, dear. I have a note from Julia; she will be here in a day or two."

He did not speak a word, but kissed me repeatedly, and then went away.

October 20.—Julia Beaufort has been here a few days; she is quite a child, but she has never suffered. How pretty she is! I like to watch her. What a lover Alton is! his eyes continually stray in my direction; if I leave the room he follows me. Sometimes he sits at Julia's feet, sometimes beside her, with his arm about her, but he always appears absent, dreaming, and asks her, "Am I not dull, missy? You do not really think me worth the having, I know; if you do, what will happen? I only know how to care for old Alicias—ailing sisters. Let me go, Julia."

"I would, if it were not for parting from this same Alicia. I have accepted you on her account; she is dearer than you to me."

---

29. These lines from "A Farewell to Home" by H.G.A. appeared in the same issue of *Friendship's Offering* (1837).

"Then I love you, child."

And I know that *they* love each other with a gentle affection, though there is a shadow upon it; but that will pass. Love will have its way. George Sand says, upon the bones of the dead, or upon a bed of roses, it is all the same to lovers. The drama here refreshes me. One way I see that I have failed in the story I am writing; that is, they teach me so. Alton loves Julia enough to make her his wife and the mother of his children; the desire to possess another woman will not enter into his heart. Yet, deep in the core of that noble heart is an undying love and regret for *me*. Every fibre of his soul recognizes me as his mate. What a pity! Yet he will be happy. Farewell, children; you have not seen me cry.

October 28.—Gray skies, gray sea, gray boughs. The winds rise and wail so, and we have long dull rains. Julia went away yesterday. The wedding is arranged. She cried terribly when she kissed me, and said she had never been so happy—what a girl's reason for weeping! I promised to be with her; but I have a conviction that if I leave this house I shall never return to it. What does that matter, though? I am on the last chapters of my book; I ventured to read two or three of the later ones to Julia. She clapped her hands at first, then grew silent; as I read on her delicate cheek crimsoned, her eyes blazed, she moved near me, took my hand, and kissed it. I refused to read her more.

"Oh, sister!" she cried, "how dare you tell the truth about us women? And, where have you lived, what have you done?"

"Does knowledge imply a wandering up and down the space of continents, and the speaking of French and Italian?"

"Not that," she stammered; "but I thought that you had been so entirely apart every way from the common herd. I did not know that one could create without experience."

"Nor can one; like Ulysses, I am a part of all that I have seen;[30] and much good it has done me, hasn't it?"

"I do not understand you, dear Alicia; does Alton?"

"Yes."

"Oh, I am so afraid of him—and you too. Thank you for giving me your written thoughts, though; I shall never forget them."

Now I am glad that she knows a thought of mine. I went about the house after she had gone, Alton having taken his departure for the woods with his gun, and never liked the rooms so little, they were so empty, desolate, and dark. I shut two or three entirely. "Next year," I said to myself. Then I packed some boxes of nicknacks and put labels to them—that was dreary too; and I was glad to hear Alton's tramp and cheery whistle.

30. Ulysses, or Odysseus, was the hero of Homer's epic *The Odyssey*. In Tennyson's poem "Ulysses" (1842), Ulysses says this line.

November 2.—Alicia Raymond—her mark.

Suddenly Alton ordains that we leave. Into a pigeon-hole goes this journal. I shall leave this room habitable—that is, I will have nothing set in order. Helen may do that for me.

This was Alicia's last record.

Helen told me that Alicia died abroad. When her brother Alton returned to this country she, Helen, was sent for, and the old house, with Alicia's papers and last wishes, given to her.

"You should have seen," said Helen, in conclusion, "Alicia's room—the one where you found her journal. When I opened the shutters to let the light in I could not for a moment persuade myself that Alicia or Alton would not presently enter, the bustle and presence of an occupation were so evident. Alton's cigar ashes and newspaper and an open book were on one table. At another I saw Alicia's little work-basket, with bits of muslin hanging from it; a vase of flowers arranged by her hands the day she left, probably, now black and rough; a pair of slippers were under her chair beside it, with blue rosettes. At the desk were loose papers, letters, boxes, and a tied-up bunch of grasses—fallen to seed and scattered like dust; the chairs were opposite each other, or in groups, as if company had lately sat in them, and the sofa-pillows were tumbled where some one had been resting. It was like a mirage. Then it grew terribly painful. It was a long time before I threw away the flower-stalks even; but you know that some material things must be taken care of, and I was forced to let in air and sunshine. As you know, also, I have never looked into Alicia's papers. Now what do you think of her?"

"I think if there were more minds among us equal to themselves, as hers appears to have been equal to *her* highest needs, we should have a better literature. I doubt whether she would ever have been induced to publish any thing."

"But is it not a pity she should be lost to the world?"

"She has her world in Alton, in you, and will have in me. Did Alton marry Julia?"

"Yes; and she cherishes Alicia's memory tenderly."

"That is enough."

Source: Harper's New Monthly Magazine (1870)

Nameless Pain

I should be happy with my lot:
A wife and mother—is it not

Enough for me to be content?
What other blessing could be sent?

A quiet house, and homely ways,
That make each day like other days;
I only see Time's shadow now
Darken the hair on baby's brow!

No world's work ever comes to me,
No beggar brings his misery;
I have no power, no healing art
With bruisèd soul or broken heart.

I read the poets of the age,
'T is lotus-eating in a cage;
I study Art, but Art is dead
To one who clamors to be fed

With milk from Nature's rugged breast,
Who longs for Labor's lusty rest.
O foolish wish! I still should pine
If any other lot were mine.

Source: Poems (1895)

❧ EMILY DICKINSON (1830–1886)

Emily Dickinson lived nearly her entire life in Amherst, Massachusetts, with the exception of a year away at school. She lived relatively quietly, filling her days with visitors, gardening, baking, and, of course, writing. Of the over seventeen hundred poems Dickinson wrote, only ten are known to have been published in her lifetime. She did not need to contribute to her family's income and was reluctant to submit her work to editing. Instead, Dickinson shared some of her poems with friends and family members, often in her letters. She also wrote to Thomas Wentworth Higginson, an editor at the Atlantic Monthly, *after his article "Letters to a Young Contributor" appeared in 1862. His advice to her was not particularly encouraging. In lieu of publication, Dickinson collected over eight hundred poems in more than forty hand-sewn books or fascicles, a project that some scholars see as a form of self-editing. After her death, her sister Lavinia discovered the poems and enlisted the aid of Mabel Todd Loomis and Higginson, who together edited three volumes of Dickinson's poetry published in the 1890s. Turn-of-the-century critics considered her an untutored poet who had not mastered the rudiments of grammar and punctuation, even though Loomis and Higginson had regularized punctuation and capitalization. The reaction exemplifies how female poets were often viewed as uneducated and thus incapable of greatness, a theme of Constance Fenimore Woolson's story "'Miss Grief'" (1880). With the advent of modernism in the early decades of the twentieth century, Dickinson's poetry began to be viewed as anticipating imagism and modern alienation. Although she has long been hailed as the only significant American female poet of the nineteenth century, recent scholarship has excavated the many layers of resonance between her work and that of her female contemporaries, whom she read carefully.*

260

[1861]
I'm Nobody! Who are you?
Are you - Nobody - too?
Then there's a pair of us!
Dont tell! they'd advertise - you know!

How dreary - to be - Somebody!
How public - like a Frog -
To tell one's name - the livelong June -
To an admiring Bog!

268

[1861]
Why - do they shut me out of Heaven?
Did I sing - too loud?
But - I can say a little "minor"
Timid as a Bird!

Would'nt the Angels try me -
Just - once - more -
Just - see - if I troubled them -
But dont - shut the door!

Oh, if I - were the Gentleman
In the "White Robe"[1] -
And they - were the little Hand - that knocked -
Could - I - forbid?

324

[1862]
Put up my lute!
What of - my Music!
Since the sole ear I cared to charm -
Passive - as Granite - laps my music -
Sobbing - will suit - as well as psalm!

Would but the "Memnon"[2] of the Desert -
Teach me the strain
That vanquished Him -
When He - surrendered to the Sunrise -
Maybe - that - would awaken - them!

1. In the Resurrection of Christ, the angel of the Lord descended from heaven in a "raiment white as snow" (Matthew 28:3).
2. The statue of Memnon, son of Aurora, at Thebes was said to produce a sound like the snap of a musical string when the rays of the morning sun (or Aurora) fell upon it.

348

[1862]
I would not paint - a picture -
I'd rather be the One
It's bright impossibility
To dwell - delicious - on -
And wonder how the fingers feel
Whose rare - celestial - stir -
Evokes so sweet a torment -
Such sumptuous - Despair -

I would not talk, like Cornets -
I'd rather be the One
Raised softly to the Ceilings -
And out, and easy on -
Through Villages of Ether -
Myself endued Balloon
By but a lip of Metal -
The pier to my Pontoon -

Nor would I be a Poet -
It's finer - Own the Ear -
Enamored - impotent - content -
The License to revere,
A privilege so awful
What would the Dower be,
Had I the Art to stun myself
With Bolts - of Melody!

380

[1862]
All the letters I can write
Are not fair as this -
Syllables of Velvet -
Sentences of Plush,
Depths of Ruby, undrained,
Hid, Lip, for Thee -

Play it were a Humming Bird -
And just sipped - me -

445

[1862]
They shut me up in Prose -
As when a little Girl
They put me in the Closet -
Because they liked me "still" -

Still! Could themself have peeped -
And seen my Brain - go round -
They might as wise have lodged a Bird
For Treason - in the Pound -

Himself has but to will
And easy as a Star
Look down opon Captivity -
And laugh - No more have I -

446

[1862]
This was a Poet -
It is That
Distills amazing sense
From Ordinary Meanings -
And Attar[3] so immense

From the familiar species
That perished by the Door -
We wonder it was not Ourselves
Arrested it - before -

Of Pictures, the Discloser -
The Poet - it is He -

3. Fragrant essence of a rose.

Entitles Us - by Contrast -
To ceaseless Poverty -

Of Portion - so unconscious -
The Robbing - could not harm -
Himself - to Him - a Fortune -
Exterior - to Time -

458

[1862]
She dealt her pretty words like Blades -
How glittering they shone -
And every One unbared a Nerve
Or wantoned with a Bone -

She never deemed - she hurt -
That - is not Steel's Affair -
A vulgar grimace in the Flesh -
How ill the Creatures bear -

To Ache is human - not polite -
The Film opon the eye
Mortality's old Custom -
Just locking up - to Die -

466

[1862]
I dwell in Possibility -
A fairer House than Prose -
More numerous of Windows -
Superior - for Doors -

Of Chambers as the Cedars -
Impregnable of eye -
And for an everlasting Roof
The Gambrels⁴ of the Sky -

---

4. Type of roof.

Of Visitors - the fairest -
For Occupation - This -
The spreading wide my narrow Hands
To gather Paradise -

519

[1863]
This is my letter to the World
That never wrote to Me -
The simple News that Nature told -
With tender Majesty

Her Message is committed
To Hands I cannot see -
For love of Her - Sweet - countrymen -
Judge tenderly - of Me

533

[1863]
I reckon - When I count at all -
First - Poets - Then the Sun -
Then Summer - Then the Heaven of God -
And then - the List is done -

But, looking back - the First so seems
To Comprehend the Whole -
The Others look a needless Show -
So I write - Poets - All -

Their Summer - lasts a solid Year -
They can afford a Sun
The East - would deem extravagant -
And if the Further Heaven -

Be Beautiful as they prepare
For Those who worship Them -
It is too difficult a Grace -
To justify the Dream -

600

[1863]
Her - last Poems[5] -
Poets ended -
Silver - perished - with her Tongue -
Not on Record - bubbled Other -
Flute - or Woman - so divine -

Not unto it's Summer Morning -
Robin - uttered half the Tune
Gushed too full for the adoring -
From the Anglo-Florentine -

Late - the Praise - 'Tis dull - Conferring
On the Head too High - to Crown -
Diadem - or Ducal[6] showing -
Be it's Grave - sufficient Sign -

Nought - that We - No Poet's Kinsman -
Suffocate - with easy Wo -
What - and if Ourself a Bridegroom -
Put Her down - in Italy?

764

[1863]
My Life had stood - a Loaded Gun -
In Corners - till a Day
The Owner passed - identified -
And carried Me away -

And now We roam in Sovreign Woods -
And now We hunt the Doe -
And every time I speak for Him -
The Mountains straight reply -

5. Elizabeth Barrett Browning's *Last Poems* were published in 1862; she died in Florence, Italy, in 1861.
    6. Diadem: crown. Ducal: pertaining to a duke, here royalty.

And do I smile, such cordial light
Opon the Valley glow -
It is as a Vesuvian[7] face
Had let it's pleasure through -

And when at Night - Our good Day done -
I guard My Master's Head -
'Tis better than the Eider Duck's
Deep Pillow - to have shared -

To foe of His - I'm deadly foe -
None stir the second time -
On whom I lay a Yellow Eye[8] -
Or an emphatic Thumb -

Though I than He - may longer live
He longer must - than I -
For I have but the power to kill,
Without - the power to die -

772

[1863]
Essential Oils - are wrung -
The Attar from the Rose
Be not expressed by Suns - alone -
It is the gift of Screws -

The General Rose - decay -
But this - in Lady's Drawer
Make Summer - When the Lady lie
In Ceaseless Rosemary[9] -

7. Of volcanic power, referring to Mount Vesuvius, which erupted in Italy in 79 A.D. and destroyed Pompeii.
8. A symptom of jaundice, once believed to cause everything to appear yellow; symbolic of a prejudiced view.
9. Rosemary, as a token of remembrance, was thrown into open graves during funerals.

788

[1863]
Publication - is the Auction
Of the Mind of Man -
Poverty - be justifying
For so foul a thing

Possibly - but We - would rather
From Our Garret go
White - Unto the White Creator -
Than invest - Our Snow -

Thought belong to Him who gave it -
Then - to Him Who bear
It's Corporeal illustration - sell
The Royal Air -

In the Parcel - Be the Merchant
Of the Heavenly Grace -
But reduce no Human Spirit
To Disgrace of Price -

1009

[1865]
I was a Phebe[10] - nothing more -
A Phebe - nothing less -
The little note that others dropt
I fitted into place -

I dwelt too low that any seek -
Too shy, that any blame -
A Phebe makes a little print
Opon the Floors of Fame -

10. Phebe or Phoebe was one of the Titans, the first race of the Greek gods. Her name means "shining one," and she was the goddess of the moon. She was associated with the Oracle at Delphi and with prophesy. The phoebe is also a small brown bird that builds its nests under the eaves of a roof and thus is associated with domesticity. Its song is not melodious but a monotonous two notes.

1353

[1875]
To pile like Thunder to it's close
Then crumble grand away
While everything created hid
This - would be Poetry -

Or Love - the two coeval come -
We both and neither prove -
Experience either and consume -
For none see God and live -

Source: The Poems of Emily Dickinson, ed. R. W. Franklin (1999)

Letters to Thomas Wentworth Higginson

[received April 16, 1862]

MR. HIGGINSON,—Are you too deeply occupied to say if my verse is alive?

The mind is so near itself it cannot see, distinctly, and I have none to ask.

Should you think it breathed, and had you the leisure to tell me, I should feel quick gratitude.

If I make the mistake, that you dared to tell me would give me sincerer honor toward you.

I inclose my name, asking you, if you please, sir, to tell me what is true?

That you will not betray me it is needless to ask, since honor is its own pawn.

[received April 26, 1862]

MR. HIGGINSON,—Your kindness claimed earlier gratitude, but I was ill, and write to-day from my pillow.

Thank you for the surgery;[11] it was not so painful as I supposed. I bring you others, as you ask, though they might not differ. While my thought is undressed, I can make the distinction; but when I put them in the gown, they look alike and numb.

You asked how old I was? I made no verse, but one or two, until this winter, sir.

---

11. Presumably his editing and/or critique of the poems she had sent him with her first letter.

I had a terror since September, I could tell to none; and so I sing, as the boy does of the burying ground, because I am afraid.

You inquire my books. For poets, I have Keats, and Mr. and Mrs. Browning. For prose, Mr. Ruskin, Sir Thomas Browne, and the Revelations.[12] I went to school, but in your manner of the phrase had no education. When a little girl, I had a friend who taught me Immortality; but venturing too near, himself, he never returned. Soon after, my tutor died, and for several years, my lexicon was my only companion. Then I found one more, but he was not contented I be his scholar, so he left the land.

You ask of my companions. Hills, sir, and the sundown, and a dog large as myself, that my father bought me. They are better than beings because they know, but do not tell; and the noise in the pool at noon excels my piano.

I have a brother and sister; my mother does not care for thought, and father, too busy with his briefs to notice what we do. He buys me many books, but begs me not to read them, because he fears they joggle the mind. They are religious, except me, and address an eclipse, every morning, whom they call their "Father."

But I fear my story fatigues you. I would like to learn. Could you tell me how to grow, or is it unconveyed, like melody or witchcraft?

You speak of Mr. Whitman.[13] I never read his book, but was told that it was disgraceful.

I read Miss Prescott's Circumstance,[14] but it followed me in the dark, so I avoided her.

Two editors of journals came to my father's house this winter, and asked me for my mind, and when I asked them "why" they said I was penurious, and they would use it for the world.

I could not weigh myself, myself. My size felt small to me. I read your chapters in the Atlantic, and experienced honor for you. I was sure you would not reject a confiding question.

Is this, sir, what you asked me to tell you?   Your friend,

E. DICKINSON.

12. John Keats (1795–1821), British Romantic poet. Robert Browning (1812–1889) and Elizabeth Barrett Browning (1806–1861), Victorian poets and husband and wife. John Ruskin (1819–1900), British art critic. Sir Thomas Browne (1605–1682), British writer on religion and science. Revelations, the final book of the New Testament.

13. Walt Whitman (1819–1892), whose *Leaves of Grass* (1855) was deemed offensive for its frank depictions of sexuality.

14. Harriet Prescott [Spofford]'s short story "Circumstance" was published in the *Atlantic Monthly* in 1860. It depicted a woman who is held captive by a panther and survives by singing to it.

[received June 8, 1862]

DEAR FRIEND,—Your letter gave no drunkenness, because I tasted rum before. Domingo[15] comes but once; yet I have had few pleasures so deep as your opinion, and if I tried to thank you, my tears would block my tongue.

My dying tutor told me that he would like to live till I had been a poet, but Death was much of mob as I could master, then. And when, far afterward, a sudden light on orchards, or a new fashion in the wind troubled my attention, I felt a palsy, here, the verses just relieve.

Your second letter surprised me, and for a moment, swung. I had not supposed it. Your first gave no dishonor, because the true are not ashamed[.] I thanked you for your justice, but could not drop the bells whose jingling cooled my tramp. Perhaps the balm seemed better, because you bled me first. I smile when you suggest that I delay "to publish," that being foreign to my thought as firmament to fin.

If fame belonged to me, I could not escape her; if she did not, the longest day would pass me on the chase, and the approbation of my dog would forsake me then. My barefoot rank is better.

You think my gait "spasmodic." I am in danger, sir. You think me "uncontrolled." I have no tribunal.

Would you have time to be the "friend" you should think I need? I have a little shape: it would not crowd your desk, nor make much racket as the mouse that dents your galleries.

If I might bring you what I do—not so frequent to trouble you—and ask you if I told it clear, 't would be control to me. The sailor cannot see the North, but knows the needle can. The "hand you stretch me in the dark" I put mine in, and turn away. I have no Saxon[16] now:—

> As if I asked a common alms,
> And in my wondering hand
> A stranger pressed a kingdom,
> And I, bewildered, stand;
> As if I asked the Orient
> Had it for me a morn,
> And it should lift its purple dikes
> And shatter me with dawn!

But, will you be my preceptor, Mr. Higginson?

15. Santo Domingo was a major producer of rum.
16. By *Saxon* Dickinson means language. *Needle* refers to the needle of a compass.

[July 1862]

Could you believe me without? I had no portrait, now, but am small, like the wren; and my hair is bold, like the chestnut bur; and my eyes, like the sherry in the glass, that the guest leaves. Would this do just as well?

It often alarms father. He says death might occur, and he has moulds of all the rest, but has no mould of me; but I noticed the quick wore off those things, in a few days, and forestall the dishonor. You will think no caprice of me.

You said "Dark." I know the butterfly, and the lizard, and the orchis.[17] Are not those *your* countrymen?

I am happy to be your scholar, and will deserve the kindness I cannot repay.

If you truly consent, I recite now. Will you tell me my fault, frankly as to yourself, for I had rather wince than die. Men do not call the surgeon to commend the bone, but to set it, sir, and fracture within is more critical. And for this, preceptor, I shall bring you obedience, the blossom from my garden, and every gratitude I know.

Perhaps you smile at me. I could not stop for that. My business is circumference. An ignorance, not of customs, but if caught with the dawn, or the sunset see me, myself the only kangaroo among the beauty, sir, if you please, it afflicts me, and I thought that instruction would take it away.

Because you have much business, beside the growth of me, you will appoint, yourself, how often I shall come, without your inconvenience.

And if at any time you regret you received me, or I prove a different fabric to that you supposed, you must banish me.

When I state myself, as the representative of the verse, it does not mean me, but a supposed person.

You are true about the "perfection." To-day makes Yesterday mean.

You spoke of Pippa Passes.[18] I never heard anybody speak of Pippa Passes before. You see my posture is benighted.

To thank you baffles me. Are you perfectly powerful? Had I a pleasure you had not, I could delight to bring it.

YOUR SCHOLAR.

DEAR FRIEND,—Are these more orderly? I thank you for the truth.

I had no monarch in my life, and cannot rule myself; and when I try to organize, my little force explodes and leaves me bare and charred.

I think you called me "wayward." Will you help me improve?

17. Another word for orchid.
18. An 1841 drama by Robert Browning.

I suppose the pride that stops the breath, in the core of woods, is not of ourself.

You say I confess the little mistake, and omit the large. Because I can see orthography; but the ignorance out of sight is my preceptor's charge.

Of "shunning men and women," they talk of hallowed things, aloud, and embarrass my dog. He and I don't object to them, if they 'll exist their side. I think Carl would please you. He is dumb, and brave. I think you would like the chestnut tree I met in my walk. It hit my notice suddenly, and I thought the skies were in blossom.

Then there 's a noiseless noise in the orchard that I let persons hear.

You told me in one letter you could not come to see me "now," and I made no answer; not because I had none, but did not think myself the price that you should come so far.

I do not ask so large a pleasure, lest you might deny me.

You say, "Beyond your knowledge." You would not jest with me, because I believe you; but, preceptor, you cannot mean it?

All men say "What" to me, but I thought it a fashion.

When much in the woods, as a little girl, I was told that the snake would bite me, that I might pick a poisonous flower, or goblins kidnap me; but I went along and met no one but angels, who were far shyer of me than I could be of them, so I have n't that confidence in fraud which many exercise.

I shall observe your precept, though I don't understand it, always.

I marked a line in one verse, because I met it after I made it, and never consciously touch a paint mixed by another person.

I do not let go it, because it is mine. Have you the portrait of Mrs. Browning? Persons sent me three. If you had none, will you have mine?

YOUR SCHOLAR.

Source: Atlantic Monthly (1891)

The young Harriet Prescott burst onto the literary scene in 1859 with the publication of her story "In a Cellar" in the Atlantic Monthly. *Much of the interest in the story, which was set in France and full of intrigue, derived from the fact that a young, seemingly inexperienced woman had written it. The editors of the* Atlantic *predicted for her a glorious literary career, and though her career was lengthy and prolific, it was overshadowed by developing tastes for realism and local color. As the following poem attests, Spofford's vivid imagination led her to a decidedly romantic model of artistry. By claiming the female self as the source of creativity, this poem also deviates from representing woman in the conventional position of muse to the male artist. It features a seamstress as the model of the woman artist, a common figure in women's poetry.*

Pomegranate-Flowers

The street was narrow, close, and dark,
    And flanked with antique masonry,
The shelving eaves left for an ark
      But one long strip of summer sky.
      But one long line to bless the eye—
      The thin white cloud lay not so high,
      Only some brown bird, skimming nigh,
      From wings whence all the dew was dry
Shook down a dream of forest scents,
Of odorous blooms and sweet contents,
      Upon the weary passers-by.

Ah, few but haggard brows had part
    Below that street's uneven crown,
And there the murmurs of the mart
      Swarmed faint as hums of drowsy noon.
      With voices chiming in quaint tune
      From sun-soaked hulls long wharves adown,
      The singing sailors rough and brown
      Won far melodious renown,
Here, listening children ceasing play,
And mothers sad their well-a-way,
      In this old breezy sea-board town.

Ablaze on distant banks she knew,
    Spreading their bowls to catch the sun,
Magnificent Dutch tulips grew
    With pompous color overrun.
    By light and snow from heaven won
    Their misty web azaleas spun;
    Low lilies pale as any nun,
    Their pensile bells rang one by one;
And spicing all the summer air
Gold honeysuckles everywhere
    Their trumpets blew in unison.

Than where blood-cored carnations stood
    She fancied richer hues might be,
Scents rarer than the purple hood[1]
    Curled over in the fleur-de-lis.[2]
    Small skill in learned names had she,
    Yet whatso wealth of land or sea
    Had ever stored her memory,
    She decked its varied imagery
Where, in the highest of the row
Upon a sill more white than snow,
    She nourished a pomegranate-tree.

Some lover from a foreign clime,
    Some roving gallant of the main,
Had brought it on a gay spring-time,
    And told her of the nacar[3] stain
    The thing would wear when bloomed again.
    Therefore all garden growths in vain
    Their glowing ranks swept through her brain,
    The plant was knit by subtile chain
To all the balm of Southern zones,
The incenses of Eastern thrones,
    The tinkling hem of Aaron's train.[4]

---

1. Skunk cabbage, which appears in the Spring, a purple hood first coming up through the snow.

2. Literally, "flower of lily," a symbol of French royalty. Here an iris.

3. Reddish.

4. The ceremonial robes of Aaron, the brother of Moses in the Old Testament and the first high priest, were adorned on the hem with pomegranates and bells (Exodus 28: 33–34).

The almond shaking in the sun
    On some high place ere day begin,
Where winds of myrrh and cinnamon
      Between the tossing plumes have been,
      It called before her, and its kin
      The fragrant savage balaustine[5]
      Grown from the ruined ravelin[6]
      That tawny leopards couch them in;
But this, if rolling in from seas
It only caught the salt-fumed breeze,
    Would have a grace they might not win.

And for the fruit that it should bring,
    One globe she pictured, bright and near,
Crimson, and throughly perfuming
      All airs that brush its shining sphere.
      In its translucent atmosphere
      Afrite[7] and Princess reappear,—
      Through painted panes the scattered spear
      Of sunrise scarce so warm and clear,—
And pulped with such a golden juice,
Ambrosial,[8] that one cannot choose
    But find the thought most sumptuous cheer.

Of all fair women she was queen,
    And all her beauty, late and soon,
O'ercame you like the mellow sheen
      Of some serene autumnal noon.
      Her presence like a sweetest tune
      Accorded all your thoughts in one.
      Than last year's alder-tufts in June
      Browner, yet lustrous as a moon
Her eyes glowed on you, and her hair
With such an air as princes wear
    She trimmed black-braided in a crown.

---

5. The wild pomegranate flower. When dried it was used in medicines.
6. Railing or fence.
7. Evil demon in Muslim mythology.
8. Divinely fragrant, referring to a scent derived from heaven.

A perfect peace prepared her days,
    Few were her wants and small her care,
No weary thoughts perplexed her ways,
    She hardly knew if she were fair.
    Bent lightly at her needle there
    In that small room stair over stair,
    All fancies blithe and debonair
    She deftly wrought on fabrics rare,
All clustered moss, all drifting snow,
All trailing vines, all flowers that blow,
    Her dædal[9] fingers laid them bare.

Still at the slowly spreading leaves
    She glanced up ever and anon,
If yet the shadow of the eaves
    Had paled the dark gloss they put on.
    But while her smile like sunlight shone,
    The life danced to such blossom blown
    That all the roses ever known,
    Blanche of Provence, Noisette, or Yonne,[10]
Wore no such tint as this pale streak
That damasked[11] half the rounding cheek
    Of each bud great to bursting grown.

And when the perfect flower lay free,
    Like some great moth whose gorgeous wings
Fan o'er the husk unconsciously,
    Silken, in airy balancings,—
    She saw all gay dishevellings
    Of fairy flags, whose revellings
    Illumine night's enchanted rings.
    So royal red no blood of kings
She thought, and Summer in the room
Sealed her escutcheon[12] on their bloom,
    In the glad girl's imaginings.

   9. Poetical usage: skillful. Also a reference to Daedalus (literally, "cunning one") from Greek mythology. He was a symbol of the artist, creator of the labyrinth and wings for himself and his son Icarus.
   10. Types of French roses.
   11. Of cloth, richly woven. Damask is also a type of rose.
   12. In horticulture, a cutting of a branch with a bud, shaped like a shield.

Now, said she, in the heart of the woods
    The sweet south-winds assert their power,
And blow apart the snowy snoods
    Of trilliums in their thrice-green bower.
    Now all the swamps are flushed with dower
    Of viscid pink, where, hour by hour,
    The bees swim amorous, and a shower
    Reddens the stream where cardinals tower.
Far lost in fern of fragrant stir
Her fancies roam, for unto her
    All Nature came in this one flower.

Sometimes she set it on the ledge
    That it might not be quite forlorn
Of wind and sky, where o'er the edge,
    Some gaudy petal, slowly borne,
    Fluttered to earth in careless scorn,
    Caught, for a fallen piece of morn
    From kindling vapors loosely shorn,
    By urchins ragged and wayworn,
Who saw, high on the stone embossed,
A laughing face, a hand that tossed
    A prodigal spray just freshly torn.

What wizard hints across them fleet,—
    These heirs of all the town's thick sin,
Swift gypsies of the tortuous street,
    With childhood yet on cheek and chin!
    What voices dropping through the din
    An airy murmuring begin,—
    These floating flakes, so fine and thin,
    Were they and rock-laid earth akin?
Some woman of the gods was she,
The generous maiden in her glee?
    And did whole forests grow within?

A tissue rare as the hoar-frost,
    White as the mists spring dawns condemn,
The shadowy wrinkles round her lost,

She wrought with branch and anadem,[13]
Through the fine meshes netting them,
Pomegranate-flower and leaf and stem.
Dropping it o'er her diadem[14]
To float below her gold-stitched hem,
Some duchess through the court should sail
Hazed in the cloud of this white veil,
    As when a rain-drop mists a gem.

Her tresses once when this was done,
    —Vanished the skein, the needle bare,—
She dressed with wreaths vermilion
    Bright as a trumpet's dazzling blare.
    Nor knew that in Queen Dido's[15] hair,
    Loading the Carthaginian air,
    Ancestral blossoms flamed as fair
    As any ever hanging there.
While o'er her cheek their scarlet gleam
Shot down a vivid varying beam,
    Like sunshine on a brown-bronzed pear.

And then the veil thrown over her,
    The vapor of the snowy lace
Fell downward, as the gossamer
    Tossed from the autumn winds' wild race
    Falls round some garden-statue's grace.
    Beneath, the blushes on her face
    Fled with the Naiad's[16] shifting chase
    When flashing through a watery space.
And in the dusky mirror glanced
A splendid phantom, where there danced
    All brilliances in paler trace.

A spicery of sweet perfume,
    As if from regions rankly green

13. Wreath for the head made of flowers or leaves. Sometimes associated with the wreath bestowed upon the genius.
14. Crown or wreath of flowers or leaves for the head.
15. Dido was Queen of Carthage, ca. seventh century B.C.
16. Nymphs associated with fresh running water sources believed to have medicinal, prophetic, or inspirational powers.

And these rich hoards of bud and bloom,
  Lay every waft of air between.
  Out of some heaven's unfancied screen
  The gorgeous vision seemed to lean.
  The Oriental kings have seen
  Less beauty in their daïs-queen,
And any limner's pencil then
Had drawn the eternal love of men,
  But twice Chance will not intervene.

For soon with scarce a loving sigh
  She lifts it off half unaware,
While through the clinging folds held high,
  Arachnean in a silver snare
  Her rosy fingers nimbly fare,
  Till gathered square with dainty care.
  But still she leaves the flowery flare
  —Such as Dame Venus' self might wear—
Where first she placed them, since they blow
More bounteous color hanging so,
  And seem more native to the air.

Anon the mellow twilight came
  With breath of quiet gently freed
From sunset's felt but unseen flame.
  Then by her casement wheeled in speed
  Strange films, and half the wings indeed
  That steam in rainbows o'er the mead,
  Now magnified in mystery, lead
  Great revolutions to her heed.
And leaning out, the night o'erhead,
Wind-tossed in many a shining thread,
  Hung one long scarf of glittering brede.[17]

Then as it drew its streamers there,
  And furled its sails to fill and flaunt
Along fresh firmaments of air
  When ancient morn renewed his chant,—

17. Poetical: interwoven colors or embroidery.

She sighed in thinking on the plant
  Drooping so languidly aslant;
  Fancied some fierce noon's forest-haunt
  Where wild red things loll forth and pant,
Their golden antlers wave, and still
Sigh for a shower that shall distil
  The largess gracious nights do grant.

The oleanders in the South
  Drape gray hills with their rose, she thought,
The yellow-tasselled broom through drouth
  Bathing in half a heaven is caught.
  Jasmine and myrtle flowers are sought
  By winds that leave them fragrance-fraught.
  To them the wild bee's path is taught,
  The crystal spheres of rain are brought,
Beside them on some silent spray
The nightingales sing night away,
  The darkness wooes them in such sort.

But this, close shut beneath a roof,
  Knows not the night, the tranquil spell,
The stillness of the wildwood ouphe,[18]
  The magic dropped on moor and fell.
  No cool dew soothes its fiery shell,
  Nor any star, a red sardel,[19]
  Swings painted there as in a well.
  Dyed like a stream of muscadel
No white-skinned snake coils in its cup
To drink its soul of sweetness up,
  A honeyed hermit in his cell.

No humming-bird in emerald coat,
  Shedding the light, and bearing fain
His ebon spear, while at his throat
  The ruby corselet sparkles plain,
  On wings of misty speed astain

18. Elf or changeling.
19. A precious stone.

With amber lustres, hangs amain,
And tireless hums his happy strain;
Emperor of some primeval reign,
Over the ages sails to spill
The luscious juice of this, and thrill
Its very heart with blissful pain.

As if the flowers had taken flight
Or as the crusted gems should shoot
From hidden hollows, or as the light
Had blossomed into prisms to flute
Its secret that before was mute,
Atoms where fire and tint dispute,
No humming-birds here hunt their fruit.
No burly bee with banded suit
Here dusts him, no full ray by stealth
Sifts through it stained with warmer wealth
Where fair fierce butterflies salute.

Nor night nor day brings to my tree,
She thought, the free air's choice extremes,
But yet it grows as joyfully
And floods my chamber with its beams,
So that some tropic land it seems
Where oranges with ruddy gleams,
And aloes, whose weird flowers the creams
Of long rich centuries one deems,
Wave through the softness of the gloom,—
And these may blush a deeper bloom
Because they gladden so my dreams.

The sudden street-lights in moresque[20]
Broke through her tender murmuring,
And on her ceiling shades grotesque
Reeled in a bacchanalian[21] swing.
Then all things swam, and like a ring
Of bubbles welling from a spring

20. Moorish style.
21. Bacchus was the Roman god of wine.

Breaking in deepest coloring
Flower-spirits paid her minist'ring.
Sleep, fusing all her senses, soon
Fanned over her in drowsy rune[22]
All night long a pomegranate wing.

Source: *Atlantic Monthly* (1861)

22. Incantation, poem, or chant of magical powers.

❧ "A Weak-Minded Woman"

The writer of the following missive is unknown and signed herself only as "A Weak-Minded Woman." George W. Curtis was the author of the "Editor's Easy Chair" in Harper's New Monthly Magazine. *A similar piece by "A Disappointed Man" was published and responded to in the "Editor's Easy Chair" in October 1864. But this piece speaks specifically to the difficulties women (especially those of the lower classes and with families to care for) encountered in their attempts to become published authors. As Curtis suggests in his reply, she speaks for thousands of women yearning to improve their lives through the use of their pens. Two responses—by Susan Elston Wallace and Elizabeth Stuart Phelps—both of which are included in this anthology, were subsequently published in the magazine.*

Letter to the "Editor's Easy Chair"

A correspondent, who signs herself "A Weak-minded Woman," and who has sent two or three articles to this Magazine, which have not seemed to the editor exactly suitable for his purpose, writes to the Easy Chair of her bitter disappointment. The story which she tells will interest many, and perhaps speaks for many:

"Think of raising your head from your pillow on the dawn of a midsummer morning, startled by the sleepless consciousness that there is ever so much work to be done, and you must be up and about it. But your head aches, you have not slept and rested long enough; you are tired yet, for you were up till after ten o'clock mending your child's dress; your hands feel nerveless and very unfit to begin another round of toil. But you must stop thinking how good it would seem just to rest an hour longer. The work must be done, and you must do it alone; there is nobody to help. Why do you linger? You will be sorry when the heat comes down for every minute lost of this cool hour. Impelled by stern resolve the unwilling body moves. You are up and dressed, and run first to skim the milk. Then the fire must he made. Where is the wood? There's none in the yard, and you have already picked up all the old pieces round the fences near by. True, a man with an axe would have plenty in three minutes, but it was forgotten. Breakfast is expected at half past six; you must have some wood. Here is an old board which was 'shaky' in its prime, being now very much decayed it will break by stepping on it; draw it along and here in the barn-yard are some pieces which the cattle have broken, quite an armful in all. It has taken many minutes of precious time to get the wood, and now do you pause in going back to drink in the beauty of the morning? to look, while your soul grows larger, on the blue sky dotted and ribboned with clouds? on the wide, dewy fields and the circling woods, robed in the glory of summer? You pause not. Your eyes are fixed on the kitchen door, toward which you move rapidly in a right line. You might almost as well be an engine running through a tunnel, as far as looking on the outer world is concerned.

"Your fire is made, breakfast is cooking, and very warm it grows around the stove, and very faint you grow bending over it. Your flat-irons are heating, your birds are up crying for bread-and-butter. You sink down on the door-step, and slip their clothes on them swallowing the cool air; but there's something burning on the stove, you must breathe the hot steam again, while the cry for bread-and-butter grows more fervent. Hurry now, move your hands fast; you may get the coarse ironing done before time to set the table.

"Well, it is done, and the family are down to breakfast, but you can not eat—indeed you don't have time to eat. You know how things should be done, but you could not get every thing on the table in time; there's a spoon wanted, then water, and maybe something else. It is not a family reunion; it is to some a time to eat; to one a time to wonder if things will ever be any different; to you a time to think how they can be different; why there must be so much warm food in warm weather; and to try—vain attempt!—to simplify the day's work. But there it is, a great fact: victuals to be cooked in variety, to be placed on the table; the inevitable dish-washing, knife-scouring, sweeping, and so much besides, that no one who has not gone through it can understand it. With all your dropping and transposing you can not change the relations of things. It is as hopeless as the trials you used to make to bring out values by forming three equations of two unknown quantities.

"You keep your mouth close shut, and don't mean to complain; but after the man goes out you say to your husband, from sheer hopelessness perhaps, 'If I only had somebody to help me to-day!' Ah, you might better have kept still. He is in debt, is working hard, and he knows that you are, and it irritates him, because he can not tell how to help it; but he doesn't know that your very life is being worked in to help along. He can not know, with his strength, how utterly hopeless you feel in your weakness; so he says, 'I don't know what to do; I might as well give up one time as another; you'll have to have help, but I can hardly keep my head above water now.' How much better if you had kept still; you have taken all heart out of him for the day. So you sit with your head in your hands, while he goes to his work, and the children are out bareheaded, shouting in the sunshine.

" 'I *must* try,' you resolve, breaking away from your thoughts and going to work—'I must try writing again, and not give up till I succeed.' You have long been thinking of this, but could not get time. Now it is plain you must help yourself in some way; the time must be taken from the making and mending; there will be more rags; but let that pass. So through the hot summer days you hasten the day's work and the week's work; the washing, baking, ironing, and churning to get space to carry out your resolve, and just the hope and the effort help to take off the savageness of toil. Sometimes pen and paper lie on the pantry shelf, and you drop down in a chair there to rest five minutes and write; and sometimes, as you sit for an hour in the afternoon in your muslin dress in 'the other room,' a habit of old days that you can not get over, you write a little when no one is by. So your piece is finished after a long time and sent away, and you try not to think of it, but a small bright hope will live, hidden away in your heart, till crushed out by the truth.

"Another and another is sent to share the same fate. Yes, more than I will tell you of; and now, dear Easy Chair, would you keep trying or would you give up?

"A WEAK-MINDED WOMAN."

Where the feeling is so strong, yield to it. Write, since writing is so great a solace. But do not suppose that what you write will of course be published, and—if you can—try to think that it may not be worth publishing, much as it may have cost you.

There are thousands of women in this country like our correspondent. They have a constant yearning, for it seems to be more than a desire, not to write only but to print. They are like all the shrubs and trees and plants in spring, sprouting and budding and putting out leaves, but only now and then a flower so fine that the passer stops to remark it. . . .

Source: Harper's New Monthly Magazine (1867)

*Susan Elston was a native of Crawfordsville, Indiana. In 1852 she married Lew Wallace,
famous author of* Ben Hur *(1880), and their only child was born the following year. Her
first publication was a poem called "The Patter of Little Feet," which appeared in the*
Cincinnati Daily Gazette *on April 17, 1858, and was reprinted in* Harper's *in the "Editor's Drawer" in February 1859. It is undoubtedly the poem referred to as "My Children"
in the following essay, which Wallace wrote in response to a letter signed "A Weak-Minded
Woman." In the letter, the disheartened writer asked the editor of* Harper's New
Monthly Magazine *whether she should abandon writing. Although Wallace's response
exhorts women to "Bury pen and paper at once," she resumed her literary career over a
decade later as her husband's success grew. In the 1880s and 1890s, she published poetry
and travel essays in the* Atlantic Monthly *and the* Independent, *as well as collections of
her travel writings. She also completed her husband's autobiography after his death.*

Another Weak-Minded Woman
A Confession

I thought to join the noble army of martyrs unconfessed. I expected to die and
make no sign. But the recent letter of a "Weak-minded Woman," and kind words
of the Easy Chair,[1] have made me rise to speak. Perhaps the experience of one who
has partly succeeded where so many fail may warn others how straight is the gate
and narrow is the way to authorship, and how few there be that find it.

I do not address any who can lock themselves in libraries secure from interrup-
tion. I speak to those to whom the morning sun brings daily work; my fair countrywomen, who are so like white lilies at sixteen, yellow lilies at thirty, and alas! how
many spotted lilies at forty.

I can not remember when I did not make rhymes and little compositions. At
ten years of age I broke out in song, "Thoughts on my Rose-bush." It was written
in a cramped, pot-hooky hand, and carried to my mother. She praised my verse, but
told me to write no more; she was afraid it would make me unhappy. I wonder it
did not make *her* unhappy to read,

> My rose that's scarcely yet in bloom,
>> Its beauty charms my sight;
> Its fragrance, too, beneath the moon,
>> Still fills me with delight.

If the nightingale had answered from among the roses, I verily believe mother
would have thought my song the sweetest.

1. Editor's column in *Harper's New Monthly Magazine.*

At school I was always high in "composition," and helped others through the dreaded Friday. I loved to write on "Solitude" and "Friendship," and constitutional weakness for rhyme showed itself in abundant quotation. I wrote verses secretly and carried them in my pocket, where they were mashed into a wad Monday mornings.

While in boarding-school two years' real study kept down the afflatus. It was not dead, but sleeping. Soon after returning home, I came on an idea in Prescott's Conquest of Mexico, about the cross being a sign of worship almost universal.

"Ah," said I, "I have struck a vein; here is a new idea." I worked up five eight-line verses and sent it to *Putnam's Monthly.* I did not expect it to appear the first month—of course not; nor the second—no, indeed. Nor—so I tried to persuade my waiting soul—did I look for it in three months. The magazine came regularly; but "The Cross" I have not seen from that day to this. I was not discouraged. They had a dull "Reader" in the office; he was tired when he came on my manuscript, and tossed it into the waste-basket, without reading it at all. No wonder, when my hand-writing was so indistinct.

One day I read in the *Saturday Courier* an offer of a hundred dollars for the best story of American life. There! If I could write a "prize tale it would give me place in the literary world at once." I went to work at morning; laid my scenes in New York, a city of which I, at that time, knew precisely nothing. And, because my belongings were plain, I rioted in descriptions "perfectly splendid." My hero dwelt in a house something like a flash hotel, and gorgeous was the dress of my heroine: it would make Broadway stare. He spake as never man spake; she replied in sentimental quotations. With great care I copied the stuff and sent it to Philadelphia.

In two weeks the heavy package came back to me. The Editor had examined my manuscript, and must write that "the plot is too slight for a serial tale. He would recommend me to practice before attempting to print again, as book-making is no more a thing of inspiration than clock-making is."

Cool and kind advice; but I was stone-deaf. I threw out some hundreds of adjectives, rehashed the thing, and sent it to a religious paper in Michigan, that was like the Goldsmith family, to the last degree "poor and pious." It was accepted; but the editor could not afford to pay for such articles.

At last I saw myself in print. The story seemed wonderfully shrunken, and there were several misprints which drove me nearly crazy. But I was an "author"—therein like Shakspeare [*sic*]. In all this I had no confidant. I was shy and sensitive, and the idea of discovery put me in agony. I wrote in the attic, sitting in a broken-backed chair, with an old chest for a table.

Encouraged by this crumb of comfort, I wrote what was intended for a lively sketch of Western life, and sent it to the *Post*—Bryant's[2] paper. I aimed at the

2. William Cullen Bryant (1794–1878), American Romantic poet and editor of the *New York Post* from 1829 to 1878.

highest—beginners always do—and demanded ten dollars for my work. I presume the "Reader" of that article thought me hopelessly insane or a total idiot.

Soon after I was married. In the golden days of courtship and honey-moon, how many rhymes I made are known "To him who will understand them"—this being the flimsy veil under which Love strung my harp and taught me what to sing.

In the first six years of housekeeping and baby-tending, the *furore scribendi*[3] was pretty well kept down; but, like inherent disease, though long concealed, it is sure as death, and will come out.

One day, as I was embroidering a soft blanket, I said to myself, "My life is so narrow, so common, so poor, I will break through it once more and write a song, and see if I can not bring back some portion of the lost bloom and fresh breeze of morning." The old longing came upon me stronger than ever before; but with it a meekness altogether new. I was humble and patient, and felt weak as a little child.

Looking into my heart of hearts I wrote "My Children." Fifteen years ago baby-poetry was not so done to death as now; the subject did not seem worn out. I felt so keenly in writing that I found tears running down my face; surely, thought I, others must feel in some degree what stirs me so deeply. I dared not carry it in my pocket for fear it might be lost and I discovered. For weeks I wore it in my bosom. No deed of shame was ever hidden with more anxious care. After copying it nine times, I sent it to the *Home Journal.* Three weeks later I saw respectfully declined "My Children."

I was sorry but not hopeless. I remembered how often rejected poetry found way. I wrote it out again for a Chicago paper, and without name or date dropped it into the Post-Office at dusk. Had I been caught stealing I could not have felt more guilty as I hurried home.

The same week it appeared in fine type on the inside. No one noticed the thing, and it gradually passed out of my thoughts. One happy evening, as I was looking through *Harper's Magazine,* I found in the Drawer "My Children." I trembled from head to foot; blushing fearfully, I showed it to my husband; and when he said, "My love, I never doubted you could write poetry and prose too," I felt as if his hand had crowned me with laurel and myrtle.[4]

It was midwinter, and the snow was deep, but the sun went down in summer splendor, and daisies bloomed under my feet. For one transcendent hour I wore the robes of prophecy, and looked from shining heights into a glory yet to come. I was not a paid contributor to *Harper's Magazine,* but returns were in from the Promised

3. Latin: rage for writing.
4. Laurel and myrtle crowns were bestowed in ancient Greece upon victors in war or games and later became public symbols of recognition for various deeds, including literary genius.

Land. A breeze blew from the far hills of Beulah,[5] and for one night I feasted on grapes of Eschol.[6]

My poem was copied. I found it in an English periodical, and it came home in a bilious-looking sheet, *The Pioneer,* published in Salt Lake City. My neighbors read it, and gave me generous praise; and when a friend in Baltimore wrote, "Oh, Jane, if I had been told you wrote 'The Star-spangled Banner' I could not have been more surprised," my cup, so full before, ran over. Some years later I read "The Children's Hour,"[7] and finding a line in it identical with my own, I exclaimed, "The great musician, the sweetest of all singers, he has read my little song."

The mania for writing took complete possession of me. I sent out my sewing, and let the children have full swing in the arbor. They had a pretty high time, while I wore the ink-spot on my finger. Housekeeping went on as usual; but every thing was still as a grave, and I so absent-minded I might as well have been miles away. John came and went to his office in silence, while I fancied I heard a voice from heaven saying, "Write!" I wonder how he bore with me so long.

I wrote sketches intended to be amusing, a poem, and a long Indian story, "The Miami Lovers." The papers were usually accepted, but when I demanded wages for my work no one could afford to pay. "Pigeon-holes were crowded;" they were "over-run with just such articles;" "drawers were stuffed." I grew nervous and hollow-eyed. I could not eat, and the "Miami Lovers" murdered my sleep. The insanity ran on for five months, then the end came.

One September afternoon, as I leaned my aching head upon my hands, a light broke in upon my brain, and Common-Sense spoke:

"If a jury of twelve honest men bring sentence in a case fairly tried before them, would you abide by their verdict?"

"Certainly I would."

"You have addressed twelve editors. The sentence is, your writings are worth nothing, and the jury all agree."

It was over in an instant. I gathered my papers, walked to the kitchen, and dropped them under Biddy's tea-kettle.

"Shure! an yer after settin' the chimley afire," said she.

"No, there is not fire enough in my papers to do any damage."

But the joke was lost on Biddy.

I went through the house, and made a clean sweep. The trash was all consumed in an hour. It was equal to a spring cleaning. I washed the ink-spot away with a lemon (it was a very deep stain), called the children, tuned my guitar, and delighted them with a fandango. We had a glorious supper of wafers and honey, and a game

5. Reference to the Land of Beulah, a paradise, in John Bunyan's Christian allegory *Pilgrim's Progress* (1678).

6. From the Bible, a symbol of the land of plenty.

7. Popular poem by Henry Wadsworth Longfellow, published in 1859.

of romps afterward, and then the old songs. I believe John had a sort of instinct as to what had happened, but I knew he would never say one word; so I must speak first. That night, as I unbraided my long hair, the only beauty ever possessed by me, I said,

"John, I am done writing forever."

He came behind me and looked over my head at the haggard image in the glass before us. We stood a moment silent.

"So," he said, softly turning my face toward him, "my wife is coming home."

I burst into tears. I fell on his breast and sobbed aloud. The wife was indeed coming home.

I slept in halcyon quiet, and woke to new life. The ghosts of the "Miami Lovers" are laid forever. Peace descended upon our house, and the angel abides with us yet. I have ceased from troubling editors, and trust they are at rest.

One weakness remained—I leave nothing unconfessed: I could not burn "My Children." I had so doted on that bantling, and—it may as well be told—I dote on it still. The boy it glorifies is a tall fellow, at this moment going through the house like a young buffalo. My little girl has passed within the veil; but I hear my lost darling when I read the poor old rhymes, and they are as dear to me to-day as the first sweet words of my first sweet baby.

The impulse to write is not gone. Early dreams come back with mellow October days, and in banishing them I have something of the feeling which comes over me in listening to the dead march wailing for the burial of the brave and the beautiful. It returned in dim, vague yearnings when I saw Ristori,[8] when I heard Parepa[9] sing; but it will never possess me again. Should I yield to the influence, I would divide myself from what I love best for the sake of a pale, weak picture of emotion, which I can no more portray than I can copy the vanishing hues of sunset, the dying tints of the rainbow.

Oh, Easy Chair! I have heard you plead eloquently for woman, and I longed to tell you then, as I do now, that the gentlest act of your gentle life was to unbar the charmed gate and give me one fleeting glimpse of what lies within. The singers are there, and the harpers with their harps. Without are weeping and wailing and, I do believe, some gnashing of teeth. I try to warn weary pilgrims seeking that gate, as I stand afar off, not disconsolate, but content.

And now you have my "Experience"—Methodist, you see—will you listen to a few words of "Exhortation?"

I know you "weak-minded woman." I see your wistful eyes; I understand your

8. Adelaide Ristori (1822–1906), renowned Italian actress, who visited the United States in 1866.

9. Euphrosyne Parepa-Rosa (1836–1874), Scottish soprano, who also visited the United States in 1866–1867.

yearning heart; I watch your patient waiting. You fight seven days' battles every week. Let me take your tired hand as I speak. Bury pen and paper at once. Roll a great stone over the sepulchre, and seal it with a seal that shall remain unbroken till the coming of the Angel of the Resurrection. Do it cheerfully, and do it now. Your path is plain; you can not be author and do your duty. Take your place in the silent ranks of those

> "—who never sing,
> But die with all their music in them."[10]

If you train your sons to be men who will not lie or hunt office, and your daughters to be true and womanly as yourself, it is better than to have written "Aurora Leigh" or translated the "Inferno."[11]

"It is easy enough to preach," you say. Dear friend, I am ordained to preach, because I have first experienced.

In every human life there is something wanting. Your husband's home is not what he would like to have it; your friends are every one struggling for what they may never possess, and men feel just as we do. They, too, are bound down by circumstance, and made wretched by ambition. You and I know many a general in no way like Themistocles,[12] who finds the trophies of another will not let him sleep.

"If I could but speak like Miss Dickinson!"[13]

That way lies madness. The aloe which happened to burst into flower in our time will not blossom again in a hundred years. Should you undertake to address a town-meeting your knees would give way, you would come down in a heap, and your friends think you were struck with sudden imbecility. *You can't do it.*

If the motherly hen in your back-yard should try to follow the flight of the lark that "goes singing up to heaven's gate," what can she do? Get as high as the fence and fall on the other side, while the chickens scatter as if the hawk were come. Only this, and nothing more.

"But I would *so* love to write a little something!"

Well, my dear, I yield this much. Should the Glee Club wait on you for a campaigning song adapted to "Sparkling and Bright," it is enough. Write: the occasion and surroundings will give it value.

"I am so worn and faded."

Yes, we all are; it is pitiful. I think the secret cause is known only to the Great

10. Lines from Oliver Wendell Holmes's poem "The Voiceless," from his "Autocrat of the Breakfast Table" series (1858). The poem is specifically about women who are unable to fulfill their desires to write.

11. "Aurora Leigh" (1857), poem by Elizabeth Barrett Browning. "Inferno" refers to Dante's *Inferno* from *The Divine Comedy* (1306–1321).

12. Athenian military leader of the fifth century B.C.

13. Anna Dickinson (1842–1932), actress, lecturer, and author.

Physician. The strong women are dead. We all do fade as a leaf while men are in their summer prime. Your daughters wear your roses and lilies, and if heart and life be right the imprint on your face will make those who see understand "how angels come by their beauty."[14]

Cultivate cheerfulness; keep a funny book "lying around loose;" read the children's fairy tales and the glorious golden legends; avoid women looking for "spheres" and "missions." Listen to the children; such bright ones as yours can not live twelve hours without saying something to make you laugh. Buy a few perpetual roses; they will brighten a whole summer; and after the short crowded days of winter go into the starlight, look up to the chambers of the East, open your heart to the sweet influences of the Pleiades,[15] and remember the Land that lies beyond them.

The true reason of the growing unhappiness of women is that nearly all women write is feverish and morbid. Fanny Fern broke ground in this field; a host of sowers followed. The harvest is whitening, and you, poor child, have thrust in your sickle. As you value happiness turn your back on it and go home. Fling away ambition, or invest it in your sons.

Many women fail where men succeed because women do not support each other as men do. You are ready to stone me, but I will say it. I have heard very tame speeches in the Senate, after which Senators crowded up, and assured the speaker they had heard nothing like him since the days of Clay and Webster.[16] Of course the speaker knew they lied; but it was praise and encouragement; it was what he needed; it was delightful. I do not recommend a lie; but if you must err let it be on the pleasant side.

When Sallie Sunflower sent an essay "On Spring" to the county paper did you go and tell her she could do more and better? No. You made fun of her so it came to Sallie's ears, and she locked herself in her room and cried her eyes out. Why do you laugh at her for precisely the yearning after the ideal which you feel to-day? Weak stirrings of the same spirit which in higher natures have given us the majestic lines of Milton, the divine melodies of Mendelssohn.

Let a man commit a crime: his friends hide him, hustle him off on the early train, and stand by him to the last. Let a woman fall, and how many—I shame to think *how* many—hands are lifted to cast the first stone. I once saw a drunken woman carried through the street before a crowd of hooting boys. If some one, for the sake of all womanhood, had veiled that poor creature from the sunlight, the hand that did it would be whiter ever afterward. Nobody stirred. Why? Because we were afraid of what each other would say.

Finally, my dissatisfied sisters—(recollect I speak only to the married, I am too

14. Quote from Nathaniel Hawthorne's *The Marble Faun* (1860).

15. Star cluster in the constellation of Taurus.

16. American senators Henry Clay (1777–1852) and Daniel Webster (1782–1852), both known for their oratory.

weak to wrestle with the Giant)—let us not forget man was created first, and then woman. The colors of his life are deepest, the currents of his being strongest. I do not believe the world will ever produce a feminine Shakspeare [*sic*] or Milton, or a woman's hand write grand oratorios or create beauty like the Apollo.[17] We will vote before a great while; we may hold office; we may be angels; but we can never be men.

Tell me, were you a crowned queen, would you want a royal consort like England's, whose only aim was to sink his existence in that of the queen? I hope not. Rest assured, whatever you may do and be, your life is the second, the accompaniment to your husband's. It is "Bible doctrine," and I glory in preaching it. In the holy Trinity—I speak with awe and reverence—there is one sex. There is no mention of feminine angels. No women were called to be disciples. Only Moses and Elias appeared in the transfiguration.[18] We shall sit down with Abraham, Isaac, and Jacob.[19] Sarah, Rebecca, and Rachel will be there, but *not among the rulers.* It is the law.

Let us repeat the old, old story that made Eden Paradise. In our hands are the strings which hold the harmonies. Shall we fill the air with wailing, or wake an under-song so sweet that all who pass will pause to hear?

Source: New Harper's Monthly Magazine (1867)

17. Probably a reference to the Apollo Belvedere, an ancient marble statue that was revered for its perfect beauty.

18. In the New Testament, the Transfiguration of Jesus occurs when he is illuminated, speaks with Elijah (Elias) and Moses, and is called "son" by God.

19. The patriarchs or founders of Judaism. Their wives were Sarah, Rebecca, and Rachel. Leah was also a wife of Job, and the four are called the matriarchs of Judaism.

❧ Elizabeth Stuart Phelps (Ward) (1844–1911)

Born Mary Gray in Boston, Massachusetts, Phelps was the daughter of the popular author Elizabeth Stuart Phelps, whose name she adopted upon the latter's death in 1852. Her first story was published in the Youth's Companion *when she was thirteen. At twenty, she published her first story for adults in* Harper's New Monthly Magazine, *and in 1868, she became internationally known with the publication of her first novel,* The Gates Ajar, *which sold tens of thousands of copies and was used to sell merchandise from cigars to sheet music. Thereafter, she produced a steady stream of novels, some religious, and many concerned with social causes, particularly women's rights.* The Story of Avis *(1877) treats the problem of marriage for women with artistic talent and ambition. Phelps married Herbert Ward in 1888 and thereafter occasionally appended "Ward" to her name. Their marriage was not a happy one. "What Shall They Do?" was a sympathetic response to the letter from "A Weak-Minded Woman." In it Phelps describes a crowded literary market and goes on to survey other fields of employment for women. In the following excerpts from her autobiography, Phelps portrays her advent as an author and explains her literary theories in opposition to the vogue of masculine realism trumpeted by the influential critic William Dean Howells.*

What Shall They Do?

The tale not long ago unfolded by "a weak-minded woman" to the "Easy Chair" has fallen upon sympathetic ears.

We wish that she knew—we should like to sit down beside her in her kitchen and tell her—how our sorrowful thought has followed her through the hopeless waking, the hopeless work, the hopeless dreaming, through the whole dull, drudging day. We should like to have been there to slip the clothes upon the children, and run for the spoons and the water; we wished that we could have helped her skim the milk and make the fire—we will not offer to do the cooking, for our prophetic soul tells us that the result would be extraordinary; we make it a principle to let cooking alone, on condition that people shall let us alone, and not remind us of the typical woman who "talks French and plays the piano." But we would have gladly helped about the dusting and the dish-washing, and have planned a little that her golden hour in "the other room," in the "muslin dress," might grow into two, and the sunset find her with braver eyes and send her "strengthened on her way."

How to spend the treasured minutes, though, that is the question; we might have read to her, or we might have chatted with her; we might not, perhaps, have advised her to take the pen and paper down from the pantry-shelf. Then, perhaps, we might.

And this brings us to the point. "A weak-minded woman" is one of many, and their name is legion. Consumed with little wearing cares, their girlish dreams ended in a struggle for bread-and-butter—a steady disquiet aching through the days and nights, and a steady, baffled, disappointing effort to write it away—is not that about it?

To be sure they have not asked our advice, and may think that we don't know any more about the matter than they do, and very likely we don't; but if we think we do it answers the purpose. Perhaps the "Easy Chair" may be right in saying: "When the feeling is so strong, yield to it." Yet we venture to doubt whether this is always a safe rule.

As a general thing, it is next to impossible for a woman with the care of a family on her hands to be a successful writer. The majority of the exceptions made their literary reputation before marriage, and if they choose, may lie on their oars and drift on it. We assume that a woman at the head of a home proposes to take care of that home to begin with. If the husband and children have the go-by, and the magazine editors have the stories, we have nothing to say to her. She has no right to a place in the ranks of authorship. She has not come in by the door into the sheep-fold, but has climbed up some other way. Away down in some inner chamber of her heart she will find, if she make diligent search, a handwriting on the wall, but it is not our business to stop and translate it to her just now.

It is no easy matter to keep the "holy fire burning in the holy place,"[1] yet never be out of kindlings for the kitchen stove, nor forget to tell Bridget about the furnace dampers, nor let the baby have the match-box to play with. It is worse than a "Conflict of Ages." Women whose consciences would not let them be any thing but generous wives, and mothers faithful unto death, have had to give it up and lay by the pen forever. Women have died, too, in the struggle to bring the opposing forces into thorough, symmetrical union.

It can be done, to be sure; but it needs one or both of two things: the physical strength of an Amazon and talent of the highest order. They are the geniuses of the world, as a rule, who "make it pay" in any sense. "Le jeu ne vaut pas la chaudelle," for ordinary women.

If the magazines will not publish your stories it is a natural inference that you are not exactly a genius, is it not? It is of no use to suggest Keats, or talk about "mute, inglorious Miltons," or cast glances up at Wordsworth, "knowing that he should be unpopular, but knowing too that he should be immortal."[2] All that did very well for Keats and Wordsworth, but you and I may rest content that if nobody will publish for us we don't write any thing that is worth publishing. "Unappreciated genius" may be an obsolete fact; but in these days, when it is as easy to get into

---

1. Gail Hamilton, "Moving," from *Country Living and Country Thinking* (1862).
2. "Some mute inglorious Milton may here rest" is from Thomas Gray, "An Elegy Wrote in a Country Church Yard" (1751). Source of quote about Wordsworth unknown.

print as to write a letter about—to use a bit of the boys' slang—"played out"; and oh, Mr. Washington Moon, and Mr. Richard Grant White,[3] if you are frowning, why don't you give us something better?

So, good friend, looking wistfully up from among the children and the ironing-tables, don't depend on your pen to take away that persistent disquiet, or to hire an Irish girl. *Don't.* You run nine chances of bitter disappointment. Ah, we know all about it; taking the little yellow package out of the mail; hiding it in your pocket that no one may see; stealing away home heart-sick in the evening light, and up to your room to have a cry —you run nine chances of this where you have one of success. If, however, the Irish girl can come and the disquiet go, *without* depending on it, why, well and good.

Just here is room to say that we honestly believe that many women aspiring to authorship, and meeting with downright failure, might bring to themselves a little money and a good deal of pleasure, did they not fire too high. We have seen them repeatedly; women—and men too, for that matter—who have never written any thing of a more ambitious nature than a school-composition, deliberately proposing to send, and sending, their first essay or story or poem to *Harper's Magazine* or the *Atlantic.* Why, how do you expect, in your inexperience, that there will be any room for you in such quarters? Should you allow a raw cook, whom you have taken "to teach," to make her first experiments at bread-making, when you have company to dinner?

Aim lower. Send to the county papers. Lay siege to the Dailies. If they will print a story for you once in four months at three dollars a column, that is better than nothing, and will buy your summer bonnet, or take the children to the beach. If you had not exactly expected it, but brought it on rather as a side-dish in the entertainment, the success will be so much more pleasant, and the worry infinitely less. Perhaps by-and-by you will work yourself up over stepping-stones of your dead newspaper training to better things. Or perhaps you will stay where you are. In either case you will be where you belong, and should thank God and be content.

If, however, Monthlies and Weeklies and Dailies combined happen universally to "have their columns full just now, and much regret that they can not make room for your excellent article," give it up. You are only wasting time and strength and hope that, as far as money goes, would bring you in more spent in crocheting edging for the fancy stores; as far as usefulness goes, had better be given to the cheering of some other life more disheartened and crowded than your own; as far as positive, necessary comfort to yourself goes, might be better employed in company with a poem, or a picture, or your little Bible, perhaps, in certain moods, out under the apple-trees, where it is cool and still.

3. George Washington Moon was author of *The Dean's English* (1866). Richard Grant White (1822–1885) was a Shakespearean scholar and the author of *Words and Their Uses* (1870), which was a compilation of previously published articles.

It is not strange, but it is sorrowful, to see in what crowds the women, married and unmarried, flock to the gates of authorship. Here and there you see them with white hands of command turning back the ponderous golden hinges and entering in where the palms are, and the crowns. Down below they are turning away in great sad groups, shut out.

Why will people persist in utterly hopeless efforts? And why, when one thing fails, will they not try another thing?

Women have a mania for going where they are not wanted, and then complaining that nobody makes room for them.

Authorship is but one of several favored avenues of employment, which they choke up to the brim, till no one has room to breathe, much less to turn around and take courage. . . .

Source: Harper's New Monthly Magazine (1867)

Chapters from a Life [Excerpts]

My mother, whose name I am proud to wear, was the eldest daughter of professor Stuart, and inherited his intellectuality. At the time of her death she was at the first blossom of her very positive and widely-promising success as a writer of the simple home stories which took such a hold upon the popular heart. Her "Sunnyside"[4] had already reached a circulation of one hundred thousand copies, and she was following it fast—too fast—by other books for which the critics and the publishers clamored. Her last book and her last baby came together, and killed her. She lived one of those rich and piteous lives such as only gifted women know; torn by the civil war of the dual nature which can be given to women only. It was as natural for her daughter to write as to breathe; but it was impossible for her daughter to forget that a woman of intellectual power could be the most successful of mothers.

"Everybody's mother is a remarkable woman," my father used to say when he read overdrawn memoirs indited by devout children; and yet I have sometimes felt as if even the generation that knows her not would feel a certain degree of interest in the tact and power by which this unusual woman achieved the difficult reconciliation between genius and domestic life.

In our times and to our women such a problem is practical, indeed. One need not possess genius to understand it now. A career is enough.

The author of "Sunnyside," "The Angel on the Right Shoulder," and "Peep at Number Five," lived before women had careers and public sympathy in them. Her

4. Her mother, Elizabeth Stuart Phelps (1815–1852), published the novels *Sunnyside* (1851) and *A Peep at Number Five* (1852), and the short story "The Angel Over the Right Shoulder" (1852), about a woman's struggles to manage a household and develop her mind.

nature was drawn against the grain of her times and of her circumstances; and where our feet find easy walking, hers were hedged. A child's memories go for something by way of tribute to the achievement of one of those rare women of the elder time whose gifts forced her out, but whose heart held her in.

I can remember no time when I did not understand that my mother must write books because people would have and read them; but I cannot remember one hour in which her children needed her and did not find her.

My first distinct vision of this kind of a mother gives her by the nursery lamp, reading to us her own stories, written for ourselves, never meant to go beyond that little public of two, and illustrated in colored crayons by her own pencil. For her gift in this direction was of an original quality, and had she not been a writer she must have achieved something as an artist.

Perhaps it was to keep the standards up, and a little girl's filial adoration down, that these readings ended with some classic—Wordsworth, I remember most often— "We are Seven," or "Lucy Gray."

It is certain that I very early had the conviction that a mother was a being of power and importance to the world; but that the world had no business with her when we wanted her. In a word, she was a strong and lovely symmetry—a woman whose heart had not enfeebled her head, but whose head could never freeze her heart.

I hardly know which of those charming ways in which I learned to spell the word motherhood impressed me most. All seemed to go on together side by side and step by step. Now she sits correcting proof-sheets, and now she is painting apostles for the baby's first Bible lesson. Now she is writing her new book, and now she is dyeing things canary-yellow in the white-oak dye—for the professor's salary is small, and a crushing economy was in those days one of the conditions of faculty life on Andover Hill. Now—for her practical ingenuity was unlimited—she is whittling little wooden feet to stretch the children's stockings on, to save them from shrinking; and now she is reading to us from the old, red copy of Hazlitt's "British Poets," by the register, upon a winter night. Now she is a popular writer, incredulous of her first success, with her future flashing before her; and now she is a tired, tender mother, crooning to a sick child, while the MS. lies unprinted on the table, and the publishers are wishing their professor's wife were a free woman, childless and solitary, able to send copy as fast as it is wanted. The struggle killed her, but she fought till she fell.

In these different days, when,

> "Pealing, the clock of time
> Has struck the Woman's Hour,"[5]

---

5. From Phelps's poem "Victurae Salutamus" (1885), written for the first commencement at Smith College.

I have sometimes been glad, as my time came to face the long question which life puts to-day to all women who think and feel, and who care for other women and are loyal to them, that I had those early visions of my own to look upon.

When I was learning why the sun rose and the moon set, how the flowers grew and the rain fell, that God and heaven and art and letters existed, that it was intelligent to say one's prayers, and that well-bred children never told a lie, I learned that a mother can be strong and still be sweet, and sweet although she is strong; and that she whom the world and her children both have need of, is of more value to each, for this very reason. . . .

The first thing which I wrote, marking in any sense the beginning of what authors are accustomed to call their "literary career," —I dislike the phrase and wish we had a better,—was a war story.

As nearly as I can recall the facts, up to this time I had shown no literary tendency whatever, since the receipt of that check for two dollars and a half. Possibly the munificence of that honorarium seemed to me to satiate mortal ambition for years. It is true that, during my schooldays, I did perpetrate three full-grown novels in manuscript. My dearest particular intimate and I shared in this exploit, and read our chapters to each other on Saturday afternoons.

I remember that the title of one of these "books" was "The Shadow of a Lifetime." It was a double title with a heroine to it, but I forget the lady's name, or even the nature of her particular shadow. The only thing that can be said about these three volumes is, that their youthful author had the saving sense not to try the Christian temper of a publisher with their perusal.

Yet, in truth, I have never regretted the precious portion of human existence spent in their creation; for I must have written off in that way a certain amount of apprenticeship which does, in some cases, find its way into type, and devastate the endurance of a patient public.

The war story of which I speak was distinctly the beginning of anything like genuine work for me. Mr. Alden[6] tells me that it was published in January, 1864; but I think it must have been written a while before that, though not long, for its appearance quickly followed the receipt of the manuscript. The name of the story was "A Sacrifice Consumed." It was a very little story, not covering more than four or five pages in print. I sent it to "Harper's Magazine," without introduction or what young writers are accustomed to call "influence;" it was sent quite privately, without the knowledge of any friend. It was immediately accepted, and a prompt check for twenty-five dollars accompanied the acceptance. Even my father knew nothing of the venture until I carried the letter and enclosure to him. The pleasure of his expressive face was only equaled by its frank and unqualified astonishment.

6. Henry Mills Alden (1836–1919) edited *Harper's New Monthly Magazine* from 1869 to 1919.

He read the story when it came out, and, I think, was touched by it,—it was a story of a poor and plain little dressmaker, who lost her lover in the army,—and his genuine emotion gave me a kind of awed elation which has never been repeated in my experience. Ten hundred thousand unknown voices could not move me to the pride and pleasure which my father's first gentle word of approval gave to a girl who cared much to be loved and little to be praised; and the plaudits of a "career" were the last things in earth or heaven then occupying her mind.

Afterwards, I wrote with a distinct purpose, and, I think, quite steadily. I know that longer stories went, soon and often, to the old magazine, which never sent them back; and to which I am glad to pay the tribute of a gratitude that I have never outgrown. There was nothing of the stuff that heroines and geniuses are made of in a shy and self-distrustful girl, who had no faith in her own capabilities, and, indeed, at that time the smallest possible amount of interest in the subject.

It may be a humiliating fact, but it is the truth, that had my first story been refused, or even the second or the third, I should have written no more.

For the opinion of important editors, and for the sacredness of market value in literary wares, as well as in professorships or cotton cloth, I had a kind of respect at which I sometimes wonder; for I do not recall that it was ever distinctly taught me. But, assuredly, if nobody had cared for my stories enough to print them, I should have been the last person to differ from the ruling opinion, and should have bought at Warren Draper's old Andover book-store no more cheap printer's paper on which to inscribe the girlish handwriting (with the pointed letters and the big capitals) which my father, with patient pains, had caused to be taught me by a queer old traveling master with an idea. Professor Phelps, by the way, had an exquisite chirography, which none of his children, to his evident disappointment, inherited.

But the editor of "Harper's" took everything I sent him; so the pointed letters and the large capitals continued to flow towards his desk.

Long after I had achieved whatever success has been given me, this magazine returned me one of my stories—it was the only one in a lifetime. I think the editor then in power called it too tragic, or too something; it came out forthwith in the columns of another magazine that did not agree with him, and was afterwards issued, I think, in some sort of "classic" series of little books.

I was a little sorry, I know, at the time, for I had the most superstitious attachment for the magazine that, when "I was a stranger, took me in;" but it was probably necessary to break the record in this, as in all other forms of human happiness. A manuscript by any chance returned from any other quarter seemed a very inferior affliction.

Other magazines took their turn—the "Atlantic," I remember—in due course; but I shared the general awe of this magazine at that time prevailing in New England, and, having, possibly, more than my share of personal pride, did not very early venture to intrude my little risk upon that fearful lottery.

The first story of mine which appeared in the "Atlantic" was a fictitious narrative of certain psychical phenomena occurring in Connecticut, and known to me, at first hand, to be authentic. I have yet to learn that the story attracted any attention from anybody more disinterested than those few friends of the sort who, in such cases, are wont to inquire, in tones more freighted with wonder than admiration: "What! Has she got into the '*Atlantic*'?"

The "Century" came in turn, when it came into being. To this delightful magazine I have always been, and always hope to be, a contributor.

I read, with a kind of hopeless envy, histories and legends of people of our craft who "do not write for money." It must be a pleasant experience to be able to cultivate so delicate a class of motives for the privilege of doing one's best to express one's thoughts to people who care for them. Personally, I have yet to breathe the ether of such a transcendent sphere. I am proud to say that I have always been a working woman, and always had to be; though I ought to add that I am sure the proposal that my father's allowance to his daughter should cease, did not come from the father.

When the first little story appeared in "Harper's Magazine," it occurred to me, with a throb of pleasure greater than I supposed then that life could hold, that I could take care of myself, and from that day to this I have done so. . . .

I have been particularly asked, in closing these papers, to say a few words about my own theory of literary art. However unimportant one's personal fraction of achievement may be, it is built upon theory of some kind; and the theory may be considered of as much or as little interest or value as the work achieved. . . .

In a word, I believe it to be the province of the literary artist to tell the truth about the world he lives in, and I suggest that, in so far as he fails to be an accurate truth-teller, he fails to be an artist. Now there is something obviously very familiar about this simple proposition; and, turning to trace the recognition down, one is amused to perceive that here is almost the precise language of the school of writers to which one distinctly does not belong. Truth, like climate, is common property; and I venture to suggest that the issue between the two contending schools of literary art to-day is not so much one of fact as of form; or, perhaps I should rather say, not so much one of theory as of temperament in the expression of theory.

A literary artist portrays life as it is, or has been, as it might be, or as it should be. We classify him as the realist, the romanticist, or the idealist; though I am not sure but our classification is more defective than his ability to meet it. Separate, for instance, the first of these clauses from the formulation. Let us say, it is the duty of the artist in fiction to-day to paint life as it exists. With this inevitable observation who of us has any quarrel?

The quarrel arises when the artist defines his subject, and chooses his medium. The conflict begins when the artist proffers his personal impression as to what life is. "Your work," said Hall Caine before the Century Club, "is what you are."[7] Just here, I venture to suggest, lies the only important, uncontested field left in a too familiar war. Most of the controversy between our schools of art goes "firing wild," because it fails to perceive the true relations of this one simple feature of resistance.

We are all agreed, I submit, that we should picture life as it is. If I may return to the definite words,—our difference is not so much one of artistic theory as of the personal equation. Our book reveals what life is to us. Life is to us what we are.

Mr. Howells, in his charming papers on literary Boston,[8] has given us some of the latest phrases of the school of art whose chief exponent in America he undoubtedly is. Of our great New Englanders—Hawthorne, Emerson, Longfellow, Lowell, Whittier, Holmes, Mrs. Stowe[9]—he says: "Their art was Puritan. So far as it was impressed . . . it was marred by the intense ethicism that pervaded . . . and still characterizes the New England mind . . . They still helplessly pointed the moral in all they did. It was in poetry and in romance that they excelled. In the novel, so far as they attempted it, they failed . . . New England yet lacks her novelist, because it was her instinct and her conscience to be true to an ideal of life rather than to life itself." Of the greatest of American novels, he concluded by saying that "it is an address to the conscience and not to the taste; to the ethical sense, not the æsthetical sense."

This is not the place, nor does it offer the space, in which to reply with anything which I should call thoroughness to such a view of the nature of art. But it seems to be the place for me to suggest, at least, so much as this:—Since art implies the truthful and conscientious study of life as it is, we contend that to be a radically defective view of art which would preclude from it the ruling constituents of life. Moral character is to human life what air is to the natural world;—it is elemental. . . .

"Helplessly to point the moral" is the last thing needful or artistic. The moral takes care of itself. Life is moral struggle. Portray the struggle, and you need write no tract. In so far as you feel obliged to write the tract, your work is not well done. One of the greatest works of fiction ever given to the world in any tongue was "Les Misérables." Are those five books the less novels because they raised the mortal cry of the despised and rejected against the deafness of the world? By the majesty of a great art, No!

Did Victor Hugo write a tract? He told an immortal story. Hold beside it the

7. Hall Caine (1853–1931) was a British novelist. The Century Club was a private, all-male club for artists and authors founded in New York in 1847.

8. William Dean Howells (1837–1920), often referred to as the Dean of American Letters, published essays on literary Boston in *Harper's New Monthly Magazine* and collected them in *Literary Friends and Acquaintance* (1900).

9. Nathaniel Hawthorne (1804–1864), Ralph Waldo Emerson (1803–1882), Henry Wadsworth Longfellow (1807–1882), James Russell Lowell (1819–1891), John Greenleaf Whittier (1807–1892), Oliver Wendell Holmes, Sr. (1809–1894), and Harriet Beecher Stowe (1811–1896).

sketches and pastels, the etchings, the studies in dialect, the adoration of the incident, the dissection of the cadaver, which form the fashion in the ateliers of our schools to-day!

It has seemed to me, to return to the personal question, that so far as one is able to command attention at all, one's first duty in the effort to become a literary artist is to portray the most important, not altogether the least important, features of the world he lives in.

The last thirty years in America have pulsated with moral struggle. No phase of society has escaped it. It has ranged from social experiment to religious cataclysm, and to national upheaval. I suggest that even moral reforms, even civic renovations, might have their proper position in the artistic representation of a given age or stage of life. I submit that even the religious nature may be fit material for a work of art, which shall not be refused the name of a novel *for that reason*. Such expressions of "ethicism" are phases of human life, are elements of human nature.

Therefore, they are lawful material for any artist who chooses them; who understands them; and whose art is sufficient for their control. If he has sacrificed truth or beauty to didactics, he is, in so far, no artist. But because he selects for his canvas—whether from mere personal aptitude, or from a color sense, which leads him to prefer the stronger values—the moral elements of life, he shall not *for that reason* be denied the name of artist. "Omit Eternity in your estimate of area," said a great mathematician, "and your solution is wrong." Omit the true proportions of moral responsibility in your estimate of beauty, you who paint for "Art's sake," and your art is in error. . . .

Source: Chapters from a Life (1896)

❧ Adah Isaacs Menken (1835–1868)

Although little is known about her today, Adah Isaacs Menken was a trans-Atlantic celebrity and nineteenth-century sex symbol. Likely born in New Orleans, she was an actress famous for her sexually charged and semi-nude performances, as well as a poet and artist. Her ethnic background is unclear; at various times she claimed she was Jewish, Spanish, Creole, African American, and white. She also reported that her real name was Adelaide McCord and Adelaide Thomas, although her birth name was probably Ada Bertha Theodore. She created her pen and stage name from that of her second husband, Alexander Isaacs Menken, and was married at least four times. Infelicia (1868), her only collection of poetry, appeared a week after her death. Her passionate poetry conveyed the influence of Walt Whitman, who called her "another woman born too soon." Menken flouted gender conventions in her life as well as her poetry, claiming the romantic inspiration of genius without regard to the limitations of womanhood. "Where power exists, it cannot be suppressed," she writes in "Genius."

Miserimus[1]

"Sounding through the silent dimness
    Where I faint and weary lay,
Spake a poet: 'I will lead thee
    To the land of song to-day.'"

I.

O Bards! weak heritors of passion and of pain!

Dwellers in the shadowy Palace of Dreams!

With your unmated souls flying insanely at the stars!

Why have you led me lonely and desolate to the Deathless Hill of Song?

You promised that I should ring trancing shivers of rapt melody down to the dumb earth.

You promised that its echoes should vibrate till Time's circles met in old Eternity.

You promised that I should gather the stars like blossoms to my white bosom.

You promised that I should create a new moon of Poesy.

You promised that the wild wings of my soul should shimmer through the dusky locks of the clouds, like burning arrows, down into the deep heart of the dim world.

---

1. *Miserrimus* (Menken omits the second *r*), Latin for most pitiful, unfortunate, or wretched.

But, O Bards! sentinels on the Lonely Hill, why breaks there yet no Day to me?

II.

O lonely watchers for the Light! how long must I grope with my dead eyes in the sand?

Only the red fire of Genius, that narrows up life's chances to the black path that crawls on to the dizzy clouds.

The wailing music that spreads its pinions to the tremble of the wind, has crumbled off to silence.

From the steep ideal the quivering soul falls in its lonely sorrow like an unmated star from the blue heights of Heaven into the dark sea.

O Genius! is this thy promise?

O Bards! is this all?

Dreams of Beauty

Visions of Beauty, of Light, and of Love,
    Born in the soul of a Dream,
Lost, like the phantom-bird under the dove,
    When she flies over a stream—

Come ye through portals where angel wings droop,
    Moved by the heaven of sleep?
Or, are ye mockeries, crazing a soul,
    Doomed with its waking to weep?

I could believe ye were shadows of earth,
    Echoes of hopes that are vain,
But for the music ye bring to my heart,
    Waking its sunshine again.

And ye are fleeting. All vainly I strive
    Beauties like thine to portray;
Forth from my pencil the bright picture starts,
    And—ye have faded away.

Like to a bird that soars up from the spray,
    When we would fetter its wing;

Like to the song that spurns Memory's grasp
    When the voice yearneth to sing;

Like the cloud-glory that sunset lights up,
    When the storm bursts from its height;
Like the sheet-silver that rolls on the sea,
    When it is touched by the night—

Bright, evanescent, ye come and are gone,
    Visions of mystical birth;
Art that could paint you was never vouchsafed
    Unto the children of earth.

Yet in my soul there's a longing to tell
    All you have seemed unto me,
That unto others a glimpse of the skies
    You in their sorrow might be.

Vain is the wish. Better hope to describe
    All that the spirit desires,
When through a cloud of vague fancies and schemes
    Flash the Promethean fires.

Let me then think of ye, Visions of Light,
    Not as the tissue of dreams,
But as realities destined to be
    Bright in Futurity's beams.

Ideals formed by a standard of earth
    Sink at Reality's shrine
Into the human and weak like ourselves,
    Losing the essence divine;

But the fair pictures that fall from above
    On the heart's mirror sublime
Carry a signature written in tints,
    Bright with the future of time.

And the heart, catching them, yieldeth a spark
    Under each stroke of the rod—

Sparks that fly upward and light the New Life,
    Burning an incense to God!

Genius

"Where'er there's a life to be kindled by love,
    Wherever a soul to inspire,
Strike this key-note of God that trembles above
    Night's silver-tongued voices of fire."

Genius is power.

The power that grasps in the universe, that dives out beyond space, and grapples with the starry worlds of heaven.

If genius achieves nothing, shows us no results, it is so much the less genius.

The man who is constantly fearing a lion in his path is a coward.

The man or woman whom excessive caution holds back from striking the anvil with earnest endeavour, is poor and cowardly of purpose.

The required step must be taken to reach the goal, though a precipice be the result.

Work must be done, and the result left to God.

The soul that is in earnest, will not stop to count the cost.

Circumstances cannot control genius: it will nestle with them: its power will bend and break them to its path.

This very audacity is divine.

Jesus of Nazareth did not ask the consent of the high priests in the temple when he drove out the "moneychangers;" but, impelled by inspiration, he knotted the cords and drove them hence.

Genius will find room for itself, or it is none.

Men and women, in all grades of life, do their utmost.

If they do little, it is because they have no capacity to do more.

I hear people speak of "unfortunate genius," of "poets who never penned their inspirations;" that

"Some mute inglorious Milton here may rest;"[2]

of "unappreciated talent," and "malignant stars," and other contradictory things.

It is all nonsense.

Where power exists, it cannot be suppressed any more than the earthquake can be smothered.

2. Thomas Gray, "An Elegy Wrote in a Country Church Yard" (1751).

As well attempt to seal up the crater of Vesuvius as to hide God's given power of the soul.

> "You may as well forbid the mountain pines
> To wag their high tops, and to make no noise
> When they are fretten with the gusts of heaven,"[3]

as to hush the voice of genius.

There is no such thing as unfortunate genius.

If a man or woman is fit for work, God appoints the field.

He does more; He points to the earth with her mountains, oceans, and cataracts, and says to man, *"Be great!"*

He points to the eternal dome of heaven and its blazing worlds, and says: "Bound out thy life with beauty."

He points to the myriads of down-trodden, suffering men and women, and says: "Work with me for the redemption of these, my children."

He lures, and incites, and thrusts greatness upon men, and they will not take the gift.

Genius, on the contrary, loves toil, impediment, and poverty; for from these it gains its strength, throws off the shadows, and lifts its proud head to immortality.

Neglect is but the fiat to an undying future.

To be popular is to be endorsed in the To-day and forgotten in the To-morrow.

It is the mess of pottage that alienates the birthright.[4]

Genius that succumbs to misfortune, that allows itself to be blotted by the slime of slander—and other serpents that infest society—is so much the less genius.

The weak man or woman who stoops to whine over neglect, and poverty, and the snarls of the world, gives the sign of his or her own littleness.

Genius is power.

The eternal power that can silence worlds with its voice, and battle to the death ten thousand arméd Hercules.

Then make way for this God-crowned Spirit of Night, that was born in that Continuing City, but lives in lowly and down-trodden souls!

Fling out the banner!

Its broad folds of sunshine will wave over the turret and dome, and over the thunder of oceans on to eternity.

---

3. William Shakespeare, *The Merchant of Venice* (1596–1598).
4. In Genesis 25:29–34, Esau sells his birthright for a "mess of pottage," or lentil stew.

"Fling it out, fling it out o'er the din of the world!
  Make way for this banner of flame,
That streams from the mast-head of ages unfurled,
  And inscribed by the deathless in name.
And thus through the years of eternity's flight,
  This insignia of soul shall prevail,
The centre of glory, the focus of light;
  O Genius! proud Genius, all hail!"[5]

Source: Infelicia (1868)

5. Apparently, Menken's own composition.

🍂 Sarah Orne Jewett (1849–1909)

Sarah Orne Jewett, the daughter of a wealthy physician in South Berwick, Maine, began submitting stories to prominent magazines in 1867 under the names Alice Eliot, Sarah Sweet, and A. C. Eliot. She was published in the Atlantic Monthly *in 1869 and culti-vated a serious career as an author, never having to depend upon her writing for a living. Her book* Country of the Pointed Firs *(1896) is considered a masterpiece of American regionalist literature. As her letters to Horace Scudder, an* Atlantic *editor, suggest, she sought the advice of influential men at the outset of her career. As she developed as a writer, however, she was firm in her own theories of literature and shared them freely, such as in the letter to Frederick M. Hopkins, an editorial assistant for* Harper's Monthly *and* Munsey's. *She also was the center of a supportive community of women writers, including Annie Fields, with whom she lived and traveled in a "Boston marriage" for eighteen years. Her mentorship of Willa Cather convinced the younger writer to give up editing and devote herself to authorship.*

Letters

South Berwick, Maine
November 30, 1869

Dear Sir [Horace Scudder]:

Thank you for your kind note and especially for your criticisms on my two stories. They will help me, I know. You were right about "Mr. Bruce"[1] and if I were talking instead of writing I would tell you of ever so many things that might have been very different. I couldn't expect it to be perfect. In the first place I couldn't write a perfect story, and, secondly, I didn't try very hard on that. I wrote it in two evenings after ten, when I was supposed to be in bed and sound asleep, and I copied it in part of another day. That's all the work I "laid out" on it. It was last August and I was nineteen then, but now I'm twenty. So you see you are "an old hand" and I "a novice" after all. Do you remember in "Mr. Bruce" I made Elly say that, like Miss Alcott's Jo,[2] she had the habit of "falling into a vortex?" That's myself, but I mean to be more sensible. I mean to write this winter and I think you will know of it.

I like the *Riverside M*[*agazine*] so much, and what you have written, and you are delightful to have dear old Hans Andersen. I don't see the *Riverside* regularly though. I'm not a bit grown up if I am twenty and I like my children's books just as

---

1. "Mr. Bruce" appeared anonymously in the *Atlantic Monthly* in 1869.
2. Jo March in Louisa May Alcott's *Little Women* (1868). Alcott also used the expression "falling into a vortex" to refer to herself in her journals.

well as ever I did, and I read them just the same. I'd like to see the "Buttons" in print; you said the 18th, I think. It's a dreadful thing to have been born very lazy, isn't it, Mr. Scudder? For I might write ever so much; it's very easy for me, and when I have been so successful in what I have written. I ought to study—which I never did in my life hardly, except reading, and I ought to try harder and perhaps by and by I shall know something I can write really well.

There was no need for me to write this note and I'm a silly girl. I know it. But your letter was very nice and you are kind to be interested in my stories. So I beg your pardon and will never do so any more.

You said you had seen my name before. It was some verses—"The Old Doll"— two ~~or three~~ years ago, I think. I must hunt them up. I believe they were very silly.

> Yours very respectfully and gratefully,
> "Alice Eliot"

South Berwick, Maine
July 1, 1873

My dear Mr. Scudder:

You have always been so kind to me that I cannot help thinking of you as one of my friends, and I have a question to ask which I am sure you will be able to answer. So I ask it without making elaborate apologies. Will you tell me about keeping the copyright of my stories? Someone asked me not long ago if I would like to have them published in book form, and, though I did not care to tell him "yes," it has suggested to me that perhaps I might like to have someone else take them one of these days. And I know there is something about a thing's being "copyrighted" or not, which may hinder their being used over again. At any rate, I should like to know if there is anything for me to do about it.

I have been writing for the *Independent* since I saw you. Not very much, however, for I don't think I need the practice of writing so much as I need study, and care in other ways. I think you advised me long ago not to write too much, or to grow careless? I am getting quite ambitious and really feel that writing is my work— my business perhaps; and it is so much better than making a mere amusement of it as I used.

I sent you some sketches I gave a paper published at our Hospital Fair in Portland, not long ago. I am really trying to be very much in earnest and to do the best I can, and I know you will wish me "good luck." I have had nothing to complain of, for the editors have never proved to be dragons, and I even find I have achieved a small reputation already. I am glad to have something to do in the world and something which may prove very helpful and useful if I care to make it so, which I certainly do. But I am disposed to long-windedness! If you will tell me with the least possible trouble to yourself how I can have my stories copyrighted, or "keep the copyright" I believe one should say—or if it is not necessary, I shall thank you exceedingly, both for that and for your other kindnesses.

> Yrs very sincerely,
> Sarah O. Jewett

South Berwick, Maine
July 13, 1873

My dear Mr. Scudder:

In the first place, I think this letter will need no answer. Does not this announcement help you to begin to read it with a pleasanter feeling? The truth is I wish to talk to you a little about my writing. I am more than glad to have you criticise me. I know I must need it very much and I realize the disadvantage of never hearing anything about my stories except from my friends, who do not write themselves, and are not unexceptionable authorities upon any strictly literary question. I do know several literary people quite well, but whenever they read anything of mine I know that they look down from their pinnacles in a benignant way and think it very well done "for her," as the country people say. And all this is not what I want. Then it is a disadvantage that I should have been so successful in getting my nonsense printed!

I am so glad to have you show me where I fail, for I wish to gain as fast as possible and I must know definitely what to do. But Mr. Scudder, I think my chief fault is my being too young and knowing so little! Those sketches I sent you were carefully written. Of course they were experiments and I could perhaps have made them better if they could have been longer. Those first stories of mine were written with as little thought and care as one could possibly give and write them at all. Lately I have chosen my words and revised as well as I knew how; though I always write impulsively—very fast and without much plan. And, strange to say, this same fault shows itself in my painting, for the more I worked over pictures the stiffer and more hopeless they grew. I have one or two little marine views I scratched off to use up paint and they are bright and real and have an individuality—just as the "Cannon Dresses"[3] did. That is the dearest and best thing I have ever written. "The Shore House," which Mr. Howells has,[4] reminds me of it and comes next. I wrote

3. Jewett published "The Girl With the Cannon Dresses" in *Riverside Magazine* in August 1870.

4. William Dean Howells was the editor of the *Atlantic Monthly,* in which Jewett's "The Shore House" did not appear until September 1873.

it in the same way and I think it has the same reality. I believe the only thing he found fault with was that I did not make more of it. "The characters were good enough for me to say a great deal more of them."

But I don't believe I could write a long story as he suggested, and you advise me in this last letter. In the first place, I have no dramatic talent. The story would have no plot. I should have to fill it out with descriptions of character and meditations. It seems to me I can furnish the theatre, and show you the actors, and the scenery, and the audience, but there never is any play! I could write you entertaining letters perhaps, from some desirable house where I was in most charming company, but I couldn't make a story about it. I seem to get very much bewildered when I try to make these come in for secondary parts. And what shall be done with such a girl? For I wish to keep on writing, and to do the very best I can.

It is rather discouraging to find I lose my best manner by studying hard and growing older and wiser! Copying one's self has usually proved disastrous. Shall not I let myself alone and not try definitely for this trick of speech or that, and hope that I shall grow into a sufficient respectability as the years go on? I do not know how much real talent I have as yet, how much there is in me to be relied upon as original and effective in writing. I am certain I could not write one of the usual magazine stories. If the editors will take the sketchy kind and people like to read them, is not it as well to do that and do it successfully as to make hopeless efforts to achieve something in another line which runs much higher? You know the spirit in which I say this, for you know my writing has until very lately been done merely for the pleasure of it. It is not a bread and butter affair with me, though such a spendthrift as I could not fail to be glad of money, which has in most instances been lightly earned. I don't wish to ignore such a gift as this, God has given me. I have not the slightest conceit on account of it, indeed, I believe it frightens me more than it pleases me.

Now it has been a great satisfaction to have said all this to you. Please look upon it as a slight tribute to your critical merits which no one can appreciate more heartily than I, and remember that I told you in the beginning there would be no questions which would need answering.

Thank you for telling me of your engagement, though I had heard of it long ago from some Boston friend and I had half a mind to speak of it when I was writing you. I am very glad now to send you my best wishes. I shall like exceedingly to see Miss Owen,[5] and I congratulate you both with all my heart.

Yours most sincerely,
Sarah O. Jewett

5. Scudder married Grace Owen later that year.

South Berwick, Maine
May 22, 1893

My dear Sir [Frederick M. Hopkins]:

I often keep up this average of writing but while I can keep even to a higher average for a week or so, I am not a steady worker like Mr. Howells, for instance, and I am apt to have long spaces between these seasons of writing, when I do hardly any writing at all except many letters, and occasional pages of memoranda. Sometimes I have written sketches of 6000 or 7000 words in a single day. Of course that is exceptional, but I am apt to be at work during five or six weeks and then stop, except that I am always thinking about my work.

This is all I can say about my irregular fashions of getting my sketches done.

About the other matter—I certainly never expressed myself in those words about my town friends and neighbours. You know there is a saying of Plato's that the best thing one can do for the people of a State is to make them acquainted with each other, and it was some instinctive feeling of this sort which led me to wish that the town and country people were less suspicious of one another. When I was writing the Deephaven sketches[6] not long after I was twenty and was beginning my *Atlantic* work, it was just the time when people were beginning to come into the country for the summer in such great numbers. It has certainly been a great means of broadening both townsfolk and country folk. I think nothing has done so much for New England in the last decade; it accounts for most of the enlargement and great gain that New England has certainly made, as if there had been a fine scattering or sowing broadcast of both thought and money! But twenty years ago city-people and country-people were a little suspicious of each other—and, more than that, the only New Englander generally recognized in literature was the caricatured Yankee.

I tried to follow Mrs. Stowe in those delightful early chapters of *The Pearl of Orr's Island*[7] in writing about people of rustic life just as they were. Now there are a great many stories with this intention, but twenty years ago there were hardly any. "Human nature is the same the world over" but somehow the caricature of the Yankee, the Irishman, the Frenchman takes its place first, and afterwards comes a more true and sympathetic rendering. This is a most interesting subject, is it not?

Pardon so long a letter, which I have been obliged to write in great haste, and believe me

Yours sincerely,
S. O. Jewett

Source: Sarah Orne Jewett Letters, ed. Richard Cary (1967)

6. *Deephaven* (1877) was comprised of a series of related sketches, which first appeared in the *Atlantic Monthly,* about the visit of two Bostonian women to the New England countryside.

7. Harriet Beecher Stowe's *The Pearl of Orr's Island* (1862) was set in rural Maine.

148 Charles Street, Boston, Mass.,
Sunday, 13th of *December* [1908].

My dear Willa [Cather],—I have been thinking about you and hoping that things are going well. I cannot help saying what I think about your writing and its being hindered by such incessant, important, responsible work as you have in your hands now.[8] I do think that it is impossible for you to work so hard and yet have your gifts mature as they should—when one's first working power has spent itself nothing ever brings it back just the same, and I do wish in my heart that the force of this very year could have gone into three or four stories. In the "Troll-Garden" the Sculptor's Funeral[9] stands alone a head higher than the rest, and it is to that level you must hold and take for a starting-point. You are older now than that book in general; you have been living and reading and knowing new types; but if you don't keep and guard and mature your force, and above all, have time and quiet to perfect your work, you will be writing things not much better than you did five years ago. This you are anxiously saying to yourself! but I am wondering how to get at the right conditions. I want you to be surer of your backgrounds,—you have your Nebraska life,—a child's Virginia, and now an intimate knowledge of what we are pleased to call the "Bohemia" of newspaper and magazine-office life. These are uncommon equipment, but you don't see them yet quite enough from the outside,— you stand right in the middle of each of them when you write, without having the standpoint of the looker-on who takes them each in their relations to letters, to the world. Your good schooling and your knowledge of "the best that has been thought and said in the world,"[10] as Matthew Arnold put it, have helped you, but these you wish and need to deepen and enrich still more. You must find a quiet place near the best companions (not those who admire and wonder at everything one does, but those who know the good things with delight!). You do need reassurance,—every artist does!—but you need still more to feel "responsible for the state of your conscience" (your literary conscience, we can just now limit that quotation to), and you need to dream your dreams and go on to new and more shining ideals, to be aware of "the gleam" and to follow it; your vivid, exciting companionship in the office must not be your audience, you must find your own quiet centre of life, and write from that to the world that holds offices, and all society, all Bohemia; the city, the country—in short, you must write to the human heart, the great consciousness that all humanity goes to make up. Otherwise what might be strength in a writer is only crudeness, and what might be insight is only observation; sentiment falls to senti-

8. Cather was the editor of *McClure's* magazine.
9. Cather's first collection of stories, *The Troll Garden* (1905), in which "The Sculptor's Funeral" appeared. Many of the stories feature artists or musicians, most of them male.
10. From *Culture and Anarchy* (1869) by Matthew Arnold, a prominent British cultural theorist. This famous quote demarcated high culture from low or mass culture.

mentality—you can write about life, but never write life itself. And to write and work on this level, we must live on it—we must at least recognize it and defer to it at every step. We must be ourselves, but we must be our best selves. If we have patience with cheapness and thinness, as Christians must, we must know that it *is* cheapness and not make believe about it. To work in silence and with all one's heart, that is the writer's lot; he is the only artist who must be a solitary, and yet needs the widest outlook upon the world. But you have been growing I feel sure in the very days when you felt most hindered, and this will be counted to you. You need to have time to yourself and time to read and add to your recognitions. I do not know when a letter has grown so long and written itself so easily, but I have been full of thought about you. You will let me hear again from you before long?

Source: The Letters of Sarah Orne Jewett, ed. Annie Fields (1911)

ঌ Lucy Larcom (1824–1893)

Lucy Larcom, who was born in Beverly, Massachusetts, first gained notoriety as one of the mill girls who published in the Lowell Offering. *She was encouraged by the famous abolitionist poet John Greenleaf Whittier to devote herself to a literary career, which she did in 1862 after many years as a teacher. Larcom chose never to marry. She supported herself, in part, by editing the children's magazine* Our Young Folks *from 1865 to 1874. Her long career as a poet culminated in the publication of her complete* Poetical Works *in 1884. Her poem "Weaving" draws from her years working the looms in Lowell and responds to Tennyson's "The Lady of Shalott" (1833)—as Elizabeth Stoddard's "Before the Mirror" does—utilizing weaving as a metaphor for creativity or poetry. The excerpts from Larcom's autobiography describe her first literary aspirations and her experiences with* The Lowell Offering.

Weaving

All day she stands before her loom;
   The flying shuttles come and go:
By grassy fields, and trees in bloom,
   She sees the winding river flow.
And fancy's shuttle flieth wide,
And faster than the waters glide.

Is she entangled in her dreams,
   Like that fair weaver of Shalott,
Who left her mystic mirror's gleams,
   To gaze on light Sir Lancelot?
Her heart, a mirror sadly true,
Brings gloomier visions into view.

"I weave, and weave, the livelong day:
   The woof is strong, the warp is good:
I weave, to be my mother's stay;
   I weave, to win my daily food:
But ever as I weave," saith she,
"The world of women haunteth me.

"The river glides along, one thread
   In nature's mesh, so beautiful!
The stars are woven in; the red

Of sunrise; and the rain-cloud dull.
Each seems a separate wonder wrought;
Each blends with some more wondrous thought.

"So, at the loom of life, we weave
   Our separate shreds, that varying fall,
Some stained, some fair; and, passing, leave
   To God the gathering up of all,
In that full pattern, wherein man
Works blindly out the eternal plan.

"In his vast work, for good or ill,
   The undone and the done he blends.
With whatsoever woof we fill,
   To our weak hands His might He lends,
And gives the threads beneath His eye
The texture of eternity.

"Wind on, by willow and by pine,
   Thou blue, untroubled Merrimack![1]
Afar, by sunnier streams than thine,
   My sisters toil, with foreheads black;
And water with their blood this root,
Whereof we gather bounteous fruit.

"There be sad women, sick and poor;
   And those who walk in garments soiled:
Their shame, their sorrow, I endure;
   By their defect my hope is foiled:
The blot they bear is on my name;
Who sins, and I am not to blame?

"And how much of your wrong is mine,
   Dark women slaving at the South?
Of your stolen grapes I quaff the wine;
   The bread you starve for fills my mouth:
The beam unwinds, but every thread
With blood of strangled souls is red.

---

   1. River that flows through Massachusetts, past Lowell, source of power for the mills.

"If this be so, we win and wear
　　A Nessus-robe[2] of poisoned cloth;
Or weave them shrouds they may not wear,—
　　Fathers and brothers falling both
On ghastly, death-sown fields, that lie
Beneath the tearless Southern sky.

"Alas! the weft has lost its white.
　　It grows a hideous tapestry,
That pictures war's abhorrent sight:—
　　Unroll not, web of destiny!
Be the dark volume left unread,—
The tale untold,—the curse unsaid!"

So up and down before her loom
　　She paces on, and to and fro,
Till sunset fills the dusty room,
　　And makes the water redly glow,
As if the Merrimack's calm flood
Were changed into a stream of blood.

Too soon fulfilled, and all too true
　　The words she murmured as she wrought:
But, weary weaver, not to you
　　Alone was war's stern message brought:
"Woman!" it knelled from heart to heart,
"Thy sister's keeper know thou art!"

Source: Poems (1869)

A New England Girlhood [Excerpts]

. . . I never cared much for machinery. The buzzing and hissing and whizzing of pulleys and rollers and spindles and flyers around me often grew tiresome. I could not see into their complications, or feel interested in them. But in a room below us we were sometimes allowed to peer in through a sort of blind door at the great water-wheel that carried the works of the whole mill. It was so huge that we could

2. In Greek mythology, Hercules's wife innocently gave him a robe tainted with the centaur Nessus's blood, which led to Hercules's death.

only watch a few of its spokes at a time, and part of its dripping rim, moving with a slow, measured strength through the darkness that shut it in. It impressed me with something of the awe which comes to us in thinking of the great Power which keeps the mechanism of the universe in motion. Even now, the remembrance of its large, mysterious movement, in which every little motion of every noisy little wheel was involved, brings back to me a verse from one of my favorite hymns:—

"Our lives through various scenes are drawn,
    And vexed by trifling cares,
While Thine eternal thought moves on
    Thy undisturbed affairs."

There were compensations for being shut in to daily toil so early. The mill itself had its lessons for us. But it was not, and could not be, the right sort of life for a child, and we were happy in the knowledge that, at the longest, our employment was only to be temporary.

When I took my next three months at the grammar school, everything there was changed, and I too was changed. The teachers were kind, and thorough in their instruction; and my mind seemed to have been ploughed up during that year of work, so that knowledge took root in it easily. It was a great delight to me to study, and at the end of the three months the master told me that I was prepared for the high school.

But alas! I could not go. The little money I could earn—one dollar a week, besides the price of my board—was needed in the family, and I must return to the mill. It was a severe disappointment to me, though I did not say so at home. I did not at all accept the conclusion of a neighbor whom I heard talking about it with my mother. His daughter was going to the high school, and my mother was telling him how sorry she was that I could not.

"Oh," he said, in a soothing tone, "my girl has n't got any such head-piece as yours has. Your girl does n't need to go."

Of course I knew that whatever sort of a "head-piece" I had, I did need and want just that very opportunity to study. I think the resolution was then formed, inwardly, that I *would* go to school again, some time, whatever happened. I went back to my work, but now without enthusiasm. I had looked through an open door that I was not willing to see shut upon me.

I began to reflect upon life rather seriously for a girl of twelve or thirteen. What was I here for? What could I make of myself? Must I submit to be carried along with the current, and do just what everybody else did? No: I knew I should not do that, for there was a certain Myself who was always starting up with her own original plan or aspiration before me, and who was quite indifferent as to what people generally thought.

Well, I would find out what this Myself was good for, and that she should be!

It was but the presumption of extreme youth. How gladly would I know now, after these long years, just why I was sent into the world, and whether I have in any degree fulfilled the purpose of my being!

In the older times it was seldom said to little girls, as it always has been said to boys, that they ought to have some definite plan, while they were children, what to be and do when they were grown up. There was usually but one path open before them, to become good wives and housekeepers. And the ambition of most girls was to follow their mothers' footsteps in this direction; a natural and laudable ambition. But girls, as well as boys, must often have been conscious of their own peculiar capabilities,—must have desired to cultivate and make use of their individual powers. When I was growing up, they had already begun to be encouraged to do so. We were often told that it was our duty to develop any talent we might possess, or at least to learn how to do some one thing which the world needed, or which would make it a pleasanter world.

When I thought what I should best like to do, my first dream—almost a baby's dream—about it was that it would be a fine thing to be a schoolteacher, like Aunt Hannah. Afterward, when I heard that there were artists, I wished I could some time be one. A slate and pencil, to draw pictures, was my first request whenever a day's ailment kept me at home from school; and I rather enjoyed being a little ill, for the sake of amusing myself in that way. The wish grew up with me; but there were no good drawing-teachers in those days, and if there had been, the cost of instruction would have been beyond the family means. My sister Emilie, however, who saw my taste and shared it herself, did her best to assist me, furnishing me with pencil and paper and paint-box.

If I could only make a rose bloom on paper, I thought I should be happy! or if I could at last succeed in drawing the outline of winter-stripped boughs as I saw them against the sky, it seemed to me that I should be willing to spend years in trying. I did try a little, and very often. Jack Frost was my most inspiring teacher. His sketches on the bedroom window-pane in cold mornings were my ideal studies of Swiss scenery, crags and peaks and chalets and fir-trees,—and graceful tracery of ferns, like those that grew in the woods where we went huckleberrying, all blended together by his touch of enchantment. I wondered whether human fingers ever succeeded in imitating that lovely work.

The taste has followed me all my life through, but I could never indulge it except as a recreation. I was not to be an artist, and I am rather glad that I was hindered, for I had even stronger inclinations in other directions; and art, really noble art, requires the entire devotion of a lifetime.

I seldom thought seriously of becoming an author, although it seemed to me that anybody who had written a book would have a right to feel very proud. But I believed that a person must be exceedingly wise, before presuming to attempt it: although now and then I thought I could feel ideas growing in my mind that it might be worth while to put into a book,—if I lived and studied until I was forty or fifty years old.

I wrote my little verses, to be sure, but that was nothing; they just grew. They were the same as breathing or singing. I could not help writing them, and I thought and dreamed a great many that were never put on paper. They seemed to fly into my mind and away again, like birds going with a carol through the air. It seemed strange to me that people should notice them, or should think my writing verses anything peculiar; for I supposed that they were in everybody's mind, just as they were in mine, and that anybody could write them who chose.

One day I heard a relative say to my mother,—

"Keep what she writes till she grows up, and perhaps she will get money for it. I have heard of somebody who earned a thousand dollars by writing poetry."

It sounded so absurd to me. Money for writing verses! One dollar would be as ridiculous as a thousand. I should as soon have thought of being paid for thinking! My mother, fortunately, was sensible enough never to flatter me or let me be flattered about my scribbling. It never was allowed to hinder any work I had to do. I crept away into a corner to write what came into my head, just as I ran away to play; and I looked upon it only as my most agreeable amusement, never thinking of preserving anything which did not of itself stay in my memory. This too was well, for the time did not come when I could afford to look upon verse-writing as an occupation. Through my life, it has only been permitted to me as an aside from other more pressing employments. Whether I should have written better verses had circumstances left me free to do what I chose, it is impossible now to know.

All my thoughts about my future sent me back to Aunt Hannah and my first infantile idea of being a teacher. I foresaw that I should be that before I could be or do any thing else. It had been impressed upon me that I must make myself useful in the world, and certainly one could be useful who could "keep school" as Aunt Hannah did. I did not see anything else for a girl to do who wanted to use her brains as well as her hands. So the plan of preparing myself to be a teacher gradually and almost unconsciously shaped itself in my mind as the only practicable one. I could earn my living in that way,—an all-important consideration.

I liked the thought of self-support, but I would have chosen some artistic or beautiful work if I could. I had no especial aptitude for teaching, and no absorbing wish to be a teacher, but it seemed to me that I might succeed if I tried. What I did like about it was that one must know something first. I must acquire knowledge before I could impart it, and that was just what I wanted. I could be a student, wherever I was and whatever else I had to be or do, and I would!

I knew I should write; I could not help doing that, for my hand seemed instinctively to move towards pen and paper in moments of leisure. But to write anything worth while, I must have mental cultivation; so, in preparing myself to teach, I could also be preparing myself to write.

This was the plan that indefinitely shaped itself in my mind as I returned to my work in the spinning-room, and which I followed out, not without many breaks and hindrances and neglects, during the next six or seven years,—to learn all I could, so that I should be fit to teach or to write, as the way opened. And it turned out that fifteen or twenty of my best years were given to teaching. . . .

Childhood, however, is not easily defrauded of its birthright, and mine soon reasserted itself. At home I was among children of my own age, for some cousins and other acquaintances had come to live and work with us. We had our evening frolics and entertainments together, and we always made the most of our brief holiday hours. We had also with us now the sister Emilie of my fairy-tale memories, who had grown into a strong, earnest-hearted woman. We all looked up to her as our model, and the ideal of our heroine-worship. . . .

I think she was determined that we should not be mentally defrauded by the circumstances which had made it necessary for us to begin so early to win our daily bread. This remark applies especially to me, as my older sisters (only two or three of them had come to Lowell) soon drifted away from us into their own new homes or occupations, and she and I were left together amid the whir of spindles and wheels.

One thing she planned for us, her younger housemates,—a dozen or so of cousins, friends, and sisters, some attending school, and some at work in the mill,—was a little fortnightly paper [the *Diving Bell*], to be filled with our original contributions, she herself acting as editor. . . .

Our small venture set some of us imagining what larger possibilities might be before us in the far future. We talked over the things we should like to do when we should be women out in the active world; and the author of the shoe-story horrified us by declaring that she meant to be distinguished when she grew up for something, even if it was for something bad! She did go so far in a bad way as to plagiarize a long poem in a subsequent number of the "Diving Bell"; but the editor found her out, and we all thought that a reproof from Emilie was sufficient punishment.

I do not know whether it was fortunate or unfortunate for me that I had not, by nature, what is called literary ambition. I knew that I had a knack at rhyming, and I knew that I enjoyed nothing better than to try to put thoughts and words together, in any way. But I did it for the pleasure of rhyming and writing, indifferent as to what might come of it. For any one who could take hold of every-day, practical work, and carry it on successfully, I had a profound respect. To be what is called "capable" seemed to me better worth while than merely to have a taste or talent for writing, perhaps because I was conscious of my deficiencies in the former respect. But certainly the world needs deeds more than it needs words. I should never have been willing to be *only* a writer, without using my hands to some good purpose besides.

My sister, however, told me that here was a talent which I had no right to ne-glect, and which I ought to make the most of. I believed in her; I thought she understood me better than I understood myself; and it was a comfort to be assured that my scribbling was not wholly a waste of time. So I used pencil and paper in every spare minute I could find.

Our little home-journal went bravely on through twelve numbers. Its yellow manuscript pages occasionally meet my eyes when I am rummaging among my old papers, with the half-conscious look of a waif that knows it has no right to its escape from the waters of oblivion.

While it was in progress my sister Emilie became acquainted with a family of bright girls, near neighbors of ours, who proposed that we should join with them, and form a little society for writing and discussion, to meet fortnightly at their house. We met,—I think I was the youngest of the group,—prepared a Constitu-tion and By-Laws, and named ourselves "The Improvement Circle." If I remember rightly, my sister was our first president. The older ones talked and wrote on many subjects quite above me. I was shrinkingly bashful, as half-grown girls usually are, but I wrote my little essays and read them, and listened to the rest, and enjoyed it all exceedingly. Out of this little "Improvement Circle" grew the larger one whence issued the "Lowell Offering,"[3] a year or two later.

At this time I had learned to do a spinner's work, and I obtained permission to tend some frames that stood directly in front of the river-windows, with only them and the wall behind me, extending half the length of the mill,—and one young woman beside me, at the farther end of the row. She was a sober, mature person, who scarcely thought it worth her while to speak often to a child like me; and I was, when with strangers, rather a reserved girl; so I kept myself occupied with the river, my work, and my thoughts. And the river and my thoughts flowed on together, the happiest of companions. Like a loitering pilgrim, it sparkled up to me in recogni-tion as it glided along, and bore away my little frets and fatigues on its bosom. When the work "went well," I sat in the window-seat, and let my fancies fly whither they would,—downward to the sea, or upward to the hills that hid the mountain-cradle of the Merrimack.

The printed regulations forbade us to bring books into the mill, so I made my window-seat into a small library of poetry, pasting its side all over with newspaper clippings. In those days we had only weekly papers, and they had always a "poet's corner," where standard writers were well represented, with anonymous ones, also. I was not, of course, much of a critic. I chose my verses for their sentiment, and because I wanted to commit them to memory; sometimes it was a long poem, sometimes a hymn, sometimes only a stray verse. . . .

3. Magazine published from 1840 to 1845 in Lowell, Massachusetts, by the female operatives in the mills.

. . . When I returned to Lowell, at about sixteen, I found my sister Emilie interested in the "Operatives' Magazine,"[4] and we both contributed to it regularly, until it was merged in the "Lowell Offering," to which we then transferred our writing efforts. It did not occur to us to call these efforts "literary." I know that I wrote just as I did for our little "Diving Bell,"—as a sort of pastime, and because my daily toil was mechanical, and furnished no occupation for my thoughts. Perhaps the fact that most of us wrote in this way accounted for the rather sketchy and fragmentary character of our "Magazine." It gave evidence that we thought, and that we thought upon solid and serious matters; but the criticism of one of our superintendents upon it, very kindly given, was undoubtedly just: "It has plenty of pith, but it lacks point."

The "Offering" had always more of the literary spirit and touch. It was, indeed, for the first two years, edited by a gentleman of acknowledged literary ability. But people seemed to be more interested in it after it passed entirely into the hands of the girls themselves.

The "Operatives' Magazine" had a decidedly religious tone. We who wrote for it were loyal to our Puritanic antecedents, and considered it all-important that our lightest actions should be moved by some earnest impulse from behind. We might write playfully, but there must be conscience and reverence somewhere within it all. We had been taught, and we believed, that idle words were a sin, whether spoken or written. This, no doubt, gave us a gravity of expression rather unnatural to youth.

In looking over the bound volume of this magazine, I am amused at the grown-up style of thought assumed by myself, probably its very youngest contributor. I wrote a dissertation on "Fame," quoting from Pollok, Cowper, and Milton, and ending with Diedrich Knickerbocker's definition of immortal fame,—"Half a page of dirty paper."[5] For other titles I had "Thoughts on Beauty"; "Gentility"; "Sympathy," etc. . . .

It is a very youthful weakness to exaggerate passing moods into deep experiences, and if we put them down on paper, we get a fine opportunity of laughing at ourselves, if we live to outgrow them, as most of us do. I think I must have had a frequent fancy that I was not long for this world. Perhaps I thought an early death rather picturesque; many young people do. There is a certain kind of poetry that fosters this idea; that delights in imaginary youthful victims, and has, reciprocally, its youthful devotees. One of my blank verse poems in the "Offering" is entitled "The Early Doomed." It begins,—

And must I die? The world is bright to me,
And everything that looks upon me, smiles.

4. Another magazine published by the Lowell mill girls.
5. Robert Pollok (ca. 1798–1827), Scottish poet; William Cowper (1731–1800), English poet; John Milton (1608–1674), English poet; Diedrich Knickerbocker, fictional historian who narrates Washington Irving's *A History of New York* (1809), from which the quote comes.

Another poem is headed "Memento Mori;" and another, entitled a "Song in June," which ought to be cheerful, goes off into the doleful request to somebody, or anybody, to

Weave me a shroud in the month of June!

I was, perhaps, healthier than the average girl, and had no predisposition to a premature decline; and in reviewing these absurdities of my pen, I feel like saying to any young girl who inclines to rhyme, "Don't sentimentalize! Write more of what you see than of what you feel, and let your feelings realize themselves to others in the shape of worthy actions. Then they will be natural, and will furnish you with something worth writing." . . .

Source: A New England Girlhood, Outlined from Memory (1889)

❦ Mary E. Bryan (1838–1913)

Mary E. Bryan, who, according to Ida Raymond, in Southland Writers *(1870), was widely considered "the most gifted female writer which the South has produced," grew up on a Florida plantation. When she was twelve, her family moved to Thomasville, Georgia, where she went to school and published poems and stories in a local newspaper. After marrying at sixteen, Bryan moved to Louisiana, but within a year her father brought her home again, and she continued her studies. During this period she was a regular writer for southern periodicals as well as an editor. While editing the* Southern Field and Fireside, *she also contributed stories, poems, and essays, including "How Should Women Write?" which critiques the tendency of women writers to shy away from unfeminine topics. She returned to Louisiana, and during the Civil War Bryan maintained the plantation in her husband's absence. After the war, to earn money for her family, including three children, she edited magazines in Atlanta and New York and wrote numerous novels.*

How Should Women Write?

The idea of women writing books! There were no prophets in the days of King John[1] to predict an event so far removed from probability. The women of the household sat by their distaffs,[2] or toiled in the fields, or busied themselves in roasting and brewing for their guzzling lords. If ever a poetic vision or a half-defined thought floated through their minds, they sang it out to their busy wheels, or murmured it in rude sentences to lull the babies upon their bosoms, or silently wove it into their lives to manifest itself in patient love and gentleness. And it was all as it should have been; there was need for nothing more. Physical labor was then all that was required of woman; and to "act well her part," meant but to perform the domestic duties which were given her. Life was less complex then than now—the intellectual part of man's twofold nature being but unequally developed, while the absence of labor-saving implements demanded a greater amount of manual toil from men as well as from women.

It is different now. Modern ingenuity and Protean appliances of machinery have lessened the necessity of actual physical labor; and, in the constant progress of the human race, new fields have been opened, and new social needs and requirements are calling for workers in other and higher departments.

There is a cry now for intellectual food through the length and breadth of the land. The old oracles of the past, the mummied literary remains of a dead age, will

---

1. John was King of England from 1199 to 1216.
2. Wool or flax was wound around a distaff, part of a spinning wheel.

not satisfy a generation that is pressing so vigorously forward. They want books imbued with the strong vitality and energy of the present. And as it is a moving, hurrying, changing time, with new influences and opinions constantly rising like stars above the horizon, men want books to keep pace with their progress—nay, to go before and guide them, as the pillar of fire and cloud did the Israelites in the desert. So they want books for every year, for every month—mirrors to "catch the manners living as they rise,"[3] lenses to concentrate the rays of the new stars that dawn upon them.

There is a call for workers; and woman, true to her mission as the helpmeet for man, steps forward to take her part in the intellectual labor, as she did when only manual toil was required at her hands. The pen has become the mighty instrument of reform and rebuke; the press is the teacher and the preacher of the world; and it is not only the privilege, but the duty of woman to aid in extending this influence of letters, and in supplying the intellectual demands of society, when she has been endowed with the power. Let her assure herself that she has been called to the task, and then grasp her pen firmly, with the stimulating consciousness that she is performing the work assigned to her.

Thus is apparent what has been gradually admitted, that it is woman's duty to write—but how and what? This is yet a mooted question. Men, after much demur and hesitation, have given women liberty to write; but they cannot yet consent to allow them full freedom. They may flutter out of the cage, but it must be with clipped wings; they may hop about the smooth-shaven lawn, but must, on no account, fly. With metaphysics they have nothing to do; it is too deep a sea for their lead to sound; nor must they grapple with those great social and moral problems with which every strong soul is now wrestling. They must not go beyond the surface of life, lest they should stir the impure sediment that lurks beneath. They may whiten the outside of the sepulchre, but must not soil their kidded[4] hands by essaying to cleanse the inside of its rottenness and dead men's bones.

Nature, indeed, is given them to fustianize[5] over, and religion allowed them as their chief capital—the orthodox religion, that says its prayers out of a prayer-book, and goes to church on Sabbaths; but on no account the higher, truer religion, that, despising cant and hypocrisy, and scorning forms and conventionalisms, seeks to cure, not to cloak the plague-spots of society—the self-forgetting, self-abnegating religion that shrinks not from following in the steps of Christ, that curls not its lip at the touch of poverty and shame, nor fears to call crime by its right name, though it wear a gilded mask, nor to cry out earnestly and bravely, "Away with it! away with it!" No! not such religion as this. It is *unfeminine;* women have no business with it

3. Alexander Pope, *An Essay on Man* (1733–1734).
4. Covered with kid, or lambskin, gloves, signifying daintiness or delicacy.
5. To write in a coarse or plain manner.

whatever, though they may ring changes as often as they please upon the "crowns of gold," the "jasper walls," and "seraph harps."[6]

Having prescribed these bounds to the female pen, men are the first to condemn her efforts as tame and commonplace, because they lack earnestness and strength.

If she writes of birds, of flowers, sunshine, and *id omne genus,* as did Amelia Welby,[7] noses are elevated superbly, and the effusions are said to smack of bread and butter.

If love, religion, and domestic obligations are her theme, as with Mrs. Hentz, "namby-pamby" is the word contemptuously applied to her productions. If, like Mrs. Southworth, she reproduces Mrs. Radcliffe in her possibility-scorning romances, her nonsensical clap-trap is said to be "beneath criticism;" and if, with Patty Pepper, she gossips harmlessly of fashions and fashionables, of the opera and Laura Keene's, of watering-places, lectures, and a railroad trip, she is "*pish*"-ed aside as silly and childish; while those who seek to go beyond the boundary-line are put down with the stigma of "*strong-minded.*" Fanny Fern,[8] who, though actuated by no fixed purpose, was yet more earnest than the majority of her sisterhood, heard the word hissed in her ears whenever she essayed to strike a blow at the root of social sin and inconsistency, and had whatever there was of noble and philanthropic impulse in her nature annihilated by the epithets of "bold" and "indelicate," which were hurled at her like poisoned arrows.

It will not do. Such dallying with surface-bubbles, as we find in much of our periodical literature, might have sufficed for another age, but not for this. We want a deeper troubling of the waters, that we may go down into the pool and be healed. It is an earnest age we live in. Life means more than it did in other days; it is an intense reality, crowded thick with eager, questioning thoughts and passionate resolves; with burning aspirations and agonized doubts. There are active influences at work, all tending to one grand object—moral, social, and physical advancement. The pen is the compass-needle that points to this pole. Shall woman dream on violet banks, while this great work of reformation is needing her talents and her

6. "Crowns of gold": part of the Arc of the Covenant (Ex. 25:11); "jasper walls": the New Jerusalem was to have walls of precious stones, including jasper (Rev. 21:19); "seraph harps": angels' harps.

7. *Id omne genus,* Latin for everything of the sort. Amelia B. Welby (1819–1852), popular poet from Louisville, Kentucky.

8. Caroline Lee Hentz (1800–1856), southern domestic novelist (included in this anthology); E.D.E.N. Southworth (1819–1899), southern sensational novelist (included in this anthology); Ann Radcliffe (1764–1823), English novelist most known for the supernatural romance *The Mysteries of Udolpho* (1794); "Patty Pepper" is probably a creation of Bryan's; Laura Keene (1826–1873), actress and theater manager, was born in England and emigrated to New York in 1852; Fanny Fern (Sarah Willis Parton) (1811–1872), northern author (included in this volume).

energies? Shall she prate prettily of moonlight, music, love, and flowers, while the world of stern, staring, pressing realities of wrong and woe, of shame and toil, surrounds her? Shall she stifle the voice in her soul for fear of being sneered at as *strong-minded,* and shall her great heart throb and heave as did the mountain of Æsop, only to bring forth such insignificant mice[9]—such productions—more paltry in purpose than in style and conception—which she gives to the world as the offspring of her brain?

It will not long be so. Women are already forming higher standards for themselves, learning that genius has no sex, and that, so the truth be told, it matters not whether the pen is wielded by a masculine or a female hand. The active, earnest, fearless spirit of the age, which sends the blood thrilling through the veins of women, will flow out through their pens, and give color to the pictures they delineate, to the principles they affirm. Literature must embody the prominent feeling of the age on which it is engrafted. It is only an isolated, excepted spirit, like Keats's, which can close its eyes to outward influences, and, amid the roar of gathering political storms, and the distant thunderings of the French Revolution, lie down among the sweet, wild English flowers, and dream out its dream of the old Greek beauty.[10]

How should a woman write? I answer, as men, as all should write to whom the power of expression has been given—*honestly and without fear.* Let them write what they feel and think, even if there be errors in the thought and the feeling—better that than the lifeless inanities of which literature, and especially periodical literature, furnishes so many deplorable samples.

Our opinions on ethical and social questions change continually as the mind develops, and the light of knowledge shines more broadly through the far-off opening in the labyrinth of inquiry through which we wander, seeking for truth. Thus, even when writers are most honest, their opinions, written at different times, often appear contradictory. This the discerning reader will readily understand. He will know that in ascending the ladder, upon whose top the angels stand, the prospect widens and changes continually as newer heights are won. Emerson, indeed, tells us that "a foolish consistency is the hobgoblin of little minds. With consistency, a great soul has simply nothing to do. Speak what you think now in hard words; and to-morrow, speak what to-morrow thinks in hard words again, though it contradict everything you said to-day."[11]

This is strong—perhaps too unqualified; but even inconsistency is better than

---

9. In Aesop's fable "The Mountain and the Mouse," a large crowd gathers to witness a mountain groaning and heaving in labor and is disappointed when only a mouse is produced.

10. British Romantic poet John Keats's "Ode on a Grecian Urn" (1820), the classic meditation on the timelessness of beauty.

11. From Ralph Waldo Emerson's essay "Self-Reliance" (1841).

the dull, donkey-like obstinacy which refuses to move from one position, though the wooing spirit of inquiry beckon it onward, and winged speculation tempt it to scale the clouds.

Still, there should be in writing, as in acting, a fixed and distinct purpose to which everything should tend. If this be to elevate and refine the human race, the purpose will gradually and unconsciously work out its own accomplishment. Not, indeed, through didactic homilies[12] only; every image of beauty or sublimity crystallized in words, every philosophic truth, and every thought that has a tendency to expand the mind or enlarge the range of spiritual vision, will aid in advancing this purpose, will be as oil to the lamp we carry to light the footsteps of others.

As to the subjects that should be written upon, they are many and varied; there is no exhausting them while nature teems with beauty—while men live, and act, and love, and suffer—while the murmurs of the great ocean of the *Infinite* come to us in times when the soul is stillest, like music that is played too far off for us to catch the tune. Broad fields of thought lie before us, traversed, indeed, by many feet, but each season brings fresh fruits to gather and new flowers to crop.

Genius, like light, shines upon all things—upon the muck-heap as upon the gilded cupola.

As to the wrong and wretchedness which the novelist lays bare—it will not be denied that such really exists in this sin-beleaguered world. Wherefore shrink and cover our eyes when these social ulcers are probed? Better earnestly endeavor to eradicate the evil, than seek to conceal or ignore its existence. Be sure this will not prevent it eating deeper and deeper into the heart.

Genius, when true and earnest, will not be circumscribed. No power shall say to it: "Thus far shalt thou go, and no farther." Its province is, in part, to daguerreotype the shifting influences, feelings, and tendencies at work in the age in which it exists—and sin, and grief, and suffering, as well as hope, and love, and joy, and star-eyed aspiration, pass across its pages as phantoms across the charmed mirror of the magician. Genius thrills along "the electric chain wherewith we are darkly bound,"[13] from the highest to the lowest link of the social ligature; for true genius is Christlike; *it scorns nothing;* calls nothing that God made common or unclean, because of its great yearning over mankind, its longing to lift them up from the sordid things of sense in which they grovel to its own higher and purer intellectual or spiritual atmosphere. The noblest woman of us all, Mrs. Elizabeth Browning,[14] whom I hold to have written, in "Aurora Leigh," the greatest book of this century,—the greatest, not from the wealth of its imagery, or the vigor of its thoughts, but because of the moral grandeur of its purpose,—Mrs. Browning, I say, has not shrunk from

12. Sermons meant to instruct audiences on spiritual matters.
13. Line from Lord Byron's *Childe Harold's Pilgrimage* (1812).
14. Elizabeth Barrett Browning (1806–1861), most revered British female poet and author of *Aurora Leigh* (1857), an autobiographical *Künstlerroman* in blank verse.

going down, with her purity encircling her, like the halo around the Saviour's head, to the abodes of shame and degradation for materials to aid in elucidating the serious truths she seeks to impress for sorrowful examples of the evils for which she endeavors to find some remedy. She is led to this through that love which is inseparable from the higher order of genius. That noblest form of genius which generates the truest poetry—the poetry of feeling rather than of imagination—warm with human life, but uncolored by voluptuous passion—is strongly connected with love. Not the sentiment which dances through the world to the music of marriage-bells; but that divine, self-ignoring, universal love of which the inspired apostle wrote so burningly, when, caught up in the fiery chariot of the Holy Ghost, he looked down upon the selfish considerations of common humanity: the love (or charity) "which beareth all things, endureth all things, which suffereth long and is kind,"[15]—the love which, looking to heaven, stretches its arms to enfold the whole human brotherhood.

This is the love which, hand in hand with genius, is yet to work out the redemption of society. I have faith to believe it; and sometimes, when the tide of hope and enthusiasm is high, I have thought that woman, with the patience and the long-suffering of her love, the purity of her intellect, her instinctive sympathy and her soul of poetry, might be God's chosen instrument in this work of gradual reformation, this reconciling of the harsh contrasts in society that jar so upon our sense of harmony, this righting of the grievous wrongs and evils over which we weep and pray, this final uniting of men into one common brotherhood by the bonds of sympathy and affection.

It may be but a Utopian dream; but the faith is better than hopelessness; it is elevating and cheering to believe it. It is well to aspire, though the aspiration be unfulfilled. It is better to look up at the stars, though they dazzle, than down at the vermin beneath our feet.

Source: Southland Writers, ed. Ida Raymond (1870)

15. 1 Cor. 13:7.

ꮦ Margaret Junkin Preston (1820–1897)

Remembered primarily for her pro-Confederacy poetry, Margaret Junkin Preston was born and raised in Pennsylvania until 1848, when her father moved the family to Lexington, Virginia. As a professor's daughter, she received a thorough education, including instruction in Greek and Latin. In 1857, Margaret Junkin married John Preston, who became a major in the Confederacy. They had two children. Although Margaret had begun publishing stories and poems in literary magazines in the 1850s, she stopped writing after her marriage because her husband disapproved. During the Civil War, however, he allowed her to write poetry honoring her brother-in law "Stonewall" Jackson and other fallen heroes, as well as her long poem Beechenbrook: Rhyme of the War *(1865). In the 1870s, she published verse on less political themes in northern magazines. Her husband edited and collected many of these later poems in book form. "Erinna's Spinning" describes the struggle between poetry and women's duties, while "Art's Limitations" comments on the state of national poetry (as does Emma Lazarus's poem "How Long").*

Erinna's Spinning[1]

The Lesbian[2] youths are all abroad to-day,
Filling the vales with joyance. Up and down
The festive streets, with roses garlanded,
Go hand in hand, fair Mytilené's[3] daughters.

Slaves follow, bearing baskets overheaped
With laurels, myrtles, lilies, hyacinths,
And all the world of flowers, wherewith to deck
The May-day altar of the dear "Good Goddess."[4]

And pranksome children, spilling on the paths
Acanthus blooms from out their laden'd arms,
Come shouting after—mad with hey-day glee,
Making fit ending to the gay procession.

---

1. Classic authors mention but one poem by this friend and cotemporary of Sappho—"The Distaff." Her mother, it is said, frowning upon her literary proclivities, held her, despite her protestations, remorselessly to her monotonous work. [Preston's note.]

2. Of the Greek isle Lesbos, birthplace of Sappho, Greek lyric poet of the sixth century B.C., widely considered the greatest female poet before the modern era.

3. City on Lesbos.

4. In ancient Rome, the "Good Goddess," a deity of fertility and healing, was celebrated in early May in a festival of only women. Preston probably means the Greek goddess Maia.

Sweet Goddess! frown not on me, tho' I bring
No votive wreath to hang above thy shrine;
For—"See, Erinna," my stern mother saith,
"Thou gaddest not abroad with idle maidens.

"The flowers will blow as well, unhelped of thee—
The fruits fall in due season—tho' no trains
Of dallying girls thus waste the sunshine hours,
That wiser thrift should give to wheel and distaff."[5]

And so I bide at home, day after day,
Because my mother wills it: but my heart
Steals after my companions, while I keep
Time to their dances with my droning spindle.

I hear Alcæus[6] strike his lyric string—
I catch our Sappho's answering choric song,
On some high festival—and all my soul
Flutters to spring beyond the bars that cage it.

O, for the freedom of the flowers!—I feel
Tumultuous stirs, even as the quickening earth
Feels in her bosom now, the tremulous life
Of all her myriads of unsheathing blossoms.

But like a frost, the nipping voice grates harsh:
—"Hence with thy tablets, girl! The Gods above
Made thee a woman—formed for household needs,
For wifely handiwork and ministration:

"Banish forever from thy foolish heart,
These vain outreachings. If thou strive to snatch
At man's high attributes—thy mad essay
O'erthrown, will only leave thee less a woman.

"Do what thou wilt—strip off thy maiden gear,
Wrestle with athletes—hurl the warlike dart—

5. Part of a spinning wheel around which wool or flax is wound.
6. Greek poet of the sixth century B.C., who may have been a lover of Sappho and exchanged poems with her.

Spin forth the discus: in the Isthmian games[7]
Enroll thyself amid the sleek-limb'd runners—

"Or seize the Delphian lyre and try thy skill,
Or measure dithrambs with Æolian[8] bards,—
And for thy pains—confess thyself undone
Ever and always, gauged by manhood's stature."

If I make answer that chaste Artemis
Is wise as Pythias, or the Queen of heaven
Is strong of will as proud Olympian Jove,[9]
She hastes to silence me with quick impatience.

"—What man of men was ever fain to sit
Uplooking in a *woman's* face, and learn
Aught other lore than love?" I answer low,
"A woman taught her craft once to a hero!"

She chafes—"I am beholden for thy hint!
The stylus fits *thee* as the spindle did
The hand of Hercules, who sat unsex'd,
Struck for his dulness by Omphalé's slipper."[10]

Then comes the taunt—"What youth of Lesbos, stout
And lithe of limb—as ripe for war as peace,
Versed in the rhythms of Chian's mighty seer,
Will think to choose *thee* for thy trick of singing?

"Nay—talk to him of soft Milesian wool—
Of Colchian linens[11]—rose or saffron dyes—

7. In ancient Greece, athletic contests in which males participated, like the Olympian games.
8. Delphian: of Delphi, a town in ancient Greece on Mount Parnassus, containing the sanctuary of Apollo. Dithyramb: Greek choric hymn, usually in honor of Dionysus. Æolean: of Æolus, mythic god of the winds.
9. Artemis was the huntress of Greek mythology. Pythias was the wife of Aristotle, one of the foremost philosophers of ancient Greece. The "Queen of heaven" refers to Hera, wife of Zeus, also known as Jove, the ruler of heaven. "Olympian Jove" was the statue by Phidias counted as one of the seven wonders of the world. Mount Olympus was the home of the gods.
10. For three years Hercules was a slave of Omphale, queen of Lydia. She made him wear women's clothes and sit and spin among her ladies, striking him with her slipper when he was clumsy. They later married and she bore his son.
11. Much-prized wool and linen of ancient Greece.

Of patterns for thy newest silken web—
Of viands—wines; the youth is fond to listen.

" 'This maid'—he murmurs to his inner self,
'Could order well all housely offices,
Could rule discreetly the small realm of home,
Could rear, control and wisely guide my children.' "

And thus she ends: "Erinna, be advised:
Let Lesbian virgins sing, let Sappho write,
Mindless of wifehood's ripen'd disciplines—
Thou—leave thy scrolls, and keep thee to thy spinning."

But what care I for wifehood?—I, so young!—
—For matron dignities?—they clog and cling:
—For petty talk?—*Are olives fine this year?*
"Are figs full-formed?"—Beshrew my mother's wisdom!

I'd give them all for Sappho's wreath of bay[12]—
Forego them all for room to sing out full
The wild, dumb questionings of my haunted soul,
And so forever leave my weary spinning.

Source: The Galaxy (1870)

Art's Limitations

This rich, rank Age—does it breed giants now—
Dantes or Michaels, Raphaels, Shakespeares? Nay!
Its culture is of other sort to-day.
From the stanch stem (too ready to allow
Growths that divide the strength that should endow
The one tall trunk) who firmly lops away,
With wise reserve, such shoots as lead astray
The wasted sap to some collateral bough?

Had Dante chiselled stone, had Angelo
Intrigued with courts, had Shakespeare dulled his pen

12. Public tribute for victory or achievement.

With critic gauge of Chaucer, Drummond, Ben[13]—
What lack there were of that life-giving shade,
Which these high-tower'd, centurial oaks have made,
Where walk the happy nations to and fro!

Source: The Galaxy (1877)

13. Geoffrey Chaucer (c.1343–1400), author of *The Canterbury Tales.* William Drummond of Hawthornden (1585–1649) and Benjamin Jonson (1572–1637) were lesser writers of Shakespeare's day.

🍂 Mary Kyle Dallas (1830–1897)

The following essay, signed "M.K.D.," was most likely penned by Mary Kyle Dallas, "the well-known writer in Bonner's Ledger*" (J. C. Derby,* Fifty Years Among Authors, Books, and Publishers*). Dallas also published novels, and her short fiction appeared in* Lippincott's, Godey's Lady's Book, Frank Leslie's Illustrated, *and* Harper's New Monthly Magazine. *Her most famous work was a parody of George du Maurier's* Trilby *(1894), called* Billtry *(1895). She explained that her novel explored "the reverse of the question . . . 'what might have been'—had the bachelor artists of the Parisian studios been bachelor girls of Gotham, and their model masculine instead of feminine." Her obituary in the* New York Times *identifies her birthplace as Philadelphia and her residence as New York City. At the age of twenty she married an artist, Jacob A. Dallas, who only lived for a year and a half. Their son died shortly thereafter. At the time of her death, she was living with her three sisters and a nephew. The following essay is a bold challenge to women writers to have the courage to write "the truth," in spite of the world's disapproval.*

Women in Literature

Even when women have power and talent enough to enable them to do remarkably well in the ranks of literature, there is something in the very fact that they are women which prevents them from writing those startling yet excellent things which make a reputation in a week, and yet live for generations. This is partly because such work is generally an advance into new ground, and we are not intended for pioneers, though we may follow in the march and do as much good as the humble vivandiere[1] does upon the field of battle, but the great cause is this: we *dare not* say or write so many things.

The thought struck me, as I read over for the twentieth time a certain popular poem that always makes me hold my breath in a sort of frightened delight, that if a woman could have written this—and since a woman understood it so well, why not?—she would never have found courage to publish it; moreover, that one would not wish a woman one loved to have written it, after all.

There are wonderful things that women might write—good women, who have never met with any odd adventures—just by looking into their own hearts and writing down the truth. But they will never be put down upon paper; or if they are, they will never get to press. All scribbling women destroy those of their productions that have in them most true passion, lest some one might chance to see the treasured thoughts written down, and only publish those trivialities, which Madam

---

1. A person who feeds the army.

Grundy[2] accepts as proper, and which editors mean to pay for when they say, "We shall strive to make these columns peculiarly acceptable to the ladies." And we sign our names without a blush to skim-milk love stories, in which the latest fashions and the most poignant emotions are mixed up together, to poetry written on the principle that where every other line rhymes the production cannot be prose, and to demented declarations of our intention to vote, and scarcely ever to anything more. Not so much that we cannot, as that we do not dare, or if we dare, will not, write our hearts out. In a little while no woman upon earth will vail [*sic*] her face from man's eyes, not even the young Turkish maiden; but as long as this world shall last, woman will strive to vail her heart from all eyes but her own, and when she writes anything more than a fashion column, generally expresses the sentiments men have expressed, or those of some clique of women who think to order. And so an original woman's book, with real women in it, and with a woman's actual thoughts stamped upon the pages, is the rarest of all literary productions.

Charlotte Brontë gave us one in "Villette." I have never read another.

Source: New York Ledger (1871)

2. Symbol of the tyranny of propriety. She first appeared in Thomas Morton's play *Speed the Plough* (1798), in which characters ask, "What will Mrs. Grundy say?"

❧ EMMA LAZARUS (1849–1887)

Although she wrote the famous lines inscribed on the Statue of Liberty ("Give me your tired, your poor, / Your huddled masses yearning to breathe free"), Emma Lazarus is today almost entirely unknown. She was born into a wealthy Jewish family in New York City and received a strong classical education. She never married. In 1911, Edmund Clarence Stedman wrote in his profile of her in Genius and Other Essays *that she was the "natural companion to scholars and thinkers." Her father encouraged her work as a translator, critic, and writer of poetry and fiction, and she gained the attention and friendship of Ralph Waldo Emerson and Henry James, as well as other members of the male literary elite. She felt conflicted about her gender and her art, and often portrayed artists and poets as male. Nonetheless, she devoted herself to her poetry in her early years and near the end of her life was an outspoken advocate of a homeland for Jews in Palestine.*

How Long

How long, and yet how long,
Our leaders will we hail from over seas,
Masters and kings from feudal monarchies,
   And mock their ancient song
With echoes weak of foreign melodies?

   That distant isle mist-wreathed,
Mantled in unimaginable green,
Too long hath been our mistress and our queen.
   Our fathers have bequeathed
Too deep a love for her, our hearts within.

   She made the whole world ring
With the brave exploits of her children strong,
And with the matchless music of her song.
   Too late, too late we cling
To alien legends, and their strains prolong.

   This fresh young world I see,
With heroes, cities, legends of her own;
With a new race of men, and overblown
   By winds from sea to sea,
Decked with the majesty of every zone.

    I see the glittering tops
Of snow-peaked mounts, the wid'ning vale's expanse,
Large prairies where free herds of horses prance,
    Exhaustless wealth of crops,
In vast, magnificent extravagance.

    These grand, exuberant plains,
These stately rivers, each with many a mouth,
The exquisite beauty of the soft-aired south,
    The boundless seas of grains,
Luxuriant forests' lush and splendid growth.

    The distant siren-song
Of the green island in the eastern sea,
Is not the lay for this new chivalry.
    It is not free and strong
To chant on prairies 'neath this brilliant sky.

    The echo faints and fails;
It suiteth not, upon this western plain,
Our voice or spirit; we should stir again
    The wilderness, and make the vales
Resound unto a yet unheard-of strain.

Source: Admetus and Other Poems (1871)

Critic and Poet
An Apologue

(*"Poetry must be simple, sensuous, or impassioned; this man is neither simple, sensuous, nor impassioned; therefore he is not a poet."*)

No man had ever heard a nightingale,
When once a keen-eyed naturalist was stirred
To study and define—*what is a bird,*
To classify by rote and book, nor fail
To mark its structure and to note the scale
Whereon its song might possibly be heard.
Thus far, no farther;—so he spake the word.
When of a sudden,—hark, the nightingale!

Oh deeper, higher than he could divine
That all-unearthly, untaught strain! He saw
The plain, brown warbler, unabashed. "Not mine"
(He cried) "the error of this fatal flaw.
No bird is this, it soars beyond my line,
Were it a bird, 'twould answer to my law."

Echoes

Late-born and woman-souled I dare not hope,
The freshness of the elder lays, the might
Of manly, modern passion shall alight
Upon my Muse's lips, nor may I cope
(Who veiled and screened by womanhood must grope)
With the world's strong-armed warriors and recite
The dangers, wounds, and triumphs of the fight;
Twanging the full-stringed lyre through all its scope.
But if thou ever in some lake-floored cave
O'erbrowed by rocks, a wild voice wooed and heard,
Answering at once from heaven and earth and wave,
Lending elf-music to thy harshest word,
Misprize thou not these echoes that belong
To one in love with solitude and song.

Life and Art

Not while the fever of the blood is strong,
The heart throbs loud, the eyes are veiled, no less
With passion than with tears, the Muse shall bless
The poet-soul to help and soothe with song.
Not then she bids his trembling lips express
The aching gladness, the voluptuous pain.
Life is his poem then; flesh, sense, and brain
One full-stringed lyre attuned to happiness.
But when the dream is done, the pulses fail,
The day's illusion, with the day's sun set,
He, lonely in the twilight, sees the pale
Divine Consoler, featured like Regret,

Enter and clasp his hand and kiss his brow.
Then his lips ope to sing—as mine do now.

Source: The Poems of Emma Lazarus (1889)

❧ Ina Coolbrith (1841–1928)

Born in the Mormon settlement of Nauvoo, Illinois, Josephine Donna Smith was a niece of Joseph Smith, the founder of the Mormon Church. Her mother called her Ina. In 1846, after her widowed mother married a non-Mormon, the family moved to Saint Louis and renounced Mormonism. They moved to California in 1851, and at fifteen Ina started publishing her poetry in the Los Angeles Star. *She married at seventeen but was divorced by twenty. Changing her name to Ina Donna Coolbrith, she moved to San Francisco, where she met Bret Harte and Charles Warren Stoddard. With them she started the* Overland Monthly Magazine, *a periodical whose aim was to rival the eastern literary establishment. She published sixty-eight of her poems there during its run from 1868 to 1875. In 1874, in order to provide for family members, Coolbrith became a librarian. Upon her death, the* New York Times *called her "the Sappho of the West." Her poetry reflects her deep attachment to the landscape and her desire to establish the West as significant in America's literary culture. In her poem "California," described in the introduction below, the land itself calls for its "master" poet. Although Coolbrith does not claim to be that poet, the Whitmanian tone of the poem is nonetheless striking.*

At the Hill's Base

O singers, singing up the laureled[1] height
   Whereon song dwells—with thoughts to rhyme that run
   As flowers unfold and gladden to the sun—
    Have ye no room for one
Whose soul uplift with longing infinite,
    Findeth in song alone
The perfect meed[2] and measure of delight?

Like to a reed in some still river-bed
   That grew, with drowsy lotus-leaves afloat—
A reed some child hath plucked and fashioned
Flute-wise, to take within the young mouth's red,
   And blow one shrill, clear note;

Lo, such am I! Upon the crownéd hill,
   For one so lacking skill
Have ye no room, O singers, at whose feet

1. In ancient Greece, laurel wreathes were public symbols of literary achievement.
2. Reward.

      The lowliest place were sweet?
    No space where one that can not sing, indeed,
    May pipe the slender music of the reed,
        O, thou divinest song,
      That I have loved so long! ·

Source: Overland Monthly Magazine (1872)

At the Hill's Base[3]

O Singers, up the heights of gold
    Whereon Song dwells—with thoughts that run
To music, as the flowers unfold
    And gladden to the sun,

Is there, amid the fadeless bloom
    Of rose and bay,[4] low at your feet,
A little room, O ye, with whom
    The lowliest place were sweet?

A reed within some river-bed
    That grew, with drifting weeds afloat,
A reed by rude hands fashionëd
    To pipe one slender note,—

Lo, such am I! yet crave the grace
    To rest with thee, divinest Song,
A moment's space within the ways
    That I have loved so long!

California

Was it the sigh and shiver of the leaves?
Was it the murmur of the meadow brook,
That in and out the reeds and water weeds

---

3. This poem is substantially altered from its original magazine publication, thus both versions are included here for comparison. Both strike the familiar note of the poet's humility, yet the line about her lack of skill was struck in the later version.

4. In ancient Greece, wreaths of bay leaves were public tributes to victory or achievement.

Slipped silverly, and on their tremulous keys
Uttered her many melodies? Or voice
Of the far sea, red with the sunset gold,
That sang within her shining shores, and sang
Within the Gate, that in the sunset shone
A gate of fire against the outer world?

For, ever as I turned the magic page
Of that old song the old, blind singer sang
Unto the world, when it and song were young—
The ripple of the reeds, or odorous,
Soft sigh of leaves, or voice of the far sea—
A mystical, low murmur, tremulous
Upon the wind, came in with musk of rose,
The salt breath of the waves, and far, faint smell
Of laurel up the slopes of Tamalpais[5]. . . . [in original]

"Am I less fair, am I less fair than these,
      Daughters of far-off seas?
Daughters of far-off shores,—bleak, over-blown
With foam of fretful tides, with wail and moan
Of waves, that toss wild hands, that clasp and beat
Wild, desolate hands above the lonely sands,
Printed no more with pressure of their feet:
That chase no more the light feet flying swift
      Up golden sands, nor lift
Foam fingers white unto their garment hem,
      And flowing hair of them.

"For these are dead: the fair, great queens are dead!
The long hair's gold a dust the wind bloweth
      Wherever it may list;
      The curvëd lips, that kissed
Heroes and kings of men, a dust that breath,
Nor speech, nor laughter, ever quickeneth;
      And all the glory sped
From the large, marvelous eyes, the light whereof
Wrought wonder in their hearts,—desire, and love!
      And wrought not any good:

5. Peak visible from San Francisco.

But strife, and curses of the gods, and flood,
    And fire and battle-death!
    Am I less fair, less fair,
    Because that my hands bear
Neither a sword, nor any flaming brand,
To blacken and make desolate my land,
But on my brows are leaves of olive boughs,
    And in mine arms a dove![6]

"Sea-born and goddess, blossom of the foam,
Pale Aphrodite,[7] shadowy as a mist
    Not any sun hath kissed!
    Tawny of limb *I* roam,
The dusks of forests dark within my hair;
    The far Yosemite,[8]
For garment and for covering of me,
    Wove the white foam and mist,
The amber and the rose and amethyst
Of her wild fountains, shaken loose in air.
And I am of the hills and of the sea:
Strong with the strength of my great hills, and calm
With calm of the fair sea, whose billowy gold
Girdles the land whose queen and love I am!
    Lo! am I less than thou,
That with a sound of lyres, and harp-playing,
    Not any voice doth sing
The beauty of mine eyelids and my brow?
Nor hymn in all my fair and gracious ways,
    And lengths of golden days,
The measure and the music of my praise?

    "Ah, what indeed is this
Old land beyond the seas, that ye should miss
For her the grace and majesty of mine?
    Are not the fruit and vine
Fair on my hills, and in my vales the rose?
    The palm-tree and the pine

6. The olive branch and dove are symbols of peace.
7. Greek goddess of love and beauty, who was born amid sea foam.
8. The Yosemite Valley in California is known for its giant sequoia forests and waterfalls. It became a national park in 1890.

Strike hands together under the same skies
   In every wind that blows.
   What clearer heavens can shine
Above the land whereon the shadow lies
Of her dead glory, and her slaughtered kings,
   And lost, evanished gods?
   Upon my fresh green sods
No king has walked to curse and desolate:
But in the valleys Freedom sits and sings,
   And on the heights above;
Upon her brows the leaves of olive boughs,
   And in her arms a dove;
And the great hills are pure, undesecrate,
   White with their snows untrod,
And mighty with the presence of their God!

   "Hearken, how many years
I sat alone, I sat alone and heard
   Only the silence stirred
By wind and leaf, by clash of grassy spears,
And singing bird that called to singing bird.
   Heard but the savage tongue
Of my brown savage children, that among
The hills and valleys chased the buck and doe,
   And round the wigwam fires
Chanted wild songs of their wild savage sires,
And danced their wild, weird dances to and fro,
And wrought their beaded robes of buffalo.
   Day following upon day,
Saw but the panther crouched upon the limb,
   Smooth serpents, swift and slim,
Slip through the reeds and grasses, and the bear
   Crush through his tangled lair
Of chapparal,[9] upon the startled prey!

   "Listen, how I have seen
Flash of strange fires in gorge and black ravine;
Heard the sharp clang of steel, that came to drain
   The mountain's golden vein—

---

9. Regions of scrub in the Southwest.

And laughed and sang, and sang and laughed again,
Because that 'now,' I said, 'I shall be known!
　I shall not sit alone;
But reach my hands unto my sister lands!
　And they? Will they not turn
Old, wondering dim eyes to me, and yearn—
　Aye, they will yearn, in sooth,
To my glad beauty, and my glad fresh youth!'

　"What matters though the morn
Redden upon my singing fields of corn!
What matters though the wind's unresting feet
　Ripple the gold of wheat,
　And my vales run with wine,
　And on these hills of mine
The orchard boughs droop heavy with ripe fruit?
　When with nor sound of lute
Nor lyre, doth any singer chant and sing
　Me, in my life's fair spring:
The matin song of me in my young day?
But all my lays and legends fade away
From lake and mountain to the farther hem
Of sea, and there be none to gather them.

　"Lo! I have waited long!
How longer yet must my strung harp be dumb,
　Ere its great master come?
Till the fair singer comes to wake the strong,
Rapt chords of it unto the new, glad song!
　Him a diviner speech
　My song-birds wait to teach:
　The secrets of the field
　My blossoms will not yield
　To other hands than his;
　And, lingering for this,
My laurels lend the glory of their boughs
　To crown no narrower brows.
For on his lips must wisdom sit with youth,
And in his eyes, and on the lids thereof,
　The light of a great love—
　And on his forehead, truth!" . . . [in original]

Was it the wind, or the soft sigh of leaves,
Or sound of singing waters? Lo, I looked,
And saw the silvery ripples of the brook,
The fruit upon the hills, the waving trees,
And mellow fields of harvest; saw the Gate
Burn in the sunset; the thin thread of mist
Creep white across the Saucelito hills;[10]
Till the day darkened down the ocean rim,
The sunset purple slipped from Tamalpais,
And bay and sky were bright with sudden stars.

Source: Songs From the Golden Gate (1895)

Introduction to *California*

I have always believed that the Poet of the New World—of the World—was to come out of the West—from California. Why not? Would it be more strange that this broad land by the shores of the vast Pacific should produce the Supreme Singer, than that a little Island of the far Atlantic should have given birth to the Bard of Avon[11]—to that kinglier brow than ever wore a crown?

For California is a Poem! The land of romance, of mystery, of worship, of beauty and of Song. It chants from her snow-crested, cloud-bannered mountain-ranges; it hymns thro' her forests of sky-reaching pine and sequoia; it ripples in her flowered and fruited valleys; it thunders from her fountains pouring, as it were, from the very waters above the firmament; it anthems from the deeps of the mightiest ocean of the world; and echoes ever in the syllables of her own strangely beautiful name,—California.

The spell of enchantment which she wove about me from the day when—a little child—I entered her borders thro' the rocky mountain-pass from the long trail across the great plains, was not lessened by the after-vision of the Southland grape and fig, orange and pomegranate,—or the (so-called) deserts of sand and cacti, which the spring months covered with a carpet of bloom rivalling the richest dyes of the Persian looms. Rather has it increased with the passing of time.

And then she is, as our brothers of France would say, of such a Bigness; is so stupendous! Surely, of her, greatness only should be born: why not the greatest of all,—the Master Singer?

With all this mind-enwoven, it was but natural, when in after years I was asked

---

10. In the San Francisco Bay area.
11. William Shakespeare.

by the University of California to contribute a poem for its Commencement Day, that I should seek to voice my belief. How inadequate the expression to the inner song only I may fully realize. Yet am I glad that the first Commencement Poem to be written by a woman for any university, is of, and bears the name of California.

Source: California (1918)

❧ FRANCES HARPER (1825–1911)

Frances Ellen Watkins was born a free black in Baltimore, Maryland. She first worked as a domestic, then became a teacher. Throughout the 1850s, she was active in the abolitionist movement as a writer and lecturer, traveling throughout the North. She married a farmer in 1860 and had a daughter. When she was widowed in 1864, she returned to her career as an activist. After the abolition of slavery, Harper committed herself to other important causes, including women's suffrage, temperance, and anti-lynching. Harper's poetry was a natural extension of her public life lecturing on the evils of slavery and the rights of women. She often read her poems as part of her lectures and published them in journals devoted to the antislavery cause. Her poetry used sentimental techniques to elicit readers' sympathy and spur them to action. As the following poem and sketch attest, Harper's view of authorship meshed with her desire to help effect social change. Her novel Iola Leroy; or Shadows Uplifted *(1892) also features an African American woman who devotes herself to the uplift of her race.*

Fancy Etchings

"Why! aunt Jane this is delightful. I was saying that I hoped you would come this morning, and lo! you are here; a pleasant exemplification of the beautiful adage, talk of the angels and they will show their wings."

"Well, darling, I am glad that you have leisure to sit awhile with me; I feared that you would be engaged in house cleaning, and that I would find you too busy to have a pleasant little chat."

"Oh, no, I shall not commence that job till next week, and were I in the midst of it, I do not think I should be too busy to give you hearty welcome; so just let me take your things and give you this easy chair, and I do hope that we will have an uninterrupted morning."

"Well, Jenny, I am at your disposal; hand me my knitting, darling, if you please. Do you remember this satchel?"

"I should think I did, when some of the pleasantest memories of my childhood are connected with it. Don't you remember how we children used to ransack it for gum-drops and pepper mints, and how you used to shake your head and say you feared the little rogues loved your satchel better than they loved you."

"Do I remember it? Ah, you and your sister Anna lifted too many shadows from my lonely widowed life, and scattered too much sunshine around my path for me to forget those pleasant days of yore."

"And these pleasant interviews which we now have, only seem to me like a lengthening out of those warm bright days of childhood, days gilded with love and flecked with gladness."

"Yes, Jenny, I feel that the love I bear you, strengthens with my years, and you are far dearer to me than when tired of play you used to nestle in my arms and fall to sleep! and one reason is that you have so pleasantly surprised me."

"How so, Aunty?"

"Why, Jenny, when you returned from college having graduated with such high honors, I feared that you might think Aunty is too old fashioned for companionship, and that I should lose my loving, little girl in the accomplished woman; but instead of that I retained them both."

"Ah, Aunty, you don't know how much your love was a stimulus to my exertions; and one of my first thoughts after graduating was, how this will please Aunty. Aunty I want to be a poet, to earn and take my place among the poets of the nineteenth century; but with all the glowing enthusiasms that light up my life I cannot help thinking, that more valuable than the soarings of genius are the tender nestlings of love. Genius may charm the intellect, but love will refresh the spirit."

"I am glad, Jenny, that you feel so, for I think the intellect that will best help our race must be heart supplied: but do you think by being a poet you can best serve our people?"

"I think, Aunty, the best way to serve humanity, is by looking within ourselves, and becoming acquainted with our powers and capacities. The fact is we should all go to work and make the most of ourselves, and we cannot do that without helping others."

"And so having sounded the depths of your inner life, you have come to the conclusion that you have talent or genius for poetry."

"Aunty, do you remember that poem I wrote some months since which you and others admired so? To me that poem was a revelation, I learned from it that I had power to create, and it gave me faith in myself, and I think faith in one's self is an element, of success. Perhaps you think this is egotism."

"Oh no, I do not think that consciousness of one's ability to perform certain things, is egotism. If a woman is beautiful it is not vanity for her to know what the looking glass constantly reveals. A knowledge of powers and capacities should be an incentive to growth and not a stimulus for vain glory; but, Jenny, what do you expect to accomplish among our people by being a poet?"

"Aunty I want to learn myself and be able to teach others to strive to make the highest ideal, the most truly real of our lives[.]"

"But, Jenny, will not such an endeavor be love's labor lost?[1] what time will our people have in their weary working every day life to listen to your songs?"

"It is just because our lives are apt to be so hard and dry, that I would scatter the flowers of poetry around our paths; and would if I could amid life's sad discords introduce the most entrancing strains of melody. I would teach men and women to

---

1. *Love's Labour's Lost* (1594–1595) is a play by Shakespeare.

love noble deeds by setting them to the music, of fitly spoken words. The first throb of interest that a person feels in the recital of a noble deed, a deed of high and holy worth, the first glow of admiration for suffering virtue, or thrill of joy in the triumph of goodness, forms a dividing line between the sensuous and material and the spiritual and progressive. I think poetry is one of the great agents of culture, civilization and refinement. What grander poetry can you find than among the ancient Hebrews; and to-day the Aryan race with all the splendor of its attainments and the magnificence of its culture; still lights the lamp of its devotion at Semitic altars. Ages have passed since the blind beggar of Chios[2] was denied a pension, in his native place, but his poetry is still green in the world's memory."

Source: Christian Recorder (1873)

Songs for the People

Let me make the songs for the people,
  Songs for the old and young;
Songs to stir like a battle-cry
  Wherever they are sung.

Not for the clashing of sabres,
  For carnage nor for strife;
But songs to thrill the hearts of men
  With more abundant life.

Let me make the songs for the weary,
  Amid life's fever and fret,
Till hearts shall relax their tension,
  And careworn brows forget.

Let me sing for little children,
  Before their footsteps stray,
Sweet anthems of love and duty,
  To float o'er life's highway.

I would sing for the poor and aged,
  When shadows dim their sight;

---

2. Homer, great epic poet of ancient Greece.

Of the bright and restful mansions,
  Where there shall be no night.

Our world, so worn and weary,
  Needs music, pure and strong
To hush the jangle and discords
  Of sorrow, pain, and wrong.

Music to soothe all its sorrow,
  Till war and crime shall cease;
And the hearts of men grown tender
  Girdle the world with peace.

Source: Poems (1895)

❧ REBECCA HARDING DAVIS (1831–1910)

Rebecca Harding was raised in Wheeling, Virginia (now West Virginia), where she helped her mother care for their large family. Except for four years away from home at Washington Female Seminary, she was educated at home. Although she had contributed articles to the Wheeling newspaper, Harding was completely unknown until 1861, when her story "Life in the Iron Mills" was published in the Atlantic Monthly, *bringing her the recognition of the nation's literary elite. She was invited to Boston and Concord, where she met Nathaniel Hawthorne, Ralph Waldo Emerson, and others. Her story also caught the attention of Clarke Davis, a Philadelphia journalist, who initiated a courtship via correspondence. After their marriage in 1863 and the subsequent births of three children, Rebecca continued her literary career with a greater interest in her ability to earn an income. The difficulties creative women faced was a prominent theme of her fiction. In "Marcia," told from a successful writer's perspective, an untutored young woman looks to authorship as a way to escape the prison of marriage and a rural, domestic life.*

Marcia

One winter morning a few years ago the mail brought me a roll of MS.[1] (with one stamp too many, as if to bribe the post to care for so precious a thing) and a letter. Every publisher, editor, or even the obscurest of writers receives such packages so often as to know them at a glance. Half a dozen poems and a story—a blur of sunsets, duchesses, violets, bad French, and worse English; not a solid grain of common-sense, not a hint of reality or even of possibility, in the whole of it. The letter—truth in every word: formal, hard, practical, and the meaning of it a woman's cry for bread for her hungry children. Each woman who writes such a letter fancies she is the first, that its pathos will move hard-hearted editors, and that the extent of her need will supply the lack of wit, wisdom, or even grammar in her verses or story. Such appeals pour in literally by the thousand every year to every publishing office. The sickly daughter of a poor family; the wife of a drunken husband; a widow; children that must be fed and clothed. What was the critic's honest opinion of her work? how much would it bring in dollars and cents? etc., etc.

I did not open the letter that day. When we reach middle age we have learned, through rough experiences, how many tragedies there are in our street or under our own roof which will be none the better for our handling, and are apt, selfishly, to try to escape the hearing of them.

---

1. Manuscripts.

This letter, however, when I opened it next morning, proved to be not of a tragical sort. The writer was "not dependent on her pen for support;" she "had vowed herself to literature;" she "was resolved to assist in the Progress of humanity." Scarcely had I laid down the letter when I was told that she waited below to see me. The card she sent up was a bit of the fly-leaf of a book, cut oblong with scissors, and the name—Miss Barr—written in imitation of engraving. Her back was toward me when I came down, and I had time to read the same sham stylishness written all over her thin little person. The sleazy black silk was looped in the prevailing fashion, a sweeping white plume drooped from the cheap hat, and on her hands were washed cotton gloves.

Instead of the wizened features of the "dead beat" which I expected, she turned on me a child's face: an ugly face, I believe other women called it, but one of the most innocent and honest in the world. Her brown eyes met yours eagerly, full of a joyous good-fellowship for every thing and every body alive. She poured out her story, too, in a light-hearted way, and in the lowest, friendliest of voices. To see the girl was to be her ally. "People will do any thing for me—but publish my manuscripts," she said.

She came from Mississippi; had been the only white child on a poor plantation on the banks of the Yazoo. "I have only had such teaching as my mother could give: she had but two years with a governess. We had no books nor newspapers, except an occasional copy of a magazine sent to us by friends in the North." Her mother was the one central figure in the world to her then. In our after-intercourse she talked of her continually. "She is a little woman—less than I; but she has one of the finest minds in the world," she would cry. "The sight of any thing beautiful or the sound of music sways her as the wind does a reed. But she never was twenty miles from the plantation; she has read nothing, knows nothing. My father thinks women are like mares—only useful to bring forth children. My mother's children all died in babyhood but me. There she has lived all her life, with the swamp on one side and the forest of live-oak on the other: nothing to do, nothing to think of. Oh, it was frightful! With a mind like hers, any woman would go mad, with that eternal forest and swamp, and the graves of her dead babies just in sight! She rubbed snuff a good deal to quiet herself, but of late years she has taken opium."

"And you?"

"I left her. I hoped to do something for us both. My mind is not of as high order as hers, but it is very different from that of most women. I shall succeed some day," in the most matter-of-fact tones. "As soon as I knew that I was a poet I determined to come to Philadelphia and go straight to real publishers and real editors. In my country nobody had ever seen a man who had written a book. Ever since I came here I find how hard it is to find out any thing about the business of authorship. Medicine, or law, or blacksmithing—every body knows the workings of those trades, but people with pens in their hands keep the secret of their craft like Freemasons,"[2] laughing.

"You came alone?"

"Quite alone. I hired a little room over a baker's shop in Pine Street. They are a very decent couple, the baker and his wife. I board myself, and send out my manuscripts. They always come back to me."

"Where do you send them?"

"Oh, every where. I can show you printed forms of rejection from every magazine and literary newspaper in the country," opening and shutting again a black sachel [*sic*] on her lap. "I have written three novels, and sent them to the ——s' and ——s'. They sent them back as unavailable. But they never read them. I trick them this a-way: I put a loose blue thread between the third and fourth pages of the manuscript, and it is always there when it comes back." Her voice broke a little, but she winked her brown eyes and laughed bravely.

"How long have you been here?"

"Three years."

"Impossible! You are but a child."

"I am twenty. I had an article published once in a Sunday paper," producing a slip about two inches long.

Three years, and only that little grain of success! She had supported herself meanwhile, as I learned afterward, by sewing men's socks for a firm in Germantown.

"You are ready to give up now?"

"No; not if it were ten years instead of three."

Yet I can swear there was not a drop of New England blood in her little body. One was certain, against all reason, that she would succeed. When even such puny creatures as this take the world by the throat in that fashion, they are sure to conquer it.

Her books and poems must, I think, have seemed unique to any editor. The spelling was atrocious; the errors of grammar in every line beyond remedy. The lowest pupil in our public schools would have detected her ignorance on the first page. There was, too, in all she said or wrote an occasional gross indecency, such as a child might show: her life on the plantation explained it. Like Juliet, she spoke the language of her nurse.[3] But even Shakespeare's nurse and Juliet would not be allowed nowadays to chatter at will in the pages of a family magazine.

But in all her ignorance, mistakes, and weaknesses there was no trace of imitation. She plagiarized nobody. There was none of the usual talk of countesses,

2. All-male fraternal organization famous for its secrecy.
3. In Shakespeare's *Romeo and Juliet* (1595–1596), Juliet's nurse spoke an earthy dialect.

heather, larks, or emotions of which she knew nothing. She painted over and over again her own home on the Yazoo: the hot still sunshine, the silence of noon, the swamp, the slimy living things in the stagnant ponds, the semi-tropical forest, the house and negro quarters, with all their dirt and dreary monotony. It was a picture which remained in the mind strong and vivid as a desert by Gérôme or a moor by Boughton.[4]

There could be but one kind of advice to give her—to put away pen and ink, and for three years at least devote herself to hard study. She would, of course, have none of such counsel. The popular belief in the wings of genius, which can carry it over hard work and all such obstacles as ignorance of grammar or even the spelling-book, found in her a marked example. Work was for commonplace talent, not for those whose veins were full of the divine ichor.[5]

Meanwhile she went on sewing socks, and sending off her great yellow envelopes, with stamps to bring them back.

"Stamps and paper count up so fast!" she said, with a laugh, into which had grown a pitiful quaver. She would take not a penny of aid. "I shall not starve. When the time has come for me to know that I have failed, I can go back to my own country and live like the other women there."

Meanwhile her case very nearly reached starvation. I remember few things more pathetic than the damp, forlorn little figure in a shabby water-proof, black sachel in hand, which used to come to my door through the snows and drenching rains that winter. Her shoes were broken, and her hands shriveled blue with cold. But a plated gilt chain or a scarlet ribbon used to flaunt somewhere over the meagre, scant poverty. Sometimes she brought news with her. She had work given her—to collect a column of jokes for a Sunday paper, by which she made three dollars a week. But she lost it from trying to insert her own matter, which could not well be reckoned as funny sayings. One day she came flushed with excitement. Somebody had taken her through the Academy of Design and a private gallery of engravings then on exhibition. She had a keen, just eye for form and color, and the feeling of a true artist for both.

"That is what I could have done," she said, after keeping silence a long while. "But what chance had I? I never even saw a picture at home, except those which were cut out of illustrated papers. There seemed to be no way for me but to write."

It was suggested to her that she might find the other way even now. Painting, designing, wood-engraving, were expressions for a woman's mind, even though, like her own, it was "one of the finest in the world."

She did not smile. "It is too late," she said. "I will go on as I have begun. But it is a pity my mother and I had not known of such things."

4. Jean-Léon Gérôme (1824–1904), neoclassical French painter, and George Henry Boughton (1833–1905), Anglo-American painter famous for Puritan and Dutch scenes.
5. Fluid supposed to flow in the veins of the Greek gods.

After that her light-hearted courage seemed to give way. She persevered, but it was with dogged, indomitable resolution, and little hope.

One day in the spring I was summoned to see a visitor on business. I found a tall, lank young man stalking up and down the room, the most noticeable point about him the shock of red hair and whisker falling over his neck and greasy coat collar. The face was that of an ignorant, small-minded man. But it was candid and not sensual.

He came straight toward me. "Is Marcia Barr here?"

"No; she has been gone for an hour."

He damned his luck in a white heat of rage, which must, I thought, have required some time to kindle. Indeed, I found he had been pacing up and down the street half the morning, having seen her come in. She had gone out by a side door.

"I caught a glimpse of her half a mile off. I have come to Philadelphia three times this year to find her. Good God! how rank poor she is! Where does she live?"

I could not tell him, as Marcia had long ago left the baker's, and changed her quarters every month.

"And I reckon I'll have to wait until she comes hyah again. Tell her it's Zack Biron, the overseer's son, on—on business."

He was not long in unveiling his business, which any woman would soon have guessed. He had come to bring Marcia home and marry her. He had always "wanted her," and the old colonel, her father, had promised he should marry her provided he could bring her back from her mad flight. The colonel was dead, and he was now "runnin' the plantation for ole madam. She's no better than a walkin' corpse, with that damned drug she chews. She can't keep still now: walks, walks incessant about the place, with her eyes set an' the skin clingin' to her bones. I couldn't 'a borne it, I ashuah you, but for the sake of findin' Marcia."

Two months passed, in which he haunted the house. But Marcia did not come. She had begun to frequent newspaper offices, and occasionally was given a trifling bit of work by the managers of the reporting corps—a description of the dresses at a Männerchor[6] ball to write, or a puff[7] of some coming play, etc. She came at last to tell me of what she had done.

"It is miserable work. I would rather sew the heels of stockings; but the stocking looms have stopped, and I must live a little longer, at any rate. I think I have something to say, if people only would hear it."

I told her of Biron and his chase for her.

"I saw him outside the window the last time I was here. That was the reason I went out by the side street. I knew he was looking for me. You will not tell him I have been here?"

6. German men's singing club.
7. Positive review.

"But, Marcia, the man seems honest and kindly—"

"If he found me," in the same quiet tone, "he would marry me and take me back to the plantation."

"And you are not ready to give up?"

"No, I will not give up. I shall get into the right groove at last," with the infectious little laugh which nobody could resist.

The water-proof cloak was worn down quite into the cotton by this time, and the straw hat had been darned around the ragged edge. But there was a cheap red rose in it. Her cheek-bones showed high, and her eyes shone out of black hollows.

"No, I have no cough, and I don't need medicine," she said, irritably, when questioned. "I have had plenty of offers of help. But I'd rather steal than take alms." She rose hastily and buttoned her cloak.

"This man Biron waits only a word to come to you. He is faithful as a dog."

She nodded carelessly. Biron, or a return to her old home, held no part in her world, it was plain to see.

I was out of the city for several months. A few weeks after my return I saw in the evening paper one day, in the usual list of crimes and casualties, an item headed "*Pitiable Case.*—A young woman named Burr was arrested yesterday on charge of theft, and taken to the Central Station. About eleven o'clock the other women in the cell where she was confined perceiving that she lay on a bench breathing in a stertorous[8] manner, summoned Lieutenant Pardy, who found life to be almost extinct. A physician was called, who discovered that the woman had swallowed some poisonous drug. With her first breath of returning consciousness she protested her innocence of the charge. She appears to have been in an extreme state of want. But little hope is entertained of her recovery. Miss Burr is favorably known, we believe, as a writer of some ability for the daily press."

In spite of the difference of name, it must be Marcia.

When we reached the Central Station we were told that her discharge was already procured. She had friends who knew what wires to work. In the outer room were half a dozen young men, reporters, a foreman of a printing-room, and one or two women, dramatic or musical critics. There is as eager an *esprit de corps* among that class of journalists as among actors. They were all talking loudly, and zealous in defense of "little Marty," as they called her, whom they declared to be "a dunce so far as head went, but pure and guileless as a child."

"I knew she was devilishly hard up," said one, "but never suspected she was starving. She would not borrow a dollar, she had that pride in her."

Marcia was still in the cell, lying on an iron stretcher. The Mississippian, Biron, was with her, kneeling on the floor in his shirt sleeves, chafing her hand. He had taken off his coat to wrap about her.

---

8. Irregular.

"I've a good Quaker nurse and a room ready for her at the Continental the minute she can be moved," he whispered. "Look a-here!" turning down the poor bit of lace and red ribbon at her throat, his big hairy hand shaking. "Them bones is a'most through the skin! The doctor says it's hunger—hunger! And *I* was eatin' three solid meals a day—like a beast!"

Hunger had almost done its work. There was but a feeble flicker of life left in the emaciated little body; not enough to know or speak to us when at last she opened her dull eyes.

"None o' them folks need consarn themselves any furder about her," said Biron, savagely. "She'll come home to her own now, thank God, and be done with rubbishy book-makers. Mrs. Biron will live like a lady."

Two or three weeks later, the most splendid of hired phaetons stopped at my door, and Mr. and Mrs. Biron sent up their cards. Mr. Biron was glowing with happiness. It asserted itself offensively somehow in the very jingling of his watch chain and tie of his cravat.

"We return immediately to the plantation," he said, grandiloquently. "I reckon largely on the effect of her native air in restorin' Mrs. Biron to health."

Marcia was magnificent in silk and plumes, the costliest that her owner's money could buy. Her little face was pale, however, and she looked nobody in the eye.

"We leave for the South to-morrow," she said, calmly, "and I shall not return to Philadelphia. I have no wish to return."

"Shall I send you books or papers, Marcia?"

"No, I thank you; nothing."

When they rose to go, her husband said, "Mrs. Biron has some—rubbish she wishes to leave with you. Hyah!" calling out of the window. "You nigger, bring that thah bag!"

It was the old black sachel. Marcia took it in her white-gloved hands, half opened it, shut it quickly, came up closer.

"These are my manuscripts," she said. "Will you burn them for me? All: do not leave a line, a word. I could not do it."

I took the sachel, and they departed. Mr. Biron was vehement in his protestations of friendship and invitations to visit the plantation. But Marcia did not say a word, even of farewell.

Source: Harper's New Monthly Magazine (1876)

🍂 LORETA JANETA VELÁZQUEZ (1842–?)

Loreta Janeta Velázquez was born in Havana, Cuba, to a Spanish father and an American-French mother. She had a privileged childhood and was sent to New Orleans to be educated. There she married an army officer who joined the Confederacy in 1861; she disguised herself as a soldier to join him. After his death, she fought in many of the war's major battles, was wounded, and acted as a spy. Velázquez wrote her memoir to assist in the support of her only child, just as Harriet Wilson wrote her book Our Nig *to support her son. Velázquez's memoir included many sensational adventures, leading some to accuse her of fabrication. Nonetheless, it is one of only two autobiographies of their Civil War experiences written by female soldiers, and the only one by a Latina. Virtually all that is known of her life comes from her own account, which was undoubtedly influenced by what she admitted was her own tendency to romanticize her experiences. Scholars have found no records of her life after the publication of her book.*

Author's Prefatory Notice to *The Woman in Battle*

If I expected by this story of my adventures to achieve any literary reputation, I might be disposed, on account of its many faults of style, to ask the indulgence of those who will do me the honor to undertake its perusal. As, however, I only attempted authorship because I had, as others assured me, and as I myself believed, something to tell that was worth telling, I have been more concerned about the matter than the manner of my book, and I hope that the narrative will prove of sufficient interest to compensate for a lack of literary elegance in the setting forth. Mine has been a life too busily occupied in other matters for me to cultivate the graces of authorship; and the best I can hope to do is to relate my story with simplicity and truth, and then let it find its fate, whether it be praise or condemnation.

The composition of this book has been a labor of love, and yet one of no ordinary difficulties. The loss of my notes has compelled me to rely entirely upon my memory; and memory is apt to be very treacherous, especially when, after a number of years, one endeavors to relate in their proper sequence a long series of complicated transactions. Besides, I have been compelled to write hurriedly, and in the intervals of pressing business, the necessities I have been under of earning my daily bread being such as could not be disregarded, even for the purpose of winning the laurels of authorship. To speak plainly, however, I care little for laurels of any kind just now, and am much more anxious for the money that I hope this book will bring in to me than I am for the praises of either critics or public. The money I want badly, while praise, although it will not be ungratifying, I am sufficiently philosophical to get along very comfortably without.

I do not know what the good people who will read this book will think of me.

My career has differed materially from that of most women; and some things that I have done have shocked persons for whom I have every respect, however much my ideas of propriety may differ from theirs. I can only say, however, that in my opinion there was nothing essentially improper in my putting on the uniform of a Confederate officer for the purpose of taking an active part in the war; and, as when on the field of battle, in camp, and during long and toilsome marches, I endeavored, not without success, to display a courage and fortitude not inferior to the most courageous of the men around me, and as I never did aught to disgrace the uniform I wore, but, on the contrary, won the hearty commendation of my comrades, I feel that I have nothing to be ashamed of. Had I believed that my book needed any apologies on this score, it would never have been written; and, having written it, I am willing to submit my conduct to the judgment of the public, with a confidence that I will at least receive due credit for the motives by which I was animated.

In the preparation of this book for the press, I have been greatly aided by the gentleman who has consented to act as my editor. Although during the war he was on the other side, he has interested himself most heartily in assisting me to get my narrative into the best shape for presentation to the public, and has shown a remarkable skill in detecting and correcting errors into which I had inadvertently fallen. I take pleasure in acknowledging my indebtedness to him.

The book, such as it is,—and I have tried to make it all that such a book should be by telling my story in as plain, straightforward, and unpretending a style as I could command,—is now, for good or ill, out of my hands, and my adopted country people will have to decide for themselves whether the writing of it was worth the while or not.

Source: The Woman in Battle: A Narrative of the Exploits, Adventures, and Travels of Madame Loreta Janeta Velázquez, Otherwise Known as Lieutenant Harry T. Buford, Confederate States Army (1876)

Frances Elizabeth Caroline Willard was born in Churchville, New York, but raised in Janesville, Wisconsin. She preferred to be called "Frank" and wore boys' clothing. She was educated at home before going on to become valedictorian of her class at North Western Female College in Evanston, Illinois. She taught for many years and rose to the presidency of Evanston College for Ladies. She later became dean of the Women's College of Northwestern University and was engaged to the university's president. However, she broke off the engagement for fear of losing her independence. After a trip to Europe in 1868, she devoted herself to the causes of women's rights and temperance, resigning her post at Northwestern in 1874. She traveled the country as a lecturer and activist and is most well known for her position as president of the Woman's Christian Temperance Union, which she held from 1879 until her death. The following letter was published anonymously, but Willard claimed authorship of it in her Glimpses of Fifty Years: The Autobiography of an American Woman *(1889). Although remembered today for the faux pas Mark Twain committed in a speech that appeared to mock the literary lions Emerson, Longfellow, and others, the* Atlantic Monthly's *dinner at the Hotel Brunswick in Boston celebrating its twentieth anniversary and John Greenleaf Whittier's seventieth birthday caused some protest at the time for its exclusion of women. Fifty-seven men attended the exclusive event, but no women were invited, even though many had been instrumental to the magazine's success. As Willard's letter makes clear, the magazine and its highly publicized events were perceived as having the power to grant American literary "citizenship" or withhold it from its female contributors.*

The Atlantic-Whittier Dinner—A Woman's Thoughts Thereof

To the Editors of the Boston Daily Advertiser:—

Some of us feel as though our own mothers had received a slight; a few of us have cried, and many stormed, but I alone am left to tell thee. In the republic of letters, if nowhere else, woman is a citizen. Parnassus[1] seats gods and goddesses on the same throne; the Muses are feminine, the entire nine of them. Alongside facts like these set the Brunswick banqueting-table, with a guest at its head accustomed to see women honored equally with men in his Quaker home and church,[2] and down the sides of the groaning board, among the "contributors to the Atlantic," see the brilliant women of that guild conspicuous only for their absence!

Astræa at the Capital, forsooth! Dear Bard of Freedom,[3] what did you think

1. Mountain in Delphi; home of the Muses in Greek mythology.
2. John Greenleaf Whittier (1807–1892) was a Quaker poet. Quakers were known for their recognition of women's equality with men.
3. Astræa: Greek goddess of justice. Bard of Freedom: Whittier was known for his antislavery poetry.

about Astræa's absence from your birthday *fête*? "Assuredly," we thought, glancing along the columns radiant with the wit and wisdom of the feast, "there will be letters of regret, showing that all the leading contributors were at least invited," but the hope proved vain. "Then most assuredly," we gasped, "the publishers or editors will give some explanation of all this,—some recognition of services so splendid, some brief phrase, at least, to redeem the very dome of American brain from the charge of an obliviousness not explainable by any law of mind yet ascertained?" But no; from generous publisher and genial editor to grotesque humorist, all combined "to let expressive silence muse their praise." The only reference to the gentler sex that anywhere creeps in is this: "When the after-dinner speaking began the women who were staying in the hotel entered and were favored with seats."

Indeed! But who had *earned* a seat at Whittier's own right hand? Who but Harriet Beecher Stowe, one of the chief contributors to the Atlantic? And Harriet Prescott Spofford, Rebecca Harding Davis, Gail Hamilton, Elizabeth Stuart Phelps, Mrs. Whitney, Harriet W. Preston and Louisa M. Alcott—were they not "to the manner born"?[4] Among the sweet singers, ought Rose Terry and Lucy Larcom, Celia Thaxter, Florence Percy and "H. H." to have been overlooked? And Mrs. S. M. B. Piatt—why should she not have had an invitation and sent a poem, as well as John?[5] Yet this is Boston, that sat on her three hills and ruled the world! And those are the Bostonians—so broad, so liberal and so just!

And Colonel Higginson[6] was there, and he forgot us, too! Ah me, this is the unkindest cut of all!

Hopeless as seems the task, we must still seek an explanation of this uncomely state of things. Was it because "women are angels" that "the contributors" belonging to that celestial class were not invited to nor mentioned at a banquet in honor of a total abstainer before whom were set (in delicate compliment of course) eight kinds of wine? Was it because Eve, being "first in transgression" (as tempter in chief at the first dinner) her sons determined she should never more sit down beside them at the convivial board? Or was it that *prestige* of sex is not yet offset by the chivalry of justice even among the liberals?

If it were not Boston we should say, "I wot it is through ignorance ye did it." But as it is, we dismiss the subject with the mild reproof in sorrow, not in anger. "My brethren, these things ought not so to be!"

[Signed]   A FEW AMONG MANY.
Parnassusville, Dec. 18, 1877.

Source: Boston Daily Advertiser (1877)

4. All well-known female American authors published in the *Atlantic,* in addition to those whose names follow. "To the manner born": naturally suited for.

5. "H. H." is Helen Hunt Jackson (1830–1885). Sarah Piatt's husband, John, was also a poet.

6. Thomas Wentworth Higginson (1823–1911), an editor at the *Atlantic,* was known for his encouragement of women writers, most famously today of Emily Dickinson.

The following response to women's exclusion from the dinner commemorating the Atlantic Monthly's *twentieth anniversary and the poet John Greenleaf Whittier's seventieth birthday appeared in a Western newspaper. Scholar Susan Coultrap-McQuin believes that Gail Hamilton was likely its author. It satirically portrays a nervous Mr. Houghton (publisher of the* Atlantic) *as he realizes his mistake in alienating his female contributors, who have the power to leave the magazine and take their readers with them.*

Mr. Houghton's Mistake

"We are glad to learn that the lady contributors to the *Atlantic,* who did not attend the Whittier dinner were not disappointed. Indeed, they had intended all along not to be present, and they so indicated to Mr. Houghton in letters written the very day before the dinner. 'I hear it intimated,' writes Mrs. Stowe, 'that I am to be selected to sit at the right hand of Mr. Whittier. Now, my dear Mr. Houghton, while I am deeply grateful for the compliment, I cannot accept. I believe in the largest freedom for everybody, and I am sure the gentlemen who participate in the festivities would not be pleased to have their programme embarrassed by the presence of ladies. He, he! I suppose you know what I mean. One of these days, perhaps, the ladies of the *Atlantic* will have a dinner, and I think they are selfish enough to desire to be alone.'"

Mr. Houghton read the letter and said, passing his hand through his hair, "I think I have forgotten something. I detect sarcasm in this."

"I am glad, Mr. Houghton," wrote Harriet Prescott Spofford, "that you have decided not to call the ladies from their sylvan solitude. I am deeply engaged in studying the peculiarities of some rushes that grow upon the banks of the beautiful river that rolls by my door, crystallized at present, by the way—I mean the river—in the mellowest moonlight that ever sifted its gold upon a beautiful world; so I couldn't attend anyhow. Thank you for sending no invitation. It would have embarrassed me greatly.

"Have you heard that Mrs. Stowe is about to give a dinner? Are you aware that there is to be a new ladies' magazine? But I cannot write more. Thank you again, and good-bye."

"I am quite confident," said Mr. Houghton, looking worried, "that there is an inadvertence somewhere. It's very singular I did'nt [*sic*] think of these ladies before." He turned wearily and opened a letter from Gail Hamilton.

"Well, my boy," wrote this lady, "so you're going to give a dinner, are you? To Mr. Whittier, the dearest and best for whom my soul longeth? And without us? I didn't think it of you, Mr. Houghton. I was about to say I didn't think anything of you, but I won't. You can thank your true goodness for that. O, say nothing of that last check. Seriously, however, I don't blame you. If there's anything unpleasant in this world, it is a woman in a wide house—I mean in a banquet hall. I will not stop to argue the wine question;[1] I have no liquid by me to create the necessary inspiration. I suppose it would do no good either—you men are determined to have your own way always, and ours as often as possible. I write to say that I won't come, and to insist that Mr. Whittier and the rest shall not break their hearts over it. Sufficient is it on these occasions to break bread, and, perhaps, also heads. I have just seen a circular in behalf of a new ladies' magazine. Have you seen it? Excuse me now. I have an engagement to spank the Administration at this very moment. Do you know, by the way, that Mrs. Spofford is about to give a grand dinner to the lady contributors of the *Atlantic*?"

"Alas! for my stupidity!" remarked Mr. Houghton, his face growing pale, and his knees knocking together. "This great moral earthquake will be after me next."

"Oh, Mr. Houghton," wrote H. H.,[2] enthusiastically, "I am so pleased to hear of the honor to grand old Mr. Whittier. My pleasure is only exceeded by my joy that I am not to be there. I should be highly honored by being permitted to be in such company, of course, but I am timid, and I fear that literary men do 'cut up' dreadfully—you will pardon the expression—on these occasions. Do you know, Mr. Houghton, that Gail Hamilton talks of starting a magazine? and they do say that there is to be a grand literary reunion at her house, or rather at the house of Mr. Blaine.[3] I shall not be able to send you anything for some time to come."

"Merciful Heavens!" exclaimed Mr. Houghton, "this must be a conspiracy. They are all of them pleased, and yet they all seem to be contemplating the worst kind of retaliation. I do not understand this!"

He turned with a sigh to a letter from Philadelphia. "You will accept my regrets," said Rebecca Harding Davis. "I cannot possibly be present. I have not received my invitation[,] but of course it has been delayed in the mail. However, none of that brilliant gathering will feel my absence. I am not so presuming as to suppose that such a slight vacancy in so immense a place will be noticeable. And I do know, Mr. Houghton, that gentlemen delight to be by themselves at times. I hear Helen Hunt and Louisa M. Alcott have put their heads together in behalf of a ladies' magazine

1. Prov. 21:9: "It is better to dwell in a corner of the housetop, than with a brawling woman in a wide house." "Wine question": Men of the literary elite held dinners at which wine was served, an excuse often given for not inviting women.

2. Helen Hunt Jackson (1830–1885), American writer known as "H. H." She also published fiction under the name "Saxe Holm."

3. James G. Blaine (1830–1893), U.S. senator from Maine. Gail Hamilton lived with him and his wife, her cousin, in Washington, D.C.

and I understand that Rose Terry is to give a dinner to several well-known writers of the gentler sex. Such a magazine might be profitable, and I know the dinner would be delightful."

"Now this is dreadful" said Mr. Houghton, striking the desk with his clenched hand. "I have actually been applying the paper-cutter to my own nose. It is the stupidest thing I ever did in my life. Why, oh! why could I not have seen this result before?" He thought very fast a moment, and then his face brightened and he laughed right out. "I have it!" he exclaimed. "Two months hence there shall be a dinner to the lady contributors of the *Atlantic Monthly.* It shall be given in honor of Gail Hamilton's seventieth birthday."

Source: J. C. Derby, *Fifty Years Among Authors, Books, and Publishers* (1884)

❧ Constance Fenimore Woolson (1840–1894)

Constance Fenimore Woolson was born in Claremont, New Hampshire, but grew up in Cleveland, Ohio. After her father's death in 1869, she began to publish, capitalizing on her middle name, given to her in honor of her great-uncle, James Fenimore Cooper. During the Reconstruction era, she and her mother traveled throughout the South, as Woolson honed her skills as an astute observer of inter-regional encounters. After her mother died in 1879, Woolson moved to Europe. Her short stories and novels of the 1880s and 1890s were compared to the work of Henry James and George Eliot. Nonetheless, throughout her career, Woolson was an outsider to the inner circles of the transatlantic literary world. Her death, likely a suicide, in Venice in 1894 was a shock to her friends and many readers. "'Miss Grief'" is a scathing critique of the male dominance of the literary world and anticipates some of the difficulties Woolson would have gaining the respect of James, whom she met shortly after writing this story and who became a close friend. With similarities to Emily Dickinson, the heroine of Elizabeth Stoddard's "Collected by a Valetudinarian," and Rebecca Harding Davis's "Marcia," Woolson's protagonist refuses to have her work altered to fit it for publication and thus has to make her peace with obscurity.

"Miss Grief"

"A conceited fool" is a not uncommon expression. Now, I know that I am not a fool, but I also know that I am conceited. But, candidly, can it be helped if one happens to be young, well and strong, passably good-looking, with some money that one has inherited and more that one has earned—in all, enough to make life comfortable—and if upon this foundation rests also the pleasant superstructure of a literary success? The success is deserved, I think: certainly it was not lightly gained. Yet even with this I fully appreciate its rarity. Thus, I find myself very well entertained in life: I have all I wish in the way of society, and a deep, though of course carefully concealed, satisfaction in my own little fame; which fame I foster by a gentle system of non-interference. I know that I am spoken of as "that quiet young fellow who writes those delightful little studies of society, you know;" and I live up to that definition.[1]

A year ago I was in Rome, and enjoying life particularly. I had a large number of my acquaintances there, both American and English, and no day passed without its invitation. Of course I understood it: it is seldom that you find a literary man who is good-tempered, well-dressed, sufficiently provided with money, and amiably

1. This description suggests a similarity to the writer Henry James (1843–1916), whom Woolson had attempted to meet within a week of her arrival in Europe in late 1879. They finally met in late April 1880, about the time "'Miss Grief'" was appearing in the May issue of *Lippincott's*.

obedient to all the rules and requirements of "society." "When found, make a note of it;"[2] and the note was generally an invitation.

One evening, upon returning to my lodgings, my man Simpson informed me that a person had called in the afternoon, and upon learning that I was absent had left not a card, but her name—"Miss Grief." The title lingered—Miss Grief! "Grief has not so far visited me here," I said to myself, dismissing Simpson and seeking my little balcony for a final smoke, "and she shall not now. I shall take care to be 'not at home' to her if she continues to call." And then I fell to thinking of Ethelind Abercrombie, in whose society I had spent that and many evenings: they were golden thoughts.

The next day there was an excursion; it was late when I reached my rooms, and again Simpson informed me that Miss Grief had called.

"Is she coming continuously?" I said, half to myself.

"Yes, sir: she mentioned that she should call again."

"How does she look?"

"Well, sir, a lady, but not so prosperous as she was, I should say," answered Simpson, discreetly.

"Young?"

"No, sir."

"Alone?"

"A maid with her, sir."

But once outside in my little high-up balcony with my cigar, I again forgot Miss Grief and whatever she might represent. Who would not forget in that moonlight, with Ethelind Abercrombie's face to remember?

The stranger came a third time, and I was absent; then she let two days pass, and began again. It grew to be a regular dialogue between Simpson and myself when I came in at night: "Grief today?"

"Yes, sir."

"What time?"

"Four, sir."

"Happy the man," I thought, "who can keep her confined to a particular hour!"

But I should not have treated my visitor so cavalierly if I had not felt sure that she was eccentric and unconventional—qualities extremely tiresome in a woman no longer young or attractive, and without money to gild them over. If she were not eccentric she would not have persisted in coming to my door day after day in this silent way, without stating her errand, leaving a note, or presenting her credentials in any shape. I made up my mind that she had something to sell—a bit of carving or some intaglio supposed to be antique. It was known that I had a fancy for oddities. I said to myself, "She has read or heard of my 'Old Gold' story, or else 'The

2. From Charles Dickens's *Dombey and Sons* (1846–1848).

Buried God,' and she thinks me an idealizing ignoramus upon whom she can impose. Her sepulchral name is at least not Italian: probably she is a sharp country-woman of mine, turning, by means of aesthetic lies an honest penny when she can."

She had called seven times during a period of two weeks without seeing me, when one day I happened to be at home in the afternoon, owing to a pouring rain and a fit of doubt concerning Miss Abercrombie. For I had constructed a careful theory of that young lady's characteristics in my own mind, and she had lived up to it delightfully until the previous evening, when with one word she had blown it to atoms and taken flight, leaving me standing, as it were, on a desolate shore, with nothing but a handful of mistaken inductions wherewith to console myself. I do not know a more exasperating frame of mind, at least for a constructor of theories. I could not write, and so I took up a French novel (I model myself a little on Balzac).[3] I had been turning over its pages but a few moments when Simpson knocked, and, entering softly, said, with just a shadow of a smile on his well-trained face, "Miss Grief." I briefly consigned Miss Grief to all the Furies,[4] and then, as he still lingered—perhaps not knowing where they resided—I asked where the visitor was.

"Outside, sir—in the hall. I told her I would see if you were at home."

"She must be unpleasantly wet if she had no carriage."

"No carriage, sir: they always come on foot. I think she *is* a little damp, sir."

"Well, let her in, but I don't want the maid. I may as well see her now, I suppose, and end the affair."

"Yes, sir."

I did not put down my book. My visitor should have a hearing, but not much more: she had sacrificed her womanly claims by her persistent attacks upon my door. Presently Simpson ushered her in. "Miss Grief," he said, and then went out, closing the curtain behind him.

A woman—yes, a lady—but shabby, unattractive, and more than middle-aged.

I rose, bowed slightly, and then dropped into my chair again, still keeping the book in my hand. "Miss Grief?" I said interrogatively as I indicated a seat with my eyebrows.

"Not Grief," she answered—"Crief: my name is Crief."

She sat down, and I saw that she held a small flat box.

"Not carving, then," I thought—"probably old lace, something that belonged to Tullia or Lucrezia Borgia."[5] But as she did not speak I found myself obliged to begin: "You have been here, I think, once or twice before?"

3. French writer Honoré de Balzac (1799–1850) was a founder of Realism. James's work was often compared to his.

4. In Greek and Roman mythology, the goddesses of revenge.

5. Tullia D'Aragona (c. 1510–1556) was an Italian courtesan, and author Lucrezia Borgia (1480–1519) was the daughter of the man who would become Pope Alexander VI and his mistress.

"Seven times: this is the eighth."

A silence.

"I am often out: indeed, I may say that I am never in," I remarked carelessly.

"Yes: you have many friends."

"Who will perhaps buy old lace," I mentally added. But this time I too remained silent: why should I trouble myself to draw her out? She had sought me: let her advance her idea, whatever it was, now that entrance was gained.

But Miss Grief (I preferred to call her so) did not look as though she could advance anything: her black gown, damp with rain, seemed to retreat fearfully to her thin self, while her thin self retreated as far as possible from me, from the chair, from everything. Her eyes were cast down: an old-fashioned lace veil with a heavy border shaded her face. She looked at the floor, and I looked at her.

I grew a little impatient, but I made up my mind that I would continue silent and see how long a time she would consider necessary to give due effect to her little pantomime. Comedy? Or was it tragedy? I suppose full five minutes passed thus in our double silence; and that is a long time when two persons are sitting opposite each other alone in a small still room.

At last my visitor, without raising her eyes, said slowly, "You are very happy, are you not, with youth, health, friends, riches, fame?"

It was a singular beginning. Her voice was clear, low and very sweet as she thus enumerated my advantages one by one in a list. I was attracted by it, but repelled by her words, which seemed to me flattery both dull and bold.

"Thanks," I said, "for your kindness, but I fear it is undeserved. I seldom discuss myself even when with my friends."

"I am your friend," replied Miss Grief. Then, after a moment, she added slowly, "I have read every word you have written."

I curled the edges of my book indifferently: I am not a fop, I hope, but—others have said the same.

"What is more, I know much of it by heart," continued my visitor. "Wait: I will show you;" and then, without pause, she began to repeat something of mine word for word, just as I had written it. On she went, and I—listened. I intended interrupting her after a moment, but I did not, because she was reciting so well, and also because I felt a desire gaining upon me to see what she would make of a certain conversation which I knew was coming—a conversation between two of my characters which was, to say the least, sphinx-like, and somewhat incandescent as well. What won me a little, too, was the fact that the scene she was reciting (it was hardly more than that, although called a story) was secretly my favorite among all the sketches from my pen with which a gracious public had been favored. I never said so, but it was; and I had always felt a wondering annoyance that the aforesaid public, while kindly praising beyond their worth other attempts of mine, had never noticed the higher purpose of this little shaft, aimed not at the balconies and lighted windows of society, but straight up toward the distant stars. So she went on, and presently reached the conversation: my two people began to talk. She had raised her eyes now, and was looking at me soberly as she gave the words of the woman, quiet, gentle, cold, and the replies of the man, bitter, hot, and scathing. Her very voice changed, and took, although always sweetly, the different tones required, while no point of meaning, however small, no breath of delicate emphasis which I had meant, but which the dull types could not give, escaped appreciative and full, almost overfull, recognition which startled me. For she had understood me—understood me almost better than I had understood myself. It seemed to me that while I had labored to interpret partially a psychological riddle, she, coming after, had comprehended its bearings better than I had, although confining herself strictly to my own words and emphasis. The scene ended (and it ended rather suddenly), she dropped her eyes, and moved her hand nervously to and fro over the box she held: her gloves were old and shabby, her hands small.

I was secretly much surprised by what I had heard, but my ill-humor was deep-seated that day, and I still felt sure, besides, that the box contained something that I was expected to buy.

"You recite remarkably well," I said carelessly, "and I am much flattered also by your appreciation of my efforts. But it is not, I presume, to that alone that I owe the pleasure of this visit?"

"Yes," she answered, still looking down, "it is, for if you had not written that scene I should not have sought you. Your other sketches are interiors—exquisitely painted and delicately finished, but of small scope. *This* is a sketch in a few bold, masterly lines—work of entirely different spirit and purpose."

I was nettled by her insight. "You have bestowed so much of your kind attention upon me that I feel your debtor," I said, conventionally. "It may be that there is something I can do for you—connected, possibly, with that little box?"

It was a little impertinent, but it was true, for she answered, "Yes."

I smiled, but her eyes were cast down and she did not see the smile.

"What I have to show you is a manuscript," she said after a pause which I did not break: "it is a drama. I thought that perhaps you would read it."

"An authoress! This is worse than old lace," I said to myself in dismay.—Then, aloud, "My opinion would be worth nothing, Miss Crief."

"Not in a business way, I know. But it might be—an assistance personally." Her voice had sunk to a whisper: outside, the rain was pouring steadily down. She was a very depressing object to me as she sat there with her box.

"I hardly think I have the time at present—" I began.

She had raised her eyes and was looking at me: then, when I paused, she rose and came suddenly toward my chair. "Yes, you will read it," she said with her hand on my arm—"you will read it. Look at this room; look at yourself; look at all you have. Then look at me, and have pity."

I had risen, for she held my arm, and her damp skirt was brushing my knees.

Her large dark eyes looked intently into mine as she went on: "I have no shame in asking. Why should I have? It is my last endeavor, but a calm and well-considered one. If you refuse I shall go away, knowing that Fate has willed it so. And I shall be content."

"She is mad," I thought. But she did not look so, and she had spoken quietly, even gently.—"Sit down," I said, moving away from her. I felt as if I had been magnetized, but it was only the nearness of her eyes to mine, and their intensity. I drew forward a chair, but she remained standing.

"I cannot," she said in the same sweet, gentle tone, "unless you promise."

"Very well, I promise; only sit down."

As I took her arm to lead her to the chair I perceived that she was trembling, but her face continued unmoved.

"You do not, of course, wish me to look at your manuscript now?" I said, temporizing: "it would be much better to leave it. Give me your address, and I will return it to you with my written opinion; though, I repeat, the latter will be of no use to you. It is the opinion of an editor or publisher that you want."

"It shall be as you please. And I will go in a moment," said Miss Grief, pressing her palms together, as if trying to control the tremor that had seized her slight frame.

She looked so pallid that I thought of offering her a glass of wine: then I remembered that if I did it might be a bait to bring her there again, and this I was desirous to prevent. She rose while the thought was passing through my mind. Her pasteboard box lay on the chair she had first occupied: she took it, wrote an address on the cover, laid it down, and then, bowing, with a little air of formality, drew her black shawl around her shoulders and turned toward the door.

I followed, after touching the bell. "You will hear from me by letter," I said.

Simpson opened the door, and I caught a glimpse of the maid, who was waiting in the anteroom. She was an old woman, shorter than her mistress, equally thin, and dressed like her in rusty black. As the door opened she turned toward it a pair of small, dim blue eyes with a look of furtive suspense. Simpson dropped the curtain, shutting me into the inner room: he had no intention of allowing me to accompany my visitor farther. But I had the curiosity to go to a bay-window in an angle from whence I could command the street-door, and presently I saw them issue forth in the rain and walk away side by side, the mistress, being the taller, holding the umbrella: probably there was not much difference in rank between persons so poor and forlorn as these.

It grew dark. I was invited out for the evening, and I knew that if I went I should meet Miss Abercrombie. I said to myself that I would not go. I got out my paper for writing, I made my preparations for a quiet evening at home with myself; but it was of no use. It all ended slavishly in my going. At the last allowable moment

I presented myself, and—as a punishment for my vacillation, I suppose—I never passed a more disagreeable evening. I drove homeward in a vixenish temper: it was foggy without, and very foggy within. What Ethelind really was, now that she had broken through my elaborately-built theories, I was not able to decide. There was, to tell the truth, a certain young Englishman— But that is apart from this story.

I reached home, went up to my rooms, and had a supper. It was to console myself: I am obliged to console myself scientifically once in a while. I was walking up and down afterward, smoking and feeling somewhat better, when my eye fell upon the pasteboard box. I took it up: on the cover was written an address which showed that my visitor must have walked a long distance in order to see me: "A. Crief."—"A Grief," I thought; "and so she is. I positively believe she has brought all this trouble upon me: she has the evil eye." I took out the manuscript and looked at it. It was in the form of a little volume, and clearly written: on the cover was the word "Armor" in German text, and underneath a pen-and-ink sketch of a helmet, breastplate and shield.

"Grief certainly needs armor," I said to myself, sitting down by the table and turning over the pages. "I may as well look over the thing now: I could not be in a worse mood." And then I began to read.

Early the next morning Simpson took a note from me to the given address, returning with the following reply: "No; I prefer to come to you; at four; A. CRIEF." These words, with their three semicolons, were written in pencil upon a piece of coarse printing-paper, but the handwriting was as clear and delicate as that of the manuscript in ink.

"What sort of a place was it, Simpson?"

"Very poor, sir, but I did not go all the way up. The elder person came down, sir, took the note, and requested me to wait where I was."

"You had no chance, then, to make inquiries?" I said, knowing full well that he had emptied the entire neighborhood of any information it might possess concerning these two lodgers.

"Well, sir, you know how these foreigners will talk, whether one wants to hear or not. But it seems that these two persons have been there but a few weeks: they live alone, and are uncommonly silent and reserved. The people round there call them something that signifies 'the Madames American, thin and dumb.'"

At four the "Madames American" arrived: it was raining again, and they came on foot under their old umbrella. The maid waited in the anteroom, and Miss Grief was ushered into my bachelor's parlor, which was library and dining-room in one. I had thought that I should meet her with great deference, but she looked so forlorn that my deference changed to pity. It was the woman that impressed me then, more than the writer—the fragile, nerveless body more than the inspired mind. For it was inspired: I had sat up half the night over her drama, and had felt thrilled through and through more than once by its earnestness, passion and power.

No one could have been more surprised than I was to find myself thus enthusiastic. I thought I had outgrown that sort of thing. And one would have supposed, too (I myself should have supposed so the day before), that the faults of the drama, which were many and prominent, would have chilled any liking I might have felt, I being a writer myself, and therefore critical; for writers are as apt to make much of the "how," rather than the "what," as painters, who, it is well known, prefer an exquisitely rendered representation of a commonplace theme to an imperfectly executed picture of even the most striking subject.

But in this case, on the contrary, the scattered rays of splendor in Miss Grief's drama had made me forget the dark spots, which were numerous and disfiguring; or, rather, the splendor had made me anxious to have the spots removed. And this also was a philanthropic state very unusual with me. Regarding unsuccessful writers, my motto had been "Væ victis!"[6]

My visitor took a seat and folded her hands: I could see, in spite of her quiet manner, that she was in breathless suspense. It seemed so pitiful that she should be trembling there before me—a woman so much older than I was, a woman who possessed the divine spark of genius, which I was by no means sure, in spite of my success, had been granted to me—that I felt as if I ought to go down on my knees before her and entreat her to take her proper place of supremacy at once. But there! one does not go down on one's knees combustively, as it were, before a woman over fifty, plain in feature, thin, dejected, and ill-dressed. I contented myself with taking her hands (in their miserable old gloves) in mine, while I said cordially, "Miss Crief, your drama seems to me full of original power. It has roused my enthusiasm: I sat up half the night reading it."

The hands I held shook, but something (perhaps a shame for having evaded the knees business) made me tighten my hold and bestow upon her also a reassuring smile. She looked at me for a moment, and then, suddenly and noiselessly, tears rose and rolled down her cheeks. I dropped her hands and retreated. I had not thought her tearful: on the contrary, her voice and face had seemed rigidly controlled. But now here she was bending herself over the side of the chair with her head resting on her arms, not sobbing aloud, but her whole frame shaken by the strength of her emotion. I rushed for a glass of wine: I pressed her to take it. I did not quite know what to do, but, putting myself in her place, I decided to praise the drama; and praise it I did. I do not know when I have used so many adjectives. She raised her head and began to wipe her eyes.

"Do take the wine," I said, interrupting myself in my cataract of language.

"I dare not," she answered: then added humbly, "that is, unless you have a biscuit here or a bit of bread."

I found some biscuit: she ate two, and then slowly drank the wine while I re-

6. Latin: Woe to the conquered!

sumed my verbal Niagara. Under its influence—and that of the wine too, perhaps—she began to show new life. It was not that she looked radiant—she could not—but simply that she looked warm. I now perceived what had been the principal discomfort of her appearance heretofore: it was that she had looked all the time as if suffering from cold.

At last I could think of nothing more to say, and stopped. I really admired the drama, but I thought I had exerted myself sufficiently as an anti-hysteric, and that adjectives enough, for the present at least, had been administered. She had put down her empty wine-glass, and was resting her hands on the broad cushioned arms of her chair with a sort of expanded content.

"You must pardon my tears," she said, smiling: "it was the revulsion of feeling. My life was at a low ebb: if your sentence had been against me it would have been my end."

"Your end?"

"Yes, the end of my life: I should have destroyed myself."

"Then you would have been a weak as well as wicked woman," I said in a tone of disgust: I do hate sensationalism.

"Oh no, you know nothing about it. I should have destroyed only this poor worn tenement of clay. But I can well understand how *you* would look upon it. Regarding the desirableness of life the prince and the beggar may have different opinions.—We will say no more of it, but talk of the drama instead." As she spoke the word "drama" a triumphant brightness came into her eyes.

I took the manuscript from a drawer and sat down beside her. "I suppose you know that there are faults," I said, expecting ready acquiescence.

"I was not aware that there were any," was her gentle reply.

Here was a beginning! After all my interest in her—and, I may say under the circumstances, my kindness—she received me in this way! However, my belief in her genius was too sincere to be altered by her whimsies; so I persevered. "Let us go over it together," I said. "Shall I read it to you, or will you read it to me?"

"I will not read it, but recite it."

"That will never do: you will recite it so well that we shall see only the good points, and what we have to concern ourselves with now is the bad ones."

"I will recite it," she repeated.

"Now, Miss Crief," I said bluntly, "for what purpose did you come to me? Certainly not merely to recite: I am no stage-manager. In plain English, was it not your idea that I might help you in obtaining a publisher?"

"Yes, yes," she answered, looking at me apprehensively, all her old manner returning.

I followed up my advantage, opened the little paper volume and began. I first took the drama line by line, and spoke of the faults of expression and structure: then I turned back and touched upon two or three glaring impossibilities in the plot. "Your absorbed interest in the motive of the whole no doubt made you forget these blemishes," I said apologetically.

But, to my surprise, I found that she did not see the blemishes—that she appreciated nothing I had said, comprehended nothing. Such unaccountable obtuseness puzzled me. I began again, going over the whole with even greater minuteness and care. I worked hard: the perspiration stood in beads upon my forehead as I struggled with her—what shall I call it—obstinacy? But it was not exactly obstinacy. She simply could not see the faults of her own work, any more than a blind man can see the smoke that dims a patch of blue sky. When I had finished my task the second time she still remained as gently impassive as before. I leaned back in my chair exhausted, and looked at her.

Even then she did not seem to comprehend (whether she agreed with it or not) what I must be thinking. "It is such a heaven to me that you like it!" she murmured dreamily, breaking the silence. Then, with more animation, "And *now* you will let me recite it?"

I was too weary to oppose her: she threw aside her shawl and bonnet, and, standing in the centre of the room, began.

And she carried me along with her: all the strong passages were doubly strong when spoken, and the faults, which seemed nothing to her, were made by her earnestness to seem nothing to me, at least for that moment. When it was ended she stood looking at me with a triumphant smile.

"Yes," I said, "I like it, and you see that I do. But I like it because my taste is peculiar. To me originality and force are everything—perhaps because I have them not to any marked degree myself—but the world at large will not overlook as I do your absolutely barbarous shortcomings on account of them. Will you trust me to go over the drama and correct it at my pleasure?" This was a vast deal for me to offer: I was surprised at myself.

"No," she answered softly, still smiling. "There shall not be so much as a comma altered." Then she sat down and fell into a reverie as though she were alone.

"Have you written anything else?" I said after a while, when I had become tired of the silence.

"Yes."

"Can I see it? Or is it *them*?"

"It is *them*. Yes, you can see all."

"I will call upon you for the purpose."

"No, you must not," she said, coming back to the present nervously: "I prefer to come to you."

At this moment Simpson entered to light the room, and busied himself rather longer than was necessary over the task. When he finally went out I saw that my visitor's manner had sunk into its former depression: the presence of the servant seemed to have chilled her.

"When did you say I might come?" I repeated, ignoring her refusal.

"I did not say it. It would be impossible."

"Well, then, when will you come here?" There was, I fear, a trace of fatigue in my tone.

"At your good pleasure, sir," she answered humbly.

My chivalry was touched by this: after all, she was a woman. "Come to-morrow," I said. "By the way, come and dine with me then: why not?" I was curious to see what she would reply.

"Why not, indeed? Yes, I will come. I am forty-three: I might have been your mother."

This was not quite true, as I am over thirty; but I look young, while she—Well, I had thought her over fifty. "I can hardly call you 'mother' but we might compromise upon 'aunt,'" I said, laughing. "Aunt what?"

"My name is Aaronna," she gravely answered. "My father was much disappointed that I was not a boy, and gave me as nearly as possible the name he had prepared—Aaron."

"Then come and dine with me to-morrow, and bring with you the other manuscripts, Aaronna," I said, amused at the quaint sound of the name. On the whole, I did not like "aunt."

"I will come," she answered. It was twilight and still raining, but she refused all offers of escort or carriage, departing with her maid, as she had come, under the brown umbrella.

The next day we had the dinner. Simpson was astonished—and more than astonished,—grieved when I told him that he was to dine with the maid; but he could not complain in words, since my own guest, the mistress, was hardly more attractive. When our preparations were complete I could not help laughing: the two prim little tables, one in the parlor and one in the anteroom, and Simpson disapprovingly going back and forth between them, were irresistible.

I greeted my guest hilariously when she arrived, and, fortunately, her manner was not quite so depressed as usual: I could never have accorded myself with a tearful mood. I had thought that perhaps she would make, for the occasion, some change in her attire: I have never known a woman who had not some scrap of finery, however small, in reserve for that unexpected occasion of which she is ever dreaming. But no: Miss Grief wore the same black gown, unadorned and unaltered. I was glad that there was no rain that day, so that the skirt did not at least look so damp and rheumatic.

She ate quietly, almost furtively, yet with a good appetite, and she did not refuse the wine. Then, when the meal was over and Simpson had removed the dishes, I asked for the new manuscripts. She gave me an old green copybook filled with short poems, and a prose sketch by itself: I lit a cigar and sat down at my desk to look them over.

"Perhaps you will try a cigarette?" I suggested, more for amusement than anything else, for there was not a shade of Bohemianism about her: her whole appearance was puritanical.

"I have not yet succeeded in learning to smoke."

"You have tried?" I said, turning round.

"Yes: Serena and I tried, but we did not succeed."

"Serena is your maid?"

"She lives with me."

I was seized with inward laughter, and began hastily to look over her manuscripts with my back toward her, so that she might not see it. A vision had risen before me of those two forlorn women, alone in their room with locked doors, patiently trying to acquire the smoker's art.

But my attention was soon absorbed by the papers before me. Such a fantastic collection of words, lines and epithets I had never before seen, or even in dreams imagined. In truth, they were like the work of dreams: they were *Kubla Khan*[7] only more so. Here and there was radiance like the flash of a diamond, but each poem, almost each verse and line, was marred by some fault or lack which seemed wilful [*sic*] perversity, like the work of an evil sprite. It was like a case of jeweller's wares set before you, with each ring unfinished, each bracelet too large or too small for its purpose, each breastpin without its fastening, each necklace purposely broken. I turned the pages, marvelling. When about half an hour had passed, and I was leaning back for a moment to light another cigar, I glanced toward my visitor. She was behind me, in an easy-chair before my small fire, and she was—fast asleep! In the relaxation of her unconsciousness I was struck anew by the poverty her appearance expressed: her feet were visible, and I saw the miserable worn old shoes which hitherto she had kept concealed.

After looking at her for a moment I returned to my task and took up the prose story: in prose she must be more reasonable. She was less fantastic perhaps, but hardly more reasonable. The story was that of a profligate and commonplace man forced by two of his friends, in order not to break the heart of a dying girl who loves him, to live up to a high imaginary ideal of himself which her pure but mistaken mind has formed. He has a handsome face and sweet voice, and repeats what they tell him. Her long, slow decline and happy death, and his own inward ennui and profound weariness of the rôle he has to play, made the vivid points of the story. So far, well enough, but here was the trouble: through the whole narrative moved another character, a physician of tender heart and exquisite mercy, who practised murder as a fine art, and was regarded (by the author) as a second Messiah! This was monstrous. I read it through twice, and threw it down: then, fatigued, I turned

7. Dream-like poem published in 1816 by Samuel Taylor Coleridge, who claimed to have written it under the influence of opium.

round and leaned back, waiting for her to wake. I could see her profile against the dark hue of the easy-chair.

Presently she seemed to feel my gaze, for she stirred, then opened her eyes. "I have been asleep," she said, rising hurriedly.

"No harm in that, Aaronna."

But she was deeply embarrassed and troubled, much more so than the occasion required; so much so, indeed, that I turned the conversation back upon the manuscripts as a diversion. "I cannot stand that doctor of yours," I said, indicating the prose story: "no one would. You must cut him out."

Her self-possession returned as if by magic. "Certainly not," she answered haughtily.

"Oh, if you do not care— I had labored under the impression that you were anxious these things should find a purchaser."

"I am, I am," she said, her manner changing to deep humility with wonderful rapidity. With such alternations of feeling as this sweeping over her like great waves, no wonder she was old before her time.

"Then you must take out that doctor."

"I am willing, but do not know how," she answered, pressing her hands together helplessly. "In my mind he belongs to the story so closely that he cannot be separated from it."

Here Simpson entered, bringing a note for me: it was a line from Mrs. Abercrombie inviting me for that evening—an unexpected gathering, and therefore likely to be all the more agreeable. My heart bounded in spite of me: I forgot Miss Grief and her manuscripts for the moment as completely as though they had never existed. But, bodily, being still in the same room with her, her speech brought me back to the present.

"You have had good news?" she said.

"Oh no, nothing especial—merely an invitation."

"But good news also," she repeated. "And now, as for me, I must go."

Not supposing that she would stay much later in any case, I had that morning ordered a carriage to come for her at about that hour. I told her this. She made no reply beyond putting on her bonnet and shawl.

"You will hear from me soon," I said: "I shall do all I can for you."

She had reached the door, but before opening it she stopped, turned and extended her hand. "You are good," she said: "I give you thanks. Do not think me ungrateful or envious. It is only that you are young, and I am so—so old." Then she opened the door and passed through the anteroom without pause, her maid accompanying her and Simpson with gladness lighting the way. They were gone. I dressed hastily and went out—to continue my studies in psychology.

Time passed: I was busy, amused and perhaps a little excited (sometimes psychology is delightful). But, although much occupied with my own affairs, I did not altogether neglect my self-imposed task regarding Miss Grief. I began by sending her prose story to a friend, the editor of a monthly magazine, with a letter making a strong plea for its admittance. It should have a chance first on its own merits. Then I forwarded the drama to a publisher, also an acquaintance, a man with a taste for phantasms and a soul above mere common popularity, as his own coffers knew to their cost. This done, I waited with conscience clear.

Four weeks passed. During this waiting period I heard nothing from Miss Grief. At last one morning came a letter from my editor. "The story has force, but I cannot stand that doctor," he wrote. "Let her cut him out, and I might print it." Just what I myself had said. The package lay there on my table, travel-worn and grimed: a returned manuscript is, I think, the most melancholy object on earth. I decided to wait, before writing to Aaronna, until the second letter was received. A week later it came. "Armor" was declined. The publisher had been "impressed" by the power displayed in certain passages, but the "impossibilities of the plot" rendered it "unavailable for publication"—in fact, would "bury it in ridicule" if brought before the public, a public "lamentably" fond of amusement, "seeking it, undaunted, even in the cannon's mouth." I doubt if he knew himself what he meant. But one thing, at any rate, was clear: "Armor" was declined.

Now, I am, as I have remarked before, a little obstinate. I was determined that Miss Grief's work should be received. I would alter and improve it myself, without letting her know: the end justified the means. Surely the sieve of my own good taste, whose mesh had been pronounced so fine and delicate, would serve for two. I began, and utterly failed.

I set to work first upon "Armor." I amended, altered, left out, put in, pieced, condensed, lengthened: I did my best, and all to no avail. I could not succeed in completing anything that satisfied me, or that approached, in truth, Miss Grief's own work just as it stood. I suppose I went over that manuscript twenty times: I covered sheets of paper with my copies. But the obstinate drama refused to be corrected: as it was it must stand or fall.

Wearied and annoyed, I threw it aside and took up the prose story: that would be easier. But, to my surprise, I found that that apparently gentle "doctor" would not out: he was so closely interwoven with every part of the tale that to take him out was like taking out one especial figure in a carpet: that is impossible unless you unravel the whole. At last I did unravel the whole, and then the story was no longer good, or Aaronna's: it was weak, and mine. All this took time, for of course I had much to do in connection with my own life and tasks. But, although slowly and at my leisure, I really did try my best as regarded Miss Grief, and without success. I was forced at last to make up my mind that either my own powers were not equal to the task, or else that her perversities were as essential a part of her work as her inspirations, and not to be separated from it. Once during this period I showed two of the short poems to Ethelind, withholding of course the writer's name. "They were written by a woman," I explained.

"Her mind must have been disordered, poor thing!" Ethelind said in her gentle way when she returned them—"at least, judging by these. They are hopelessly mixed and vague."

Now, they were not vague so much as vast. But I knew that I could not make Ethelind comprehend it, and (so complex a creature is man) I do not know that I wanted her to comprehend it. These were the only ones in the whole collection that I would have shown her, and I was rather glad that she did not like even these. Not that poor Aaronna's poems were evil: they were simply unrestrained, large, vast, like the skies or the wind. Ethelind was bounded on all sides, like a violet in a garden-bed. And I liked her so.

One afternoon, about the time when I was beginning to see that I could not "improve" Miss Grief, I came upon the maid. I was driving, and she had stopped on the crossing to let the carriage pass. I recognized her at a glance (by her general forlornness), and called to the driver to stop. "How is Miss Crief?" I said. "I have been intending to write to her for some time."

"And your note, when it comes," answered the old woman on the crosswalk fiercely, "she shall not see."

"What?"

"I say she shall not see it. Your patronizing face shows that you have no good news, and you shall not rack and stab her any more on *this* earth, please God, while I have authority."

"Who has racked or stabbed her, Serena?"

"Serena, indeed! Rubbish! I'm no Serena: I'm her aunt. And as to who has racked and stabbed her, I say you, *you*—YOU literary men!" She had put her old head inside my carriage, and flung out these words at me in a shrill, menacing tone. "But she shall die in peace in spite of you," she continued. "Vampires! you take her ideas and fatten on them, and leave her to starve. You know you do—*you* who have had her poor manuscripts these months and months!"

"Is she ill?" I asked in real concern, gathering that much at least from the incoherent tirade.

"She is dying," answered the desolate old creature, her voice softening and her dim eyes filling with tears.

"Oh, I trust not. Perhaps something can be done. Can I help you in any way?"

"In all ways if you would," she said, breaking down and beginning to sob weakly, with her head resting on the sill of the carriage-window. "Oh, what have we not been through together, we two! Piece by piece I have sold all."

I am good-hearted enough, but I do not like to have old women weeping across my carriage-door. I suggested, therefore, that she should come inside and let me take her home. Her shabby old skirt was soon beside me, and, following her directions, the driver turned toward one of the most wretched quarters of the city, the abode of poverty, crowded and unclean. Here, in a large bare chamber up many flights of stairs, I found Miss Grief.

As I entered I was startled: I thought she was dead. There seemed no life present until she opened her eyes, and even then they rested upon us vaguely, as though she did not know who we were. But as I approached a sudden light came into them: she recognized me, and this sudden animation, this return of the soul to the windows of the almost deserted body, was the most wonderful thing I ever saw. "You have good news of the drama?" she whispered as I bent over her: "tell me. I *know* you have good news."

What was I to answer? Pray, what would you have answered, puritan?

"Yes, I have good news, Aaronna," I said. "The drama will appear." (And who knows? Perhaps it will in some other world.)

She smiled, and her now brilliant eyes did not leave my face.

"He knows I'm your aunt: I told him," said the old woman, coming to the bedside.

"Did you?" whispered Miss Grief, still gazing at me with a smile. "Then please, dear Aunt Martha, give me something to eat."

Aunt Martha hurried across the room, and I followed her. "It's the first time she's asked for food in weeks," she said in a husky tone.

She opened a cupboard-door vaguely, but I could see nothing within. "What have you for her?" I asked with some impatience, though in a low voice.

"Please God, nothing!" answered the poor old woman, hiding her reply and her tears behind the broad cupboard-door. "I was going out to get a little something when I met you."

"Good Heavens! is it money you need? Here, take this and send; or go yourself in the carriage waiting below."

She hurried out breathless, and I went back to the bedside, much disturbed by what I had seen and heard. But Miss Grief's eyes were full of life, and as I sat down beside her she whispered earnestly, "Tell me."

And I did tell her—a romance invented for the occasion. I venture to say that none of my published sketches could compare with it. As for the lie involved, it will stand among my few good deeds, I know, at the judgment-bar.

And she was satisfied. "I have never known what it was," she whispered, "to be fully happy until now." She closed her eyes, and when the lids fell I again thought that she had passed away. But no, there was still pulsation in her small, thin wrist. As she perceived my touch she smiled. "Yes, I am happy," she said again, although without audible sound.

The old aunt returned: food was prepared, and she took some. I myself went out after wine that should be rich and pure. She rallied a little, but I did not leave her: her eyes dwelt upon me and compelled me to stay, or rather my conscience compelled me. It was a damp night, and I had a little fire made. The wine, fruit, flowers, and candles I had ordered made the bare place for the time being bright and fragrant. Aunt Martha dozed in her chair from sheer fatigue—she had watched many nights—but Miss Grief was awake, and I sat beside her.

"I make you my executor," she murmured, "as to the drama. But my other manuscripts place, when I am gone, under my head, and let them be buried with me. They are not many—those you have and these. See!"

I followed her gesture, and saw under her pillows the edges of two more copy-books like the one I had. "Do not look at them—my poor dead children!" she said tenderly. "Let them depart with me—unread as I have been."

Later she whispered, "Did you wonder why I came to you? It was the contrast. You were young—strong—rich—praised—loved—successful: all that I was not. I wanted to look at you—and imagine how it would feel. You had success—but I had the greater power. Tell me: did I not have it?"

"Yes, Aaronna."

"It is all in the past now. But I am satisfied."

After another pause she said with a faint smile, "Do you remember when I fell asleep in your parlor? It was the good and rich food. It was so long since I had had food like that!"

I took her hand and held it, conscience-stricken, but now she hardly seemed to perceive my touch. "And the smoking?" she whispered. "Do you remember how you laughed? I saw it. But I had heard that smoking soothed—that one was no longer tired and hungry—with a cigar."

In little whispers of this sort, separated by long rests and pauses, the night passed. Once she asked if her aunt was asleep, and when I answered in the affirmative she said, "Help her to return home—to America: the drama will pay for it. I ought never to have brought her away."

I promised, and she resumed her bright-eyed silence.

I think she did not speak again. Toward morning the change came, and soon after sunrise, with her old aunt kneeling by her side, she passed away.

All was arranged as she had wished. Her manuscripts, covered with violets, formed her pillow. No one followed her to the grave save her aunt and myself: I thought she would prefer it so. Her name was not "Crief," after all, but "Moncrief:" I saw it written out by Aunt Martha for the coffin-plate, as follows: "Aaronna Mon-crief, aged forty-three years, two months, and eight days."

I never knew more of her history than is written here. If there was more that I might have learned, it remained unlearned, for I did not ask.

And the drama? I keep it here in this locked case. I could have had it published at my own expense, but I think that now she knows its faults herself and would not like it.

I keep it, and, once in a while, I read it over—not as a *memento mori*[8] exactly, but rather as a memento of my own good fortune, for which I should continually give thanks. The want of one grain made all her work void, and that one grain was given to me. She, with the greater power, failed—I, with the less, succeeded. But no praise is due to me for that. When I die "Armor" is to be destroyed unread: not even Ethelind is to see it. For women will misunderstand each other; and, dear and precious to me as my sweet wife is, I could not bear that she or any one should cast so much as a thought of scorn upon the memory of the writer, upon my poor dead, "unavailable," unaccepted "Miss Grief."

Source: Lippincott's (1880)

8. Latin: Reminder of one's mortality.

❧ Mary Mann (1806–1887)

Mary Peabody Mann was the wife of educator and Congressman Horace Mann as well as the sister of the reformer Elizabeth Palmer Peabody and Sophia Peabody Hawthorne, wife of Nathaniel Hawthorne. Mary Mann met Sarah Winnemucca (1841–1891) during the latter's lecture tour in Boston in 1883. Mann and her sister Elizabeth encouraged Sarah to publish her lectures, and Mann helped to edit them. Life Among the Piutes *was the first book published in the United States by a Native American. As with slave narratives, many Native American texts were edited and/or prefaced by influential whites, whose authority lent authenticity for a reading public skeptical of the literacy and intelligence of nonwhites.*

Editor's Preface to *Life Among the Piutes*

My editing has consisted in copying the original manuscript in correct orthography and punctuation, with occasional emendations by the author, of a book which is an heroic act on the part of the writer. Mrs. Hopkins came to the East from the Pacific coast with the courageous purpose of telling in detail to the mass of our people, "extenuating nothing and setting down naught in malice," the story of her people's trials. Finding that in extemporaneous speech she could only speak at one time of a few points, she determined to write out the most important part of what she wished to say. In fighting with her literary deficiencies she loses some of the fervid eloquence which her extraordinary colloquial command of the English language enables her to utter, but I am confident that no one would desire that her own original words should be altered. It is the first outbreak of the American Indian in human literature, and has a single aim—*to tell the truth* as it lies in the heart and mind of a true patriot, and one whose knowledge of the two races gives her an opportunity of comparing them justly. At this moment, when the United States seem waking up to their duty to the original possessors of our immense territory, it is of the first importance to hear what only an Indian and an Indian woman can tell. To tell it was her own deep impulse, and the dying charge given her by her father, the truly parental chief of his beloved tribe.

Source: *Life Among the Piutes: Their Wrongs and Claims,* by Sarah Winnemucca (1883)

Susette La Flesche was an Omaha Indian from Nebraska and the first published Native American author. She was educated at a reservation mission school and a New Jersey finishing school. In 1879 she became a vocal advocate for the right of the Poncas (her mother's tribe) to stay in their homeland and thus began her public career as a lecturer, author, and artist. She toured the East coast with Standing Bear (the Ponca chief) and Omaha Herald correspondent Thomas H. Tibbles, whom she would marry in 1881. She also testified before the U.S. Senate in 1880. Her lectures inspired the writer Helen Hunt Jackson to join the cause for Native American rights. Bright Eyes traveled and lectured for many years with her husband, published many essays and short stories, and worked as a journalist, editor, and artist. In the following piece, she relates the centrality of story-telling for a "people with no literature" and questions, as Zitkala-Ša later would, the superiority of white literature and culture.

Introduction to "Omaha Legends and Tent-Stories"

To the readers of Wide Awake: These legends, a few of which I have translated, are nearly the same in every tribe—a little varied, it is true—but substantially the same, which shows, I think, that they are of common origin.

These which I have translated, are as told by the Omaha tribe. I have written them down just as they were told to me by my father, mother and grandmother, only of course I have translated them into English.

I wish I could have written the music of the songs. I think they are beautiful. I have heard some of your finest singers, but nothing I ever heard from them has touched me so profoundly as the singing of the Indians. The tears fill my eyes as I listen to their wild, weird singing, and I can never seem to tell myself why.

Among the Omahas, and I suppose in all the tribes, there are men and women, who, though they are not professional story tellers, yet as they can tell stories and legends so much better than any one else, are often invited by families to come visiting for the sole purpose of story-telling. The best story-teller that I know of in the tribe is "Onidabi." Last winter our family took a four days' journey, and with us travelled this man. Evening after evening we gathered round the fire to hear him tell stories, the tent so full that it could not hold another person, and we laughed till the tears came as he told story after story in rapid succession, with such inimitable gestures and changes of tone, that it would have been a study for any of your most accomplished elocutionists, and one by which they might have profited. Any one standing outside the tent and not knowing what was going on within, would have declared that he heard a conversation carried on by several people, when in reality it was only one person speaking, so perfectly did he imitate the tones of old men, women and children. He did not have to say of his characters, "the old man said this, the young warrior this," or "the little boy said this," but we knew at once by the tone of his voice, who was speaking. When we went to bed at night we would be as tired from laughing as though we had been hard at work all day.

My mother told me that one of the stories I have written out, was told her by an old man when she was a little child, and that it was her delight after coaxing her mother to get a nice supper, to go to the old man's tent and invite him to supper. When he came she would wait on him herself, and when he had finished eating, she would say: "Grandfather, please tell me a story!" The old man would pretend to be very reluctant at first, for the pleasure of having her coax him, and then he would comply with story after story from those strange legends, while she listened with rapt attention, until my grandmother bade her get ready for bed.

I never read any of your "Mother Goose Rhymes" until I was grown up, and I used to be inclined to feel sorry sometimes that I had missed them in my childhood; but if I had known them, I should probably have never known the nursery stories of my own people, and so I am satisfied.

My grandmother tells exactly the same old stories and sings the same queer little songs to my sister's children that she used to sing to us when we were babies, and only yesterday when I asked her to tell me a story, she laughed at me, and made up a funny little song which she sang to her great grandson, aged six months, telling him about his big auntie who wanted to be told a story as though she were a baby like him.

How often I have fallen asleep when a child, with my arms tight around my grandmother's neck, while she told me a story, only I did not fall asleep till the story was finished. When thinking of those old days—so happy and free, when we slept night after night in a tent on the wide trackless prairie, with nothing but the skies above us and the earth beneath; with nothing to make us afraid; not even knowing that we were not civilized, or were ordered to be by the government; not even knowing that there were such beings as white men; happy in our freedom and our love for each other—I often wonder if there is anything in your civilization which will make good to us what we have lost. I sometimes think not, unless it be the wider, fuller knowledge of God and his Word. But I am straying from my subject. Thinking of these legends brought back the old days so vividly. I wish I could gather up all the old legends and nursery songs so that they could live after we were dead, but some of them are so fragmentary and nonsensical that I hesitate.

In reading these legends, I hope my readers will try to imagine themselves in a tent, with the firelight flaming up now and then, throwing weird effects of light and shadow on the eager listening faces, and seeming to sympathize and keep pace with the story; and how we have had only these legends and stories in place of your science and literature. After all, that is only what your forefathers had before the days of books, and perhaps remembering that will make your thoughts more charitable toward a people having no literature.

These legends have never been published, with the exception of one which was published in *The Critic*. I have taken them down fresh from the lips of my father, mother and grandmother. I suppose legends something like them have been published from time to time by people from other tribes. These are Omaha legends.

Source: Wide Awake (1883)

❧ ALICE WILLIAMS BROTHERTON (1848–1930)

Alice Williams was born in Indiana and soon moved to Cincinnati, Ohio, where she spent the rest of her life. She married in 1876 and had three children. She contributed mostly poetry but also some prose to many of the high culture literary magazines from the 1870s through the 1890s. In a profile for the magazine The Writer *in 1894, Mary E. Cardwill wrote, "Much of her best work has been done with her babes about her, sitting in her lap or clinging to her gown." The first two poems included here wrestle with the desires of a mother for poetic recognition. "Exit Poetry" humorously laments the changes in poetic style and taste as the century came to a close.*

To E. M. T.

A brief way up Parnassus'[1] slope,
   Only, I may go:
Held by clasp of little fingers,
Cooing cry that with me lingers,
   To the vale below.

Another treads where I may not,
   Strikes the ringing lyre;[2]
Another reaches the charmed spot
   Of my heart's desire.

O fair soul, a little way
   I bear you company;
Then with "God speed!" back once more,
Heart in me with longing sore,
   Eyes tear-dim, I flee.

See, the embers on the hearth
   I must make to glow;
What time you climb the mountain slope,
   Singing as you go.

---

1. Mountain in Delphi, Greece; home of the Muses in Greek mythology. Widely used as a metaphor for poetic inspiration and literary honors.
2. In antiquity, the lyre was played to accompany recitations of poetry; thus it was often used as a metaphor for poetry.

You may chant before the shrine,
    I— croon lullabies.
You may tend the fire divine;
Ah, for me, that spark must shine
    In my baby's eyes!

Source: Atlantic Monthly (1887)

Woman and Artist

I thought to win me a name
    Should ring in the ear of the world!—
How can I work with small pink fists
    About my fingers curled?

Then adieu to name and to fame!
    They scarce are worth at the best
One touch of this wet little, warm little mouth
    With its lips against my breast.

Source: The Century (1887)

Exit Poetry

Alack, poor Phœbus,[3] shut up shop,
    And send the Muses packing!
Our old-time ways of turning lays[4]
    In rules were sadly lacking.
Instead of "light that never was
    On sea or land"[5] beholden,
They turn on verse electric light;
    And scout our methods olden.

The veriest freshman of the schools
    Now threatens to surpass us:

3. Literally, "radiant one," another name for Apollo, Greek god of poetry, music, and learning.
4. Simple narrative poetry.
5. Line from William Wordsworth's "Elegiac Stanzas, Suggested by a Picture of Peele Castle, In a Storm, Painted by Sir George Beaumont" (1807), referring to the artist's skill.

They 've got an Inclined Plane[6] to lift
   The rhymer up Parnassus.
They 've turned your Fount of Castaly[7]
   To steam to furnish "power,"
And handbooks of Poetics make
   A poet in an hour!

The simple song, from simpler heart,
   To law once bade defiance,
But verse no more can be an art—
   They 've changed it to a science.
Since half the bards are pedants grown,
   And half are college fellows,
The minstrel's occupation's gone
   As surely as Othello's![8]

Said Phœbus: "Bards began to sing
   Ere handbooks of Poetics
Set all the world to tinkering
   A sort of rhymed athletics.
What boots it that from dawn to dark
   You spend the hours rehearsing
This ground-and-lofty tumbling, or
   The Del Sarte[9] drill in versing?

"Until some spark of fire divine
   Has set the heart aglow, it
Is not the rules of all the schools
   Will ever make a poet!
No, no, we 'll rhyme and chime it still
   In that good old-time fashion
Which gave instead of rule and saw
   Just melody and passion.

6. Simple construction used to lift an object more easily. Brotherton is using the term to connote a type of shortcut up Mount Parnassus.

7. Fountain on Parnassus sacred to the Muses; source of poetic inspiration.

8. In Shakespeare's *Othello* (1604), when Othello learns of Desdemona's infidelity, he declares, "Othello's occupation's gone."

9. François Delsarte (1811–1871) established set rules for coordinating voice and physical gesture in dramatic expression. Brotherton here refers to the rigidity and mechanical nature of these rules applied to a creative act.

"First—*catch your thought,* then bend the ear
    And set the lyre repeating
The tunes which still through earth and sky,
    Through heart and brain, go beating:
The rhythms to which the billows sway
    And which the flowers nod in,
To which the planets circle aye
    And the first stars praised God in!"

Ah, no—too late! The day 's gone by:
    Our simple themes romantic
Might on Parnassus win a place,
    But scarce will suit *The Atl-nt-c*![10]
Who breaks the lock-step of the gang
    Is lashed for being venture-y,
Or at the best will hardly find
    His verses *fin du C-nt-ry.*[11]

Wait, if you will, for better days;
    Ambrosia and nectar[12]
Are cheap, but bread and butter dear;
    Starvation is no specter.
Leave nature's music to the wind,
    The ocean wave and birdie:
The lyre is out of date—I mean
    To buy a hurdy-gurdy![13]

Source: The Century (1893)

10. The *Atlantic Monthly* was among the foremost U.S. literary magazines.
11. The *Century,* another important literary magazine, in which this poem appeared. Also a play on the phrase *fin de siècle,* French for end of the century.
12. Food and drink of the gods in Greek mythology.
13. A stringed instrument that produces music by the turn of a crank.

Born and raised in New York state, Mary Hallock Foote was trained first as an artist and was a successful illustrator in the 1870s, illustrating books by Henry Wadsworth Longfellow and Nathaniel Hawthorne. After her marriage to a mining engineer, Arthur DeWint Foote, in 1876, the couple moved to a mining camp in California and had a son. Foote's first story about California was published in the Atlantic Monthly *in 1881. Many of her stories reflect her ambivalence about her hard life in the West. The heroine of her story "The Fate of a Voice" (1886) is a singer who loses her voice and regains it only after she decides to marry and give up her ambition for renown. In the following piece, Foote, like Ina Coolbrith, looks forward to a home-grown author who will truly represent the West in literature. After stints in Colorado, Idaho, and Mexico, the Footes returned in 1895 to California, where Mary concentrated on her writing. In their final years, they returned East.*

"Introductory" to "The Last Assembly Ball: A Pseudo-Romance of the Far West"

The East generalizes the West much as England has the habit of generalizing America; taking note of picturesque outward differences, easily perceived across a breadth of continent. Among other unsafe assumptions, the East has decided that nothing can be freer and simpler than the social life of the far West, exemplified by the flannel shirt and the flowing necktie, the absence of polish on boots and manners.

As a matter of experience, no society is so puzzling in its relations, so exacting in its demands upon self-restraint, as one which has no methods, which is yet in the stage of fermentation. Middle age has decided, or has learned to dispense with, many things which youth continues to fash itself about; and the older societies, with all their perpetuated grooves and deep-rooted complexities, are freer and more cheerful than the new.

In constructing a pioneer community one must add to the native, Western-born element the "tenderfoot" element, so called, self-conscious, new to surrounding standards, warped by disappointment or excited by success, torn, femininely speaking, between a past not yet abandoned and a present reluctantly accepted. Add, generally, the want of homogeneity in a population hastily recruited from divers [*sic*] States, cities, nationalities, with a surplus of youth, energy, incapacity, or misfortune to dispose of; add the melancholy of a land oppressed by too much nature,—not mother nature of the Christian poets, but nature of the dark old mythologies,—the spectacle of a creation indeed scarcely more than six days old. When Adam's celestial visitor (in the seventh book of "Paradise Lost")[1] condescends

---

1. Epic poem by John Milton first published in 1667.

to relate how the world was first created, he gives an astonishing picture of the sixth and last great act; when the earth brought forth the living creature after its kind regardless of zones and habitudes, crawling, wriggling, pawing from the sod, rent to favor the transmission. Life on the surface could not have been simple, for a few days at least, after that violent and promiscuous birth.

The life of the West historically, like the story of Man, is an epic, a song tale of grand meanings. Socially, it is a genesis, a formless record of beginnings, tragic, grotesque, sorrowful, unrelated, except as illustrations of a tendency towards confusion and failure, with contrasting lights of character and high personal achievement. The only successful characterizations of it in literature have treated it in this episodic manner.

But looking forward to the story in periods, the West has a future, socially, of enormous promise. It has all the elements of greatness, when it shall have passed the period of uncouth strivings and that later stage of material satisfaction which is the sequel to the age of force. The East denies it modesty, but there is a humility which apes pride as well as a pride which apes humility. It has never been denied generosity, charity, devotedness, humor of a peculiarly effective quality, a desire for self-improvement, unconquerable, often pathetic, courage, and enthusiasm. It has that admixture of contrasting national types which gives us the golden thread of genius. Finally, the New South is seeking its future there—not a future of conquest, but of patience and hard work.

The West is not to be measured by home-sick tales from an Eastern point of view. The true note will be struck when the alien touch no longer blunts the chord, groping for futile harmonies, through morbid minor strains; when we have our novelist of the Pacific slope, cosmopolite by blood, acclimated through more than one generation to the heavy air of the plains, bred in the traditions of an older civilization—or, better still, with a wild note as frank as that which comes to us from the sad northern steppe.

Source: Century Magazine (1889)

❧ HELEN GRAY CONE (1859–1934)

Helen Gray Cone was a prolific poet and a literary scholar. She attended the New York Normal College and then became a professor of English there. She was later a professor at Hunter College. She co-edited with Jeannette L. Gilder Pen Portraits of Literary Women *(1887) and in the following essay provided the most comprehensive assessment in the nineteenth century of American women's literary history. Her almost exclusive focus on white writers reflects her era's disregard for the contributions of nonwhite writers to American literature.*

Woman in American Literature

I am obnoxious to each carping tongue
That says my hand a needle better fits.

.   .   .   .

Men can do best, and women know it well;
Preëminence in each and all is yours,
Yet grant some small acknowledgment of ours.
> —*Anne Bradstreet, 1640.*[1]

Let us be wise, and not impede the soul. Let her work as she will. Let us have one creative energy, one incessant revelation. Let it take what form it will, and let us not bind it by the past to man or woman.—*Margaret Fuller, 1844.*[2]

It is difficult to disengage a single thread from the living web of a nation's literature. The interplay of influences is such that the product spun from the heart and brain of woman alone must, when thus disengaged, lose something of its significance. In criticism a classification based upon sex is necessarily misleading and inexact. As far as difference between the literary work of women and that of men is created by difference of environment and training it may be regarded as accidental; while the really essential difference, resulting from the general law that the work of woman shall somehow subtly express womanhood, not only varies widely in degree with the individual worker, but is, in certain lines of production, almost ungraspable by criticism. We cannot rear walls which shall separate literature into departments, upon a principle elusive as the air. "It is no more the order of nature that the espe-

---

1. From "The Prologue" in *The Tenth Muse Lately Sprung Up in America* (1650), the first volume of poetry published by a resident of North America. Authors mentioned in this essay will not be footnoted when they appear in this anthology.

2. From "The Great Lawsuit. Man versus Men. Woman Versus Women," published in the *Dial* in 1843.

cially feminine element should be incarnated pure in any form, than that the masculine energy should exist unmingled with it in any form."[3] The experiment which, Lowell tells us, Nature tried in shaping the genius of Hawthorne,[4] she repeats and reverses at will.

In practice the evil effects which have followed the separate consideration of woman's work in literature are sufficiently plain. The debasement of the coin of criticism is a fatal measure. The dearest foe of the woman artist in the past has been the suave and chivalrous critic, who, judging all "female writers" by a special standard, has easily bestowed the unearned wreath.

The present paper is grounded, it will be seen, upon no preference for the Shaker-meeting arrangement[5] which prevailed so long in our American temple of the Muses. It has seemed desirable, in a historical review of the work of women in this country, to follow the course of their effort in the field of literature; to note the occasional impediments of the stream, its sudden accessions of force, its general tendency, and its gradual widening.

The colonial period has, of course, little to give us. The professional literary woman was then unknown. The verses of Mrs. Anne Bradstreet, called in flattery "the tenth Muse,"[6] were "the fruit but of some few hours curtailed from her sleep and other refreshments." The negro girl Phillis Wheatley,[7] whose poetical efforts had been published under aristocratic patronage in England, when robbed of her mistress by death "resorted to marriage"— not to literature —"as the only alternative of destitution." Mrs. Mercy Warren was never obliged to seek support from that sharp-pointed pen which copied so cleverly the satiric style of Pope,[8] and which has left voluminous records of the Revolution. She too wrote her tragedies "for amusement, in the solitary hours when her friends were abroad."

Miss Hannah Adams, born in Massachusetts in 1755, may be accepted as the first American woman who made literature her profession. Her appearance as a pioneer in this country corresponds closely in time with that of Mary Wollstonecraft in England. She wrote, at seventy-seven, the story of her life. Her account sets forth clearly the difficulties which in her youth had to be dealt with by a woman

3. With slight alteration from Fuller's "The Great Lawsuit."

4. James Russell Lowell (1819–1891), American poet and critic. Nathaniel Hawthorne (1804–1864), author of *The Scarlet Letter* (1850) and widely considered America's greatest literary genius.

5. Men and women sat on separate sides of the church during Shaker services.

6. From the title of Bradstreet's collection of poetry. In Greek mythology there were nine Muses who inspired mortals to create the various arts. The following quote is from the collection's preface by James Woodbridge.

7. Phillis Wheatley (c. 1753–1784) was a slave who gained fame for her accomplished poetry. The following quote is from Rufus Griswold, *The Female Poets of America* (1849).

8. Alexander Pope (1688–1744), English poet and satirist. The following quote is from Rufus Griswold, *The Female Poets of America* (1849).

seriously undertaking authorship. Ill health, which forbade her attending school, was an individual disadvantage; but she remarks incidentally on the defectiveness of the country school, where girls learned only to write and cipher, and were in summer "instructed by females in reading, sewing, and other kinds of work. . . . I remember that my first idea of the happiness of heaven was of a place where we should find our thirst for knowledge fully gratified."[9] How pathetically the old woman recalls the longing of the eager girl! All her life she labored against odds; learning, however, the rudiments of Latin, Greek, geography, and logic, "with indescribable pleasure and avidity," from some gentlemen boarding at her father's house. Becoming interested in religious controversy, she formed the plan of compiling a "View of Religions"; not at first hoping to derive what she calls "emolument" from the work. To win bread she relied at this time upon spinning, sewing, or knitting, and, during the Revolutionary war, on the weaving of bobbin lace; afterwards falling back on her scant classical resources to teach young gentlemen Latin and Greek. Meanwhile the compilation went on. "Reading much religious controversy," observes Miss Adams, "must be extremely trying to a female, whose mind, instead of being strengthened by those studies which exercise the judgment and give stability to the character, is debilitated by reading romances and novels." This sense of disadvantage, of the meekly accepted burden of sex, pervades the autobiography; it seems the story of a patient cripple. When the long task was done her inexperience made her the dupe of a dishonest printer; and, although the book sold well, her only compensation was fifty copies, for which she was obliged herself to find purchasers, having previously procured four hundred subscribers. Fortunately she had the copyright; and before the publication of a second edition she chanced to make the acquaintance of a clerical good Samaritan, who transacted the business for her. The "emolument" derived from this second edition at last enabled her to pay her debts, and to put out a small sum upon interest. Her "History of New England," in the preparation of which her eyesight was nearly sacrificed, met with a good sale; but an abridgment of it brought her nothing, on account of the failure of the printer. She sold the copyright of her "Evidences of Christianity" for one hundred dollars in books.

This, then, is our starting-point—evident character and ability, at a disadvantage both in production and in the disposal of the product; imperfect educational equipment; and a hopeless consciousness of inferiority, amounting almost to an inability to stand upright mentally.

Susanna Rowson, who wrote the popular "Charlotte Temple," may be classed as an American novelist, though not born in this country. She appears also as a

---

9. Hannah Adams (1755–1831), historian. Mary Wollstonecraft (1759–1797), English writer and feminist. Quotes below from *A Memoir of Miss Hannah Adams* (1832).

writer of patriotic songs, an actress, a teacher, and the compiler of a dictionary and other school-books. "The Coquette; or, the History of Eliza Wharton," by Hannah Webster Foster,[10] was another prime favorite among the formal novels of the day.

Kind Miss Hannah Adams, in her old age, chanced to praise a certain metrical effort, unpromisingly labeled "Jephthah's Rash Vow," put forth by a girl of sixteen, Miss Caroline Howard.[11] Here occurs an indicative touch. "When I learned," says this commended Miss Caroline, "that my verses had been surreptitiously printed in a newspaper, I wept bitterly, and was as alarmed as if I had been detected in man's apparel." Such was the feeling with which the singing-robes were donned by a maiden in 1810—a state of affairs soon to be replaced by a general fashion of feminine singing-robes of rather cheap material. During the second quarter of the present century conditions somewhat improved, and production greatly increased. "There was a wide manifestation of that which bears to pure ideality an inferior relationship," writes Mr. Stedman of the general body of our literature at this period. In 1848 Dr. Griswold reports that "women among us are taking a leading part"; that "the proportion of female writers at this moment in America far exceeds that which the present or any other age in England exhibits."[12] Awful moment in America! one is led to exclaim by a survey of the poetic field. Alas, the verse of those "Tokens," and "Keepsakes," and "Forget-Me-Nots," and "Magnolias," and all the rest of the annuals,[13] all glorious without in their red or white Turkey morocco and gilding! Alas, the flocks of quasi swan-singers! They have sailed away down the river of Time, chanting with a monotonous mournfulness. We need not speak of them at length. One of them early wrote about the Genius of Oblivion;[14] most of them wrote for it. It was not their fault that their toil increased the sum of the "Literature suited to Desolate Islands."[15] The time was out of joint. Sentimentalism infected both continents. It was natural enough that the infection should seize most strongly upon those who were weakened by an intellectual best-parlor atmosphere, with small chance of free out-of-door currents. They had their reward. Their crude constituencies were proud of them; and not all wrought without "emolument," though it need hardly be said that verse-making was not and is not, as a rule, a remunerative

10. *Charlotte Temple* (1791) by Susanna Rowson (1762–1824) and *The Coquette* (1797) by Hannah Webster Foster (1758–1840) were the two most popular American novels of the eighteenth century.

11. Caroline Howard Gilman (1794–1888). Gilman recounted the anecdote, including the following quote, in John S. Hart's *Female Prose Writers of America* (1866).

12. Edmund Clarence Stedman, *Poets of America* (1885). Rufus Griswold did not include the quoted statement in the first edition of *The Female Poets of America* (1849). It first appeared in the second edition published in 1853.

13. Literary annuals or "gift books" were produced yearly for the Christmas season chiefly from the 1820s to the 1850s and were hospitable to women writers. They were beautifully bound, often in "Turkey morocco," a high-quality leather.

14. Sarah J. Hale, *The Genius of Oblivion* (1823).

15. James Russell Lowell, "A Fable for Critics" (1848), a satire of American authors.

occupation. Some names survive, held in the memory of the public by a few small, sweet songs on simple themes, probably undervalued by their authors, but floating now like flowers above the tide that has swallowed so many pretentious, sand-based structures.

Mrs. Lydia H. Sigourney, the most prolific poetess of the period, was hailed as "the American Mrs. Hemans."[16] A gentle and pious womanhood shone through her verse; but her books are undisturbed and dusty in the libraries now, and likely to remain so. Maria Gowen Brooks—"Maria del Occidente"—was, on the other hand, not popular at home; but put forth a far stronger claim than Mrs. Sigourney, and won indeed somewhat disproportionate praises abroad. "Southey says 'Zophiel; or, The Bride of Seven,' is by some Yankee woman," writes Charles Lamb; "as if there had ever been a woman capable of anything so great!"[17] One is glad that we need not now consider as the acme of woman's poetic achievement this metrical narrative of the loves of the angels; nevertheless, it is on the whole a remarkably sustained work, with a gorgeousness of coloring which might perhaps be traced to its author's Celtic strain.

As Mrs. Samuel Gilman, Caroline Howard, of whom we have already spoken, carried the New England spirit into a Southern home, and there wrote not only verses, but sketches and tales, much in the manner of her sisters who never left the Puritan nest, though dealing at times with material strange to them, as in her "Recollections of a Southern Matron." With the women of New England lies our chief concern, until a date comparatively recent. A strong, thinking, working race—all know the type; granite rock, out of its crevices the unexpected harebells trembling here and there. As writers they have a general resemblance; in one case a little more mica and glitter, in another more harebells than usual. Mrs. Sigourney, for instance, presents an azure predominance of the flowery, on a basis of the practical. Think of her fifty-seven volumes—copious verse, religious and sentimental; sketches of travel; didactic "Letters to Mothers," "Letters to Young Ladies"; the charmingly garrulous "Letters of Life," published after her death. Quantity, dilution, diffusiveness, the dispersion of energy in a variety of aims—these were the order of the day. Lydia Maria Child wrote more than thirty-five books and pamphlets, beginning with the apotheosis of the aboriginal American in romance, ending in the good fight with slavery, and taking in by the way domestic economy, the progress of religious ideas, and the Athens of Pericles,[18] somewhat romanticized. Firm granite here, not without ferns of tenderest grace. It is very curious and impressive, the self-reliant dignity

16. Felicia Hemans (1793–1835), British poet.

17. Quoted in the biography of Brooks in the 1879 edition of *Zóphiël: Or, The Bride of Seven*. Robert Southey (1774–1843), English Romantic poet and poet laureate who helped Brooks publish her book. Charles Lamb (1775–1834), English essayist.

18. Child's romance *Philothea* (1836) was set in Athens, Greece, during the era of Pericles (c. 495–429 B.C.), statesman and general.

with which these noble matrons circumambulate the whole field of literature with errant feet, but with a character central and composed. They *are* "something better than their verse," and also than their prose. Why was it that the dispersive tendency of the time showed itself especially in the literary effort of women? Perhaps the scattering, haphazard kind of education then commonly bestowed upon girls helped to bring about such a condition of things. Efficient work, in literature as in other professions, is dependent in a degree upon preparation; not indeed upon the actual amount of knowledge possessed, but upon the training of the mind to sure action, and the vitality of the spark of intellectual life communicated in early days. To the desultory and aimless education of girls at this period, and their continual servitude to the sampler, all will testify. "My education," says Mrs. Gilman, "was exceedingly irregular, a perpetual passing from school to school. I drew a very little and worked 'The Babes in the Wood' on white satin, with floss silk." By and by, however, she "was initiated into Latin," studied Watts's "Logic"[19] by herself, and joined a private class in French. Lydia Huntley (Mrs. Sigourney) fared somewhat better, pursuing mathematics, though she admits that too little time was accorded to the subject, and being instructed in "the *belles-lettres* studies" by competent teachers. Her school education ceased at thirteen; she afterwards worked alone over history and mental philosophy, had tutors in Latin and French, and even dipped into Hebrew, under clerical guidance. This has a deceptively advanced sound; we are to learn presently that she was sent away to boarding-school, where she applied herself to "embroidery of historical scenes, filigree, and other finger-works."[20] (May we not find a connection between this kind of training and the production of dramatic characters as lifelike as those figures in floss silk? Was it not a natural result, that corresponding "embroidery of historical scenes" performed by the feminine pen?) Lydia Maria Francis (Mrs. Child), "apart from her brother's companionship, had, as usual, a very unequal share of educational opportunities; attending only the public schools,"— the public schools of the century in its teens,—"with one year at a private seminary."[21] Catherine [*sic*] Sedgwick, "reared in an atmosphere of high intelligence," still confesses, "I have all my life felt the want of more systematic training."[22]

Another cause of the scattering, unmethodical supply may have been the vagueness of the demand. America was not quite sure what it was proper to expect of the "female writer"; and perhaps that lady herself had a lingering feudal idea that she could hold literary territory only on condition of stout pen service in the cause of the domestic virtues and pudding. "In those days," says Thomas Wentworth Higginson, "it seemed to be held necessary for American women to work their passage

19. Isaac Watts's *Logic* (1724), a popular textbook.
20. Sigourney, *Letters of Life* (1866).
21. Thomas Wentworth Higginson, "Lydia Maria Child," in *Eminent Women of the Age*, edited by James Parton (1869). The quote in the next paragraph is also from this essay.
22. Mary Dewey, ed., *Life and Letters of Catharine Maria Sedgwick* (1871).

into literature by first compiling a cookery book." Thus we have Mrs. Child's "Frugal Housewife"; and we find clever Eliza Leslie,[23] of Philadelphia, putting forth "Seventy-five Receipts" before she ventures upon her humorous and satirical "Pencil Sketches." The culinary tradition was carried on, somewhat later, by Catherine Beecher, with her "Domestic Receipt Book";[24] and we have indeed most modern instances in the excellent "Common-sense Series" of the novelist "Marion Harland,"[25] and in Mrs. Whitney's "Just How."[26] Perhaps, however, it is not fancy that these wear the kitchen apron with a difference.

In addition to lack of training, and to the vague nature of the public demand, a third cause operated against symmetrical artistic development among the women of those electric days preceding the civil war. That struggle between the art instinct and the desire for reform, which is not likely to cease entirely until the coming of the golden year, was then at its height. Both men and women were drawn into the maelstrom of the antislavery conflict; yet to a few men the artist's single aim seemed still possible—to Longfellow, to Hawthorne. Similar examples are lacking among contemporary women. Essential womanhood, *"das Ewigweibliche,"* seems at this point unusually clear in the work of women; the passion for conduct, the enthusiasm for abstract justice, not less than the potential motherhood that yearns over all suffering. The strong Hebraic element in the spiritual life of New England women in particular tended to withdraw them from the service of pure art at this period. "My natural inclinations," wrote Lydia Maria Child, "drew me much more strongly towards literature and the arts than towards reform, and the weight of conscience was needed to turn the scale."[27]

Mrs. Child and Miss Sedgwick, chosen favorites of the public, stand forth as typical figures. Both have the art instinct, both the desire for reform: in Mrs. Child the latter decidedly triumphs, in spite of her romances; in Miss Sedgwick the former, though less decidedly, in spite of her incidental preachments. She wrote "without any purpose or hope to slay giants," aiming merely "to supply mediocre readers with small moral hints on various subjects that come up in daily life." It is interesting to note just what public favor meant materially to the most popular women writers of those days. Miss Sedgwick, at a time when she had reached high-water mark, wrote in reply to one who expected her to acquire a fortune, that she found it impossible to make much out of novel-writing while cheap editions of English

23. Eliza Leslie (1787–1858) published her first cookbook in 1828; she would write eight others. *Pencil Sketches* appeared in 1833.

24. Catherine Beecher (1800–1878) was the sister of Harriet Beecher Stowe and an educator as well as author of *Miss Beecher's Domestic Receipt Book* (1846) and other works.

25. Mary Virginia Terhune (1830–1922) was a popular novelist who published as Marion Harland. The series mentioned began in 1871 with *Common Sense in the Household.*

26. A. D. T. Whitney (1824–1906), a popular author of girls' books, wrote *Just How: A Key to The Cook-Books* (1878).

27. Quoted in Higginson, "Lydia Maria Child."

novels filled the market. "I may go on," she says, "earning a few hundred dollars a year, and precious few too."[28] One could not even earn the "precious few" without observing certain laws of silence. The "Appeal in Behalf of that Class of Americans called Africans" seriously lessened the income of Mrs. Child. That dubious America of 1833 was decided on one point—this was not what she expected of the "female writer." She was willing to be instructed by a woman—about the polishing of furniture and the education of daughters.

And now there arises before us another figure, of striking singularity and power. Margaret Fuller never appeared as a candidate for popular favor. On the polishing of furniture she was absolutely silent; nor, though she professed "high respect for those who 'cook something good,' and create and preserve fair order in houses,"[29] did she ever fulfil [sic] the understood duty of woman by publishing a cookery book. On the education of daughters she had, however, a vital word to say; demanding for them "a far wider and more generous culture."[30] Her own education had been of an exceptional character; she was fortunate in its depth and solidity, though unfortunate in the forcing process that had made her a hard student at six years old. Her equipment was superior to that of any American woman who had previously entered the field of literature; and hers was a powerful genius, but, by the irony of fate, a genius not prompt to clothe itself in the written word. As to the inspiration of her speech all seem to agree; but one who knew her well has spoken of the "singular embarrassment and hesitation induced by the attempt to commit her thoughts to paper." The reader of the sibylline leaves she scattered about her in her strange career receives the constant impression of hampered power, of force that has never found its proper outlet. In "Woman in the Nineteenth Century" there is certainly something of that "shoreless Asiatic dreaminess" complained of by Carlyle;[31] but there are also to be found rich words, fit, like those of Emerson, for "gold nails in temples to hang trophies on."[32] The critical Scotchman himself subsequently owned that "some of her Papers are the undeniable utterances of a true heroic mind; altogether unique, so far as I know, among the Writing Women of this generation; rare enough, too, God knows, among the Writing Men." She accomplished comparatively little that can be shown or reckoned. Her mission was "to free, arouse, dilate."[33] Those who immediately responded were few; and as the circle of her influence has widened through their lives the source of the original impulse has been unnamed and forgotten. But if we are disposed to rank a fragmentary great-

28. *Life and Letters of Catharine Maria Sedgwick.*

29. Margaret Fuller, *Woman in the Nineteenth Century* (1845).

30. Margaret Fuller, "The Wrongs of American Women. The Duty of American Women," *New York Tribune* (1845).

31. Thomas Carlyle (1795–1881), Scottish historian and essayist. This quote and quote below from *The Correspondence of Thomas Carlyle to Ralph Waldo Emerson, 1834–1872* (1883).

32. Lowell, "Fable for Critics."

33. Walt Whitman, "Democratic Vistas" (1868).

ness above a narrow perfection, to value loftiness of aim more than the complete attainment of an inferior object, we must set Margaret Fuller, despite all errors of judgment, all faults of style, very high among the "Writing Women" of America. It is time that, ceasing to discuss her personal traits, we dwell only upon the permanent and essential in her whose mind was fixed upon the permanent, the essential. Her place in our literature is her own; it has not been filled, nor does it seem likely to be. The particular kind of force which she exhibited—in so far as it was not individual—stands a chance in our own day of being drawn into the educational field, now that the "wider and more generous culture" which she claimed has been accorded to women.

We may trace from the early publications of Lydia Maria Francis and Catherine [*sic*] Sedgwick the special line along which women have worked most successfully. It is in fiction that they have wrought with the greatest vigor and freedom, and in that important class of fiction which reflects faithfully the national life, broadly or in sectional phases. In 1821 Miss Francis, a girl of nineteen, wrote "Hobomok," a rather crude novel of colonial Massachusetts, with an Indian hero. Those were the times of the pseudo-American school, the heyday of what Mr. Stedman has called "the supposititious Indian."[34] To the sanguine "Hobomok" seemed to foreshadow a feminine Cooper,[35] and its author put forth in the following year "The Rebels," a novel of Boston before the Revolution. A more effective worker on this line, however, was Miss Sedgwick, whose "New England Tale"—a simple little story, originally intended as a tract—was published in 1822, and at once drew attention, in spite of a certain thinness, by its recognizable home flavor. The plain presentation of New England life in "Redwood," her succeeding book, interests and convinces the reader of to-day. Some worthless elements of plot, now out of date, are introduced; but age cannot wither nor custom stale the fresh reality of the most memorable figure—that manly soul Miss Deborah, a character as distinct as Scott himself could have made her. "Hope Leslie," "Clarence," and "The Linwoods" followed; then the briefer tales supplying "small moral hints," such as the "Poor Rich Man and Rich Poor Man." All are genuine, wholesome, deserving of the hearty welcome they received. "Wise, clear, and kindly," one must echo the verdict of Margaret Fuller on our gentle pioneer in native fiction; we may look back with pride on her "speech moderate and sane, but never palsied by fear or skeptical caution"; on herself, "a fine example of the independent and beneficent existence that intellect and character can give to women."[36] The least studied among her pathetic scenes are admirable; and she displays some healthy humor, though not as much as her charming letters indicate that she possessed. A recent writer has ranked her work in one

34. Stedman, *Poets of America* (1885).
35. James Fenimore Cooper (1789–1851). The first installment in his popular Leatherstocking series was published in 1823.
36. Margaret Fuller, *Woman in the Nineteenth Century* (1845).

respect above that of Cooper, pronouncing it more truly calculated to effect "the emancipation of the American mind from foreign types."

Miss Sedgwick, past threescore, was still in the literary harness when the woman who was destined to bring the novel of New England to a fuller development reached fame at a bound with "Uncle Tom's Cabin." At last the artist's instinct and the purpose of the reformer were fused, as far as they are capable of fusion, in a story that still holds its reader, whether passive or protesting, with the grip of the master-hand. The inborn powers of Mrs. Stowe were fortunately developed in a home atmosphere that supplied deficiencies in training. Fate was kind in providing occasional stimulants for the feminine mind, though an adequate and regular supply was customarily withheld. Miss Sedgwick attributes an especial quickening force to the valuable selections read aloud by her father to his family; Miss Francis,[37] as we have seen, owed much to the conversation of her brother. To Harriet Beecher was granted, outside her inspiring home circle, an extra stimulus in the early influence of the enthusiastic teacher whose portrait she has given us in the Jonathan Rossiter of "Oldtown Folks." A close knowledge of Scott's[38] novels from her girlhood had its effect in shaping her methods of narration. She knew her Bible—perpetual fountain feeding the noblest streams of English literature—as Ruskin[39] knew his. Residence for years near the Ohio border had familiarized her with some of the darkest aspects of slavery; so that when the passage of the Fugitive Slave Law[40] roused her to the task of exhibiting the system in operation, she was as fully prepared to execute that task as a woman of New England birth and traditions well could be. Since the war Southern writers, producing with the ease of intimacy works steeped in the spirit of the South, have taught us much concerning negro character and manners, and have accustomed us to an accurate reproduction of dialect. The sublimity of Uncle Tom has been tried by the reality of the not less lovable Uncle Remus.[41] But whatever blemishes or extravagances may appear to a critical eye in the great antislavery novel, it still beats with that intense life which nearly forty years ago awoke a deep responsive thrill in the repressed heart of the North. We are at present chiefly concerned with its immense practical success. It was a "shot heard round the world." Ten thousand copies were sold in a few days; over three hundred thousand in a year; eight power presses were kept running day and night to supply the continual demand. The British Museum now contains thirty-five complete editions in English, and translations exist in at least twenty

37. Maiden name of Lydia Maria Child.
38. Sir Walter Scott (1771–1832), popular Scottish historical novelist.
39. John Ruskin (1819–1900), English art critic.
40. The Fugitive Slave Law of 1850 made it illegal for Americans to harbor escaped slaves or assist in their flight to freedom. The law galvanized public opinion in the North against slavery.
41. Created by Joel Chandler Harris in 1880, Uncle Remus was a storytelling slave. His stories included the Br'er Rabbit and Tar Baby folktales.

different languages. "Never did any American work have such success," exclaims Mrs. Child, in one of her enthusiastic letters. "It has done much to command respect for the faculties of woman."[42] The influences are, indeed, broad and general which have since that day removed all restrictions tending to impress inferiority on the woman writer, so that the distinction of sex is lost in the distinction of schools. Yet a special influence may be attributed to this single marked manifestation of force, to this imposing popular triumph. In the face of the fact that the one American book which had stormed Europe was the work of a woman, the old tone of patronage became ridiculous, the old sense of ordained and inevitable weakness on the part of the "female writer" became obsolete. Women henceforth, whatever their personal feelings in regard to the much-discussed book, were enabled, consciously or unconsciously, to hold the pen more firmly, to move it more freely. In New England fiction what a leap from the work of Miss Sedgwick, worthy as it is, to that of Mrs. Stowe! The field whence a few hardy growths were peeping seems to have been overflowed by a fertilizing river, so rich is its new yield. It is "the soul of Down East" that we find in "The Minister's Wooing" and "Oldtown Folks." Things spiritual are grasped with the insight of kinship, externals are drawn with the certainty of life-long acquaintance. If we glance at the humorous side of the picture, surely no hand that ever wrought could have bettered one smile-provoking line in the familiar figure of Sam Lawson, the village do-nothing. There is a free-handedness in the treatment of this character not often found in more recent conscientious studies of local types; it is as a painting beside photographs. A certain inequality, it may be admitted, appears in the range of Mrs. Stowe's productions. They form links, more or less shining, between a time of confused and groping effort on the part of women and a time of definitely directed aims, of a concentration that has, inevitably, its own drawbacks.

The encouragement of the great magazines, from the first friendly to women writers, is an important factor in their development. "Harper's" dates from 1850; "The Atlantic Monthly," in 1857, opened a new outlet for literary work of a high grade. Here appeared many of the short stories of Rose Terry,[43] depicting the life of New England; unsurpassable in their fidelity to nature, their spontaneous flow, their grim humor, pathos, tragedy. In the pages of "The Atlantic," too, suddenly flashed into sight the brilliant exotics of Harriet Prescott, who holds among American women a position as singular as that of Poe[44] among men. Her characters have their being in some remote, gorgeous sunset-land; we feel that the Boston Common of "Azarian" is based upon a cloud rather than solid Yankee earth, and the author can scarce pluck a May flower but it turns at her touch to something rich

42. *Letters of Lydia Maria Child* (1882).
43. Maiden name of Rose Terry Cooke.
44. Maiden name of Harriet Prescott Spofford, whose exotic Romanticism echoed that of Edgar Allan Poe (1809–1849).

and strange. Native flavor there is in some of her shorter stories, such as "The South Breaker" and "Knitting Sale-Socks"; but a sudden waft of foreign spices is sure to mingle with the sea-wind or the inland lilac-scents. "The Amber Gods" and "The Thief in the Night" skillfully involve the reader in a dazzling web of deceptive strength.

In "Temple House," "Two Men," and "The Morgesons," the peculiarly powerful works of Mrs. Stoddard, the central figures do not seem necessarily of any particular time or country. Their local habitation, however, is impressively painted; with a few swift, vigorous strokes the old coast towns spring up before us; the very savor of the air is imparted. Minor characters strongly smack of the soil; old Cuth, in "Two Men," dying "silently and firmly, like a wolf"; Elsa, in the same book. There are scenes of a superb fierce power—that of the wreck in "Temple House," for instance. The curt and repressed style, the ironic humor of Mrs. Stoddard, serve to grapple her work to the memory as with hooks of steel; it is as remote as possible from the conventional notion of woman's writing.

The old conflict between the reformer's passion and the art instinct is renewed in the novels and stories of Elizabeth Stuart Phelps, who possesses the artist's responsiveness in a high degree, with but little of the artist's restraint. Exquisitely sensitive to the significant beauty of the world, she is no less sensitive to the appeal of human pain. In "Hedged In" and "The Silent Partner," in her stories of the squalid tenement and the storm-beaten coast, her literary work reflects, point for point, her personal work for the fallen, the toiling, and the tempted. Her passionate sympathy gives her a power of thrilling, of commanding the tribute of tears, which is all her own. An enthusiast for womanhood, she has given us in "The Story of Avis" and "Dr. Zay" striking studies of complementary themes; "Avis," despite certain flaws of style to which objection is trite, remaining the greater, as it is the sadder, book. All Miss Phelps's stories strike root into New England, though it is not precisely Mrs. Cooke's New England of iron farmers and stony farms; and none strikes deeper root than "Avis," a natural product of the intellectual region whence "Woman in the Nineteenth Century" sprang thirty years before. No other woman, among writers who have arisen since the war, has received in such fullness the spiritual inheritance of New England's past.

The changes brought about by the influx of foreigners into the factory towns of the East are reflected in the pages of Miss Phelps, particularly in "The Silent Partner." A recent worker of the same vein is Lillie Chace Wyman,[45] whose short stories, collected under the symbolic title "Poverty Grass," are marked by sincerity and simple power. Sarah Orne Jewett roams the old pastures, gathering many pungent handfuls of the familiar flowers and herbs that retain for us their homely precious-

---

45. Lillie Chace Wyman (1847–1929), writer whose fiction promoted equality among the races and exposed the cruelties of the factory system.

ness. She is attracted also by the life of the coast. Without vigorous movement, her sketches and stories have always an individual, delicate picturesqueness, the quality of a small, clear water-color. "A Country Doctor" is to be noted for its very quiet and true presentation of a symmetrical womanhood, naturally drawn towards the large helpfulness of professional life.

A novel which has lately aroused much discussion, the "John Ward, Preacher," of Margaret Deland,[46] is, although its scene is laid in Pennsylvania, a legitimate growth of New England in its problem and its central character. The orthodox idea of eternal future punishment receives a treatment somewhat similar to that applied by Miss Phelps in "The Gates Ajar" to the conventional heaven. The hero seems a revisitant Thomas Shepard,[47] or other stern yet tender Puritan of the past, miraculously set down in a modern environment. The incisiveness of portions of "John Ward," as well as the grace of its side scenes, gives promise of still more valuable coming contributions to American fiction by the poet of the charming "Old Garden." A yet later New England production is the book of stories by Mary E. Wilkins, "A Humble Romance," a work brimful of vigor and human nature.

We need not now enter into the circumstances tending to the misdirection of intellectual effort which so affected the work of Southern women in literature that for some time they produced little of enduring value. These causes have been of late fully set forth by a writer of the new South, Thomas Nelson Page,[48] who in naming the women of Southern birth or residence most prominent as novelists before the civil war places Mrs. Terhune in a class by herself. "Like the others, she has used the Southern life as material, but has exhibited a literary sense of far higher order, and an artistic touch." Mrs. Rebecca Harding Davis, a native of West Virginia, has chosen a Pennsylvanian background for some of her best work; producing, perhaps, nothing stronger than "Life in the Iron Mills," published long since in "The Atlantic"—a story distantly akin to those of Miss Phelps and the author of "Poverty Grass." The hopeless heart-hunger of the poor has seldom been so passionately pictured. A distinguishing characteristic of the work of Mrs. Davis is her Browning-like[49] insistence on the rare test-moments of life. If, as in the complicated war-time novel "Waiting for the Verdict,"—a work of high intention,—the characters come out startlingly well in the sudden lights flashed upon them, the writer's idealism is tonic and uplifting.

It was a woman of the North who pictured, in a series of brief tales and sketches

---

46. Margaret Deland (1857–1945), prolific novelist and short story writer.

47. Thomas Shepard (1605–1649), Puritan minister.

48. Thomas Nelson Page (1853–1922), novelist who promoted an idealized view of the Old South. Following quote is from his essay "Authorship in the South Before the Civil War" first published in *Lippincott's* (1889).

49. Either Elizabeth Barrett Browning (1806–1861) or Robert Browning (1812–1889), British poets.

full of insight, the desolate South at the close of the civil war—Constance Fenimore Woolson, the most broadly national of our women novelists. Her feeling for local color is quick and true; and though she has especially identified herself with the Lake country and with Florida, one is left with the impression that her assimilative powers would enable her to reproduce as successfully the traits of any other quarter of the Union. Few American writers of fiction have given evidence of such breadth, so full a sense of the possibilities of the varied and complex life of our wide land. Robust, capable, mature—these seem fitting words to apply to the author of "Anne," of "East Angels," of the excellent short stories in "Rodman the Keeper." Women have reason for pride in a representative novelist whose genius is trained and controlled, without being tamed or dispirited.

Similar surefootedness and mastery of means are displayed by Mary Hallock Foote in her picturesque Western stories, such as "The Led-Horse Claim: a Romance of a Mining Camp," and "John Bodewin's Testimony"—in which a certain gracefulness takes the place of the fuller warmth of Miss Woolson. One is apt to name the two writers together, since they represent the most supple and practiced talent just now exercised by women in the department of fiction.

Mrs. Frances Hodgson Burnett,[50] English by birth and education, and influenced by the Dickens[51] tradition, though reflecting the tone of her environment wherever fate may lead her, touches American literature chiefly on the Southern side, through "Louisiana" and "Esmeralda." Despite the ambitious character of her novel of Washington society, "Through One Administration," her most durable work is either thoroughly English or belongs to the international school. This particular branch of fiction we cannot now pause to note, though conscious that such books as the beautiful "Guenn" of Blanche Willis Howard[52] have their own distinct value.

A truly native flower, though gathered in a field so unfamiliar as to wear a seemingly foreign charm, is Mrs. Jackson's[53] poetic "Ramona." A book instinct with passionate purpose, intensely alive and involving the reader in its movement, it yet contains an idyl of singular loveliness, the perfection of which lends the force of contrast to the pathetic close. A novel of reform, into which a great and generous soul poured its gathered strength, it none the less possesses artistic distinction. Something is, of course, due to the charm of atmosphere, the beauty of the back-

---

50. Frances Hodgson Burnett (1849–1924) is best known today for her children's fiction, including *The Secret Garden* (1909).

51. Charles Dickens (1812–1870), English novelist famous for his gritty and humorous portrayals of life in Victorian London.

52. Blanche Willis Howard (1847–1898) published many novels from the 1870s until her death.

53. Helen Hunt Jackson (1830–1885) was a prolific poet and fiction writer who also published under the names H. H. and Saxe Holm. Her novel *Ramona* (1884) attacked the treatment of Native Americans.

ground against which the plot naturally placed itself; more, to the trained hand, the pen pliant with long and free exercise; most, to the poet-heart. "Ramona" stands as the most finished, though not the most striking, example that what American women have done notably in literature they have done nobly.

The magazine-reading world has hardly recovered yet from its shock of surprise on discovering the author of "In the Tennessee Mountains," a book of short stories projecting the lines on which the writer has since advanced in "The Prophet of the Great Smoky Mountains" and "The Despot of Broomsedge Cove." Why did Miss Murfree[54] prefer to begin her literary career under the masculine name of "Charles Egbert Craddock"? Probably for the same reason as George Sand, George Eliot, Currer Bell; a reason stated by a stanch advocate of women, in words that form a convenient answer to the common sneer, "Not because they wished to be men, but because they wished for an unbiased judgment as artists."[55] The world has grown so much more enlightened on this point that the biased critic is now the exception, and the biased editor is a myth. The precaution of disguise cannot much longer remain a necessity, if, indeed, it was necessary in the case of Miss Murfree.

From whatever cause adopted, the mask was a completely deceptive one. Mr. Craddock's vivid portrayal of life among the Tennessee mountains was fairly discussed and welcomed as a valuable and characteristic contribution from the South; and nobody hinted then that the subtle poetic element and the tendency to subordinate human interest to scenery were indications of the writer's sex. The few cherishers of the fading superstition that women are without humor laughed heartily and unsuspiciously over the droll situations, the quaint sayings of the mountaineers. Once more the *reductio ad absurdum*[56] has been applied to the notion of ordained, invariable, and discernible difference between the literary work of men and that of women. The method certainly defers to dullness; but it also affords food for amusement to the ironically inclined.

This review, cursory and incomplete as it is, of the chief accomplishment of American women in native fiction, serves to bring out the fact that they have during the last forty years supplied to our literature an element of great and genuine value; and that while their productions have of course varied in power and richness, they have steadily gained in art. How wide the gap between "Hobomok" and "Ramona"![57] During the latter half of the period the product gives no general evi-

54. Mary Noailles Murfree (1850–1922) published her stories of the Tennessee mountains under the name Charles Egbert Craddock. Thomas Bailey Aldrich, editor of the *Atlantic Monthly*, was shocked when Murfree appeared at the magazine's offices and introduced herself as Craddock.

55. Thomas Wentworth Higginson, "Why Women Write Under the Names of Men," in *Women and Men* (1888).

56. Latin: reduction to the absurd. Refers to an argument that is proved by showing the absurdity of its opposite.

57. Lydia Maria Child's *Hobomok* (1824), an historical novel, and Helen Hunt Jackson's *Ramona* (1884), a reform novel, were both about Native Americans.

dence of limitation; and the writers would certainly be placed, except for the purposes of this article, among their brother authors, in classes determined by method, local background, or any other basis of arrangement which is artistic rather than personal. In exceptional cases a reviewer perhaps exclaims upon certain faults as "womanish"; but the cry is too hasty; the faults are those of individuals, in either sex. It is possible to match them from the work of men, and to adduce examples of women's work entirely free from them. Colonel Higginson has pointed out that the ivory miniature method in favor with some of our masculine artists is that of Jane Austen.[58] Wherein do Miss Sprague's "Earnest Trifler" or "The Daughter of Henry Sage Rittenhouse" display more salient indications of sex than works of similar scope by Mr. Henry James?[59]

"The almost entire disappearance of the distinctively woman's novel"— that is, the novel designed expressly for feminine readers, such as "The Wide, Wide World" and "The Lamplighter"— has lately been commented upon.[60] It is to be observed that this species—chiefly produced in the past by women, as the Warner sisters, Maria S. Cummins, Elizabeth Payson Prentiss, the excellent Miss McIntosh[61]—has become nearly extinct at the very time when women are supplying a larger proportion of fiction than ever before; and, further, that the comparatively few "domestic semi-pious" novels, very popular in late years, have been of masculine production. The original and suggestive, though perhaps at times over-subtle, work of Mrs. Whitney, thoroughly impregnated with the New England spirit, and portraying with insight various phases of girlhood, takes another rank. Whatever may be concluded from the decadence of fiction, written of women, for women, by women, it is certainly probable that women will remain, as a rule, the best writers for girls. In connection with this subject must be mentioned the widely known and appreciated stories of Louisa M. Alcott, "Little Women" and its successors, which "have not only been reprinted and largely sold in England, but also translated into several foreign languages, and thus published with persistent success." We are told that when "Little Men" was issued "its publication was delayed until the publishers were prepared to fill advance orders for fifty thousand copies."

A like popularity is to be noted of the spirited and artistic "Hans Brinker; or, the Silver Skates," of Mrs. Mary Mapes Dodge,[62] which "has had a very large cir-

---

58. In "The Literary Pendulum," first published in the *Library Magazine* (1887), Higginson credited Jane Austen with founding the school of realism then so prominent among male writers.

59. Mary Aplin Sprague (1849–?). Henry James (1843–1916), American Realist author.

60. O. B. Bunce, "Literature for Women," the *Critic* (1889).

61. Susan Warner (1819–1885), author of *The Wide, Wide World* (1851), Anna Warner (1827–1915), Maria Susanna Cummins (1827–1866), author of *The Lamplighter* (1854), Elizabeth Payson Prentiss (1818–1878), and Maria McIntosh (1803–1878) were authors of popular religious novels for women.

62. Mary Mapes Dodge (1831–1905), children's writer and editor of *St. Nicholas,* a popular children's magazine.

culation in America; has passed through several editions in England; and has been published in French at Paris, in German at Leipsic, in Russian at St. Petersburg, and in Italian at Rome. . . . The crowning tribute to its excellence is its perennial sale in Holland in a Dutch edition."[63] No name in our juvenile literature so "brings a perfume in the mention" as that of Mrs. Dodge, who for years has been as "the very pulse of the machine" in the making of that magazine for children, which is not only an ever new delight, but a genuine educational power.

In poetry the abundant work of women during the last half-century shows a development corresponding to that traced in the field of fiction. As the flood of sentimentalism slowly receded hopeful signs began to appear—the rather vague tints of a bow of poetical promise. The varying verse of Mrs. Oakes Smith, Mrs. Kinney, Elizabeth Lloyd Howell, and Harriet Winslow Sewall[64] represents, in different degrees, a general advance. The "little vagrant pen" of Frances Sargent Osgood, as she confessed, "wandered lightly down the paper," but its fanciful turns had now and then a swift, capricious grace. The poems of Sarah Helen Whitman, belonging to the landscape school of Bryant, are of marked value, as are also the deeply earnest productions of Mrs. Anna Lynch Botta, which display a new distinctness of motive, possibly attributable to the influence of Longfellow.[65] The same influence is felt in some of the early work of Alice Cary, whose individual strain of melancholy melody clings to remembrance, its charm stubbornly outliving our critical recognition of defects due, in great measure, to over-production. Emily Judson sometimes touched finely the familiar chords, as in the well-known poem of motherhood, "My Bird." The tender "Morning Glory" of Maria White Lowell,[66] whose poems are characterized by a delicate and childlike simplicity, will be remembered.

In 1873 a critic, not generally deemed too favorable to growths of the present day, recorded the opinion that there was "more force and originality—in other words, more genius—in the living female poets of America than in all their predecessors, from Mistress Anne Bradstreet down. At any rate there is a wider range of thought in their verse, and infinitely more art."[67] For the change first noted by Mr. Stoddard there is no accounting; the tides of genius are incalculable. The other gains, like those in fiction, are to be accounted for partly by the law of evolution working through our whole literature, by the influence of sounder models and of a

63. Lucia Gilbert Runkle, "Mary Mapes Dodge," in *Our Famous Women* (1883).
64. Elizabeth C. Kinney (1810–1889), Elizabeth Lloyd Howell (1811–1896), and Harriet Winslow Sewall (1819–1889).
65. Sarah Helen Whitman (1803–1878), Anna Lynch Botta (1815–1891), and Henry Wadsworth Longfellow (1807–1882).
66. Emily C. Judson (1817–1854), who wrote under the pseudonym Fanny Forester, and Maria White Lowell (1821–1853).
67. Richard Henry Stoddard (1825–1903), preface to the 1873 edition of *Female Poets of America*, edited by Rufus Griswold.

truer criticism, and by the winnowing processes of the magazines; partly, also, by the altered position and improved education of women in general—not necessarily of the individual, since change in the atmosphere may have important results in cases where other conditions remain unchanged.

The poems of Mrs. Howe express true womanly aspiration, and a high scorn of unworthiness, but their strongest characteristic is the fervent patriotism which breathes through the famous "Battle Hymn of the Republic." The clear, hopeful "orchard notes"[68] of Lucy Larcom,—it is impossible to refrain from quoting Mr. Stedman's perfect phrase,— first heard long since, have grown more mellow with advancing years.

The dramatic lyric took new force and naturalness in the hands of Rose Terry Cooke, and turned fiery in those of Mrs. Stoddard, whose contemplative poems also have an eminent sad dignity of style. The fine-spun subjective verse of Mrs. Piatt flashes at times with felicities, as a web with dewdrops. Many names appear upon the honorable roll: Mrs. Fields, Mrs. Spofford,—whose rich nature reveals itself in verse as in the novel,—Mrs. Margaret J. Preston, Mrs. Mary Ashley Townsend; Elizabeth Akers Allen, Julia C. R. Dorr, Mrs. Stowe, Mrs. Whitney, Mrs. Dodge, Mrs. Moulton; Mrs. Thaxter,[69]—the sea's true lover, who has devoted herself to the faithful expression of a single phase of natural beauty,—Mrs. Mary E. Bradley, Kate Putnam Osgood, Nora Perry, Mary N. Prescott, and Harriet McEwen Kimball;[70] Mary Clemmer Hudson, Margaret E. Sangster, Miss Bushnell, "Susan Coolidge," "Howard Glyndon," "Stuart Sterne," Charlotte Fiske Bates,[71] May Riley Smith, Ella Dietz, Mary Ainge de Vere, Edna Dean Proctor, the Goodale sisters, Miss Coolbrith, Miss Shinn, "Owen Innsly," Elizabeth Stuart Phelps, and Alice Wellington Rollins.[72] There is a kind of white fire in the best of the subtle verses of "H. H."[73]—a diamond light, enhanced by careful cutting. Generally impersonal, the author's individuality yet lives in them to an unusual degree. We may recognize

68. Edmund Clarence Stedman, *Poets of America* (1885).

69. Annie Adams Fields (1834–1915), Mary Ashley Townsend (1832–1901), Elizabeth Akers Allen (1832–1911), Julia C. R. Dorr (1825–1913), Louise Chandler Moulton (1835–1908), and Celia Thaxter (1835–1894).

70. Mary E. Bradley (1835–1898); Kate Putnam Osgood (1841–1910); Nora Perry (1831–1896); Mary Newmarch Prescott (1849–1888), sister of Harriet Prescott Spofford; Harriet McEwen Kimball (1834–1917).

71. Mary Clemmer Hudson (1839–1884), known as the poet and critic Mary Clemmer; Margaret E. Sangster (1838–1912), poet and editor of *Harper's Bazaar*; Frances Louisa Bushnell (1834–1899); Susan Coolidge (1835–1905). Laura Redden Searing (1839–1923) wrote patriotic Civil War poetry under the pseudonym Howard Glyndon. Gertrude Bloede (1845–1905) published as Stuart Sterne. Charlotte Fiske Bates (1838–1916).

72. May Riley Smith (1842?–1927); Ella Dietz Clymer (1856–?); Mary Ainge de Vere (?–?); Edna Dean Proctor (1829–1923); Elaine Goodale Eastman (1863–1953) and Dora Reed Goodale (1866–1953); Milicent Washburn Shinn (1858–1940), an editor of the *Overland Monthly*. Owen Innsly was the pseudonym of Lucy White Jennison (1850–?). Alice Wellington Rollins (1847–1897).

73. Helen Hunt Jackson.

also in the Jewish poems of Emma Lazarus, especially in "By the Waters of Baby-lon," and the powerful fourteenth-century tragedy, "The Dance to Death," "the precious life-blood of a master spirit, embalmed and treasured up on purpose to a life beyond life."[74] The poems of Edith M. Thomas, with their exquisite workman-ship, mark the high attainment of woman in the mastery of poetic form, and exhale some breath of that fragrance which clings to the work of the young Keats. Miss Hutchinson's "Songs and Lyrics" have also rare quality. The graceful verse of Mrs. Deland has been quick to win the ear of the public. Louise Imogen Guiney,[75] some-times straining the voice, has nevertheless contributed to the general chorus notes of unusual fullness and strength.

In other branches of literature, to which comparatively few women have chosen to devote themselves, an increasing thoroughness is apparent, a growing tendency to specialism. The irresponsible feminine free lance, with her gay dash at all sub-jects, and her alliterative pen name dancing in every mêlée like a brilliant pennon, has gone over into the more appropriate field of journalism. The calmly adequate literary matron of all work is an admirable type of the past, no longer developed by the new conditions. The articles of the late Lucy M. Mitchell on sculpture, and of Mrs. Schuyler van Rensselaer on art and architecture; the historical work of Mar-tha J. Lamb and of the lamented Mary L. Booth, the latter also an indefatigable translator; the studies of Helen Campbell in social science; the translations of Har-riet Waters Preston[76]—these few examples are typical of the determination and concentration of woman's work at the present day. We notice in each new issue of a magazine the well-known specialists. Miss Thomas has given herself to the inter-pretation of nature, in prose as in verse; "Olive Thorne" Miller to the loving study of bird life. Mrs. Jackson,[77] the most versatile of later writers, possessed the rare combination of versatility and thoroughness in such measure that we might almost copy Hartley Coleridge's saying of Harriet Martineau,[78] and call her a specialist about everything; but her name will be associated with the earnest presentation of the wrongs of the Indian, as that of Emma Lazarus with the impassioned defense of the rights of the Jew.

The just and genial Colonel Higginson expresses disappointment that woman's advance in literature has not been more marked since the establishment of the

74. John Milton wrote in *Areopagitica* (1644), "A good book is the precious life-blood . . . "

75. Edith M. Thomas (1854–1925). Ellen Mackay Hutchinson (Cortissoz) (?–?) edited with Edmund Clarence Stedman the eleven-volume *Library of American Literature* (1888–1889). Louise Imogen Guiney (1861–1920).

76. Lucy Myers Wright Mitchell (1845–1888), Mariana Griswold van Rensselaer (1851–1934), Martha J. Lamb (1829–1893), Mary Louise Booth (1831–1899), Helen Campbell (1839–1918), and Harriet Waters Preston (1836–1911), a prolific literary critic.

77. Edith M. Thomas (1854–1925), Olive Thorne Miller (1831–1918), and Helen Hunt Jackson.

78. Hartley Coleridge (1796–1849), English writer. Harriet Martineau (1802–1876), English feminist writer.

women's colleges. "It is," he says, "considerable and substantial; yet in view of the completeness with which literary work is now thrown open to women, and their equality as to pay, there is room for some surprise that it is not greater."[79]

The proper fruit of the women's colleges in literature has, in fact, not yet ripened. It may at first seem strangely delayed, yet reflection suggests the reasons. An unavoidable self-consciousness hampers the first workers under a new dispensation. It might appear at a casual glance that those released from the burden of a retarding tradition were ready at once for the race, but the weight has only been exchanged for the lighter burden of the unfamiliar. College-bred women of the highest type have accepted, with grave conscientiousness, new social responsibilities as the concomitant of their new opportunities.

> Pealing, the clock of Time
> Has struck the Woman's hour;
> We hear it on our knees,

wrote Miss Phelps for the graduates of Smith College ten years ago.[80] That the summons has indeed been reverently heard and faithfully obeyed, those who have followed the work of the Association of Collegiate Alumnæ can testify. The deed, and not the word, engages the energy of the college woman of to-day; but as these institutions grow into the life of our land that life will be everywhere enriched, and the word must follow in happy time. Individual genius for literature is sure, sooner or later, to appear within the constantly widening circle of those fairly equipped for its exercise. It would be idle to expect that the cases in which native power and an adequate preparation go hand in hand will be frequent, since they are infrequent among men. The desirable thing was, that this rare development should be made a possibility among women. It is possible to-day; some golden morrow will make it a reality.

Source: The Century (1890)

79. Higginson, "More Thorough Work Visible," in *Women and Men* (1888).

80. Elizabeth Stuart Phelps's poem "Victuræ Salutamus," *Songs of the Silent World and Other Poems* (1884). The title of the poem, which Phelps wrote for Smith's first commencement, has been translated by Carol Farley Kessler as, "We women, who are about to attain our goal, call upon you."

❧ Mary Livermore (1820–1905)

Born and raised in Boston, Mary Ashton Rice was well educated and began teaching in her teens. She married Reverend Daniel Livermore in 1845 and embarked on a life of charitable work and authorship. During the stormy years before the war, the Livermores planned to move to the battleground of Kansas, yet ended up in Chicago, where Mary raised their two children and served as associate editor of the periodical her husband had purchased. Shortly after the war began, she became director of the northwestern branch of the U.S. Sanitary Commission, coordinating volunteers and the distribution of donated goods to soldiers in the field. After the war, her family moved back to the Boston area. She was a leader in the temperance and suffrage movements and edited the suffragist Woman's Journal. *Her memoir,* My Story of the War, *is one of the most well-known accounts of women's involvement in the Civil War. Her desire to record women's contributions as well as her accounts of how writing was intertwined with her relief work suggest how the war transformed women's writing lives.*

Preface to *My Story of the War*

At the close of the war, I was importuned to publish my experiences and reminiscences in connection with the hospitals and the relief work of the Sanitary Commission.[1] But I declined to do so. A horror of the war still enwrapped the country. The salvation of the nation had been purchased with the blood of her sons, and she was still in the throes of anguish because of her bereavement. The people had turned with relief to the employments of peaceful life, eager to forget the fearful years of battle and carnage. I put away all mementoes of the exceptional life I had led, and re-entered with gladness upon the duties connected with my home and family, giving my leisure, as before the war, to charitable work and literary pursuits. I expected this quiet and happy order of things would continue to the end.

It has been otherwise ordered. The twenty-odd years that have passed since the bells rang in the long prayer for peace have been unlike any of which I had ever dreamed. They have been packed with work, have brought me in contact with people and events of national importance, have afforded me extended opportunities of travel in my own country and Europe, and have given me a largeness and variety of experience not often gained by a woman. The sun of my life is now sloping swiftly to the west, the years that I have travelled lie stretching in long array behind me, and I am approaching the time when one lives much in memory. I have again been asked to write for publication my story of the war and its relief work, and this time the request has found me favorably disposed to the undertaking.

---

1. Founded in 1861 to provide relief for soldiers and promote healthy conditions in the camps, the Sanitary Commission was largely comprised of female volunteers.

The public ear has listened eagerly to the stories of the great battles of the war of the rebellion, told by the master spirits who conducted them, and who led the hosts of freedom to victory. The plan of the campaigns, the division of the forces, and the parts assigned to the various officers in command, the topography of the battle-fields, the personal prowess and heroism developed in the hotly contested struggle, and the jubilant victory which resulted, whose pæans of joy drowned the cries of the wounded and the wails of bereavement—of these histories the people have not grown weary. Every detail of Fort Donelson and Vicksburg, Antietam and Gettysburg, and the surrender of Appomattox[2] is eagerly sought and devoured with zest. Millions of readers bend over the thrilling autobiographies of Grant, Sherman, Logan,[3] and other great captains of the memorable war, when, on the top wave of a nation's righteous wrath with slavery, four million of slaves were lifted to the level of freemen.

But there is a paucity of histories of the private soldier, of sketches of the rank and file. These have not been written, partly because of the modesty of the men whose experiences were worth narrating, and partly because they were not favorably circumstanced for extensive observation. There is a whole world of thrilling and heroic deed and endeavor, of lofty patience, silent endurance and sacrifice, con- nected with the soldiers of the army, of which the world will always remain igno- rant. It cannot be told. Neither can the deeds of nobleness performed by the people who remained at home, and who stood loyally by the government in its every hour of extremity. They measured their ready aid by the nation's need, and, in their con- secration to the cause of national unity and freedom, outran all outward demands made upon them.

The patriotism of men, the solemn joyfulness with which they gave of their possessions and of themselves, the unfaltering faith which no disaster could shake and no treachery enfeeble, who has told us of these, in detail? Who has fully nar- rated the consecrated and organized work of women, who strengthened the sinews of the nation with their unflagging enthusiasm, and bridged over the chasm between civil and military life, by infusing homogeneousness of feeling into the army and the people, "keeping the men in the field civilians, and making the people at home, of both sexes, half soldiers"?[4] It can never be understood save by those who lived

2. Fort Donelson in Tennessee was the first major victory for northern troops in the Civil War. Vicksburg, Mississippi, was the site of a great victory for Gen. Ulysses S. Grant. Antietam in Maryland was the first major battle on northern soil. The Battle of Gettysburg, in Pennsylvania, was the deadliest of the war and the turning point for northern forces. Appomattox, Virginia, was the site of the Confederate surrender at the close of the war.

3. Ulysses S. Grant (1822–1885), William Tecumseh Sherman (1820–1891), and John Alexander Logan (1826–1886), major U.S. generals.

4. Henry W. Bellows, president of the U.S. Sanitary Commission, in his introduction to Linus Pierpont Brockett and Mary C. Vaughan's *Woman's Work in the Civil War: A Record of Heroism, Patriotism, and Patience* (1867).

through that period, when one year counted more in the history of noble development than a half-score of ordinary years of buying and selling, building and furnishing, visiting and feasting. If this book shall in any way help to supply the deficiency I have indicated, my purpose will be accomplished.

I am largely indebted to my husband and friends for the materials from which this book has been made. My own tendency is to destroy the records of my past, as soon as an event or experience has ended. I have had little taste for preserving records, journals, memoranda, and letters, and am never hampered with this sort of *impedimenta.* "Let the dead past bury its dead!"[5] has been one of my cherished mottoes. The duty of the hour, the work of the "living present," has enthralled me, rather than contemplation of the past. But, in this instance, what I have been careless of preserving, my kindred and friends have held in trust for me.

For more than a dozen years, covering the entire period of the war, I was associated with my husband in the editorship of his paper, published in Chicago. For its columns I wrote sketches of all events, that were interesting or inspiring, in connection with the Sanitary Commission. Its readers were informed of every phase of its relief work, as soon as it was undertaken, and of its special calls for aid. And when I went to the hospitals on errands connected with the sick, wounded and dying, or made trips into the army in charge of sanitary stores, for whose disbursement I was held responsible, I always corresponded for the press. And no issue of my husband's paper appeared, when I was thus engaged, that did not contain long letters from the front, packed with narrations of facts and events, for which I knew its readers were eagerly looking.

I sent similar letters to other periodicals in the Northwest, wrote war sketches for magazines struggling for existence, edited the monthly bulletins of the Chicago Branch of the Commission, which were its means of communication with its four thousand Aid Societies, wrote its circular letters appealing for specific and immediate aid, wrote for its contributors a detailed history of the first great Sanitary Fair, which proved the inspiration and model of those which followed it, dictated and penned letters by the thousand from the rooms of the Commission, which were inspired by the emergencies of the time, and which have been largely preserved by the individuals and societies to whom they were addressed, answered every soldier's letter that I received, whether I had ever heard of him or not, wrote letters by the hundred to their friends at home, by the bedside of sick, wounded and dying soldiers, and in behalf of those who had died—in short, notwithstanding the herculean[6] work imposed on me, as on all women at the head of the Branch Commissions, I

5. From "A Psalm of Life" (1839) by Henry Wadsworth Longfellow. "Living present" is also a quote from the poem.

6. From the Greek mythological hero, Heracles, who embodied great strength and virile masculinity.

accomplished more with my pen during the four years of the war than during any similar period of time before or since.

Whatever of mine was published, or whatever related to my work during the war, my husband preserved in chronological order, as he did all memoranda or diaries made by me. And whatever letters came to me from the army, or from civilians working in the interest of the country, he saved from destruction. When to these were added my personal letters to friends, which after twenty years were returned, in response to an appeal for them, copies of circulars, bulletins, reports, crude magazine sketches, synopses of addresses, all inspired by the one absorbing topic of the time—the war for the Union, and its brave soldiers, with their anxious and suffering families,—I was embarrassed by the enormous bulk of the collection. It was no small task to collate and arrange the appalling mass of documents, and to decide what would be of present interest, and what had been made valueless by the lapse of years.

At last the book is completed, and is now presented to the public. In no sense does it purport to be a history. It is a collection of experiences and reminiscences, more interesting to me in the retrospect than at the time of their occurrence. For then all who loved their native land, and strove to save it from disintegration, carried its woes on their hearts like a personal bereavement, and only lived through the awful anguish by the help of the mighty panacea of absorbing work for others. No one is more keenly alive than I to the defects of this volume. But any farther attempt at improvement would result, I fear, in its entire withdrawal. And as I have something to say in behalf of the common soldiers, most of them veritable Philip Sidneys[7] in their heroism and unselfishness, and of that noble army of women who worked untiringly for the right, while the war lasted, "exerting a greater moral force on the nation than the army that carried loaded muskets,"[8] I hasten to save my work from destruction, by placing it beyond my reach, in the hands of the publisher.

May it receive a warm welcome from the "Boys in Blue,"[9] whose thinning ranks can never know an increase, and from my surviving co-workers in the Sanitary Commission, whose beloved comradeship is one of the priceless possessions of which the covetous years have not wholly bereft me.

Source: My Story of the War: A Woman's Narrative of Four Years' Personal Experience As Nurse in the Union Army, and in Relief Work at Home, in Hospitals, Camps, and at the Front, During the War of Rebellion (1890)

---

7. Philip Sidney (1554–1586) was an important author as well as a loyal courtier during the reign of Elizabeth I.

8. Bellows, introduction to *Woman's Work in the Civil War.*

9. Union soldiers wore blue uniforms.

Best known for her stories of impoverished New England women, Mary Wilkins grew up in Massachusetts during years of declining prosperity. After her sister's and her mother's deaths, she began to write in 1880 and supported herself by her pen until she married Charles Manning Freeman in 1902. Their marriage, although initially happy, turned sour as he resumed his heavy drinking. They separated in 1922. Mary Wilkins Freeman's reputation as one of the foremost American authors of her day suffered in later years when she wrote supernatural and historical romance fiction. Nonetheless, in 1926 she was one of the first women admitted to the National Institute of Arts and Letters, and upon her death the Academy of Arts and Sciences dedicated its bronze doors to "Mary E. Wilkins Freeman and the Women Writers of America." "The Poetess" celebrates, as does Elizabeth Stoddard's "Collected by a Valetudinarian," the solitude of the woman writer devoted to her craft. Yet Freeman's story focuses on a sentimental poet who takes to heart the disdain of the male literary elite, here represented by her minister.

A Poetess

The garden-patch at the right of the house was all a gay spangle with sweet-pease and red-flowering beans, and flanked with feathery asparagus. A woman in blue was moving about there. Another woman, in a black bonnet, stood at the front door of the house. She knocked and waited. She could not see from where she stood the blue-clad woman in the garden. The house was very close to the road, from which a tall evergreen hedge separated it, and the view to the side was in a measure cut off.

The front door was open; the woman had to reach to knock on it, as it swung into the entry. She was a small woman and quite young, with a bright alertness about her which had almost the effect of prettiness. It was to her what greenness and crispness are to a plant. She poked her little face forward, and her sharp pretty eyes took in the entry and a room at the left, of which the door stood open. The entry was small and square and unfurnished, except for a well-rubbed old card-table against the back wall. The room was full of green light from the tall hedge, and bristling with grasses and flowers and asparagus stalks.

"Betsey, you there?" called the woman. When she spoke, a yellow canary, whose cage hung beside the front door, began to chirp and twitter.

"Betsey, you there?" the woman called again. The bird's chirps came in a quick volley; then he began to trill and sing.

"She ain't there," said the woman. She turned and went out of the yard through the gap in the hedge; then she looked around. She caught sight of the blue figure in the garden. "There she is," said she.

She went around the house to the garden. She wore a gay cashmere-patterned calico dress with her mourning bonnet, and she held it carefully away from the dewy grass and vines.

The other woman did not notice her until she was close to her and said, "Good-mornin', Betsey." Then she started and turned around.

"Why, Mis' Caxton! That you?" said she.

"Yes. I've been standin' at your door for the last half-hour. I was jest goin' away when I caught sight of you out here."

In spite of her brisk speech her manner was subdued. She drew down the corners of her mouth sadly.

"I declare I'm dreadful sorry you had to stan' there so long!" said the other woman.

She set a pan partly filled with beans on the ground, wiped her hands, which were damp and green from the wet vines, on her apron, then extended her right one with a solemn and sympathetic air.

"It don't make much odds, Betsey," replied Mrs. Caxton. "I ain't got much to take up my time nowadays." She sighed heavily as she shook hands, and the other echoed her.

"We'll go right in now. I'm dreadful sorry you stood there so long," said Betsey.

"You'd better finish pickin' your beans."

"No; I wa'n't goin' to pick any more. I was jest goin' in."

"I declare, Betsey Dole, I shouldn't think you'd got enough for a cat!" said Mrs. Caxton, eying the pan.

"I've got pretty near all there is. I guess I've got more flowerin' beans than eatin' ones, anyway."

"I should think you had," said Mrs. Caxton, surveying the row of bean poles topped with swarms of delicate red flowers. "I should think they were pretty near all flowerin' ones. Had any pease?"

"I didn't have more'n three or four messes. I guess I planted sweet-pease mostly. I don't know hardly how I happened to."

"Had any summer squash?"

"Two or three. There's some more set, if they ever get ripe. I planted some gourds. I think they look real pretty on the kitchen shelf in the winter."

"I should think you'd got a sage bed big enough for the whole town."

"Well, I have got a pretty good sized one. I always liked them blue sage-blows. You'd better hold up your dress real careful goin' through here, Mis' Caxton, or you'll get it wet."

The two women picked their way through the dewy grass, around a corner of the hedge, and Betsey ushered her visitor into the house.

"Set right down in the rockin-chair," said she. "I'll jest carry these beans out into the kitchen."

"I should think you'd better get another pan and string 'em, or you won't get 'em done for dinner."

"Well, mebbe I will, if you'll excuse it, Mis' Caxton. The beans had ought to boil quite a while; they're pretty old."

Betsey went into the kitchen and returned with a pan and an old knife. She seated herself opposite Mrs. Caxton, and began to string and cut the beans.

"If I was in your place I shouldn't feel as if I'd got enough to boil a kettle for," said Mrs. Caxton, eying the beans. "I should 'most have thought when you didn't have any more room for a garden than you've got that you'd planted more real beans and pease instead of so many flowerin' ones. I'd rather have a good mess of green pease boiled with a piece of salt pork than all the sweet-pease you could give me. I like flowers well enough, but I never set up for a butterfly, an' I want some thing else to live on." She looked at Betsey with pensive superiority.

Betsey was near-sighted; she had to bend low over the beans in order to string them. She was fifty years old, but she wore her streaky light hair in curls like a young girl. The curls hung over her faded cheeks and almost concealed them. Once in a while she flung them back with a childish gesture which sat strangely upon her.

"I dare say you're in the rights of it," she said, meekly.

"I know I am. You folks that write poetry wouldn't have a single thing to eat growin' if they were left alone. And that brings to mind what I come for. I've been thinkin' about it ever since—our—little Willie—left us." Mrs. Caxton's manner was suddenly full of shamefaced dramatic fervor, her eyes reddened with tears.

Betsey looked up inquiringly, throwing back her curls. Her face took on unconsciously lines of grief so like the other woman's that she looked like her for the minute.

"I thought maybe," Mrs. Caxton went on, tremulously, "you'd be willin' to—write a few lines."

"Of course I will, Mis' Caxton. I'll be glad to, if I can do 'em to suit you," Betsey said, tearfully.

"I thought jest a few—lines. You could mention how—handsome he was, and good, and I never had to punish him but once in his life, and how pleased he was with his little new suit, and what a sufferer he was, and—how we hope he is at rest—in a better land."

"I'll try, Mis' Caxton, I'll try," sobbed Betsey. The two women wept together for a few minutes.

"It seems as if—I couldn't have it so sometimes," Mrs. Caxton said, brokenly. "I keep thinkin' he's in the other—room. Every time I go back home when I've been away it's like—losin' him again. Oh, it don't seem as if I could go home and not find him there—it don't, it don't! Oh, you don't know anything about it, Betsey. You never had any children!"

"I don't s'pose I do, Mis' Caxton; I don't s'pose I do."

Presently Mrs. Caxton wiped her eyes. "I've been thinkin'," said she, keeping her mouth steady with an effort, "that it would be real pretty to have—some lines printed on some sheets of white paper with a neat black border. I'd like to send some to my folks, and one to the Perkinses in Brigham, and there's a good many others I thought would value 'em."

"I'll do jest the best I can, Mis' Caxton, an' be glad to. It's little enough anybody can do at such times."

Mrs. Caxton broke out weeping again. "Oh, it's true, it's true, Betsey!" she sobbed. "Nobody can do anything, and nothin' amounts to anything—poetry or anything else—when he's *gone*. Nothin' can bring him back. Oh, what shall I do, what shall I do?"

Mrs. Caxton dried her tears again, and arose to take leave. "Well, I must be goin', or Wilson won't have any dinner," she said, with an effort at self-control.

"Well, I'll do jest the best I can with the poetry," said Betsey. "I'll write it this afternoon." She had set down her pan of beans and was standing beside Mrs. Caxton. She reached up and straightened her black bonnet, which had slipped backward.

"I've got to get a pin," said Mrs. Caxton, tearfully. "I can't keep it anywheres. It drags right off my head, the veil is so heavy."

Betsey went to the door with her visitor. "It's dreadful dusty, ain't it?" she remarked, in that sad, contemptuous tone with which one speaks of discomforts in the presence of affliction.

"Terrible," replied Mrs. Caxton. "I wouldn't wear my black dress in it nohow; a black bonnet is bad enough. This dress is 'most too good. It's enough to spoil everything. Well, I'm much obliged to you, Betsey, for bein' willin' to do that."

"I'll do jest the best I can, Mis' Caxton."

After Betsey had watched her visitor out of the yard she returned to the sitting-room and took up the pan of beans. She looked doubtfully at the handful of beans all nicely strung and cut up. "I declare I don't know what to do," said she. "Seems as if I should kind of relish these, but it's goin' to take some time to cook 'em, tendin' the fire an' everything, an' I'd ought to go to work on that poetry. Then, there's another thing, if I have 'em to-day, I can't to-morrow. Mebbe I shall take more comfort thinkin' about 'em. I guess I'll leave 'em over till to-morrow."

Betsey carried the pan of beans out into the kitchen and set them away in the pantry. She stood scrutinizing the shelves like a veritable Mother Hubbard. There was a plate containing three or four potatoes and a slice of cold boiled pork, and a spoonful of red jelly in a tumbler; that was all the food in sight. Betsey stooped and lifted the lid from an earthen jar on the floor. She took out two slices of bread. "There!" said she. "I'll have this bread and that jelly this noon, an' to-night I'll have a kind of dinner-supper with them potatoes warmed up with the pork. An' then I can sit right down an' go to work on that poetry."

It was scarcely eleven o'clock, and not time for dinner. Betsey returned to the sitting-room, got an old black portfolio and pen and ink out of the chimney cupboard, and seated herself to work. She meditated, and wrote one line, then another. Now and then she read aloud what she had written with a solemn intonation. She sat there thinking and writing, and the time went on. The twelve-o'clock bell rang, but she never noticed it; she had quite forgotten the bread and jelly. The long curls drooped over her cheeks; her thin yellow hand, cramped around the pen, moved slowly and fitfully over the paper. The light in the room was dim and green, like the light in an arbor, from the tall hedge before the windows. Great plumy bunches of asparagus waved over the tops of the looking-glass; a framed sampler,[1] a steel engraving of a female head taken from some old magazine, and sheaves of dried grasses hung on or were fastened to the walls; vases and tumblers of flowers stood on the shelf and table. The air was heavy and sweet.

Betsey in this room, bending over her portfolio, looked like the very genius of gentle, old-fashioned, sentimental poetry. It seemed as if one, given the premises of herself and the room, could easily deduce what she would write, and read without seeing those lines wherein flowers rhymed sweetly with vernal bowers, home with beyond the tomb, and heaven with even.

The summer afternoon wore on. It grew warmer and closer; the air was full of the rasping babble of insects, with the cicadas shrilling over them; now and then a team passed, and a dust cloud floated over the top of the hedge; the canary at the door chirped and trilled, and Betsey wrote poor little Willie Caxton's obituary poetry.

Tears stood in her pale blue eyes; occasionally they rolled down her cheeks, and she wiped them away. She kept her handkerchief in her lap with her portfolio. When she looked away from the paper she seemed to see two childish forms in the room—one purely human, a boy clad in his little girl petticoats, with a fair chubby face; the other in a little straight white night-gown, with long, shining wings, and the same face. Betsey had not enough imagination to change the face. Little Willie Caxton's angel was still himself to her, although decked in the paraphernalia of the resurrection.

"I s'pose I can't feel about it nor write about it anything the way I could if I'd had any children of my own an' lost 'em. I s'pose it *would* have come home to me different," Betsey murmured once, sniffing. A soft color flamed up under her curls at the thought. For a second the room seemed all aslant with white wings, and smiling with the faces of children that had never been. Betsey straightened herself as if she were trying to be dignified to her inner consciousness. "That's one trouble I've been clear of, anyhow," said she; "an' I guess I can enter into her feelin's considerable."

1. Earlier in the century, young women were taught to embroider decorative samplers, which often included the alphabet and religious or moral sayings, as proof of their skill with the needle.

She glanced at a great pink shell on the shelf, and remembered how she had often given it to the dead child to play with when he had been in with his mother, and how he had put it to his ear to hear the sea.

"Dear little fellow!" she sobbed, and sat awhile with her handkerchief at her face.

Betsey wrote her poem upon backs of old letters and odd scraps of paper. She found it difficult to procure enough paper for fair copies of her poems when composed; she was forced to be very economical with the first draft. Her portfolio was piled with a loose litter of written papers when she at length arose and stretched her stiff limbs. It was near sunset; men with dinner-pails were tramping past the gate, going home from their work.

Betsey laid the portfolio on the table. "There! I've wrote sixteen verses," said she, "an' I guess I've got everything in. I guess she'll think that's enough. I can copy it off nice to-morrow. I can't see to-night to do it, anyhow."

There were red spots on Betsey's cheeks; her knees were unsteady when she walked. She went into the kitchen and made a fire, and set on the tea-kettle. "I guess I won't warm up them potatoes to-night," said she; "I'll have the bread an' jelly, an' save 'em for breakfast. Somehow I don't seem to feel so much like 'em as I did, an' fried potatoes is apt to lay heavy at night."

When the kettle boiled, Betsey drank her cup of tea and soaked her slice of bread in it; then she put away her cup and saucer and plate, and went out to water her garden. The weather was so dry and hot it had to be watered every night. Betsey had to carry the water from a neighbor's well: her own was dry. Back and forth she went in the deepening twilight, her slender body strained to one side with the heavy water pail, until the garden-mould looked dark and wet. Then she took in the canary-bird, locked up her house, and soon her light went out. Often on these summer nights Betsey went to bed without lighting a lamp at all. There was no moon, but it was a beautiful starlight night. She lay awake nearly all night, thinking over her poem. She altered several lines in her mind.

She arose early, made herself a cup of tea, and warmed over the potatoes, then sat down to copy the poem. She wrote it out on both sides of note-paper, in a neat, cramped hand. It was the middle of the afternoon before it was finished. She had been obliged to stop work and cook the beans for dinner, although she begrudged the time. When the poem was fairly copied, she rolled it neatly and tied it with a bit of black ribbon; then she made herself ready to carry it to Mrs. Caxton's.

It was a hot afternoon. Betsey went down the street in her thinnest dress—an old delaine, with delicate bunches of faded flowers on a faded green ground. There was a narrow green belt ribbon around her long waist. She wore a green barége bonnet, stiffened with rattans, scooping over her face, with her curls pushed forward over her thin cheeks in two bunches, and she carried a small green parasol with a jointed handle. Her costume was obsolete, even in the little country village where she lived. She had worn it every summer for the last twenty years. She made no more change in her attire than the old perennials in her garden. She had no money with which to buy new clothes, and the old satisfied her. She had come to regard them as being as unalterably a part of herself as her body.

Betsey went on, setting her slim, cloth-gaitered feet daintily in the hot sand of the road. She carried her roll of poetry in a black-mitted hand. She walked rather slowly. She was not very strong; there was a limp feeling in her knees; her face, under the green shade of her bonnet, was pale and moist with the heat.

She was glad to reach Mrs. Caxton's and sit down in her parlor, damp and cool and dark as twilight, for the blinds and curtains had been drawn all day. Not a breath of the fervid out-door air had penetrated it.

"Come right in this way; it's cooler than the sittin'-room," Mrs. Caxton said; and Betsey sank into the hair-cloth rocker and waved a palm-leaf fan.

Mrs. Caxton sat close to the window in the dim light, and read the poem. She took out her handkerchief and wiped her eyes as she read. "It's beautiful, beautiful," she said, tearfully, when she had finished. "It's jest as comfortin' as it can be, and you worked that in about his new suit so nice. I feel real obliged to you, Betsey, and you shall have one of the printed ones when they're done. I'm goin' to see to it right off."

Betsey flushed and smiled. It was to her as if her poem had been approved and accepted by one of the great magazines. She had the pride and self-wonderment of recognized genius. She went home buoyantly, under the wilting sun, after her call was done. When she reached home there was no one to whom she could tell her triumph, but the hot spicy breath of the evergreen hedge and the fervent sweetness of the sweet-pease seemed to greet her like the voices of friends.

She could scarcely wait for the printed poem. Mrs. Caxton brought it, and she inspected it, neatly printed in its black border. She was quite overcome with innocent pride.

"Well, I don't know but it does read pretty well," said she.

"It's beautiful," said Mrs. Caxton, fervently. "Mr. White said he never read anything any more touchin', when I carried it to him to print. I think folks are goin' to think a good deal of havin' it. I've had two dozen printed."

It was to Betsey like a large edition of a book. She had written obituary poems before, but never one had been printed in this sumptuous fashion. "I declare I think it would look pretty framed!" said she.

"Well, I don't know but it would," said Mrs. Caxton. "Anybody might have a neat little black frame, and it would look real appropriate."

"I wonder how much it would cost?" said Betsey.

After Mrs. Caxton had gone, she sat long, staring admiringly at the poem, and speculating as to the cost of a frame. "There ain't no use; I can't have it nohow, not if it don't cost more'n a quarter of a dollar," said she.

Then she put the poem away and got her supper. Nobody knew how frugal Betsey Dole's suppers and breakfasts and dinners were. Nearly all her food in the summer came from the scanty vegetables which flourished between the flowers in her garden. She ate scarcely more than her canary-bird, and sang as assiduously. Her income was almost infinitesimal: the interest at a low per cent. of a tiny sum in the village savings-bank, the remnant of her father's little hoard after his funeral expenses had been paid. Betsey had lived upon it for twenty years, and considered herself well-to-do. She had never received a cent for her poems; she had not thought of such a thing as possible. The appearance of this last in such shape was worth more to her than its words represented in as many dollars.

Betsey kept the poem pinned on the wall under the looking-glass; if any one came in, she tried with delicate hints to call attention to it. It was two weeks after she received it that the downfall of her innocent pride came.

One afternoon Mrs. Caxton called. It was raining hard. Betsey could scarcely believe it was she when she went to the door and found her standing there.

"Why, Mis' Caxton!" said she. "Ain't you wet to your skin?"

"Yes, I guess I be, pretty near. I s'pose I hadn't ought to come 'way down here in such a soak; but I went into Sarah Rogers's a minute after dinner, and something she said made me so mad, I made up my mind I'd come down here and tell you about it if I got drowned." Mrs. Caxton was out of breath; rain-drops trickled from her hair over her face; she stood in the door and shut her umbrella with a vicious shake to scatter the water from it. "I don't know what you're goin' to do with this," said she; "it's drippin'."

"I'll take it out an' put it in the kitchen sink."

"Well, I'll take off my shawl here too, and you can hang it out in the kitchen. I spread this shawl out. I thought it would keep the rain off me some. I know one thing, I'm goin' to have a water-proof if I live."

When the two women were seated in the sitting-room, Mrs. Caxton was quiet for a moment. There was a hesitating look on her face, fresh with the moist wind, with strands of wet hair clinging to the temples.

"I don't know as I had ought to tell you," she said, doubtfully.

"Why hadn't you ought to?"

"Well, I don't care; I'm goin' to, anyhow. I think you'd ought to know, an' it ain't so bad for you as it is for me. It don't begin to be. I put considerable money into 'em. I think Mr. White was pretty high, myself."

Betsey looked scared. "What is it?" she asked, in a weak voice.

"*Sarah Rogers says that the minister told her Ida that that poetry you wrote was jest as poor as it could be, an' it was in dreadful bad taste to have it printed an' sent round that way.* What do you think of that?"

Betsey did not reply. She sat looking at Mrs. Caxton as a victim whom the first blow had not killed might look at her executioner. Her face was like a pale wedge of ice between her curls.

Mrs. Caxton went on. "Yes, she said that right to my face, word for word. An' there was something else. She said the minister said that you had never wrote anything that could be called poetry, an' it was a dreadful waste of time. I don't s'pose he thought 'twas comin' back to you. You know he goes with Ida Rogers, an' I s'pose he said it to her kind of confidential when she showed him the poetry. There! I gave Sarah Rogers one of them nice printed ones, an' she acted glad enough to have it. Bad taste! H'm! If anybody wants to say anything against that beautiful poetry, printed with that nice black border, they can. I don't care if it's the minister, or who it is. I don't care if he does write poetry himself, an' has had some printed in a magazine. Maybe his ain't quite so fine as he thinks 'tis. Maybe them magazine folks jest took his for lack of something better. I'd like to have you send that poetry there. Bad taste! I jest got right up. 'Sarah Rogers,' says I, 'I hope you won't never do anything your self in any worse taste.' I trembled so I could hardly speak, and I made up my mind I'd come right straight over here."

Mrs. Caxton went on and on. Betsey sat listening, and saying nothing. She looked ghastly. Just before Mrs. Caxton went home she noticed it. "Why, Betsey Dole," she cried, "you look as white as a sheet. You ain't takin' it to heart as much as all that comes to, I hope. Goodness, I wish I hadn't told you!"

"I'd a good deal ruther you told me," replied Betsey, with a certain dignity. She looked at Mrs. Caxton. Her back was as stiff as if she were bound to a stake.

"Well, I thought you would," said Mrs. Caxton, uneasily; "and you're dreadful silly if you take it to heart, Betsey, that's all I've got to say. Goodness, I guess I don't, and it's full as hard on me as 'tis on you!"

Mrs. Caxton arose to go. Betsey brought her shawl and umbrella from the kitchen, and helped her off. Mrs. Caxton turned on the door-step and looked back at Betsey's white face. "Now don't go to thinkin' about it any more," said she. "I ain't goin' to. It ain't worth mindin'. Everybody knows what Sarah Rogers is. Good-by."

"Good-by, Mis' Caxton," said Betsey. She went back into the sitting-room. It was a cold rain, and the room was gloomy and chilly. She stood looking out of the window, watching the rain pelt on the hedge. The bird-cage hung at the other window. The bird watched her with his head on one side; then he begun to chirp.

Suddenly Betsey faced about, and began talking. It was not as if she were talking to herself; it seemed as if she recognized some other presence in the room. "I'd like to know if it's fair," said she. "I'd like to know if you think it's fair. Had I ought to have been born with the wantin' to write poetry if I couldn't write it—had I? Had I ought to have been let to write all my life, an' not know before there wa'n't any use in it? Would it be fair if that canary-bird there, that 'ain't never done anything but sing, should turn out not to be singin'? Would it, I'd like to know? S'pose them sweet-pease shouldn't be smellin' the right way? I ain't been dealt with as fair as they have. I'd like to know if I have."

The bird trilled and trilled. It was as if the golden down on his throat bubbled. Betsey went across the room to a cupboard beside the chimney. On the shelves were neatly stacked newspapers and little white rolls of writing-paper. Betsey began clearing the shelves. She took out the newspapers first, got the scissors, and cut a poem neatly out of the corners of each. Then she took up the clipped poems and the white rolls in her apron, and carried them into the kitchen. She cleaned out the stove carefully, removing every trace of ashes; then she put in the papers, and set them on fire. She stood watching them as their edges curled and blackened, then leaped into flame. Her face twisted as if the fire were curling over it also. Other women might have burned their lovers' letters in agony of heart. Betsey had never had any lover, but she was burning all the love-letters that had passed between her and life. When the flames died out she got a blue china sugar-bowl from the pantry and dipped the ashes into it with one of her thin silver teaspoons; then she put on the cover and set it away in the sitting-room cupboard.

The bird, who had been silent while she was out, began chirping again. Betsey went back to the pantry and got a lump of sugar, which she stuck between the cage wires. She looked at the clock on the kitchen shelf as she went by. It was after six. "I guess I don't want any supper to-night," she muttered.

She sat down by the window again. The bird pecked at his sugar. Betsey shivered and coughed. She had coughed more or less for years. People said she had the old-fashioned consumption.[2] She sat at the window until it was quite dark; then she went to bed in her little bedroom out of the sitting-room. She shivered so she could not hold herself upright crossing the room. She coughed a great deal in the night.

Betsey was always an early riser. She was up at five the next morning. The sun shone, but it was very cold for the season. The leaves showed white in a north wind, and the flowers looked brighter than usual, though they were bent with the rain of the day before. Betsey went out in the garden to straighten her sweet-pease.

Coming back, a neighbor passing in the street eyed her curiously. "Why, Betsey, you sick?" said she.

"No; I'm kinder chilly, that's all," replied Betsey.

But the woman went home and reported that Betsey Dole looked dreadfully, and she didn't believe she'd ever see another summer.

It was now late August. Before October it was quite generally recognized that Betsey Dole's life was nearly over. She had no relatives, and hired nurses were rare in this little village. Mrs. Caxton came voluntarily and took care of her, only going

2. Tuberculosis.

home to prepare her husband's meals. Betsey's bed was moved into the sitting-room, and the neighbors came every day to see her, and brought little delicacies. Betsey had talked very little all her life; she talked less now, and there was a reticence about her which somewhat intimidated the other women. They would look pityingly and solemnly at her, and whisper in the entry when they went out.

Betsey never complained; but she kept asking if the minister had got home. He had been called away by his mother's illness, and returned only a week before Betsey died.

He came over at once to see her. Mrs. Caxton ushered him in one afternoon.

"Here's Mr. Lang come to see you, Betsey," said she, in the tone she would have used toward a little child. She placed the rocking-chair for the minister, and was about to seat herself, when Betsey spoke:

"Would you mind goin' out in the kitchen jest a few minutes, Mis' Caxton?" said she.

Mrs. Caxton arose, and went out with an embarrassed trot. Then there was silence. The minister was a young man—a country boy who had worked his way through a country college. He was gaunt and awkward, but sturdy in his loose black clothes. He had a homely, impetuous face, with a good forehead.

He looked at Betsey's gentle, wasted face sunken in the pillow, framed by its clusters of curls; finally he began to speak in the stilted fashion, yet with a certain force by reason of his unpolished honesty, about her spiritual welfare. Betsey listened quietly; now and then she assented. She had been a church member for years. It seemed new to the young man that this elderly maiden, drawing near the end of her simple, innocent life, had indeed her lamp, which no strong winds of temptation had ever met, well trimmed and burning.[3]

When he paused, Betsey spoke. "Will you go to the cupboard side of the chimney and bring me the blue sugar-bowl on the top shelf?" said she, feebly.

The young man stared at her a minute; then he went to the cupboard, and brought the sugar-bowl to her. He held it, and Betsey took off the lid with her weak hand. "Do you see what's in there?" said she.

"It looks like ashes."

"It's—the ashes of all—the poetry I—ever wrote."

"Why, what made you burn it, Miss Dole?"

"I found out it wa'n't worth nothin'."

The minister looked at her in a bewildered way. He began to question if she were not wandering in her mind. He did not once suspect his own connection with the matter.

3. In Matthew 25.1–13, the parable of the ten maidens, Jesus compares the soul's readiness for salvation to the ten virgins who awaited the arrival of the bridegroom. Those who wasted their oil went to buy more and missed him. Those who kept their wicks trimmed were ready to meet him.

Betsey fastened her eager, sunken eyes upon his face. "What I want to know is—if you'll 'tend to—havin' this—buried with me."

The minister recoiled. He thought to himself that she certainly was wandering.

"No, I ain't out of my head," said Betsey. "I know what I'm sayin'. Maybe it's queer soundin', but it's a notion I've took. If you'll—'tend to it, I shall be—much obliged. I don't know anybody else I can ask."

"Well, I'll attend to it, if you wish me to, Miss Dole," said the minister, in a serious, perplexed manner. She replaced the lid on the sugar-bowl, and left it in his hands.

"Well, I shall be much obliged if you will 'tend to it; an' now there's something else," said she.

"What is it, Miss Dole?"

She hesitated a moment. "You write poetry, don't you?"

The minister colored. "Why, yes; a little sometimes."

"It's good poetry, ain't it? They printed some in a magazine."

The minister laughed confusedly. "Well, Miss Dole, I don't know how good poetry it may be, but they did print some in a magazine."

Betsey lay looking at him. "I never wrote none that was—good," she whispered, presently; "but I've been thinkin'—if you would jest write a few—lines about me—afterward— I've been thinkin' that—mebbe my—dyin' was goin' to make me—a good subject for—poetry, if I never wrote none. If you would jest write a few lines."

The minister stood holding the sugar-bowl; he was quite pale with bewilderment and sympathy. "I'll—do the best I can, Miss Dole," he stammered.

"I'll be much obliged," said Betsey, as if the sense of grateful obligation was immortal like herself. She smiled, and the sweetness of the smile was as evident through the drawn lines of her mouth as the old red in the leaves of a withered rose. The sun was setting; a red beam flashed softly over the top of the hedge and lay along the opposite wall; then the bird in his cage began to chirp. He chirped faster and faster until he trilled into a triumphant song.

Source: Harper's New Monthly Magazine (1890)

❧ ANNA JULIA COOPER (1858–1964)

Anna Julia Haywood was born a slave in Raleigh, North Carolina. After emancipation, at the age of nine, she received a scholarship to attend a school for freed slaves, eventually graduating from Oberlin College in 1884 and earning a Ph.D. from the University of Paris in 1924. Throughout her life she was a lecturer and social activist, as well as a dedicated teacher at the high school and college levels. She married George A. Cooper in 1877, but he died in 1879, and she remained single for the rest of her life so that she could continue her teaching (married women had to give up their posts). She was a prominent proponent of civil rights, a theme explored in her seminal work A Voice From the South, *which includes an argument for the pivotal role of African American women in racial progress as well as an assessment of race in American literature, an excerpt of which is included here.*

Our Raison D'Être[1]

In the clash and clatter of our American Conflict, it has been said that the South remains Silent. Like the Sphinx[2] she inspires vociferous disputation, but herself takes little part in the noisy controversy. One muffled strain in the Silent South, a jarring chord and a vague and uncomprehended cadenza has been and still is the Negro. And of that muffled chord, the one mute and voiceless note has been the sadly expectant Black Woman,

> An infant crying in the night,
> An infant crying for the light;
> And with *no language—but a cry.*[3]

The colored man's inheritance and apportionment is still the sombre crux, the perplexing *cul de sac*[4] of the nation,—the dumb skeleton in the closet provoking ceaseless harangues, indeed, but little understood and seldom consulted. Attorneys for the plaintiff and attorneys for the defendant, with bungling *gaucherie*[5] have analyzed and dissected, theorized and synthesized with sublime ignorance or pathetic misapprehension of counsel from the black client. One important witness has not yet been heard from. The summing up of the evidence deposed, and the charge to the jury have been made—but no word from the Black Woman.

---

1. French: reason for existence.
2. The Great Sphinx of Giza in Egypt, a statue of a lion with a human head. The mystery of its meaning persists.
3. Lines from Alfred Lord Tennyson's "In Memoriam" (1850).
4. French: impasse or dead end.
5. French: tactless or awkward act.

It is because I believe the American people to be conscientiously committed to a fair trial and ungarbled evidence, and because I feel it essential to a perfect understanding and an equitable verdict that truth from *each* standpoint be presented at the bar,—that this little Voice, has been added to the already full chorus. The "other side" has not been represented by one who "lives there." And not many can more sensibly realize and more accurately tell the weight and the fret of the "long dull pain" than the open-eyed but hitherto voiceless Black Woman of America.

The feverish agitation, the perfervid energy, the busy objectivity of the more turbulent life of our men serves, it may be, at once to cloud or color their vision somewhat, and as well to relieve the smart and deaden the pain for them. Their voice is in consequence not always temperate and calm, and at the same time radically corrective and sanatory. At any rate, as our Caucasian barristers are not to blame if they cannot *quite* put themselves in the dark man's place, neither should the dark man be wholly expected fully and adequately to reproduce the exact Voice of the Black Woman.

Delicately sensitive at every pore to social atmospheric conditions, her calorimeter may well be studied in the interest of accuracy and fairness in diagnosing what is often conceded to be a "puzzling" case. If these broken utterances can in any way help to a clearer vision and a truer pulse-beat in studying our Nation's Problem, this Voice by a Black Woman of the South will not have been raised in vain.

The Negro as Presented in American Literature

. . . By a rough classification, authors may be separated into two groups: first, those in whom the artistic or poetic instinct is uppermost—those who write to please— or rather who write because *they* please; who simply paint what they see, as naturally, as instinctively, and as irresistibly as the bird sings—with no thought of an audience—singing because it loves to sing,—singing because God, nature, truth sings through it. For such writers, to be true to themselves and true to Nature is the only canon.[6] They cannot warp a character or distort a fact in order to prove a point. They have nothing to prove. All who care to, may listen while they make the woods resound with their glad sweet carolling; and the listeners may draw their own conclusions as to the meaning of the cadences of this minor strain, or that hushed and almost awful note of rage or despair. And the myriad-minded multitude attribute their myriad-fold impressions to the myriad-minded soul by which they have severally been enchanted, each in his own way according to what he brings to the witching auditorium. But the singer sings on with his hat before his face, unmindful, it may be unconscious, of the varied strains reproduced from him

6. Law.

in the multitudinous echoes of the crowd. Such was Shakespeare, such was George Eliot, such was Robert Browning. Such, in America, was Poe, was Bryant, was Longfellow; and such, in his own degree perhaps, is Mr. Howells.[7]

In the second group belong the preachers,—whether of righteousness or unrighteousness,—all who have an idea to propagate, no matter in what form their talent enables them to clothe it, whether poem, novel, or sermon,— all those writers with a purpose or a lesson, who catch you by the buttonhole and pommel you over the shoulder till you are forced to give assent in order to escape their vociferations; or they may lure you into listening with the soft music of the siren's tongue— no matter what the expedient to catch and hold your attention, they mean to fetter you with their one idea, whatever it is, and make you, if possible, ride their hobby. In this group I would place Milton in much of his writing, Carlyle in all of his, often our own Whittier, the great reformer-poet, and Lowell; together with such novelists as E. P. Roe, Bellamy, Tourgee[8] and some others.

Now in my judgment writings of the first class will be the ones to withstand the ravages of time. 'Isms' have their day and pass away. New necessities arise with new conditions and the emphasis has to be shifted to suit the times. No finite mind can grasp and give out the whole circle of truth. We do well if we can illuminate just the tiny arc which we occupy and should be glad that the next generation will not need the lessons we try so assiduously to hammer into this. In the evolution of society, as the great soul of humanity builds it "more lofty chambers," the old shell and slough of didactic teaching must be left behind and forgotten. . . .

Now owing to the problematical position at present occupied by descendants of Africans in the American social polity,—growing, I presume, out of the continued indecision in the mind of the more powerful descendants of the Saxons as to whether it is expedient to apply the maxims of their religion to their civil and political relationships,—most of the writers who have hitherto attempted a portrayal of life and customs among the darker race have belonged to our class II: they have all, more or less, had a point to prove or a mission to accomplish, and thus their art has been almost uniformly perverted to serve their ends; and, to add to their disadvantage, most, if not all the writers on this line have been but partially acquainted with the life they wished to delineate and through sheer ignorance oft-times, as well as from design occasionally, have not been able to put themselves in the darker man's place. The art of "thinking one's self imaginatively into the experi-

7. William Shakespeare (1594–1616); George Eliot, pen name of Marian Evans (1819–1880), British novelist; Robert Browning (1812–1889), British poet; Edgar Allan Poe (1809–1849), critic, poet, and fiction writer; William Cullen Bryant (1794–1878), poet; Henry Wadsworth Longfellow (1807–1882), poet; and William Dean Howells (1837–1920), critic and Realist writer.

8. John Milton (1608–1674), English poet; Thomas Carlyle (1795–1881), Scottish historian and essayist; John Greenleaf Whittier (1807–1892), American poet; James Russell Lowell (1819–1891), American poet and critic; Edward Payson Roe (1838–1888); Edward Bellamy (1850–1898); and Albion Tourgée (1838–1905).

ences of others" is not given to all, and it is impossible to acquire it without a background and a substratum of sympathetic knowledge. Without this power our portraits are but death's heads or caricatures and no amount of cudgeling can put into them the movement and reality of life. Not many have had Mrs. Stowe's power because not many have studied with Mrs. Stowe's humility and love. They forget that underneath the black man's form and behavior there is the great bed-rock of humanity, the key to which is the same that unlocks every tribe and kindred of the nations of earth. Some have taken up the subject with a view to establishing evidences of ready formulated theories and preconceptions; and, blinded by their prejudices and antipathies, have altogether abjured all candid and careful study. Others with flippant indifference have performed a few psychological experiments on their cooks and coachmen, and with astounding egotism, and powers of generalization positively bewildering, forthwith aspire to enlighten the world with dissertations on racial traits of the Negro. A few with really kind intentions and a sincere desire for information have approached the subject as a clumsy microscopist, not quite at home with his instrument, might study a new order of beetle or bug. Not having focused closely enough to obtain a clear-cut view, they begin by telling you that all colored people look exactly alike and end by noting down every chance contortion or idiosyncrasy as a race characteristic. . . .

After this cursory glance at a few contributions which have peculiarly emphasized one phase of our literature during the last decade or two, I am brought to the conclusion that an authentic portrait, at once aesthetic and true to life, presenting the black man as a free American citizen, not the humble slave of *Uncle Tom's Cabin*—but the *man,* divinely struggling and aspiring yet tragically warped and distorted by the adverse winds of circumstance, has not yet been painted. It is my opinion that the canvas awaits the brush of the colored man himself. It is a pathetic—a fearful arraignment of America's conditions of life, that instead of that enrichment from the years and days, the summers and springs under which, as Browning says,

"The flowers turn double and the leaves turn flowers,—"9

the black man's native and original flowers have in this country been all hardened and sharpened into thorns and spurs. In literature we have no artists for art's sake. Albery A. Whitman in *"Twasinta's Seminoles"* and *"Not a Man and Yet a Man"* is almost the only poet who has attempted a more sustained note than the lyrics of Mrs. Harper,10 and even that note is almost a wail.

The fact is, a sense of freedom in mind as well as in body is necessary to the appreciative and inspiring pursuit of the beautiful. A bird cannot warble out his

9. Line from Robert Browning's "Cleon" in *Men and Women* (1856).
10. Albery Allson Whitman (1851–1901) and Frances Harper (1825–1911), African American poets.

fullest and most joyous notes while the wires of his cage are pricking and cramping him at every heart beat. His tones become only the shrill and poignant protest of rage and despair. And so the black man's vexations and chafing environment, even since his physical emancipation has given him speech, has goaded him into the eloquence and fire of oratory rather than the genial warmth and cheery glow of either poetry or romance. And pity 'tis, 'tis true. A race that has produced for America the only folk-lore and folk songs of native growth, a race which has grown the most original and unique assemblage of fable and myth to be found on the continent, a race which has suggested and inspired almost the only distinctive American note which could chain the attention and charm the ear of the outside world—has as yet found no mouthpiece of its own to unify and perpetuate its wondrous whisperings—no painter-poet to distil in the alembic of his own imagination the gorgeous dyes, the luxuriant juices of this rich and tropical vegetation. It was the glory of Chaucer[11] that he justified the English language to itself—that he took the homely and hitherto despised Saxon elements and ideas, and lovingly wove them into an artistic product which even Norman conceit and uppishness might be glad to acknowledge and imitate. The only man who is doing the same for Negro folklore is one not to the manner born. Joel Chandler Harris[12] has made himself rich and famous by simply standing around among the black railroad hands and cotton pickers of the South and compiling the simple and dramatic dialogues which fall from their lips. What I hope to see before I die is a black man honestly and appreciatively portraying both the Negro as he is, and the white man, occasionally, as seen from the Negro's standpoint.

There is an old proverb "The devil is always painted *black*—by white painters." And what is needed, perhaps, to reverse the picture of the lordly man slaying the lion, is for the lion to turn painter.

Then too we need the calm clear judgment of ourselves and of others born of a disenchantment similar to that of a little girl I know in the South, who was once being laboriously held up over the shoulders of a surging throng to catch her first glimpse of a real live president. "Why Nunny," she cried half reproachfully, as she strained her little neck to see—"*It's nuffin but a man!*"

When we have been sized up and written down by others, we need not feel that the last word is said and the oracles sealed. "It's nuffin but a man." And there are many gifts the giftie may gie us, far better than seeing ourselves as others see us—and one is that of Bion's[13] maxim "*Know Thyself.*" Keep true to your own ideals. Be not ashamed of what is homely and your own. Speak out and speak honestly. Be

---

11. Geoffrey Chaucer (1340–1400), author of *The Canterbury Tales* (c. 1375–1400).

12. Joel Chandler Harris (1848–1908), white Southern author of the Uncle Remus stories.

13. "Gifts the giftie may gie us . . . ": adapted from Robert Burns's "To a Louse" (1786). Bion (ca. 335–ca. 245 B.C.), Greek philosopher.

true to yourself and to the message God and Nature meant you to deliver. The young David cannot fight in Saul's unwieldy armor.[14] Let him simply therefore gird his loins, take up his own parable and tell this would-be great American nation "*A chile's amang ye takin' notes;*"[15] and when men act the part of cowards or wild beasts, this great silent but open-eyed constituency has a standard by which they are being tried. Know thyself, and know those around at their true weight of solid intrinsic manhood without being dazzled by the fact that littleness of soul is often gilded with wealth, power and intellect. There can be no nobility but that of soul, and no catalogue of adventitious circumstances can wipe out the stain or palliate the meanness of inflicting one ruthless, cruel wrong. 'Tis not only safer, but nobler, grander, diviner,

> "To be that which we destroy
> Than, by destruction, dwell in doubtful joy."[16]

With this platform to stand on we can with clear eye weigh what is written and estimate what is done and ourselves paint what is true with the calm spirit of those who know their cause is right and who believe there is a God who judgeth the nations.

Source: A Voice from the South (1892)

14. David, a follower of King Saul in the Old Testament, killed Goliath with a single stone from his sling.
15. Line from Robert Burns, "Tam O' Shanter" (1789).
16. Shakespeare, *Macbeth* (ca. 1606).

E. Pauline Johnson (1861–1913)

Emily Pauline Johnson (Tekahionwake) was born in Ontario, Canada, to a Mohawk father and a white mother. According to John Gavin, editor of Canadian Poets *(1916), she "early showed a marked tendency towards the reading and writing of rhymes," although her formal education was limited. From 1892 to 1907, she supported herself by traveling throughout North America and England, performing plays and reciting her verse. She published three books of poetry as well as stories and travel essays in popular periodicals. Her poetry is celebrated in Canada to this day. In the following article, she laments the ways that Native American women had been stereotyped in literature, suggesting that voices like her own were needed to correct false impressions that had a damning effect on "the Redman[, who] has suffered enough."*

A Strong Race Opinion: On the Indian Girl in Modern Fiction

Every race in the world enjoys its own peculiar characteristics, but it scarcely follows that every individual of a nation must possess these prescribed singularities, or otherwise forfeit in the eyes of the world their nationality. Individual personality is one of the most charming things to be met with, either in the flesh and blood existence, or upon the pages of fiction, and it matters little to what race an author's heroine belongs, if he makes her character distinct, unique and natural.

The American book heroine of to-day is vari-colored as to personality and action. The author does not consider it necessary to the development of her character, and the plot of the story to insist upon her having American-colored eyes, an American carriage, an American voice, American motives, and an American mode of dying; he allows her to evolve an individuality ungoverned by nationalisms—but the outcome of impulse and nature and a general womanishness.

Not so the Indian girl in modern fiction, the author permits her character no such spontaneity, she must not be one of womankind at large, neither must she have an originality, a singularity that is not definitely "Indian." I quote "Indian" as there seems to be an impression amongst authors that such a thing as tribal distinction does not exist amongst the North American aborigines.

Tribal Distinctions

The term "Indian" signifies about as much as the term "European," but I cannot recall ever having read a story where the heroine was described as "a European." The Indian girl we meet in cold type, however, is rarely distressed by having to belong to any tribe, or to reflect any tribal characteristics. She is merely a wholesale sort of admixture of any band existing between the Mic Macs of Gaspe and the Kwaw-

Kewiths of British Columbia,[1] yet strange to say, that notwithstanding the numerous tribes, with their aggregate numbers reaching more than 122,000 souls in Canada alone, our Canadian authors can cull from this huge revenue of character, but one Indian girl, and stranger still that this lonely little heroine never had a prototype in breathing flesh-and-blood existence!

It is a deplorable fact, but there is only one of her. The story-writer who can create a new kind of Indian girl, or better still portray a "real live" Indian girl will do something in Canadian literature that has never been done, but once. The general author gives the reader the impression that he has concocted the plot, created his characters, arranged his action, and at the last moment has been seized with the idea that the regulation Indian maiden will make a very harmonious background whereon to paint his pen picture that he, never having met this interesting individual, stretches forth his hand to his library shelves, grasps the first Canadian novelist he sees, reads up his subject, and duplicates it in his own work.

After a half dozen writers have done this, the reader might as well leave the tale unread as far as the interest touches upon the Indian character, for an unvarying experience tells him that this convenient personage will repeat herself with monotonous accuracy. He knows what she did and how she died in other romances by other romancers, and she will do and die likewise in this, (she always does die, and one feels relieved that it is so, for she is too unhealthy and too unnatural to live).

THE INEVITABLE "WINONA"

The rendition of herself and her doings gains no variety in the pens of manifold authors, and the last thing that they will ever think of will be to study "The Indian Girl" from life, for the being we read of is the offspring of the writer's imagination and never existed outside the book covers that her name decorates. Yes, there is only one of her, and her name is "Winona." Once or twice she has borne another appellation, but it always has a "Winona" sound about it. Even Charles Mair,[2] in that masterpiece of Canadian-Indian romances, "Tecumseh," could not resist "Winona." We meet her as a Shawnee, as a Sioux, as a Huron, and then, her tribe unnamed, in the vicinity of Brockville.[3]

She is never dignified by being permitted to own a surname, although, extraordinary to note, her father is always a chief, and, had he ever existed, would doubtless have been as conservative as his contemporaries about the usual significance that his people attach to family name and lineage.

1. Native tribes from Quebec and British Columbia, Canada, respectively.

2. Charles Mair (1838–1927), Canadian poet. His 1886 verse play *Tecumseh* was a huge success in Toronto.

3. The Shawnee lived in Ohio, Western Virginia, and Pennsylvania until they were driven to Oklahoma in the mid-1800s; the Sioux were spread from Minnesota and the Dakotas to Nebraska and Canada; the Huron were from the Great Lakes region of the United States and Canada. Brockville is a city in Ontario.

In addition to this most glaring error this surnameless creation is possessed with a suicidal mania. Her unhappy, self-sacrificing life becomes such a burden, both to herself and the author that this is the only means by which they can extricate themselves from a lamentable tangle, though, as a matter of fact suicide is an evil positively unknown among Indians. To-day there may be rare instances where a man crazed by liquor might destroy his own life, but in the periods from whence "Winona's" character is sketched self-destruction was unheard of. This seems to be a fallacy which the best American writers have fallen a prey to. Even Helen Hunt Jackson, in her powerful and beautiful romance of "Ramona,"[4] has weakened her work deplorably by having no less than three Indians suicide while maddened by their national wrongs and personal grief.

To Be Crossed in Love Her Lot

But the hardest fortune that the Indian girl in fiction meets with is the inevitable doom that shadows her love affairs. She is always desperately in love with the young white hero, who in turn is grateful to her for services rendered the garrison in general and himself in particular during red days of war. In short, she is so much wrapped up in him that she is treacherous to her own people, tells falsehoods to her father and the other chiefs of her tribe, and otherwise makes herself detestable and dishonorable. Of course, this white hero never marries her! Will some critic who understands human nature, and particularly the nature of authors, please tell the reading public why marriage with the Indian girl is so despised in books and so general in real life? Will this good far-seeing critic also tell us why the book-made Indian makes all the love advances to the white gentleman, though the real wild Indian girl (by the way, we are never given any stories of educated girls, though there are many such throughout Canada) is the most retiring, reticent, non-committal being in existence!

Captain Richardson, in that inimitable novel, "Wacousta,"[5] scarcely goes as far in this particular as his followers. To be sure he has his Indian heroine fall madly in love with young de Haldimar, a passion which it goes without saying he does not reciprocate, but which he plays upon to the extent of making her a traitor to Pontiac inasmuch as she betrays the secret of one of the cleverest intrigues of war known in the history of America, namely, the scheme to capture Fort Detroit through the means of an exhibition game of lacrosse. In addition to this de Haldimar makes a cat's paw of the girl, using her as a means of communication between his fiancee and himself, and so the excellent author permits his Indian girl to get herself despised by her own nation and disliked by the reader. Unnecessary to state, that as

4. Helen Hunt Jackson's *Ramona* (1884) indicted Americans for their treatment of Native Americans.

5. John Richardson's novel *Wacousta* (1832) was influenced by James Fenimore Cooper's Leatherstocking novels and is set at Fort Detroit, a French fort in the location of present-day Detroit.

usual the gallant white marries his fair lady, who the poor little red girl has assisted him to recover. . . .

A CHANCE FOR CANADIAN WRITERS

Perhaps, sometimes an Indian romance may be written by someone who will be clever enough to portray national character without ever having come in contact with it. Such things have been done, for are we not told that Tom Moore had never set foot in Persia before he wrote Lalla Rookh?[6] and those who best know what they affirm declare that remarkable poem as a faithful and accurate delineation of Oriental scenery, life and character. But such things are rare, half of our authors who write up Indian stuff have never been on an Indian reserve in their lives, have never met a "real live" Redman, have never even read Parkman, Schoolcraft or Catten;[7] what wonder that their conception of a people they are ignorant of, save by hearsay, is dwarfed, erroneous and delusive.

And here follows the thought—do authors who write Indian romances love the nation they endeavor successfully or unsuccessfully to describe? Do they, like Tecumseh, say, "And I, who love your nation, which is just, when deeds deserve it,"[8] or is the Indian introduced into literature but to lend a dash of vivid coloring to an otherwise tame and somber picture of colonial life: it looks suspiciously like the latter reason, or why should the Indian always get beaten in the battles of romance, or the Indian girl get inevitably the cold shoulder in the wars of love?

Surely the Redman has lost enough, has suffered enough without additional losses and sorrows being heaped upon him in romance. There are many combats he has won in history from the extinction of the Jesuit Fathers at Lake Simcoe to Cut Knife Creek.[9] There are many girls who have placed dainty red feet figuratively upon the white man's neck from the days of Pocahontas to those of little "Bright Eyes,"[10] who captured all Washington a few seasons ago. Let us not only hear, but read something of the North American Indian "besting" some one at least once in a decade, and above all things let the Indian girl of fiction develop from the "dog-

6. British poet Sir Thomas Moore's wildly popular *Lalla Rookh* (1817) was a series of verse stories set in Persia.

7. American historian Francis Parkman (1823–1893), American geologist and ethnologist Henry Schoolcraft (1793–1864), and American artist and author George Catlin (1796–1872) were known for their documentary studies of Native American tribes. By "Catten," Johnson must mean Catlin.

8. From Charles Mair, *Tecumseh*. Tecumseh (c. 1768–1813), a Shawnee leader, urged intertribal unity in resistance to whites.

9. In the late 1640s, Iroquois drove Jesuit missionaries from the shores of Lake Simcoe in Ontario. On May 2, 1885, a band of Cree and Assiniboine warriors defeated Canadian soldiers at Cut Knife Creek in Saskatchewan.

10. Susette La Flesche Tibbles.

like," "fawnlike," "deer-footed," "fire-eyed," "crouching," "submissive" book heroine into something of the quiet, sweet womanly woman she is, if wild, or the every-
day, natural, laughing girl she is, if cultivated and educated, let her be the italics,[11]
even if the author is not competent to give her tribal characteristics.

Source: Toronto Sunday Globe (1892)

11. Other reprints of this essay read, "let her be natural, even if . . . " But the original text reads,
"let her be the italics," the meaning of which is unclear.

❧ Elia Wilkinson Peattie (1862–1935)

Elia Wilkinson was born in Kalamazoo, Michigan, and moved to Chicago when she was young. After her 1883 marriage to the journalist Robert Burns Peattie, with whom she would have three sons, she became a reporter for the Chicago newspapers. In 1888 the family moved to Omaha, Nebraska, where Robert edited and Elia wrote for the Omaha World-Herald. *Elia also published her short stories in many national magazines, including* The Century *and* Harper's Monthly, *and wrote numerous books. She was an early promoter of Willa Cather and a friend to Kate M. Cleary, another Nebraska writer, about whom she wrote the following article. Although ostensibly about Cleary, this piece is a tribute to all women writers (although particularly those on the Western frontier) who managed households as well as kept up their literary activities. As such, then, it is a more hopeful account of a woman attempting to pursue a combination of domesticity and literature than that provided by "A Weak-Minded Woman."*

A Bohemian in Nebraska
A Peep at a Home Which Is a Slice out of Bohemia

A Wife and a Mother Who Finds Time to Turn Out Poems, Humor and Fiction

It's not very often that a woman is a bohemian—a genuine bohemian. And it must be confessed that Nebraska is not the place where one would go to look for a woman of that kind, and certainly he would not journey all day along the Burlington road, over the prairie, to the tiny town of Hubbell—the quietest place, with prohibition politics—to find such a woman.

Yet, there is one there. Perhaps some night you will get in that little town, lying down among its hills, about midnight. The place will be black as Erebus.[1] Everyone of the busy, simple-living folk of the hamlet will be in bed. But up the dark, straight street one light will be shining, and it will show you inside—for the curtain is always up—a group of people in a room which does not in the least look like a room of a quiet Nebraska farming village.

It is lined with books. It has a typewriter in it, and a writing desk, and a jolly big stove, and some chairs and sofas designed for loafing. And it has pictures not at all of the sort you would expect to find out on the prairie—little sketches of clever artists, old engravings, souvenirs of occasions, mementoes of famous folks. There never was a more informal room—never. It's a room where you say good things if it is in you to do it. There's something in the atmosphere of the place that brings the humor out of you. And when you get in one of those comfortable chairs with a

---

1. In Greek mythology, Erebus, the son of Chaos, is the personification of darkness.

glass of beer in your hand, and no particular care whether it is time to go to bed or not, and the Chicago, New York and Omaha papers at your elbow, and new books and magazines yet to be cut[2] lying near, and the memory of a dinner that was very much more than good—that was daring and scientific in its way—then suddenly, bohemia has come to you, and the Nebraska prairie with its hard working, quiet living people seem very far away.

The big world of letters is around you, the world of Puck[3] has come to you. You laugh with all those who have ever, by laughing, made themselves famous. You feel as if the spirits of all those who were cleverest that ever you have known, had come out with you over the wind-racked plains, and were there, drinking beer and laughing, too.

It's the mistress of the place that brings all this about. She is a woman not unknown in this state to those who keep track of such small literature as Nebraska can turn out. Her name is Kate McPhelim Cleary . . .

But even the four babies, and the careful study of the household art has not put a stop to Mrs. Cleary's literary work. She writes romantic tales for the story papers; she contributes some of the brightest jokes that appear in Puck, she sends delightful sketches to the Chicago Tribune, and she occasionally writes verses. Perhaps she would do all of this work more earnestly if she did not do it so easily. What I mean to say is, that she has no definite aim in view. She does not care whether she "succeeds" or not. She wants to live as happily as possible, and she writes because she enjoys it, not because she has an ambition to write. She does without thought or care work which slower witted persons would spend sleepless nights over. And after she has done it she thinks no more about it, but sells it if she happens to want the money for anything, and if she doesn't she lets it lie in her drawer. It is, however, to persons just so careless of success that it is apt to come. Perhaps she would write more persistently if there was need for doing so from a monetary point of view. But since there is no such need, and as she has everything she wants, writing is taken up only as a form of amusement. It is valued more because it brings her into association with clever people all over the country than for any other reason. And her correspondence is of the sort that keeps her constantly in touch with eastern cities, and that gives to her days a pleasant excitement. Some charming people have been entertained in that little house up the quiet Hubbell street, and the gay little ponies that race over the hills with the family phaeton[4] have introduced some distinguished visitors to the Nebraska hills.

To find a life so full, so interesting, so entertaining and—bohemian—for there

2. In the bookbinding process, sheets were folded but not trimmed. So the reader had to cut a new book's "leaves," or pages, along the edges.
3. *Puck* magazine, published from 1871 to 1918, was known for its political cartoons. Kate Cleary published many pieces in the magazine.
4. A horse-drawn carriage with four wheels.

is no other word for it—out on the Nebraska prairies, has never ceased to be an astonishment to me. And I hope I have not in any way betrayed the confidence imposed in me telling something of the inner life of this peculiar home. And I think it would not be possible to mention that home without mentioning also the genial, kindly, generous and most hospitable gentleman who is at the head of it, and whose friendship is worthy of anybody's winning. . . .

There is one thing that distinguishes this home from most of those out on the prairies, and that is good cooking. I don't mean that the cooking in most Nebraska farming communities is not good in its simple way. But I mean when Mrs. Cleary found herself stranded, as it were, in mid-plains, and confronted by the deplorably small bill of fare of a country town, that she set about making a scientific cuisine. In all the arts of salad making, roasting, deviling, baking, preserving and mixing, she is a connoisseur—and more, she is original. It would be absurd to commend all of her methods to the busy farm woman who has neither time nor money for making fine dishes, but I am sure the isolated life out on the plains would take to itself a little more charm if other women would do as Mrs. Cleary has, and make a study of how to use cream and eggs, poultry and pork, vegetables and the native fruit. It's a great art; and it takes brains of a good sort—so no one need scorn it because of the idea that it is not intellectual.

All this may not be to the point, and may seem very vacuous and discursive; but I really think it will be a good thing for some of our serious, hard-working American women to know how humor, imagination, ability and adaptability can illuminate our lonely western life.

For say what you may, there is a little ache in the hearts of every one of us for the "place back east" which we left. In this state are hundreds of thousands of homesick people. It is inevitable. We did not grow up together here. And the new home, the new friends, however dear, cannot be quite like those we were born to. The Plymouth women used to weep when the Mayflower spread its white sails and turned toward "home," yet not one faltered, not one went with her. On them, unknown to themselves, was placed the destiny of conquering this continent. And westward still have come the pilgrims, and the subjugation of the continent is yet far from complete. And we, here in the west, a vast company of strangers from many lands, look at each other with eyes of longing, appealing for closer friendship, stronger interests, dearer compensations.

And so I think that anyone who has broken down the obstacles, who has proved that the art of living is not a thing controlled by environment and circumstances, is a fine example to us all.

And in the home in Hubbell that I have told you of such an example may be found.

Source: Omaha World-Herald (1893)

&. Annie Nathan Meyer (1867–1951)

Annie Nathan was a native of New York City, a member of an elite Jewish family, and a distant cousin of Emma Lazarus. In 1887 she married Dr. Alfred Meyer, whom she claimed was "entirely sympathetic with my literary ambitions." Having encountered obstacles in her pursuit of a higher education at Columbia College, she founded Barnard College in 1889 and served as a trustee until 1942. Beginning in 1888, Meyer published essays, stories, novels, and plays (three of which were produced on Broadway), fulfilling her childhood ambition to become an author. Her works often focused on the difficulties women faced as they attempted to combine marriage and a career. She also edited Woman's Work in America *(1891) and chaired the literary committee of the Women's Congress at the World's Fair in 1893, for which she wrote the following essay. She tackles here the question of whether or not women's writing is inherently different from men's, taking a different position than that of Sarah Hale in her "Editor's Table" column (1857).*

Woman's Place in Letters

I am going to begin by telling you something very pleasant. An officer of the A. A. W. told me the other day that when the association first began to hold congresses, twenty-one years ago, they had great difficulty in keeping the annual reports down to anything like the necessary economical limit. All the speakers were so very anxious to see themselves in print, and so unaccustomed to it, that any attempt at condensation was fiercely resented, while to omit a paper was to offend deeply. "We have difficulty with our reports now," she continued, "but it is a difficulty of another kind. A difficulty in securing a sufficient number of the addresses to make a respectable showing; for the women who address the annual congresses today are loath to give their papers for the report, because they can command their own price in the leading magazines." We know that women are writing a great deal today, and are doing some very good work. They are doing so much that it would be absurd to attempt to treat this subject fully. I shall merely, therefore, look at certain phases of the subject. I am interested particularly in the question: Has woman something specific, something *sui generis*[1] to contribute to literature? One of our women writers tells us: "Once let woman wield the pen and thoughts will be put into books that have never been put there before, or at least some of the old things will be told from a side never before dreamed of.["] Unfortunately I am so constituted that when I encounter an interesting theory I always ask myself, Is it true? It is so easy to be philosophical and learned if one does not happen to be hampered by knowing very much about one's subject. We are told by Browning, Sludge the medium:

---

1. Latin: unique, in its own class.

"Don't let truth's lump rot stagnant for the lack of a timely helpful lie to leaven it."[2] But I think on the contrary, with Ameil, that "An error is dangerous just according to the amount of truth it may contain."[3]

Much as I would be interested in believing that woman, with the pen in her hand, has turned a new page of life before us, candor compels me to admit that if there is such a thing as sex in literature, I have not succeeded in discovering it. I look about me and observe that the very subjects upon which one would naturally expect women to throw a new light have really inspired the masterpieces of men. No woman, burning with the sense of wrong, could have painted the injustice of the social code of morals more forcibly, more tragically than Thomas Hardy did in his "Test [*sic*] of the d'Urbervilles."[4] No woman, eager to reconstruct and ennoble our ideal of marital obligation, could have held up its pitiable sham and conventionality with more inspired pen than was wielded by Henrik Ibsen in his "Ghosts and Doll-house" [*sic*].[5] Could any woman have depicted more sympathetically the hard, dull life of the faithful woman of the fields and prairies than Hamlin Garland and Major Kirkland and Bret Harte have done it?[6] There was a little anonymous story that appeared in the "Century" a couple of years ago—I think it was called "A Common Story"—and I remember every one, myself included, was certain that only a woman could have written it, because only a woman could possibly have had the necessary insight. It revealed the love story of an old maid, and it struck a note that must have vibrated in every woman's heart. Yet this story was by that gifted young man, Walcott Balestier.[7] I have heard various receipts for discovering the sex of an author, but have seen them all go down ingloriously before the simple strategy of the *nom de plume.* It was generally conceded that no one but a man could have painted the rugged solemnity of the Tennessee Mountains and the primitive poetry of the lives of the mountaineers as Charles Egbert Craddock did. At least it was conceded, before Mary Murfree[8] modestly appeared before the startled eyes of the editor of the "Atlantic Monthly;" and I am sure that the claims of a certain man to

2. From Robert Browning's "Mr. Sludge, 'the Medium,'" from *Dramatis Personae* (1864).

3. With slight alteration from *Amiel's Journal: The Journal Intime of Henri-Frédéric Amiel*, translated by Mrs. Humphrey Ward (1885).

4. Thomas Hardy's novel *Tess of the d'Urbervilles* (1891) was scandalous for its insistence that its fallen heroine was an innocent victim of social forces.

5. Henrik Ibsen's play *Ghosts* (published in English, 1890) features a woman and her son who suffer the aftereffects of her husband's infidelity and syphilis. His play *A Doll's House* (published in English, 1889) portrays a woman's refusal to stay in her unhappy marriage.

6. Hamlin Garland (1860–1940) from Wisconsin, Joseph Kirkland (1830–1893) from Chicago, and Bret Harte (1836–1902) from California portrayed frontier women sympathetically.

7. Wolcott Balestier (1861–1891), American writer, most famous for coauthoring *The Naulahka* (1892) with Rudyard Kipling, who married his sister.

8. Mary Noailles Murfree (1850–1922) used the pseudonym of Charles Egbert Craddock. Thomas Bailey Aldrich was shocked when she appeared at the *Atlantic's* office and introduced herself as Craddock.

the novels of George Eliot were immensely strengthened by the current view that it would be absurd to abscribe [*sic*] the simple, vigorous strength of "Adam Bede" to the hand of a woman. When we turn to those that would theorize about woman's place in the republic of letters, what ideas do we find current: First, and I think this reasoning is not entirely unfamiliar to you; we hear them say: "Woman is the heart, and man the mind. Woman stands for the emotions and man for the intellect." Therefore we should find that women may write charming love stories, but that it will be impossible for them to reveal any intellectual grasp; impossible for them to probe down into the deeper problems of life.

What do we find as an actual fact? We find the men critics showering anathemas at the authors of "Robert Elsmere" and "John Ward, Preacher,"[9] for bringing into the domain of a novel serious problems and non-emotional material that properly belong rather to the domain of philosophy or theology. Then, of course, we are told that women lack the broad sympathy that is so necessary to the novelist of today. As Mrs. Browning's Romney tells Aurora, "Women are sympathetic to the personal pangs, but hard to general suffering."[10] And yet, think of the exquisitely tender delineation of the forbidding New England old maid by Mary Wilkins, and those two great stories that immortalized the wrongs of two races, "Uncle Tom's Cabin" and "Romola."[11] Then we are told that it is easy for women to write on fashionable society or of the village sewing circles, but in the very nature of things women are limited in their scope. It is impossible for them to depict the rough primitive life of the fields and mines, and yet right here in America we have Mary Hallock Foote, Octave Thanet, and Miss Elliot,[12] the author of "Jerry," and so many others who seem to have gone straight down to the soil for inspiration. Then, of course, women have not had what are called "experiences." How can a woman in her sheltered innocence know anything of certain phases of life, or if she does possess sufficient imagination, how will she treat it? Surely she can only give us what some one has called: "The moral harshness of copy-book maxims,"[13] and yet with what passion and fire Mrs. Humphery Ward has given us the Parisian episode in the life of David Grieve; and think of Elizabeth Stewart Phelps' powerful and pitiful

9. Novels by Mrs. Humphrey Ward (Mary Arnold) (1851–1920) and Margaret Deland (1857–1945), respectively, which provoked religious controversy.

10. Elizabeth Barrett Browning, *Aurora Leigh* (1856), a novel in verse that tells the story of a young woman's commitment to poetry despite the arguments of her beloved, Romney, against women's ability to write great poetry.

11. George Eliot's *Romola* (1863) was set during the Italian Renaissance. Meyer undoubtedly means Helen Hunt Jackson's novel *Ramona* (1884), which portrayed the wrongs inflicted on Native Americans.

12. Octave Thanet, the pseudonym of Alice French (1850–1934), from Iowa; and Sarah Barnwell Elliot (1848–1928) from Tennessee.

13. Source of quote unknown. Copy books were volumes containing models of handwriting, which were often trite moralistic expressions.

story, "Hedged In," and the breadth and insight of Olive Schreiner.[14] I am sure no one has dealt with the character of a guilty woman more exquisitely, more tactfully, more sympathetically, and yet with more powerful irony and pathos than Mrs. K. Clifford did with her Mrs. North in her story, "Aunt Anne."[15] While her Mrs. Walter Hibbert is a capital hit at the timid attitude of the average "good woman."

I heard the other day that Mr. Brander Mathews[16] so keenly misses the sense of humor in woman that he has resolved the next time he marries to marry a man. No, I am not going to get angry about it, it hits Mrs. Mathews so much harder than it hits me; nor am I going to assist Mr. Mathews to prove his cause by taking his skit too seriously. But I cannot resist just a reference to the delightful quality of the humor of Agnes Repplier, Mary Wilkins, Sarah Orme [sic] Jewett, Mrs. W. K. Clifford, and Mrs. Craigie,[17] who is generally known by her pen name of John Oliver Hobbs. The humor of the last is so subtle, so whimsical, and so utterly pervasive that I have a suspicion in my mind that Mr. Mathews, in his ignorance of the *nom de plume,* was thinking of taking a certain Mr. John Oliver Hobbs as that second wife.

Let me here say something in connection with that terrible tirade that was launched forth by a certain Molly Elliott Seawall,[18] a writer herself of novels of no common order. She said: "If all that women have ever done in literature was swept out of existence, the world would not lose a single masterpiece." I was amused the other day by a lady saying that it was our own dear president, Mrs. May Wright Sewall,[19] who was the author of this attack. "Do you think," I said, when I had recovered from laughter sufficiently to speak, "that the president of the Woman's International Council could say such things without suffering impeachment?"

I am not discouraged by such remarks, although I think it absurd to say that women had produced no masterpieces, yet I am perfectly willing to admit that they have produced no genius of the very highest rank, the rank of Dante and Shakespeare and Milton and Goethe.[20] But do you know the same thing precisely has been said of American literature? It is [sic] not interesting that they say both of

---

14. Mrs. Humphrey Ward's *The History of David Grieve* (1892). Elizabeth Stuart Phelps's *Hedged In* (1870) was about a prostitute. Olive Schreiner's (1855–1920) best-known work was the autobiography *The Story of an African Farm* (1883).

15. *Aunt Anne* (1892) by Lucy Lane Clifford (1846–1929), a.k.a. Mrs. W. K. Clifford, British writer.

16. Brander Matthews (1852–1929), American critic and Columbia literature professor.

17. Agnes Repplier (1855–1950), witty American essayist; Mrs. Pearl Mary Teresa Craigie (1867–1906), popular novelist, who was born in America but lived her adult life in England.

18. Molly Elliott Seawall (dates unknown) was an American novelist and correspondent for the *Washington Post.*

19. May Wright Sewall (1844–1920), women's rights and peace activist.

20. Dante Alighieri (1265–1321), Italian poet; William Shakespeare (1594–1616), English dramatist; John Milton (1608–1674), English poet; and Johann Wolfgang von Goethe (1749–1832), German poet and dramatist.

American literature and woman's literature, if I may coin the phrase, that it has produced some clever and delightful writers, but no genius of the very highest rank. Mr. James Bryce[21] has a good deal to say of this on his work on America, and he puts a good deal of the onus on the shoulders of our hurried, interrupted, unrestful life. But he thinks that America in time will settle down to create the highest kind of literature. That the time will come when America (and the same thing is true of woman) will no longer feel the necessity of proving her right to be. I am cheered by the words of Emerson: "The scholar of the first age received into him the world around; brooded thereon; and uttered it again. * * * It came into him life; it went out from him truth and poetry."[22]

Well, woman is still in her first age. She is slowly awakening from a long sleep, and is just beginning to look about her and see the world around. She is still brooding thereon. I am sure the time is not far distant when she shall translate life into forms of perfect truth and poetry.

Source: The Congress of Women: Held in the Woman's Building, World's Columbian Exposition, Chicago, U. S. A., 1893, With Portraits, Biographies and Addresses (1894)

21. James Bryce (1838–1922), British politician and historian, author of *The American Commonwealth* (1888).
22. Ralph Waldo Emerson's "The American Scholar" (1837).

Gertrude Bustill Mossell (1855–1948)

Gertrude Bustill was a native of Philadelphia and a member of a wealthy and socially active family. She received an extensive education and was a teacher before her marriage in 1883 to Dr. Nathan Frances Mossell. Her primary occupation, however, was journalism. She wrote for several prominent African American periodicals such as the New York Freeman, *the* Indianapolis World, Woman's Era, *and the* Colored American Magazine. *Her landmark book* The Work of Afro-American Women, *which chronicled the accomplishments of black women in various fields, was published under her married name Mrs. N. F. Mossell. The first essay from this work, reprinted below, provides a history of black women's journalism as well as advice to aspiring journalists. "A Lofty Study" offers practical advice on how to set up "a quiet nook to write in," thirty-five years before Virginia Woolf published her famous essay "A Room of One's Own." During the rest of Gertrude Mossell's life, she focused on civic activities and helping her husband found the Frederick Douglass Memorial Hospital in Philadelphia. She also raised two daughters.*

Our Women in Journalism

The heredity and environment of women has for many ages circumscribed them to a certain routine both of work and play. In this century, sometimes called the "Nineteenth Century," but often the "Women's Century," there has been a yielding of the barriers that surround her life. In the school, the church, the state, her value as a co-operative is being widely discussed. The co-education of the sexes, the higher education of woman, has given to her life a strong impetus in the line of literary effort. Perhaps this can be more strongly felt in the profession of journalism than in any other. On every hand journals published by women and for women are multiplying. The corps of lady writers employed on most of our popular magazines and papers is quite as large as the male contingent and often more popular if not as scholarly. We can realize what this generation would have lost if the cry of "blue stocking"[1] had checked the ambition of our present women writers. The women of our race have become vitalized by the strong literary current that surrounds them. The number is daily increasing of those who write commendably readable articles for various journals published by the race. There was a day when an Afro-American woman of the greatest refinement and culture could aspire no higher than the dressmaker's art, or later who would rise higher in the scale could be a teacher, and there the top round of higher employment was reached. But we have fallen on brighter days, we retain largely the old employments and have added to this literary work and its special line of journalistic effort.

New lines are being marked out by us; notice "Aunt Lindy" and "Dr. Sevier" in

---

1. An epithet for learned or literary women.

the *Review*.[2] The success of this line of effort is assured and we hail it with joy. Our women have a great work to do in this generation; the ones who walked before us could not do it, they had no education. The ones who come after us will expect to walk in pleasant paths of our marking out. Journalism offers many inducements, it gives to a great extent work at home; sex and race are no bar, often they need not be known; literary work never employs all one's time, for we cannot write as we would wash dishes. Again, our quickness of perception, tact, intuition, help to guide us to the popular taste; her ingenuity, the enthusiasm woman has for all she attempts, are in her favor. Again, we have come on the world of action in a century replete with mechanical means for increasing efficiency; woman suffrage is about to dawn. Our men are too much hampered by their contentions with their white brothers to afford to stop and fight their black sisters, so we slip in and glide along quietly. We are out of the thick of the fight. Lookers-on in Venice, we have time to think over our thoughts, and carry out our purposes; we have everything to encourage us in this line of effort, and so far I have found nothing to discourage an earnest worker. All who will do good work can get a hearing in our best Afro-American journals. In the large cities especially of the North we have here and there found openings on white journals. More will come as more are prepared to fill them and when it will have become no novelty to be dreaded by editor or fellow-reporters. To women starting in literary work I would say, Write upon the subjects that lie nearest your heart; by that means you will be most likely to convince others. Be original in title, conception and plan. Read and study continuously. Study the style of articles, of journals. Discuss methods with those who are able to give advice. Every branch of life-work is now being divided into special lines and the literary field shares in the plan marked out by other lines of work; so much is this the case that the name of Cable, or Tourgee, or Haygood, suggests at once southern Negro life; Edward Atkinsson, food; Prof. Shaler,[3] scientific research, and so on ad infinitum. Our literati would do well to follow the same plan; it may have its disadvantages, but it certainly also has its advantages. To those who aspire to become journalists we only give the old rule, enter the office, begin at the lowest round and try to learn each department of work well. Be thankful for suggestions and criticism, make friends, choose if possible your editor, your paper, be loyal to both, work for the interest of both. See that your own paper gets the best, the latest news. If a new idea comes to you, even if it is

2. Victoria Earle (Matthews), "Aunt Lindy: A Story Founded on Real Life" (1891) was published in the *A.M.E. Church Review*, a quarterly published by the African Methodist Episcopal Church. *Dr. Sevier* (1884) was a novel about prison reform by George Washington Cable (1844–1925) first serialized in *The Century*.

3. Cable often wrote about the legacy of slavery, including in his controversial "The Freedman's Case in Equity" (1885). Albion Tourgée (1838–1905) was the author of the Reconstruction novel *A Fool's Errand* (1879). Atticus Green Haygood (1839–1896) wrote *Our Brother In Black: His Freedom and His Future* (1881). Edward Atkinson (1827–1905) invented the Aladdin oven and was one of the authors of *The Science of Nutrition* (1896). Nathaniel Southgate Shaler (1841–1906) was a professor of geology and paleontology at Harvard as well as a prolific writer on evolution.

out of your line of work, talk over it with him. Study papers, from the design at the top, the headings, the advertisements, up to the editorials. Have an intelligent comprehension of every department of work on the paper. As a reporter I believe a lady has the advantage of the masculine reporter in many respects. She can gain more readily as an interviewer access to both sexes. Women know best how to deal with women and the inborn chivalry of a gentleman leads him to grant her request when a man might have been repulsed without compunction. In seven years' experience as an interviewer on two white papers I have never met with a refusal from either sex or race. If at first for some reason they declined, eventually I gained my point. Another pleasant feature of this as of all other employment is its comradeship; one can always find a helper in a fellow-worker. I have received some such kind, helpful letters; one from Mrs. Marion McBride, President of New England Women's Press Association comes to my mind; another from Mrs. Henry Highland Garnet of N. Y. Here and there pleasant tokens of esteem and co-operation greet me. I have been thanked heartily in many strange places, by many new and unaccustomed voices, for helpful words spoken in the long ago. To the women of my race, the daughters of an oppressed people, I say a bright future awaits you. Let us each try to be a lamp in the pathway of the co-laborer a guide to the footsteps of the generation that must follow. Let us make, if we can, the rough places smooth; let us write naught that need cause a blush to rise to our cheek even in old age. Let us feel the magnitude of the work, its vast possibilities for good or ill. Let us strive ever not to be famous, but to be wisely helpful, leaders and guides for those who look eagerly for the daily or weekly feast that we set before them.

Doing this, our reward must surely come. And when at some future day we shall desire to start a women's journal, by our women, for our women, we will have built up for ourselves a bulwark of strength; we will be able to lead well because we have learned to follow. May these few words, allied to the bright and shining examples of such women as Mrs. Frances Ellen Watkins Harper, Mrs. Fanny Jackson Coppin, Mrs. Sara M. Douglass,[4] and other consistent, industrious workers, serve as a stimulus to some one who is strong of will, but weak of purpose, or to another whose aspiration is to become a journalist, but who fears to launch her little bark on the waves of its tempestuous sea.

A Lofty Study

In these days of universal scribbling, when almost every one writes for fame or money, many people who are not reaping large pecuniary profits from their work

4. Fanny Jackson Coppin (1837–1913) was the first African American woman to become a school principal. Sarah Mapps Douglass (1806–1882) was an abolitionist and educator.

do not feel justified in making any outlay to gratify the necessities of their labors in literature.

Every one engaged in literary work, even if but to a limited extent, feels greatly the need of a quiet nook to write in. Each portion of the home seems to have its clearly defined use, that will prevent their achieving the desired result. A few weeks ago, in the course of my travels, I came across an excellent idea carried into practical operation, that had accomplished the much-desired result of a quiet spot for literary work, without the disarrangement of a single portion of the household economy. In calling at the house of a member of the Society of Friends,[5] I was ushered first into the main library on the first floor. Not finding in it the article sought, the owner invited me to walk upstairs to an upper library. I continued my ascent until we reached the attic. This had been utilized in such a way that it formed a comfortable and acceptable study. I made a mental note of my surroundings. The room was a large sloping attic chamber. It contained two windows, one opening on a roof; another faced the door: a skylight had been cut directly overhead, in the middle of the room. Around the ceiling on the side that was not sloping ran a line of tiny closets with glass doors. Another side had open shelves. On the sloping side, drawers rose from the floor a convenient distance. The remaining corner had a desk built in the wall; it was large and substantial, containing many drawers. Two small portable tables were close at hand near the centre.

An easy chair, an old-fashioned sofa with a large square cushion for a pillow, completed the furniture of this unassuming study. Neatness, order, comfort reigned supreme. Not a sound from the busy street reached us. It was so quiet, so peaceful, the air was so fresh and pure, it seemed like living in a new atmosphere.

I just sat down and wondered why I had never thought of this very room for a study. Almost every family has an unused attic, dark, sloping, given up to odds and ends. Now let it be papered with a creamy paper, with narrow stripes, giving the impression of height; a crimson velvety border. Paint the woodwork a darker shade of yellow, hang a buff and crimson portière[6] at the door. Put in an open grate; next widen the windowsills, and place on them boxes of flowering plants. Get an easy chair, a desk that suits your height, and place by its side a revolving bookcase, with the books most used in it. Let an adjustable lamp stand by its side, and with a nice old-fashioned sofa, well supplied with cushions, you will have a study that a queen might envy you. Bright, airy, cheerful, and almost noiseless, not easy of access to those who would come only to disturb, and far enough away to be cosy and inviting, conferring a certain privilege on the invited guest.

These suggestions can be improved upon, but the one central idea, a place to one's self without disturbing the household economy, would be gained.

5. Quakers.
6. Heavy curtain for a doorway.

Even when there is a library in the home, it is used by the whole family, and if the husband is literary in his tastes, he often desires to occupy it exclusively at the very time you have leisure, perhaps. Men are so often educated to work alone that even sympathetic companionship annoys. Very selfish, we say, but we often find it so—and therefore the necessity of a study of one's own.

If even this odd room cannot be utilized for your purposes, have at least your own corner in some cheerful room. A friend who edits a special department in a *weekly* has in her own chamber a desk with plenty of drawers and small separate compartments. The desk just fits in an alcove of the room, with a revolving-chair in front. What a satisfaction to put everything in order, turn the key, and feel that all is safe—no busy hands, no stray breeze can carry away or disarrange some choice idea kept for the future delectation of the public! Besides this, one who writes much generally finds that she can write best at some certain spot. Ideas come more rapidly, sentences take more lucid forms. Very often the least change from that position will break up the train of thought.

Source: The Work of Afro-American Women (1894)

🐦 Kate M. Cleary (1863–1905)

Kate McPhelim was born in New Brunswick, Canada, to Irish parents and was well educated at convent schools. In the late 1870s, after her father's death, the family moved back to Ireland and then to Chicago. Kate, her mother, and her brother all published poetry and stories as a way to survive. In 1884, Kate published her first novel, married Michael Cleary, and moved to the frontier town of Hubbell, Nebraska, where he ran a lumber and coal business. As Elia Wilkinson Peattie's "A Bohemian in Nebraska" describes, Kate Cleary concentrated on her home and six children as well as writing for pleasure during these years. In the late 1890s, she lost two children to typhoid fever, became addicted to morphine after a postpartum illness, and returned to Chicago with her family. Through her hardships, she continued to write humorous poems and sketches as well as harshly realistic fiction, much of which reflects her ambivalence about life in the West. She died in an insane asylum after years of battling her addiction. The following sketch is a humorous critique of the tendency to downplay women writers' literary achievements in favor of their domestic accomplishments.

The New Man

"Here" she said impressively, "I have a book personally descriptive of American female writers and their admirable contributions to literature."

"I shall take it—," he began,

She beamed, and opened her order-book

"— if," he continued, suavely, "it does not say of a certain writer: 'She is prouder of her pork pies than of her poems.'"

"I—I believe in one biography there is mention of something of that sort."

"Is there an assertion that another author pays attention to every detail of her house-work, and takes particular pains that dust shall never be permitted to gather in her domain?"

"I—I think there is."

"Does one paragraph declare that a well-known novelist makes a boast of darning her table damask with number one hundred and fifty thread?"

"I recall a reference to that effect."

"And is it averred of another celebrity that she fashions and re-models her gowns with such skill that her neighbors and associates believe them Parisian-made?"

"That is, indeed, said of a brilliant poetess."

"And is it also asserted in any part that a popular woman of the pen takes more pleasure, in the knowledge that the suppers prepared in the chafing-dish[1] by her own hands are exceedingly successful, than in the popularity of her novels?"

---

1. A dish supported by a tripod with coals underneath, used for dishes that would burn when exposed to direct heat.

"There"—(*faintly*)—"is something of the sort."

"So I supposed. When you bring me a book, dealing with what women have done in literature, without any apology for their having presumed to do it, I shall gladly buy the volume. I have not read that Ruskin put his ability for chopping kindling-wood above his brilliant criticism. I never heard that the chief argument in favor of Howells was his deftness in putting up stove-pipes. It is yet to be announced that Riley[2] takes less pride in his poems than in whitewashing a cellar. There may be people who think that a compensatory domestic sop should be offered to the Cerberus[3] of mediocrity by every woman who ventures to send her soul beyond the four walls of the kitchen. But such people would not buy the book, anyway. They would borrow it. They shall not borrow it from me. Good-morning!"

Source: Puck (1895)

2. John Ruskin (1819–1900), English art critic. William Dean Howells (1837–1920), American author, editor, and literary critic. James Whitcomb Riley (1849–1916), popular poet from Indiana.

3. A sop is a gift or bribe to appease the recipient. In Greek mythology, Cerberus was the three-headed beast who guarded the entrance to Hades (Hell), making sure that the dead could enter but not exit. A common expression, to give a sop to Cerberus, means to stop his mouth for the moment.

🐚 ALICE DUNBAR-NELSON (1875–1935)

Alice Ruth Moore was a light-skinned, middle-class Creole of color from New Orleans. She attended Cornell, Columbia, and the University of Pennsylvania, and taught school for many years. Her early publications attracted the attention of the famous poet Paul Lawrence Dunbar. The two wed in 1898, but Alice left Paul in 1902. In 1916, she married Robert J. Nelson, with whom she edited the Wilmington Advocate *and* Masterpieces of Negro Eloquence *(1914). Before 1900, Dunbar-Nelson's writings (mostly poetry, sketches, and local stories) had primarily featured white or racially indiscriminate characters, but after the turn of the century, they conveyed a stronger sense of her African American identity. A social activist in her journalism and poetry, she was associated with the Harlem Renaissance. The following pieces from her first book participate in the mainstream dialogues about women and art and concern, in particular, the question of fame and the dilemma between marriage and a creative career.*

Three Thoughts

FIRST

   How few of us
In all the world's great, ceaseless struggling strife,
Go to our work with gladsome, buoyant step,
And love it for its sake, whate'er it be.
Because it is a labor, or, mayhap,
Some sweet, peculiar art of God's own gift;
And not the promise of the world's slow smile
Of recognition, or of mammon's[1] gilded grasp.
Alas, how few, in inspiration's dazzling flash,
Or spiritual sense of world's beyond the dome
Of circling blue around this weary earth,
Can bask, and know the God-given grace
Of genius' fire that flows and permeates
The virgin mind alone; the soul in which
The love of earth hath tainted not.
The love of art and art alone. . . .

---

1. A false god in the New Testament; greed or desire for wealth.

At Eventide

All day had she watched and waited for his coming, and still her strained ears caught no sounds of the footsteps she loved and longed to hear. All day while the great sun panted on his way around the brazen skies; all day while the busy world throbbed its mighty engines of labor, nor witted of the breaking hearts in its midst. And now when the eve had come, and the sun sank slowly to rest, casting his red rays over the earth he loved, and bidding tired nature a gentle radiant good-night, she still watched and waited. Waited while the young moon shone silvery in the crimson flush of the eastern sky, while the one bright star trembled as he strove to near his love; waited while the hum of soul-wearing traffic died in the distant streets, and the merry voices of happy children floated to her ears.

And still he came not. What kept him from her side? Had he learned the cold lesson of self-control, or found one other thing more potent than love? Had some cruel chain of circumstances forced him to disobey her bidding—or—did he love another? But no, she smiles triumphantly, he could not having known and loved her.

Sitting in the deep imbrasure of the window through which the distant wave sounds of city life floated to her, the pages of her life seemed to turn back, and she read the almost forgotten tale of long ago, the story of their love. In those days his wish had been her law; his smile her sun; his frown her wretchedness. Within his arms, earth seemed a far-away dream of empty nothingness, and when his lips touched and clung to hers, sweet with the perfume of the South they floated away into a Paradise of enfolding space, where Time and Death and the woes of this great earth are naught, only these two—and love, the almighty.

And so their happiness drifted slowly across the sea of Time until it struck a cruel rock, whose sharp teeth showed not above the dimpled waves; and where once had been a craft of strength and beauty, now was only a hideous wreck. For the Tempter had come into this Eden, and soon his foul whisper found place in her heart.

And the Tempter's name was Ambition.

Often had the praises and plaudits of men rang in her ears when her sweet voice sang to her chosen friends, often had the tears evoked by her songs of love and hope and trust, thrilled her breast faintly, as the young bird stirs in its nest under the loving mother's wing, but he had clasped his arms around her, and that was enough. But one day the Tempter whispered, "Why waste such talent; bring that beauty of voice before the world and see men bow in homage, and women envy and praise. Come forth and follow me."

But she put him fiercely aside, and cried, "I want no homage but his, I want no envy from any one."

Still the whisper stayed in her heart, nor would the honeyed words of praise be gone, even when he kissed her, and thanked the gods for this pearl of great price.

Then as time fled on, the tiny whisper grew into a great roar, and all the praise of men, and the sweet words of women, filled her brain, and what had once been her aversion became a great desire, and caused her brow to grow thoughtful, and her eyes moody.

But when she spoke to him of this new love, he smiled and said, "My wife must be mine, and mine alone. I want not a woman whom the world claims, and shouts her name abroad. My wife and my home must by [*sic*] inviolate." And again as of yore, his wish controlled her—but only for a while.

Then the tiny whisper grown into the great roar urging her on, became a mighty wind which drove her before it, nor could she turn aside from the path of ambition, but swept on, and conquered.

Ah, sweet, sweet the exultation of the victor! Dear the plaudits of the admiring world; wild the joy, when queen of song, admired of men, she stood upon the pinacle of fame! And he? True to his old convictions, turned sadly from the woman who placed the admiration of the world before his love and the happiness of his home—and went out from her life broken-hearted, disappointed, miserable.

All these things, and more, she thought upon in the first flush of eventide, as the bold, young star climbed toward his lady-love, the moon, all these things, and what had come to pass after the victory.

For there came a day when the world wearied of its toy, and turned with shouts of joy, and wreaths of fresh laurels[2] for the new star. Then came disappointments and miseries crowding fast upon her; the sorrows which a loving heart knows when its [*sic*] finds its idols faithless. Then the love for him which she had once repressed arose in all its strength which had gained during the long struggle with the world, arose and overwhelmed her with its might, and filled her soul with an unutterable longing for peace and rest and him.

She wrote to him and told him all her heart, and begged of him to come back to her, for Fame was but an empty bubble[3] while love was supreme and the only happiness, after all. And now she waited while the crimson and gold of the west grew dark, and gray and lowering.

Hark! She hears his loved step. He comes, ah, joy of heaven he comes! Soon will he clasp her in his arms, and there on his bosom shall she know peace and rest and love.

As he enters the door she hastens to meet him, the love-light shining in her tired eyes, her soft rounded arms out-stretched to meet him. But he folds her not in his

2. Laurel was sacred to the Greek sun god Apollo, the patron of music and poetry. Thus the wreath of laurel symbolized public recognition for artistic achievement.

3. James Grainger, "Ode to Solitude" (1755): "What is fame? an empty bubble."

embrace, nor yet does he look with love into her upturned eyes; the voice she loves, ah so well, breaks upon the dusky silence, pitiless, stern.

"Most faithless of faithless women, think you that like the toy of a fickle child I can be thrown aside, then picked up again? Think you that I can take a soiled lily[4] to my bosom? Think you that I can cherish the gaudy sun-flower that ever turns to the broad, brazen glare of the uncaring sun, rather than the modest shrinking, violet?[5] Nay, be not deceived, I loved you once, but that love you killed in its youth and beauty leaving me to stand and weep alone over its grave. I came to-night, not to kiss you, and to forgive you as you entreat, but to tell that you I have wed another."

The pitiless voice ceased, and she was alone in the dusky silence; alone in all the shame and agony and grief of unrequited love and worthless fame. Alone to writhe and groan in despair while the roseate flush of eventide passed into the coldness of midnight.

Oh faithless woman, oh, faithless man! How frail the memory of thy binding vows, thy blissful hours of love! Are they forgotten? Only the record of broken hearts and loveless lives will show.

Source: Violets and Other Tales (1895)

4. The lily was a symbol of a woman's chastity.
5. The violet was a symbol of modesty or a woman's faithfulness.

Victoria Smith was born a slave in Georgia. After Emancipation, she moved with her mother and four of her siblings to Virginia and later to New York, where she received some formal education. She married William E. Matthews in 1879, although their union was likely unhappy. Shortly thereafter, she began working as a journalist, publishing under the name "Victoria Earle" or other pseudonyms in African American journals as well as mainstream newspapers, such as the New York Times. *She also wrote fiction, but her greatest influence was as a clubwoman and social worker. She held a prominent position in the National Association of Colored Women and helped found a mission for African American women in New York. Matthews gave her lecture "The Value of Race Literature" at the National Conference of Colored Women in 1895. It was not published until 1986 but is considered a key document in the history of African American criticism. Like Anna Julia Cooper's "The Negro in Literature," it chronicles the prejudiced portrayals of African Americans in white literature and calls for self-representation. The portion concerning the contributions of women writers is reprinted here.*

The Value of Race Literature

. . . And now comes the question, What part shall we women play in the Race Literature of the future? I shall best answer that question by calling your attention to the glorious part which they have already performed in the columns of the "Woman's Era," edited by Josephine St. P. Ruffin.[1]

Here within the compass of one small journal we have struck out a new line of departure—a journal, a record of Race interests gathered from all parts of the United States, carefully selected, moistened, winnowed and garnered by the ablest intellects of educated colored women, shrinking at no lofty theme, shirking no serious duty, aiming at every possible excellence, and determined to do their part in the future uplifting of the race.

If twenty women, by their concentrated efforts in one literary movement, can meet with such success as has engendered, planned out, and so successfully consummated this convention, what much more glorious results, what wider spread success, what grander diffusion of mental light will not come forth at the bidding of the enlarged hosts of women writers, already called into being by the stimulus of your efforts?

And here let me speak one word for my journalistic sisters who have already

1. Josephine St. Pierre Ruffin (1842–1924) was a journalist and women's and civil rights activist. In 1890 she helped found the *Woman's Era,* the first newspaper for African American women, and served as its editor until 1897.

entered the broad arena of journalism. Before the "Woman's Era" had come into existence, no one except themselves can appreciate the bitter experience and sore disappointments under which they have at all times been compelled to pursue their chosen vocations.

If their brothers of the press have had their difficulties to contend with, I am here as a sister journalist to state, from the fullness of knowledge, that their task has been an easy one compared with that of the colored woman in journalism.

Woman's part in Race Literature, as in Race building,[2] is the most important part and has been so in all ages. It is for her to receive impressions and transmit them. All through the most remote epochs she has done her share in literature. When not an active singer like Sappho,[3] she has been the means of producing poets, statesmen, and historians, understandingly as Napoleon's mother worked on Homeric tapestry while bearing the future conqueror of the world.[4]

When living up to her highest development, woman has done much to make lasting history, by her stimulating influence and there can be no greater responsibility than that, and this is the highest privilege granted to her by the Creator of the Universe. . .

Source: Massachusetts Review (1986)

2. After the demise of slavery and Reconstruction, African American elites promoted the idea of "uplifting the race," what Matthews here calls "Race building." The goal was civic equality to be gained by the recognition of blacks' common humanity with whites. The means to achieving such recognition were education, middle-class values and status, and public eloquence. Matthews argues in her lecture that literary accomplishments will play a central role as well.

3. Greek lyric poet of the sixth century B.C., widely considered the greatest female poet before the modern era.

4. Legend had it that when Napoleon was born he was wrapped in a tapestry depicting battles from Homer's *Iliad*.

≈ Sarah Piatt (1836–1919)

A daughter of the Kentucky planter class, Sarah Morgan Bryan was well educated and began to publish her poetry in local newspapers in 1855. She married the poet John James Piatt in 1861. They had eight children, only two of whom lived to adulthood. Her husband served as her editor and agent, helping her gain access to the most prestigious literary magazines. However, despite her prolific career, her poetry was not well received due to its often enigmatic or critical themes and irregular rhythms. Today Piatt's poetry is gaining renewed recognition for its anticipation of modernism. The following poems depict the powers and the sorrows of artists and poets. In "A Mistake in the Bird-Market," Piatt inverts the outcome of traditional Persian fables in which the more unusual song of the nightingale is preferred to the predictable, familiar song of the more common bird.[1] Like "Tabitha," Fanny Fern, Thrace Talmon, and Elizabeth Stoddard, Piatt thus laments the fate of the unfeminine woman writer.

A Wood Bird's Whim

Hollow of a dead man's breast,
   In a mighty wood—
Here's a place to make a nest
   And to warm a brood!

Bees through its caressing vines,
   Honey-heavy, flit;
Every star of God that shines
   Sees the way to it.

Buds which at their beauty blush
   Weep their dews out here;
And the snake—I pray you, hush!
   Something slides a-near.

Was he poet?—he to whom
   All these things have paid
Reverent rites in sacred gloom,
   Loving, not afraid?

---

1. Retellings of these fables can be found in G. Moir Bussey, *Fables Original and Selected; By the most Esteemed European and Oriental Authors* (1842), 277–79.

He was poet. What dark whim
  Set his heart to wings?—
Oh, the song that wasted him
  Now the wild bird sings!

Source: The Century (1897)

A Mistake in the Bird-Market

A Persian in the market-place
  Longed for, and so took home, a wren.
Yes, his was but a common case;
  Such always are the ways of men!

Once his, the brown bird pleased him not;
  Almost he wished it would take wing.
He loosed the cage-door, and forgot
  The dark, unsinging, lonely thing.

Night came, and touched with wind and dew
  (Alone there in the dim moonshine)
A rose that at the window grew—
  And oh, that sudden song divine!

His children started from their sleep,
  Their Orient eyes with rapture lit;
Their pale young mother hid to weep;
  Their father did not care a whit.

He only heard the impassioned wail
  From that small prison overhead.
"My wren is but a nightingale!²
  I'll wring its noisy throat!" he said.

Source: The Century (1898)

2. A small reddish-brown thrush known for its beautiful song; however only the male sings (a mating song) while the female is silent. Ironically, in Greek mythology and later literature, the nightingale had been used to signify a female singer or poet.

✿ KATE CHOPIN (1851–1904)

Katherine O'Flaherty, raised in a wealthy St. Louis family and educated at the Sacred Heart Convent, married Oscar Chopin, a successful New Orleans cotton broker, in 1870. For nine years, the couple enjoyed a prosperous life in New Orleans with their six children until Oscar's business failed. After his death in 1882, Kate briefly took over the management of their northern Louisiana plantation, but in 1884, she returned with her children to St. Louis, where she lived for the rest of her life. It was her family doctor who noticed the fine writing in her letters and encouraged her to try her hand at fiction. She published her first story in 1889, producing thereafter a hundred stories and sketches as well as two novels. Her novel The Awakening *(1899) is today considered a classic in women's fiction, although it initially received mixed reviews, some condemning the novel's want of morality. Some have speculated that this negative response influenced Chopin to cease her career. In the following essay, she describes her method of writing and her reluctance to consider herself an "author."*

Untitled Essay

On certain brisk, bright days I like to walk from my home near Thirty-fourth street, down to the shopping district. After a few such experiments I begin to fancy that I have the walking habit. Doubtless I convey the same impression to acquaintances who see me from the car window "hot-footing" it down Olive street or Washington avenue. But in my sub-consciousness, as my friend Mrs. R—— would say, I know that I have not the walking habit.

Eight or nine years ago I began to write stories—short stories which appeared in the magazines, and I forthwith began to suspect I had the writing habit. The public shared this impression, and called me an author. Since then, though I have written many short stories and a novel or two, I am forced to admit that I have not the writing habit. But it is hard to make people with the questioning habit believe this.

"Now, where, when, why, what do you write?" are some of the questions that I remember. How do I write? On a lapboard with a block of paper, a stub pen and a bottle of ink bought at the corner grocery, which keeps the best in town.

Where do I write? In a Morris chair[1] beside the window, where I can see a few trees and a patch of sky, more or less blue.

When do I write? I am greatly tempted here to use slang and reply "any old time," but that would lend a tone of levity to this bit of confidence, whose serious-

---

1. A reclining chair designed by William Morris (1834–1896), a founder of the Arts and Craft movement.

ness I want to keep intact if possible. So I shall say I write in the morning, when not too strongly drawn to struggle with the intricacies of a pattern, and in the afternoon, if the temptation to try a new furniture polish on an old table leg is not too powerful to be denied; sometimes at night, though as I grow older I am more and more inclined to believe that night was made for sleep.

"Why do I write?" is a question which I have often asked myself and never very satisfactorily answered. Story-writing—at least with me—is the spontaneous expression of impressions gathered goodness knows where. To seek the source, the impulse of a story is like tearing a flower to pieces for wantonness.

What do I write? Well, not everything that comes into my head, but much of what I have written lies between the covers of my books.

There are stories that seem to write themselves, and others which positively refuse to be written—which no amount of coaxing can bring to anything. I do not believe any writer has ever made a "portrait" in fiction. A trick, a mannerism, a physical trait or mental characteristic go a very short way towards portraying the complete individual in real life who suggests the individual in the writer's imagination. The "material" of a writer is to the last degree uncertain, and I fear not marketable. I have been told stories which were looked upon as veritable gold mines by the generous narrators who placed them at my disposal. I have been taken to spots supposed to be alive with local color. I have been introduced to excruciating characters with frank permission to use them as I liked, but never, in any single instance, has such material been of the slightest service. I am completely at the mercy of unconscious selection. To such an extent is this true, that what is called the polishing up process has always proved disastrous to my work, and I avoid it, preferring the integrity of crudities to artificialities.

How hard it is for one's acquaintances and friends to realize that one's books are to be taken seriously, and that they are subject to the same laws which govern the existence of others' books! I have a son who is growing wroth[2] over the question: "Where can I find your mother's books, or latest book?"

"The very next time any one asks me that question," he exclaimed excitedly, "I am going to tell them to try the stock yards!"

I hope he won't. He might thus offend a possible buyer. Politeness, besides being a virtue, is sometimes an art. I am often met with the same question, and I always try to be polite. "My latest book? Why, you will find it, no doubt, at the bookseller's or the libraries."

"The libraries! Oh, no, they don't keep it." She hadn't thought of the bookseller's. It's real hard to think of everything! Sometimes I feel as if I should like to get a good, remunerative job to do the thinking for some people. This may sound conceited, but it isn't. If I had space (I have plenty of time; time is my own, but

2. Indignant.

space belongs to the Post-Dispatch), I should like to demonstrate satisfactorily that it is not conceited.

I trust it will not be giving away professional secrets to say that many readers would be surprised, perhaps shocked, at the questions which some newspaper editors will put to a defenseless woman under the guise of flattery.

For instance: "How many children have you?" This form is subtle and greatly to be commended in dealing with women of shy and retiring propensities. A woman's reluctance to speak of her children has not yet been chronicled. I have a good many, but they'd be simply wild if I dragged them into this. I might say something of those who are at a safe distance—the idol of my soul in Kentucky; the light of my eye off in Colorado; the treasure of his mother's heart in Louisiana—but I mistrust the form of their displeasure, with poisoned candy going through the mails.

"Do you smoke cigarettes?" is a question which I consider impertinent, and I think most women will agree with me. Suppose I do smoke cigarettes? Am I going to tell it out in meeting?[3] Suppose I don't smoke cigarettes. Am I going to admit such a reflection upon my artistic integrity, and thereby bring upon myself the contempt of the guild?

In answering questions in which an editor believes his readers to be interested, the victim cannot take herself too seriously.

Source: St. Louis Post-Dispatch (1899)

3. Reference to Quakers' practice of sitting silent in meeting until moved by the Spirit to speak.

⁊ PAULINE HOPKINS (1859–1930)

Pauline Elizabeth Hopkins was born in Portland, Maine, and raised in Boston, where she attended the Girls' High School. She began her literary career in 1880 as a playwright and performed in her own plays as a member of her family's acting troupe. After a decade as a stenographer and lecturer, she began to publish fiction in 1900. Hopkins wrote for the Colored American Magazine, *the most influential African American literary magazine of its time, and served for a time as its editor. She is most well known today as the author of* Contending Forces *(1900), a historical romance featuring Sappho Clark, an octoroon orphan who struggles to overcome a past marked by rape and forced prostitution.* Contending Forces *is a political novel that condemns the sexual exploitation of black women and the lynching of black men. As her preface to the novel shows, Hopkins saw fiction as a vehicle for social change, and she believed that African Americans had to speak for themselves rather than rely on whites to take up their cause.*

Preface to *Contending Forces*

In giving this little romance expression in print, I am not actuated by a desire for notoriety or for profit, but to do all that I can in an humble way to raise the stigma of degradation from my race.

While I make no apology for my somewhat abrupt and daring venture within the wide field of romantic literature, I ask the kind indulgence of the generous public for the many crudities which I know appear in the work, and their approval of whatever may impress them as being of value to the Negro race and to the world at large.

The colored race has historians, lecturers, ministers, poets, judges and lawyers,—men of brilliant intellects who have arrested the favorable attention of this busy, energetic nation. But, after all, it is the simple, homely tale, unassumingly told, which cements the bond of brotherhood among all classes and all complexions.

Fiction is of great value to any people as a preserver of manners and customs—religious, political and social. It is a record of growth and development from generation to generation. *No one will do this for us; we must ourselves develop the men and women who will faithfully portray the inmost thoughts and feelings of the Negro with all the fire and romance which lie dormant in our history,* and, as yet, unrecognized by writers of the Anglo-Saxon race.

The incidents portrayed in the early chapters of the book actually occurred. Ample proof of this may be found in the archives of the courthouse at Newberne, N. C., and at the national seat of government, Washington, D. C.

In these days of mob violence, when lynch-law is raising its head like a venomous monster, more particularly in the southern portion of the great American republic, the retrospective mind will dwell upon the history of the past, seeking there a solution of these monstrous outbreaks under a government founded upon the greatest and brightest of principles for the elevation of mankind. While we ponder the philosophy of cause and effect, the world is horrified by a fresh outbreak, and the shocked mind wonders that in this—the brightest epoch of the Christian era— *such things are.*

Mob-law is nothing new. Southern sentiment has not been changed; the old ideas close in analogy to the spirit of the buccaneers, who formed in many instances the first settlers of the Southland, still prevail, and break forth clothed in new forms to force the whole republic to an acceptance of its principles.

"Rule or ruin" is the motto which is committing the most beautiful portion of our glorious country to a cruel revival of piratical methods; and, finally, to the introduction of *Anarchy.* Is this not so? Let us compare the happenings of one hundred—two hundred years ago, with those of today. The difference between then and now, if any there be, is so slight as to be scarcely worth mentioning. The atrocity of the acts committed one hundred years ago are duplicated today, when slavery is supposed no longer to exist.

I have tried to tell an impartial story, leaving it to the reader to draw conclusions. I have tried to portray our hard struggles here in the North to obtain a respectable living and a partial education. I have presented both sides of the dark picture—lynching and concubinage—truthfully and without vituperation, pleading for that justice of heart and mind for my people which the Anglo-Saxon in America never withholds from suffering humanity.

In Chapter XIII. I have used for the address of the Hon. Herbert Clapp the statements and accusations made against the Negro by ex-Governor Northen of Georgia,[1] in his memorable address before the Congregational Club at Tremont Temple, Boston, Mass., May 22, 1899. In Chapter XV. I have made Will Smith's argument in answer to the Hon. Herbert Clapp a combination of the best points made by well-known public speakers in the United States—white and black—in defense of the Negro. I feel my own deficiencies too strongly to attempt original composition on this subject at this crisis in the history of the Negro in the United States. I have introduced enough of the exquisitely droll humor peculiar to the Negro (a work like this would not be complete without it) to give a bright touch to an otherwise gruesome subject.

Source: Contending Forces: A Romance Illustrative of Negro Life North and South (1900)

---

1. William Jonathan Northen (1835–1913) was a conservative Democratic governor of Georgia from 1890 to 1894. Although he repeatedly advocated the enactment of anti-lynch laws, which were not passed, he was also viewed as paternalistic toward African Americans. He spoke on the "white man's view" of conditions for African Americans in the South to the Congregational Club in Boston on May 22, 1889. Booker T. Washington was asked to speak on the "black man's view." See his letter to Washington, Feb. 24, 1899, in *The Booker T. Washington Papers,* vol. 5 (1976).

🐦 PRISCILLA JANE THOMPSON (1871–1942)

A native of Ohio, Thompson never married and lived with her sister, Clara, who was also a poet. She wrote in the introduction to her self-published volume, Gleanings of Quiet Hours *(1907), "if in any of these humble and simple rhymes, a passage or thought may chance prove a medium, through which the race may be elevated, or benefited, if only in the private mind of some reader, the writer feels, that her efforts is [sic] fully repaid." "The Muse's Favor" and "The Song" pay tribute to the beauty of African American women, who have been left out of the tradition of poetry.*

The Muse's Favor

Oh Muse! I crave a favor,
   Grant but this one unto me;
Thou hast always been indulgent—
   So I boldly come to thee.

For oft I list thy singing—
   And the accents, sweet and clear,
Like the rhythmic flow of waters,
   Fall on my ecstatic ear.

But of Caucasia's daughters,
   So oft I've heard thy lay,[1]
That the music, too familiar—
   Falls in sheer monotony.

And now, oh Muse exalted!
   Exchange this old song staid,
For an equally deserving—
   The oft slighted, Afric maids.

The Muse, with smiles, consenting,
   Runs her hand the strings along,
And the harp, as bound by duty—
Rings out with the tardy song.

---

1. Simple narrative poem.

The Song

Oh, foully slighted Ethiope maid!
With patience, bearing rude upbraid,
With sweet, refined, retiring, grace,
And sunshine ling'ring in thy face,
With eyes bedewed and pityingly,
   I sing of thee, I sing of thee.

Thy dark and misty curly hair,
In small, neat, braids entwineth fair,
Like clusters of rich, shining, jet,
All wrapt in mist, when sun is set;
Fair maid, I gaze admiringly,
   And sing of thee, and sing of thee.

Thy smooth and silky, dusky skin,
Thine eyes of sloe, thy dimple chin,
That pure and simple heart of thine,
'Tis these that make thee half divine;
Oh maid! I gaze admiringly,
And sing of thee, and sing of thee.

Oh modest maid, with beauty rare,
Whoe'er hath praised thy lithe form, fair?
Thy tender mein,[2] thy fairy tread—
Thy winsome face and queenly head?
Naught of thy due in verse I see,
   All pityingly I sing of thee.

Who've dared to laud thee 'fore the world,
And face the stigma of a churl?[3]
Or brook the fiery, deep, disdain—
Their portion, who defend thy name?
Oh maiden, wronged so cowardly,
   I boldly, loudly, sing of thee.

Who've stood the test of chastity,
Through slav'ry's blasting tyranny,

2. Misspelling of "mien," which refers to the look, bearing, or conduct of a person.
3. A term of contempt; a rude, low-bred person.

And kept the while, their virtuous grace,
To instill in a trampled race?
Fair maid, thy equal few may see;
Thrice honored I, to sing of thee.

Let cowards fear thy name to praise,
Let scoffers seek thee but to raze;[4]
Despite their foul, ignoble, jeers,
A worthy model thou appear,
Enrobed in love and purity;
   Oh who dare blush, to sing of thee?

And now, oh maid, forgive I pray,
The tardiness of my poor lay;
The weight of wrongs unto thee done—
Did paralize my falt'ring tongue;
'Twas my mute, innate, sympathy,—
   That staid this song, I sing to thee.

Source: Ethiope Lays (1900)

   4. To cut, erase, or destroy.

❧ ZITKALA-ŠA (1876–1938)

Born Gertrude Simmons, Zitkala-Ša was a member of the Yankton Sioux tribe in South Dakota. In her youth, she endured a painful separation from her mother while attending a Quaker-run boarding school in Indiana. She later attended college, becoming a teacher and an accomplished violinist. In 1900, she adopted a Lakota nom de plume Zitkala-Ša (Red Bird), under which she published three autobiographical essays in the Atlantic Monthly. *In the passages excerpted below, she conveys her painful transition from a traditional story-telling culture to white "civilization," a text-based culture. She later married Raymond T. Bonnin and worked with him on behalf of Native American rights for the rest of her life, editing for a time the* American Indian Magazine *and publishing collections of Native American folktales, through which she sought to preserve the oral traditions of her people.*

Impressions of an Indian Childhood

THE LEGENDS

During the summer days, my mother built her fire in the shadow of our wigwam.

In the early morning our simple breakfast was spread upon the grass west of our tepee. At the farthest point of the shade my mother sat beside her fire, toasting a savory piece of dried meat. Near her, I sat upon my feet, eating my dried meat with unleavened bread, and drinking strong black coffee.

The morning meal was our quiet hour, when we two were entirely alone. At noon, several who chanced to be passing by stopped to rest, and to share our luncheon with us, for they were sure of our hospitality.

My uncle, whose death my mother ever lamented, was one of our nation's bravest warriors. His name was on the lips of old men when talking of the proud feats of valor; and it was mentioned by younger men, too, in connection with deeds of gallantry. Old women praised him for his kindness toward them; young women held him up as an ideal to their sweethearts. Every one loved him, and my mother worshiped his memory. Thus it happened that even strangers were sure of welcome in our lodge, if they but asked a favor in my uncle's name.

Though I heard many strange experiences related by these wayfarers, I loved best the evening meal, for that was the time old legends were told. I was always glad when the sun hung low in the west, for then my mother sent me to invite the neighboring old men and women to eat supper with us. Running all the way to the wigwams, I halted shyly at the entrances. Sometimes I stood long moments without saying a word. It was not any fear that made me so dumb when out upon such a happy errand; nor was it that I wished to withhold the invitation, for it was all I could do to observe this very proper silence. But it was a sensing of the atmosphere, to assure myself that I should not hinder other plans. My mother used to say to me, as I was almost bounding away for the old people: "Wait a moment before you invite any one. If other plans are being discussed, do not interfere, but go elsewhere."

The old folks knew the meaning of my pauses; and often they coaxed my confidence by asking, "What do you seek, little granddaughter?"

"My mother says you are to come to our tepee this evening," I instantly exploded, and breathed the freer afterwards.

"Yes, yes, gladly, gladly I shall come!" each replied. Rising at once and carrying their blankets across one shoulder, they flocked leisurely from their various wigwams toward our dwelling.

My mission done, I ran back, skipping and jumping with delight. All out of breath, I told my mother almost the exact words of the answers to my invitation. Frequently she asked, "What were they doing when you entered their tepee?" This taught me to remember all I saw at a single glance. Often I told my mother my impressions without being questioned.

While in the neighboring wigwams sometimes an old Indian woman asked me, "What is your mother doing?" Unless my mother had cautioned me not to tell, I generally answered her questions without reserve.

At the arrival of our guests I sat close to my mother, and did not leave her side without first asking her consent. I ate my supper in quiet, listening patiently to the talk of the old people, wishing all the time that they would begin the stories I loved best. At last, when I could not wait any longer, I whispered in my mother's ear, "Ask them to tell an Iktomi[1] story, mother."

Soothing my impatience, my mother said aloud, "My little daughter is anxious to hear your legends." By this time all were through eating, and the evening was fast deepening into twilight.

As each in turn began to tell a legend, I pillowed my head in my mother's lap; and lying flat upon my back, I watched the stars as they peeped down upon me, one by one. The increasing interest of the tale aroused me, and I sat up eagerly listening for every word. The old women made funny remarks, and laughed so heartily that I could not help joining them.

The distant howling of a pack of wolves or the hooting of an owl in the river bottom frightened me, and I nestled into my mother's lap. She added some dry sticks to the open fire, and the bright flames leaped up into the faces of the old folks as they sat around in a great circle. . . .

---

1. A shape-shifting deity in Lakota mythology who usually appears as a spider. Zitkala-Ša would tell many of these stories in her collection *Old Indian Legends* (1901).

An Indian Teacher Among Indians

RETROSPECTION

Leaving my mother, I returned to the school in the East. As months passed over me, I slowly comprehended that the large army of white teachers in Indian schools had a larger missionary creed than I had suspected.

It was one which included self-preservation quite as much as Indian education. When I saw an opium-eater holding a position as teacher of Indians, I did not understand what good was expected, until a Christian in power replied that this pumpkin-colored creature had a feeble mother to support. An inebriate paleface sat stupid in a doctor's chair, while Indian patients carried their ailments to untimely graves, because his fair wife was dependent upon him for her daily food.

I find it hard to count that white man a teacher who tortured an ambitious Indian youth by frequently reminding the brave changeling that he was nothing but a "government pauper."

Though I burned with indignation upon discovering on every side instances no less shameful than those I have mentioned, there was no present help. Even the few rare ones who have worked nobly for my race were powerless to choose workmen like themselves. To be sure, a man was sent from the Great Father[2] to inspect Indian schools, but what he saw was usually the students' sample work *made* for exhibition. I was nettled by this sly cunning of the workmen who hoodwinked the Indian's pale Father at Washington.

My illness, which prevented the conclusion of my college course, together with my mother's stories of the encroaching frontier settlers, left me in no mood to strain my eyes in searching for latent good in my white co-workers.

At this stage of my own evolution, I was ready to curse men of small capacity for being the dwarfs their God had made them. In the process of my education I had lost all consciousness of the nature world about me. Thus, when a hidden rage took me to the small white-walled prison which I then called my room, I unknowingly turned away from my one salvation.

Alone in my room, I sat like the petrified Indian woman of whom my mother used to tell me. I wished my heart's burdens would turn me to unfeeling stone. But alive, in my tomb, I was destitute!

For the white man's papers I had given up my faith in the Great Spirit.[3] For these same papers I had forgotten the healing in trees and brooks. On account of my mother's simple view of life, and my lack of any, I gave her up, also. I made no

---

2. Nineteenth-century Native Americans often used the term "Great Father" to refer to the U.S. president.

3. In Native American religions, the Great Spirit is the supreme creator who, unlike the Christian God, is embodied in the natural world.

friends among the race of people I loathed. Like a slender tree, I had been uprooted from my mother, nature, and God. I was shorn of my branches, which had waved in sympathy and love for home and friends. The natural coat of bark which had protected my oversensitive nature was scraped off to the very quick.

Now a cold bare pole I seemed to be, planted in a strange earth. Still, I seemed to hope a day would come when my mute aching head, reared upward to the sky, would flash a zigzag lightning across the heavens. With this dream of vent for a long-pent consciousness, I walked again amid the crowds.

At last, one weary day in the school-room, a new idea presented itself to me. It was a new way of solving the problem of my inner self. I liked it. Thus I resigned my position as teacher; and now I am in an Eastern city, following the long course of study I have set for myself. Now, as I look back upon the recent past, I see it from a distance, as a whole. I remember how, from morning till evening, many specimens of civilized peoples visited the Indian school. The city folks with canes and eyeglasses, the countrymen with sunburnt cheeks and clumsy feet, forgot their relative social ranks in an ignorant curiosity. Both sorts of these Christian palefaces were alike astounded at seeing the children of savage warriors so docile and industrious.

As answers to their shallow inquiries they received the students' sample work to look upon. Examining the neatly figured pages, and gazing upon the Indian girls and boys bending over their books, the white visitors walked out of the schoolhouse well satisfied: they were educating the children of the red man! They were paying a liberal fee to the government employees in whose able hands lay the small forest of Indian timber.

In this fashion many have passed idly through the Indian schools during the last decade, afterward to boast of their charity to the North American Indian. But few there are who have paused to question whether real life or long-lasting death lies beneath this semblance of civilization.

Source: Atlantic Monthly (1900)

❧ HENRIETTA CORDELIA RAY (1849–1916)

Henrietta Cordelia Ray was born in New York City and became a teacher after receiving a master's degree from the University of the City of New York in 1891. Her father was a well-known minister, abolitionist, and newspaper editor. She lived her entire life with her sister, Florence, who was also a teacher. She began to publish her poetry in the 1880s, and many of the verses collected in Poems *(1910) initially appeared before the turn of the century. They reflect her extensive education and participate in the genteel tradition of poetry without specific reference to her African American race.*

The Poet's Ideal

"Spirit! what art thou erecting
On the heights of contemplation,
Where the vistas blue and shadowy,
Fade in airy clouds away?
At the fane of meditation
Art thou bowed to-day?"

"Lo! I climbed in floating ether
When the first tints of the dawning,
O'er the pale stars chaste in grandeur,
Shed a stream of liquid light;
In the azure calm of morning
Gleamed a vision bright.

"Twas air-fashioned: faint, dissolving,
Seemed its statuesque proportions,
Yet imperious and majestic
Were its gestures and its mien;
And all beauty seemed distortions
To this,—fairest ever seen.

"Round its head a circlet shaping,
Wove a cloud its golden tissues,
Where these words were writ in splendor:
'Ideal Beauty is my name;
I from life draw finest issues,
Wouldst thou do the same?'

"Poised aloft on heights serenest,
There she stands,—that radiant vision.
At the fane of meditation,
Wouldst thou know, O questioner?
Lo! I bow in calm decision,
Yield my thoughts to her.

"'Mid the vistas blue and shadowy,
'Mid the ether iris-tinted,
I erect Ideal Perfection,
And then worship at her shrine;
To the poet she has hinted
Sense of things divine."

Aspiration

We climb the slopes of life with throbbing heart,
And eager pulse, like children toward a star.
Sweet siren music cometh from afar,
To lure us on meanwhile. Responsive start
The nightingales to richer song than Art
Can ever teach. No passing shadows mar
Awhile the dewy skies; no inner jar
Of conflict bids us with our quest to part.
We see adown the distance, rainbow-arched,
What melting aisles of liquid light and bloom!
We hasten, tremulous, with lips all parched,
And eyes wide-stretched, nor dream of coming gloom.
Enough that something held almost divine
Within us ever stirs. Can we repine?

Source: Poems (1910)

🍃 Onoto Watanna (Winnifred Eaton) (1875–1954)

Winnifred Eaton was born to a Chinese mother and English father in Montreal, Canada. She and her sister, Edith Eaton, both became writers and took differing paths to reconciling their Chinese ancestry with American prejudices. While Edith adopted the Chinese pen name "Sui Sin Far," Winnifred took a Japanese pseudonym, "Onoto Watanna," presumably because the Japanese were viewed more favorably than the much-denigrated Chinese. Sui Sin Far's writings worked to dismantle stereotypes of Chinese immigrants, while Onoto Watanna's works, mostly romance novels, capitalized on the vogue of the exotic Far East. Onoto Watanna began to publish stories at the age of fourteen, and her first novel, which came out in 1899, was the first published by an Asian American. In 1901, after five years in Chicago, she moved to New York to pursue a full-time career as an author. She lived there until 1917. A prolific and popular novelist, Watanna also worked as a screenwriter for Hollywood in the 1920s. She was married twice and had four children. The following essay (which does not accurately represent her age) describes her early struggling-author days in New York.

Starving and Writing in New York

I was not quite eighteen years old when I made my entrance into New York City. I had a letter from Mr. S—— editor of Frank Leslie's Magazine. Instead of the usual printed rejection slip, Mr. S—— had written me a quarter page letter, in which he expressed an interest in my work and suggested that I should let his magazine see whatever else I had written besides the short story "regretfully returned."

Upon my arrival in New York City, I did not wait to secure lodgings, but went straight from the train, bag in hand, to the Frank Leslie office. Having explained to the editor who I was,—it was plain he had forgotten that letter he had written me—I said:

" — and you wrote me to let you see anything else I have written, and so—"

I opened my bag. He leaped to his feet, threw up his hands, and shouted at the top of his voice:

"Help! Help!"

In rushed half-a-dozen clerks and editors, and the wild looking Mr. S—— pointed dramatically to that bag of mine, which was brim full to the top with manuscripts.

With a vague idea that I was about to be arrested for some crime or another, I burst into tears. I bawled as hard and heartily as only a husky youngster can, with the result that that outrageous mirth was silenced, and Mr. S——, alternately wringing his hands and running them through his hair, implored me to stop weeping. He said:

"Now don't cry! Don't cry, I say! Don't cry! For heaven's sakes, don't cry! Stop it, I say! I'll buy a story from you—it's all right. There, there now—stop crying. Shut up, do!"

In later years, Mr. S—— and I occasionally met, and he never failed to recall that amusing episode, and he told his friends that I had blackmailed him into buying my first story from me with tears.

Whatever I lacked in talent, I made up in pertinacity. I was determined, by hook or crook, by fair means or foul, to get my stories and poems read and published. When driven by extreme necessity, however, I was forced to seek employment. I would take a temporary position in an office, and hold the position until such time as a story would be sold, and I was again in funds. One such position I obtained in the office of the K— Publishing Company, and before I had been there a week, by a fortunate, or unfortunate, coincidence, I was elevated to the position of private secretary to Mr. K— —, the president. He was a big, lanky, sandy-haired man, with large freckles on his nose. He reminded me a bit of Bob Fitzsimmons,[1] with whom I once had shaken hands when in Chicago, a crushing experience that I never forgot.

SOME EVADED CENSORS

In those days, I picked up a most precarious sort of living in New York. I wrote and wrote and wrote, and I was undaunted by the unflattering return of my manuscripts by every mail. One or two, it is true, did slip by the censors, and the thrills I then enjoyed, and the much needed checks, more than compensated for the many weeks and months of drought. Curiously enough, in spite of privations, that, looking back upon them now, seem to me appalling, when considered in connection with an extremely young and ignorant girl, my heart was always light and my head teemed with plots and ideas.

I lived with two other girls in a dingy room on the top floor of a house on East Sixteenth St., between Union Square and Third Avenue. My two roommates were as penniless and improvident as I, but we managed to exist, and even squeeze a measure of fun out of life. Our jobs were always uncertain, but each staked the other when the other was "broke." That plan worked very well, except when we were all "broke" at the same time. Then we were sore put to make two ends meet.

Jocelyn, or "Jossy" as we called her, the oldest of our trio, was a dark-eyed girl from the sunny South. She had a voice like a mellow bell, and was studying vocal culture. At least, she studied it when she had the price and a piano to practise on. Jossy would have $5 in hand, to pay for a month's rent of a piano. When the month was up, the piano people would begin to dun, and they would keep on dunning for

---

1. Robert James Fitzsimmons (1863–1917) was a boxer from New Zealand who won three world champion titles.

a month, and sometimes two months; then they would take the piano away; but, you see, she would have had the piano for two or three months at the price of one.

Jocelyn was an outlaw from home, because of her operatic aspirations. She was a practical young person, who always seemed out of place in our rackety-packety room.

Anna Andison, my other room-mate, was an overwhelmingly beautiful girl of Danish birth. She had milk-white skin, as soft and smooth as a baby's, a neck and throat that were our envy and despair, and hair such as the daughter of a Viking might have possessed. It was so thick and long, that when she took it down, it fell nearly to the bottom of her skirt, and was dead gold in color. Her eyes were very large, with big, white, sleepy lids, and they were as blue as a Danish lake. Simple, trusting, empty eyes they were—the kind men—some men—plunge into.

Anna was built on a grand scale, and her feet and hands were of a size to match her great, graceful body. *I* had discovered Anna. She was holding down a perfectly respectable position as waitress at Bamberger's on Third Ave. when I assured her that she was destined for greater things. I knew a man who knew a stage hand who knew the stage director at Weber & Fields Theatre. To this man, I piloted my willing Anna. The thing worked like a charm. Anna secured her first job in the chorus. From that moment she had but one ambition in life—to remain in said chorus. Just as she had been entirely satisfied to wait on table for the rest of her natural days, so now Anna was satisfied to remain in the chorus. Unfortunately the various managers for whom she worked, did not always share Anna's ambition, and for two reasons she was invariably fired from one musical show after another. The first was the heaviness of her hand, which resented familiarity from those in authority over her; and the second was her utter inability to move with the agility peculiar to the chorus girl race. . . .

OUR EFFORTS TO GET A "SQUARE"

So there we were, the three of us, making two ends meet on practically nothing, and using our wits a good part of the time to save us from starvation. Some of the ways and means we resorted to, it is true, might not have been considered ethical by our more affluent sisters, but poverty, in a way, is a state of warfare, and we are assured that "All is fair in love and war." Some of the devices for obtaining a square, or half or even a quarter of a square meal were ingenious and very often disastrous. Most of our efforts however met with unqualified success. Youth and bright wits are a combination that Fate finds it hard to beat.

For instance: On the first—the parlor—floor of our residence, there dwelt a prosperous man of whose wealth and generosity and susceptibility toward the weaker sex, we heard much from our sometimes garrulous landlady. He had cast a sentimental and appraising eye on our Anna, and had made sufficient inquiries concerning her to induce our landlady to climb the four flights of stairs to our room to tell us all about it.

From that day, the man on the parlor floor was marked as a possible meal ticket, not merely for Anna, but for us. We aided and abetted by every means in our power his suit, or rather, I should say, our suit. In due time he invited Anna to go to a dinner and dance with him. Anna accepted, of course. I had told her to, and she was an obedient and grateful creature and looked upon me, humbly, in the light of a benefactor.

The three of us then put our heads together to consider the problem of a dress for Anna, for Anna possessed but one, and that hardly of a kind calculated to charm a desirable suitor. Accordingly I generously tendered to Anna my own sole party frock. It was pink and fluffy, and I was small and dark, and, therefore, showed up well in it. At that time, I weighed about a hundred pounds. Anna tipped the scales at close to a hundred and eighty. Jossy, however, was a genius with the needle. She let down that dress at least a half a foot. I, then, took Anna in hand, and, attaching her by her corset strings to the bed, I bade her pull. She pulled as hard as only a great Dane could. Presently we had her firmly encased in that dress, and, like proud mothers, we led her below to her waiting man.

That evening Jossy and I spent talking over the things we liked best to eat. I was partial to lobsters, welsh rabbit, hot dogs, chop suey, pancakes, pastry, sardines, pickles, spaghetti, and cheese. Jossy said that the mere thought of a rare porterhouse steak entirely surrounded by onions made her teeth water. As for mushrooms—the thought of mushrooms and corn made Jossy so homesick that she was ready to give up her musical career, till I talked her out of it, or, rather back to it.

We Wait for Anna

Talking about food aggravated our situation, and we hungrily watched the clock for Anna to return. She had given us her solemn word of honor—crossed her neck and crossed her heart, wished she might die a horrible death if she didn't, etc.—that she would order without stint at the dinner hour, and that she would stow away in her own ample insides only one third of the dinner. The remaining two-thirds she was to surreptitiously confine to the capacious bag with which we had provided her and which was to mask as a handkerchief holder.

At ten, there was no sign of Anna, so Jossy suggested that we should go and look for her. She declared that, in a way, we were Anna's guardians and chaperones and it was not proper for a young and innocent girl to be out alone at night with a man. They never did such things in Tennessee, Jocelyn assured me solemnly.

So we two sallied forth, and arrived duly at the dance hall, which was above a well-known German restaurant of the East Side. We were some time in discovering our Anna, for she was backed up against a wall, hidden by a solid mass of admiring and besieging males. I could see at once that my dress had made a hit. Foremost in this crowd of Anna's admirers was the man from the parlor floor.

ANNA "BUSTS" AT THE BACK

As we approached nearer to this mob we saw that Anna was in evident trouble. As soon as she saw us, a guttural exclamation of appeal escaped her lips. Whenever Anna was unduly moved by emotion or excitement, she invariably forgot the exquisite accent I was painstakingly teaching her, and lapsed into a sort of English version of her mother tongue. Now as we pushed our way through the crowd and came directly to her, she whispered hoarsely in my ear;

"I ban busted!"

"You ban what?" I whispered back, hoarsely also.

"I ban busted. I ban busted on dam corset, and I ban busted on dam dress on dam back."

I know that backless evening gowns are now the vogue, but it was not so in my young days. I realized at once the fatal sensation and disgrace that would befall us should Anna turn around. Jocelyn, the practical and resourceful in all crises, pushed me aside, and hissed:

"Faint! Faint! Faint, you fool! Don't you understand? I say, faint! Faint, you big slob. Fall over. Pretend to die!"

A MEAL TICKET AT LAST

When at last it percolated through Anna's skull that a swoon might save the day for us, she fell promptly backward with such a crash that I am sure she nearly broke the arm of the man from the parlor floor, who nobly sprang to her rescue.

There she lay in a dead faint on the floor, her rosy face upturned and her ruby lips parted widely as she breathed through them stertorously.

Luckily for our fortunes, soon after this, the Dutch delicatessen man on Third Avenue fell passionately in love with Anna, and for a time we lived upon the fat of the land. I made up a rhyme which we sang to the tune of "Just before the Battle, Mother." Jossy would sit at the head of the stairs when Anna's beau was calling, and she would croon in her deep, heart-reaching contralto:

"Don't forget the cheese, my darling,
    Don't forget the bread and jam;
Don't forget the pickles, Anna,
    And the piece of Ham.
Goodbye, Anna, we shall never,
    Eat a bit till you get back,
But you'll not forget us, Anna,
    When you fill your little sack."

Source: Maclean's Magazine (1922)

🍃 GRACE KING (1852–1932)

Grace King was a member of an upper-class New Orleans family and, although Protestant, was educated at a convent school. However, the Civil War reversed her family's fortunes. The family struggled, and King and her sisters, who never married, were forced to depend upon their brother. When the World's Fair, called the World Cotton Centennial Exposition, was held in New Orleans in 1884, King met many influential northern writers and editors, such as Julia Ward Howe and Richard Watson Gilder, editor of the Century. As she later explained in her autobiography, she began to write in earnest after Gilder challenged her to write what she considered a more faithful portrayal of New Orleans Creoles than that produced by the popular writer George Washington Cable. King went on to publish several volumes of fiction set in New Orleans as well as histories of the city.

Memories of a Southern Woman of Letters [Excerpts]

It must not be inferred that we had no literary lights of our own in New Orleans. We had among us names that we boldly and with naïve assurance put forward when questioned by strangers. . . .

Out of this mosaic came much good entertainment and the opportunity that proved to be the opening door to my future life. When my name was announced in due course of routine for a paper,[1] I shrank back in consternation from the ordeal and had to be coaxed and persuaded by my friends to stand in the group of the previous brave volunteers. When I saw there was no escape from it, I went home miserable, but at the same time determined to stand the test for which, in truth, I had been waiting secretly.

The next morning after breakfast I sat down with pencil and paper and wrote out my thoughts on a subject that had been interesting me, "The Heroines of Fiction," a review of the different ladies we read about in English, French, and German novels. A rather caustic review it must have been, and an arrogant one. I read it at the club meeting in a trembling voice and could hardly believe my ears when I heard expressions of compliment and applause. It seemed to please everyone. The next morning Henry Austin[2] called upon me and asked permission to send it North to his paper. I consented with misgivings. Eventually it was copied in full in an English paper, which Austin brought me with a hearty exhortation to push on, that this was a good beginning. He did not convince me.

---

1. King was a member of the Pan Gnostics literary club, which was started by Julia Ward Howe while she was visiting New Orleans as head of the Woman's Department of the Cotton Centennial. King was asked to present a paper to the club.
2. Henry Willard Austin (1858–1912) was a Boston poet and journalist.

And then, suddenly and unexpectedly, there was opened to me the path leading out of and beyond the life I was living, to the life of my secret hopes and prayers, for which I had been long and humbly waiting.

Richard Watson Gilder,[3] the editor of the *Century Magazine,* was one of the most important visitors that the Exposition brought us. I knew him only vaguely; not as an editor, but as a poet of distinction in American letters. I met him at a little gathering in one of our clubs during the carnival season. He, of course, did not know me, and I could not perceive any desire on his part to know me, a perfectly reasonable attitude for a great man of letters to an insignificant creature. All that I can remember of the important meeting is that we were assembled in the reception room of the Pickwick Club, a group of about a dozen friends, whose names I do not recall, and Mr. Gilder. My brother, Branch, was present, and, as ever, was the life and soul of the party. He was devoting himself to a beautiful young lady, one of the belles of New Orleans, who, with her father, joined us.

As we were standing around in a desultory fashion, Branch had the brilliant idea of inviting us all to a supper. I whispered to him to give Mr. Gilder a special invitation. This he did so tactfully that Mr. Gilder seemed to be the guest of honor. He joined us with evident pleasure. He was a small man as I remember him, with a wonderful head, and eyes that once seen could never be forgotten—so large and luminous and keen withal. After supper, which was gay and bright in the trivial way of society, we separated to go home, and Mr. Gilder paired off with me.

As we strolled along to my home, not many blocks away, he spoke of his stay in the city. "New Orleans," he said, "holds a very sad memory for me." The young brother of his wife, an officer in the Union army, had died here, and his funeral had been grossly insulted by a lady of the city who from her gallery had publicly laughed and jeered at it.

I was shocked into a heartfelt exclamation of sympathy and hastened to explain—at least I hope I did, for in truth I remember only what he said. The lady was the wife of a distinguished lawyer, then in the Confederacy. She was on her front gallery overlooking the street, playing with a child, and without thinking, laughed aloud at some antic of the child at the unfortunate moment when a funeral was passing by, a military funeral.

She was arrested the next day and brought before General Butler,[4] who would accept no excuses or apologies but condemned her forthwith to imprisonment and solitary confinement on Ship Island, an isolated and desolate patch of sand in the

3. Richard Watson Gilder (1844–1909) was a poet and editor of the *Century* from 1881 until his death. He published works by Mark Twain and George Washington Cable.

4. Gen. Benjamin Butler (1818–1893) was the commander of the Union forces that occupied New Orleans in 1862. His notorious "woman's order" declared that any woman showing contempt for a Union soldier would be treated as "a woman of the town plying her avocation," or a prostitute.

Gulf of Mexico, or rather an outlet of the Gulf, Lake Pontchartrain, garrisoned at that time by a Negro corps. The prisoner had no other woman with her, and was left, as General Butler wished her to be, in the power and under the domination of Negroes. This constituted the bitter humiliation of her imprisonment, as her fellow citizens felt and proclaimed to the civilized world. Mr. Gilder did not allude to this, only to the heartless insult to the dead body of his brother-in-law.

After this depressing beginning he proceeded to ask questions of me about the inimical stand taken by the people of New Orleans against George Cable[5] and his works.

I hastened to enlighten him to the effect that Cable proclaimed his preference for colored people over white and assumed the inevitable superiority—according to his theories—of quadroons over the Creoles.[6] He was a native of New Orleans and had been well treated by its people, and yet he stabbed the city in the back, as we felt, in a dastardly way to please the Northern press.

While I was speaking in all earnestness and desire to inform him I could feel a cold atmosphere emanating from him and chilling me to the bone. He listened to me with icy indifference, and the rest of our walk was accomplished in silence, except for one remark. "Why," he said, "if Cable is so false to you, why do not some of you write better?"

The shot told. I had nothing to say. I reached the door of our home and shook hands with him. I did not see him again for years.

"Why, why, do we not write our side?" I asked myself furiously at home before going to bed. "Are we to submit to Cable's libels in resignation?" I could not sleep that night for thinking of Gilder's rankling taunt.

The next morning I was resolved to do at least my share in our defense, a mighty small share I felt it to be, possibly a hopeless effort. Brave with the courage of desperation, I got paper and pencil, and on the writing-table in my bedroom wrote my first story, with not an idea in my brain except that I must write it or forfeit all my allegiance to self-respect.

My pencil started off by itself, and before I was really aware of what I was doing, I was describing the old St. Louis Institute where I had been educated. I had always realized that the school was unique in a picturesque way, and that my fellow students, Creoles, were peculiarly interesting. The story shaped itself through the description of our annual Commencement Day with its great concert and distribu-

5. George Washington Cable (1844–1925) was a novelist who had garnered exceptional acclaim from northern readers for his depiction of his native New Orleans. However, many white locals felt that he had portrayed them unfavorably.

6. Quadroons: persons of one-quarter African ancestry. Creoles: people of European, African, and/or Native American ancestry born in the New World colonies. Here King refers to the class of people of French and/or Spanish descent in Louisiana, as distinguished from people of color and from the Americans who immigrated to Louisiana after the Louisiana Purchase in 1803.

tion of prizes. The quadroon woman, Marcelite, I took from life, as also the head of the *Institut,* Madame la Reveillière, who was the old beloved and respected Madame Lavillebeuvre.

I could not write fast enough, I remember, and finished the story in one sitting. The next day I copied it. I said to myself, "I will show Mr. Gilder that we in New Orleans can at least make an effort to show what we are; we are not entirely dependent upon Mr. George Cable's pen!"

I showed the little story to my sisters in a defiant spurt of courage, and then I enveloped it, without signing it, and mailed it to Mr. Gilder. I was determined that he should not trace it to me, to avoid personal humiliation when it was refused, for I was certain it would be refused immediately.

There was an old bookseller and antique dealer at the corner of our street, a remarkable old man, who collected books, pictures, and the débris of old houses—pictures, cut glass, and silver. His name was Hawkins. He looked upon himself as a friend of the family, and he was in addition a great friend of Judge Gayarré's,[7] whom he admired and with whom he kept in touch. So to Hawkins I directed that my manuscript be returned, after telling him all about it. He was pleased to be my intermediary, and this led to a good many pleasant visits to his shop and much interesting conversation during the following years. After allowing the necessary time for the post, I went to Mr. Hawkins and, as I expected, received my story back without a word of comment. . . .

Curiously, as things happen now and then, on the very day that my story was returned to me from the *Century Magazine,* I received a letter from Mr. Warner,[8] who had heard of my "Heroines of Fiction," in which he reproached me for not giving him the pleasure of forwarding it to a publisher, assuring me of his willingness to serve me in any literary way. Accordingly, I wrote him all the circumstances that had plunged me into writing a story and sent him my rejected manuscript.

The dénouement came punctually a week later. It was an overwhelming surprise, an incredible one. Mr. Warner wrote that after reading my story he was convinced that it was good and that it should be published. He had taken it with him to New York, where *Harper's Magazine* business called him, and had shown it to his good friend, Mr. Alden,[9] the editor of the magazine, who asked that it be left with him; he would look at it later.

Mr. Warner left the manuscript on Mr. Alden's desk and took his departure. On reaching the street he ran upon his friend, Professor Sloane,[10] the editor of the *New*

7. Charles Gayarré (1805–1895), New Orleans historian, lawyer, judge, and author, as well as King's friend.

8. Charles Dudley Warner (1829–1900), author and member of the editorial staff at *Harper's Monthly.*

9. Henry Mills Alden (1836–1919) edited *Harper's New Monthly Magazine* from 1869 until his death.

10. James Renwick Wilson Sloane (1833–1886).

Princeton Review, that was being revived. He told Warner that the first number was ready for publication except for a good story which he was seeking. In a flash Warner saw his opportunity. "I have the very story for you," he said; "wait a moment."

He turned, ran up the Harper steps, and went into Alden's office. Alden was not there, but on the corner of his desk lay the manuscript, just as he had left it. Seizing it at once, he went to the street, where Sloane was waiting for him. He gave him the manuscript. Sloane liked the story and published it without more ado in his first number. I received one hundred and fifty dollars for it, which almost stunned me. It was the first check I had ever received. In fact, the first one I had ever seen.

The little story, "Monsieur Motte" was well received. It pleased the public, the quiet, unsensational public of the eighties. My anonymity was strictly guarded. I repulsed sensitively all efforts to fasten authorship upon me. A year elapsed before I acknowledged "Monsieur Motte" as mine.

In the meantime Mr. Alden was provoked by Mr. Warner's action in giving to the *New Princeton Review* a story that should have gone to *Harper's Magazine.* To placate him, Mr. Warner offered my next story to him and wrote me to get another story ready. I did it at once, "Bayou L'Ombre," a little episode that I had heard on the plantation. . . .

How simple it all seemed to me, this coming of the answer to my inward hopes and dreams, the secret wish that I had not revealed to another, even to my mother.

I was full of stories all ready to be written out. I did not have to invent them; they were in my mind, waiting only for the pen to transcribe them. They were simply my experiences. Fortunately they pleased both publishers and readers.

Source: Memories of a Southern Woman of Letters (1932)

Acknowledgments

First and foremost I wish to thank Beverly Anne Hall Rude, my mother, for her generous aid in compiling this anthology. She cheered me on in all of my efforts, exhibited boundless interest in my work, and donated to this project more hours than I can count of free labor, scanning, typing, and editing documents. Without her this book would not have been possible. Thus, I wish to dedicate it to her.

For further assistance in editing and proofing, I am grateful to Julia Smith and Megan Cian. For his interest in the project and his support each step of the way, particularly his unwavering understanding of the delays caused by Hurricane Katrina, I wish to thank Michael Lonegro at the Johns Hopkins University Press. I am also grateful for the thorough evaluations provided by Paula Bennett and the anonymous reviewer. My heartfelt thanks, as well, to the interlibrary loan staff of Earl K. Long Library at the University of New Orleans. Without their hard work tracking down sources, this project would not have been possible. My sincere thanks to the many individuals who answered my queries about biographical and source information.

Financial assistance in the form of summer stipends from the College of Liberal Arts and the English Department at the University of New Orleans are much appreciated.

Lastly, I wish to thank my husband and daughter for their tolerance of the many hours I spent away from them while working on this project.

Poems by Emily Dickinson are reprinted by permission of the publishers and the Trustees of Amherst College from *The Poems of Emily Dickinson: Reading Edition,* Ralph W. Franklin, ed., Cambridge, MA: The Belknap Press of Harvard University Press. Copyright © 1998, 1999 by the President and Fellows of Harvard College. Copyright © 1951, 1955, 1979, 1983 by the President and Fellows of Harvard College.

Letters by Augusta Jane Evans to Rachel Lyons are reprinted from Rebecca Grant Sexton, ed., *A Southern Woman of Letters: The Correspondence of Augusta Jane Evans Wilson* (University of South Carolina Press, 2002), by permission of the publisher.

Letters by Harriet Jacobs to Amy Post are printed by permission of the Post Family Papers, Department of Rare Books and Special Collections, University of Rochester Library.

Letters by Sarah Orne Jewett to Horace Scudder and to Frederick M. Hopkins are reprinted by permission of Colby College.

"The Value of Race Literature" by Victoria Earle Matthews is reprinted by permission from *Massachusetts Review* 27, no. 2 (Summer 1986).

List of Authors

Contents by Genre

Autobiography

Essays, Editorials, and Criticism

Fiction and Sketch

Letters and Journals

Poetry

Prefaces and Conclusions

Selected Contents by Theme

Activism / Social Causes

Advice to Aspiring Writers

African American Literature and Writers

Literary Aesthetics and Theories

Literary Histories and Criticism

Love, Marriage, and Motherhood

Native American Literature

Nature

Poetry as Theme

Western Literature and Writers